The Complete Poems of
CHRISTINA ROSSETTI

The Complete Poems of CHRISTINA ROSSETTI

A VARIORUM EDITION

VOLUME III

Edited, with Textual Notes and Introductions, by

R. W. CRUMP

LOUISIANA STATE UNIVERSITY PRESS

BATON ROUGE & LONDON

Manufactured in the United States of America
First printing
99 98 97 96 95 94 93 92 91 90   5 4 3 2 1

Designer: Laura Roubique Gleason
Typeface: Baskerville
Typesetter: G&S Typesetters, Inc.
Printer and binder: Thomson-Shore, Inc.

LIBRARY OF CONGRESS CATALOGING-IN-PUBLICATION DATA

(Revised for vol. 3)

Rossetti, Christina Georgina, 1830–1894.
  The complete poems of Christina Rossetti.

  A variorum ed.
  Includes bibliographical references and indexes.
  I. Crump, R. W. (Rebecca W.), 1944–
II. Title.
PR5237.A1   1979   821'.8   78-5571
ISBN 0-8071-0358-6 (v. 1)
ISBN 0-8071-1246-1 (v. 2)

The paper in this book meets the guidelines for permanence and durability of the Committee on Production Guidelines for Book Longevity of the Council on Library Resources. ∞

Table of Contents

III Unpublished Poems

Acknowledgments

It is a pleasure to express my continued gratitude to all of the libraries, institutions, and private collectors named in the list of holograph poems, for their generous assistance and kind permission to use their books and manuscripts. I remain indebted to all others whose help is acknowledged in Volumes I and II, especially Harold F. Rossetti, Mrs. Geoffrey Dennis, and Mrs. Roderic O'Conor, for permission to print the unpublished material of Christina Rossetti. In addition, I am grateful to Edgar F. Harden, professor of English, Simon Fraser University, Burnaby, British Columbia, for informing me of the location of the 1893 *Verses* manuscript, and to David S. Goodes, Walpole Librarian, the King's School, Canterbury, for assistance in obtaining a photocopy of that manuscript. J. Michael Smethurst, Director General, Humanities and Social Sciences, the British Library, kindly helped me obtain the texts of Christina Rossetti's poems published in *"New and Old:" For Seed-Time and Harvest*. John Easterly, Production Editor, Louisiana State University Press, provided valuable assistance in producing this volume. A fellowship from the National Endowment for the Humanities, with a supplement from the Louisiana State University College of Arts and Sciences (David B. Harned, Dean), enabled me to complete this volume.

The Complete Poems of
CHRISTINA ROSSETTI

Holograph Poems

Beinecke Rare Book and Manuscript Library, Yale University,
New Haven, Connecticut
  Manuscript of "A Bird Song"
  Fourteen numbered pages containing six poems: "Symbols,"
    "Something like Truth" ["Sleep at Sea"], "Easter Even,"
    "The Watchers," "Once," and "Long Enough" ["Dream-
    Love"]

Henry W. and Albert A. Berg Collection, New York Public
Library, New York City
  Cancelled leaves of pp. 55–56 of *Verses* (1847), containing
    holograph changes incorporated into the printed text

Bodleian Library, Oxford, England
  Nine notebooks of poems, 1845–1856
  Manuscripts of "The Offering of the New Law, the One
    Oblation once Offered" and "Heaven overarches"

British Library, London, England
  Seven notebooks of poems, 1842–1845, 1856–1866
  Bound holograph volume of *Sing-Song*
  Bound holograph of *Il rosseggiar dell' Oriente*
  Manuscripts of *Valentines from C.G.R.*, 1876–1886
  Manuscripts of "Sleeping at Last," "A Song of Flight,"
    "An Apple-Gathering," "By way of Remembrance,"
    "Counterblast on Penny Trumpet," "He and She," "Hymn
    after Gabriele Rossetti," "Mirrors of Life and Death," "My
    Mouse," and "To my Mother on her Birthday"
  Manuscript of "Hear what the mournful linnets say" in
    Maria Francesca Rossetti's handwriting

Brown University Library, Providence, Rhode Island
  Manuscript of "A Year's Windfalls"

Mrs. Geoffrey Dennis, Woodstock, England
 Notebook of poems, 1859–1860
 One of Christina's copies of *Sing-Song* (1872) with her
  holographs of the poems added in the second edition
  of *Sing-Song* (1893)
 Manuscript of "Michael F. M. Rossetti"

Duke University Library, Durham, North Carolina
 Manuscript of "Methinks the ills of life I fain would shun"

Christopher Erb, Bayonne, New Jersey
 Manuscript of "One Sea-Side Grave"

Historical Society of Pennsylvania, Philadelphia
 Letter containing the first stanza of "Passing Away"

Houghton Library, Harvard University, Cambridge,
  Massachusetts
 Manuscript of "A Ballad of Boding"

Humanities Research Center, University of Texas at Austin
 Notebook containing *A Pageant and Other Poems*
 Manuscripts of "Song" ["She sat and sang alway"], "Three
  Seasons," "An Echo from Willowwood," and "The Way of
  the World"
 Letter containing the first stanza of "Up-Hill"

Huntington Library, San Marino, California
 Notebook containing *Maude: Prose and Verse*
 Manuscripts of *Later Life: A Double Sonnet of Sonnets*
 Manuscripts of "Behold the Man," "Up-Hill," and part of
  "At Home"

Iowa State Department of History and Archives, Des Moines
 Two pages from Christina's rough draft of "The Months:
  A Pageant"

The King's School, Canterbury, England
 Notebook containing *Verses* (1893)

Mrs. Roderic O'Conor, Henley-on-Thames, England
 One of Christina's copies of *Sing-Song* (1872), containing her
  Italian translations of the poems, and the poems added in
  the second edition of *Sing-Song* (1893)

Pierpont Morgan Library, New York City
  Manuscript of "A Dirge"
  Manuscript of "Song" ["When I am dead my dearest"] and
    part of "What Sappho would have said had her leap cured
    instead of killing her"
Open Collection, Princeton University Library, Princeton, New
  Jersey
  Manuscripts of "Autumn," "A Coast Nightmare," "A Discov-
    ery," "An Escape," "A Hopeless Case," "My Old Friends,"
    "A Prospective Meeting," "Reflection," "A Return,"
    "Rivals," "River Thames," "Ruin," "Solitude," "A Study,"
    "Summer," "Sunshine," "Winter. A Christmas Carol," "A
    Year's Windfalls," "4th May morning," and "Gone to his
    rest"
Rossetti Collection of Janet Camp Troxell, Princeton University
  Library
  Rough drafts of eighteen *bouts-rimés* sonnets
  Rough draft of lines 25–28 of "The German-French Cam-
    paign. 1870–1871"
  Manuscripts of "A Christmas Carol ["A Holy Heavenly
    Chime"], "Cor Mio," "De Profundis," "Hadrian's Death-
    Song Translated," "Heaven overarches," "Husband and
    Wife," "Imitated from the Arpa Evangelica: Page 121,"
    "In resurrection is it awfuller" ["By way of Remem-
    brance"], "L'Uommibatto," "Meeting," "Parted," "Si ri-
    manda la tocca-caldaja," "Time and Opportunity," "Hope
    in Grief," and "The Succession of Kings"
  Partial manuscript of "Summer" ["Come, cuckoo, come"]
  Manuscript containing deleted partial stanzas of three
    poems, including "The Key-Note" and "The Descent from
    the Cross"
  Manuscript of the first three stanzas of "A Christmas Carol"
    ["Before the paling of the stars"]
  Manuscript of the first stanza of "Up-Hill"
  Manuscript of the short story "Commonplace," containing
    "In July" and "Love hath a name of Death"
Harold F. Rossetti, London, England
  Manuscript of "Sonnets are full of love"

Kenneth Spencer Research Library, University of Kansas,
Lawrence
    Manuscript of "The whole head is sick, and the whole heart
        faint" and the last three lines of "The Trees' Counselling"
    Manuscript of the first four stanzas of "A true Story"

Robert H. Taylor Collection, Princeton University Library, New
Jersey
    Letter containing "Mr. and Mrs. Scott, and I" (on indefinite
        deposit at the Princeton University Library)

University of British Columbia Library, Vancouver, Canada
    Letters containing Christina's Italian translations of "Bread
        and milk for breakfast," "Hear what the mournful linnets
        say," "O sailor come ashore," "The horses of the sea," "Oh
        fair to see," and "If a pig wore a wig"
    Letters containing "A roundel seems to fit a round of days,"
        "Pity the sorrows of a poor old dog" ["A Word for the
        Dumb"], "The two Rossettis (brothers they)," "In prog-
        ress," and part of "A sonnet and a love sonnet from me"

University of Kentucky Libraries, Lexington
    Manuscript of "Roses and Roses" ["Where shall I find a
        white rose blowing"]

Editions and Reprints

In order to be certain that the absence of end-of-line punctuation was not the result of imperfect inking in each printed text recorded in the notes, I collated several copies of each text. A complete list including anthologies, journals, newspapers, and other works containing authoritative texts that are used in this volume would be very long; the list below is therefore limited to the editions and reprints of Christina Rossetti's works. An *a* after the date of publication indicates an American edition, and parentheses enclose the dates of reprints. Reprints are cited in the textual notes only where they show a new variant; the variants designated 1885r and 1896s are recorded only if they differ from the first editions published in those years (r = Christina Rossetti's own annotated copy, s = special edition).

1847   *Verses: Dedicated to Her Mother.* London: privately printed
        at G. Polidori's, 1847.
            Copy owned by Mrs. Roderic O'Conor, with Christina's
                holograph corrections
            University of Texas Library, PR5237.V4.1847.HRC,
                copy 3, containing drawings by Dante Gabriel
                Rossetti and Christina's holograph corrections
            University of Texas Library, Wp.R734.847v

1870   *Commonplace, and Other Short Stories.* London: F. S. Ellis,
        1870.
            Princeton University Library, 3913.1.333.11
            Harvard University Library, EC85.R7354.870C

1870a   *Commonplace, A Tale of To-day; and Other Stories.* Boston:
        Roberts Brothers, 1870.
            Library of Congress, PZ3.R737C.2
            Harvard University Library, KD4278

1874   *Annus Domini: A Prayer for Each Day of the Year, Founded on
        a Text of Holy Scripture.* Oxford and London: James Parker
        and Co., 1874.
            Princeton University Library, *EC85.R7354.874a, with
            Christina's holograph marginalia
            Harvard University Library, EC85.R7354.874a

1881   *Called to be Saints: The Minor Festivals Devotionally Studied.*
        London: Society for Promoting Christian Knowledge;
        New York: E. and J. B. Young, [1881].
            Boston University Theology Library, 242.3.R73c
            Harvard University Library, *EC.85.R7354.881c
            Yale University Library, Mrg78.R73

1885   *Time Flies: A Reading Diary.* London: Society for Promot-
        ing Christian Knowledge, 1885.
            University of Georgia Library, BV832.R74.1885
            University of Virginia, BV832.R74

1885r *Time Flies: A Reading Diary.* London: Society for Promot-
        ing Christian Knowledge, 1885.
            University of Texas Library, MS file (Rossetti, CG)
            Works B, containing Christina's holograph
            marginalia

1886a *Time Flies: A Reading Diary.* Boston: Roberts Brothers,
        1886.
            Oberlin College Library, 242.R735
            University of Chicago Library, PR5237.T5.1886

(1890) *Time Flies: A Reading Diary.* London: Society for Promot-
        ing Christian Knowledge, 1890.
            Library of Congress, BV4832.R74.1890
            Yale University Library, Ip.R734.885Tb

1892   *The Face of the Deep: A Devotional Commentary on the Apoca-
        lypse.* London: Society for Promoting Christian Knowl-
        edge; New York: E. and J. B. Young, 1892.
            Florida State University Library, Hum.BS.2825.R65
            Harvard University Library, *EC85.R7354.892f
            University of Wisconsin Library, BS.2825.R65

(1893) *The Face of the Deep: A Devotional Commentary on the Apocalypse.* Second edition. London: Society for Promoting Christian Knowledge; New York: E. and J. B. Young, 1893.
    Princeton University Library, Ex5298.786.1893
    College of Puget Sound Library, 228.R735f

1896 *New Poems, Hitherto Unpublished or Uncollected.* Edited by William Michael Rossetti. London and New York: Macmillan, 1896.
    Harvard University Library, Keats*EC8 K2262, Za895rb
    Princeton University Library, 3913.1.367
    University of Texas Library, ApR 734 896nba

1896s *New Poems, Hitherto Unpublished or Uncollected.* Edited by William Michael Rossetti. London: Macmillan, 1896. Special edition of one hundred large paper copies printed in January, 1896.
    Princeton University Library, 3913.1.367.11 (#35)
    University of Texas Library, HANLEY R734n (#76)

1897 *Maude: A Story for Girls.* London: James Bowden, 1897.
    Library of Congress, PZ3.R737M
    Princeton University Library, Ex.3913.1.362.11

1897a *Maude: Prose & Verse by Christina Rossetti; 1850.* Chicago: Herbert S. Stone, 1897.
    Library of Congress, PZ3.R737M.2
    Princeton University Library, 3913.1.362

1904 *The Poetical Works of Christina Georgina Rossetti, with Memoir and Notes by William Michael Rossetti.* London: Macmillan, 1904.
    Louisiana State University Library, 828.R734pXr
    The editor's own copy

Introduction

The present volume, containing the poems Christina did not include in her published collections of poetry, is divided into three main sections. In the first are the poems she published separately in anthologies, periodicals, or her own prose works, such as *Commonplace, and Other Short Stories;* the poems are presented in order of publication. The second group consists of the privately printed poems—including, most notably, those from the 1847 *Verses: Dedicated to Her Mother*—arranged in order of private printing. The extant poems that Christina never published make up the third and by far the largest section of Volume III. Within this category, I have maintained the integrity of groups of manuscripts. The groups of fair copy manuscripts are presented first, beginning with her notebooks of poetry (dating from 1842 to 1866), followed by the poems from the 1850 notebook of *Maude: Prose & Verse,* the poems in *Il rosseggiar dell' Oriente* (1862–1868), the four *By way of Remembrance* poems (1870), and finally Christina's Valentine poems to her mother (1876–1886). Following the groups of fair copy manuscripts is the group of rough draft *bouts-rimés* sonnets (written probably in 1847–1848) and the group of Italian translations of *Sing-Song* (1872) written in the margins of one of her copies of that book. The more than twenty extant separate manuscripts of poems are presented next, in roughly chronological order (most of those manuscripts are not dated). Part III concludes with the poems no longer extant in manuscript form; for most of them, the text is taken from William Michael Rossetti's editions.[1]

In establishing the text for each poem, I chose the basic text (or copy-text) according to the following order of preference: latest au-

---

1. I was unable to locate two poems named but not presented by William Michael Rossetti in *The Poetical Works of Christina Georgina Rossetti* (London: Macmillan and Co., 1904): "Verses to W. B. Scott (dos-à-dos)" (p. xliii), and "Aegisthus" (p. 491).

thorial fair copy manuscript; authorial rough draft; manuscript in the handwriting of Christina's sister Maria or their mother; earliest published or privately printed version during the author's lifetime; nonauthorial source (usually Christina's brother William Michael Rossetti). For each poem in this volume, the basic text is named in the headnote to the textual notes at the back of the book. As in Volumes I and II, all the works consulted in determining the final text of the poem are listed in the headnote, and any changes made in the basic text are recorded in the textual notes. The present edition thus furnishes an eclectic text, which, unlike any single authoritative version, is based on a consideration of Christina's extant manuscripts, letters, editions, and individual printings of her poems in journals and anthologies.

Appendix A records the extant indexes from Christina's notebooks of poetry, including the 1893 *Verses* notebook. Two of her notebooks do not contain indexes: the 1859–1860 notebook owned by Mrs. Geoffrey Dennis, and the 1864–1866 notebook in the British Library.

I *Separately Published Poems*

DEATH'S CHILL BETWEEN.

Chide not; let me breathe a little,
   For I shall not mourn him long.
Tho' the life-cord was so brittle
   The love-cord was very strong.
5   I would wake a little space
   Till I find a sleeping-place.

You can go, I shall not weep;
   You can go unto your rest;
My heart-ache is all too deep,
10   And too sore my throbbing breast.
Can sobs be, or angry tears,
Where are neither hopes nor fears?

Tho' with you I am alone,
   And must be so everywhere,
15   I will make no useless moan;
   None shall say: "She could not bear;"
While life lasts I will be strong,
But I shall not struggle long.

Listen, listen! everywhere
20   A low voice is calling me,
And a step is on the stair,
   And one comes ye do not see.
Listen, listen! evermore
A dim hand knocks at the door.

25   Hear me: he is come again;
   My own dearest is come back.

Bring him in from the cold rain;
    Bring wine, and let nothing lack.
Thou and I will rest together,
30   Love, until the sunny weather.

I will shelter thee from harm,
    Hide thee from all heaviness;
Come to me, and keep thee warm
    By my side in quietness.
35   I will lull thee to thy sleep
With sweet songs; we will not weep.

Who hath talked of weeping? yet
    There is something at my heart
Gnawing, I would fain forget,
40   And an aching and a smart—
Ah my Mother, 'tis in vain,
For he is not come again.

HEART'S CHILL BETWEEN.

I did not chide him, tho' I knew
    That he was false to me:
Chide the exhaling of the dew,
    The ebbing of the sea,
5   The fading of a rosy hue,
    But not inconstancy.

Why strive for love when love is o'er?
    Why bind a restive heart?
He never knew the pain I bore
10   In saying: "We must part;
Let us be friends, and nothing more":—
    Oh woman's shallow art!

But it is over, it is done;
    I hardly heed it now;
15   So many weary years have run
    Since then, I think not how
Things might have been; but greet each one
    With an unruffled brow.

What time I am where others be
20   My heart seems very calm,
Stone calm; but if all go from me
    There comes a vague alarm,
A shrinking in the memory
    From some forgotten harm.

25   And often thro' the long long night
    Waking when none are near,
I feel my heart beat fast with fright,
    Yet know not what I fear.
Oh how I long to see the light
30   And the sweet birds to hear!

To have the sun upon my face,
    To look up through the trees,
To walk forth in the open space,
    And listen to the breeze,
35   And not to dream the burial place
    Is clogging my weak knees.

Sometimes I can nor weep nor pray,
    But am half stupified;
And then all those who see me say
40   Mine eyes are opened wide,
And that my wits seem gone away:—
    Ah would that I had died!

Would I could die and be at peace,
    Or living could forget;
45   My grief nor grows nor doth decrease,
    But ever is:—and yet
Methinks now that all this shall cease
    Before the sun shall set.

Repining.

She sat alway thro' the long day
Spinning the weary thread away;
And ever said in undertone:
"Come; that I be no more alone."

5   From early dawn to set of sun
Working, her task was still undone;
And the long thread seemed to increase
Even while she spun and did not cease.
She heard the gentle turtle dove
10   Tell to its mate a tale of love;
She saw the glancing swallows fly,
Ever a social company;
She knew each bird upon its nest
Had cheering songs to bring it rest;
15   None lived alone, save only she;
The wheel went round more wearily;
She wept, and said in undertone:
"Come; that I be no more alone."
Day followed day; and still she sighed
20   For love, and was not satisfied;
Until one night, when the moon-light
Turned all the trees to silver white,
She heard, what ne'er she heard before,
A steady hand undo the door.
25   The nightingale since set of sun
Her throbbing music had not done,
And she had listened silently;
But now the wind had changed, and she
Heard the sweet song no more, but heard
30   Beside her bed a whispered word:
"Damsel, rise up; be not afraid,
"For I am come at last;" it said.

She trembled tho' the voice was mild,
She trembled like a frightened child,
35   Till she looked up, and then she saw
The unknown speaker without awe.
He seemed a fair young man, his eyes
Beaming with serious charities;
His cheek was white, but hardly pale;
40   And a dim glory, like a veil,
Hovered about his head, and shone
Thro' the whole room, till night was gone.

So her fear fled; and then she said,
Leaning upon her quiet bed:
45 "Now thou art come I prithee stay,
"That I may see thee in the day,
"And learn to know thy voice, and hear
"It evermore calling me near."
He answered: "Rise, and follow me."
50 But she looked upwards wonderingly:
"And whither would'st thou go friend? stay
"Until the dawning of the day."
But he said: "The wind ceaseth, Maid;
"Of chill nor damp be thou afraid."
55 She bound her hair up from the floor,
And passed in silence from the door.

So they went forth together, he
Helping her forward tenderly.
The hedges bowed beneath his hand;
60 Forth from the streams came the dry land
As they passed over; evermore
The pallid moonbeams shone before,
And the wind hushed, and nothing stirred;
Not even a solitary bird
65 Scared by their footsteps fluttered by,
Where aspen trees stood steadily.

As they went on, at length a sound
Came trembling on the air around;
The undistinguishable hum
70 Of life; voices that go and come
Of busy men and the child's sweet
High laugh, and noise of trampling feet.

Then he said: "Wilt thou go and see?"
And she made answer joyfully:
75 "The noise of life, of human life,
"Of dear communion without strife,
"Of converse held 'twixt friend and friend;
"Is it not here our path shall end?"

He led her on a little way
80   Until they reached a hillock: "Stay."

It was a village in a plain.
High mountains screened it from the rain
And stormy wind; and nigh at hand
A bubbling streamlet flowed, o'er sand
85   Pebbly and fine; and sent life up
Green succous stalk and flower cup.

Gradually, day's harbinger,
A chilly wind began to stir.
It seemed a gentle powerless breeze
90   That scarcely rustled thro' the trees;
And yet it touched the mountain's head,
And the paths man might never tread.
But hearken! in the quiet weather
Do all the streams flow down together?
95   No, 'tis a sound more terrible
Than tho' a thousand rivers fell.
The everlasting ice and snow
Were loosened then, but not to flow;
With a loud crash like solid thunder
100 The avalanche came, burying under
The village; turning life and breath
And rest and joy and plans to death.

"Oh let us fly, for pity fly,
"Let us go hence friend, thou and I.
105 "There must be many regions yet
"Where these things make not desolate."

He looked upon her seriously;
Then said: "Arise, and follow me."
The path that lay before them was
110 Nigh covered over with long grass,
And many slimy things and slow
Trailed on between the roots below.
The moon looked dimmer than before;
And shadowy cloudlets floating o'er

115   Its face, sometimes quite hid its light,
       And filled the skies with deeper night.

       At last, as they went on, the noise
       Was heard of the sea's mighty voice;
       And soon the ocean could be seen
120   In its long restlessness serene.
       Upon its breast a vessel rode
       That drowsily appeared to nod
       As the great billows rose and fell,
       And swelled to sink, and sank to swell.

125   Meanwhile the strong wind had come forth
       From the chill regions of the North;
       The mighty wind invisible.
       And the low waves began to swell;
       And the sky darkened overhead;
130   And the moon once looked forth, then fled
       Behind dark clouds; while here and there
       The lightning shone out in the air;
       And the approaching thunder rolled
       With angry pealings manifold.
135   How many vows were made; and prayers
       That in safe times were cold and scarce.
       Still all availed not; and at length
       The waves arose in all their strength,
       And fought against the ship, and filled
140   The ship; then were the clouds unsealed,
       And the rains hurried forth and beat
       On every side and over it.

       Some clung together; and some kept
       A long stern silence; and some wept.
145   Many, half crazed, looked on in wonder
       As the strong timbers rent asunder;
       Friends forgot friends; foes fled to foes;
       And still the water rose and rose.

       "Ah woe is me! whom I have seen
150   "Are now as tho' they had not been.

"In the earth there is room for birth,
"And there are graves enough in earth;
"Why should the cold sea, tempest torn,
"Bury those whom it hath not borne?"

155 He answered not, and they went on.
The glory of the heavens was gone;
The moon gleamed not, nor any Star;
Cold winds were rustling near and far;
And from the trees the dry leaves fell
160 With a sad sound unspeakable.

The air was cold; till from the South
A gust blew hot like sudden drouth
Into their faces, and a light
Glowing and red shone thro' the night.

165 A mighty city full of flame,
And death, and sounds without a name!
Amid the black and blinding smoke
The people, as one man, awoke.
Oh happy they who yesterday
170 On the long journey went away;
Whose pallid lips, smiling and chill,
While the flames scorch them smile on still;
Who murmur not, who tremble not
When the bier crackles fiery hot;
175 Who dying said in love's increase:
"Lord, let Thy servant part in peace."

Those in the town could see and hear
A shaded river flowing near.
The broad deep bed could hardly hold
180 Its plenteous waters calm and cold.
Was flame wrapped all the city wall,
The city gates were flame wrapped all.

What was man's strength, what puissance then?
Women were mighty as strong men.
185 Some knelt in prayer believing still,
Resigned unto a righteous will,
Bowing beneath the chastening rod,

Lost to the world, but found of God.
Some prayed for friend, for child, for wife;
190 Some prayed for faith; some prayed for life;
While some, proud even in death, hope gone,
Steadfast and still stood looking on.

"Death, death! oh let us fly from death,
"Where'er we go it followeth.
195 "All these are dead; and we alone
"Remain to weep for what is gone.
"What is this thing, thus hurriedly
"To pass into eternity?
"To leave the earth so full of mirth?
200 "To lose the profit of our birth?
"To die and be no more? to cease,
"Having numbness that is not peace?
"Let us go hence: and even if thus
"Death everywhere must go with us,
205 "Let us not see the change, but see
"Those who have been or still shall be."

He sighed, and they went on together.
Beneath their feet did the grass wither;
Across the heaven, high overhead,
210 Dark misty clouds floated and fled;
And in their bosom was the thunder;
And angry lightnings flashed out under,
Forkèd and red and menacing;
Far off the wind was muttering;
215 It seemed to tell, not understood,
Strange secrets to the listening wood.

Upon its wings it bore the scent
Of blood of a great armament;
Then saw they how on either side
220 Fields were downtrodden far and wide;
That morning at the break of day,
Two nations had gone forth to slay.

As a man soweth, so he reaps.
The field was full of bleeding heaps;

225 Ghastly corpses of men and horses
That met death at a thousand sources;
Cold limbs and putrifying flesh;
Long love-locks clotted to a mesh
That stifled; stiffened mouths beneath
230 Staring eyes that had looked on death.

But these were dead; these felt no more
The anguish of the wounds they bore.
Behold; they shall not sigh again,
Nor justly fear, nor hope in vain.
235 What if none wept above them; is
The sleeper less at rest for this?
Is not the young child's slumber sweet
When no man watcheth over it?

These had deep calm: but all around
240 There was a deadly smothered sound,
The choking cry of agony
From wounded men who could not die.
Who watched the black wing of the raven
Rise like a cloud 'twixt them and heaven,
245 And in the distance, flying fast,
Beheld the eagle come at last.

She knelt down in her agony:
"O Lord, it is enough;" said she:
"My heart's prayer putteth me to shame;
250 "Let me return to whence I came.
"Thou, Who for love's sake didst reprove,
"Forgive me, for the sake of love."

NEW ENIGMAS.

Name any gentleman you spy,
And there's a chance that he is I;
Go out to angle, and you may
Catch me on a propitious day:
5 Booted and spurred, their journey ended,

The weary are by me befriended:
If roasted meat should be your wish,
I am more needful than a dish:
I am acknowledgedly poor:
10   Yet my resources are no fewer
Than all the trades; there is not one
But I profess, beneath the sun:
I bear a part in many a game;
My worth may change, I am the same.
15   Sometimes, by you expelled, I roam
Forth from the sanctuary of home.

CHARADES.

My *first* is no proof of my *second*,
    Though my second's a proof of my first:
If I were my *whole* I should tell you
    Quite freely my best and my worst.

5   One clue more: if you fail to discover
    My meaning, you're blind as a mole;
But if you will frankly confess it,
    You show yourself clearly my *whole*.

THE ROSE.

O Rose, thou flower of flowers, thou fragrant wonder,
    Who shall describe thee in thy ruddy prime;
    Thy perfect fulness in the summer time;
When the pale leaves blushingly part asunder
5   And show the warm red heart lies glowing under?
    Thou shouldst bloom surely in some sunny clime,
    Untouched by blights and chilly Winter's rime,
Where lightnings never flash, nor peals the thunder.
And yet in happier spheres they cannot need thee
10   So much as we do with our weight of woe;

Perhaps they would not tend, perhaps not heed thee,
    And thou wouldst lonely and neglected grow;
And He Who is All-Wise, He hath decreed thee
    To gladden earth and cheer all hearts below.

The Trees' Counselling.

I was strolling sorrowfully
    Thro' the corn fields and the meadows;
The stream sounded melancholy,
    And I walked among the shadows;
5   While the ancient forest trees
    Talked together in the breeze;
In the breeze that waved and blew them,
With a strange weird rustle thro' them.

Said the oak unto the others
10   In a leafy voice and pleasant:
"Here we all are equal brothers,
    "Here we have nor lord nor peasant.
"Summer, Autumn, Winter, Spring,
"Pass in happy following.
15 "Little winds may whistle by us,
"Little birds may overfly us;

"But the sun still waits in heaven
    "To look down on us in splendour;
"When he goes the moon is given,
20   "Full of rays that he doth lend her:
"And tho' sometimes in the night
"Mists may hide her from our sight,
"She comes out in the calm weather,
"With the glorious stars together."

25 From the fruitage, from the blossom,
    From the trees came no denying;
Then my heart said in my bosom:
    "Wherefore art thou sad and sighing?
"Learn contentment from this wood

30   "That proclaimeth all states good;
     "Go not from it as it found thee;
     "Turn thyself and gaze around thee."

     And I turned: behold the shading
       But showed forth the light more clearly;
35   The wild bees were honey-lading;
       The stream sounded hushing merely,
     And the wind not murmuring
     Seemed, but gently whispering:
     "Get thee patience; and thy spirit
40   "Shall discern in all things merit."

"Behold, I stand at the door and knock."

     Who standeth at the gate?—A woman old,
       A widow from the husband of her love:
     "O Lady, stay; this wind is piercing cold,
       Oh look at the keen frosty moon above;
5   I have no home, am hungry, feeble, poor:"—
       "I'm really very sorry, but I can
       Do nothing for you, there's the clergyman,"—
     The Lady said, and shivering closed the door.

     Who standeth at the gate?—Way-worn and pale,
10   A grey-haired man asks charity again:
     "Kind Lady, I have journeyed far, and fail
       Thro' weariness; for I have begged in vain
     Some shelter, and can find no lodging-place:"—
       She answered: "There's the Workhouse very near,
15   Go, for they'll certainly receive you there:"—
     Then shut the door against his pleading face.

     Who standeth at the gate?—a stunted child,
       Her sunk eyes sharpened with precocious care:
     "O Lady, save me from a home defiled,
20   From shameful sights and sounds that taint the air.
     Take pity on me, teach me something good;"—
       "For shame, why don't you work instead of cry?—

   I keep no young impostors here, not I;"—
   She slammed the door, indignant where she stood.

25 Who standeth at the gate, and will be heard?—
    Arise, O woman, from thy comforts now:
   Go forth again to speak the careless word,
    The cruel word unjust, with hardened brow.
   But Who is This, That standeth not to pray
30   As once, but terrible to judge thy sin?
    This, Whom thou wouldst not succour, nor take in,
   Nor teach, but leave to perish by the way?—

   "Thou didst it not unto the least of these,
    And in them hast not done it unto Me.
35 Thou wast as a princess, rich and at ease,
    Now sit in dust and howl for poverty.
   Three times I stood beseeching at thy gate,
    Three times I came to bless thy soul and save:
   But now I come to judge for what I gave,
40 And now at length thy sorrow is too late."

   Gianni my friend and I both strove to excel,
   But, missing better, settled down in well.
   Both fail, indeed; but not alike we fail—
   My forte being Venus' face, and his a dragon's tail.

The Offering of the New Law, the One Oblation once Offered.

"Sacrifice and Offering Thou wouldest not, but a BODY hast Thou prepared Me."

   Once I thought to sit so high
   In the Palace of the sky;
   Now I thank God for His Grace,
  If I may fill the lowest place.

5 Once I thought to scale so soon
   Heights above the changing moon;

Now I thank God for delay—
Today, it yet is called today.

While I stumble, halt and blind,
10   Lo! He waiteth to be kind;
Bless me soon, or bless me slow,
Except He bless, I let not go.

Once for earth I laid my plan,
Once I leaned on strength of man,
15   When my hope was swept aside,
I stayed my broken heart on pride:

Broken reed hath pierced my hand;
Fell my house I built on sand;
Roofless, wounded, maimed by sin,
20   Fightings without, and fears within:

Yet, a tree, He feeds my root;
Yet, a branch, He prunes for fruit;
Yet, a sheep, these eves and morns,
He seeks for me among the thorns.

25   With Thine Image stamped of old,
Find Thy coin more choice than gold;
Known to Thee by name, recall
To Thee Thy home-sick prodigal.

Sacrifice and Offering
30   None there is that I can bring;
None, save what is Thine alone:
I bring Thee, Lord, but of Thine Own—

Broken Body, Blood Outpoured,
These I bring, my God, my Lord;
35   Wine of Life, and Living Bread,
With these for me Thy Board is spread.

The eleventh hour.

Faint and worn and aged
    One stands knocking at a gate,

Tho' no light shines in the casement,
Knocking tho' so late.
5   It has struck eleven
In the courts of Heaven,
Yet he still doth knock and wait.

While no answer cometh
From the heavenly hill,
10   Blessed Angels wonder
At his earnest will.
Hope and fear but quicken
While the shadows thicken;
He is knocking knocking still.

15   Grim the gate unopened
Stands with bar and lock,
Yet within the unseen Porter
Hearkens to the knock.
Doing and undoing,
20   Faint and yet pursuing,
This man's feet are on the Rock.

With a cry unceasing
Knocketh prayeth he:—
"Lord, have mercy on me
25   "When I cry to Thee."—
With a knock unceasing
And a cry increasing:—
"O my Lord, remember me."

Still the Porter standeth,
30   Love-constrained He standeth near,
While the cry increaseth
Of that love and fear:—
"Jesus look upon me;
"Christ hast Thou foregone me?
35   "If I must, I perish here."—

Faint the knocking ceases,
Faint the cry and call:
Is he lost indeed for ever,

Shut without the wall?—
40 Mighty Arms surround him,
Arms that sought and found him,
Held withheld and bore thro' all.—

O celestial mansion
Open wide the door:
45 Crown and robes of whiteness,
Stone inscribed before,
Flocking Angels bear them;
Stretch thy hand and wear them,
Sit thou down for evermore.

I know you not.

O Christ the Vine with living Fruit,
The twelvefold fruited Tree of Life,
The Balm in Gilead after strife,
The valley Lily and the Rose:
5 Stronger than Lebanon, Thou Root,
Sweeter than clustered grapes, Thou Vine;
Oh Best, Thou Vineyard of red Wine
Keeping Thy best Wine till the close.

Pearl of great price Thyself alone
10 And ruddier than the ruby Thou,
Most precious lightening Jasper Stone,
Head of the corner spurned before;
Fair Gate of pearl, Thyself the Door,
Clear golden Street, Thyself the Way,
15 By Thee we journey toward Thee now
Thro' Thee shall enter Heaven one day.

I thirst for Thee, full Fount and Flood,
My heart calls Thine as deep to deep:
Dost Thou forget Thy sweat and pain,
20 Thy provocation on the Cross?
Heart pierced for me, vouchsafe to keep
The purchase of Thy lavished Blood;

The gain is Thine Lord if I gain,
Or if I lose Thine Own the loss.

25 At midnight, saith the parable,
A cry was made, the Bridegroom came:
Those who were ready entered in;
The rest shut out in death and shame
Strove all too late that feast to win
30 Their die was cast and fixed their lot,
A gulph divided heaven from hell,
The Bridegroom said, 'I know you not.'

But Who is This That shuts the door
And saith 'I know you not' to them?
35 I see the wounded Hands and Side,
The Brow thorn-tortured long ago:
Yea, This Who grieved and bled and died,
This Same is He Who must condemn;
He called, but they refused to know,
40 So now He hears their cry no more.

A Christmas Carol.

Before the paling of the stars
    Before the winter morn
Before the earliest cockcrow
    Jesus Christ was born:
5   Born in a stable
    Cradled in a manger,
In the world His Hands had made
    Born a Stranger.

Priest and King lay fast asleep
10   In Jerusalem,
Young and Old lay fast asleep
    In crowded Bethlehem:
Saint and Angel Ox and Ass
    Kept a watch together

15   Before the Christmas daybreak
     In the winter weather.

Jesus on His Mother's breast
    In the stable cold,
Spotless Lamb of God was He
20   Shepherd of the Fold:
Let us kneel with Mary Maid
    With Joseph bent and hoary
With Saint and Angel Ox and Ass
    To hail the King of Glory.

Easter Even.

There is nothing more that they can do
    For all their rage and boast;
Caiaphas with his blaspheming crew,
    Herod with his host,

5   Pontius Pilate in his judgment hall
    Judging their Judge and his,
Or he who led them all and passed them all
    Arch-Judas with his kiss.

The sepulchre made sure with ponderous stone
10   Seal that same stone, O priest;
It may be thou shalt block the Holy One
    From rising in the east:

Set a watch about the sepulchre
    To watch on pain of death;
15   They must hold fast the stone if One should stir
    And shake it from beneath.

God Almighty He can break a seal,
    And roll away a stone;
Can grind the proud in dust who would not kneel,
20   And crush the mighty one.

There is nothing more that they can do
   For all their passionate care,
Those who sit in dust, the blessed few,
   And weep and rend their hair.

25   Peter, Thomas, Mary Magdalen,
   The Virgin unreproved,
Joseph with Nicodemus foremost men,
   And John the well-beloved.

Bring your finest linen and your spice,
30   Swathe the Sacred Dead,
Bind with careful hands and piteous eyes
   The napkin round His Head;

Lay Him in the garden rock to rest;
   Rest you the Sabbath length:
35   The Sun That went down crimson in the west
   Shall rise renewed in strength.

God Almighty shall give joy for pain,
   Shall comfort him who grieves:
Lo, He with joy shall doubtless come again
40   And with Him bring His sheaves.

Come unto Me.

Oh for the time gone by when thought of Christ
   Made His yoke easy and His burden light;
   When my heart stirred within me at the sight
Of Altar spread for awful Eucharist;
5   When all my hopes His promises sufficed;
   When my soul watched for Him by day by night;
   When my lamp lightened, and my robe was white,
And all seemed loss except the Pearl unpriced.
Yet since He calls me still with tender call,
10   Since He remembers Whom I half forgot,
   I even will run my race and bear my lot:
For Faith the walls of Jericho cast down,

And Hope to whoso runs holds forth a crown,
And Love is Christ, and Christ is All in all.

Ash Wednesday.

Jesus, do I love Thee?
Thou art far above me,
Seated out of sight
Hid in heavenly light
5 Of most highest height.
Martyred hosts implore Thee,
Seraphs fall before Thee,
Angels and Archangels,
Cherub throngs adore Thee;
10 Blessed she that bore Thee!—
All the Saints approve Thee,
All the Virgins love Thee.
I show as a blot
Blood hath cleansed not,
15 As a barren spot
In Thy fruitful lot.
I, figtree fruit-unbearing,
Thou, Righteous Judge unsparing:
What canst Thou do more to me
20 That shall not more undo me?
Thy Justice hath a sound:
"Why cumbereth it the ground?"
Thy Love with stirrings stronger
Pleads: "Give it one year longer."
25 Thou giv'st me time: but who
Save Thou, shall give me dew,
Shall feed my root with Blood
And stir my sap for good?—
Oh by Thy gifts that shame me
30 Give more lest they condemn me:
Good Lord, I ask much of Thee,
But most I ask to love Thee:

Kind Lord, be mindful of me,
Love me and make me love Thee.

SPRING FANCIES.

I.

Gone were but the Winter,
   Come were but the Spring,
I would go to a covert
   Where the birds sing
5   Ding ding, ding a ding.

Where in the whitethorn
   Singeth the thrush,
And the robin sings
   In a holly bush
10   With his breast ablush.

Full of fresh scents
   Are the budding boughs,
Arching high over
   A cool green house
15   Where doves coo the arouse.

There the sun shineth
   Most shadily;
There sounds an echo
   Of the far sea,
20   Tho' far off it be.

II.

All the world is out in leaf,
   Half the world in flower,
Faint the rainbow comes and goes
   In a sunny shower;
25   Earth has waited weeks and weeks
   For this special hour.

All the world is making love;
  Bird to bird in bushes,
Beast to beast in glades, and frog
30   To frog among the rushes:
Wake, O south wind sweet with spice
  Wake the rose to blushes.

All the world is full of change;
  Tomorrow may be dreary:
35 Life breaks forth, to right and left
  Pipe the woodnotes cheery—
Nevertheless there lie the dead
  Fast asleep and weary—

III.

If it's weary work to live,
40   It will rest us to lie dead,
With a stone at the tired feet
  And a stone at the tired head.

In the waxing April days
  Half the world will stir and sing,
45 But half the world will slug and rot
  For all the sap of spring.

"LAST NIGHT."

Where were you last night? I watched at the gate;
I went down early, I stayed down late.
  Were you snug at home, I should like to know,
Or were you in the coppice wheedling Kate?

5 She's a fine girl, with a fine clear skin;
Easy to woo, perhaps not hard to win.
  Speak up like a man and tell me the truth:
I'm not one to grow downhearted and thin.

If you love her best speak up like a man;
10 It's not I will stand in the light of your plan:

Some girls might cry and scold you a bit
And say they couldn't bear it; but I can.

Love was pleasant enough, and the days went fast;
Pleasant while it lasted, but it needn't last;
15   Awhile on the wax and awhile on the wane,
Now dropped away into the past.

Was it pleasant to you? to me it was;
Now clean gone as an image from glass,
    As a goodly rainbow that fades away,
20 As dew that steams upwards from the grass,

As the first spring day, or the last summer day,
As the sunset flush that leaves heaven grey,
    As a flame burnt out for lack of oil
Which no pains relight or ever may.

25 Good luck to Kate and good luck to you,
I guess she'll be kind when you come to woo;
    I wish her a pretty face that will last,
I wish her a husband steady and true.

Hate you? not I, my very good friend;
30 All things begin and all have an end.
    But let broken be broken; I put no faith
In quacks who set up to patch and mend.

Just my love and one word to Kate:
Not to let time slip if she means to mate;—
35 For even such a thing has been known
As to miss the chance while we weigh and wait.

PETER GRUMP.

If underneath the water
    You comb your golden hair
With a golden comb, my daughter,
    Oh, would that I were there.

5   If underneath the wave
You fill a slimy grave,
Would that I, who could not save,
    Might share.

FORSS.

If my love Hero queens it
10   In summer Fairyland,
What would I be
    But the ring on her hand?
Her cheek when she leans it
    Would lean on me:—
15   Or sweet, bitter-sweet,
    The flower that she wore
When we parted, to meet
    On the hither shore
Anymore? nevermore.

Helen Grey.

Because one loves you, Helen Grey,
    Is that a reason you should pout
    And like a March wind veer about
And frown and say your shrewish say?
5   Don't strain the cord until it snaps,
    Don't split the sound heart with your wedge,
    Don't cut your fingers with the edge
Of your keen wit: you may perhaps.

Because you're handsome, Helen Grey,
10   Is that a reason to be proud?
    Your eyes are bold, your laugh is loud,
Your steps go mincing on their way:
But so you miss that modest charm
    Which is the surest charm of all;
15   Take heed; you yet may trip and fall,
And no man care to stretch his arm.

Stoop from your cold height, Helen Grey,
  Come down and take a lowlier place;
  Come down to fill it now with grace;
20 Come down you must perforce some day:
For years cannot be kept at bay,
  And fading years will make you old;
  Then in their turn will men seem cold,
When you yourself are nipped and grey.

If.

If he would come today today today,
  Oh what a day today would be;
But now he's away, miles and miles away
  From me across the sea.

5 O little bird flying flying flying
  To your nest in the warm west,
Tell him as you pass that I am dying,
  As you pass home to your nest.

I have a sister, I have a brother,
10 A faithful hound, a tame white dove;
But I had another, once I had another,
  And I miss him my love, my love.

In this weary world it is so cold so cold
  While I sit here all alone
15 I would not like to wait and to grow old
  But just to be dead and gone.

Make me fair when I lie dead on my bed,
  Fair where I am lying;
Perhaps he may come and look upon me dead
20 He for whom I am dying.

Dig my grave for two with a stone to show it
  And on the stone write my name:
If he never comes I shall never know it
  But sleep on all the same.

Seasons.

Oh the cheerful budding-time
   When thorn-hedges turn to green;
When new leaves of elm and lime
   Cleave and shed their winter screen:
5 Tender lambs are born and baa,
   North wind finds no snow to bring,
Vigorous nature laughs Haha
   In the miracle of spring.

Oh the gorgeous blossom-days
10   When broad flag-flowers drink and blow;
In and out in summer blaze
   Dragonflies flash to and fro:
Ashen branches hang out keys,
   Oaks put forth the rosy shoot,
15 Wandering herds wax sleek at ease,
   Lovely blossoms end in fruit.

Oh the shouting harvest-weeks:
   Mother Earth grown fat with sheaves;
Thrifty gleaner finds who seeks:
20   Russet golden pomp of leaves
Crowns the woods, to fall at length;
   Bracing winds are felt to stir,
Ocean gathers up her strength,
   Beasts renew their dwindled fur.

25 Oh the starving winter-lapse,
   Ice-bound, hunger-pinched and dim:
Dormant roots recal their saps,
   Empty nests show black and grim,
Short-lived sunshine gives no heat,
30   Undue buds are nipped by frost,
Snow sets forth a windingsheet
   And all hope of life seems lost.

HENRY HARDIMAN,
AGED 55.

Affliction sore long time he bore,
 Physicians were in vain,
Till God did please his soul release,
 And ease him of his pain.

Within the Veil.

She holds a lily in her hand,
Where long ranks of Angels stand;
A silver lily for her wand.

All her hair falls sweeping down,
5   Her hair that is a golden brown;
A crown beneath her golden crown.

Blooms a rose-bush at her knee,
Good to smell and good to see;
It bears a rose for her, for me:

10   Her rose a blossom richly grown,
My rose a bud not fully blown
But sure one day to be mine own.

Paradise: in a Symbol.

Golden-winged, silver-winged,
 Winged with flashing flame,
Such a flight of birds I saw,
 Birds without a name:
5   Singing songs in their own tongue
 (Song of songs) they came.

One to another calling,
 Each answering each,
One to another calling
10   In their proper speech:

High above my head they wheeled,
    Far out of reach.

On wings of flame they went and came
    With a cadenced clang,
15 Their silver wings tinkled,
    Their golden wings rang,
The wind it whistled thro' their wings
    Where in heaven they sang.

They flashed and they darted
20   Awhile before mine eyes,
Mounting mounting mounting still
    In haste to scale the skies,
Birds without a nest on earth,
    Birds of Paradise.

25 Where the moon riseth not
    Nor sun seeks the west,
There to sing their glory
    Which they sing at rest,
There to sing their love-song
30   When they sing their best:

Not in any garden
    That mortal foot hath trod,
Not in any flowering tree
    That springs from earthly sod,
35 But in the garden where they dwell
    The Paradise of God.

In July
No goodbye;
In Augùst
Part we must.

Love hath a name of Death:
He gives a breath
And takes away.

Lo we beneath his sway
5 Grow like a flower;
To bloom an hour,
To droop a day,
And fade away.

Tu scendi dalle stelle, O Re del Cielo,
E vieni in una grotta al freddo al gelo:
    O Bambino mio divino
    Io Ti voglio sempre amar!
5   O Dio beato
E quanto Ti costò l'avermi amato.

Alas my Lord,
How should I wrestle all the livelong night
With Thee my God, my Strength and my Delight?

How can it need
5 So agonized an effort and a strain
To make Thy Face of Mercy shine again?

How can it need
Such wringing out of breathless prayer to move
Thee to Thy wonted Love, when Thou art Love?

10   Yet Abraham
So hung about Thine Arm outstretched and bared,
That for ten righteous Sodom had been spared.

Yet Jacob did
So hold Thee by the clenched hand of prayer
15 That he prevailed, and Thou didst bless him there.

Elias prayed,
And sealed the founts of Heaven; he prayed again
And lo, Thy Blessing fell in showers of rain.

Gulped by the fish,
20 As by the pit, lost Jonah made his moan;
And Thou forgavest, waiting to atone.

All Nineveh
Fasting and girt in sackcloth raised a cry,
Which moved Thee ere the day of grace went by.

25   Thy Church prayed on
And on for blessed Peter in his strait,
Till opened of its own accord the gate.

Yea, Thou my God
Hast prayed all night, and in the garden prayed
30   Even while, like melting wax, Thy strength was made.

Alas for him
Who faints, despite Thy Pattern, King of Saints:
Alas, alas, for me, the one that faints.

Lord, give us strength
35   To hold Thee fast, until we hear Thy Voice
Which Thine own know, who hearing It rejoice.

Lord, give us strength
To hold Thee fast until we see Thy Face,
Full Fountain of all Rapture and all Grace.

40   But when our strength
Shall be made weakness, and our bodies clay,
Hold Thou us fast, and give us sleep till day.

AN ALPHABET.

A is the Alphabet, A at its head;
    A is an Antelope, agile to run.
B is the Baker Boy bringing the bread,
    Or black Bear and brown Bear, both begging for bun.

5   C is a Cornflower come with the corn;
    C is a Cat with a comical look.
D is a dinner which Dahlias adorn;
    D is a Duchess who dines with a Duke.

E is an elegant eloquent Earl;
10   E is an Egg whence an Eaglet emerges.

F is a Falcon, with feathers to furl;
F is a Fountain of full foaming surges.

G is the Gander, the Gosling, the Goose;
G is a Garnet in girdle of gold.
15   H is a Heartsease, harmonious of hues;
H is a huge Hammer, heavy to hold.

I is an Idler who idles on ice;
I am I—who will say I am not I?
J is a Jacinth, a jewel of price;
20   J is a Jay, full of joy in July.

K is a King, or a Kaiser still higher;
K is a Kitten, or quaint Kangaroo.
L is a Lute or a lovely-toned Lyre;
L is a Lily all laden with dew.

25   M is a Meadow where Meadowsweet blows;
M is a Mountain made dim by a mist.
N is a Nut—in a nutshell it grows—
Or a Nest full of Nightingales singing—oh list!

O is an Opal, with only one spark;
30   O is an Olive, with oil on its skin.
P is a Pony, a pet in a park;
P is the Point of a Pen or a Pin.

Q is a Quail, quick-chirping at morn;
Q is a Quince quite ripe and near dropping.
35   R is a Rose, rosy red on a thorn;
R is a red-breasted Robin come hopping.

S is a Snow-storm that sweeps o'er the Sea;
S is the Song that the swift Swallows sing.
T is the Tea-table set out for tea;
40   T is a Tiger with terrible spring.

U, the Umbrella, went up in a shower;
Or Unit is useful with ten to unite.
V is a Violet veined in the flower;
V is a Viper of venomous bite.

45 W stands for the water-bred Whale;
Stands for the wonderful Wax-work so gay.
X, or XX, or XXX is ale,
Or Policeman X, exercised day after day.

Y is a yellow Yacht, yellow its boat;
50 Y is the Yucca, the Yam, or the Yew.
Z is a Zebra, zigzagged his coat,
Or Zebu, or Zoöphyte, seen at the Zoo.

Husband and Wife.

"Oh kiss me once before I go,
"To make amends for sorrow;
"Oh kiss me once before we part
"Who shall not meet tomorrow.

5 "And I was wrong to urge your will,
"And wrong to mar your life;
"But kiss me once before we part,
"Because you are my wife."

She turned her head and tossed her head
10 And puckered up her brow:
"I never kissed you yet," said she,
"And I'll not kiss you now.

"Tho' I'm your wife by might and right
"And forsworn marriage vow,
15 "I never loved you yet," said she,
"And I don't love you now."

So he went sailing on the sea,
And she sat crossed and dumb
While he went sailing on the sea
20 Where the storm winds come.

He'd been away a month and day
Counting from morn to morn:

And many buds had turned to leaves
And many lambs were born

25   And many buds had turned to flowers
For Spring was in a glow,
When she was laid upon her bed
As white and cold as snow.

"Oh let me kiss my baby once,
30   "Once before I die;
"And bring it sometimes to my grave
"To teach it where I lie.

"And tell my husband when he comes
"Safe home from sea,
35   "To love the baby that I leave
"If ever he loved me:

"And tell him, not for might or right
"Or forsworn marriage vow
"But for the helpless baby's sake,
40   "I would have kissed him now."

MICHAEL F. M. ROSSETTI.
Born April 22nd, 1881; Died January 24th, 1883.

A holy Innocent gone home
Without so much as one sharp wounding word:
A blessed Michael in heaven's lofty dome
Without a sword.

========

5   Brief dawn and noon and setting time!
Our rapid-rounding moon has fled:
A black eclipse before the prime
Has swallowed up that shining head.
Eternity holds up her lookingglass:—
10   The eclipse of Time will pass,
And all that lovely light return to sight.

========

I watch the showers and think of flowers:
Alas, my flower that shows no fruit!
My snowdrop plucked, my daisy shoot
15   Plucked from the root.

Soon Spring will shower, the world will flower,
A world of buds will promise fruit,
Pear trees will shoot and apples shoot
Sound at the root.

20   Bud of an hour, far off you flower;
My bud, far off you ripen fruit;
My prettiest bud, my straightest shoot
Sweet at the root.

The youngest bud of five,
25   The least lamb of the fold,—
Bud not to blossom, yet to thrive
Away from cold.

Lamb which we shall not see
Leap at its pretty pranks,
30   Our lamb at rest and full of glee
On heavenly banks.

A SICK CHILD'S MEDITATION

Pain and weariness, aching eyes and head,
   Pain and weariness all the day and night:
Yet the pillow's soft on my smooth soft bed,
   And fresh air blows in, and mother shades the light.

5   Thou, O Lord, in pain hadst no pillow soft,
   In Thy weary pain, in Thine agony:
But a cross of shame held Thee up aloft
   Where Thy very mother could do nought for Thee.

I would gaze on Thee, on Thy patient face;
10   Make me like Thyself, patient, sweet, at peace;

Make my days all love, and my nights all praise,
    Till all days and nights and patient sufferings cease.

Love is all happiness, love is all beauty,
    Love is the crown of flaxen heads and hoary,
Love is the only everlasting duty,
    And love is chronicled in endless story
5   And kindles endless glory.

A handy Mole who plied no shovel
To excavate his vaulted hovel,
While hard at work met in mid-furrow
An Earthworm boring out his burrow.
5   Our Mole had dined and must grow thinner
Before he gulped a second dinner,
And on no other terms cared he
To meet a worm of low degree.
The Mole turned on his blindest eye
10   Passing that base mechanic by;
The Worm entrenched in actual blindness
Ignored or kindness or unkindness;
Each wrought his own exclusive tunnel
To reach his own exclusive funnel.

15   A plough its flawless track pursuing
Involved them in one common ruin.
Where now the mine and countermine,
The dined-on and the one to dine?
The impartial ploughshare of extinction
20   Annulled them all without distinction.

"One swallow does not make a summer."

A Rose which spied one swallow
Made haste to blush and blow:
"Others are sure to follow:"
Ah no, not so!

5   The wandering clouds still owe
    A few fresh flakes of snow,
    Chill fog must fill the hollow,
    Before the bird-stream flow
    In flood across the main
10   And winter's woe
    End in glad summer come again.
    Then thousand flowers may blossom by the shore,
    But that Rose never more.

    Contemptuous of his home beyond
    The village and the village pond,
    A large-souled Frog who spurned each byeway,
    Hopped along the imperial highway.

5   Nor grunting pig nor barking dog
    Could disconcert so great a frog.
    The morning dew was lingering yet
    His sides to cool, his tongue to wet;
    The night dew when the night should come
10   A travelled frog would send him home.

    Not so, alas! the wayside grass
    Sees him no more:—not so, alas!

    A broadwheeled waggon unawares
    Ran him down, his joys, his cares.
15   From dying choke one feeble croak
    The Frog's perpetual silence broke:
    "Ye buoyant Frogs, ye great and small,
    Even I am mortal after all.
    My road to Fame turns out a wry way:
20   I perish on this hideous highway,—
    Oh for my old familiar byeway!"

    The choking Frog sobbed and was gone:
    The waggoner strode whistling on.

    Unconscious of the carnage done,
25   Whistling that waggoner strode on,
    Whistling (it may have happened so)

"A Froggy would a-wooing go:"
A hypothetic frog trolled he
Obtuse to a reality.

30   O rich and poor, O great and small,
Such oversights beset us all:
The mangled frog abides incog,
The uninteresting actual frog;
The hypothetic frog alone
35   Is the one frog we dwell upon.

A Word for the Dumb.

Pity the sorrows of a poor old Dog
    Who wags his tail a-begging in his need:
Despise not even the sorrows of a Frog,
    God's creature too, and that's enough to plead:
5   Spare Puss who trusts us purring on our hearth:
    Spare Bunny once so frisky and so free:
Spare all the harmless tenants of the earth:
    Spare, and be spared:—or who shall plead for thee?

CARDINAL NEWMAN.
"In the grave, whither thou goest."

O weary Champion of the Cross, lie still:
    Sleep thou at length the all-embracing sleep:
    Long was thy sowing day, rest now and reap:
Thy fast was long, feast now thy spirit's fill.
5   Yea, take thy fill of love, because thy will
    Chose love not in the shallows but the deep:
    Thy tides were springtides, set against the neap
Of calmer souls: thy flood rebuked their rill.
Now night has come to thee—please God, of rest:
10   So some time must it come to every man;

To first and last, where many last are first.
Now fixed and finished thine eternal plan,
Thy best has done its best, thy worst its worst:
Thy best its best, please God, thy best its best.

An Echo from Willowwood.
"O ye, all ye that walk in Willowwood."
D. G. Rossetti.

Two gazed into a pool, he gazed and she,
   Not hand in hand, yet heart in heart, I think,
   Pale and reluctant on the water's brink,
As on the brink of parting which must be.
5   Each eyed the other's aspect, she and he,
   Each felt one hungering heart leap up and sink,
   Each tasted bitterness which both must drink,
There on the brink of life's dividing sea.
Lilies upon the surface, deep below
10   Two wistful faces craving each for each,
   Resolute and reluctant without speech:—
A sudden ripple made the faces flow
   One moment joined, to vanish out of reach:
   So those hearts joined, and ah! were parted so.

"YEA, I HAVE A GOODLY HERITAGE."

My vineyard that is mine I have to keep,
   Pruning for fruit the pleasant twigs and leaves.
Tend thou thy cornfield: one day thou shalt reap
   In joy thy ripened sheaves.

5   Or if thine be an orchard, graft and prop
   Food-bearing trees each watered in its place:
Or if a garden, let it yield for crop
   Sweet herbs and herb of grace.

But if my lot be sand where nothing grows?—
10   Nay, who hath said it? Tune a thankful psalm:
For tho' thy desert bloom not as the rose,
     It yet can rear thy palm.

A Death of a First-born.
JANUARY 14th, 1892.

One young life lost, two happy young lives blighted,
     With earthward eyes we see:
With eyes uplifted, keener, farther-sighted,
     We look, O Lord, to Thee.

5   Grief hears a funeral knell: hope hears the ringing
     Of birthday bells on high;
Faith, hope, and love make answer with soft singing,
     Half carol and half cry.

Stoop to console us, Christ, Sole Consolation,
10   While dust returns to dust;
Until that blessed day when all Thy Nation
     Shall rise up of the Just.

"FAINT, YET PURSUING."

1.

Beyond this shadow and this turbulent sea,
     Shadow of death and turbulent sea of death,
Lies all we long to have or long to be:—
     Take heart, tired man, toil on with lessening breath,
5   Lay violent hands on heaven's high treasury,
     Be what you long to be thro' life-long scathe:
A little while hope leans on charity,
     A little while charity heartens faith.
A little while: and then what further while?
10   One while that ends not and that wearies not,
     For ever new whilst evermore the same:
     All things made new bear each a sweet new name;

Man's lot of death has turned to life his lot,
And tearful charity to love's own smile.

2.

Press onward, quickened souls, who mounting move,
  Press onward, upward, fire with mounting fire;
  Gathering volume of untold desire
Press upward, homeward, dove with mounting dove.
5 Point me the excellent way that leads above;
  Woo me with sequent will, me too to aspire;
  With sequent heart to follow higher and higher,
To follow all who follow on to love.
Up the high steep, across the golden sill,
10   Up out of shadows into very light,
    Up out of dwindling life to life aglow,
  I watch you, my beloved, out of sight;—
Sight fails me, and my heart is watching still:
  My heart fails, yet I follow on to know.

What will it be, O my soul, what will it be
To touch the long-raced-for goal, to handle and see,
To rest in the joy of joys, in the joy of the blest,
To rest and revive and rejoice, to rejoice and to rest!

Lord, Thou art fulness, I am emptiness:
Yet hear my heart speak in its speechlessness
Extolling Thine unuttered loveliness.

O Lord, I cannot plead my love of Thee:
I plead Thy love of me;—
The shallow conduit hails the unfathomed sea.

Faith and Hope are wings to Love,
Silver wings to golden dove.

A SORROWFUL SIGH OF A PRISONER.

Lord, comest Thou to me?
  My heart is cold and dead:
Alas that such a heart should be
  The place to lay Thy head!

"I sit a queen, and am no widow, and shall see no
            sorrow"—
Yea, scarlet woman, today: but not yea at all tomorrow.
Scarlet queen on a scarlet throne all today without sorrow,
Bethink thee: today must end; there is no end of
            tomorrow.

Passing away the bliss,
  The anguish passing away:
Thus it is
    Today.

5   Clean past away the sorrow,
  The pleasure brought back to stay:
Thus and this
    Tomorrow.

Love builds a nest on earth and waits for rest,
Love sends to heaven the warm heart from its breast,
Looks to be blest and is already blest,
And testifies: "God's Will is alway best."

Jesus alone:—if thus it were to me;
Yet thus it cannot be;
Lord, I have all things if I have but Thee.

Jesus and all:—precious His bounties are,
5   Yet He more precious far;
Day's-eyes are many, one the Morning Star.

Jesus my all:—so let me rest in love,
Thy peaceable poor dove,
Some time below till timeless time above.

The Way of the World.

A boat that sails upon the sea;
   Sails far and far and far away:
Who sail in her sing songs of glee,
   Or watch and pray.

5 A boat that drifts upon the sea
   Silent and void to sun and air:
Who sailed in her have ended glee
   And watch and prayer.

BOOKS IN THE RUNNING BROOKS.

"It is enough, enough," one said,
   At play among the flowers:
"I spy a rose upon the thorn,
   A rainbow in the showers;
5 I hear a merry chime of bells
   Ring out the passing hours."—
     Soft springs the fountain
       From the daisied ground:
     Softly falling on the moss
10   Without a sound.

"It is enough," she said, and fixed
   Calm eyes upon the sky:
"I watch a flitting tender cloud
   Just like a dove go by;
15 A lark is rising from the grass;
   A wren is building nigh."—
     Softly the fountain
       Threads its silver way,

        Screened by the scented bloom
20   Of whitest may.

"Enough?" she whispered to herself,
   As doubting: "Is it so?
Enough to wear the roses fair?
   Oh sweetest flowers that blow:—
25 Oh yes, it surely is enough,
   My happy home below."—
      A shadow stretcheth
        From the hither shore:
      Those waters darken
30   More and more and more.

"It is enough," she says; but with
   A listless, weary moan:
"Enough," if mixing with her friends;
   "Enough," if left alone.
35 But to herself: "Not yet enough,
   This suffering, to atone?"—
      The cold black waters
        Seem to stagnate there;
      Without a single wave,
40   Or breath of air.

And now she says: "It is enough,"
   Half languid and half stirred:
"Enough," to silence and to sound,
   Thorn, blossom, soaring bird:
45 "Enough," she says; but with a lack
   Of something in the word.—
      Defiled and turbid
        See the waters pass;
      Half light, half shadow,
50   Struggling thro' the grass.

Ah, will it ever dawn, that day
   When calm for good or ill
Her heart shall say: "It is enough,
   For Thou art with me still;

55   It is enough, O Lord my God,
        Thine only blessed Will."—
          Then shall the fountain sing
          And flow to rest;
          Clear as the sun track
60   To the purple West.

GONE BEFORE

She was most like a rose, when it flushes rarest;
She was most like a lily, when it blows fairest;
She was most like a violet, sweetest on the bank:
Now she's only like the snow cold and blank
5   After the sun sank.

She left us in the early days, she would not linger
For orange blossoms in her hair, or ring on finger:
Did she deem windy grass more good than these?
Now the turf that's between us and the hedging trees
10   Might as well be seas.

I had trained a branch she shelters not under,
I had reared a flower she snapped asunder:
In the bush and on the stately bough
Birds sing; she who watched them track the plough
15   Cannot hear them now.

Every bird has a nest hidden somewhere
For itself and its mate and joys that come there,
Tho' it soar to the clouds, finding there its rest:
You sang in the height, but no more with eager breast
20   Stoop to your own nest.

If I could win you back from heaven-gate lofty,
Perhaps you would but grieve returning softly:
Surely they would miss you in the blessed throng,
Miss your sweet voice in their sweetest song,
25   Reckon time too long.

Earth is not good enough for you, my sweet, my sweetest;
Life on earth seemed long to you tho' to me fleetest.
I would not wish you back if a wish would do:
Only love I long for heaven with you
30   Heart-pierced thro' and thro'.

II *Privately Printed Poems*

THE DEAD CITY.

Once I rambled in a wood
With a careless hardihood,
Heeding not the tangled way;
Labyrinths around me lay,
5   But for them I never stood.

On, still on, I wandered on,
And the sun above me shone;
And the birds around me winging
With their everlasting singing
10   Made me feel not quite alone.

In the branches of the trees,
Murmured like the hum of bees
The low sound of happy breezes,
Whose sweet voice that never ceases
15   Lulls the heart to perfect ease.

Streamlets bubbled all around
On the green and fertile ground,
Thro' the rushes and the grass,
Like a sheet of liquid glass,
20   With a soft and trickling sound.

And I went, I went on faster,
Contemplating no disaster;
And I plucked ripe blackberries,
But the birds with envious eyes
25   Came and stole them from their master:

For the birds here were all tame;
Some with bodies like a flame,

Some that glanced the branches thro'
Pure and colourless as dew;
30   Fearlessly to me they came.

Before me no mortal stood
In the mazes of that wood;
Before me the birds had never
Seen a man, but dwelt for ever
35   In a happy solitude;

Happy solitude, and blest
With beatitude of rest;
Where the woods are ever vernal,
And the life and joy eternal,
40   Without Death's or Sorrow's test.

Oh most blessed solitude!
Oh most full beatitude!
Where are quiet without strife,
And imperishable life,
45   Nothing marred, and all things good.

And the bright sun, life begetting,
Never rising, never setting,
Shining warmly overhead,
Nor too pallid, nor too red,
50   Lulled me to a sweet forgetting,

Sweet forgetting of the time:
And I listened for no chime
Which might warn me to begone;
But I wandered on, still on,
55   'Neath the boughs of oak and lime.

Know I not how long I strayed
In the pleasant leafy shade;
But the trees had gradually
Grown more rare, the air more free,
60   The sun hotter overhead.

Soon the birds no more were seen
Glancing thro' the living green;

And a blight had passed upon
All the trees; and the pale sun
65   Shone with a strange lurid sheen.

Then a darkness spread around:
I saw nought, I heard no sound;
Solid darkness overhead,
With a trembling cautious tread
70   Passed I o'er the unseen ground.

But at length a pallid light
Broke upon my searching sight;
A pale solitary ray,
Like a star at dawn of day
75   Ere the sun is hot and bright.

Towards its faintly glimmering beam
I went on as in a dream;
A strange dream of hope and fear!
And I saw as I drew near
80   'Twas in truth no planet's gleam;

But a lamp above a gate
Shone in solitary state
O'er a desert drear and cold,
O'er a heap of ruins old,
85   O'er a scene most desolate.

By that gate I entered lone
A fair city of white stone;
And a lovely light to see
Dawned, and spread most gradually
90   Till the air grew warm and shone.

Thro' the splendid streets I strayed
In that radiance without shade,
Yet I heard no human sound;
All was still and silent round
95   As a city of the dead.

All the doors were open wide;
Lattices on every side

In the wind swung to and fro;
Wind that whispered very low:
100 Go and see the end of pride.

With a fixed determination
Entered I each habitation,
But they all were tenantless;
All was utter loneliness,
105 All was deathless desolation.

In the noiseless market-place
Was no care-worn busy face;
There were none to buy or sell,
None to listen or to tell,
110 In this silent emptiness.

Thro' the city on I went
Full of awe and wonderment;
Still the light around me shone,
And I wandered on, still on,
115 In my great astonishment,

Till at length I reached a place
Where amid an ample space
Rose a palace for a king;
Golden was the turreting,
120 And of solid gold the base.

The great porch was ivory,
And the steps were ebony;
Diamond and chrysoprase
Set the pillars in a blaze,
125 Capitalled with jewelry.

None was there to bar my way—
And the breezes seemed to say:
Touch not these, but pass them by,
Pressing onwards: therefore I
130 Entered in and made no stay.

All around was desolate:
I went on; a silent state

Reigned in each deserted room,
And I hastened thro' the gloom
135   Till I reached an outer gate.

Soon a shady avenue
Blossom-perfumed, met my view.
Here and there the sun-beams fell
On pure founts, whose sudden swell
140   Up from marble basins flew.

Every tree was fresh and green;
Not a withered leaf was seen
Thro' the veil of flowers and fruit;
Strong and sapful were the root,
145   The top boughs, and all between.

Vines were climbing everywhere
Full of purple grapes and fair:
And far off I saw the corn
With its heavy head down borne,
150   By the odour-laden air.

Who shall strip the bending vine?
Who shall tread the press for wine?
Who shall bring the harvest in
When the pallid ears begin
155   In the sun to glow and shine?

On I went, alone, alone,
Till I saw a tent that shone
With each bright and lustrous hue;
It was trimmed with jewels too,
160   And with flowers; not one was gone.

Then the breezes whispered me:
Enter in, and look, and see
How for luxury and pride
A great multitude have died:—
165   And I entered tremblingly.

Lo, a splendid banquet laid
In the cool and pleasant shade.

Mighty tables, every thing
Of sweet Nature's furnishing
170 That was rich and rare, displayed;

And each strange and luscious cate
Practised Art makes delicate;
With a thousand fair devices
Full of odours and of spices;
175 And a warm voluptuous state.

All the vessels were of gold
Set with gems of worth untold.
In the midst a fountain rose
Of pure milk, whose rippling flows
180 In a silver basin rolled.

In green emerald baskets were
Sun-red apples, streaked, and fair;
Here the nectarine and peach
And ripe plum lay, and on each
185 The bloom rested every where.

Grapes were hanging overhead,
Purple, pale, and ruby-red;
And in panniers all around
Yellow melons shone, fresh found,
190 With the dew upon them spread.

And the apricot and pear
And the pulpy fig were there;
Cherries and dark mulberries,
Bunchy currants, strawberries,
195 And the lemon wan and fair.

And unnumbered others too,
Fruits of every size and hue,
Juicy in their ripe perfection,
Cool beneath the cool reflection
200 Of the curtains' skyey blue.

All the floor was strewn with flowers
Fresh from sunshine and from showers,

Roses, lilies, jessamine;
And the ivy ran between
205 Like a thought in happy hours.

And this feast too lacked no guest
With its warm delicious rest;
With its couches softly sinking,
And its glow, not made for thinking,
210 But for careless joy at best.

Many banquetters were there,
Wrinkled age, the young, the fair;
In the splendid revelry
Flushing cheek and kindling eye
215 Told of gladness without care.

Yet no laughter rang around,
Yet they uttered forth no sound;
With the smile upon his face
Each sat moveless in his place,
220 Silently, as if spell-bound.

The low whispering voice was gone,
And I felt awed and alone.
In my great astonishment
To the feasters up I went—
225 Lo, they all were turned to stone.

Yea they all were statue-cold,
Men and women, young and old;
With the life-like look and smile
And the flush; and all the while
230 The hard fingers kept their hold.

Here a little child was sitting
With a merry glance, befitting
Happy age and heedless heart;
There a young man sat apart
235 With a forward look unweeting.

Nigh them was a maiden fair;
And the ringlets of her hair

Round her slender fingers twined;
And she blushed as she reclined,
240   Knowing that her love was there.

Here a dead man sat to sup,
In his hand a drinking cup;
Wine cup of the heavy gold,
Human hand stony and cold,
245   And no life-breath struggling up.

There a mother lay, and smiled
Down upon her infant child;
Happy child and happy mother
Laughing back to one another
250   With a gladness undefiled.

Here an old man slept, worn out
With the revelry and rout;
Here a strong man sat and gazed
On a girl, whose eyes upraised
255   No more wandered round about.

And none broke the stillness, none;
I was the sole living one.
And methought that silently
Many seemed to look on me
260   With strange stedfast eyes that shone.

Full of fear I would have fled;
Full of fear I bent my head,
Shutting out each stony guest:—
When I looked again the feast
265   And the tent had vanished.

Yes, once more I stood alone
Where the happy sunlight shone
And a gentle wind was sighing,
And the little birds were flying,
270   And the dreariness was gone.

All these things that I have said
Awed me, and made me afraid.

What was I that I should see
So much hidden mystery?
275 And I straightway knelt and prayed.

The Water Spirit's Song.

In the silent hour of even,
When the stars are in the heaven,
When in the azure cloudless sky
The moon beams forth all lustrously,
5 When over hill and over vale
Is wafted the sweet-scented gale,
When murmurs thro' the forest trees
The cool, refreshing, evening breeze,
When the nightingale's wild melody
10 Is waking herb and flower and tree,
From their perfumed and soft repose,
To list the praises of the rose;
When the ocean sleeps deceitfully,
When the waves are resting quietly,
15 I spread my bright wings, and fly far away
To my beautiful sister's mansion gay:
I leave behind me rock and mountain,
I leave behind me rill and fountain,
And I dive far down in the murmuring sea,
20 Where my fair sister welcomes me joyously;
For she's Queen of Ocean for ever and ever,
And I of each fountain and still lake and river.

She dwells in a palace of coral
Of diamond and pearl;
25 And in each jewelled chamber the fishes
Their scaly length unfurl;
And the sun can dart no light
On the depths beneath the sea;
But the ruby there shines bright
30 And sparkles brilliantly;

No mortal e'er trod on the surface
    Of the adamantine floor;
No human being e'er passed the bound
    Of the pearl-encrusted door.
35 But the mermaidens sing plaintively
    Beneath the deep blue ocean,
And to their song the green fishes dance
    With undulating motion.
And the cold bright moon looks down on us
40   With her fixed unchanging smile;
'Neath her chilly glance the mermaids dance
    Upon each coral isle;
And her beams she laves in the briny waves
    With loving constancy;
45 And she never ceases with light caresses
    To soothe the swelling sea;
All night on us she softly shines
    With a fond and tender gaze,
Till the sun blushes red from his ocean bed
50   And sends forth his warming rays.
And then she flies to other skies
    Till the sun has run his race,
And again the day to the night's soft sway
    To the moon and stars gives place.

55 And when the bright sun doth arise,
To tinge with gold the vaulted skies,
When the nightingale no longer sings,
And the blush rose forth its odour flings,
When the breath of morn is rustling through
60 The trees, and kissing away the dew,
When the sea casts up its foam and spray,
And greets the fresh gale that speeds away,
I fly back to my home in the rushing cascade—
By the silvery streamlet my dark hair I braid,
65 And then when the sun once more sinks in the ocean,
I glide with a floating and passionless motion,
To my sister 'neath the boundless sea
And with her till morn dwell joyously.

The Song of the Star.

I am a star dwelling on high
In the azure of the vaulted sky.
I shine on the land and I shine on the sea,
And the little breezes talk to me.
5   The waves rise towards me every one
And forget the brightness of the sun:
The growing grass springs up towards me
And forgets the day's fertility.
My face is light, and my beam is life,
10 And my passionless being hath no strife.
In me no love is turned to hate,
No fulness is made desolate;
Here is no hope, no fear, no grief,
Here is no pain and no relief;
15 Nor birth nor death hath part in me,
But a profound tranquillity.
The blossoms that bloomed yesterday
Unaltered shall bloom on today,
And on the morrow shall not fade.
20 Within the everlasting shade
The fountain gushing up for ever
Flows on to the eternal river,
That, running by a reedy shore,
Bubbles, bubbles evermore.
25 The happy birds sing in the trees
To the music of the southern breeze;
And they fear no lack of food,
Chirping in the underwood;
For ripe seeds and berried bushes
30 Serve the finches and the thrushes,
And all feathered fowls that dwell
In that shade majestical.
Beyond all clouds and all mistiness
I float in the strength of my loveliness;
35 And I move round the sun with a measured motion
In the blue expanse of the skyey ocean;
And I hear the song of the Angel throng

In a river of extasy flow along,
Without a pausing, without a hushing,
40   Like an everlasting fountain's gushing
That of its own will bubbles up
From a white untainted cup.
Countless planets float round me
Differing all in majesty;
45   Smaller some, and some more great,
Amethystine, roseate,
Golden, silvery, glowing blue,
Hueless, and of every hue.
Each and all, both great and small,
50   With a cadence musical,
Shoot out rays of glowing praise,
Never ending, but always
Hymning the Creator's might
Who hath filled them full of light.
55   Pealing through eternity,
Filling out immensity,
Sun and moon and stars together,
In heights where is no cloudy weather;
Where is nor storm, nor mist, nor rain;
60   Where night goeth not to come again.
On, and on, and on for ever,
Never ceasing, sinking never,
Voiceless adorations rise
To the Heaven above the skies.
65   We all chant with a holy harmony,
No discord marreth our melody;
Here are no strifes nor envyings,
But each with love joyously sings,
For ever and ever floating free
70   In the azure light of infinity.

Summer.

Hark to the song of greeting! the tall trees
Murmur their welcome in the southern breeze.

Amid the thickest foliage many a bird
Sits singing, their shrill matins scarcely heard
5   One by one, but all together
Welcoming the sunny weather.
In every bower hums a bee
Fluttering melodiously.
Murmurs joy in every brook,
10   Rippling with a pleasant look.
What greet they with their guileless bliss?
What welcome with a song like this?

See in the south a radiant form,
        Her fair head crowned with roses;
15   From her bright foot-path flies the storm;
        Upon her breast reposes
Many an unconfinèd tress,
Golden, glossy, motionless.
Face and form are love and light,
20   Soft ineffably, yet bright.
All her path is strewn with flowers,
Round her float the laughing Hours,
Heaven and earth make joyful din,
Welcoming sweet Summer in.

25   And now she alights on the Earth
        To play with her children the flowers;
She touches the stems, and the buds have birth,
        And gently she trains them in bowers.
And the bees and the birds are glad,
30   And the wind catches warmth from her breath,
And around her is nothing sad,
        Nor any traces of death.
See now she lays her down
With roses for her crown,
35   With jessamine and myrtle
Forming her fragrant kirtle;
Conquered by softest slumbers
No more the hours she numbers,
The hours that intervene
40   Ere she may wing her flight

Far from this smiling scene
With all her love and light,
And leave the flowers and the summer bowers
To wither in autumn and winter hours.

45   And must they wither then?
Their life and their perfume
Sinking so soon again
Into their earthy tomb?
Let us bind her as she lies
50   Ere the fleeting moment flies;
Hand, and foot and arm and bosom,
With a chain of bud and blossom;
Twine red roses round her hands,
Round her feet twine myrtle bands.
55   Heap up flowers higher, higher,
Tulips like a glowing fire,
Clematis of milky whiteness,
Sweet geraniums' varied brightness,
Honeysuckle, commeline,
60   Roses, myrtles, jessamine;
Heap them higher, bloom on bloom,
Bury her as in a tomb.

But alas! they are withered all,
And how can dead flowers bind her?
65   She pushes away her pall,
And she leaves the dead behind her:
And she flies across the seas
To gladden for a time
The blossoms and the bees
70   Of some far distant clime.

To my Mother on her Birthday.

Today's your natal day
Sweet flowers I bring;
Mother accept I pray,
My offering.

5   And may you happy live,
      And long us bless;
    Receiving as you give
      Great happiness.

The Ruined Cross.

She wreathed bright flower-wreaths in her hair,
    And all men smiled as she passed by:
And she smiled too, for now she knew
    That her last hour was nigh.

5   Soft radiance shone upon her path,
      Her step was fearless, free and light;
Her cheek was flushed with burning red,
      Her azure eye was bright.

On, on, still on, she hurried on,
10   For in the wind she heard a knell,
And to her ear the water's splash
    Was as a dying bell.

And in the flowers she saw decay,
    And saw decay in every tree;
15   And change was written on the sun,
    And change upon the sea.

She might not pause upon the road,
    Lest Death should claim his promised bride
Ere yet her longing was fulfilled,
20   Her young heart satisfied.

The sun arose, the sun went down,
    The moonbeams on the waters shone
How many times! yet paused she not,
    But ever journeyed on.

25   And still, tho' toilsome was the way,
    The colour flushed her sunken cheek;
Nor dimmed the azure of her eye,
    Nor waxed her purpose weak.

At length she reached a lonely spot, . . .
30   Why trembled she? why turned she pale?
A ruined Cross stood in the midst
    Of a most quiet vale.

A Cross o'ergrown with moss and flowers,
    A cross fast sinking to decay;
35   The Cross she knew, the Cross she loved
    In childhood's happy day.

And she had journeyed many miles,
    Morning and eve untiringly,
To look again upon that Cross,
40   To look again and die.

She knelt within its sacred shade,
    And hung her garland on the stone;
Her azure eyes were bright with tears
    Of love and joy unknown.

45   And there she knelt, and there she prayed
    Until her heart was satisfied;—
The ancient Cross is standing yet,
    The youthful wanderer died.

Eva.

(From Maturin's "Woman.")

Yes, I loved him all too well,
    And my punishment is just,
But its greatness who can tell?
    Still I have a stedfast trust
5   That the sorrow shall not last,
And the trial shall be past,
And my faith shall anchor fast.

Lord, Thou knowest, I have said,
    All is good that comes from Thee;
10   Unto Thee I bow my head.
    I have not repented me.

Still, oh! still 'tis bitter ill;
Still I have a stubborn will,
And my heart is haughty still:

15 Haughty in its humbleness;
        Proud in its idolatry;
    Let the loved heel gall and press
        On my neck: so it should be.
    'Twas in madness that I spake it:
20 Let him leave my heart or take it,
    Let him heal my heart or break it;

    But it still shall be for him,
        It shall love him only still.—
    Nay, it was no passing whim,
25   But a woman's stedfast will.
    And this word is aye returning:
    And I cannot quell the yearning
    That in breast and brain is burning.

    Tears of mine may quench it never,
30   Bitter tears shed all alone;
    Dropping, dropping, dropping ever
        For the thought of him that's gone:
    Dropping when none see or know.
    Woe is me! they only flow
35 For the joys of long ago.

    Foolish one, were it not fitter
        For thyself to mourn and pray?
    Tho' thy Father's cup be bitter,
        Put it not from thee away.
40 It is good and meet and right.
    Yea, if darksome be the night,
    The day dawn shall be more bright.

    Hast thou too much time, in sooth,
        For the work of penitence,
45 That thou wastest tears and youth
        Mourning one who is gone hence?
    For thyself cry out and weep

Ere that thou lie down and sleep,
And for ever silence keep.

50 Humbly strive to enter in
        By the strait and narrow gate;
    Strive the courts of Heaven to win,
        Where nought maketh desolate;
    Where are none to come and go;
55 Where no tears may ever flow;
    Where nor death may be, nor woe.

    And in prayer think thou of him
        Who hath left thee sad and lone.
    Pray that earth's light may grow dim,
60   So to him Heaven's light be shown.
    Pray that, all thy sins forgiven,
    Pray that, from his errors shriven,
    Ye may meet at length in Heaven.

Love ephemeral.

    Love is sweet, and so are flowers
    Blooming in bright summer bowers;
    So are waters, clear and pure,
    In some hidden fountain's store;
5   So is the soft southern breeze
    Sighing low among the trees;
    So is the bright queen of heaven,
    Reigning in the quiet even:
    Yet the pallid moon may breed
10 Madness in man's feeble seed;
    And the wind's soft influence
    Often breathes the pestilence;
    And the waves may sullied be
    As they hurry to the sea;
15 Flowers soon must fade away—
    Love endures but for a day.

Burial Anthem.

Flesh of our flesh—bone of our bone—
  (For thou and we in Christ are one)
Thy soul unto its rest hath flown,
And thou has left us all alone
5   Our weary race to run
In doubt, and want, and sin, and pain,
Whilst thou wilt never sin again.
For us remaineth heaviness;
Thou never more shalt feel distress,
10   For thou hast found repose
Beside the bright eternal river
That clear and pure flows on for ever,
  And sings as on it flows.
And it is better far for thee
15   To reach at once thy rest,
Than share with us earth's misery,
  Or tainted joy at best;
Brother, we will not mourn for thee,
  Although our hearts be weary
20 Of struggling with our enemy,
  When all around is dreary.
But we will pray that still we may
Press onward in the narrow way
With a calm thankful resignation,
25 And joy in this our desolation.
And we will hope at length to be
With our Great Head, and, friend! with thee
  Beside that river blest.

Sappho.

I sigh at day-dawn, and I sigh
When the dull day is passing by.
I sigh at evening, and again
I sigh when night brings sleep to men.

5   Oh! it were better far to die
     Than thus for ever mourn and sigh,
     And in death's dreamless sleep to be
     Unconscious that none weep for me;
     Eased from my weight of heaviness,
10   Forgetful of forgetfulness,
     Resting from pain and care and sorrow
     Thro' the long night that knows no morrow;
     Living unloved, to die unknown,
     Unwept, untended and alone.

Tasso and Leonora.

A glorious vision hovers o'er his soul,
    Gilding the prison and the weary bed
    Though hard the pillow placed beneath his head;
Though brackish be the water in the bowl
5   Beside him; he can see the planets roll
    In glowing adoration, without dread;
    Knowing how, by unerring wisdom led,
They struggle not against the strong control.
When suddenly a star shoots from the skies,
10   Than all the other stars more purely bright,
Replete with heavenly loves and harmonies;
    He starts:—what meets his full awakening sight?
Lo! Leonora with large humid eyes,
    Gazing upon him in the misty light.

ON THE DEATH OF A CAT,
A FRIEND OF MINE, AGED TEN YEARS AND A HALF.

Who shall tell the lady's grief
When her Cat was past relief?
Who shall number the hot tears
Shed o'er her, beloved for years?

5   Who shall say the dark dismay
     Which her dying caused that day?

     Come, ye Muses, one and all,
     Come obedient to my call.
     Come and mourn, with tuneful breath,
10   Each one for a separate death;
     And while you in numbers sigh,
     I will sing her elegy.

     Of a noble race she came,
     And Grimalkin was her name.
15   Young and old full many a mouse
     Felt the prowess of her house:
     Weak and strong full many a rat
     Cowered beneath her crushing pat:
     And the birds around the place
20   Shrank from her too close embrace.
     But one night, reft of her strength,
     She laid down and died at length:
     Lay a kitten by her side,
     In whose life the mother died.
25   Spare her line and lineage,
     Guard her kitten's tender age,
     And that kitten's name as wide
     Shall be known as her's that died.

     And whoever passes by
30   The poor grave where Puss doth lie,
     Softly, softly let him tread,
     Nor disturb her narrow bed.

Mother and Child.

"What art thou thinking of," said the Mother,
   "What art thou thinking of my child?"
"I was thinking of Heaven," he answered her,
   And looked up in her face and smiled.

5   "And what didst thou think of Heaven?" she said;
        "Tell me, my little one!"
      "Oh . . , I thought that there the flowers never fade,
        That there never sets the sun."

      "And wouldst thou love to go thither, my child?
10   Thither wouldst thou love to go?
      And leave the pretty flowers that wither,
        And the sun that sets below?"

      "Oh, I would be glad to go there, mother,
        To go and live there now;
15   And I would pray for thy coming, mother,
        My mother, wouldst not thou?"

FAIR MARGARET.

"Fair Margaret sat in her bower window,
    Combing her yellow hair;
There she spied sweet William and his bride
    As they were a riding near."—*Old Ballad.*

      The faith of years is broken,
      The fate of years is spoken,
            Years past, and years to come;
      I pity and I scorn thee,
5   I would not now adorn me
            For thy false bridal home.

      Yet thou, perfidious wooer,
      Thou yet mayst be the ruer,
            For thou mayst meet with one
10   Who will not love thee really,
      But cast kind glances merely
            That thou mayst be undone.

      Soft eyes, and dark, and flashing,
      Thy hopes may yet be dashing,
15   Thou yet mayst be deceived;
      And then think on her sadly,

Whom once thou grievedst gladly,
   Ere thou thyself wast grieved.

And if despair should seize thee,
20 And urge thee to release thee
   From weariness and life,
Oh! think on her who'll languish,
Bearing the bitter anguish
   Of a heart's bitter strife.

25 For, though I may not love thee,
Though calm as heaven above me,
   My thoughts of thee must be,
I cannot break so lightly
The chain that bound me tightly,
30   *Once* bound my soul to thee.

Earth and Heaven.

Water calmly flowing,
Sun-light deeply glowing,
Swans some river riding,
That is gently gliding
5 By the fresh green rushes;
The sweet rose that blushes,
Hyacinths whose dow'r
Is both scent and flow'r,
Skylark's soaring motion,
10 Sun-rise from the ocean,
Jewels that lie sparkling
'Neath the waters darkling,
Sea-weed, coral, amber,
Flow'rs that climb and clamber,
15 Or more lowly flourish
Where the earth may nourish;
All these are beautiful,
Of beauty Earth is full:—
Say, to our promised Heaven
20 Can greater charms be given?

Yes; for aye in Heav'n doth dwell
Glowing, indestructible,
What here below finds tainted birth
In the corrupted sons of Earth;
25   For, filling there and satisfying
Man's soul unchanging and undying,
Earth's fleeting joys and beauties far above,
In Heaven is Love.

Love attacked.

Love is more sweet than flowers,
    But sooner dying;
Warmer than sunny hours,
    But faster flying;

5   Softer than music's whispers
    Springing with day
To murmur till the vespers,
    Then die away;

More kind than friendship's greeting,
10   But as untrue,
Brighter than hope, but fleeting
    More swiftly too;

Like breath of summer breezes
    Gently it sighs,
15   But soon, alas! one ceases,
    The other dies;

And like an inundation
    It leaves behind
An utter desolation
20   Of heart and mind.

Who then would court Love's presence,
    If here below
It can but be the essence
    Of restless woe?

25 Returned or unrequited
    'Tis still the same;
The flame was never lighted,
    Or sinks the flame.

Yet all, both fools and sages,
30   Have felt its power,
In distant lands and ages,
    Here, at this hour.

Then what from fear and weeping
    Shall give me rest?
35 Oh tell me, ye who sleeping
    At length are blest!

In answer to my crying
    Sounds like incense
Rose from the earth, replying,
40   Indifference.

Love defended.

Who extols a wilderness?
    Who hath praised indifference?
Foolish one, thy words are sweet,
    But devoid of sense.

5 As the man who ne'er hath seen,
    Or as he who cannot hear,
Is the heart that hath no part
    In Love's hope and fear.

True, the blind do not perceive
10   The unsightly things around;
True, the deaf man trembleth not
    At an awful sound.

But the face of Heaven and Earth,
    And the murmur of the main,
15 Surely are a recompense
    For a little pain.

So, tho' Love may not be free
   Always from a taint of grief,
If its sting is very sharp,
20   Great is its relief.

Divine and Human Pleading.

"I would the saints could hear our prayers!
   If such a thing might be,
O blessed Mary Magdalene,
   I would appeal to thee!

5   "For once in lowly penitence
   Thy head was bowed with shame;
But now thou hast a glorious place,
   And hast an unknown name."

So mused a trembling contrite man,
10   So mused he wearily;
By angels borne his thoughts appeared
   Before the Throne on high.
      *   *   *   *   *   *
The calm, still night was at its noon,
   And all men were at rest,
15   When came before the sleeper's eyes
   A vision of the blest.

A woman stood beside his bed,
   Her breath was fragrance all;
Round her the light was very bright,
20   The air was musical.

Her footsteps shone upon the stars,
   Her robe was spotless white;
Her breast was radiant with the Cross,
   Her head with living light.

25   Her eyes beamed with a sacred fire;
   And on her shoulders fair,

From underneath her golden crown
    Clustered her golden hair.

Yet on her bosom her white hands
30   Were folded quietly;
Yet was her glorious head bowed low
    In deep humility.

Long time she looked upon the ground;
    Then raising her bright eyes
35   Her voice came forth as sweet and soft
    As music when it dies.

"O thou who in thy secret hour
    Hast dared to think that aught
Is faulty in God's perfect plan,
40   And perfect in thy thought!

"Thou who the pleadings would'st prefer
    Of one sin-stained like me
To His Who is the Lord of Life,
    To His Who died for thee!

45   "In mercy I am sent from Heaven:
    Be timely wise, and learn
To seek His love Who waits for thee,
    Inviting thy return.

"Well know I His long-suffering
50   And intercession's worth;
My guilt was as a heavy chain
    That bound me to the earth.

"It was a clog upon my feet,
    To keep me from Life's path;
55   It was a stain upon my hands,
    A curse upon my hearth.

"But there is mighty Power and Grace
    Can loose the heavy chain,
Can free the feet, can cleanse the hands,
60   Can purge the hearth again.

"Weeping I sought the Lord of Life,
    Bowed with my shame and sin;
And then unto my wondering heart
    Love's searching fire came in.

65   "It was with deep repentance,
    I knelt down at His Feet
Who can change the sorrow into joy,
    The bitter into sweet.

"I had cast away my jewels
70   And my rich attire;
And my breast was filled with a holy flame,
    And my heart with a holy fire.

"My tears were more precious
    Than my precious pearls;—
75   My tears that fell upon His Feet
    As I wiped Them with my curls.

"My youth and my beauty
    Were budding to their prime;
But I wept for the great transgression,
80   The sin of other time.

"Trembling betwixt hope and fear,
    I sought the King of Heaven;
Forsook the evil of my ways,
    Loved much, and was forgiven.

85   "In hope and fear I went to Him,
    He broke and healed my heart;
No man was there to intercede;
    As I was, so thou art."

TO MY FRIEND ELIZABETH.
with some Postage Stamps towards a collection.

Sweetest Elizabeth, accept I pray
These lowly stamps I send in homage true;

One hundred humble servants in their way
Are not to be despised, though poor to view.
5 Their livery of red and black, nor gay,
Nor sober all, is typical of you,
In whom are gravity and gladness mixed.
Thought here, smiles there; perfection lies betwixt.

AMORE E DOVERE.

Chiami il mio core
Crudele, altero,
No, non è vero,
    Crudel non è:
5 T'amo, t'amai,—
    E tu lo sai,—
    Men del dovere,
    Ma più di me.

    O ruscelletto,
10   Dì al Dio d'Amore
    Che questo petto,
    Che questo core,
    A lui ricetto
        Più non darà.
15 L'alme tradisce
    Senza rimorso;
    Non compatisce,
    Non dà soccorso,
    E si nudrisce
20   Di crudeltà.

    T'intendo, ti lagni,
        Mio povero core;
    T'intendo, l'amore
        Si lagna di me.
25 Deh! placati alfine;
    Mi pungon le spine
    Che vengon da te.

Amore e Dispetto.

O grande Amor possente
  Che reggi la mia mente,
  Odi l'umíl preghiera
  D'un tristo tuo fedel:
5 Deh fa che Lisa altiera
  Più non mi sia crudel.

Un giorno essendo stanco
  Posai sull' erba il fianco;
  Mesto pensando a quella
10 Che questo cor ferì,
Oh quanto sembò bella,
  Guardommi, e poi fuggì,

Quindì la vidi andare
  Con lievi passi al mare;
15 E parve sì pietosa
  Che dissi alfin: Chi sa!
Forse, non più sdegnosa,
  Verso di me sarà.

Timido allora io sorsi,
20 E ad incontrarla corsi;
  Mi vide, e gli occhi lenti
  Chinando, si arrossì;
Ed io sclamai: Deh senti,
  Lisa, pietà—così

25 Volea seguir; ma intanto
  Mi venne al ciglio il pianto;
  E mi confuse i detti
  Un tenero sospir;
Poi muto alquanto stetti,
30 Ed ella prese a dir:

Amar non voglio alcuno,
  E s'io volessi, l'uno
  Tu non saresti. E poi
  Tacendo, se ne andò.—

35   Se servo più mi vuoi,
     Amor, tu dei far ciò;

    Spirar le devi in core
     Sensi d'un puro amore;
     Chè se ciò far non puoi,
40   O se non vuoi ciò far,
     Io sprezzo i lacci tuoi,
     E più non voglio amar.

Love and Hope.

    Love for ever dwells in Heaven,
     Hope entereth not there.
    To despairing man Love's given,
     Hope dwells not with despair.
5   Love reigneth high, and reigneth low, and reigneth
     everywhere.

    In the inmost heart Love dwelleth,
     It may not quenchèd be;
    E'en when the life-blood welleth
     Its fond effects we see.
10   In the name that leaves the lips the last, fades last from
     memory.

    And when we shall awaken
     Ascending to the sky,
    Tho' Hope shall have forsaken,
     Sweet Love shall never die.
15   For perfect Love, and perfect bliss, shall be our lot on
     high.

Serenade.

Come, wander forth with me! the orange flowers
Breathe faintest perfume from the summer bowers.
Come, wander forth with me! the moon on high

Shines proudly in a flood of brilliancy.
5   Around her car each burning star
Gleams like a beacon from afar;
The night-wind scarce disturbs the sea
As it sighs forth so languidly,
Laden with sweetness like a bee;
10 And all is still, below, above,
Save murmurs of the turtle dove,
That murmurs ever of its love:
For now 'tis the hour, the balmy hour
When the strains of love have chiefly power;
15 When the maid looks forth from her latticed bower,
With a gentle yielding smile,
Donning her mantle all the while.
Now the moon beams down on high
From her halo brilliantly;
20 By the dark clouds unencumbered
That once o'er her pale face slumbered.
Far from her mild rays flutters Folly,
For on them floats calm Melancholy.
A passionless sadness without dread,
25 Like the thought of those we loved long dead,
Full of hope and chastened joy,
Heavenly without earth's alloy.
Listen, dearest! all is quiet,
Slumb'ring the world's toil and riot,
30 And all is fair in earth and sky and sea,
Come, wander forth with me!

The Rose.

Gentle, gentle river
    Hurrying along
With a sparkle ever,
    And a murmured song,
5   Pause in thine onward motion,
    Fast flowing toward the ocean,

And give this rose from me
To haughty Coralie.

Tell her that love's symbol,
10 The deep blushing rose,
Doth in all resemble
That it would disclose.
Untended, shortly thriving
There'll soon be no reviving;
15 But nursed with kindliness
'T will cheer life's wilderness.

Present and Future.

What is life that we should love it,
  Cherishing it evermore,
Never prizing aught above it,
  Ever loath to give it o'er?
5 Is it goodness? Is it gladness?
Nay, 'tis more of sin and sadness,
  Nay, of weariness 'tis more.

Earthly joys are very fleeting—
  Earthly sorrows very long;—
10 Parting ever follows meeting,
  Night succeeds to even-song.
Storms may darken in the morning,
And eclipse the sun's bright dawning,
  And the chilly gloom prolong.

15 But though clouds may screen and hide it
  The sun shines for evermore;
Then bear grief in hope: abide it,
  Knowing that it must give o'er:
And the darkness shall flee from us,
20 And the sun beam down upon us
  Ever glowing more and more.

WILL THESE HANDS NE'ER BE CLEAN?

And who is this lies prostrate at thy feet?
And is he dead, thou man of wrath and pride?
    Yes, now thy vengeance is complete,
        Thy hate is satisfied.
5   What had he done to merit this of thee?
Who gave thee power to take away his life?
    Oh deeply-rooted direful enmity
        That ended in long strife!
See where he grasped thy mantle as he fell,
10 Staining it with his blood; how terrible
Must be the payment due for this in hell!

And dost thou think to go and see no more
Thy bleeding victim, now the struggle's o'er?
    To find out peace in other lands,
15   And wash the red mark from thy hands?
It shall not be; for everywhere
He shall be with thee; and the air
Shall smell of blood, and on the wind
His groans pursue thee close behind.
20 When waking he shall stand before thee;
And when at length sleep shall come o'er thee,
    Powerless to move, alive to dream,
    So dreadful shall thy visions seem
    That thou shalt own them even to be
25   More hateful than reality
What time thou stoopest down to drink
Of limpid waters, thou shalt think
It is thy foe's blood bubbles up
From the polluted fountain's cup,
30 That stains thy lip, that cries to Heaven
For vengeance—and it shall be given.

And when thy friends shall question thee,
"Why art thou changed so heavily?"
Trembling and fearful thou shalt say
35 "I am not changed," and turn away;

For such an outcast shalt thou be
Thou wilt not dare ask sympathy.

And so thy life will pass, and day by day
The current of existence flow away;
40   And though to thee earth shall be hell, and breath
Vengeance, yet thou shalt tremble more at death.
And one by one thy friends will learn to fear thee,
And thou shalt live without a hope to cheer thee;
Lonely amid a thousand, chained though free,
45   The curse of memory shall cling to thee:
Ages may pass away, worlds rise and set—
   But thou shalt not forget.

SIR EUSTACE GREY.
See Crabbe.

When I die, oh lay me low
Where the greenest grasses grow;
Where the happy stream meanders;
Where the deer securely wanders;
5   Where the sweet birds sit and sing
In the branches quivering;
Where the violets spring to die,
And the breezes passing by,
Laden with their fragrant breath,
10   Scarcely seem to tell of death;
Where the sun can dart no ray
In the noon-tide of his day;
Where upon the fertile ground
   Broods an everlasting shade,
15   And a strange, mysterious sound
   By the rustling boughs is made,
And all's quiet, meet for one
Whose long, toilsome race is run.
O'er my grave the turf extend,
20   But beside me lay no friend,

And above me place no stone;
I would lie there all alone,
Unremembered or unknown.
Soon forgotten, none will taunt me;
25   Soon forgetting, none will haunt me
Of the ghosts of former pleasures
Meted out with scanty measures.
Resting from all human passion,
From earth's hate and its compassion,
30   From its hope and fear, from love
Stedfast as the stars above,
That shine clearly down for ever
On some cold, unglowing river;
By my faith and hope sure lighted
35   Through the darkness of the tomb;
And by Heavenly Love requited
For whatever love was slighted,
And whatever joy was blighted
By earth's coldness and its gloom,
40   In the grave I'll rest secure
Till the appointed time is o'er,
And the work of love is done,
And the great sin; and the sun
Sets in night to rise no more.
45   What is life but toil and riot?
What is death but rest and quiet?
Life is but a dream of trouble,
Death calm sleep from visions free;
Life is but a bursting bubble,
50   Death is immortality.

THE TIME OF WAITING.

Life is fleeting, joy is fleeting,
Coldness follows love and greeting,
Parting still succeeds to meeting.

If I say, "Rejoice today,"
5   Sorrow meets me in the way,
I cannot my will obey.

If I say, "My grief shall cease;
Now then I will live in peace:"
My cares instantly increase.

10   When I look up to the sky,
Thinking to see light on high,
Clouds my searching glance defy.

When I look upon the earth
For the flowers that should have birth,
15   I find dreariness and dearth.

And the wind sighs on for ever,
Murmurs still the flowing river,
On the graves the sun-beams quiver.

And destruction waxes bold,
20   And the earth is growing old,
And I tremble in the cold.

And my weariness increases
To an ache that never ceases,
And a pain that ne'er decreases.

25   And the times are turbulent,
And the Holy Church is rent,
And who tremble or repent?

And loud cries do ever rise
To the portals of the skies
30   From our earthly miseries;

From love slighted, not requited;
From high hope that should have lighted
All our path up, now benighted;

From the woes of human kind;
35   From the darkness of the mind;
From all anguish undefined;

From the heart that's crushed and sinking;
From the brain grown blank with thinking;
From the spirit sorrow drinking.

40 All cry out with pleading strong:
"Vengeance, Lord; how long, how long
Shall we suffer this great wrong?"

And the pleading and the cry
Of earth's sons are heard on high,
45 And are noted verily.

When this world shall be no more,
The Oppressors shall endure
The great Vengeance, which is sure.

And the sinful shall remain
50 To an endless death and pain;
But the good shall live again,

Never more to be oppressed;
Balm shall heal the bleeding breast,
And the weary be at rest.

55 All shall vanish of dejection,
Grief, and fear, and imperfection,
In that glorious Resurrection.

Heed not then a night of sorrow,
If the dawning of the morrow
60 From past grief fresh beams shall borrow.

Thankful for whate'er is given,
Strive we, as we ne'er have striven,
For love's sake to be forgiven.

Then, the dark clouds opening,
65 Ev'n to us the sun shall bring
Gladness; and sweet flowers shall spring.

For Christ's guiding Love alway,
For the everlasting Day,
For meek patience, let us pray.

Charity.

I praised the myrtle and the rose,
    At sunrise in their beauty vying;
I passed them at the short day's close,
    And both were dying.

5   The summer sun his rays was throwing
    Brightly; yet ere I sought my rest,
His last cold ray, more deeply glowing,
    Died in the west.

After this bleak world's stormy weather,
10   All, all, save Love alone, shall die;
For Faith and Hope shall merge together
    In Charity.

The Dead Bride.

There she lay so still and pale,
    With her bridal robes around her:
Joy is fleeting—life is frail—
    Death had found her.

5   Gone for ever: gone away
    From the love and light of earth;
Gone for ever: who shall say
    Where her second birth?

Had her life been good and kind?
10   Had her heart been meek and pure?
Was she of a lowly mind,
    Ready to endure?

Did she still console the sad,
    Soothe the widow's anguish wild,
15   Make the poor and needy glad,
    Tend the orphan child?

Who shall say what hope and fear
   Crowded in her short life's span?
If the love of God was dear,
20   Or the love of man?

Happy bride if single-hearted
   Her first love to God was given;
If from this world she departed
   But to dwell in Heaven;

25 If her faith on Heaven was fixed,
   And her hope; if love's pure worth
Made her rich indeed, unmixed
   With the dross of earth.

But alas! if tainted pleasure
30   Won her heart and held it here,
Where is now her failing treasure,
   All her gladness where? . . . . .

Hush, too curious questioner;
   Hush and think thine own sins o'er:
35 Little canst thou learn from her;
   For we know no more

Than that there she lies all pale
   With her bridal robes around her:
Joy is fleeting—life is frail—
40   Death hath found her.

LIFE OUT OF DEATH.

"Now I've said all I would, mother;
   My head is on thy breast,
And I feel I can die without a sigh,
   And sink into my rest.

5 "And if ever you weep o'er my grave, mother,
   Weep not for doubt or sadness;
I shall fall asleep in pain and in grief,
   But wake to perfect gladness."

Mourn not, thou mother of the dead,
10   That in her youth she died;
for He was with her then Who said:
    "Ye that in me abide,
Ask what ye will, it shall be given;
Faith, hope, and love on earth, and Love and Joy in
    Heaven."

The solitary Rose.

O happy Rose, red Rose, that bloomest lonely
    Where there are none to gather while they love thee;
That art perfumed by thine own fragrance only,
    Resting like incense round thee and above thee;—
5   Thou hearest nought save some pure stream that flows,
        O happy Rose.

What tho' for thee no nightingales are singing?
    They chant one eve, but hush them in the morning.
Near thee no little moths and bees are winging
10   To steal thy honey when the day is dawning;—
Thou keep'st thy sweetness till the twilight's close,
        O happy Rose.

Then rest in peace, thou lone and lovely flower;
    Yea be thou glad, knowing that none are near thee
15   To mar thy beauty in a wanton hour,
    And scatter all thy leaves, nor deign to wear thee.
Securely in thy solitude repose,
        O happy Rose.

Lady Isabella.

Lady Isabella,
    Thou art gone away,
Leaving earth's darksome trouble,
    To rest until the Day.

5   From thy youth and beauty,
      From each loving friend,
    Thou art gone to the land of sure repose,
      Where fears and sorrows end.

    Thou wert pure whilst with us;
10   Now, we trust, in Heaven,
    All thy tears are wiped away,
      All thy sins forgiven.

    Who would wish thee back again
      But to share our sorrow?
15   Who would grudge thine hour of rest,
      Ere the coming morrow?

    Let us rejoice the rather
      That thou hast reached that shore,
    Whilst yet thy soul was spotless,
20   And thy young spirit pure.

    And if thy crown be brighter
      By but one little ray,
    Why wish to dim its lustre? . .
      Oh! rather let us pray
25   That when we are most fitted
      We too may pass away.

THE DREAM.

    Rest, rest; the troubled breast
    Panteth evermore for rest:—
    Be it sleep, or be it death,
    Rest is all it coveteth.

5   Tell me, dost thou remember the old time
      We sat together by that sunny stream,
    And dreamed our happiness was too sublime
      Only to be a dream?

Gazing, till steadfast gazing made us blind,
10 We watched the fishes leaping at their play;
Thinking our love too tender and too kind
    Ever to pass away.

And some of all our thoughts were true at least
    What time we thought together by that stream;
15 THY happiness has evermore increased,—
    MY love was not a dream.

And now that thou art gone, I often sit
    On its green margin, for thou once wert there;
And see the clouds that, floating over it,
20   Darken the quiet air.

Yes, oftentimes I sit beside it now,
    Harkning the wavelets ripple o'er the sands;
Until again I hear thy whispered vow
    And feel thy pressing hands.

25 Then the bright sun seems to stand still in heaven,
    The stream sings gladly as it onward flows,
The rushes grow more green, the grass more even,
    Blossoms the budding rose.

I say: "It is a joy-dream; I will take it;
30   He is not gone; he will return to me."
What found'st thou in my heart that thou should'st break
        it?—
    How have I injured thee?

Oh! I am weary of life's passing show,—
    Its pageant and its pain.
35 I would I could lie down lone in my woe,
    Ne'er to rise up again;
I would I could lie down where none might know;
    For truly love is vain.
Truly love's vain; but oh! how vainer still
40   Is that which is not love, but seems;
Concealed indifference, a covered ill,
    A very dream of dreams.

The Dying Man to his Betrothed.

One word—'tis all I ask of thee;
    One word—and that is little now
That I have learned thy wrong of me;
    And thou too art unfaithful—thou!—
5   O thou sweet poison, sweetest death,
    O honey between serpent's teeth,
    Breathe on me with thy scorching breath!

The last poor hope is fleeting now,
    And with it life is ebbing fast;
10 I gaze upon thy cold white brow,
    And loathe and love thee to the last.
    And still thou keepest silence—still
    Thou look'st on me—for good or ill
    Speak out, that I may know thy will.

15 Thou weepest, woman, and art pale!
    Weep not, for thou shalt soon be free;
My life is ending like a tale
    That was—but never more shall be.
    O blessed moments, ye fleet fast,
20 And soon the latest shall be past,
    And she will be content at last.

Nay, tremble not—I have not cursed
    Thy house or mine, or thee or me;
The moment that I saw thee first,
25   The moment that I first loved thee,
    Curse them! alas!—I can but bless,
    In this mine hour of heaviness;—
    Nay, sob not so in thy distress!

I have been harsh, thou sayst of me;—
30   God knows my heart was never so;
It never could be so to thee—
        And now it is too late—I know
    Thy grief—forgive me, love! 'tis o'er,
    For I shall never trouble more
35 Thy life that was so calm before.

I pardon thee—mayst thou be blest!
　　Say, wilt thou sometimes think of me?
Oh may I, from my happy rest,
　　Still look with love on thine and thee,
40　And may I pray for thee alway,
And for thy Love still may I pray,
Waiting the everlasting Day.

Stoop over me—ah! this is death!
　　I scarce can see thee at my side;
45　Stoop lower—let me feel thy breath,
　　O thou, mine own, my promised bride!
Pardon me, love—I pardon thee,
And may our pardon sealèd be
Throughout the long eternity.

50　The pains of death my senses cover:—
　　Oh! for His Sake Who died for men,
Be thou more true to this thy lover
　　Than thou hast been to me—Amen!
And if he chide thee wrongfully,
55　One little moment think on me,
And thou wilt bear it patiently.

And now, O God, I turn to Thee:
　　Thou Only, Father, canst not fail;
Lord, Thou hast tried and broken me,
60　　And yet Thy Mercy shall prevail.
Saviour, through Thee I am forgiven—
Do Thou receive my soul, blood-shriven,
O Christ, Who art the Gate of Heaven!

The Martyr.

See, the sun hath risen!
　Lead her from the prison;
She is young and tender, lead her tenderly:
　　May no fear subdue her,
5　　　Lest the Saints be fewer,
Lest her place in Heaven be lost eternally.

Forth she came, not trembling,
No, nor yet dissembling
An o'erwhelming terror weighing her down—down;
10   Little, little heeding
Earth, but inly pleading
For the strength to triumph and to win a crown.

All her might was rallied
To her heart; not pallid
15 Was her cheek, but glowing with a glorious red,
Glorious red and saintly,
Never paling faintly,
But still flushing, kindling still, without thought of dread.

On she went, on faster,
20   Trusting in her Master,
Feeling that His Eye watched o'er her lovingly;
He would prove and try her,
But would not deny her,
When her soul had pass'd, for His sake, patiently.

25   "Christ," she said, "receive me,
Let no terrors grieve me,
Take my soul and guard it with Thy heavenly cares:
Take my soul and guard it,
Take it and reward it
30 With the Love Thou bearest for the love it bears."

Quickened with a fire
Of sublime desire,
She looked up to Heaven, and she cried aloud,
"Death, I do entreat thee,
35   Come! I go to meet thee;
Wrap me in the whiteness of a virgin shroud."

On she went, hope-laden;
Happy, happy maiden!
Never more to tremble, and to weep no more:
40   All her sins forgiven,
Straight the path to Heaven
Through the glowing fire lay her feet before.

On she went, on quickly,
And her breath came thickly,
45   With the longing to see God coming pantingly:
Now the fire is kindled,
And her flesh has dwindled
Unto dust;—her soul is mounting up on high:

Higher, higher mounting,
50   The swift moments counting,
Fear is left beneath her, and the chastening rod:
Tears no more shall blind her,
Trouble lies behind her,
Satisfied with hopeful rest, and replete with God.

The End of Time.

Thou who art dreary
With a cureless woe,
Thou who art weary
Of all things below,
5   Thou who art weeping
By the loved sick-bed,
Thou who art keeping
Watches o'er the dead,
Hope, hope! old Time flies fast upon his way,
10   And soon will cease the night, and soon will dawn the day.

The rose blooms brightly,
But it fades ere night;
And youth flies lightly,
Yet how sure its flight!
15   And still the river
Merges in the sea,
And death reigns ever
Whilst old Time shall be;
Yet hope! old Time flies fast upon his way,
20   And soon will cease the night, and soon will dawn the day.

       All we most cherish
         In this world below,
       What tho' it perish?
         It has aye been so.
25   So thro' all ages
         It has ever been
       To fools and sages,
         Noble men and mean:
    Yet hope, still hope! for Time flies on his way,
30   And soon will end the night, and soon will dawn the day.

       All of each nation
         Shall that morning see
       With exultation
         Or with misery:
35   From watery slumbers,
         From the opening sod,
       Shall rise up numbers
         To be judged by God.
    Then hope and fear, for Time speeds on his way,
40   And soon must end the night, and soon must dawn the
       day.

Resurrection Eve.

    He resteth: weep not!
    The living sleep not
    With so much calm:
    He hears no chiding
5   And no deriding,
    Hath joy for sorrow,
    For night hath morrow,
    For wounds hath balm,
    For life's strange riot
10 Hath death and quiet.
    Who would recall him
    Of those that love him?

    No fears appal him,
    No ills befal him;
15 There's nought above him
    Save turf and flowers
    And pleasant grass.
    Pass the swift hours,
    How swiftly pass!
20 The hours of slumber
    He doth not number;
    Grey hours of morning
    Ere the day's dawning:
    Brightened by gleams
25 Of the sun-beams,
    By the foreseeing
    Of Resurrection,
    Of glorious being,
    Of full perfection,
30 Of sins forgiven
    Before the face
    Of men and spirits;
    Of God in Heaven,
    The Resting Place
35 That he inherits.

ZARA.
SEE MATURIN'S "WOMEN."

Now the pain beginneth and the word is spoken;—
    Hark unto the tolling of the churchyard chime!—
Once my heart was gladsome, now my heart is broken,—
    Once my love was noble, now it is a crime.

5   But the fear is over; yea, what now shall pain me?
    Arm thee in thy sorrow, O most Desolate!
Weariness and weakness, these shall now sustain me,—
    Pride and bitter grieving, burning love and hate.

Yea, the fear is over, the strong fear and trembling;
10   I can doubt no longer, he is gone indeed.
Rend thy hair, lost woman, weep without dissembling;
    The heart torn forth from it, shall the breast not bleed?

Happy she who looketh on his beauty's glory!
Happy she who listeneth to his gentle word!
15   Yet, O happy maiden, sorrow lies before thee;
    Greeting hath been given, parting must be heard.

He shall leave thee also, he who now hath left me,
    With a weary spirit and an aching heart;
Thou shalt be bereaved by him who hath bereft me;
20   Thou hast sucked the honey,—feel the stinging's smart.

Let the cold gaze on him, let the heartless hear him,
    For he shall not hurt them, they are safe in sooth:
But let loving women shun that man and fear him,
    Full of cruel kindness and devoid of ruth.

25   When ye call upon him, hope for no replying;
    When ye gaze upon him, think not he will look;
Hope not for his pity when your heart is sighing;
    Such another, waiting, weeping, he forsook.

Hath the Heaven no thunder wherewith to denounce
        him?
30   Hath the Heaven no lightning wherewith to chastise?
O my heart and spirit, O my soul, renounce him
    Who hath called for vengeance from the distant skies.

Vengeance which pursues thee, vengeance which shall
        find thee,
    Crushing thy false spirit, scathing thy fair limb:—
35   O ye thunders deafen, O ye lightnings blind me,
    Winds and storms from heaven, strike me but spare
        him.

I forgive thee, dearest, cruel, I forgive thee;—
    May thy cup of sorrow be poured out for me;
Though the dregs be bitter yet they shall not grieve me,
40   Knowing that I drink them, O my love, for thee.

Versi.

Figlia, la madre disse:
   Guardati dall' Amore;
   È crudo, è traditore,—
   Che vuoi saper di più?
5 Non fargli mai sperare
   D'entrare nel tuo petto;
   Chè chi gli diè ricetto
   Sempre tradito fu.

Colla sua benda al ciglio
10   È un bel fanciullo, è vero:
   Ma sempre è menzognero;
   Ma sempre tradirà.
Semplice tu se fidi
   Nel riso suo fallace;
15   Tu perderai la pace
   Nè mai ritornerà.

Ma vedo: già sei stanca
   Del mio parlar prudente;
   Già volgi nella mente
20   Il quando, il come, e il chi.
Odimi: i detti miei
   Già sai se son sinceri;
   E se son falsi o veri
   Saprai per prova un dì.

L'Incognita.

Nobil rosa ancor non crebbe
   Senza spine in sullo stelo:
Se vi fosse allor sarebbe
   Atta immagine di te.
5 È la luna in mezzo al cielo
   Bella è ver, ma passeggiera:
   Passa ancor la Primavera:
   Ah! l'immagin tua dov' è?

Purpurea rosa
Dolce, odorosa,
È molto bella,
Ma pur non è,
5   O mia Nigella,
Rival di te.

Donna nel velo,
Fior sullo stelo,
Ciascun l'amore
10   Reclama a se:
Ma passa il fiore,
Tu resti a me.

Soul rudderless, unbraced,
The Body's friend and guest,
Whither away today?
Unsuppled, pale, discased,
5   Dumb to thy wonted jest.

Animuccia, vagantuccia, morbiduccia,
    Oste del corpo e suora,
    Ove or farai dimora?
Palliduccia, irrigidita, svestituccia,
5   Non più scherzante or ora.

III Unpublished Poems

Heaven.

1.

What is heaven? 'tis a country
  Far away from mortal ken;
'Tis a land, where, by God's bounty,
  After death live righteous men.

2.

5 That that blest land I may enter,
    Is my humble, earnest cry;
Lord! admit me to Thy presence,
    Lord! admit me, or I die.

Hymn.

To the God Who reigns on high,
To th'Eternal Majesty,
To the Blessed Trinity
    Glory on earth be giv'n;
5 In the sea, and in the sky,
    And in the highest heav'n.

Corydon's Lament and Resolution.

1.

I have wept and I have sighed;
  Chloe will not be my bride.

I have sighed and I have wept,
She hath not her promise kept.

2.

5   I have grieved and I have mourned;
She hath not my love returned.
I have mourned and I have grieved;
She hath not my pains relieved.

3.

But her pride I'll mortify,
10   For her love I will not die.
Amaryllis fair I'll wed,
Nor one tear for Chloe shed.

Rosalind.

She sat upon a mountain,
    And gazed upon the sea;
Beside her crouched a stag-hound,
    A boy stood at her knee.

5   She fixed upon the ocean
    An agonizèd stare—
The ship is fast receding—
    Her husband off they bear.

"Oh, robbers! take some pity
10   Upon my helpless state:
Restore him to my fond arms!
    Leave me not desolate!"

They heed not her entreaties,
    They list not to her prayer;
15   The ship is fast receding—
    Her husband off they bear.

"Oh Captain! take these jewels
    That grace my hair of jet;
And ne'er in my devotion
20   To bless thee I'll forget."

Then sudden cried the pirate,
    "Lady, your prayers are vain;
When as my bride I sought you,
    You heeded not my pain.

25   "Now for the grief I suffered
    I'll compensated be"—
He said; and hurled her husband
    Into the raging sea.

Upon her snow-white bosom
30   Sank down that Lady's head;—
"I join thee, dearest Arthur"—
    Fair Rosalind is dead.

Pitia a Damone.

Ah non chiamarlo pena,
    È gioia quel ch'io sento;
Io morirò contento
    Se morirò per te.
5   È fervido diletto
    Quel che mi sta nel petto;
Per te la morte istessa
    Terribile non è.

The Faithless Shepherdess.

1

There once was a time when I loved,
    'Tis gone to return never more;
My shepherdess faithless has proved,
    The maiden I once did adore.

2

5   And now we are parted for ever,
   And gone are my hopes and my fears,
To forget Phillis false I'll endeavour,
   And arrest all these fast-flowing tears.

3

   Yet wherever I turn I must think
10   Of her who is faithless to me;
I stand by the rivulet's brink,
   And the play of its waters I see.

4

'Twas there I first told her my love,
   And she blushingly bade me hope still,
15 And the moon looking down from above
   Seemed to smile on the murmuring rill;

5

On the rill that was murm'ring of love
   To its beautiful mistress in heaven,
The moon seeming to speak far above
20   Of the rays that in token she'd given;

6

In token of love never-ending,
   And pure as when first 'twas avowed,
As long as that stream should be sending
   Soft sighs to its Queen in the cloud.

7

25 And false Phillis swore that she'd ever
   Keep faithful her pure heart to me,
That she'd think of another love never,
   So long as the rill true should be.

8

The rill to its love true remains,
30   The moon still smiles on it from heaven,
But from you I've experienced sharp pains,
That the rill to the moon ne'er has given.

9

And now we are parted for ever,
    And gone are my hopes and my fears;
35   To forget Phillis false I'll endeavour,
    And arrest all these fast-flowing tears.

Ariadne to Theseus.

1

Sunlight to the river,
    Moonlight to the sea,
As false and as fleeting
    Thou hast been to me.

2

5   And I've been like the lily
    That to the summer clings,
Or like the nightingale
    That to the sweet rose sings:

3

That wooing never ceases
10   For her indifference,
And never his beloved flower
    Reproaching will incense.

4

But thou more cruel than the rose
    Hast left me faithlessly,

15   To mourn for ever and alone
         Over thy perfidy.

                   5

      Soft breezes! waft him not
         Across the wide wide sea;
      Ingulph, just waves of Ocean!
20   The wretch who flies from me.

                   6

      Ah no! 'tis vain! Affection
         For my false love still remains:
      Blow, breezes! Peace, ye waters!
         Revenge not ye my pains!

                   7

25   May happiness attend thee,
         Who hast ta'en from me all joy!
      Be thine unmixèd pleasure;
         Be mine the sad alloy!

On Albina.

The roses lingered in her cheeks,
   When fair Albina fainted;
Oh! gentle Reader, could it be
   That fair Albina painted?

A Hymn for Christmas Day.

The Shepherds watch their flocks by night,
Beneath the moon's unclouded light,
All around is calm and still,
Save the murm'ring of the rill:

5 When lo! a form of light appears,
   And on the awe-struck Shepherds' ears
   Are words, of peace and comfort flowing
   From lips with love celestial glowing.
   Spiritual forms are breaking
10 Through the gloom, their voices taking
   Part in the adoring song
   Of the bright angelic throng.
   Wondering the Shepherds bend
   Their steps to Bethlehem, and wend
15 To a poor and crowded inn:—
   Tremblingly their way they win
   To the stable, where they find
   The Redeemer of mankind,
   Just born into this world of danger,
20 Lying in an humble manger.
   And they spread abroad each word
   Which that joyful night they'd heard,
   And they glorified the name
   Of their gracious God, Who came
25 Himself to save from endless woe
   The offspring of this world below.

Love and Death.

"Our bark's on the water; come down, come down,
I'll weave for thy fair head a leafy crown,
And in it I'll blend the roses bright,
With asphodel woven of faint sunlight.
5 But more precious than these I'll twine the pearls
In the flowing locks of thy chestnut curls;
And the gem and the flow'r from wave and from tree
Shall form a bright diadem, Bianca, for thee.
The sea is calm, and I will guard thee;
10 Oh what, sweet love, should thus retard thee?
Descend, fairest maiden, descend to the sea,
And sail o'er the motionless waters with me."
The sound of his last words was scarcely o'er,

When beside him she stood on the ocean shore.
15 Lightly she entered the gondola,
And gaily her lover followed her—
But for them it had been happier
Had they quietly lain in their beds all night,
Nor sailed forth 'neath the moonbeam's deceitful light.
20 Smoothly, swiftly the gondolier rowed along,
The splash of his oars keeping time to his song;
'Twas an old tale of hope and of fear and of danger,
Of the loves of a noble princess and a stranger;
How they fled, and were married one fine summer night,
25 And their days glided on in one stream of delight.
But oh! wherefore trembles that lady fair?
The lightning gleams forth through the heavy air;
The thunder peals loudly, the low wind is wailing,
And the heart of the lady for terror is failing.
30 But Gonsalvo around her his left arm clasped tightly,
And he fought with the sea that was foaming so whitely;
All vain are his struggles—the billows rise higher,
The thunder is pealing, the sky seems on fire,
The wild wind is howling, the lightning ne'er ceases—
35 He still clasps his love, but his strength fast decreases—
Fair Bianca has fainted; she hears not the wind,
Nor the splash of the rain; to the lightning she's blind—
She knows not that down to the depths of the sea
She's dragging her love irresistibly:
40 Gonsalvo's efforts have fainter grown,
And she hangs on his arm like a heavy stone;—
And now o'er them rolls each mighty wave—
In the sea they have found a common grave.

Despair.

1

Up rose the moon in glory,
    And glittered on the sea;
Up rose the stars around her,
    Making the darkness flee.

2

5   The nightingale's wild warbling
    Rang in the far-off wood;
    When in his Father's castle
    A mournful figure stood.

3

    His heart was almost bursting,
10   He madly beat his breast;
    As, in low plaintive accents,
    His grief he thus exprest.

4

    "Stars, shroud yourselves in darkness!
    Pale moon, withdraw thy light!
15   Let darkness hide the ocean
    For ever from my sight;

5

    "Hide cottage, town and city;—
    Appear no more, thou Sun!
    But let in foreign countries
20   Thy cheering race be run.

6

    "For I have lost my loved one!
    Low lies she in her grave!
    Speak not to me of pleasure,
    For her I could not save.

7

25   "Hark to the distant murmur
    As waves break on the shore"—
    When lo! a light came flashing
    Along the corridor.

8

The mystic form that bore it
30   He scarcely could discern;
Its flowing robe was blackness—
Higher the flame doth burn—

9

He cried, "What art thou, Spirit
So luminous and bright?"
35   A voice said, "I'm the maid, Sir,
A bringing in the light."

Forget Me Not.

1

"Forget me not! Forget me not!"
The maiden once did say,
When to some far-off battle-field
Her lover sped away.

2

5   "Forget me not! Forget me not!"
Says now the chamber-maid
When the traveller on his journey
No more will be delayed.

Easter Morning.

1

The sun arises from the sea,
And all around his rays is flinging,
The flowers are opening on the lea,
The merry birds are singing.

2

⁵ The summer breeze is rustling past,
  Sweet scents are gathering around it,
The rivulet is flowing fast,
  Beside the banks that bound it.

3

All nature seemeth to rejoice,
¹⁰ In the returning summer weather;
Let us with nature raise our voice,
  And harmonise together.

4

But not alone for summer skies
  Shall praise unto our God be given:
¹⁵ This day our Saviour did arise,
  And oped the gate of heaven.

5

To sinful man, if only he
  His errings will confess with sorrow,
Then, after earth's night-misery,
  Shall dawn a glorious morrow:

6

A blissful bright eternity
  Bought by the rising of the Giver,
To Whom all praise, all honour be,
  For ever and for ever.

A Tirsi.

Chiami il mio core
Crudele, altero;

No, non è vero,
   Crudel non è.
5 T'amo, t'amai,
   E tu lo sai,
Men del dovere,
   Ma più di me.

The Last Words of St. Telemachus.

There is a sound of weeping; wherefore weep
   That I should sleep?
Oh! wherefore mourn that I at last should be
   At liberty?
5 One only grief yet lingers at my heart—
   That we must part:
Part—! and perchance we never more may meet
   In converse sweet!
The memory of all thy gentle ways,
10   Kind without praise—
And of thy loving acts, scarce seen before,
   Now numbered o'er,
Weigh me to earth clinging about my heart—
   And must we part?
15 Yet still my trust in God shall stedfast be—
   By faith I see
Through the long vista of eternal years,
   Free from all fears,
Thee by my side in calm unchanging rest,
20   For ever blest!

Lord Thomas and fair Margaret.

1

Fair Marg'ret sat in her bower,
   Unbraiding of her hair,
When entered in Lord Thomas' ghost,
   And gave her greeting fair.

2

5   "Oh how pale thou art, my love," she said,
    "Oh how pale thou art to see!
    Once thine eye was bright, and thy cheek was red;
    Why comest thou so to me?"

3

    "Oh fair Marg'ret, oh sweet Marg'ret,
10   I murderèd have been—
    They have ta'en my body for love of thee,
    And cast it in a stream.

4

    "Oh fair Marg'ret, oh sweet Marg'ret,
    We aye maun parted be,
15   If thou wilt not bind up thy yellow hair,
    And quickly follow me."

5

    Up and ris fair Marg'ret,
    And quickly followed him;
    As the moon was the colour of his face,
20   And the colour of his limb.

6

    The ghost he fled, the ghost he sped,
    The ghost he ran and glided,
    And still fair Margaret pursued,
    Though never to be brided.

7

25   The ghost he sped, the ghost he fled,
    Ploughed land and hillocks over,
    And still fair Margaret pursued.
    After her flying lover.

8

Away, away "without stop or stay,"
30   Till they came to waters running,
"I canna stay, I maun away,
    For fast the day is coming.

9

"Oh fair Marg'ret, oh sweet Marg'ret,
    We now maun parted be,
35   If in the last trail thou shalt go through
    Thy heart should fail in thee."

10

On glided the ghost, while the starry host
    Glittered down on the sleeping stream;
O'er the waves glided he impalpably,
40   Then vanished like a dream.

11

Fair Margaret still followed him,
    Till she sank amid the wave;
Thus died for each other these lovers true,
    And were joinèd in the grave.

Lines to my Grandfather.

Dear Grandpapa,
        To be obedient,
    I'll try and write a letter;
Which (as I hope you'll deem expedient)
5   Must serve for lack of better.

My muse of late was not prolific,
    And sometimes I must feel

To make a verse a task terrific
   Rather of woe than weal.

10   As I have met with no adventure
   Of wonder and refulgence,
   I must write plain things at a venture
   And trust to your indulgence.

The apple-tree is showing
15   Its blossom of bright red
With a soft colour glowing
   Upon its leafy bed.

The pear-tree's pure white blossom
   Like stainless snow is seen;
20   And all earth's genial bosom
   Is clothed with varied green.

The fragrant may is blooming,
   The yellow cowslip blows;
Among its leaves entombing
25   Peeps forth the pale primrose.

The kingcup flowers and daisies
   Are opening hard by;
And many another raises
   Its head, to please and die.

30   I love the gay wild flowers
   Waving in fresh spring air;
Give me uncultured bowers
   Before the bright parterre!

And now my letter is concluded,
35   To do well I have striven;
And though news is well-nigh excluded,
   I hope to be forgiven.

With love to all the beautiful,
   And those who cannot slaughter,
40   I sign myself,
         your dutiful,
     Affectionate Granddaughter.

Charade.

My first may be the firstborn,
  The second child may be;
My second is a texture light
  And elegant to see:
5   My whole do those too often write
  Who are from talent free.

Hope in Grief.

Tell me not that death of grief
Is the only sure relief.
Tell me not that hope when dead
Leaves a void that nought can fill,
5   Gnawings that may not be fed.
Tell me not there is no skill
That can bind the breaking heart,
That can soothe the bitter smart,
When we find ourselves betrayed,
10   When we find ourselves forsaken,
By those for whom we would have laid
Our young lives down, nor wished to waken.
Say not that life is to all
But a gaily coloured pall,
15   Hiding with its deceitful glow
The hearts that break beneath it,
Engulphing as they anguished flow
The scalding tears that seethe it.
Say not, vain this world's turmoil,
20   Vain its trouble and its toil,
All its hopes and fears are vain,
Long, unmitigated pain.
What though we should be deceived
By the friend that we love best?
25   All in this world have been grieved,
Yet many have found rest.
Our present life is as the night,

Our future as the morning light:
Surely the night will pass away,
30 And surely will uprise the day.

Lisetta all' Amante.

Perdona al primo eccesso
    D'un tenero dolore;
    A te promisi il core,
        E vo' serbarlo a te.
5 Ma dimmi, e mi consola:
    M'ami tu ancor, cor mio?
    Se a te fedel son io,
        Sarai fedele a me?

Chè se nell' alma ingrata
10   Pensi ad abbandonarmi,
    Anch'io saprò scordarmi
        D'un amator crudel.
    Ma crederlo non voglio;
    Ma non lo vo' pensare;
15   Chè nol potrei lasciare,
        Chè gli sarei fedel.

Song.

I saw her; she was lovely,
    And bright her eyes of blue,
Whilst merrily her white white hands
    Over the harp-strings flew.
5 I saw her and I loved her,
    I loved her for my pain,
For her heart was given to another
    Not to return again.

Again I saw her pacing
10   Down the cathedral aisle;
The bridal wreath was in her hair,

And on her lips a smile;
A quiet smile and holy,
Meet for a holy place,
15   A smile of certain happiness
That lighted up her face.

And once, once more I saw her,
Kneeling beside a bed;
The bright sun's rays were shining there,
20   And shone upon the dead;
From the body of her husband
Earth's gloom they chased away,
And she gazed on him without a tear,
And hailed the coming day.

Praise of Love.

And shall Love cease? Ask thine own heart, O Woman,
Thy heart that beats restlessly on for ever!
All earthly things shall pass away and human,
But Love's divine: annihilated never,
5   It binds and nought shall sever.

Oh! it is Love makes the world habitable,
Love is a foretaste of our promised Heaven;
Though sometimes robed in white, sometimes in sable,
It still is Love, and still some joy is given,
10   Although the heart be riven.

And who would give Love's joy to 'scape its paining?
Yea, who would lose its sorrow and its gladness?
Then let us bear its griefs without complaining:—
This only earthly passion is not madness,
15   Nor leads to dearth and sadness.

Love is all happiness, Love is all beauty,
Love is the crown of flaxen heads and hoary,
Love is the only everlasting duty,
And Love is chronicled in endless story,
20   And leads to endless glory.

"I have fought a good fight."

"Who art thou that comest with a stedfast face
Thro' the hushed arena to the burying-place?"
"I am one whose footprints marked upon the sand
Cry in blood for vengeance on a guilty land."

5   "How are these thy garments white as whitest snow
Tho' thy blood hath touched them in its overflow?"
"My blood cannot stain them, nor my tears make white;
One than I more mighty, He hath made them bright."

"Say, do thy wounds pain thee open every one,
10 Wounds that now are glowing clearer than the sun?"
"Nay, they are my gladness unalloyed by grief;
Like a desert fountain, or a long relief."

"When the lion had thee in his deadly clasp,
Was there then no terror in thy stifled gasp?"
15 "Tho' I felt the crushing, and the grinding teeth,
He was with me ever, He Who comforteth."

"Didst thou hear the shouting, as of a great flood,
Crying out for vengeance, crying out for blood?"
"I heard it in silence, and was not afraid,
20 While for the mad people silently I prayed."

"Did their hate not move thee? art thou heedless then
Of the fear of children and the curse of men?"
"God looked down upon me from the Heaven above,
And I did not tremble, happy in His Love."

Wishes:
Sonnet.

Oh! would that I were very far away
  Among the lanes, with hedges all around,
  Happily listening to the dreamy sound
Of distant sheep-bells, smelling the new hay
5 And all the wild-flowers scattered in my way:

Or would that I were lying on some mound
Where shade and butterflies and thyme abound,
Beneath the trees, upon a sunny day:
Or would I strolled beside the mighty sea,
10   The sea before, and the tall cliffs behind;
While winds from the warm south might tell to me
How health and joy for all men are designed:—
But be I where I may, would I had thee,
And heard thy gentle voice, my Mother kind.

Eleanor.

Cherry-red her mouth was,
Morning-blue her eye,
Lady-slim her little waist
Rounded prettily;
5   And her sweet smile of gladness
Made every heart rejoice;
But sweeter even than her smile
The tones were of her voice.

Sometimes she spoke, sometimes she sang;
10   And evermore the sound
Floated, a dreamy melody,
Upon the air around;
As tho' a wind were singing
Far up beside the sun,
15   Till sound and warmth and glory
Were blended all in one.

Her hair was long and golden,
And clustered unconfined
Over a forehead high and white
20   That spoke a noble mind.
Her little hand, her little foot
Were ready evermore
To hurry forth to meet a friend;
She smiling at the door.

25   But if she sang, or if she spoke,
          'Twas music soft and grand,
      As tho' a distant singing sea
          Broke on a tuneful strand;
      As tho' a blessed Angel
30   Were singing a glad song,
      Half way between the earth and Heaven
          Joyfully borne along.

Isidora.
/See Maturin's "Melmoth."/

Love, whom I have loved too well,
    Turn thy face away from me;
For I heed nor Heaven nor Hell
    While mine eyes can look on thee.
5   Do not answer, do not speak,
    For thy voice can make me weak.

I must choose 'twixt God and man,
    And I dare not hesitate:
Oh how little is life's span,
10   And Eternity how great!
Go out from me; for I fear
Mine own strength while thou art here.

Husband, leave me; but know this:
    I would gladly give my soul
15 So that thine might dwell in bliss
        Free from the accursed control,
So that thou mightest go hence
In a hopeful penitence.

Yea, from Hell I would look up,
20   And behold thee in thy place,
Drinking of the living cup,
        With the joy-look on thy face,
And the Light that shines alone
From the Glory of the Throne.

25   But how could my endless loss
         Be thine everlasting gain?
      Shall thy palm grow from my cross?
         Shall thine ease be in my pain?
      Yea, thine own soul witnesseth
30   Thy life is not in my death.

      It were vain that I should die;
         That we thus should perish both;
      Thou would'st gain no peace thereby;
         And in truth I should be loath
35   By the loss of my salvation
      To increase thy condemnation.

      Little infant, his and mine,
         Would that I were as thou art;
      Nothing breaks that sleep of thine,
40   And ah! nothing breaks thy heart;
      And thou knowest nought of strife,
      The heart's death for the soul's life.

      None misdoubt thee; none misdeem
         Of thy wishes and thy will.
45   All thy thoughts are what they seem,
         Very pure and very still;
      And thou fearest not the voice
      That once made thy heart rejoice.

      Oh how calm thou art, my child!
50   I could almost envy thee.
      Thou hast neither wept nor smiled,
         Thou that sleepest quietly.
      Would I also were at rest
      With the one that I love best.

55   Husband, go. I dare not hearken
         To thy words, or look upon
      Those despairing eyes that darken
         Down on me—but he is gone.
      Nay, come back; and be my fate
60   As thou wilt—it is too late.

I have conquered; it is done;
  Yea, the death-struggle is o'er,
And the hopeless quiet won!—
  I shall see his face no more!—
65 And mine eyes are waxing dim
Now they cannot look on him.

And my heart-pulses are growing
  Very weak; and thro' my whole
Life-blood a slow chill is going:—
70   Blessed Saviour, take my soul
To Thy Paradise and care;—
Paradise, will he be there?

The Novice.

I love one, and he loveth me:
Who sayeth this? who deemeth this?
And is this thought a cause of bliss,
  Or source of misery?

5 The loved may die, or he may change:
And if he die thou art bereft;
Or if he alter, nought is left
  Save life that seemeth strange.

A weary life, a hopeless life,
10 Full of all ill and fear-oppressed;
A weary life that looks for rest
  Alone after death's strife.

And love's joy hath no quiet even;
It evermore is variable.
15 Its gladness is like war in Hell,
  More than repose in Heaven.

Yea, it is as a poison cup
That holds one quick fire-draught within;
For when the life seems to begin
20   The slow death looketh up.

Then bring me to a solitude
Where love may neither come nor go;
Where very peaceful waters flow,
    And roots are found for food;

25 Where the wild honey-bee booms by;
And trees and bushes freely give
Ripe fruit and nuts; there I would live,
    And there I fain would die.

There Autumn leaves may make my grave,
30 And little birds sing over it;
And there cool twilight winds may flit
    And shadowy branches wave.

Immalee:
/See Maturin's "Melmoth."/

Sonnet.

I gather thyme upon the sunny hills,
    And its pure fragrance ever gladdens me,
    And in my mind having tranquillity
I smile to see how my green basket fills.
5   And by clear streams I gather daffodils;
    And in dim woods find out the cherry-tree,
    And take its fruit, and the wild strawberry,
And nuts, and honey; and live free from ills.
I dwell on the green earth, 'neath the blue sky,
10   Birds are my friends, and leaves my rustling roof;
The deer are not afraid of me, and I
    Hear the wild goat, and hail its hastening hoof;
The squirrels sit perked as I pass them by,
    And even the watchful hare stands not aloof.

Lady Isabella.

Heart warm as Summer, fresh as Spring,
Gracious as Autumn's harvesting,
Pure as the Winter snows; as white

A hand as lilies in sun-light;
5   Eyes glorious as a midnight star;
Hair shining as the chestnuts are;
A step firm and majestical;
A voice singing and musical;
A soft expression, kind address;
10   Tears for another's heaviness;
Bright looks; an action full of grace;
A perfect form, a perfect face;
All these become a woman well,
And these had Lady Isabelle.

Night and Death.

Now the sun-lit hours are o'er,
Rise up from thy shadowy shore,
Happy Night, whom Chaos bore.

Better is the peaceful treasure
5   Of thy musings without measure,
Than the day's unquiet pleasure.

Bring the holy moon; so pale
She herself seems but a veil
For the sun, where no clouds sail.

10   Bring the stars, thy progeny;
Each a little lamp on high
To light up an azure sky.

Sounds incomprehensible
In the shining planets dwell
15   Of thy sister Queen to tell.

Of that sister Nature saith,
She hath power o'er life and breath;
And her name is written Death.

She is fairer far than thou;
20   Grief her head can never bow,
Joy is stamped upon her brow.

She is full of gentleness,
And of faith and hope; distress
Finds in her forgetfulness.

25   In her arms who lieth down
Never more is seen to frown,
Tho' he wore a thorny crown.

Whoso sigheth in unrest
If his head lean on her breast
30   Witnesseth she is the best.

All the riches of the earth
Weighed by her are nothing worth;
She is the eternal birth.

In her treasure-house are found
35   Stored abundantly around
Almsdeeds done without a sound;

Long forbearance; patient will;
Fortitude in midst of ill;
Hope, when even fear grew still;

40   Kindness given again for hate;
Hearts resigned tho' desolate;
Meekness, which is truly great;

Bitter tears of penitence;
Changeless love's omnipotence:—
45   And nought lacketh recompense.

In her house no tainted thing
Winneth any entering;
There the poor have comforting.

There they wait a little time
50   Till the angel-uttered chime
Sound the eternal matin-prime.

Then, upraised in joyfulness,
They shall know her; and confess
She is blessed and doth bless.

55   When earth's fleeting day is flown
All created things shall own,
Death is Life, and Death alone.

"Young men aye were fickle found
Since summer trees were leafy."

Go in peace my Beloved; tho' never again
Shall I feel in thy presence strange joy and sweet pain;
Go in peace my Beloved; perhaps thou may'st yet
Find a young heart to love thee that need not forget.

5   In glory and beauty and smiles thou shalt go,
And I shall remain in my wearisome woe.
Oh! thine is the rose on a bright summer morn
Full of perfume and blushes;—and mine is the thorn.

And thine is the sun-light, and mine is the cloud;
10   And thine is the feasting, and mine is the shroud.
And thou shalt have gladness and honour's increase;
And I in my cool silent grave shall have peace.

But so it is fitting, and so let it be;
The praise be thy portion, the shame be for me.
15   Ah! why should I chide thee and struggle in vain?
For love, once recalled, is not given again.

Thy word is forgotten, and broken thy vow;
If I pray or reproach thee thou heedest not now.
I would I could hate thee, false love; but in truth
20   How can I abhor the delight of my youth?

Oh! happy the maiden whose beautiful strength
Shall win thy proud heart and subdue it at length!
Yet tho' she be true, what hath she more than I?
She may live but for thee, and for thee I shall die.

25   The faith which endures and is mighty in death
Is more real, to my thinking, than words which are
       breath.

There are many fair women will court thee and live;
But who, broken-hearted, will die and forgive?

By the love that I bear thee, the hopes that are flown,
30 The heart that lies bleeding, the life left alone,—
Remember, remember the dear vanished time,
In thy far-distant country and sun-gladdened clime.

The Lotus-Eaters:
Ulysses to Penelope.

In a far-distant land they dwell,
    Incomprehensible,
Who love the shadow more than light,
    More than the sun the moon,
5   Cool evening more than noon,
Pale silver more than gold that glitters bright.
A dark cloud overhangs their land
    Like a mighty hand,
Never moving from above it;
10 A cool shade and moist and dim,
With a twilight-purple rim,
    And they love it.
And sometimes it giveth rain,
But soon it ceaseth as before,
15 And earth drieth up again;
Then the dews rise more and more,
Till it filleth, dropping o'er;
But no forked lightnings flit,
And no thunders roll in it.
20 Thro' the land a river flows;
With a sleepy sound it goes;
Such a drowsy noise, in sooth,
Those who will not listen, hear not;
But if one is wakeful, fear not;
25 It shall lull him to repose,
Bringing back the dream's of youth.
Hemlock groweth, poppy bloweth

In the fields where no man moweth;
And the vine is full of wine
30 And are full of milk the kine,
And the hares are all secure,
And the birds are wild no more,
And the forest-trees wax old,
And winds stir, or hot, or cold,
35 And yet no man taketh care,
All things resting everywhere.

Sonnet
from the Psalms.

All thro' the livelong night I lay awake
   Watering my couch with tears of heaviness.
   None stood beside me in my sore distress;—
Then cried I to my heart: If thou wilt, break,
5 But be thou still; no moaning will I make,
   Nor ask man's help, nor kneel that he may bless.
   So I kept silence in my haughtiness,
Till lo! the fire was kindled, and I spake
Saying: Oh that I had wings like to a dove,
10   Then would I flee away and be at rest:
I would not pray for friends, or hope, or love,
   But still the weary throbbing of my breast;
And, gazing on the changeless heavens above,
   Witness that such a quietness is best.

Song.

The stream moaneth as it floweth,
The wind sigheth as it bloweth,
Leaves are falling, Autumn goeth,
   Winter cometh back again;
5 And the air is very chilly,
And the country rough and hilly,
   And I shiver in the rain.

Who will help me? Who will love me?
Heaven sets forth no light above me;
10   Ancient memories reprove me,
Long-forgotten feelings move me,
    I am full of heaviness.
Earth is cold, too cold the sea;
Whither shall I turn and flee?
15   Is there any hope for me?
Any ease for my heart-aching?
Any sleep that hath no waking?
Any night without day-breaking?
    Any rest from weariness?
20   Hark! the wind is answering:
    Hark! the running stream replieth:
    There is rest for him that dieth;
    In the grave whoever lieth
Nevermore hath sorrowing.
25   Holy slumber, holy quiet,
Close the eyes and still the riot;
And the brain forgets its thought,
    And the heart forgets its beating.—
    Earth and earthly things are fleeting,
30   There is what all men have sought;
Long, unchangeable repose,
Lulling us from many woes.

A Counsel.

Oh weep for the glory departed
    That comes not again;
And weep for the friends hollow-hearted
    Ye cared for in vain;
5   And weep for the roses that perished
    Ere Summer had fled;
For hopes that ye vainly have cherished;—
    But not for the dead.

Nay mourn not for them: they have ended
10   All labours and woes;
Their hopes now of glory are blended
   With perfect repose.
And tell me, this thing that is given,
   Shall it not suffice?
15 They wait for the gladness of Heaven,
   And have Paradise.

The World's Harmonies.

Oh listen, listen; for the Earth
   Hath silent melody;
Green grasses are her lively chords,
   And blossoms; and each tree,
5 Chestnut and oak and sycamore,
   Makes solemn harmony.

Oh listen, listen; for the Sea
   Is calling unto us;
Her notes are the broad liquid waves
10   Mighty and glorious.
Lo, the first man and the last man
   Hath heard, shall hearken thus.

The Sun on which men cannot look
   Its splendour is so strong;
15 Which wakeneth life and giveth life
   Rolling in light along,
From day-dawn to dim eventide
   Sings the eternal song.

And the Moon taketh up the hymn,
20   And the Stars answer all;
And all the Clouds and all the Winds
   And all the Dews that fall
And Frost and fertilizing Rain
   Are mutely musical.

25 Fishes and Beasts and feathered Fowl
       Swell the eternal chant,
    That riseth through the lower air,
       Over the rainbow slant,
    Up through the unseen palace-gates,
30   Fearlessly jubilant.

    Before the everlasting Throne
       It is acceptable;
    It hath no pause or faltering;
       The Angels know it well;
35 Yea, in the highest heaven of heavens
       Its sound is audible.

    Yet than the voice of the whole World
       There is a sweeter voice,
    That maketh all the Cherubim
40   And Seraphim rejoice;
    That all the blessèd Spirits hail
       With undivided choice;

    That crieth at the golden door
       And gaineth entrance in;
45 That the palm-branch and radiant crown
       And glorious throne may win;—
    The lowly prayer of a poor man
       Who turneth from his sin.

Lines
given with a Penwiper.

    I have compassion on the carpeting,
       And on your back I have compassion too.
    The splendid Brussels web is suffering
       In the dimmed lustre of each glowing hue;
5   And you the everlasting altering
       Of your position with strange aches must rue.
    Behold, I come the carpet to preserve,
    And save your spine from a continual curve.

The last Answer.

She turned round to me with her steadfast eyes:
    "I tell you I have looked upon the dead;
    "Have kissed the brow and the cold lips;" she said;
    "Have called upon the sleeper to arise;
5 "He loved me, yet he stirred not; on this wise,
    "Not bowing in weak agony my head,
    "But all too sure of what life is, to dread,
    "Learned I that love and hope are fallacies."
    She gazed quite calmly on me; and I felt
10   Awed and astonished and almost afraid:
    For what was I to have admonished her?
    Then, being full of doubt and fear, I knelt,
    And tears came to my eyes even as I prayed:
    But she, meanwhile, only grew statelier.

One of the Dead.

Paler, not quite so fair as in her life,
    She lies upon the bed, perfectly still;
    Her little hands clasped with a patient will
    Upon her bosom, swelling without strife;
5 An honoured virgin, a most blameless wife.
    The roses lean upon the window sill,
    That she trained once; their sweets the hot air fill,
    And make the death-apartment odour-rife.
    Her meek white hands folded upon her breast,
10   Her gentle eyes closed in the long last sleep,
    She lieth down in her unbroken rest;
    Her kin, kneeling around, a vigil keep,
    Venting their grief in low sobs unrepressed:—
    Friends, she but slumbers, wherefore do ye weep?

"The whole head is sick, and the whole heart faint."

Woe for the young who say that life is long,
    Who turn from the sun-rising to the west,

Who feel no pleasure and can find no rest,
Who in the morning sigh for evensong.
5   Their hearts weary because of this world's wrong,
Yearn with a thousand longings unexpressed;
They have a wound no mortal ever drest,
An ill than all earth's remedies more strong.
For them the fount of gladness hath run dry,
10   And in all nature is no pleasant thing;
For them there is no glory in the sky,
No sweetness in the breezes' murmuring;
They say: The peace of heaven is placed too high,
And this earth changeth and is perishing.

"I do set My bow in the cloud."

The roses bloom too late for me;
The violets I shall not see;
Even the snowdrops will not come
Till I have passed from home to home;
5   From home on earth to home in heaven,
Here penitent and there forgiven.

Mourn not, my Father, that I seek
One Who is strong when I am weak.
Through the dark passage, verily,
10   His rod and staff shall comfort me;
He shall support me in the strife
Of death, that dieth into life;
He shall support me; He receive
My soul when I begin to live,
15   And more than I can ask for give.

He from the heaven-gates built above
Hath looked on me in perfect love.
From the heaven-walls to me He calls
To come and dwell within those walls;
20   With Cherubim and Seraphim
And Angels; yea, beholding Him.

His care for me is more than mine,
Father; His love is more than thine.
Sickness and death I have from thee,
25   From Him have immortality.
He giveth gladness where He will,
Yet chasteneth His belovèd still.

Then tell me; is it not enough
To feel that when the path is rough,
30   And the sky dark, and the rain cold,
His promise standeth as of old?
When heaven and earth have passed away,
Only His righteous word shall stay,
And we shall know His will is best.
35   Behold; He is a Haven Rest,
A Sheltering Rock, a Hiding Place,
For runners steadfast in the race;
Who, toiling for a little space,
Had light through faith when sight grew dim,
40   And offered all their world to Him.

"O Death where is thy Sting?"

She sleepeth: would ye wake her if ye could?
    Is her face sad that ye should pity her?
    Did Death come to her like a messenger
From a far land where is not any good?
I tell ye nay: but, having understood
    That God is Love, Death was her harbinger

[The rest of the manuscript is missing from the notebook.]

Undine.

She did not answer him again
    But walked straight to the door;
Her hand nor trembled on the lock,

Nor her foot on the floor,
5   But as she stood up steadily
She turned, and looked once more.

She turned, and looked on him once more:
Her face was very pale;
And from her forehead her long hair
10   Fell back like a thick veil;
But, though her lips grew white, the fire
Of her eyes did not fail.

Then as she fixed her eyes on him
Old thoughts came back again
15   Of the dear rambles long ago
Through meadow-land and lane,
When all the woods were full of flowers,
And all the fields of grain.

When all the birds were full of song
20   Except the turtle dove;
And that sat cooing tenderly
In the green boughs above;
When they hoped the same hopes, and when
He told her of his love.

25   Old memories came back to her
Of what once made her glad,
Till her heart seemed to stand quite still,
And every pulse she had:
Then the blood rose up to her brain
30   And she was almost mad.

Yet still she stood there steadily
And looked him in the face;
There was no tear upon her cheek;
Upon her brow no trace
35   Of the agonizing strife within,
The shame and the disgrace.

And so she stayed a little while
Until she turned once more,

Without a single sob or sigh;
40   But her heart felt quite sore:
The spirit had been broken, and
     The hope of life was o'er.

Lady Montrevor.

(See Maturin's "Wild Irish Boy.")

I do not look for love that is a dream:
     I only seek for courage to be still;
     To bear my grief with an unbending will,
And when I am a-weary not to seem.
5   Let the round world roll on; let the sun beam;
     Let the wind blow, and let the rivers fill
     The everlasting sea; and on the hill
The palms almost touch heaven, as children deem.
And though young Spring and Summer pass away,
10   And Autumn and cold Winter come again;
     And though my soul, being tired of its pain,
Pass from the ancient earth; and though my clay
     Return to dust; my tongue shall not complain:
No man shall mock me after this my day.

Floral Teaching.

O ye red-blushing summer roses, ye
     Who are like queens, crowned with a rich perfume,
     In whose deep heart there is no shade of gloom,
Who are a pasture for the honey-bee;
5   Surely your days and nights pass happily:
     And when the earth, your mother, doth resume
     Your little lives, do ye not think the tomb
Is full of soft leaves and looks pleasantly?
So be it with me: through life so may I deem
10   That this world's course is ordered well, and give
My help to others and my loving heed.

Then when the day comes that it is decreed
  I am to die, may I not cease to live,
But rest awhile waiting the morning beam.

"Death is swallowed up in Victory."

"Tell me: doth it not grieve thee to lie here,
  And see the cornfields waving not for thee,
  Just in the waxing Summer of the year?"

"I fade from earth; and lo! along with me
5   The season that I love will fade away:
  How should I look for Autumn longingly?"

"Yet Autumn beareth fruit whilst day by day
  The leaves grow browner with a mellow hue,
  Declining to a beautiful decay."

10 "Decay is death, with which I have to do,
  And see it near; behold, it is more good
  Than length of days and length of sorrow too."

"But thy heart hath not dwelt in solitude:
  Many have loved and love thee; dost not heed
15   Free love, for which in vain have others sued?"

"I thirst for love, love is mine only need,
  Love such as none hath borne me, nor can bear,
  True love that prompteth thought and word and deed."

"Here it is not: why seek it otherwhere?
20   Nay, bow thy head, and own that on this earth
  Are many goodly things, and sweet, and fair."

"There are tears in man's laughter; in his mirth
  There is a fearful forward look; and lo!
  An infant's cry gives token of its birth."

25 "I mark the ocean of Time ebb and flow:
  He who hath care one day, and is perplext
  Tomorrow may have joy in place of woe."

"Evil becomes good; and to this annext
   Good becomes evil; speak of it no more;
30   My heart is wearied and my spirit vext."

"Is there no place it grieves thee to give o'er?
   Is there no home thou lov'st, and so wouldst fain
   Tarry a little longer at the door?"

"I must go hence and not return again;   '
35   But the friends whom I have shall come to me,
   And dwell together with me safe from pain."

"Where is that mansion mortals cannot see?
   Behold the tombs are full of worms; shalt thou
   Rise thence and soar up skywards gloriously?"

40   "Even as the planets shine we know not how,
   We shall be raised then; changed, yet still the same;
   Being made like Christ; yea, being as He is now."

"Thither thou goest whence no man ever came:
   Death's voyagers return not; and in Death
45   There is no room for speech or sigh or fame."

"There is room for repose that comforteth;
   There weariness is not; and there content
   Broodeth for ever, and hope hovereth."

"When the stars fall, and when the graves are rent,
50   Shalt thou have safety? shalt thou look for life
   When the great light of the broad sun is spent?"

"These elements shall consummate their strife,
   This heaven and earth shall shrivel like a scroll
   And then be re-created, beauty-rife."

55   "Who shall abide it when from pole to pole
   The world's foundations shall be overthrown?
   Who shall abide to scan the perfect whole?"

"He who hath strength given to him, not his own;
   He who hath faith in that which is not seen,
60   And patient hope; who trusts in love alone."

"Yet thou! the death-struggle must intervene
Ere thou win rest; think better of it; think
Of all that is and shall be, and hath been."

"The cup my Father giveth me to drink,
65   Shall I not take it meekly? though my heart
Tremble a moment, it shall never shrink."

"Satan will wrestle with thee, when thou art
In the last agony; and Death will bring
Sins to remembrance ere thy spirit part."

70   "In that great hour of unknown suffering
God shall be with me, and His arm made bare
Shall fight for me: yea, underneath His wing
I shall lie safe at rest and freed from care."

Death.

"The grave-worm revels now"
Upon the pure white brow,
And on the eyes so dead and dim,
And on each putrifying limb,
5   And on the neck 'neath the long hair;
Now from the rosy lips
He damp corruption sips,
Banquetting everywhere.
Creeping up and down through the silken tresses
10   That once were smoothed by her husband's caresses,
In her mouth, and on her breast
Where the babe might never rest
In giving birth to whom she lost her life;
She gave all and she gave in vain,
15   Nor saw the purchase of her pain,
Poor mother and poor wife.

Was she too young to die?
Nay, young in sorrow and in years,
Her heart was old in faith and love;

20   Her eyes were ever fixed above,
     They were not dimmed by tears.
     And as the time went swiftly by
     She was even as a stately palm
     Beside still waters, where a dove
25   Broodeth in perfect calm.
     Yea, she was as a gentle breeze
     To which a thousand tones are given;
     To tell of freshness to the trees,
     Of roses to the honey-bees,
30   Of Summer to the distant seas,
     And unto all of Heaven.

     They rest together in one grave,
     The mother and her infant child,
     The holy and the undefiled:
35   Let none weep that ye could not save
     So much of beauty from the earth;
     It is not death ye see, though they
     Pass into foulness and decay;
     It is the second birth.

A Hopeless Case.
(Nydia.)

     All night I dream of that which cannot be:
         And early in the morning I awake
         My whole heart saddened for a vision's sake.
     I in my sleep have joy; but woe is me!
5   Thro' the long day the shadowy pleasures flee
         And are not: wherefore I would gladly take
         Some warm and poppied potion that might make
     My slumbers long which pass so pleasantly.
     And if I slept and never woke again,
10   But dreamed on with a happy consciousness
     Of grass and flowers and perfect rest from pain,
     I would leave hope a thousand times found vain,

And own a twilight solitude doth bless
Shut in from cold and wind and storm of rain.

Ellen Middleton.

Raise me; undraw the curtain; that is well.
   Put up the casement; I would see once more
   The golden sun-set flooding sea and shore;
And hearken to the solemn evening-bell
5   That ringeth out my spirit like a knell.
   The tree of love a bitter fruitage bore,
   Sweet at the rind but rotten at the core,
Pointing to heaven and bringing down to hell.
I will not name His name, lest the young life
10   That dieth at my heart should live again;
Strengthening me to renew the weary strife
   That ceaseth,—is this death? It is not pain.
Write on my grave: Here lieth a lone wife
   Whose faith was hidden and whose love was vain.

St. Andrew's Church.

   I listen to the holy antheming
That riseth in thy walls continually,
What while the organ pealeth solemnly
   And white-robed men and boys stand up to sing.
5   I ask my heart with a sad questioning:
"What lov'st thou here?" and my heart answers me:
"Within the shadows of this sanctuary
   To watch and pray is a most blessed thing."
To watch and pray, false heart? it is not so:
10   Vanity enters with thee, and thy love
Soars not to Heaven, but grovelleth below.
Vanity keepeth guard, lest good should reach
   Thy hardness; not the echoes from above
Can rule thy stubborn feelings or can teach.

Grown Cold.
Sonnet.

An old man asked me: What is Love? I turned
  In mirth away, and would not answer him;
  He filled a cup of wine up to the brim,
And yet no sparkling in its depths discerned.
5 Methought a death fire in his weak eyes burned
  While he beholding brightness called it dim;
  He sat and chuckled: 'twas a ghastly whim
In one whose spirit had so little learned.
So shall it be with me; but so not I
10 Shall question: certainly the blessèd thought
Of Love shall linger, when itself is gone.
  Oh nest of thorns for dove to brood upon!
    Oh painful throbbings of a heart untaught
To rest when all its gladness goeth by!

Zara.
(see Maturin's "Women.")

The pale sad face of her I wronged
  Upbraids and follows me for ever:
The silent mouth grows many-tongued
  To chide me; like some solemn river
5 Whose every wave hath found a tone
To reason of one truth alone.

She loved and was beloved again:
  Why did I spoil her paradise?
Oh fleeting joy and lasting pain!
10 Oh folly of the heart and eyes!
I loved him more than all; and he,
He also hath forsaken me.

How have I wearied thee false friend?
  Answer me, wherein have I erred
15 That so our happy loves should end?

Was it in thought, or deed, or word?
My soul lay bare to thee; disclose
The hidden fountain of my woes.

The Lady Moon is all too bright
20   Loftily seated in the skies.
They say that love once dimmed her light,
    But surely such are poets' lies.
Who knoweth that she ever shone
On rosy cheeked Endymion?

25   Narcissus looked on his own shade,
    And sickened for its loveliness.
Grasping, he saw its beauties fade
    And stretch out into nothingness.
He died, rejecting his own good,
30   And Echo mourned in solitude.

But wherefore am I left alone?
    What was my sin, to merit this?
Of all my friends there is not one
    I slighted in my happiness,
35   My joyful days—oh, very white
One face pursues me day and night.

She loved him even as I love,
    For she is dying for his sake.
Oh happy hope that looks above!
40   Oh happy heart that still can break!
I cannot die, though hope is dead;
He spurned me, and my heart but bled.

Therefore because she did not speak,
    Being strong to die and make no sign;
45   Because her courage waxed not weak,
    Strengthened with love as with new wine;
Because she stooped not while she bore,
He will return to her once more.

Perhaps he still may bring her health,
50   May call her colour back again;
While I shall pine in fame and wealth,

Owning that such as these are vain,
And envying her happier fate:—
And yet methinks it is too late.

55 Thou doubly false to her and me,
        Boast of her death and my despair.
Boast if thou canst: on land, on sea,
        I will be with thee everywhere;
My soul, let loose by mine own deed,
60 Shall make thee fear who would'st not heed.

Come, thou glad hour of vengeance, come,
        When I may dog him evermore,
May track him to his distant home:
        Yea, though he flee from shore to shore
65 I will be there, the pallid ghost
Of love and hope for ever lost.

Old memories shall make him sad,
        And thin his hair and change his mien;
He shall remember what he had,
70   And dream of what he might have been,
Till he shall long for death; yet shrink
From the cold cup that I shall drink.

Who drinketh of that potent draught
        May never set it down again.
75 What matter if one wept or laughed?
        It killeth joy and numbeth pain:
It hath sleep for the sorrowful,
And for the sick a perfect lull.

A drowsy lull, a heavy sleep:
80   Haply it may give such to me:
And if my grave place were dug deep
        Beneath the cold earth, verily
Such quietness I would not break,
Not for my cherished vengeance' sake.

85 Bring me the cup: behold, I choose
        For all my portion nothingness.
Bring me the cup: I would not lose

One drop of its forgetfulness.
On the grave brink I turn and think
90   Of thee, before I stoop to drink.

When the glad Summer time is past
   Shalt thou not weary of thy life
And turn to seek that home at last
   Where never enters fear nor strife?
95   Yea, at length, in the Autumn weather,
Shall not we twain repose together?

Ruin.

Amid the shade of a deserted hall
   I stand and think on much that hath been lost.
   How long it is since other step has cross'd
This time-worn floor; that tapestry is all
5   Worm-eaten; and those columns rise up tall
   Yet crumbling to decay; where banners toss'd
   Thin spiders' webs hang now; and bitter frost
Has even killed the flowers upon the wall.
Yet once this was a home brim full of life,
10   Full of the hopes and fears and love of youth,
   Full of love's language speaking without sound:
Here honour was enshrined and kindly truth;
   Hither the young lord brought his blushing wife,
   And here her bridal garlands were unbound.

I sit among green shady valleys oft
   Listening to echo-winds sighing of woe;
   The grass and flowers are strong and sweet below,
Yea, I am tired and the smooth turf is soft.
5   I sit and think and never look aloft
   Save to the tops of a tall poplar row
   That glisten in the wind, whispering low
Of sudden sorrow reaching those who laughed.

A very drowsy fountain bubbles near
10   Catching pale sunbeams o'er it wandering;
Its waters are so clear the stones look through:—
Then sitting by its lazy stream I hear
    Silence more loud than any other thing,
What time the trees weep o'er me honeydew.

Listen, and I will tell you of a face
    Not lovely, but made beautiful by mind;
    Lighted up with dark eyes in which you find
All womanly affections have their place;
5   Upon her even brow there is no trace
    Of passion; many fragrant blossoms bind
    Her hair glossy and golden; like a blind
It shadows her round cheeks blush full of grace.
I know now how it *is*, but it *was* so:
10   And when I think upon her bosom heaving,
    And her full glistening eyes looking on me
When the poor bird was struggling; I still see
    The throbbing tenderness, the virgin glow,
    And dream on, not at rest and yet believing.

Wouldst thou give me a heavy jewelled crown
    And purple mantle and embroidered vest?
    Dear Child, the colours of the glorious west
Are far more gorgeous when the sun sinks down.
5   The diadem would only make me frown
    With its own weight; nay, give me for my crest
    Pale violets dreaming in perfect rest,
Or rather leaves withered to Autumn brown.
A purple flowing mantle would but hinder
10   My careless walk, and an embroidered robe
Would shame me: what is the best man who stepped
On earth, more than the naked worm that crept
    Over its surface? Earth shall be a cinder;
    Where shall be then the beauty of the globe?

I said within myself: I am a fool
 To sigh ever for that which being gone
 Cannot return: the sun shines as it shone;
 Rejoice:—but who can be made glad by rule?
5 My heart and soul and spirit are no tool
 To play with and direct; my cheek is wan
 With memory; and ever and anon
I weep feeling life is a weary school.
There is much noise and bustle in the street;
10 It used to be so, and it is so now;
All are the same, and will be many a year.
 Spirit, that canst not break and wilt not bow,
Fear not the cold, thou who hast borne the heat;—
Die if thou wilt; but what hast thou to fear?

Methinks the ills of life I fain would shun;
 But then I must shun life which is a blank:
 Even in my childhood oft my spirit sank
Thinking of all that had still to be done.
5 Among my many friends there is not one
 Like her with whom I sat upon the bank
 Willow-o'er-shadowed; from whose lips I drank
A love more pure than streams that sing and run.
But many times that joy has cost a sigh;
10 And many times I in my heart have sought
For the old comfort, and not found it yet:
Surely in that calm day when I shall die
 The painful thought will be a blessed thought,
And I shall sorrow that I must forget.

Strange voices sing among the planets which
 Move on for ever; in the old sea's foam
 There is a prophecy; in Heaven's blue dome
Great beacon fires are lighted; black as pitch
5 Is night, and yet star jewels make it rich;
 And if the moon lights up her cloudy home
 The darkness flees, and forth strange gleamings roam

Lighting up hill and vale and mound and ditch.
Earth is full of all questions that all ask;
10   And she alone of heavy silence full
Answereth not: what is it severeth
Us from the spirits that we would be with?
    Or is it that our fleshly ear is dull,
And our own shadow hides light with a mask?

"Sleep, sleep, happy child;
"All creation slept and smiled."
            Blake.

Sleep, sleep, happy one;
Thy night is but just begun.
Sleep in peace; still angels keep
Holy watches o'er thy sleep.

5   Softest breasts are pillowing,
Softest wings are shadowing
Thy calm slumber; little child,
Sleep in thy white robes undefiled.

There is no more aching now
10   In thy heart or in thy brow.
The red blood upon thy breast
Cannot scare away thy rest.

Though thy hands are clasped as when
A man thou prayedst among men,
15   Thy pains are lulled, thy tears are dried,
And thy wants are satisfied.

Sleep, sleep; what quietness
After the world's noise is this!
Sleep on, where the hush and shade
20   Like a veil are round thee laid.

At thy head a cross is hewn
Whereon shines the Advent moon:
Through all the hours of the night
Its shadow rests on thee aright.

25   In temptation thou wert firm;
     Now have patience with the worm.
     Yet a little while, and he
     And death and sin shall bow to thee.

     Yet a little while, and thou
30   Shalt have a crown upon thy brow,
     And a palm branch in thy hand
     Where the holy angels stand.

     Sleep, sleep, till the chime
     Sound of the last matin prime:
35   Sleep on until the morn
     Of another Advent dawn.

What Sappho would have said had her leap cured instead of killing her.

     Love, Love, that having found a heart
         And left it, leav'st it desolate;—
         Love, Love, that art more strong than Hate,
     More lasting and more full of art;—
5   O blessèd Love, return, return,
     Brighten the flame that needs must burn.

     Among the stately lilies pale,
         Among the roses flushing red,
         I seek a flower meet for my head,
10   A wreath wherewith to bind my veil:
     I seek in vain; a shadow-pain
     Lies on my heart; and all in vain.

     The rose hath too much life in it;
         The lily is too much at rest.
15   Surely a blighted rose were best,
     Or cankered lily flower more fit;
     Or purple violet, withering
     While yet the year is in its spring.

I walk down by the river side
20   Where the low willows touch the stream;
   Beneath the ripple and sun-gleam
The slippery cold fishes glide,
Where flags and reeds and rushes lave
Their roots in the unsullied wave.

25 Methinks this is a drowsy place:
   Disturb me not; I fain would sleep:
   The very winds and waters keep
Their voices under; and the race
Of Time seems to stand still, for here
30 Is night or twilight all the year.

A very holy hushedness
   Broods here for ever: like a dove
   That, having built its nest above
A quiet place, feels the excess
35 Of calm sufficient, and would fain
Not wake, but drowse on without pain.

And slumbering on its mossy nest
   Haply hath dreams of pleasant Spring;
   And in its vision prunes its wing
40 And takes swift flight, yet is at rest.
Yea, is at rest: and still the calm
Is wrapped around it like a charm.

I would have quiet too in truth,
   And here will sojourn for a while.
45   Lo; I have wandered many a mile,
Till I am foot-sore in my youth.
I will lie down; and quite forget
The doubts and fears that haunt me yet.

My pillow underneath my head
50   Shall be green grass; thick fragrant leaves
   My canopy; the spider weaves
Meet curtains for my narrow bed;
And the dew can but cool my brow
That is so dry and burning now.

55   Ah, would that it could reach my heart,
          And fill the void that is so dry
          And aches and aches;—but what am I
      To shrink from my self-purchased part?
      It is in vain; is all in vain;
60   I must go forth and bear my pain.

      Must bear my pain, till Love shall turn
          To me in pity and come back.
          His footsteps left a smouldering track
      When he went forth, that still doth burn.
65   Oh come again, thou pain divine,
      Fill me and make me wholly thine.

On Keats.

      A garden in a garden: a green spot
          Where all is green: most fitting slumber-place
          For the strong man grown weary of a race
      Soon over. Unto him a goodly lot
5   Hath fallen in fertile ground; there thorns are not,
          But his own daisies: silence, full of grace,
          Surely hath shed a quiet on his face:
      His earth is but sweet leaves that fall and rot.
      What was his record of himself, ere he
10   Went from us? *Here lies one whose name was writ
          In water:* while the chilly shadows flit
              Of sweet Saint Agnes' Eve; while basil springs,
              His name, in every humble heart that sings,
      Shall be a fountain of love, verily.

Have Patience.

      The goblets all are broken,
          The pleasant wine is spilt,
          The songs cease; if thou wilt,
      Listen, and hear truth spoken.

5   We take thought for the morrow,
            And know not we shall see it;
        We look on death with sorrow,
            And cannot flee it.
        Youth passes like the lightning,
10   Not to return again;
        Just for a little bright'ning
            The confines of a plain;
        Gilding the spires, and whitening
            The grave-stones and the slain.
15   Youth passes like the odour
            From the white rose's cup,
            When the hot sun drinks up
        The dew that overflowed her:
        Then life forsakes the petals
20   That had been very fair;
            No beauty lingers there,
                And no bee settles.
        But when the rose is dead,
            And the leaves fallen;
25   And when the earth has spread
            A snow-white pall on;
        The thorn remains, once hidden
            By the green growth above it;
        A darksome guest unbidden,
30   With none to love it.
        Manhood is turbulent,
            And old age tires;
        That, hath no still content,
            This, no desires.
35   The present hath even less
            Joy than the past,
                And more cares fret it:—
        Life is a weariness
            From first to last:—
40   Let us forget it.
        Fill high and deep:—but how?
        The goblets all are broken.

Nay then, have patience now:
  For this is but a token
45 We soon shall have no need
  Of such to cheer us:
The palm-branches, decreed,
And crowns, to be our meed,
  Are very near us.

To Lalla, reading my verses topsy-turvy.

Darling little Cousin,
  With your thoughtful look
Reading topsy-turvy
  From a printed book

5 English hieroglyphics,
  More mysterious
To you, than Egyptian
  Ones would be to us;—

Leave off for a minute
10   Studying, and say
What is the impression
  That those marks convey?

Only solemn silence,
  And a wondering smile:
15 But your eyes are lifted
  Unto mine the while.

In their gaze so steady
  I can surely trace
That a happy spirit
20   Lighteth up your face.

Tender, happy spirit,
  Innocent and pure;
Teaching more than science,
  And than learning more.

25   How should I give answer
        To that asking look?
     Darling little Cousin
        Go back to your book.

     Read on: if you knew it,
30   You have cause to boast:—
     You are much the wisest,
        Though I know the most.

Sonnet.

     Some say that love and joy are one: and so
        They are indeed in heaven, but not on earth.
        Our hearts are made too narrow for the girth
     Of love, which is infinity; below
5   The portion we can compass may bring woe;
        Of this the Church bears witness from her birth:
        And though a throne in heaven be more than worth
     Tears, it *is* pain that makes them overflow.
     Think of the utter grief that fell on them
10   Who knew that they should see his face no more,
        When, strong in faith and love, he went before,
     Bound in the spirit, to Jerusalem,
        And yet the bitter parting scarcely bore,
     Though burning for a martyr's diadem.

The last *Complaint.*

     Woe is me! an old man said
     Stretched upon his dying bed:
     Woe is me! for life is short;
     And one hour cannot be bought
5   With great treasure or long thought.
     What have all my days been worth?

Weary labour without gain,
Pleasure ending in much pain,
Planting that brought forth no fruit,
10   Tree of life struck at the root,
Were my portion from my birth:
But my cold heart sickeneth
Shrinking from the touch of death;
And I fain would have again
15   Toil and weariness and pain
For a short time more on earth.
Yet the time was troublesome,
And the days lagged slowly on;
Surely it is better so:
20   And I cannot grieve to go
Hence. How fast the shadows come:—
Light and darkness both grow wan:—
Is that fire? it is not heat.
Cover up my face and feet;
25   Stand back; do not speak to me:
I would think how it will be
When the sun is blotted from
My existence, and the worm
Dwells with me as friend with friend
30   For a certain measured term.
But his term will have an end:
Then I shall be quite alone,
Quite alone without a sound;
For no wind beneath the ground
35   Can come jarring bone with bone.
Without eyes I shall behold
Darkness, and shall feel the cold
Without nerves, or brain, or flesh;—
Oh sweet air that blowest fresh;
40   Oh sweet stars that glimmer through
The dim casement;—I shall soon
Have a sod instead of you.
Draw the curtains, while I wake
Who shall sleep; and let me lie

45 In the blackness, till I die;
For I cannot bear to take
My last look of the clear moon.

Have you forgotten?

Have you forgotten how one Summer night
   We wandered forth together with the moon,
   While warm winds hummed to us a sleepy tune?
Have you forgotten how you praised both light
5 And darkness; not embarrassed yet not quite
   At ease? and how you said the glare of noon
   Less pleased you than the stars? but very soon
You blushed, and seemed to doubt if you were right.
We wandered far and took no note of time;
10   Till on the air there came the distant call
Of church bells: we turned hastily, and yet
Ere we reached home sounded a second chime.
   But what; have you indeed forgotten all?
Ah how then is it I cannot forget?

A Christmas Carol,
(on the stroke of Midnight.)

Thank God, thank God, we do believe,
Thank God that this is Christmas Eve.
Even as we kneel upon this day,
Even so the ancient legends say
5 Nearly two thousand years ago
The stalled ox knelt, and even so
The ass knelt full of praise which they
Could not express, while we can pray.
Thank God, thank God, for Christ was born
10 Ages ago, as on this morn:
In the snow-season undefiled

God came to earth a little Child;
He put His ancient glory by
To live for us, and then to die.

15   How shall we thank God? how shall we
Thank Him and praise Him worthily?
What will He have Who loved us thus,
What presents will He take from us?
Will He take gold, or precious heap
20   Of gems, or shall we rather steep
The air with incense, or bring myrrh?
What man will be our messenger
To go to Him and ask His Will?
Which having learned we will fulfil
25   Tho' He choose all we most prefer:—
What man will be our messenger?

Thank God, thank God, the Man is found,
Sure-footed, knowing well the ground:
He knows the road, for this the way
30   He travelled once, as on this day.
He is our Messenger; beside,
He is our Door, and Path, and Guide;
He also is our Offering,
He is the Gift that we must bring.
35   Let us kneel down with one accord
And render thanks unto the Lord:
For unto us a Child is born
Upon this happy Christmas morn;
For unto us a Son is given,
40   Firstborn of God and Heir of Heaven.

For Advent.

Sweet sweet sound of distant waters falling
    On a parched and thirsty plain;
Sweet sweet song of soaring skylark, calling
    On the sun to shine again;

5   Perfume of the rose, only the fresher
        For past fertilizing rain;
    Pearls amid the sea, a hidden treasure
        For some daring hand to gain;—
    Better, dearer than all these
10   Is the earth beneath the trees:
        Of a much more priceless worth
        Is the old, brown, common earth.

    Little snow-white lamb piteously bleating
        For thy mother far away;
15   Saddest, sweetest nightingale retreating
        With thy sorrow from the day;
    Weary fawn whom night has overtaken,
        From the herd gone quite astray;
    Dove whose nest was rifled and forsaken
20   In the budding month of May;—
        Roost upon the leafy trees;
        Lie on earth and take your ease:
        Death is better far than birth,
        You shall turn again to earth.

25   Listen to the never pausing murmur
        Of the waves that fret the shore:
    See the ancient pine that stands the firmer
        For the storm-shock that it bore;
    And the moon her silver chalice filling
30   With light from the great sun's store;
    And the stars which deck our temple's ceiling
        As the flowers deck its floor;
        Look and hearken while you may,
        For these things shall pass away:
35   All these things shall fail and cease;
        Let us wait the end in peace.

    Let us wait the end in peace; for truly
        That shall cease which was before:
    Let us see our lamps are lighted, duly
40   Fed with oil, nor wanting more:
    Let us pray while yet the Lord will hear us,

For the time is almost o'er;
Yea, the end of all is very near us;
Yea, the Judge is at the door.
45   Let us pray now while we may;
It will be too late to pray
When the quick and dead shall all
Rise at the last trumpet call.

Two Pursuits.

A voice said: "Follow, follow:" and I rose
And followed far into the dreamy night,
Turning my back upon the pleasant light.
It led me where the bluest water flows,
5   And would not let me drink; where the corn grows
I dared not pause, but went uncheered by sight
Or touch; until at length in evil plight
It left me, wearied out with many woes.
Some time I sat as one bereft of sense:
10   But soon another voice from very far
Called: "Follow, follow:" and I rose again.
Now on my night has dawned a blessèd star;
Kind, steady hands my sinking steps sustain,
And will not leave me till I shall go hence.

Looking forward.

Sleep, let me sleep, for I am sick of care;
Sleep, let me sleep, for my pain wearies me.
Shut out the light; thicken the heavy air
With drowsy incense; let a distant stream
5   Of music lull me, languid as a dream,
Soft as the whisper of a Summer sea.

Pluck me no rose that groweth on a thorn,
Nor myrtle white and cold as snow in June,

Fit for a virgin on her marriage morn:
10 But bring me poppies brimmed with sleepy death,
And ivy choking what it garlandeth,
And primroses that open to the moon.

Listen, the music swells into a song,
A simple song I loved in days of yore;
15   The echoes take it up and up along
The hills, and the wind blows it back again.—
Peace, peace, there is a memory in that strain
Of happy days that shall return no more.

Oh peace, your music wakeneth old thought,
20 But not old hope that made my life so sweet,
Only the longing that must end in nought.
Have patience with me, friends, a little while:
For soon where you shall dance and sing and smile,
My quickened dust may blossom at your feet.

25   Sweet thought that I may yet live and grow green,
That leaves may yet spring from the withered root,
And buds and flowers and berries half unseen;
Then if you haply muse upon the past,
Say this: Poor child, she hath her wish at last;
30 Barren through life, but in death bearing fruit.

Life hidden.

Roses and lilies grow above the place
Where she sleeps the long sleep that doth not dream.
If we could look upon her hidden face
Nor shadow would be there nor garish gleam
5   Of light: her life is lapsing like a stream
That makes no noise but floweth on apace
Seawards; while many a shade and shady beam
Vary the ripples in their gliding chase.
She doth not see, but knows: she doth not feel,
10   And yet is sensible: she hears no sound,

Yet counts the flight of time and doth not err.
Peace far and near; peace to ourselves and her:
  Her body is at peace in holy ground,
Her spirit is at peace where Angels kneel.

Queen Rose.

The jessamine shows like a star;
  The lilies sway like sceptres slim;
Fair clematis from near and far
  Sets forth its wayward tangled whim;
5   Curved meadowsweet blooms rich and dim;—
But yet a rose is fairer far.

The jessamine is odorous; so
  Maid lilies are, and clematis;
And where tall meadowsweet flowers grow
10   A rare and subtle perfume is;—
  What can there be more choice than these?—
A rose when it doth bud and blow.

Let others choose sweet jessamine,
  Or weave their lily crown aright,
15 And let who love it pluck and twine
  Loose clematis; or draw delight
  From meadowsweet's clustry downy white;—
The rose, the perfect rose be mine.

How one chose.

"Beyond the sea, in a green land
  Where only rivers are;—
Beyond the clouds, in the clear sky
  Close by some quiet star;—
5   Could you not fancy there might be
A home Beloved for you and me?"

"If there were such a home my Friend
    Truly prepared for us
Full of palm branches or of crowns
10   Sun-gemmed and glorious,
How should we reach it? let us cease
From longing; let us be at peace."

"The nightingale sang yestereve;
    A sweet song singeth she:
15 Most sad and without any hope
    And full of memory;
But still methought it seemed to speak
To me of home, and bid me seek."

"The nightingale ceased ere the morn:
20   Her heart could not contain
The passion of her song, but burst
    With the loud throbbing pain.
Now she hath rest which is the best,
And now I too would be at rest."

25 "Last night I watched the mounting moon:
     Her glory was too pale
To shine thro' the black heavy clouds
    That wrapped her like a veil;
And yet with patience she passed thro'
30 The mists and reached the depths of blue."

"And when the road was travelled o'er
    And when the goal was won
A little while and all her light
    Was swallowed by the sun:
35 The weary moon must seek again;
Even so our search would be in vain."

"Yet seek with me. And if our way
    Be long and troublesome,
And if our noon be hot until
40   The chilly shadows come
Of evening;—till those shadows flee
In dawn, think Love it is with me."

"Nay seek alone: I am no mate
    For such as you, in truth:
45 My heart is old before its time;
    Yours yet is in its youth:
This home with pleasures girt about
Seek you, for I am wearied out."

Seeking rest.

My Mother said: The child is changed
    That used to be so still;
All the day long she sings, and sings,
    And seems to think no ill;
5   She laughs as if some inward joy
    Her heart would overfill.

My Sisters said: Now prithee tell
    Thy secret unto us:
Let us rejoice with thee; for all
10   Is surely prosperous,
Thou art so merry: tell us Sweet:
    We had not used thee thus.

My Mother says: What ails the child
    Lately so blythe of cheer?
15 Art sick or sorry? nay, it is
    The Winter of the year;
Wait till the Spring time comes again
    And the sweet flowers appear.

My Sisters say: Come, sit with us,
20   That we may weep with thee:
Show us thy grief that we may grieve:
    Yea, haply, if we see
Thy sorrow, we may ease it; but
    Shall share it certainly.

25 How should I share my pain, who kept
    My pleasure all my own?

My Spring will never come again;
　My pretty flowers have blown
For the last time; I can but sit
30　　And think and weep alone.

A Year Afterwards.

Things are so changed since last we met:
Come; I will show you where she lies.
Doubtless the old look fills her eyes,
And the old patient smile is set
5　　Upon her mouth: it was even so
When last I saw her stretched and still,
So pale and calm I could not weep:
The steady sweetness did not go
Thro' the long week she lay asleep,
10　　Until the dust was heaped on her.
Now many-feathered grasses grow
Above her bosom: come; I will
Show you all this, and we can talk
Going; it is a pleasant walk
15　　And the wind makes it pleasanter.

This is the very path that she
So often trod with eager feet
Tho' weary. The dusk branches meet
Above, making green fretted work,
20　　The screen between my saint and me.
There, where the softest sunbeams lurk,
Cannot you fancy she may be
Leaning down to me from her rest;
And shaking her long golden hair
25　　Thro' the thick branches to my face,
That I may feel she still is mine?—
Is not this wood a pleasant place?
To me the faintest breath of air
Seems here to whisper tenderly
30　　That she, mine own, will not forget.

It may be selfishness; and yet
I like to think her joy may not
Be perfected, although divine
In all the glory of the blest,
35 Without me: that the greenest spot
And shadiest, would not suffice,
Without me, even in Paradise.

But we must leave the wood to go
Across the sunny fields of wheat;
40 I used to fancy that the grass
And daisies loved to touch her feet.
This was the way we used to pass
Together; rain nor wind nor snow
Could hinder her, until her strength
45 Failed utterly; and when at length
She was too weak, they put her bed
Close to the window; there she lay
Counting the Church chimes one by one
For many weeks: at last a day
50 Came when her patient watch was done,
And some one told me she was dead.

Now we can see the Church tower; look,
Where the old flaky yew trees stand.
There is a certain shady nook
55 Among them, where she used to sit
When weary: I have held her hand
So often there: one day she said
That sometimes, when we sat so, she
Could fancy what being dead must be,
60 And long for it if shared by me:—
She had no cause for dreading it,
And never once conceived my dread.

This path leads to the Western door
Where the sun casts his latest beam,
65 And hard beside it is her grave.
I sowed those grasses there that wave
Like down, but would sow nothing more,

No flowers, as if her resting place
Could want for sweetness; where she is
70　Is sweetest of all sweetnesses.
If you look closely, you can trace
A Cross formed by the grass, above
Her head: and sometimes I could dream
She sees the Cross, and feels the love
75　That planted it; and prays that I
May come and share her hidden rest;
May even lie where she doth lie,
With the same turf above my breast,
And the same stars and silent sky.

Two thoughts of Death.

1.

Her heart that loved me once is rottenness
　　Now and corruption; and her life is dead
　　That was to have been one with mine she said.
The earth must lie with such a cruel stress
5　On her eyes where the white lids used to press;
　　Foul worms fill up her mouth so sweet and red;
　　Foul worms are underneath her graceful head.
Yet these, being born of her from nothingness
These worms are certainly flesh of her flesh.—
10　　How is it that the grass is rank and green,
And the dew dropping rose is brave and fresh
Above what was so sweeter far than they?
Even as her beauty hath passed quite away
　　Their's too shall be as tho' it had not been.

2.

15　So I said underneath the dusky trees:
　　But because I still loved her memory
　　I stooped to pluck a pale anemone
And lo! my hand lighted upon heartsease

Not fully blown: while with new life from these
20   Fluttered a starry moth that rapidly
Rose toward the sun: sunlighted flashed on me
Its wings that seemed to throb like heart pulses.
Far far away it flew far out of sight,
From earth and flowers of earth it passed away
25 As tho' it flew straight up into the light.
Then my heart answered me: Thou fool to say
That she is dead whose night is turned to day,
And whose day shall no more turn back to night.

Three Moments.

The Child said: "Pretty bird
"Come back and play with me."
The bird said: "It is in vain,
"For I am free.
5   "I am free, I will not stay,
"But will fly far away,
"In the woods to sing and play,
"Far away, far away."
The Child sought her Mother:
10 "I have lost my bird;" said she
Weeping bitterly:
But the Mother made her answer,
Half sighing pityingly,
Half smiling cheerily:
15 "Tho' thy bird come nevermore
"Do not weep;
"Find another playfellow
"Child, and keep
"Tears for future pain more deep."

20 "Sweet rose do not wither,"
The Girl said.
But a blight had touched its heart
And it drooped its crimson head.
In the morning it had opened

25   Full of life and bloom,
But the leaves fell one by one
Till the twilight gloom.
One by one the leaves fell
By summer winds blown from their stem;
30   They fell upon the dewy earth
Which nourished once now tainted them.
Again the young Girl wept
And sought her Mother's ear:
"My rose is dead so full of grace,
35   "The very rose I meant to place
"In the wreath that I wear."
"Nay, never weep for such as this;"
The Mother answered her:
"But weave another crown, less fair
40   "Perhaps, but fitter for thy hair.
"And keep thy tears," the Mother said:
"For something heavier."

The Woman knelt; but did not pray
Nor weep nor cry; she only said:
45   "Not this, not this:" and clasped her hands
Against her heart and bowed her head
While the great struggle shook the bed.
"Not this, not this:" tears did not fall:
"Not this:" it was all
50   She could say; no sobs would come;
The mortal grief was almost dumb.—
At length when it was over, when
She knew it was and would be so,
She cried: "Oh Mother, where are they,
55   "The tears that used to flow
"So easily? one single drop
"Might save my reason now, or stop
"My heart from breaking. Blessed tears
"Wasted in former years!"
60   Then the grave Mother made reply:
"Oh Daughter mine be of good cheer,
"Rejoicing thou canst shed no tear.

"Thy pain is almost over now.
"Once more thy heart shall throb with pain,
65   "But then shall never throb again.
"Oh happy thou who canst not weep,
"Oh happy thou!"

Once.

She was whiter than the ermine
    That half shadowed neck and hand,
And her tresses were more golden
    Than their golden band;
5   Snowy ostrich plumes she wore
Yet I almost loved her more
In the simple time before.

Then she plucked the stately lilies
    Knowing not she was more fair,
10   And she listened to the skylark
        In the morning air.
Then, a kerchief all her crown,
She looked for the acorns brown,
Bent their bough and shook them down.

15   Then she thought of Christmas holly
    And of maybloom in sweet May;
Then she loved to pick the cherries
    And to turn the hay.
She was humble then and meek,
20   And the blush upon her cheek
Told of much she could not speak.

Now she is a noble lady,
    With calm voice not overloud;
Very courteous in her action,
25   Yet you think her proud;
Much too haughty to affect;
Too indifferent to direct,
Or be angry, or suspect;
Doing all from self-respect.

Three Nuns.

1.

"Sospira questo core
　E non so dir perchè."

Shadow, shadow on the wall
　　Spread thy shelter over me;
Wrap me with a heavy pall,
　　With the dark that none may see.
5　Fold thyself around me; come:
Shut out all the troublesome
Noise of life; I would be dumb.

Shadow thou hast reached my feet,
　　Rise and cover up my head;
10　Be my stainless winding sheet,
　　Buried before I am dead.
Lay thy cool upon my breast:
Once I thought that joy was best,
Now I only care for rest.

15　By the grating of my cell
　　Sings a solitary bird;
Sweeter than the vesper bell,
　　Sweetest song was ever heard.*
Sing upon thy living tree:
20　Happy echoes answer thee,
Happy songster, sing to me.

When my yellow hair was curled
　　Though men saw and called me fair,
I was weary in the world
25　　Full of vanity and care.
Gold was left behind, curls shorn
When I came here; that same morn
Made a bride no gems adorn.

Here wrapped in my spotless veil,
30　　Curtained from intruding eyes,

*"Sweetest eyes were ever seen." E. B. Browning.

I whom prayers and fasts turn pale
        Wait the flush of Paradise.
But the vigil is so long
        My heart sickens:—sing thy song,
35   Blithe bird that canst do no wrong.

Sing on, making me forget
        Present sorrow and past sin.
Sing a little longer yet:
        Soon the matins will begin;
40   And I must turn back again
To that aching worse than pain
I must bear and not complain.

Sing, that in thy song I may
        Dream myself once more a child
45   In the green woods far away
        Plucking clematis and wild
Hyacinths, till pleasure grew
Tired, yet so was pleasure too,
Resting with no work to do.

50   In the thickest of the wood,
        I remember, long ago
How a stately oak tree stood,
        With a sluggish pool below
Almost shadowed out of sight.
55   On the waters dark as night,
Water-lilies lay like light.

There, while yet a child, I thought
        I could live as in a dream,
Secret, neither found nor sought:
60   Till the lilies on the stream,
Pure as virgin purity,
Would seem scarce too pure for me:—
Ah, but that can never be.

2.

"Sospirerà d'amore,
Ma non lo dice a me."

I loved him, yes, where was the sin?
65   I loved him with my heart and soul.
But I pressed forward to no goal,
There was no prize I strove to win.
Show me my sin that I may see:—
Throw the first stone, thou Pharisee.

70 I loved him, but I never sought
    That he should know that I was fair.
    I prayed for him; was my sin prayer?
I sacrificed, he never bought.
He nothing gave, he nothing took;
75 We never bartered look for look.

My voice rose in the sacred choir,
    The choir of Nuns; do you condemn
    Even if, when kneeling among them,
Faith, zeal and love kindled a fire
80 And I prayed for his happiness
Who knew not? was my error this?

I only prayed that in the end
    His trust and hope may not be vain.
    I prayed not we may meet again:
85 I would not let our names ascend,
No, not to Heaven, in the same breath;
Nor will I join the two in death.

Oh sweet is death; for I am weak
    And weary, and it giveth rest.
90   The Crucifix lies on my breast,
And all night long it seems to speak
Of rest; I hear it through my sleep,
And the great comfort makes me weep.

Oh sweet is death that bindeth up
95   The broken and the bleeding heart.
    The draught chilled, but a cordial part

Lurked at the bottom of the cup;
And for my patience will my Lord
Give an exceeding great reward.

100   Yea, the reward is almost won,
     A crown of glory and a palm.
     Soon I shall sing the unknown psalm;
Soon gaze on light, not on the sun;
And soon, with surer faith, shall pray
105   For him, and cease not night nor day.

My life is breaking like a cloud;
     God judgeth not as man doth judge.—
     Nay, bear with me; you need not grudge
This peace; the vows that I have vowed
110   Have all been kept: Eternal Strength
Holds me, though mine own fails at length.

Bury me in the Convent ground
     Among the flowers that are so sweet;
     And lay a green turf at my feet,
115   Where thick trees cast a gloom around.
At my head let a Cross be, white
Through the long blackness of the night.

Now kneel and pray beside my bed
     That I may sleep being free from pain:
120   And pray that I may wake again
After His Likeness, Who hath said
(Faithful is He Who promiseth,)
We shall be satisfied Therewith.

3.

"Rispondimi, cor mio,
   Perchè sospiri tu?
Risponde: Voglio Iddio,
   Sospiro per Gesù."

My heart is as a freeborn bird
125   Caged in my cruel breast,
That flutters, flutters evermore,

Nor sings, nor is at rest.
But beats against the prison bars,
As knowing its own nest
130 Far off beyond the clouded West.

My soul is as a hidden fount
Shut in by clammy clay,
That struggles with an upward moan;
Striving to force its way
135 Up through the turf, over the grass,
Up, up into the day,
Where twilight no more turneth grey.

Oh for the grapes of the True Vine
Growing in Paradise,
140 Whose tendrils join the Tree of Life
To that which maketh wise.
Growing beside the Living Well
Whose sweetest waters rise
Where tears are wiped from tearful eyes.

145 Oh for the waters of that Well
Round which the Angels stand.
Oh for the Shadow of the Rock
On my heart's weary land.
Oh for the Voice to guide me when
150 I turn to either hand,
Guiding me till I reach Heaven's strand.

Thou World from which I am come out,
Keep all thy gems and gold;
Keep thy delights and precious things,
155 Thou that art waxing old.
My heart shall beat with a new life,
When thine is dead and cold:
When thou dost fear I shall be bold.

When Earth shall pass away with all
160 Her pride and pomp of sin,
The City builded without hands
Shall safely shut me in.

All the rest is but vanity
      Which others strive to win:
165   Where their hopes end my joys begin.

I will not look upon a rose
      Though it is fair to see:
The flowers planted in Paradise
      Are budding now for me.
170   Red roses like love visible
      Are blowing on their tree,
Or white like virgin purity.

I will not look unto the sun
      Which setteth night by night:
175   In the untrodden courts of Heaven
      My crown shall be more bright.
Lo, in the New Jerusalem
      Founded and built aright
My very feet shall tread on light.

180   With foolish riches of this World
      I have bought treasure, where
Nought perisheth: for this white veil
      I gave my golden hair;
I gave the beauty of my face
185   For vigils, fasts and prayer;
I gave all for this Cross I bear.

My heart trembled when first I took
      The vows which must be kept;
At first it was a weariness
190   To watch when once I slept.
The path was rough and sharp with thorns;
      My feet bled as I stepped;
The Cross was heavy and I wept.

While still the names rang in mine ears
195   Of daughter, sister, wife;
The outside world still looked so fair
      To my weak eyes, and rife

With beauty; my heart almost failed;
    Then in the desperate strife
200 I prayed, as one who prays for life,

Until I grew to love what once
    Had been so burdensome.
So now when I am faint, because
    Hope deferred seems to numb
205 My heart, I yet can plead; and say
    Although my lips are dumb:
"The Spirit and the Bride say, Come."

Song.

We buried her among the flowers
    At falling of the leaf,
And choked back all our tears; her joy
    Could never be our grief.

5 She lies among the living flowers
    And grass, the only thing
That perishes;—or is it that
    Our Autumn was her Spring?

Doubtless, if we could see her face,
10   The smile is settled there
Which almost broke our hearts, when last
    We knelt by her in prayer.

When with tired eyes and failing breath
    And hands crossed on her breast
15 Perhaps she saw her Guardian spread
    His wings above her rest.

So she sleeps hidden in the flowers:
    But yet a little while
And we shall see her wake, and rise
20   Fair, with the selfsame smile.

The Watchers.

She fell asleep among the flowers
In the sober Autumn hours.

Three there are about her bed,
At her side and feet and head.

5   At her head standeth the Cross
For which all else she counted loss:

Still and steadfast at her feet
Doth her Guardian Angel sit:

Prayers of truest love abide
10   Wrapping her on every side.

The Holy Cross standeth alone,
Beneath the white moon, whitest stone.

Evil spirits come not near
Its shadow, shielding from all fear;

15   Once she bore it in her breast,
Now it certifies her rest.

Humble violets grow around
Its base, sweetening the grassy ground,

Leaf-hidden; so she hid from praise
20   Of men her pious holy ways.

Higher about it, twining close,
Clingeth a crimson thorny rose;

So from her heart's good seed of love
Thorns sprang below, flowers spring above.

25   Tho' yet his vigil doth not cease,
Her Angel sits in perfect peace,

With white folded wings; for she
He watches, now is pure as he.

He watches with his loving eyes
30   For the day when she shall rise;

When full of glory and of grace
She shall behold him face to face.

Tho' she is safe for ever, yet
Human love doth not forget;
35   But prays that in her deep
Grave she may sleep a blessed sleep,

Till when time and the world are past
She may find mercy at the last.

So these three do hedge her in
40   From sorrow as death does from sin.

So freed from earthly taint and pain
May they all meet in Heaven. Amen.

Annie.

Annie is fairer than her kith
    And kinder than her kin;
Her eyes are like the open heaven
    Holy and pure from sin;
5   Her heart is like an ordered house
    Good fairies harbour in;
Oh happy he who wins the love
    That I can never win.

Her sisters stand as hyacinths
10   Around the perfect rose:
They bloom and open to the full,
    My bud will scarce unclose;
They are for every butterfly
    That comes and sips and goes,
15   My bud hides in the tender green
    Most sweet and hardly shows.

Oh cruel kindness in soft eyes
    That are no more than kind,
On which I gaze my heart away
20   Till the tears make me blind.

How is it others find the way
　　That I can never find
To make her laugh that sweetest laugh
　　Which leaves all else behind?

25　Her hair is like the golden corn
　　A low wind breathes upon;
Or like the golden harvest moon
　　When all the mists are gone;
Or like a stream with golden sands
30　　On which the sun has shone
Day after day in summer time
　　Ere autumn leaves are wan.

I will not tell her that I love
　　Lest she should turn away
35　With sorrow in her tender heart
　　Which now is light and gay.
I will not tell her that I love
　　Lest she should turn and say
That we must meet no more again
40　　For many a weary day.

A Dirge.

She was as sweet as violets in the Spring,
　　As fair as any rose in Summer time:
　　　But frail are roses in their prime
　　And violets in their blossoming.
5　Even so was she:
　　And now she lies,
　　　The earth upon her fast closed eyes,
Dead in the darkness silently.

The sweet Spring violets never bud again,
10　　The roses bloom and perish in a morn:
　　　They see no second quickening lying lorn;
　　Their beauty dies as tho' in vain.
Must she die so
　　For evermore,

15 Cold as the sand upon the shore,
  As passionless for joy and woe?—

  Nay, she is worth much more than flowers that fade
   And yet shall be made fair with purple fruit;
    Branch of the Living Vine, Whose Root
20 From all eternity is laid.
  Another Sun
   Than this of our's,
   Has withered up indeed her flowers
  But ripened her grapes every one.

Song.

  It is not for her even brow
   And shining yellow hair,
  But it is for her tender eyes
   I think my love so fair;
5 Her telltale eyes that smile and weep
  As frankly as they wake and sleep.

  It is not for her rounded cheek
   I love and fain would win,
  But it is for the blush that comes
10   Straight from the heart within;
  The honest blush of maiden shame
  That blushes without thought of blame.

  So in my dreams I never hear
   Her song, although she sings
15 As if a choir of spirits swept
   From earth with throbbing wings;
  I only hear the simple voice
  Whose love makes many hearts rejoice.

A Dream.

  Oh for my love, my only love,
   Oh for my lost love far away!—

Oh that the grass were green above
   Her head or mine this weary day:—
5   The grass green in the morning grey.

She lies down in a foreign land
   And in a foreign land doth rise.
I cannot hold her by the hand;
   I cannot read her speaking eyes
10   That turned mere spoken words to lies.

This is the bough she leaned upon
   And watched the rose deep western sky,
For the last sun rays almost gone:
   I did not hear the wind pass by,
15   Nor stream; I only heard her sigh.

I saw the tears that did not fall,
   I saw the blush upon her cheek,
The trembling hand so white and small:
   She did not speak, I could not speak:—
20   Oh that strong love should make us weak.

Therefore we parted as we met,
   She on her way, and I on mine.
I think her tender heart was set
   On holier things and more Divine:—
25   We parted thus and gave no sign.

Oh that the grass were green above
   Her head or mine; so I could pray
In certain faith for her my love,
   Unchanging, all the night and day:
30   Most near altho' most far away.

"A fair World tho' a fallen."———

You tell me that the world is fair, in spite
   Of the old fall; and that I should not turn
   So to the grave, and let my spirit yearn
After the quiet of the long last night.

5 Have I then shut mine eyes against the light,
  Grief-deafened lest my spirit should discern?
  Yet how could I keep silence when I burn?
  And who can give me comfort?—hear the right.
  Have patience with the weak and sick at heart:
10 Bind up the wounded with a tender touch.
   Comfort the sad, tear-blinded as they go:—
  For tho' I failed to choose the better part,
   Were it a less unutterable woe
  If we should come to love this world too much?—

Advent.

"Come," thou dost say to Angels,
 To blessed Spirits, "Come";
"Come," to the Lambs of Thine Own flock,
 Thy little Ones, "Come home."

5 "Come," from the many-mansioned house
 The gracious word is sent,
"Come," from the ivory palaces
 Unto the Penitent.

O Lord, restore us deaf and blind,
10 Unclose our lips tho' dumb;
Then say to us, "I come with speed,"
 And we will answer, "Come."

All Saints.

They have brought gold and spices to my King,
 Incense and precious stuffs and ivory;
O holy Mother mine, what can I bring
 That so my Lord may deign to look on me?
5 They sing a sweeter song than I can sing,
 All crowned and glorified exceedingly;
I, bound on earth, weep for my trespassing,
 They sing the song of love in Heaven, set free.

Then answered me my Mother, and her voice,
10   Spake to my heart, yea, answered in my heart:
Sing, saith He, to the Heavens, to Earth, rejoice;
Thou, also, lift thy heart to Him above;
    He seeks not thine, but thee, such as thou art,
For lo! His banner over thee is Love.

"Eye hath not seen."

Our feet shall tread upon the stars
    Less bright than we.
The everlasting shore shall bound
    A fairer sea
5   Than that which cold
Now glitters in the sun like gold.

Oh good, oh blest: but who shall say
    How fair, how fair,
Is the Light-region where no cloud
10   Darkens the air,
    Where weary eyes
Rest on the green of Paradise?

There cometh not the wind, nor rain,
    Nor sun, nor snow;
15   The trees of Knowledge and of Life
    Bud there and blow,
    Their leaves and fruit
Fed from an undecaying root.

There Angels flying to and fro
20   Are not more white
Than Penitents some while ago,
    Now Saints in Light:
    Once soiled and sad;
Cleansed now and crowned, fulfilled and glad.

25   Now yearning thro' the perfect rest
    Perhaps they gaze
Earthwards upon their best beloved

In all earth's ways:
Longing, but not
30 With pain, as used to be their lot.

The hush of that beatitude
Is ages long,
Sufficing Virgins, Prophets, Saints,
Till the new song
35 Shall be sent up
From lips which drained the bitter cup.

If but the thought of Paradise
Gives joy on earth,
What shall it be to enter there
40 Thro' second birth?
To find once more
Our dearest treasure gone before?

To find the Shepherd of the Sheep,
The Lamb once slain,
45 Who leads His Own by living streams.
Never again
To thirst, or need
Aught in green pastures where they feed.

But from the Altar comes a cry
50 Awful and strong
From martyred Saints: How long, they say,
O Lord, how long
Holy and True,
Shall vengeance for our blood be due?

55 Then the Lord gives them robes of white;
And bids them stay
In patience till the time be full
For the last day:
The day of dread
60 When the last sentence shall be said.

When heaven and earth shall flee away;
And the great deep
Shall render up her dead, and earth

Her sons that sleep;
65   And day of grace
Be hid for ever from Thy Face.

Oh hide us till Thy wrath be past,
    Our grief, our shame,
With Peter and with Magdalene
70   And him whose name
    No record tells
Who by Thy promise with Thee dwells.

St. Elizabeth of Hungary.

When if ever life is sweet,
    Save in heart in all a child,
    A fair virgin undefiled
Knelt she at her Saviour's feet;
5   While she laid her royal crown,
    Thinking it too mean a thing
    For a solemn offering,
Careless on the cushions down.

Fair she was as any rose,
10   But more pale than lilies white,
Her eyes full of deep repose
    Seemed to see beyond our sight.
Hush, she is a holy thing:
    Hush, her soul is in her eyes
15   Seeking far in Paradise
For her Light, her Love, her King.

Moonshine.

Fair the sun riseth,
    Bright as bright can be,
Fair the sun shineth
    On a fair fair sea.

5   "Across the water
       "Wilt thou come with me,
       "Miles and long miles, love,
         "Over the salt sea?"—

       "If thou wilt hold me
10   "Truly by the hand,
       "I will go with thee
         "Over sea and sand.

       "If thou wilt hold me
         "That I shall not fall,
15   "I will go with thee,
         "Love, in spite of all."

       Fair the moon riseth
         On her heavenly way
       Making the waters
20   Fairer than by day.

       A little vessel
         Rocks upon the sea,
       Where stands a maiden
         Fair as fair can be.

25   Her smile rejoices
         Though her mouth is mute,
       She treads the vessel
         With her little foot.

       Truly he holds her
30   Faithful to his pledge,
       Guiding the vessel
         From the water's edge.

       Fair the moon saileth
         With her pale fair light,
35   Fair the girl gazeth
         Out into the night.

       Saith she: "Like silver
         "Shines thy hair, not gold;"—

Saith she: "I shiver
40   "In thy steady hold.

"Love," she saith weeping,
"Loose thy hold awhile,
"My heart is freezing
"In thy freezing smile."

45   The moon is hidden
By a silver cloud,
Fair as a halo
Or a maiden's shroud.

No more beseeching,
50   Ever on they go:
The vessel rocketh
Softly to and fro;

And still he holds her
That she shall not fall,
55   Till pale mists whiten
Dimly over all.

Onward and onward,
Far across the sea;
Onward and onward,
60   Pale as pale can be;

Onward and onward,
Ever hand in hand,
From sun and moon light
To another land.

"The Summer is ended."

Wreathe no more lilies in my hair,
For I am dying, Sister sweet:
Or if you will for the last time
Indeed, why make me fair
5   Once for my windingsheet.

Pluck no more roses for my breast,
For I like them fade in my prime:
Or if you will, why pluck them still
    That they may share my rest
10   Once more, for the last time.

Weep not for me when I am gone,
Dear tender one, but hope and smile:
Or if you cannot choose but weep
    A little while, weep on
15   Only a little while.

"I look for the Lord."

Our wealth has wasted all away,
    Our pleasures have found wings;
The night is long until the day,
    Lord, give us better things:
5 A ray of light in thirsty night
    And secret water springs.

Our love is dead, or sleeps, or else
    Is hidden from our eyes:
Our silent love, while no man tells
10   Or if it lives or dies.
Oh give us love, O Lord, above
    In changeless Paradise.

Our house is left us desolate,
    Even as Thy word hath said.
15 Before our face the way is great,
    Around us are the dead:
Oh guide us, save us from the grave,
    As Thou Thy saints hast led.

Lead us where pleasures evermore
20   And wealth indeed are placed,
And home on an eternal shore,
    And love that cannot waste;

Where Joy Thou art unto the heart,
And Sweetness to the taste.

Song.

I have loved you for long long years Ellen,
   On you has my heart been set;
I have loved you for long patient years,
   But you do not love me yet.

5   Oh that the sun that rose that day
   Had never and never set,
When I wooed and you did not turn away,
   Tho' you could not love me yet.

I lay lands and gold at your feet Ellen,
10   At your feet a coronet,
I lay a true heart at your feet Ellen,
   But you do not love me yet.

Oh when I too lie dead at your feet,
   And in death my heart is set,
15 Will you love me then, cold proud Ellen,
   Tho' you will not love me yet?—

A Discovery.

"I thought your search was over."—"So I thought."—
   "But you are seeking still."—"Yes, even so:
   Still seeking in mine own despite below
That which in Heaven alone is found unsought;
5 Still spending for that thing which is not bought."—
   "Then chase no more this shifting empty show."—
   "Amen: so bid a drowning man forego
The straw he clutches; will he so be taught?
You have a home where peace broods like a dove
10 Screened from the weary world's loud discontent,

You have home here, you wait for home above:
    I must unlearn the pleasant ways I went,
Must learn another hope, another love,
    And sigh indeed for home in banishment."—

From the Antique.

The wind shall lull us yet,
    The flowers shall spring above us;
And those who hate forget,
    And those forget who love us.

5   The pulse of hope shall cease,
        Of joy and of regretting:
    We twain shall sleep in peace,
        Forgotten and forgetting.

    For us no sun shall rise,
10   Nor wind rejoice, nor river,
    Where we with fast closed eyes
        Shall sleep and sleep for ever.

"The heart knoweth its own bitterness."

Weep yet a while
Weep till that day shall dawn when thou shalt smile
Watch till the day
When all save only Love shall pass away.

5   Weep, sick and lonely,
        Bow thy heart to tears,
    For none shall guess the secret
        Of thy griefs and fears.
    Weep, till the day dawn,
10 Refreshing dew:
    Weep till the spring;
    For genial showers

Bring up the flowers,
And thou shalt sing
15 In summer time of blossoming.

Heart sick and silent,
  Weep and watch in pain.
Weep for hope perished,
  Not to live again;
20 Weep for love's hope and fear
  And passion vain.
Watch till the day
When all save only love shall pass away.

Then love rejoicing
25   Shall forget to weep;
Shall hope or fear no more,
  Or watch, or sleep,
But only love and cease not,
  Deep beyond deep.
30 Now we sow love in tears,
  But then shall reap:
Have patience as the Lord's Own flock of sheep:
Have patience with His Love,
Who died below, Who lives for thee above.

"To what purpose is this waste?"

A windy shell singing upon the shore:
A lily budding in a desert place;
Blooming alone
With no companion
5 To praise its perfect perfume and its grace:
A rose crimson and blushing at the core,
Hedged in with thorns behind it and before:
A fountain in the grass,
Whose shadowy waters pass
10 Only to nourish birds and furnish food
For squirrels of the wood:

An oak deep in the forest's heart, the house
Of black-eyed tiny mouse;
Its strong roots fit for fuel roofing in
15   The hoarded nuts, acorns and grains of wheat;
Shutting them from the wind and scorching heat,
And sheltering them when the rains begin:

A precious pearl deep buried in the sea
Where none save fishes be:
20   The fullest merriest note
for which the skylark strains his silver throat,
Heard only in the sky
By other birds that fitfully
Chase one another as they fly:
25   The ripest plum down tumbled to the ground
By southern winds most musical of sound,
But by no thirsty traveller found:
Honey of wild bees in their ordered cells
Stored, not for human mouths to taste:—
30   I said, smiling superior down: What waste
Of good, where no man dwells.

This I said on a pleasant day in June
Before the sun had set, tho' a white moon
Already flaked the quiet blue
35   Which not a star looked thro.'
But still the air was warm, and drowsily
It blew into my face:
So since that same day I had wandered deep
Into the country, I sought out a place
40   For rest beneath a tree,
And very soon forgot myself in sleep:
Not so mine own words had forgotten me.
Mine eyes were opened to behold
All hidden things,
45   And mine ears heard all secret whisperings:
So my proud tongue that had been bold
To carp and to reprove,
Was silenced by the force of utter Love.

All voices of all things inanimate
50   Join with the song of Angels and the song
Of blessed Spirits, chiming with
Their Hallelujahs. One wind wakeneth
Across the sleeping sea, crisping along
The waves, and brushes thro' the great
55   Forests and tangled hedges, and calls out
Of rivers a clear sound,
And makes the ripe corn rustle on the ground,
And murmurs in a shell;
Till all their voices swell
60   Above the clouds in one loud hymn
Joining the song of Seraphim,
Or like pure incense circle round about
The walls of Heaven, or like a well-spring rise
In shady Paradise.

65   A lily blossoming unseen
Holds honey in its silver cup
Whereon a bee may sup,
Till being full she takes the rest
And stores it in her waxen nest:
70   While the fair blossom lifted up
On its one stately stem of green
Is type of her, the Undefiled,
Arrayed in white, whose eyes are mild
As a white dove's, whose garment is
75   Blood-cleansed from all impurities
And earthly taints,
Her robe the righteousness of Saints.

And other eyes than our's
Were made to look on flowers,
80   Eyes of small birds and insects small:
The deep sun-blushing rose
Round which the prickles close
Opens her bosom to them all.
The tiniest living thing
85   That soars on feathered wing,

Or crawls among the long grass out of sight,
Has just as good a right
To its appointed portion of delight
As any King.
90 Why should we grudge a hidden water stream
To birds and squirrels while we have enough?
As if a nightingale should cease to sing
Lest we should hear, or finch leafed out of sight
Warbling its fill in summer light;
95 As if sweet violets in the spring
Should cease to blow, for fear our path should seem
Less weary or less rough.

So every oak that stands a house
For skilful mouse,
100 And year by year renews its strength,
Shakes acorns from a hundred boughs
Which shall be oaks at length.

Who hath weighed the waters and shall say
What is hidden in the depths from day?
105 Pearls and precious stones and golden sands,
Wondrous weeds and blossoms rare,
Kept back from human hands,
But good and fair,
A silent praise as pain is silent prayer.
110 A hymn, an incense rising toward the skies,
As our whole life should rise;
An offering without stint from earth below,
Which Love accepteth so.

Thus is it with a warbling bird,
115 With fruit bloom-ripe and full of seed,
With honey which the wild bees draw
From flowers, and store for future need
By a perpetual law.
We want the faith that hath not seen
120 Indeed, but hath believed His truth
Who witnessed that His work was good:

So we pass cold to age from youth.
Alas for us: for we have heard
And known, but have not understood.

125 O earth, earth, earth, thou yet shalt bow
Who art so fair and lifted up,
Thou yet shalt drain the bitter cup.
Men's eyes that wait upon thee now,
All eyes shall see thee lost and mean,
130 Exposed and valued at thy worth,
While thou shalt stand ashamed and dumb.—
Ah, when the Son of Man shall come,
Shall He find faith upon the earth?—

Next of Kin.

The shadows gather round me, while you are in the sun;
My day is almost ended, but yours is just begun:
The winds are singing to us both and the streams are
         singing still,
And they fill your heart with music, but mine they cannot
         fill.

5   Your home is built in sunlight, mine in another day;
Your home is close at hand, sweet friend, but mine is far
         away:
Your bark is in the haven where you fain would be;
I must launch out into the deep, across the unknown sea.

You, white as dove or lily or spirit of the light;
10 I, stained and cold and glad to hide in the cold dark night:
You, joy to many a loving heart and light to many eyes;
I, lonely in the knowledge earth is full of vanities.

Yet when your day is over, as mine is nearly done,
And when your race is finished, as mine is almost run,
15 You, like me, shall cross your hands and bow your graceful
         head;
Yea, we twain shall sleep together in an equal bed.

"Let them rejoice in their beds."

The winds sing to us where we lie,
They sing to us a pleasant song;
Sweeter than song of mortal mouth,
Spice laden from the sunny south.
5   They say: This is not death you die;
This slumber shall not hold you long.

The north winds stir around our rest,
Their whispers speak to us and say:
Sleep yet awhile secure and deep,
10   A little while the blessed sleep;
For your inheritance is best,
And night shall yet bring forth the day.

The western winds are whispering too
Of love, with faith and hope as yet,
15   Of consummation that shall be,
Of fulness as the unfathomed sea,
When all creation shall be new
And day arise that shall not set.

But from the east a word is sent
20   To which all other words are dumb:
Lo, I come quickly, saith the Lord,
Myself thy exceeding great Reward:—
While we with thirsty hearts intent
Answer: Yea, come, Lord Jesus, come.

Portraits.

An easy lazy length of limb,
    Dark eyes and features from the south,
A short-legged meditative pipe
    Set in a supercilious mouth;
5   Ink and a pen and papers laid
    Down on a table for the night,

Beside a semi-dozing man
Who wakes to go to bed by light.

A pair of brothers brotherly,
10   Unlike and yet how much the same
In heart and high-toned intellect,
    In face and bearing, hope and aim:
Friends of the selfsame treasured friends
    And of one home the dear delight,
15   Beloved of many a loving heart
    And cherished both in mine, good night.

Whitsun Eve.

The white dove cooeth in her downy nest,
Keeping her young ones warm beneath her breast:
The white moon saileth thro' the cool clear sky,
Screened by a tender mist in passing by:
5   The white rose buds, with thorns upon its stem,
All the more precious and more dear for them:
The stream shines silver in the tufted grass,
The white clouds scarcely dim it as they pass:
Deep in the valleys lily cups are white,
10   They send up incense all the holy night:
Our souls are white, made clean in Blood once shed:
White blessed Angels watch around our bed:—
O spotless Lamb of God, still keep us so,
Thou Who wert born for us in time of snow.

What?

Strengthening as secret manna,
Fostering as clouds above,
Kind as a hovering dove,
Full as a plenteous river,

5   Our glory and our banner
     For ever and for ever.

     Dear as a dying cadence
     Of music in the drowsy night;
     Fair as the flowers which maidens
10   Pluck for an hour's delight,
     And then forget them quite.

     Gay as a cowslip meadow
     Fresh opening to the sun
     When new day is begun;
15   Soft as a sunny shadow
     When day is almost done.

     Glorious as purple twilight,
     Pleasant as budding tree,
     Untouched as any islet
20   Shrined in an unknown sea;
     Sweet as a fragrant rose amid the dew;—
     As sweet, as fruitless too.

     A bitter dream to wake from,
     But oh how pleasant while we dream;
25   A poisoned fount to take from,
     But oh how sweet the stream.

A Pause.

     They made the chamber sweet with flowers and leaves,
         And the bed sweet with flowers on which I lay;
         While my soul, love-bound, loitered on its way.
     I did not hear the birds about the eaves,
5   Nor hear the reapers talk among the sheaves:
         Only my soul kept watch from day to day,
         My thirsty soul kept watch for one away:—
     Perhaps he loves, I thought, remembers, grieves.
     At length there came the step upon the stair,
10   Upon the lock the old familiar hand:

Then first my spirit seemed to scent the air
Of Paradise; then first the tardy sand
Of time ran golden; and I felt my hair
Put on a glory, and my soul expand.

Holy Innocents.

Sleep, little Baby, sleep,
   The holy Angels love thee,
And guard thy bed and keep
   A blessed watch above thee.
5   No spirit can come near
      Nor evil beast to harm thee;
Sleep, Sweet, devoid of fear
   Where nothing need alarm thee.

The Love Which doth not sleep,
10   The eternal Arms surround thee;
The Shepherd of the sheep
   In perfect love hath found thee.
Sleep thro' the holy night
   Christ-kept from snare and sorrow
15   Until thou wake to light
   And love and warmth tomorrow.

"There remaineth therefore a rest for the people of God."

1.

"Ye have forgotten the exhortation"—

Come blessed sleep, most full, most perfect, come;
   Come sleep, if so I may forget the whole;
   Forget my body and forget my soul,
Forget how long life is and troublesome.
5   Come happy sleep to soothe my heart or numb,
   Arrest my weary spirit or control;
   Till light be dark to me from pole to pole,

And winds and echoes and low songs be dumb.
Come sleep and lap me into perfect calm,
10   Lap me from all the world and weariness:
Come secret sleep that hidest us from harm,
    Safe sheltered in a hidden cool recess:
    Come heavy dreamless sleep, and close and press
Upon mine eyes thy fingers dropping balm.

2.

"Which speaketh unto you as unto children."

15   Art thou so weary then, poor thirsty soul?
    Have patience, in due season thou shalt sleep.
    Mount yet a little while, the path is steep;
Strain yet a little while to reach the goal;
Do battle with thyself, achieve, control:
20   Till night come down with blessed slumber, deep
    As love, and seal thine eyes no more to weep
Thro' long tired vigils while the planets roll.
Have patience, for thou too shalt sleep at length,
    Lapped in the pleasant shade of Paradise.
25   My Hands That bled for thee shall close thine eyes,
    My Heart That bled for thee shall be thy Rest:
I will sustain with everlasting Strength,
    And thou, with John, shalt lie upon my Breast.

Annie.

It's not for earthly bread, Annie,
    And it's not for earthly wine,
And it's not for all thou art, Annie,
    Nor for any gift of thine:
5   It's for other food and other love
    And other gifts I pine.

I long all night and day, Annie,
    In this glorious month of June,
Tho' the roses all are blossoming
10   And the birds are all in tune:

I dream and long all night, Annie,
    Beneath the tender moon.

There is a dearer home than this
    In a land that's far away,
15 And a better crown than cankered gold,
    Or withering leaves of bay:
There's a richer love than thine, Annie,
    Must fill an endless day.

I long to be alone indeed,
20   I long to sleep at last;
To know the lifelong fever
    And sick weariness are past;
To feel the night is come indeed,
    And the gate secure and fast.

25 Oh gate of death, of the blessed night,
    That shall open not again
On this world of shame and sorrow,
    Where slow ages wax and wane,
Where are signs and seasons, days and nights,
30   And mighty winds and rain.

I long to dwell in silence,
    In twilight cool and dim:
It may be sometimes seeing
    Soft gleams of Seraphim;
35 It may be sometimes catching
    Faint echoes of their hymn.

I am tired of all the shows
    And of all the songs of earth;
I am sick of the cold sky overhead,
40   And the cold land of my birth;
I am sick for the home-land of delight
    And love and endless worth.

Is the day wearing toward the west?—
    Far off cool shadows pass,
45 A visible refreshment
    Across the sultry grass;

Far off low mists are mustering,
  A broken shifting mass.

      I know there comes a struggle
50   Before the utter calm,
And a searching pain like fire
  Before the healing balm;—
But the pain shall cease, and the struggle cease,
  And we shall take no harm.

55   Doubtless the Angels wonder
    That we can live at ease
While all around is full of change,
    Yea, full of vanities:
They wonder we can think to fill
60   Our hearts with such as these.

Still in the deepest knowledge
    Some depth is left unknown;
Still in the merriest music lurks
    A plaintive undertone;
65   Still with the closest friend some throb
    Of life is felt alone.

But vain it were to linger
    On the race we have to run,
For that which was must be again
70   Till time itself is done;
Yea, there is nothing new we know
    At all beneath the sun.

I am sick for love, and moan
    Like a solitary dove:
75   Love is as deep as hell, Annie,
    And as high as heaven above;
There's nothing in all the world, Annie,
    That can compete with love.

Time's summer breath is sweet, his sands
80   Ebb sparkling as they flow,
Yet some are sick that this should end
    Which is from long ago:—

Are not the fields already white
To harvest in the glow?—

85 God puts the sickle to the corn
And reaps it when He will
From every watered valley
And from every fruitful hill:
He holdeth time in His Right Hand,
90   To check or to fulfil.

There shall come another harvest
Than was in days of yore:
The reapers shall be Angels,
Our God shall purge the floor:—
95 No more seed-time, no more harvest,
Then for evermore.

Come, let us kneel together
Once again love, I and thou;
We have prayed apart and wept apart,
100   But may weep together now:
Once we looked back together
With our hands upon the plough.

A little while, and we must part
Again, as on that day:
105 My spirit shall go forth alone
To tread the untried way;
Then thou shalt watch alone once more,
And kneel alone to pray.

When the shadows thicken round me
110   And the silence grows apace,
And I cannot hear thy voice, Annie,
Nor look upon thy face,
Wilt thou kneel for me and plead for me
Before the Throne of Grace?—

115 So surely if my spirit
Hath knowledge while it lies
In the outer courts of Heaven,
It shall watch with longing eyes

And pray that thou mayest also come
120   To dwell in Paradise.

Seasons.

In spring time when the leaves are young,
Clear dewdrops gleam like jewels, hung
On boughs the fair birds roost among.

When summer comes with sweet unrest,
5   Birds weary of their mother's breast,
And look abroad and leave the nest.

In autumn ere the waters freeze,
The swallows fly across the seas:—
If we could fly away with these!—

10   In winter when the birds are gone,
The sun himself looks starved and wan,
And starved the snow he shines upon.

Thou sleepest where the lilies fade,
    Thou dwellest where the lilies fade not;
Sweet, when thine earthly part decayed
    Thy heavenly part decayed not.

5   Thou dwellest where the roses blow,
    The crimson roses bud and blossom;
While on thine eyes is heaped the snow,
    The snow upon thy bosom.

I wish I were a little bird
    That out of sight doth soar,
I wish I were a song once heard
    But often pondered o'er,
5   Or shadow of a lily stirred
    By wind upon the floor,
Or echo of a loving word

Worth all that went before,
Or memory of a hope deferred
10   That springs again no more.

(Two parted.)

"Sing of a love lost and forgotten,
    "Sing of a joy finished and o'er,
"Sing of a heart core-cold and rotten,
    "Sing of a hope springing no more."—
5   —"Sigh for a heart aching and sore."—

"I was most true and my own love betrayed me,
    "I was most true and she would none of me.
"Was it the cry of the world that dismayed thee?
    "Love, I had bearded the wide world for thee."
10   —"Hark to the sorrowful sound of the sea."—

"Still in my dreams she comes tender and gracious,
    "Still in my dreams love looks out of her eyes:
"Oh that the love of a dream were veracious,
    "Or that thus dreaming I might not arise!"
15   —"Oh for the silence that stilleth all sighs."—

All night I dream you love me well,
    All day I dream that you are cold:
Which is the dream? ah, who can tell,
    Ah would that it were told.

5   So I should know my certain doom,
    Know all the gladness or the pain;
So pass into the dreamless tomb,
    Or never doubt again.

(For Rosaline's Album.)

Do you hear the low winds singing,
    And streams singing on their bed?—

Very distant bells are ringing
    In a chapel for the dead:—
5   Death-pale better than life-red.

Mother, come to me in rest,
    And bring little May to see.—
Shall I bid no other guest?—
Seven slow nights have passed away
10 Over my forgotten clay:
    None must come save you and she.

Care flieth,
    Hope and fear together,
Love dieth
In the Autumn weather.

5   For a friend
    Even care is pleasant;
When fear doth end
    Hope is no more present:
Autumn silences the turtle dove;—
10 In blank Autumn who could speak of love?

(Epitaph.)

A slave yet wearing on my head a crown,
A captive from whose eyes no tears ran down,
Bound with no chain, compelled to do no work,
I fell a victim to the jealous Turk.

The P.R.B.

The P.R.B. is in its decadence:—
for Woolner in Australia cooks his chops;
And Hunt is yearning for the land of Cheops;
D. G. Rossetti shuns the vulgar optic;
5   While William M. Rossetti merely lops

His B.s in English disesteemed as Coptic;
Calm Stephens in the twilight smokes his pipe
But long the dawning of his public day;
And he at last, the champion, great Millais
10   Attaining academic opulence
Winds up his signature with A.R.A.:—
So rivers merge in the perpetual sea,
So luscious fruit must fall when over ripe,
And so the consummated P.R.B.

Seasons.

Crocuses and snowdrops wither,
Violets primroses together,
Fading with the fading spring
Before a fuller blossoming.

5   O sweet summer pass not soon,
Stay awhile the harvest moon;
O sweetest summer do not go,
For autumn's next and next the snow.

When autumn comes the days are drear,
10   It is the downfall of the year:
We heed the wind and falling leaf
More than the withered harvest sheaf.

Dreary winter come at last,
Come quickly, so be quickly past;
15   Dusk and sluggish winter wane
Till spring and sunlight dawn again.

"Who have a form of godliness."

When I am sick and tired it is God's will;
Also, God's will alone is sure and best:—
So in my weariness I find my rest,
And so in poverty I take my fill:

5   Therefore I see my good in midst of ill,
      Therefore in loneliness I build my nest;
    And thro' hot noon pant toward the shady west,
    And hope in sickening disappointment still.
    So when the times of restitution come,
10   The sweet times of refreshing come at last,
    My God shall fill my longings to the brim:
    Therefore I wait and look and long for Him;
    Not wearied tho' the work is wearisome,
      Nor fainting tho' the time be almost past.

Ballad.

Soft white lamb in the daisy meadow,
    Come hither and play with me,
For I am lonesome and I am tired
    Underneath the apple tree.

5   There's your husband if you're lonesome, lady,
      And your bed if you want for rest,
    And your baby for a playfellow
      With a soft hand for your breast.

Fair white dove in the sunshine,
10   Perched on the ashen bough,
    Come and perch by me and coo to me
      While the buds are blowing now.

I must keep my nestlings warm, lady,
      Underneath my downy breast;
15   There's your baby to coo and crow to you
      While I brood upon my nest.

Faint white rose come lie on my heart,
      Come lie there with your thorn;
    For I'll be dead at the vesper bell
20   And buried the morrow morn.

There's blood on your lily breast, lady,
      Like roses when they blow,

And there's blood upon your little hand
    That should be white as snow;
25 I will stay amid my fellows
    Where the lilies grow.

But its oh my own own little babe
    That I had you here to kiss,
And to comfort me in the strange next world
30 Tho' I slighted you so in this.

You shall kiss both cheek and chin, mother,
    And kiss me between the eyes,
Or ever the moon is on her way
    And the pleasant stars arise;
35 You shall kiss and kiss your fill, mother,
    In the nest of Paradise.

A Study. (A Soul.)

She stands as pale as Parian statues stand;
    Like Cleopatra when she turned at bay,
    And felt her strength above the Roman sway,
And felt the aspic writhing in her hand.
5 Her face is steadfast toward the shadowy land,
    For dim beyond it looms the land of day;
    Her feet are steadfast; all the arduous way
That foot-track hath not wavered on the sand.
She stands there like a beacon thro' the night,
10   A pale clear beacon where the storm-drift is;
She stands alone, a wonder deathly white;
She stands there patient, nerved with inner might,
    Indomitable in her feebleness,
Her face and will athirst against the light.

"There remaineth therefore a rest."

Very cool that bed must be
    Where our last sleep shall be slept:

There for weary vigils kept,
There for tears that we have wept,
5   Is our guerdon certainly.

Underneath the growing grass,
Underneath the living flowers,
Deeper than the sound of showers;—
There we shall not count the hours
10   By the shadows as they pass.

No more struggling then at length,
Only slumber everywhere;
Nothing more to do or bear:
We shall rest, and resting there
15   Eagle-like renew our strength.

In the grave will be no space
For the purple of the proud,
They must mingle with the crowd;
In the wrappings of a shroud
20   Jewels would be out of place.

Youth and health will be but vain,
Courage reckoned of no worth;
There a very little girth
Shall hold round what once the earth
25   Seemed too narrow to contain.

High and low and rich and poor,
All will fare alike at last:
The old promise standeth fast:
None shall care then if the past
30   Held more joys for him or fewer.

There no laughter shall be heard,
Nor the heavy sound of sighs;
Sleep shall seal the aching eyes;
All the ancient and the wise
35   There shall utter not a word.

Yet it may be we shall hear
How the mounting skylark sings

And the bell for matins rings;
  Or perhaps the whisperings
40 Of white Angels sweet and clear.

Sun or moon hath never shone
  In that hidden depth of night;
  But the souls there washed and white
  Are more fair than fairest light
45 Mortal eye hath looked upon.

The die cast whose throw is life—
  Rest complete; not one in seven—
  Souls love-perfected and shriven
  Waiting at the door of heaven,
50 Perfected from fear of strife.

What a calm when all is done,
  Wearing vigil, prayer and fast:—
  All fulfilled from first to last:—
  All the length of time gone past
55 And eternity begun.

Fear and hope and chastening rod
  Urge us on the narrow way:
  Bear we still as best we may
  Heat and burden of the day,
60 Struggling panting up to God.

"Ye have forgotten the exhortation."

Angel
Bury thy dead, dear friend,
Between the night and day;
Where depths of summer shade are cool,
And murmurs of a summer pool
5 And windy murmurs stray:—

Soul
Ah, gone away,
Ah, dear and lost delight,
Gone from me and for ever out of sight.

Angel
Bury thy dead, dear love,
10   And make his bed most fair above;
The latest buds shall still
Blow there, and the first violets too,
And there a turtle dove
Shall brood and coo:—

Soul
15   I cannot make the nest
So warm, but he may find it chill
In solitary rest.

Angel
Bury thy dead heart-deep;
Take patience till the sun be set;
20   There are no tears for him to weep,
No doubts to haunt him yet:
Take comfort, he will not forget:—

Soul
Then I will watch beside his sleep;
Will watch alone,
25   And make my moan
Because the harvest is so long to reap.

Angel
The fields are white to harvest, look and see,
Are white abundantly.
The harvest moon shines full and clear,
30   The harvest time is near,
Be of good cheer:—

Soul
Ah, woe is me;
I have no heart for harvest time,
Grown sick with hope deferred from chime to chime.

Angel
35   But One can give thee heart, thy Lord and his,
Can raise both thee and him
To shine with Seraphim

      And pasture where the eternal fountain is.
      Can give thee of that tree
40   Whose leaves are health for thee;
      Can give thee robes made clean and white,
      And love, and all delight,
      And beauty where the day turns not to night.
      Who knocketh at His door
45   And presseth in, goes out no more.
      Kneel as thou hast not knelt before—
      The time is short—and smite
      Upon thy breast and pray with all thy might:—

               Soul
      O Lord, my heart is broken for my sin:
50   Yet hasten Thine Own day
      And come away.
      Is not time full? Oh put the sickle in,
      O Lord, begin.

Guesses.

      Was it a chance that made her pause
        One moment at the opened door,
        Pale where she stood so flushed before
      As one a spirit overawes:—
5   Or might it rather be because
      She felt the grave was at our feet,
      And felt that we should no more meet
        Upon its hither side no more?

      Was it a chance that made her turn
10   One moment toward the window passing by,
        One moment with a shrinking eye
      Wherein her spirit seemed to yearn:—
      Or did her soul then first discern
      How long and rough the pathway is
15   That leads us home from vanities,
        And how it will be good to die?

There was a hill she had to pass;
  And while I watched her up the hill
  She stooped one moment hurrying still,
20 But left a rose upon the grass:
  Was it mere idleness:—or was
  Herself with her own self at strife
  Till while she chose the better life
    She felt this life has power to kill?

25 Perhaps she did it carelessly,
    Perhaps it was an idle thought;
    Or else it was the grace unbought,
  A pledge to all eternity:
  I know not yet how this may be;
30 But I shall know when face to face
  In Paradise we find a place
  And love with love that endeth not.

From the Antique.

It's a weary life, it is; she said:—
  Doubly blank in a woman's lot:
I wish and I wish I were a man;
  Or, better than any being, were not:

5 Were nothing at all in all the world,
    Not a body and not a soul;
Not so much as a grain of dust
    Or drop of water from pole to pole.

Still the world would wag on the same,
10   Still the seasons go and come;
Blossoms bloom as in days of old,
    Cherries ripen and wild bees hum.

None would miss me in all the world,
    How much less would care or weep:
15 I should be nothing; while all the rest
    Would wake and weary and fall asleep.

Three Stages.

1.

I looked for that which is not, nor can be,
    And hope deferred made my heart sick in truth;
    But years must pass before a hope of youth
        Is resigned utterly.

5   I watched and waited with a steadfast will:
    And though the object seemed to flee away
    That I so longed for; ever, day by day,
        I watched and waited still.

Sometimes I said: This thing shall be no more:
10   My expectation wearies and shall cease;
    I will resign it now and be at peace:—
        Yet never gave it o'er.

Sometimes I said: It is an empty name
    I long for; to a name why should I give
15   The peace of all the days I have to live?—
        Yet gave it all the same.

Alas, thou foolish one! alike unfit
    For healthy joy and salutary pain;
    Thou knowest the chase useless, and again
20   Turnest to follow it.

2.

My happy happy dream is finished with,
    My dream in which alone I lived so long.
My heart slept—woe is me, it wakeneth;
    Was weak—I thought it strong.

5   Oh weary wakening from a life-true dream:
    Oh pleasant dream from which I wake in pain:
I rested all my trust on things that seem,
    And all my trust is vain.

I must pull down my palace that I built,
10   Dig up the pleasure-gardens of my soul;
   Must change my laughter to sad tears for guilt,
      My freedom to control.

   Now all the cherished secrets of my heart,
      Now all my hidden hopes are turned to sin:
15   Part of my life is dead, part sick, and part
      Is all on fire within.

   The fruitless thought of what I might have been
      Hauthing me ever will not let me rest:
   A cold north wind has withered all my green,
20   My sun is in the west.

   But where my palace stood, with the same stone,
      I will uprear a shady hermitage;
   And there my spirit shall keep house alone,
      Accomplishing its age:

25   There other garden beds shall lie around
      Full of sweet-briar and incense-bearing thyme;
   There I will sit, and listen for the sound
      Of the last lingering chime.

                  3.

   I thought to deal the death-stroke at a blow,
      To give all, once for all, but nevermore;—
   Then sit to hear the low waves fret the shore,
      Or watch the silent snow.

5   "Oh rest," I thought, "in silence and the dark;
      Oh rest, if nothing else, from head to feet:
   Though I may see no more the poppied wheat,
      Or sunny soaring lark.

   "These chimes are slow, but surely strike at last;
10   This sand is slow, but surely droppeth thro';
   And much there is to suffer, much to do,
      Before the time be past.

"So will I labour, but will not rejoice:
   Will do and bear, but will not hope again;
15   Gone dead alike to pulses of quick pain,
   And pleasure's counterpoise:"

I said so in my heart, and so I thought
   My life would lapse, a tedious monotone:
   I thought to shut myself, and dwell alone
20   Unseeking and unsought.

But first I tired, and then my care grew slack;
   Till my heart slumbered, may-be wandered too:—
   I felt the sunshine glow again, and knew
   The swallow on its track;

25 All birds awoke to building in the leaves,
   All buds awoke to fulness and sweet scent,
   Ah, too, my heart woke unawares, intent
   On fruitful harvest sheaves.

Full pulse of life, that I had deemed was dead,
30   Full throb of youth, that I had deemed at rest,—
   Alas, I cannot build myself a nest,
   I cannot crown my head

With royal purple blossoms for the feast,
   Nor flush with laughter, nor exult in song;—
35   These joys may drift, as time now drifts along;
   And cease, as once they ceased.

I may pursue, and yet may not attain,
   Athirst and panting all the days I live:
   Or seem to hold, yet nerve myself to give
40   What once I gave, again.

Long looked for.

When the eye hardly sees,
   And the pulse hardly stirs,
And the heart would scarcely quicken

        Though the voice were hers:
5   Then the longing wasting fever
        Will be almost past;
        Sleep indeed come back again,
        And peace at last.

        Not till then, dear friends,
10   Not till then, most like, most dear,
        The dove will fold its wings
        To settle here.
        Then to all her coldness
        I also shall be cold,
15 Then I also have forgotten
        Our happy love of old.

        Close mine eyes with care,
        Cross my hands upon my breast,
        Let shadows and full silence
20   Tell of rest:
        For she yet may look upon me
        Too proud to speak, but know
        One heart less loves her in the world
        Than loved her long ago.

25 Strew flowers upon the bed
        And flowers upon the floor,
        Let all be sweet and comely
        When she stands at the door:
        Fair as a bridal chamber
30   For her to come into,
        When the sunny day is over
        At falling of the dew.

        If she comes, watch her not
        But careless turn aside;
35 She may weep if left alone
        With her beauty and her pride:
        She may pluck a leaf perhaps
        Or a languid violet
        When life and love are finished
40   And even I forget.

Listening.

She listened like a cushat dove
　That listens to its mate alone;
She listened like a cushat dove
　That loves but only one.

5　Not fair as men would reckon fair,
　Nor noble as they count the line;
Only as graceful as a bough
　And tendrils of the vine;
Only as noble as sweet Eve
10　Your ancestress and mine.

And downcast were her dovelike eyes,
　And downcast was her tender cheek,
Her pulses fluttered like a dove
　To hear him speak.

Zara

(see Maturin's *Women*.)

I dreamed that loving me he would love on
　Thro' life and death into eternity:
　I dreamed that love would be and be and be
As surely as the sun shines that once shone.
5　Now even that my dream is killed and gone,
　It sometimes even now returns to me;
　Not what it was, but half being memory,
And half the pain that wears my cheek so wan.
Oh bitter pain, what drug will lull the pain?
10　Oh lying memory, when shall I forget?
For why should I remember him in vain
Who hath forgotten and rejoiceth still?
　Oh bitter memory, while my heart is set
Oh love that gnaws and gnaws and cannot kill.

The last look.

Her face was like an opening rose,
   So bright to look upon;
But now it is like fallen snows,
   As cold, as dead, as wan.
5 Heaven lit with stars is more like her
   Than is this empty crust;
Deaf, dumb and blind it cannot stir
   But crumbles back to dust.

No flower be taken from her bed
10   For me, no lock be shorn;
I give her up, the early dead,
   The dead, the newly born:
If I remember her, no need
   Of formal tokens set;
15 Of hollow token lies, indeed,
   No need, if I forget.

"I have a message unto thee."
(written in sickness.)

Green sprout the grasses,
   Red blooms the mossy rose,
Blue nods the harebell
   Where purple heather blows;
5 The water lily, silver white,
Is living—fair as light;
   Sweet jasmine branches trail
   A dusky starry veil:
Each goodly is to see,
10 Comely in its degree;
I, only I, alas that this should be,
   Am ruinously pale.

New year renews the grasses,
   The crimson rose renews,

15 Brings up the breezy bluebell,
        Refreshes heath with dews;
    Then water lilies ever
    Bud fresh upon the river;
        Then jasmine lights its star
20   And spreads its arms afar:
    I only in my spring
    Can neither bud nor sing;
    I find not honey but a sting
        Though fair the blossoms are.

25 For me no downy grasses,
        For me no blossoms pluck;
    But leave them for the breezes,
        For honey bees to suck,
    For childish hands to pull
30 And pile their baskets full:
        I will not have a crown
        That soon must be laid down;
    Trust me: I cannot care
    A withering crown to wear,
35 I who may be immortally made fair
        Where autumn turns not brown.

    Spring, summer, autumn,
        Winter, all will pass,
    With tender blossoms
40   And with fruitful grass.
    Sweet days of yore
    Will pass to come no more,
        Sweet perfumes fly,
        Buds languish and go by:
45 Oh bloom that cannot last,
    Oh blossoms quite gone past,
    I yet shall feast when you shall fast,
        And live when you shall die.

    Your workday fully ended,
50   Your pleasant task being done,
    You shall finish with the stars,

    The moon and setting sun.
    You and these and time
    Shall end with the last chime;
55 For earthly solace given,
    But needed not in heaven.
      Needed not perhaps
      Thro' the eternal lapse:
    Or else, all signs fulfilled,
60 What you foreshow may yield
    Delights thro' heaven's own harvest field
      With undecaying saps.

    Young girls wear flowers,
      Young brides a flowery wreath;
65 But next we plant them
      In garden plots of death.
    Whose sleep is best?—
    The maiden's curtained rest,
      Or bride's whose hoped for sweet
70   May yet outstrip her feet?—
    Ah, what are such as these
    To death's sufficing ease—
    How long and deep that slumber is
    Where night and morning meet.

75 Dear are the blossoms
      For bride's or maiden's head,
    But dearer planted
      Around our happy dead.
    Those mind us of decay
80 And joys that slip away;
      These preach to us perfection
      And endless resurrection.
    We make our graveyards fair
    For spirit-like birds of air;
85 For Angels, may be, finding there
      Lost Eden's own delection.

    A blessing on the flowers
      That God has made so good,

From crops of jealous gardens
90   To wildlings of a wood.
They show us symbols deep
Of how to sow and reap;
    They teach us lessons plain
    Of patient harvest gain.
95   They still are telling of
God's unimagined love:—
"Oh gift," they say, "all gifts above,
"Shall it be given in vain?—

"Better you had not seen us
100   "But shared the blind man's night,
"Better you had not scented
    "Our incense of delight,
"Than only plucked to scorn
"The rosebud for its thorn:
105   "Not so the instinctive thrush
"Hymns in a holly bush.
    "Be wise betimes, and with the bee
    "Suck sweets from prickly tree
"To last when earth's are flown;
110   "So God well pleased will own
"Your work, and bless not time alone
    "But ripe eternity."

Cobwebs.

It is a land with neither night nor day,
    Nor heat nor cold, nor any wind, nor rain,
    Nor hills nor valleys; but one even plain
Stretches thro' long unbroken miles away:
5   While thro' the sluggish air a twilight grey
    Broodeth; no moons or seasons wax and wane,
    No ebb and flow are there along the main,
No bud-time no leaf-falling there for aye,
No ripple on the sea, no shifting sand,
10   No beat of wings to stir the stagnant space,

No pulse of life thro' all the loveless land:
And loveless sea; no trace of days before,
　No guarded home, no toil-won restingplace
No future hope no fear for evermore.

Unforgotten.

　Oh unforgotten!
How long ago? one spirit saith:
As long as life even unto death,
The passage of a poor frail breath.

5　　Oh unforgotten:
An unforgotten load of love,
A load of grief all griefs above,
A blank blank nest without its dove.

　As long as time is—
10　No longer? time is but a span
The dalliance space of empty man;
And is this all immortals can?—

　Ever and ever,
Beyond all time, beyond all space;—
15　*Now*, shadow darkening heart and face,—
Then, glory in a glorious place.

　Sad heart and spirit
Bowed now yea broken for a while,
Lagging and toiling mile by mile
20　Yet pressing toward the eternal smile.

　Oh joy eternal!—
Oh youth eternal without flaw!—
Thee not the blessed angels saw
Rapt in august adoring awe.

25　Not the dead have thee,
Not yet O all surpassing peace;
Not till this veiling world shall cease
And harvest yield its whole increase.

       Not the dead know thee,
30   Not dead nor living nor unborn:
       Who in the new sown field at morn
       Can measure out the harvest corn?—

       Yet they shall know thee;
       And we with them, and unborn men
35   With us, shall know and have thee when
       The single grain shall wax to ten.

An Afterthought.

       Oh lost garden Paradise:—
       Were the roses redder there
       Than they blossom otherwhere?
       Was the night's delicious shade
5   More intensely star inlaid?
       Who can tell what memories
       Of lost beloved Paradise
       Saddened Eve with sleepless eyes?—

       Fair first mother lulled to rest
10   In a choicer garden nest,
       Curtained with a softer shading
       Than thy tenderest child is laid in,
       Was the sundawn brighter far
       Than our daily sundawns are?
15   Was that love, first love of all
       Warmer, deeper, better worth
       Than has warmed poor hearts of earth
       Since the utter ruinous fall?—

       Ah supremely happy once,
20   Ah supremely broken hearted
       When her tender feet departed
       From the accustomed paths of peace:
       Catching Angel orisons
       For the last last time of all,
25   Shedding tears that would not cease
       For the bitter bitter fall.

Yet the accustomed hand for leading,
Yet the accustomed heart for love;
Sure she kept one part of Eden
30   Angels could not strip her of.
Sure the fiery messenger
Kindling for his outraged Lord,
Willing with the perfect Will,
Yet rejoiced the flaming sword
35   Chastening sore but sparing still
Shut her treasure out with her.

What became of Paradise?
Did the cedars droop at all
(Springtide hastening to the fall)
40   Missing the beloved hand—
Or did their green perfection stand
Unmoved beneath the perfect skies?—
Paradise was rapt on high,
It lies before the gate of Heaven:—
45   Eve now slumbers there forgiven,
Slumbers Rachel comforted,
Slumber all the blessed dead
Of days and months and years gone by,
A solemn swelling company.

50   They wait for us beneath the trees
Of Paradise that lap of ease:
They wait for us, till God shall please.
Oh come the day of death, that day
Of rest which cannot pass away:
55   When the last work is wrought, the last
Pang of pain is felt and past
And the blessed door made fast.

To the end.

There are lilies for her sisters—
   (Who so cold as they?)—
And heartsease for one I must not name

When I am far away.
5 I shall pluck the lady lilies
  And fancy all the rest;
I shall pluck the bright eyed heartsease
  For her sake I love the best,
As I wander on with weary feet
10 Toward the twilight shadowy west.

Oh bird that fliest eastward
  Unto that sunny land
Oh wilt thou 'light on lilies white
  Beside her whiter hand?
15 Soft summer wind that breathest
  Of perfumes and sweet spice,
Ah tell her what I dare not tell
  Of watchful waiting eyes
Of love that yet may meet again
20 In distant Paradise.

I go from earth to Heaven
  A dim uncertain road,
A houseless pilgrim thro' the world
  Unto a sure abode:
25 While evermore an Angel
  Goes with me day and night,
A ministering spirit
  From the land of light,
My holy fellow servant sent
30 To guide my steps aright.

I wonder if the Angels
  Love with such love as our's,
If for each other's sake they pluck
  And keep eternal flowers.
35 Alone I am and weary,
  Alone yet not alone:
Her soul talks with me by the way
  From tedious stone to stone,
A blessed Angel treads with me
40 The awful paths unknown.

When will the long road end in rest,
   The sick bird perch and brood?
When will my Guardian fold his wings
   At rest in the finished good?—
45 Lulling lulling me off to sleep:
   While death's strong hand doth roll
My sins behind His back,
   And my life up like a scroll,
Till thro' sleep I hear kind Angels
50   Rejoicing at the goal.

If her spirit went before me
   Up from night to day,
It would pass me like the lightning
   That kindles on its way.
55 I should feel it like the lightning
   Flashing fresh from Heaven:
I should long for Heaven sevenfold more,
   Yea and sevenfold seven;
Should pray as I have not prayed before,
60   And strive as I have not striven.

She will learn new love in Heaven
   Who is so full of love,
She will learn new depths of tenderness
   Who is tender like a dove.
65 Her heart will no more sorrow,
   Her eyes will weep no more:
Yet it may be she will yearn
   And look back from far before:
Lingering on the golden threshold
70   And leaning from the door.

"Zion said."

O Slain for love of me, canst Thou be cold,
   Be cold and far away in my distress:
     Is Thy love also changed growing less and less
That carried me thro' all the days of old?—

5   O Slain for love of me, O Love untold,
      See how I flag and fail thro' weariness:
      I flag, while sleepless foes dog me and press
    On me; behold O Lord, O Love behold.
    I am sick for home, the home of love indeed;
10   I am sick for Love, that dearest name for Thee:
    Thou Who hast bled, see how my heart doth bleed;
    Open Thy bleeding Side and let me in;
    Oh hide me in Thy Heart from doubt and sin,
      Oh take me to Thyself and comfort me.

May.

    Sweet Life is dead.—
                Not so:
      I meet him day by day,
    Where bluest fountains flow
5   And trees are white as snow
      For it is time of May.
    Even now from long ago
      He will not say me nay;
      He is most fair to see;
10 And if I wander forth, I know
      He wanders forth with me.

    But Life is dead to me;
      The worn-out year was failing
      West winds took up a wailing
15 To watch his funeral:
    Bare poplars shivered tall
    And lank vines stretched to see;
      'Twixt him and me a wall
    Was frozen of earth like stone
20 With brambles overgrown;
      Chill darkness wrapped him like a pall
    And I am left alone.

    How can you call him dead?
      He buds out everywhere:

25   In every hedgerow rank,
      On every mossgrown bank
        I find him here and there.
      He crowns my willing head
      With may flowers white and red,
30   He rears my tender heartsease bed;
        He makes my branch to bud and bear,
      And blossoms where I tread.

River Thames (?).

      There are rivers lapsing down
        Lily-laden to the sea;
      Every lily is a boat
        For bees, one, two, or three:
5   I wish there were a fairy boat
        For you, my friend, and me.

      We would rock upon the river,
        Scarcely floating by;
      Rocking rocking like the lilies,
10   You, my friend, and I;
      Rocking like the stately lilies
        Beneath the statelier sky.

      But ah, where is that river
        Whose hyacinth banks descend
15   Down to the sweeter lilies,
        Till soft their shadows blend
      Into a watery twilight?—
        And ah, where is my friend?—

A chilly night.

      I rose at the dead of night
        And went to the lattice alone
      To look for my Mother's ghost
        Where the ghostly moonlight shone.

5   My friends had failed one by one,
          Middleaged, young, and old,
      Till the ghosts were warmer to me
          Than my friends that had grown cold.

      I looked and I saw the ghosts
10   Dotting plain and mound:
      They stood in the blank moonlight
          But no shadow lay on the ground;
      They spoke without a voice
          And they leapt without a sound.

15   I called: "O my Mother dear,"—
          I sobbed: "O my Mother kind,
      Make a lonely bed for me
          And shelter it from the wind:

      "Tell the others not to come
20   To see me night or day;
      But I need not tell my friends
          To be sure to keep away."

      My Mother raised her eyes,
          They were blank and could not see;
25   Yet they held me with their stare
          While they seemed to look at me.

      She opened her mouth and spoke,
          I could not hear a word
      While my flesh crept on my bones
30   And every hair was stirred.

      She knew that I could not hear
          The message that she told
      Whether I had long to wait
          Or soon should sleep in the mould:
35   I saw her toss her shadowless hair
          And wring her hands in the cold.

      I strained to catch her words
          And she strained to make me hear,
      But never a sound of words
40   Fell on my straining ear.

From midnight to the cockcrow
  I kept my watch in pain
While the subtle ghosts grew subtler
  In the sad night on the wane.

45 From midnight to the cockcrow
  I watched till all were gone,
Some to sleep in the shifting sea
  And some under turf and stone:
Living had failed and dead had failed
50 And I was indeed alone.

"Let patience have her perfect work."

I saw a bird alone,
In its nest it sat alone,
For its mate was dead or flown
  Tho' it was early spring.
5 Hard by were buds half blown,
With cornfields freshly sown;
It could only perch and moan
  That used to sing:
Droop in sorrow left alone
10 A sad sad thing.

I saw a star alone,
In blue heaven it hung alone,
A solitary throne
  In the waste of space:
15 Where no moon glories are,
Where not a second star
Beams thro' night from near or far
  To that lone place.
Its beauties all unknown,
20 Its glories all alone
  Sad in heaven's face.

Doth the bird desire a mate,
Pine for a second mate
Whose first joy was so great

25   With its own dove?
     Doth the star supreme in night
     Desire a second light
     To make it seem less bright
     In the shrine of heavenly height
30   That is above?—
     Ah, better wait alone,
     In nest or heaven alone,
     Forsaken or unknown;
     Till time being past and gone
35   Full eternity rolls on,
     While patience reaps what it has sown
        In the harvest land of love.

A Martyr.

It is over the horrible pain,
   All is over the struggle and doubt,
She's asleep tho' her friends stand and weep,
   She's asleep while the multitudes shout,
5 Not to wake to her anguish again
   Not to wake until death is cast out.

Stoop, look at the beautiful face,
   See the smile on the satisfied mouth,
The hands crost—she hath conquered not lost,
10   She hath drunk who was fevered with drouth.
She shall sleep in her safe restingplace
   While the hawk spreads her wings toward the south.

She shall sleep while slow seasons are given,
   While daylight and darkness go round;
15 Her heart is at rest in its nest;
   Her body at rest in the ground:
She has travelled the long road to heaven,
   She sought it and now she has found.

Will you follow the track that she trod,
20   Will you tread in her footsteps, my friend?

That pathway is rough but enough
    Are the light and the balm that attend.
Do I tread in her steps, O my God,
    Shall I joy with her joy in the end?

In the Lane.

When my love came home to me
    Pleasant Summer bringing
Every tree was out in leaf
    Every bird was singing
5 Every red rose burst the bud
    On its bramble springing.

There I met her in the lane
    By those waters gleamy,
Met her toward the fall of day
10   Warm and dear and dreamy;
Did I loiter in the lane?
    None was there to see me.

Only roses in the hedge
    Lilies on the river
15 Saw our greeting fast and fond,
    Counted gift and giver,
Saw me take her to my home
    Take her home for ever.

Acme.

Sleep, unforgotten sorrow, sleep awhile;
    Make even awhile as tho' I might forget,
    Let the wound staunch thy tedious fingers fret
Till once again I look abroad and smile
5 Warmed in the sunlight: let no tears defile
    This hour's content, no conscious thorns beset
    My path; O sorrow slumber, slumber yet
A moment, rouse not yet the smouldering pile.

So shalt thou wake again with added strength
10   O unforgotten sorrow, stir again
The slackening fire, refine the lulling pain
To quickened torture and a subtler edge:
The wrung cord snaps at last; beneath the wedge
The toughest oak groans long but rends at length.

A bed of Forget-me-nots.

Is love so prone to change and rot
We are fain to rear forget-me-not
By measure in a garden plot?—

I love its growth at large and free
5   By untrod path and unlopped tree,
Or nodding by the unpruned hedge,
Or on the water's dangerous edge
Where flags and meadowsweet blow rank
With rushes on the quaking bank.

10   Love is not taught in learning's school,
Love is not parcelled out by rule;
Hath curb or call an answer got?—
So free must be forget-me-not.
Give me the flame no dampness dulls,
15   The passion of the instinctive pulse,
Love steadfast as a fixèd star,
Tender as doves with nestlings are,
More large than time, more strong than death:
This all creation travails of—
20   She groans not for a passing breath—
This is forget-me-not and love.

The Chiefest among ten thousand.

When sick of life and all the world,
How sick of all the earth but Thee,
I lift mine eyes up to the hills,

Eyes of my heart that truly see:
5 I see beyond all death and ills
Refreshing green for heart and eyes;
The golden streets and gateways pearled, ´
The living trees of paradise.

Oh that a dove's white wings I had
10 To flee away from this distress
For Thou art in the wilderness
Drawing and leading Thine Own love:
Wherefore it blossoms like a rose,
The solitary place is glad;
15 There sounds the soft voice of the dove
And there the spicy south wind blows.

Draw us, we will run after Thee;
Call us by name, the name we know;
Call her beloved who was not so,
20 Beulah and blessed Hepzibah:
That where Thou art I too may be
Bride of the Bridegroom heart to heart;
Thou God, my Love, the Fairest art
Where all things fair and lovely are.

25 From north and south from east and west
Thy sons and daughters all shall flock
Who built their house upon the Rock
And eagle-like renew their strength:
How glad and glorious is their rest
30 Whom Thou hast purged from fleshly scum,—
The long-desired is come at length,
The fulness of the time is come.

Then the new heavens and earth shall be
Where righteousness shall dwell indeed:
35 There shall be no more blight nor need
Nor barrier of the tossing sea;
No sun and moon alternating
For God shall be the Light thereof,
No sorrow more no death no sting
40 For God shall reign and God is Love.

"Look on this picture and on this."

I wish we once were wedded,—then I must be true;
You should hold my will in yours to do or to undo:
But now I hate myself Eva when I look at you.

5   You have seen her hazel eyes, her warm dark skin,
Dark hair—but oh those hazel eyes a devil is dancing in:—
You my saint lead up to heaven she lures down to sin.

Listen Eva I repent, indeed I do my love:
How should I choose a peacock and leave and grieve a
           dove?—
If I could turn my back on her and follow you above.

10   No it's not her beauty bloomed like an autumn peach,
Not her pomp of beauty too high for me to reach;
It's her eyes, her witching manner—ah the lore they teach

You are winning, well I know it, who should know but I?
You constrain me, I must yield or else must hasten by:—
15   But she, she fascinates me, I can neither fight nor fly.

She's so redundant, stately;—in truth now have you seen
Ever anywhere such beauty, such a stature, such a mien?
She may be queen of devils but she's every inch a queen.

If you sing to me, I hear her subtler sweeter still
20   Whispering in each tender cadence strangely sweet to fill
All that lacks in music all my soul and sense and will.

If you dance, tho' mine eyes follow where my hand I gave
I only see her presence like a sunny wave
I only feel her presence like a wind too strong to rave.

25   If we talk: I love you, do you love me again?—
Tho' your lips speak it's her voice I flush to hear so plain
Say: Love you? yes I love you, love can neither change
           nor wane.

But, you ask, "why struggle? I have given you up:
Take again your pledges, snap the cord and break the cup:
30   Feast you with your temptation for I in heaven will sup."—

Can I bear to think upon you strong to break not bend,
Pale with inner intense passion silent to the end,
Bear to leave you, bear to grieve you, O my dove my friend?

One short pang and you would rise a light in heaven
35 While we grovelled in the darkness mean and unforgiven
Tho' our cup of love brimmed sevenfold crowns of love
    were seven.

What shall I choose, what can I for you and her and me;
With you the haven of rest, with her the tossing miry sea;
Time's love with her, or choose with you love's all eternity.—

40 Nay, you answer coldly yet with a quivering voice:
That is over, doubt and struggle, we have sealed our choice;
Leave me to my contentment vivid with fresh hopes
    and joys.

Listening so, I hide mine eyes and fancy years to come:
You cherished in another home with no cares burdensome;
45 You straitened in a windingsheet pulseless at peace
    and dumb.

So I fancy—The new love has driven the old away;
She has found a dearer shelter a dearer stronger stay;
Perhaps now she would thank me for the freedom of
    that day.

Open house and heart barred to me alone the door;
50 Children bound to meet her, babies crow before;—
Blessed wife and blessed mother whom I may see no more.

Or I fancy—In the grave her comely body lies;
She is 'tiring for the Bridegroom till the morning star
    shall rise,
Then to shine a glory in the nuptials of the skies.

55 No more yearning tenderness, no more pale regret,
She will not look for me when the marriage guests are set,
She joys with joy eternal as we had never met.

I would that one of us were dead, were gone no more
    to meet,

Or she and I were dead together stretched here at
    your feet,
60   That she and I were strained together in one windingsheet:

Hidden away from all the world upon this bitter morn;
Hidden from all the scornful world, from all your keener
    scorn;
Secure and secret in the dark as blessed babe unborn.

A pitiless fiend is in your eyes to tempt me and to taunt:
65   If you were dead I verily believe that you would haunt
The home you loved, the man you loved, you said you
    loved—avaunt.

Why do you face me with those eyes so calm they drive
    me mad,
Too proud to droop before me and own that you are sad?
Why have you a lofty angel made me mean and cursed
    and bad?

70   How have you the heart to face me with that passion in
    your stare
Deathly silent? weep before me, rave at me in your
    despair—
If you keep patience wings will spring and a halo from
    your hair.

Yet what matters—yea what matters? your frenzy can
    but mock:
You do not hold my heart's life key to lock and to unlock,
75   The door will not unclose to you tho' long you wait
    and knock.

Have I wronged you? nay not I nor she in deed or will:
You it is alone that mingle the venomous cup and fill;
Why are you so little lovely that I cannot love you still?—

One pulse, one tone, one ringlet of her's outweighs
    the whole
80   Of you, your puny graces puny body puny soul:
You but a taste of sweetness, she an overrunning bowl.

Did I make you, that you blame me because you are not
    the best?
Not so, be wise, take patience, turn away and be at rest:
Shall I not know her lovelier who is far loveliest?—

85 See now how proud you are, like us after all, no saint;
Not so upright but that you are bowed with the old bent;
White at white-heat, tainted with the devil's special taint.

Sit you still and wring the cup drop after loathsome drop:
You have let loose a torrent it is not you can stop;
90 You have sowed a noisome field-ful, now reap the
    stinging crop.

Did you think to sit in safety, to watch me torn and tost
Struggling like a mad dog, watch her tempting
    doubly lost?
Howl you, you wretched woman, for your flimsy hopes
    are crost.

Be still, tho' you may writhe you shall hear the branding
    truth:
95 You who thought to sit in judgment on our souls forsooth,
To sit in frigid judgment on our ripe luxuriant youth.

Did I love you? never from the first cold day to this;
You are not sufficient for my aim of life, my bliss;
You are not sufficient, but I found the one that is.

100 The wine of love that warms me from this life's mortal
    chill:
Drunk with love I drink again, a thirst I drink my fill;
Lapped in love I care not doth it make alive or kill.

Then did I never love you?—ah the sting struck home
    at last;
You are drooping, fainting, dying—the worst of death
    is past;
105 A light is on your face from the nearing heaven forecast.

Never?—yes I loved you then; I loved: the word still
    charms:—

For the first time last time lie here in my heart my arms,
For the first last time as if I shielded you from harms.

I trampled you, poor dove, to death; you clung to me, I
    spurned;
110   I taunted you, I tortured you, while you sat still and
    yearned:—
Oh lesson taught in anguish but in double anguish
    learned.

For after all I loved you, loved you then, I love you yet.
Listen love I love you: see, the seal of truth is set
On my face in tears—you cannot see? then feel them wet.

115   Pause at heaven's dear gate, look back, one moment back
    to grieve;
You go home thro' death to life; but I, I still must live:
On the threshold of heaven's love, O love can you forgive?—

Fully freely fondly, with heart truth above an oath,
With eager utter pardon given unasked and nothing loth,
120   Heaping coals of fire upon our heads forgiving both.

One word more—not one: one look more—too late
    too late:—
Lapped in love she sleeps who was lashed with scorn
    and hate;
Nestling in the lap of love the dove has found a mate.

Night has come, the night of rest; day will come, that day:
125   To her glad dawn of glory kindled from the deathless ray;
To us a searching fire and strict balances to weigh.

The tearless tender eyes are closed, the tender lips
    are dumb:
I shall not see or hear them more until that day
    shall come:
Then they must speak, what will they say—what then will
    be the sum?—

130   Shall we stand upon the left and she upon the right—
We smirched with endless death and shame, she glorified
    in white:

Will she sound our accusation in intolerable light?

Be open-armed to us in love—type of another Love—
As she forgave us once below will she forgive above,
135   Enthroned to all eternity our sister friend and dove?—

"Now they desire."

There is a sleep we have not slept
  Safe in a bed unknown;
There hearts are staunched that long have wept
  Alone, or bled alone:
5 Sweet sleep that dreams not, or whose dream
  Is foretaste of the truth;
Sweet sleep whose sweets are what they seem
  Refreshing more than youth.

There is a sea whose waters clear
10   Are never tempest tost;
There is a home whose children dear
  Are saved, not one is lost:
There Cherubim and Seraphim
  And Angels dwell with Saints,
15 Whose lustre no more dwindleth dim,
  Whose ardour never faints.

There is a Love Which fills desire
  And can our love requite;
Like fire It draws our lesser fire,
20   Like greater light our light:
For It we agonize in strife
  We yearn we famish thus—
Lo, in the far off land of life
  Doth It not yearn for us?—

25 "Oh fair oh fair Jerusalem,"
  How fair how far away,
When shall we see thy Jasper Gem
  That gives thee light for day?
Thy sea of glass like fire, thy streets

30   Of glass like virgin gold,
        Thy royal Elders on their seats,
        Thy four Beasts manifold?—

        Fair city of delights, the bride
        In raiment white and clean,
35   When shall we see thee loving eyed,
        Sun girdled, happy Queen?
        Without a wrinkle or a spot,
        Blood cleansed, blood purchased once:
        In how fair ground is fallen the lot
40   Of all thy happy sons.

        Dove's eyes beneath thy parted lock,
        A dove's soft voice is thine;
        Thy nest is safe within the Rock,
        Safe in the Very Vine;
45   Thy walls salvation buildeth them
        And all thy gates are praise
        Oh fair oh fair Jerusalem
        In sevenfold day of days.

A Christmas Carol, for my Godchildren.

        The shepherds had an angel,
        The wise men had a star,
        But what have I, a little child,
        To guide me home from far,
5   Where glad stars sing together
        And singing angels are?—

        Lord Jesus is my Guardian,
        So I can nothing lack:
        The lambs lie in His Bosom
10   Along life's dangerous track;
        The wilful lambs that go astray
        He bleeding fetches back.

Lord Jesus is my Guiding Star,
　My Beacon Light in heaven:
15　He leads me step by step along
　　The path of life uneven;
　He, True Light, leads me to that land
　　Whose day shall be as seven.

　Those shepherds thro' the lonely night
20　　Sat watching by their sheep,
　Until they saw the heavenly host
　　Who neither tire nor sleep
　All singing 'Glory glory'
　　In festival they keep.

25　Christ watches me His little lamb,
　　Cares for me day and night,
　That I may be His Own in heaven:
　　So angels clad in white
　Shall sing their 'Glory, glory'
30　　For my sake in the height.

　The wise men left their country
　　To journey morn by morn
　With gold and frankincense and myrrh
　　Because the Lord was born:
35　God sent a star to guide them
　　And sent a dream to warn.

　My life is like their journey,
　　Their star is like God's Book,
　I must be like those good wise men
40　　With heavenward heart and look:
　But shall I give no gifts to God?—
　　What precious gifts they took.

　Lord I will give my love to Thee,
　　Than gold much costlier,
45　Sweeter to Thee than frankincense,
　　More prized than choicest myrrh:
　Lord make me dearer day by day,
　　Day by day holier.

Nearer and dearer day by day:
50   Till I my voice unite
And sing my 'Glory, glory'
    With angels clad in white,
All 'Glory, glory' given to Thee
Thro' all the heavenly height.

"Not yours but you."

He died for me: what can I offer Him?
    Toward Him swells incense of perpetual prayer;
    His court wear crowns and aureoles round their hair;
His ministers are subtle cherubim,
5   Ring within ring, white intense seraphim
    Leap like immortal lightnings thro' the air:
    What shall I offer Him? defiled and bare
My spirit broken and my brightness dim.—
Give Me thy youth;—I yield it to Thy rod
10   As Thou didst yield Thy prime of youth for me:—
Give Me thy life;—I give it breath by breath
    As Thou didst give Thy life so give I Thee:—
Give Me thy love;—So be it, my God, my God,
As Thou hast loved me even to bitter death.

An Answer.

[The first page of the MS is missing from the notebook.]

To make it glad with a goodly crop:
    Even so One Wiser deals with me:—
Amen, say I: if He choose to lop
    Branch after branch of my leafèd tree,
5   In its own ripe season more fruit shall be.

Tenfold fruit in the time of fruit,
    In the time of corn and wine and oil,
Sound at the core, firm at the root;

10   Repaying the years and years of toil,
        Repaying the blood that fed the soil.

Sir Winter.

Sir Winter is coming across the wide sea,
With his blustering companions, so wild and so free:
He speeds on his way, like some bold buccaneer,
And Day flies before him with faltering and fear.

5   In the front of the battle new trophies to reap,
     Mid the howl of the tempest, the roar of the deep,
Lo, he comes* with his noiseless-shod legions of snow
And nips the last buds that were lingering to blow.

Sweet blackbird is silenced with chaffinch and thrush,
10   Only waistcoated robin still chirps in the bush:
Soft sun-loving swallows have mustered in force
And winged to the spice-teaming southlands their course.

Plump housekeeper dormouse has tucked himself neat,
Just a brown ball in moss with a morsel to eat;
15   Armed hedgehog has huddled him into the hedge
While frogs miss freezing deep down in the sedge.

So sturdy Sir Winter has conquered us quite,
He has ravaged our country to left and to right:
Since we must bear his yoke for a season, we'd best
20   Try to lighten its weight on ourselves and the rest.

Soft swallows have left us alone in the lurch,
But robin sits whistling to us from his perch:
If I were red robin, I'd pipe you a tune
Would make you despise all the beauties of June.

25   But since that cannot be, let us draw round the fire,
Munch chestnuts, tell stories, and stir the blaze higher:

* Down to the * these verses are
   written by Mr. Jervis.

We'll comfort pinched robin with crumbs, little man,
Till he sings us the very best song that he can.

In an Artist's Studio.

One face looks out from all his canvasses,
    One selfsame figure sits or walks or leans;
    We found her hidden just behind those screens,
That mirror gave back all her loveliness.
5   A queen in opal or in ruby dress,
    A nameless girl in freshest summer greens,
    A saint, an angel;—every canvass means
The same one meaning, neither more nor less.
He feeds upon her face by day and night,
10   And she with true kind eyes looks back on him
Fair as the moon and joyful as the light:
    Not wan with waiting, not with sorrow dim;
Not as she is, but was when hope shone bright;
    Not as she is, but as she fills his dream.

Introspective.

I wish it were over the terrible pain,
Pang after pang again and again;
First the shattering ruining blow,
Then the probing steady and slow.

5   Did I wince? I did not faint:
My soul broke but was not bent;
Up I stand like a blasted tree
By the shore of the shivering sea.

On my boughs neither leaf nor fruit,
10   No sap in my uttermost root,
Brooding in an anguish dumb
On the short past and the long to come.

Dumb I was when the ruin fell,
Dumb I remain and will never tell:

15   O my soul I talk with thee
     But not another the sight must see.

     I did not start when the torture stung,
     I did not faint when the torture wrung;
     Let it come tenfold if come it must
20   But I will not groan when I bite the dust.

"The heart knoweth its own bitterness."

     When all the over-work of life
        Is finished once, and fast asleep
     We swerve no more beneath the knife
        But taste that silence cool and deep;
5   Forgetful of the highways rough,
        Forgetful of the thorny scourge,
        Forgetful of the tossing surge,
     Then shall we find it is enough?—

     How can we say 'enough' on earth;
10   'Enough' with such a craving heart:
     I have not found it since my birth
        But still have bartered part for part.
     I have not held and hugged the whole,
        But paid the old to gain the new;
15   Much have I paid, yet much is due,
     Till I am beggared sense and soul.

     I used to labour, used to strive
        For pleasure with a restless will:
     Now if I save my soul alive
20   All else what matters, good or ill?
     I used to dream alone, to plan
        Unspoken hopes and days to come:—
        Of all my past this is the sum:
     I will not lean on child of man.

25   To give, to give, not to receive,
        I long to pour myself, my soul,
     Not to keep back or count or leave

But king with king to give the whole:
   I long for one to stir my deep—
30   I have had enough of help and gift—
   I long for one to search and sift
Myself, to take myself and keep.

You scratch my surface with your pin;
   You stroke me smooth with hushing breath;—
35 Nay pierce, nay probe, nay dig within,
   Probe my quick core and sound my depth.
You call me with a puny call,
   You talk, you smile, you nothing do;
   How should I spend my heart on you,
40 My heart that so outweighs you all?

Your vessels are by much too strait;
   Were I to pour you could not hold,
Bear with me: I must bear to wait
   A fountain sealed thro' heat and cold.
45 Bear with me days or months or years;
   Deep must call deep until the end
   When friend shall no more envy friend
Nor vex his friend at unawares.

Not in this world of hope deferred,
50   This world of perishable stuff;—
Eye hath not seen, nor ear hath heard,
   Nor heart conceived that full 'enough':
Here moans the separating sea,
   Here harvests fail, here breaks the heart;
55   There God shall join and no man part,
I full of Christ and Christ of me.

"Reflection".

Gazing thro' her chamber window
   Sits my soul's dear soul;
Looking northward, looking southward,

Looking to the goal,
5   Looking back without control.—

I have strewn thy path, beloved,
    With plumed meadowsweet,
Iris and pale perfumed lilies,
    Roses most complete:
10   Wherefore pause on listless feet?—

But she sits and never answers;
    Gazing gazing still
On swift fountain, shadowed valley,
    Cedared sunlit hill:
15   Who can guess or read her will?

Who can guess or read the spirit
    Shrined within her eyes,
Part a longing, part a languor,
    Part a mere surprize,
20   While slow mists do rise and rise?—

Is it love she looks and longs for;
    Is it rest or peace;
Is it slumber self-forgetful
    In its utter ease;
25   Is it one or all of these?

So she sits and doth not answer
    With her dreaming eyes,
With her languid look delicious
    Almost Paradise,
30   Less than happy, over wise.

Answer me, O self-forgetful—
    Or of what beside?—
Is it day dream of a maiden,
    Vision of a bride,
35   Is it knowledge, love, or pride?

Cold she sits thro' all my kindling,
    Deaf to all I pray:
I have wasted might and wisdom,

       Wasted night and day:
40   Deaf she dreams to all I say.

       Now if I could guess her secret
         Were it worth the guess?—
       Time is lessening, hope is lessening,
         Love grows less and less:
45   What care I for *no* or *yes?*—

       I will give her stately burial,
         Tho', when she lies dead:
       For dear memory of the past time,
         Of her royal head,
50   Of the much I strove and said.

       I will give her stately burial,
         Willow branches bent;
       Have her carved in alabaster,
         As she dreamed and leant
55   While I wondered what she meant.

A Coast-Nightmare.

       I have a friend in ghostland—
         Early found, ah me, how early lost!—
       Blood-red seaweeds drip along that coastland
         By the strong sea wrenched and tossed.
5   In every creek there slopes a dead man's islet,
         And such an one in every bay;
       All unripened in the unended twilight:
         For there comes neither night nor day.

       Unripe harvest there hath none to reap it
10   From the watery misty place;
       Unripe vineyard there hath none to keep it
         In unprofitable space.
       Living flocks and herds are nowhere found there;
         Only ghosts in flocks and shoals:
15   Indistinguished hazy ghosts surround there

Meteors whirling on their poles;
Indistinguished hazy ghosts abound there;
Troops, yea swarms, of dead men's souls.—

Have they towns to live in?—
20   They have towers and towns from sea to sea;
Of each town the gates are seven;
Of one of these each ghost is free.
Civilians, soldiers, seamen,
Of one town each ghost is free:
25 They are ghastly men those ghostly freemen:
Such a sight may you not see.—

How know you that your lover
Of death's tideless waters stoops to drink?—
Me by night doth mouldy darkness cover,
30   It makes me quake to think:
All night long I feel his presence hover
Thro' the darkness black as ink.

Without a voice he tells me
The wordless secrets of death's deep:
35 If I sleep, his trumpet voice compels me
To stalk forth in my sleep:
If I wake, he hunts me like a nightmare;
I feel my hair stand up, my body creep:
Without light I see a blasting sight there,
40   See a secret I must keep.

'For one Sake.'

One passed me like a flash of lightning by
To ring clear bells of heaven beyond the stars:
Then said I: Wars and rumours of your wars
Are dull with din of what and where and why;
5 My heart is where these troubles draw not nigh:
Let me alone till heaven shall burst its bars,
Break up its fountains, roll its flashing cars

Earthwards with fire to test and purify.
Let me alone tonight, and one night more
10   Of which I shall not count the eventide;
Its morrow will not be as days before:
Let me alone to dream, perhaps to weep;
    To dream of her the imperishable bride,
Dream while I wake and dream on while I sleep.

My old Friends.

They lie at rest asleep and dead,
The dew drops cool above their head,
They knew not when past summer fled—
            Amen.

5   They lie at rest and quite forget
The hopes and fears that wring us yet;
Their eyes are set, their heart is set—
            Amen.

They lie with us, yet gone away
10   Hear nothing that we sob or say
Beneath the thorn of wintry may—
            Miserere.

Together all yet each alone,
Each laid at rest beneath his own
15   Smooth turf or white appointed stone—
            Amen.

When shall our slumbers be so deep,
And bleeding heart and eyes that weep
Lie lapped in the sufficient sleep?—
20   *Miserere.*

We dream of them: and who shall say
They never dream while far away
Of us between the night and day?—
            Sursum corda.

25   Gone far away: or it may be
      They lean toward us and hear and see
      Yea and remember more than we—
                 Amen.

      For wherefore should we deem them far
30   Who know not where those spirits are
      That shall outshine both moon and star?—
                 Hallelujah.

      Where check or change can never rise
      Deep in recovered Paradise
35   They rest world-wearied heart and eyes—
                 Jubilate.

      We hope and love with throbbing breast,
      They hope and love and are at rest:
      And yet we question which is best—
40   *Miserere.*

      Oh what is earth, that we should build
      Brief houses here, and seek concealed
      Poor treasure, and add field to field

      And heap to heap and store to store,
45   Still grasping, ever grasping more,
      While death stands knocking at our door?—
                 Cui bono?

      But one will answer: Changed and pale
      And starved at heart, I thirst I fail
50   For love, I thirst without avail—
                 Miserrima.

      Sweet love, a fountain sealed to me:
      Mere love, the sole sufficiency
      For every longing that can be—
55   *Amen.*

      Oh happy those alone whose lot
      Is love: I search from spot to spot;
      In life, in death, I find it not—
                 Miserrima.

60   Not found in life: nay, verily.
     I too have sought: come sit with me
     And grief for grief shall answer thee—
          Miserrima.

     Sit with me where the sapless leaves
65   Are fallen and sere: to one who grieves
     What cheer have last year's harvest sheaves?—
          Cui bono?

     Not found in life: yet found in death.
     I sought life as but a breath
70   There is a nest of love beneath

     The sod, a home prepared before;
     Our brethren whom one mother bore
     Live there, and toil and ache no more—
          Hallelujah.

75   Dear friends and kinsfolk great and small;
     Not lost but saved both one and all:
     They watch across the parting wall

     (Do they not watch?) and count the creep
     Of time, and sound the shallowing deep,
80   Till we in port shall also sleep—
          Hallelujah, Amen.

"Yet a little while".

     These days are long before I die:
       To sit alone upon a thorn
       Is what the nightingale forlorn
     Does night by night continually;
5   She swells her heart to extasy
     Until it bursts and she can die.

     These days are long that wane and wax:
       Waxeth and wanes the ghostly moon
       Achill and pale in cordial June;

10   What is it that she wandering lacks?
      She seems as one that aches and aches
      Most sick to wane most sick to wax.

      Of all the sad sights in the world
        The downfall of an Autumn leaf
15   Is grievous and suggesteth grief:
      Who thought when Spring was fresh unfurled
      Of this? when Spring twigs gleamed impearled
      Who thought of frost that nips the world?

      There are a hundred subtle stings
20   To prick us in our daily walk:
      A young fruit cankered on its stalk,
      A strong bird snared for all his wings,
      A nest that sang but never sings;
      Yea sight and sound and silence stings.

25   There is a lack in solitude,
      There is a load in throng of life;
      One with another genders strife,
      To be alone yet is not good:
      I know but of one neighbourhood
30   At peace and full; death's solitude.

      Sleep soundly, dears, who lulled at last
      Forget the bird and all her pains,
      Forget the moon that waxes, wanes,
      The leaf, the sting, the frostful blast;
35   Forget the troublous years that past
      In strife or ache did end at last.

      We have clear call of daily bells,
      A dimness where the anthems are,
      A chancel vault of sky and star,
40   A thunder if the organ swells:
      Alas our daily life—what else?—
      Is not in tune with daily bells.

      You have deep pause betwixt the chimes
      Of earth and heaven, a patient pause

45   Yet glad with rest by certain laws:
You look and long; while oftentimes
Precursive flush of morning climbs
And air vibrates with coming chimes.

"Only believe."

I stood by weeping
Yet a sorrowful silence keeping
While an Angel smote my love
As she lay sleeping.—

5   Is there a bed above
More fragrant than these violets
That are white like death?

White like a dove
Flowers in the blessed islets
10   Breathe sweeter breath
All fair morns and twilights.

Is the gold there
More golden than these tresses?

There heads are aureoled
15   And crowned like gold
With light most rare.

Are the bowers of Heaven
More choice than these?

To them are given
20   All odorous shady trees.
Earth's bowers are wildernesses
Compared with the recesses
Made soft there now
Nest-like twixt bough and bough.

25   Who shall live in such a nest?

Heart with heart at rest:
All they whose troubles cease

In peace:
Souls that wrestled
30   Now are nestled
There at ease:
Throng from east and west
From north and south
To plenty from the land of drouth.

35   How long must they wait?

There is a certain term
For their bodies to the worm
And their souls at Heaven-gate.
Dust to dust, clod to clod
40   These precious things of God;
Trampled underfoot by man
And beast the appointed years.

Their longest life was but a span
For birth, death, laughter, tears:
45   Is it worth while to live,
Rejoice and grieve,
Hope, fear and die?
Man with man, lie with lie,
The slow show dwindles by:
50   At last what shall we have
Besides a grave?

Lies and shows no more,
No fear, no pain,
But after hope and sleep
55   Dear joys again.
Those who sowed shall reap:
Those who bore
The cross shall wear the crown:
Those who clomb the steep
60   There shall sit down.
The Shepherd of the sheep
Feeds His flock there;

[The rest of the poem is missing from the notebook.]

"Rivals."
A Shadow of Saint Dorothea.

"Golden haired, lily white,
   "Will you pluck me lilies;
"Or will you show me where they grow,
   "Show where the summer rill is?
5 "But is your hair of gold or light,
   "And is your foot of flake or fire,
"And have you wings rolled up from sight,
   "And joy to slake desire?"—

"I pluck young flowers of Paradise,
10 "Lilies and roses red;
"A sceptre for my hand,
   "A crown to crown my golden head.
"Love makes me wise:
"I sing, I stand,
15 "I pluck palm branches in the sheltered land."—

"Is there a path to Heaven
   "My heavy foot may tread;
"And will you show that way to go,
   "That rose and lily bed?
20 "Which day of all these seven
   "Will lighten my heart of lead,
"Will purge mine eyes and make me wise
   "Alive or dead?"—

"There is a Heavenward stair—
25   "Mount, strain upwards, strain and strain—
"Each step will crumble to your foot
   "That never shall descend again.
"There grows a tree from ancient root,
"With healing leaves and twelvefold fruit,
30 "In musical Heaven air:
"Feast with me there."—

"I have a home on earth I cannot leave,
"I have a friend on earth I cannot grieve:
   "Come down to me, I cannot mount to you."—

35   "Nay choose between us both,
    "Choose as you are lief or loath:
    "You cannot keep these things and have me too."—

A Yawn.

  I grow so weary: is it death
    This awful woful weariness?
  It is a weight to heave my breath,
    A weight to wake, a weight to sleep;
5   I have no heart to work or weep.

  The sunshine teazes and the dark;
    Only the twilight dulls my grief:
  Is this the Ark, the strong safe Ark,
    Or the tempestuous drowning sea
10   Whose crested coursers foam for me?

  Why does the sea moan evermore?
    Shut out from Heaven it makes its moan,
  It frets against the boundary shore:
    All earth's full rivers cannot fill
15   The sea, that drinking thirsteth still.

  Sheer miracles of loveliness
    Lie hid in its unlooked-on bed:
  Salt passionless anemones
    Blow flower-like; just enough alive
20   To blow and propagate and thrive.

  Shells quaint with curve or spot or spike,
    Encrusted live things argus-eyed,
  All fair alike yet all unlike,
    Are born without a pang and die
25   Without a pang and so pass by.

  I would I lived without a pang:
    Oh happy they who day by day
  Quiescent neither sobbed nor sang;
    Unburdened with a what or why
30   They live and die and so pass by.

For H. P.

On the land and on the sea,
Jesus keep both you and me:

Going out and coming in,
Christ keep us both from shame and sin:

5   In this world, in the world to come,
Keep us safe and lead us home:

Today in toil, tonight in rest,
Be Best Beloved and love us best.

"Then they that feared the Lord spake often one to another."

Friend I commend to thee the narrow way:
Not because I, please God, will walk therein,
But rather for the love-feast of that day
    The exceeding prize which whoso will may win.
5   This world is old and rotting at the core
Here death's heads mock us with a toothless grin
    Here heartiest laughter leaves us spent and sore.
We heap up treasures for the fretting moth,
Our children heap our fathers heaped before,
10   But what shall profit us the cumbrous growth?
It cannot journey with us, cannot save,
Stripped in that darkness be we lief or loth
    Stripped bare to what we are from all we have,
Naked we came, naked we must return
15   To one obscure inevitable grave.
    If this the lesson is which we must learn
Taught by God's discipline of love or wrath
(To brand or purify His fire must burn)—
    Friend I commend to theee the narrow path
20   That thou and I, please God, may walk therein,

May taste and see how good is God Who hath
Loved us while hating even to death our sin.

"What good shall my life do me?"

No hope in life; yet is there hope
In death, the threshold of man's scope:
Man yearneth (as the heliotrope

For ever seeks the sun) thro' light
5   Thro' dark for Love: all read aright
Is Love for Love is infinite.

Shall not this infinite Love suffice
To feed thy dearth? Lift heart and eyes
Up to the hills, grow glad and wise.

10   The hills are glad because the sun
Kisses their round tops every one
Where silver fountains laugh and run:

Smooth pebbles shine beneath; beside
The grass, mere green, grows myriad-eyed
15   With pomp of blossoms veined or pied.

So every nest is glad whereon
The sun in tender strength has shone;
So every fruit he glows upon;

So every valley depth, whose herds
20   At pasture praise him without words;
So the winged extasies of birds.

If there be any such thing, what
Is there by sunlight betters not?—
Nothing except dead things that rot.

25   Thou then who art not dead and fit
Like blasted tree beside the pit
But for the axe that levels it,

Living show life of Love, whereof
The force wields earth and heaven above:
30 Who knows not Love begetteth Love?—

Love in the gracious rain distils;
Love moves the subtle fountain rills
To fertilize uplifted hills

And seedful vallies fertilize;
35 Love stills the hungry lion's cries
And the young raven satisfies;

Love hangs this earth in space; Love rolls
Fair worlds rejoicing on their poles
And girds them round with aureoles;

40 Love lights the sun; Love thro' the dark
Lights the moon's evanescent arc;
Same Love lights up the glow-worm's spark;

Love rears the great; Love tends the small;
Breaks off the yoke, breaks down the wall;
45 Accepteth all, fulfilleth all.

O ye who taste that Love is sweet,
Set waymarks for the doubtful feet
That stumble on in search of it.

Sing hymns of Love, that those who hear
50 Far off in pain may lend an ear
Rise up and wonder and draw near.

Lead lives of Love, that others who
Behold your lives may kindle too
With Love and cast their lots with you.

The Massacre of Perugia.

A trumpet pealed thro' France. Then Italy
Stirred, shook, from sea to sea.
Then many cities broke

Their lawful yoke.
5   Then in an evil hour
Perugia on her fort-crowned hill

[The rest of the poem is missing from the notebook.]

I have done with hope;
Have done with lies from sea to sea:
How should I lie beneath the cope
Of Heaven's star-blazoned verity?
5   I will not wear your crown tonight,
But mine own crown tomorrow morn:

[The lines of the poem preceding and following the above are miss-
ing from the notebook.]

Promises like Piecrust.

Promise me no promises,
    So will I not promise you;
Keep we both our liberties,
    Never false and never true:
5   Let us hold the die uncast,
    Free to come as free to go;
For I cannot know your past,
    And of mine what can you know?

You, so warm, may once have been
10   Warmer towards another one;
I, so cold, may once have seen
    Sunlight, once have felt the sun:
Who shall show us if it was
    Thus indeed in time of old?
15   Fades the image from the glass
    And the fortune is not told.

If you promised, you might grieve
    For lost liberty again;

If I promised, I believe
20 I should fret to break the chain:
Let us be the friends we were,
 Nothing more but nothing less;
Many thrive on frugal fare
 Who would perish of excess.

By the waters of Babylon.

By the waters of Babylon
 We sit down and weep,
Far from the pleasant land
 Where our fathers sleep;
5 Far from our Holy Place
 From which the Glory is gone;
We sit in dust and weep
 By the waters of Babylon.

By the waters of Babylon
10 The willow trees grow rank:
We hang our harps thereon
 Silent upon the bank.
Before us the days are dark,
 And dark the days that are gone;
15 We grope in the very dark
 By the waters of Babylon.

By the waters of Babylon
 We thirst for Jordan yet,
We pine for Jerusalem
20 Whereon our hearts are set:
Our priests defiled and slain,
 Our princes ashamed and gone,
Oh how should we forget
 By the waters of Babylon?

25 By the waters of Babylon
 Tho' the wicked grind the just,
Our seed shall yet strike root

And shall shoot up from the dust:
The captive shall lead captive,
30   The slave rise up and begone,
And thou too shalt sit in dust
    O daughter of Babylon.

Better so.

Fast asleep, mine own familiar friend,
  Fast asleep at last:
    Tho' the pain was strong,
    Tho' the struggle long,
5   It is past;
All thy pangs are at an end.

Whilst I weep, whilst death bells toll,
  Thou art fast asleep,
    With idle hands upon thy breast
10   And heart at rest:
  Whilst I weep
Angels sing around thy singing soul.

Who would wish thee back upon the rough
  Wearisome dangerous road?
15   Wish back thy toil-spent soul
    Just at the goal?
  My soul, praise God
For one dear soul which hath enough.

I would not fetch thee back to hope with me
20 A sickening hope deferred,
    To taste the cup that slips
    From thirsty lips:
  Hast thou not heard
What was to hear, and seen what was to see?

25 I would not speak the word if I could raise
  My dead to life:
    I would not speak
    If I could flush thy cheek

And rouse thy pulses' strife
30 And send thy feet on the once-trodden ways.

How could I meet the dear rebuke
If thou should'st say:
"O friend of little faith,
Good was my lot of death,
35 And good my day
Of rest, and good the sleep I took"—?

Our widowed Queen.

The Husband of the widow care for her,
The Father of the fatherless:
The faithful Friend, the abiding Comforter,
Watch over her to bless.

5 Full twenty years of blameless married faith,
Of love and honour questioned not,
Joys, griefs imparted: for the first time Death
Sunders the common lot.

Christ help the desolate Queen upon her throne,
10 Strengthen her hands, confirm her heart:
For she henceforth must bear a load alone
Borne until now in part.

Christ help the desolate Woman in her home,
Broken of heart, indeed bereft;
15 Shrinking from solitary days to come,
Beggared tho' much is left.

Rise up, O Sons and Daughters of the Dead,
Weep with your Mother where she weeps;
Yet not as sorrowing without hope be shed
20 Your tears: he only sleeps.

Rise up, O Sons and Daughters of the realm,
In pale reflected sorrow move;
Revere the widowed hand that holds the helm,
Love her with double love.

25   In royal patience of her soul possess'd
     May she fulfill her length of days:
    Then may her children rise and call her bless'd,
     Then may her husband praise.

In progress.

Ten years ago it seemed impossible
  That she should ever grow so calm as this,
  With self-remembrance in her warmest kiss
And dim dried eyes like an exhausted well.
5   Slow-speaking when she has some fact to tell,
  Silent with long-unbroken silences,
  Centred in self yet not unpleased to please,
Gravely monotonous like a passing bell.
Mindful of drudging daily common things,
10 Patient at pastime, patient at her work,
Wearied perhaps but strenuous certainly.
Sometimes I fancy we may one day see
  Her head shoot forth seven stars from where they lurk
And her eyes lightnings and her shoulders wings.

"Out of the deep."

Have mercy, Thou my God; mercy, my God;
  For I can hardly bear life day by day:
  Be I here or there I fret myself away:
Lo for Thy staff I have but felt Thy rod
5   Along this tedious desert path long trod.
  When will Thy judgement judge me, Yea or Nay?
  I pray for grace; but then my sins unpray
My prayer: on holy ground I fool stand shod.
While still Thou haunts't me, faint upon the cross,
10 A sorrow beyond sorrow in Thy look,
Unutterable craving for my soul.
All faithful Thou, Lord: I, not Thou, forsook
  Myself; I traitor slunk back from the goal:
Lord, I repent; help Thou my helpless loss.

For a Mercy received.

Thank God Who spared me what I feared!
  Once more I gird myself to run.
  Thy promise stands, Thou Faithful One.
Horror of darkness disappeared
5   At length; once more I see the sun,

And dare to wait in hope for Spring,
  To face and bear the Winter's cold:
  The dead cocoon shall yet unfold
And give to light the living wing;
10   There's hidden sap beneath the mould.

My God, how could my courage flag
  So long as Thou art still the same?
  For what were labour, failure, shame,
Whilst Thy sure promise doth not lag
15   And Thou dost shield me with Thy Name?

Yet am I weak, my faith is weak,
  My heart is weak that pleads with Thee:
O Thou That art not far to seek
Turn to me, hearken when I speak,
20   Stretch forth Thy Hand to succour me.

Thro' many perils have I pass'd,
  Deaths, plagues, and wonders, have I seen:
Till now Thy Hand hath held me fast:
Lord help me, hold me, to the last;
25   Still be what Thou hast always been.

Open Thy Heart of Love to me,
  Give me Thyself, keep nothing back
Even as I give myself to Thee.
  Love paid by Love doth nothing lack,
30   And Love to pay Love is not slack.

Love doth so grace and dignify
  That beggars sue as King with King
Before the Throne of Grace on high:

My God, be gracious to my cry;
35   My God, accept what gift I bring:

A heart that loves; tho' soiled and bruised,
    Yet chosen by Thee in time of yore:
Who ever came and was refused
By Thee? Do, Lord, as Thou art used
40   To do, and make me love Thee more.

Summer.

Come, cuckoo, come;
    Come again, swift swallow;
Come and welcome; where you come
    Summer's sure to follow.
5   June, the month of months,
    Flowers and fruitage brings too;
When green trees spread shadiest boughs,
    When each wild bird sings too.

May is scant and crude,
10   Generous June is riper;
Birds fall silent in July,
    June has its woodland piper:
Rocks upon the maple-top
    Homely-hearted linnet,
15 Full in hearing of his nest
    And the dear ones in it.

If the year would stand
    Still at June for ever,
With no further growth on land
20   Nor further flow of river,
If all nights were shortest nights
    And longest days were all the seven,—
This might be a merrier world
    To my mind to live in.

A Dumb Friend.

I planted a young tree when I was young;
   But now the tree is grown and I am old:
   There wintry robin shelters from the cold
     And tunes his silver tongue.

5   A green and living tree I planted it,
   A glossy-foliaged tree of evergreen:
   All thro' the noontide heat it spread a screen
     Whereunder I might sit.

But now I only watch it where it towers:
10   I, sitting at my window, watch it tossed
   By rattling gale, or silvered by the frost;
     Or, when sweet summer flowers,

Wagging its round green head with stately grace
   In tender winds that kiss it and go by:
15   It shows a green full age; and what show I?
     A faded wrinkled face.

So often have I watched it, till mine eyes
   Have filled with tears and I have ceased to see;
   That now it seems a very friend to me
20   In all my secrets wise.

A faithful pleasant friend, who year by year
   Grew with my growth and strengthened with my
       strength,
   But whose green lifetime shows a longer length:
     When I shall not sit here

25   It still will bud in spring, and shed rare leaves
   In autumn, and in summer heat give shade,
   And warmth in winter; when my bed is made
     In shade the cypress weaves.

Margery.

What shall we do with Margery?
　She lies and cries upon her bed,
　All lily-pale from foot to head,
　Her heart is sore as sore can be;
5　　Poor guileless shamefaced Margery.

A foolish girl, to love a man
　And let him know she loved him so!
She should have tried a different plan;
　Have loved, but not have let him know:
10　　Then he perhaps had loved her so.

What can we do with Margery
　Who has no relish for her food?
We'd take her with us to the sea—
　Across the sea—but where's the good?
15　　She'd fret alike on land and sea.

Yes, what the neighbours say is true:
　Girls should not make themselves so cheap.
But now it's done what can we do?
　I hear her moaning in her sleep,
20　　Moaning and sobbing in her sleep.

I think—and I'm of flesh and blood—
　Were I that man for whom she cares
　I would not cost her tears and prayers
To leave her just alone like mud,
25　　Fretting her simple heart with cares.

A year ago she was a child,
　Now she's a woman in her grief;
　The year's now at the falling leaf,
At budding of the leaves she smiled;
30　　Poor foolish harmless foolish child.

It was her own fault? so it was.
　If every own fault found us out
　Dogged us and snared us round about,

What comfort should we take because
35   Not half our due we thus wrung out?

At any rate the question stands:
     What now to do with Margery,
A weak poor creature on our hands?
     Something we must do: I'll not see
40   Her blossom fade, sweet Margery.

Perhaps a change may after all
     Prove best for her: to leave behind
Those home-sights seen time out of mind;
To get beyond the narrow wall
45   Of home, and learn home is not all.

Perhaps this way she may forget,
     Not all at once, but in a while;
May come to wonder how she set
     Her heart on this slight thing, and smile
50   At her own folly, in a while.

Yet this I say and I maintain:
     Were I the man she's fretting for
     I should my very self abhor
If I could leave her to her pain,
55   Uncomforted to tears and pain.

In Patience.

I will not faint, but trust in God
     Who this my lot hath given;
He leads me by the thorny road
     Which is the road to heaven.
5   Tho' sad my day that lasts so long,
At evening I shall have a song;
Tho' dim my day until the night,
At evening time there shall be light.

My life is but a working day
10   Whose tasks are set aright:

A while to work, a while to pray,
　And then a quiet night.
And then, please God, a quiet night
Where Saints and Angels walk in white:
15　One dreamless sleep from work and sorrow,
But re-awakening on the morrow.

Sunshine.

"There's little sunshine in my heart
　Slack to spring, lead to sink;
There's little sunshine in the world
　　I think."—

5　"There's glow of sunshine in my heart
　(Cool wind, cool the glow);
There's flood of sunshine in the world
　　I know."—

Now if of these one spoke the truth,
10　One spoke more or less:
But which was which I will not tell;—
　　You, guess.

Meeting.

If we shall live, we live;
　If we shall die, we die;
If we live, we shall meet again;
　But tonight, good bye.
5　One word, let but one be heard—
What, not one word?

If we sleep, we shall wake again
　And see tomorrow's light;
If we wake, we shall meet again;
10　But tonight, good night.
Good night, my lost and found—
Still not a sound?

    If we live, we must part;
      If we die, we part in pain;
15 If we die, we shall part
      Only to meet again.
    By those tears on either cheek,
    Tomorrow you will speak.

    To meet, worth living for;
20   Worth dying for, to meet;
    To meet, worth parting for;
      Bitter forgot in sweet.
    To meet, worth parting before
    Never to part more.

"None with Him."

    My God, to live: how didst Thou bear to live
      Preaching and teaching, toiling to and fro;
    Few men accepting what Thou hadst to give,
      Few men prepared to know
5   Thy Face, to see the truth Thou camest to show?

    My God, to die: how didst Thou bear to die
      That long slow death in weariness of pain;
    A curse and an astonishment, passed by,
      Pointed at, mocked again,
10   By men for whom Thy Blood was shed in vain?

    Whilst I do hardly bear my easy life,
      And hardly face my easy-coming death:
    I turn to flee before the tug of strife;
      And shrink with troubled breath
15   From sleep, that is not death Thy Spirit saith.

Under Willows.

    Under willows among the graves
      One was walking, ah welladay!
    Where each willow her green boughs waves

Come April prime, come May.
5 Under willows among the graves
  She met her lost love, ah welladay!
Where in Autumn each wild wind raves
And whirls sere leaves away.

He looked at her with a smile,
10 She looked at him with a sigh,
Both paused to look awhile;
  Then he passed by,
Passed by and whistled a tune;
  She stood silent and still:
15 It was the sunniest day in June,
  Yet one felt a chill.

Under willows among the graves
  I know a certain black black pool
Scarce wrinkled when Autumn raves;
20   Under the turf is cool;
Under the water it must be cold;
  Winter comes cold when Summer's past;
Though she live to be old, so old,
  She shall die at last.

A Sketch.

The blindest buzzard that I know
  Does not wear wings to spread and stir,
  Nor does my special mole wear fur
And grub among the roots below;
5   He sports a tail indeed, but then
  It's to a coat; he's man with men;
    His quill is cut to a pen.

In other points our friend's a mole,
  A buzzard, beyond scope of speech:
10   He sees not what's within his reach,
Misreads the part, ignores the whole.
  Misreads the part so reads in vain,

Ignores the whole tho' patent plain,
   Misreads both parts again.

15 My blindest buzzard that I know,
   My special mole, when will you see?
   Oh no, you must not look at me,
There's nothing hid for me to show.
   I might show facts as plain as day;
20   But since your eyes are blind, you'd say:
   Where? What? and turn away.

If I had Words.

If I had words, if I had words
   At least to vent my misery:—
But muter than the speechless herds
   I have no voice wherewith to cry.
5 I have no strength to life my hands,
   I have no heart to lift mine eye,
My soul is bound with brazen bands,
   My soul is crushed and like to die.
My thoughts that wander here and there,
10   That wander wander listlessly,
Bring nothing back to cheer my care,
   Nothing that I may live thereby.
My heart is broken in my breast,
   My breath is but a broken sigh—
15 Oh if there be a land of rest
   It is far off, it is not nigh.
If I had wings as hath a dove,
   If I had wings that I might fly,
I yet would seek the land of love
20   Where fountains run which run not dry;
Tho' there be none that road to tell,
   And long that road is verily:
Then if I lived I should do well,
   And if I died I should but die.
25 If I had wings as hath a dove
   I would not sift the what and why,

I would make haste to find out love,
   If not to find at least to try.
I would make haste to love, my rest;
30   To love, my truth that doth not lie:
Then if I lived it might be best,
   Or if I died I could but die.

What to do?

Oh my love and my own own deary!
What shall I do? my love is weary.
Sleep, O friend, on soft downy pillow,
Pass, O friend, as wind or as billow,
5   And I'll wear the willow.

No stone at his head be set,
A swelling turf be his coverlet
Bound round with a graveyard wattle;
Hedged round from the trampling cattle
10   And the children's prattle.

I myself, instead of a stone,
Will sit by him to dwindle and moan;
Sit and weep with a bitter weeping,
Sit and weep where my love lies sleeping
15   While my life goes creeping.

Young Death.

Lying adying—
Such sweet things untasted,
Such rare beauties wasted:
Her hair a hidden treasure,
5   Her voice a lost pleasure;
Her soul made void of passion;
Her body going to nothing
Though long it took to fashion,
Soon to be a loathing:
10   Her road hath no turning,

Her light is burning burning
With last feeble flashes;
Dying from the birth:
Dust to dust, earth to earth,
15   Ashes to ashes.

Lying adying—
Have done with vain sighing:
Life not lost but treasured,
God Almighty pleasured,
20   God's daughter fetched and carried,
Christ's bride betrothed and married.
Lo, in the Room, the Upper,
She shall sit down to supper,
New bathed from head to feet
25   And on Christ gazing;
Her mouth kept clean and sweet
Shall laugh and sing, God praising:
Then shall be no more weeping,
Or fear, or sorrow,
30   Or waking more, or sleeping,
Or night, or morrow,
Or cadence in the song
Of songs, or thirst, or hunger;
The strong shall rise more strong
35   And the young younger.
Our tender little dove
Meek-eyed and simple,
Our love goes home to Love;
There shall she walk in white
40   Where God shall be the Light
And God the Temple.

In a certain place.

I found Love in a certain place
Asleep and cold—or cold and dead?—
All ivory-white upon his bed

All ivory-white his face.
5   His hands were folded
On his quiet breast,
To his figure laid at rest
Chilly bed was moulded.

His hair hung lax about his brow,
10   I had not seen his face before;
Or if I saw it once, it wore
Another aspect now.
No trace of last night's sorrow,
No shadow of tomorrow;
15   All at peace (thus all sorrows cease),
All at peace.

I wondered: Were his eyes
Soft or falcon-clear?
I wondered: As he lies
20   Does he feel me near?
In silence my heart spoke
And wondered: If he woke
And found me sitting nigh him
And felt me sitting by him,
25   If life flushed to his cheek,
He living man with men,
Then if I heard him speak
Oh should I know him then?

"Cannot sweeten."

If that's water you wash your hands in
   Why is it black as ink is black?—
Because my hands are foul with my folly:
   Oh the lost time that comes not back!—

5   If that's water you bathe your feet in
   Why is it red as wine is red?—
Because my feet sought blood in their goings;
   Red red is the track they tread.—

Slew you mother or slew you father
10   That your foulness passeth not by?—
Not father and oh not mother:
I slew my love with an evil eye.—

Slew you sister or slew you brother
That in peace you have not a part?—
15   Not brother and oh not sister:
I slew my love with a hardened heart.

He loved me because he loved me,
Not for grace or beauty I had;
He loved me because he loved me;
20   For his loving me I was glad.

Yet I loved him not for his loving
While I played with his love and truth,
Not loving him for his loving,
Wasting his joy, wasting his youth.

25   I ate his life as a banquet,
I drank his life as new wine,
I fattened upon his leanness,
Mine to flourish and his to pine.

So his life fled as running water,
30   So it perished as water spilt:
If black my hands and my feet as scarlet,
Blacker redder my heart of guilt.

Cold as a stone, as hard, as heavy;
All my sighs ease it no whit,
35   All my tears make it no cleaner
Dropping dropping dropping on it.

Of my life.

I weary of my life
Thro' the long sultry day,
While happy creatures play

Their harmless lives away:—
5   What is my life?

I weary of my life
Thro' the slow tedious night,
While earth and heaven's delight
The moon walks forth in white:—
10   What is my life?

If I might I would die;
My soul should flee away
To day that is not day
Where sweet souls sing and say.—
15   If I might die!

If I might I would die;
My body out of sight,
All night that is not night
My soul should walk in white—
20   If I might die!

Yes, I too could face death and never shrink:
But it is harder to bear hated life;
To stive with hands and knees weary of strife;
     To drag the heavy chain whose every link
5   Galls to the bone; to stand upon the brink
Of the deep grave, nor drowse, though it be rife
With sleep; to hold with steady hand the knife
     Nor strike home: this is courage as I think.
Surely to suffer is more than to do:
10   To do is quickly done; to suffer is
     Longer and fuller of heart-sicknesses:
Each day's experience testifies of this:
Good deeds are many, but good lives are few;
     Thousands taste the full cup; who drains the lees?—

Would that I were a turnip white,
Or raven black,

Or miserable hack
Dragging a cab from left to right;
5   Or would I were the showman of a sight,
Or weary donkey with a laden back,
Or racer in a sack,
Or freezing traveller on an Alpine height;
Or would I were straw catching as I drown,
10   (A wretched landsman I who cannot swim,)
Or watching a lone vessel sink,
Rather than writing: I would change my pink
Gauze for a hideous yellow satin gown
With deep-cut scolloped edges and a rim.

I fancy the good fairies dressed in white,
Glancing like moon-beams through the shadows black;
Without much work to do for king or hack.
Training perhaps some twisted branch aright;
5   Or sweeping faded Autumn leaves from sight
To foster embryo life; or binding back
Stray tendrils; or in ample bean-pod sack
Bringing wild honey from the rocky height;
Or fishing for a fly lest it should drown;
10   Or teaching water-lily heads to swim,
Fearful that sudden rain might make them sink;
Or dyeing the pale rose a warmer pink;
Or wrapping lilies in their leafy gown,
Yet letting the white peep beyond the rim.—

Some ladies dress in muslin full and white,
Some gentlemen in cloth succinct and black;
Some patronise a dog-cart, some a hack,
Some think a painted clarence only right.
5   Youth is not always such a pleasing sight,
Witness a man with tassels on his back;
Or woman in a great-coat like a sack
Towering above her sex with horrid height.

If all the world were water fit to drown
10   There are some whom you would not teach to swim,
Rather enjoying if you saw them sink;
Certain old ladies dressed in girlish pink,
With roses and geraniums on their gown:—
    Go to the Bason, poke them o'er the rim.—

Autumn.

Fade tender lily,
    Fade O crimson rose,
Fade every flower
    Sweetest flower that blows.

5 Go chilly Autumn,
    Come O Winter cold;
Let the green things die away
    Into common mould.

Birth follows hard on death,
10   Life on withering:
Hasten, we shall come the sooner
    Back to pleasant Spring.

Il rosseggiar dell' Oriente
Canzoniere
"All' Amico Contano"—.

1.
Amor dormente?

Addio, diletto amico;
    A me non lece amore,
    Chè già m'uccise il core
    Amato amante.

5   Eppur per l'altra vita
          Consacro a te speranze;
          Per questa, rimembranze
          Tante e poi tante.

                    2.
          Amor Si sveglia?

       In nuova primavera
          Rinasce il genio antico;
       Amor t'insinua "Spera"—
          Pur io nol dico.

5   S' "Ama"—ti dice Amore;
          S'ei t'incoraggia, amico,
       Giurando "È tuo quel core"—
          Pur io nol dico.

       Anzi, quel cor davvero
10   Chi sa se valga un fico?
       Lo credo, almen lo spero;
          Ma pur nol dico.

                    3.
       Si rimanda la tocca-caldaja.

       Lungi da me il pensiere
          D'ereditar l'oggetto
          Ch'una fiata in petto
             Destar ti seppe amor.
5   Se più l'usar non vuoi,
          Se pur fumar nol puoi,
          Dolce ti sia dovere
             Il conservarlo ognor.

4.
"Blumine" risponde:

S'io t'incontrassi nell'eterna pace,
  Pace non più, per me saria diletto;
  S'io t'incontrassi in cerchio maledetto
Te più di me lamenterei verace.
5   Per te mia vita mezzo morta giace,
  Per te le notti veglio e bagno il letto:
  Eppur di rivederti un dì m'aspetto
In secol che riman, non che in fugace.
E perciò "Fuggi" io dico al tempo, e omai
10   "Passa pur" dico al vanitoso mondo:
Mentre mi sogno quel che dici e fai
  Ripeto in me "Doman sarà giocondo,
"Doman sarem"—ma s'ami tu lo sai,
  E se non ami a che mostrarti il fondo?—

5.
"Lassù fia caro il rivederci"—.

Dolce cor mio perduto e non perduto,
  Dolce mia vita che mi lasci in morte,
  Amico e più che amico, ti saluto.
Ricordati di me; che cieche e corte
5   Fur le speranze mie, ma furon tue:
  Non disprezzar questa mia dura sorte.
Lascia ch'io dica "Le speranze sue
  "Come le mie languiro in questo inverno"—
  Pur mi rassegnerò, quel che fue fue.
10   Lascia ch'io dica ancor "Con lui discerno
  "Giorno che spunta da gelata sera,
  "Lungo cielo al di là di breve inferno,
"Al di là dell'inverno primavera."

6.

"Non son io la rosa ma vi stetti appresso."

Casa felice ove più volte omai
   Siede il mio ben parlando e ancor ridendo,
   Donna felice che con lui sedendo
Lo allegri pur con quanto dici e fai,
5 Giardin felice dove passeggiai
   Pensando a lui, pensando e non dicendo,
   Giorno felice fia quand'io mi rendo
Laddove passeggiando a lui pensai.
Ma s'egli vi sarà quand'io vi torno,
10   S'egli m'accoglie col suo dolce riso,
Ogni uccelletto canterà dintorno,
   La rosa arrossirà nel vago viso—
Iddio ci dia in eternità quel giorno,
   Ci dia per quel giardino il paradiso.

7.

"Lassuso il caro Fiore"—.

Se t'insegnasse Iddio
   Il proprio Amor così,
   Ti cederei, cor mio,
     Al caro Fiore.
5 Il caro Fior ti chiama
   "Fammi felice un dì"—
   Il caro Fior che t'ama
     Ti chiede amore.

Quel Fiore in paradiso
10   Fiorisce ognor per te;
   Sì, rivedrai quel viso,
     Sarai contento:
Intorno al duol ch'è stato
   Domanderai "Dov'è?"—
15 Chè passerà il passato
     In un momento.

Ed io per tanta vista
   In tutta eternità,
Io qual Giovan Battista
20   Loderò Dio:
L'Amata tanto amata
   Tuo guiderdon sarà,
E l'alma tua salvata
   Sarammi il mio.

8.
Sapessi pure!

Che fai lontan da me,
   Che fai, cor mio?
   Quel che facc'io
È ch'ognor penso a te.

5 Pensando a te sorrido,
   Sospiro a te:
   E tu lontan da me
Tu pur sei fido?

9.
Iddio c'illumini!

Quando il tempo avverrà che partiremo
   Ciascun di noi per separata via,
Momento che verrà, momento estremo
   Quando che fia:

5 Calcando l'uno inusitata traccia,
   Seguendo l'altro il solito suo corso,
Non ci nasca in quel dì vergogna in faccia
   Nè in sen rimorso.

Sia che tu vada pria forte soletto,
10   O sia ch'io ti preceda in quel sentiero,

Deh ricordiamci allor d'averci detto
  Pur sempre il vero.

Quanto t'amavo e quanto! e non dovea
  Esprimer quell'amor che ti portavo:
15 Più ma assai più di quel che non dicea
  Nel cuor ti amavo.

Più di felicità, più di speranza;
  Di vita non dirò, chè è poca cosa:
Dolce-amaro tu fosti in rimembranza
20 A me gelosa.

Ma a me tu preferisti la virtude,
  La veritade, amico: e non saprai
Chi amasti alfin? Soltanto il fior si schiude
  D'un sole ai rai.

25 Se più di me la Veritade amasti,
  Gesù fu quel tuo sconosciuto Amore:—
Gesù, Che sconosciuto a lui parlasti,
  Vincigli il core.

10.

"Amicizia:
"Sirocchia son d'Amor"—.

Venga Amicizia e sia la benvenuta,
  Venga, ma non perciò sen parta Amore:
  Abitan l'uno e l'altra in gentil core
Che albergo ai pellegrini non rifiuta.
5 Ancella questa docile e compiuta,
  E quei tiranno no ma pio signore:
  Regni egli occulto nè si mostri fuore,
Essa si sveli in umiltà dovuta.
Oggi ed ancor doman per l'amicizia,
10 E posdomani ancor se pur si vuole,
  Chè dolci cose apporta e non amare:
  E venga poi, ma non con luna o sole,

Giorno d'amor, giorno di gran delizia,
    Giorno che spunta non per tramontare.

11.
"Luscious and sorrowful"—.*

Uccello-delle rose e del dolore,
    Uccel d'amore,
Felice ed infelice, quel tuo canto
    È riso o pianto?
5   Fido all'infido, tieni in freddo lido
    Spina per nido.

12.
"Oh forza irresistibile
Dell'umile preghiera"—.

Che Ti darò Gesù Signor mio buono?
Ah quello ch'amo più, quello Ti dono:
Accettalo Signor Gesù mio Dio,
Il sol mio dolce amor, anzi il cor mio;
5   Accettalo per Te, siati prezioso;
Accettalo per me, salva il mio sposo.
Non ho che lui, Signor, nol disprezzare,
Caro tienlo nel cor fra cose care.
Ricordati del dì che sulla croce
10 Pregavi Iddio così, con flebil voce,
Con anelante cor: "Questo che fanno
"Padre perdona lor, ch'essi non sanno"—:
Ei pur, Signor, non sa Quello che sdegna,
Ei pure T'amerà s'uno gl'insegna.
15 Se tutto quanto appar, che a Te non piace,
Fugace spuma in mar, nebbia fugace;
Successo o avversità, contento o duolo,

* "Did she perch thee on hand or shoulder?—"

Se tutto è vanità fuorchè Tu solo;
Se chi non prega Te nel vuoto chiama;
20   Se amore amor non è che Te non ama;—
Dona Te stesso a noi, ricchi saremo;
Poi nega quanto vuoi, chè tutto avremo:
Di mel più dolce Tu, che ben ci basti;
D'amore amabil più, Tu che ci amasti.

13.

Finestra mia orientale.
[In malattia.]

Volgo la faccia verso l'oriente,
    Verso il meriggio, ove colui dimora:—
    Ben fai che vivi ai lati dell'Aurora;
Chi teco vive par felice gente.
5   Volgo verso di te l'occhio languente,
    Lo spirito che teme e spera ancora;
    Volgiti verso quella che ti onora,
T'ama, ti brama, in core e colla mente.
Debole e stanca verso te mi volgo:
10   Che sarà mai questo che sento, amico?
Ogni cara memoria tua raccolgo
    Quanto dirti vorrei! ma pur nol dico.
Lungi da te dei giorni me ne dolgo:
    Fossimo insieme in bel paese aprico!

15   Fossimo insieme!
        Che importerebbe
    U'si facesse
        Il nostro nido?
    Cielo sarebbe
20   Quasi quel lido.

    Ah fossi teco,
        Col cor ben certo
    D'essere amato
        Come vorrebbe!

25   Sì che il deserto
    S'infiorirebbe.

    14.
  [Eppure allora venivi.]

  Oh tempo tardo e amaro!—
   Quando verrai, cor mio,
    Quando, ma quando?
  Siccome a me sei caro
5   Se cara a te foss'io
    Ti andrei cercando?

    15.
  Per Preferenza.

  Felice la tua madre,
   Le suore tue felici,
   Che senton quanto dici,
    Che vivono con te,
5 Che t'amano di dritto
   D'amor contento e saggio:
   Pur questo lor vantaggio
    Non lo vorrei per me.

  Quel grave aspetto tuo
10 Veder da quando in quando,
   Frattanto andar pensando
    "Un giorno riverrà";
  Ripeter nel mio core
   (Qual rosa è senza spine?)
15 "Ei sa che l'amo alfine—
    M'ama egli ancor?" Chi sa!

  È questo assai più dolce
   Dell'altro, al parer mio:
   Essere in ver desio

20   O tutto o nulla* a te,
      Nè troppo vo'lagnarmi
      Ch'or stai da me diviso,
      Se un giorno in Paradiso
      Festeggerai con me.

* Ma no; se non amante siimi amico:
Quel ch'io sarò per te, non tel predico.

                    16.
Oggi

      Possibil non sarebbe
          Ch'io non t'amassi, o caro:
      Chi mai si scorderebbe
          Del proprio core?
5   Se amaro il dolce fai,
          Dolce mi fai l'amaro;
      Se qualche amor mi dài,
          Ti do l'amore.

                    17.
[Se fossi andata a Hastings.]

      Ti do l'addio,
      Amico mio,
      Per settimane
          Che paion lunghe:
5   Ti raccomando
      Da quando in quando
      Circoli quadri,
          Idee bislunghe.

18.
Ripetizione.

Credea di rivederti e ancor ti aspetto;
  Di giorno in giorno ognor ti vo bramando:
Quando ti rivedrò, cor mio diletto,
    Quando ma quando?
5 Dissi e ridissi con perenne sete,
  E lo ridico e vo'ridirlo ancora,
Qual usignol che canta e si ripete
    Fino all'aurora.

19.
"Amico e più che amico mio"—.

Cor mio a cui si volge l'altro mio core
  Qual calamita al polo, e non ti trova,
  La nascita della mia vita nuova
Con pianto fu, con grida e con dolore.
5 Ma l'aspro duolo fummi precursore
  Di speranza gentil che canta e cova;
  Sì, chi prova pena amor non prova,
E quei non vive che non prova amore.
O tu che in Dio mi sei, ma dopo Iddio,
10 Tutta la terra mia ed assai del cielo,
  Pensa se non m'è duol disotto a un velo
  Parlati e non ti dir mai che ti bramo:—
Dillo tu stesso a te, dolce cor mio,
  Se pur tu m'ami dillo a te ch'io t'amo.

20.
"Nostre voluntà quieti Virtù di carità"—.

Vento gentil che verso il mezzodì
  Soffiando vai, deh porta un mio sospir,
  Dicendo ad Un quel che non debbo dir,

Con un sospir dicendogli così:
5   Quella che diede un 'No' volendo un 'Sì'
    (Volendo e non volendo—a che ridir?),
    Quella ti manda: È vanità il fiorir
Di questa vita che meniam costì.
Odi che dice e piange: È vanità
10   Questo che nasce e muore amor mondan;
      Deh leva gli occhi, io gli occhi vo'levar
    Verso il reame dove non in van
      Amasi Iddio quanto ognun possa amar
Ed il creato tutto in carità.

21.

[Se così fosse.]

Io più ti amai che non mi amasti tu:—
    Amen, se così volle Iddio Signor;
    Amen, quantunque mi si spezzi il cor,
      Signor Gesù.

5   Ma Tu che Ti ricordi e tutto sai,
      Tu che moristi per virtù d'amor,
    Nell'altro mondo donami quel cor
      Che tanto amai.

By way of Remembrance.

Remember, if I claim too much of you,
    I claim it of my brother and my friend:
    Have patience with me till the hidden end,
Bitter or sweet, in mercy shut from view.
5   Pay me my due; though I to pay your due
    Am all too poor and past what will can mend:
    Thus of your bounty you must give and lend
Still unrepaid by aught I look to do.

Still unrepaid by aught of mine on earth:
10   But overpaid, please God, when recompense
Beyond the mystic Jordan and new birth
     Is dealt to virtue as to innocence;
When Angels singing praises in their mirth
     Have borne you in their arms and fetched you hence.

Will you be there? my yearning heart has cried:
     Ah me, my love, my love, shall I be there,
     To sit down in your glory and to share
Your gladness, glowing as a virgin bride?
5   Or will another dearer, fairer-eyed,
          Sit nigher to you in your jubilee;
          And mindful one of other will you be
Borne higher and higher on joy's ebbless tide?
—Yea, if I love I will not grudge you this:
10   I too shall float upon that heavenly sea
          And sing my joyful praises without ache;
     Your overflow of joy shall gladden me,
          My whole heart shall sing praises for your sake
And find its own fulfilment in your bliss.

In resurrection is it awfuller
     That rising of the All or of the Each:
     Of all kins of all nations of all speech,
Or one by one of him and him and her?
5   When dust reanimate begins to stir
          Here, there, beyond, beyond, reach beyond reach;
          While every wave disgorges on its beach
Alive or dead-in-life some seafarer.
In resurrection, on the day of days,
10   That day of mourning throughout all the earth,
          In resurrection may we meet again:
          No more with stricken hearts to part in twain;
     As once in sorrow one, now one in mirth,
One in our resurrection songs of praise.

I love you and you know it—this at least,
   This comfort is mine own in all my pain:
   You know it and can never doubt again,
   And love's mere self is a continual feast.
5 Not oath of mine nor blessing-word of priest
   Could make my love more certain or more plain:—
   Life as a rolling moon doth wax and wane
   O weary moon, still rounding, still decreased!
   Life wanes: and when love folds his wings above
10   Tired joy, and less we feel his conscious pulse,
      Let us go fall asleep, dear Friend, in peace;—
      A little while, and age and sorrow cease;
      A little while, and love reborn annuls
   Loss and decay and death—and all is love.

Valentines from C.G.R.

Fairer than younger beauties, more beloved
   Than many a wife,—
By stress of Time's vicissitudes unmoved
   From settled calm of life,—

5 Endearing rectitude to those who watch
      The verdict of your face,
   Raising & making gracious those who catch
      A semblance of your grace:—

With kindly lips of welcome, & with pleased
10   Propitious eyes benign,
   Accept a kiss of homage from your least
      Last Valentine.

A Valentine, 1877.

Own Mother dear,
We all rejoicing here
Wait for each other,

Daughter for Mother,
5   Sister for Brother,
Till each dear face appear
Transfigured by Love's flame
Yet still the same,—
The same yet new,—
10   My face to you,
Your face to me,
Made lovelier by Love's flame
But still the same;
Most dear to see
15   In halo of Love's flame,
Because the same.

1878.

Blessed Dear & heart's Delight,
   Companion, Friend, & Mother mine
   Round whom my fears & love entwine,—
      With whom I hope to stand & sing
5   Where Angels form the outer ring
Round singing Saints who, clad in white,
Know no more of day or night
      Or death or any changeful thing,
      Or anything that is not love,
10   Human love & love Divine,—
         Bid me to that tryst above,
   Bless your Valentine.

1879.

Mother mine
Whom every year
Doth endear,
Before sweet Spring
5   (That sweetest thing
Brimfull of bliss)

Sets all the throng
Of birds a-wooing
Billing & cooing,—
10   Your Valentine
Sings you a song,
Gives you a kiss.

1880.

More shower than shine
Brings sweet St. Valentine;
Warm shine, warm shower,
Bring up sweet flower on flower:
5   Thro' shower & shine
Loves you your Valentine,
Thro' shine, thro' shower,
Thro' summer's flush, thro' Autumn's fading hour.

St. Valentine's Day
1881.

Too cold almost for hope of Spring
    Or firstfruits from the realm of flowers,
Your dauntless Valentine, I bring
    One sprig of love, and sing
5   "Love has no Winter hours"—.

If even in this world love is love
    (This wintry world which felt the Fall),
What must it be in Heaven above
    Where love to great and small
10   Is all in all?

A Valentine
1882.

My blessed Mother dozing in her chair
　　On Christmas Day seemed an embodied Love,
A comfortable Love with soft brown hair
　　Softened and silvered to a tint of dove,
5　　A better sort of Venus with an air
　　Angelical from thoughts that dwell above,
A wiser Pallas in whose body fair
　　Enshrined a blessed soul looks out thereof.
Winter brought Holly then; now Spring has brought
10　　Paler and frailer Snowdrops shivering;
And I have brought a simple humble thought
　　—I her devoted duteous Valentine—,
A lifelong thought which thrills this song I sing,
　　A lifelong love to this dear Saint of mine.

February 14. 1883.

A world of change & loss, a world of death,
Of heart & eyes that fail, of labouring breath,
Of pains to bear & painful deeds to do:—
Nevertheless a world of life to come
5　　And love; where you're at home, while in our home
Your Valentine rejoices having you.

1884.

Another year of joy & grief,
　　Another year of hope & fear:
O Mother, is life long or brief?
　　We hasten while we linger here.

5　　But since we linger, love me still
　　And bless me still, O Mother mine,
While hand in hand we scale life's hill,
　　You Guide, & I your Valentine.

1885.
St. Valentine's Day.

All the Robin Redbreasts
   Have lived the winter thro',
Jenny Wrens have pecked their fill
   And found a work to do,
5   Families of Sparrows
   Have weathered wind & storm
With Rabbit on the stony hill
   And Hare upon her form.

You & I, my Mother,
10   Have lived the winter thro',
And still we play our daily parts
   And still find work to do:
And still the cornfields flourish,
   The olive & the vine,
15   And still you reign my Queen of Hearts
   And I'm your Valentine.

1886
St. Valentine's Day.

Winter's latest snowflake is the snowdrop flower,
   Yellow crocus kindles the first flame of the Spring,
At that time appointed, at that day and hour
   When life reawakens and hope in everything.
5   Such a tender snowflake in the wintry weather,
   Such a feeble flamelet for chilled St. Valentine,—
But blest be any weather which finds us still together,
   My pleasure and my treasure O blessed Mother mine.

Ah welladay and wherefore am I here?
I sit alone all day I sit & think—

I watch the sun arise, I watch it sink
And feel no soul-light tho the day is clear
5   Surely it is a folly; it is mere
Madness to stand for ever on the brink
Of dark despair & yet not break the link
That makes me scorned who cannot be held dear.
I will have done with it; I will not stand
10   And fear on without hope & tremble thus
Look for the break of day & miss it ever
Although my heart be broken they shall never
Say: She was glad to sojourn among us
Thankful if one would take her by the hand.

Along the highroad the way is too long
Let us walk where the oak trees rise up thick
I take a crab-, you take a cherry stick
Let us go from among men to the throng
5   Of belted bees: the wild roses smell strong
And sweet; & my old dog is fain to lick
My hand: best so in good truth I am sick
Of the world; & hear silence as a song
And you I think are changed friend you who once
10   Would dance thro' the long night; a something called
From your heart; into your hid brain it sunk;
Oh listen silence maketh the air drunk
I would not give these shades that have not palled
On me, for the broad light of many suns.

And is this August weather? nay not so
With the long rain the cornfield waxeth dark.
How the cold rain comes pouring down & hark
To the chill wind whose measured pace & slow
5   Seems still to linger being loth to go.
I cannot stand beside the sea and mark
Its grandeur; it's too wet for that: no lark
In this drear season cares to sing or show.

And since its name is August all men find
10   Fire not allowable; Winter foregone
Had more of sunlight & of glad warmth more
I shall be fain to run upon the shore
And mark the rain. Hath the sun ever shone
Cheer up there can be nothing worse to mind.

From early dawn until the flush of noon
And from hot noon unto the hushèd night
I look around beholding all things bright
From the deep sun unto the silver moon
5   My heart & soul & spirit are in tune.
My sense is gladdened with an inward light.
The very clouds above my head are white
And glorious radiance shall disperse them soon.
All trees & bushes fruits & flowers bear,
10   The sea is full of life & beauty, how
The grand waves leap up—as tho' full of sense,
A better day was not I think & ne'er
Was I so full of joy as I am now.
Surely a chill shall come & this go hence

I seek among the living & I seek
Among the dead for some to love; but few
I find at last & these have quite run through
Their store of love & friendship is too weak
5   And cold for me; yet will I never speak
Telling my heart want to cold listeners who
Will wonder smiling; I can bear & do
No tears shall sully my unfurrowed cheek
So when my dust shall mix with other dust
10   When I shall have found quiet in decay
And lie at ease & cease to be & rot
Those whom I love thinking of me shall not
Grieve with a measure, saying: Now we must
Weep for a little ere we go & play.

O glorious sea that in each climbing wave
Bearest great thoughts as in a wondrous book
The ends of earth oft at thy presence shook
And not denied when thou hast stooped to crave.
5   Sometimes the mighty winds have dared to brave
Thy potency; but with a single look
Raising thy head forth from its ancient nook
Thou hast recalled the quiet thou wouldst have.
What is a ship save many a fragile stick?
10   How should it brave thy terrors when they wear
The lightning crest that maketh substance wither
Yea though the planks be seasoned well & thick
Thine anger is too hard a thing to bear:—
Thou sayest to men: go back & come not hither.

Oh thou who tell'st me that all hope is over
With lazy limbs that heavily recline
On the soft cushions; flushed & fair with wine
Scarce seeming conscious of the scents that hover
5   Round & above thee: can thy heart recover
So soon its quiet, while mine own shall pine?
Thou who canst love & not o'erstep the line
Of comfort, art thou in good truth a lover
O take away from me those chill calm glances
10   As thou hast ta'en thy heart away; & give
My heart again that must forget to wander
Thy words were worse than silence they were lances
To poison all the life I have to live
Stagnate the streams of life that should meander

Surely there is an aching void within
Man's spirit unto other men unknown
And which were it unveiled and freely shown
Would open to the sight so much of sin
5   And folly & a cry that at the din
His overbearing pride & overblown

Would quite shrink down & seem as it had grown
Humble, content to lose & not to win.
Oh that we so could hide the grief of years
10   From our own selves yea the whole guilt & trouble
And in our secret spirit look on grace;
Yet death for ever sendeth messengers
Before it conscience pricks, & were these double
They were not equal to our sin-stained face.

The spring is come again not as at first
For then it was my spring; & now a brood
Of bitter memories haunt me, & my mood
Is much changed from the time when I was nursed
5   In the still country. Oh! my heart could burst
Thinking upon the long ago: the crude
Hopes all unrealised; the flowers that strewed
My path, now changed to painful thorns & curst.
And though I know the kingcups are as fine
10   As they were then, my spirit cannot soar
As it did once: when shadows of a wood
Or thinking of a blossom that soon should
Unfold & fill the air with scent, would pour
Peace on my brow now marked with many a line.

Who shall my wandering thoughts steady & fix
When I go forth into the world and gaze
Around me, thinking on mens evil ways
I wonder in myself to see how mix
5   Evil & good; beyond the Sleepy Styx
All things shall be unravelled whoso lays
These things to heart after the settled days
Shall know all. Even as a dog that licks
Your hand whom tears chide not away nor laughter
10   So to your souls clingeth the taint of crime
Shall it be ever so? & if not why?
The river bed is full of filthy slime

And so our heart is lined with wonder: die
And having died thou shalt see all things after.

You who look on passed ages as a glass
To shadow forth the future, in your home
Peacefully dwelling little heeding some
But loving many; as the visions pass
5   Turn from them for a moment to the grass
And solemn sun & blue o'erarching dome
And in the hush of nature think on Rome
Not as it is now but as it once was.
As of the mighty dead think without hope
10   But if you will indulge a hopeful pile
Yea if you will write about it in rhyme
For if it once had a too mighty scope
To be all as the sun fails not to smile
It shall be nothing to the end of time.

Angeli al capo, al piede:
   E qual ricciuto agnello
Dormir fra lor si vede
   Il bel mio bambinello.

Amami, t'amo,
   Figliolin mio:
Cantisi, suonisi,
   Con tintinnio.
5   Mamma t'abbraccia,
   Cor suo ti chiama:
Suonisi, cantisi,
   Ama chi t'ama.

E babbo e mamma ha il nostro figliolino,
   Ricco bambino:

Ma ne conosco un altro senza padre
      E senza madre—
5   Il poverino!

S'addormentò la nostra figliolina;
      Nè si risveglierà
Per giorni e giorni assai sera o mattina:
      Ma poi si sveglierà,
5   E con cara ridente bocchettina
      Ribacerà Mammà.

Cuccurucù! cuccurucù!
      All'alba il gallo canta:
Chiccherichì! chiccherichì!
      Di rose il ciel si ammanta.
5   Cuccurucù! cuccurucù!
      Comincia un gorgheggiare:
Chiccherichì! chiccherichì!
      Risalta il sol dal mare.

Oibò, piccina
      Tutto atterrita;
La medicina
      Bever si de':—
5   Uno, due, tre,—
      Ed è finita!

Otto ore suonano:
Picchia il postino!
Ben cinque lettere
Son per Papà;
5   Una per te,
Nulla per me;
E un bigliettino
V'è per Mammà.

Nel verno accanto al fuoco
　Mangio la mia minestra;
E al pettirosso schiudo la finestra,
Ch'ei pur ne voule un poco.

5　　ovvero:—
S'affaccia un pettirosso alla finestra:—
Vieni, vieni a gustar la mia minestra!
Lana ben foderata io porto addosso,
Ma tu non porti che un corpetto rosso.

Gran freddo è infuori, e dentro è freddo un poco:
Quanto è grata una zuppa accanto al fuoco!
Mi vesto di buon panno—
Ma i poveri non hanno
5　　Zuppa da bere, o fuoco a cui sedere,
O tetto, o panni, in questo freddo intenso:
Ah mi si stringe il cor mentr'io ci penso!

Scavai la neve,—sì che scavai!
Ma fior nè foglia spuntava mai:
Scavai la rena con ansia lena,
Ma fior nè foglia spicca da rena.

5　　O vento aprico, con fiato lieve
Sveglia i fioretti, sgela la neve!
Ma non soffiare su quella rena:
Chi soffia in rena perde la lena.

Sì che il fratello s'ha falconcello,
　　E tiene un fior la suora;
Ma che, ma che riman per te,
　　Il neonato or ora?
5　　Vo' farti cocchio del mio ginocchio,
　　Minor mio figliolino;
Da capo a piè ti stringo a me,
　　Minimo piccino.

Udite, si dolgono mesti fringuelli:
Bel nido facemmo per cari gemelli,
Ma tre ragazzacci lo misero in stracci.
Fuggì primavera, s'imbruna la sera,
5   E tempo ci manca da fare un secondo
Niduncolo tondo.

Ahi culla vuota! ed ahi sepolcro pieno
    Ove le smunte foglie autunno getta!
Lo spirto aspetta in Paradiso ameno,
    Il corpo in terra aspetta.

Lugubre e vagabondo in terra e in mare,
O vento, O vento, a che non ti posare?
Ci trai la pioggia fin dall'occidente,
E la neve ci trai dal nord fremente.

Aura dolcissima, ma donde siete?—
Dinfra le mammole: non lo sapete?
Abbassi il viso ad adocchiar l'erbetta
Chi vuol trovar l'ascosa mammoletta.
5   La madreselva il dolce caldo aspetta:
Tu addolci un freddo mondo, O mammoletta.

Foss'io regina
    Tu re saresti:
    Davanti a te
        M'inchinerei.

5   Ah, foss'io re!
    Tu lo vedresti:
    Sì, che regina
        Mi ti farei.

Pesano rena e pena:
Oggi e doman son brevi:
La gioventude e un fior son cose lievi:
Ed han profondità
5   Mar magno e magna verità.

Basta una notte a maturare il fungo;
Un secol vuol la quercia, e non par lungo:
Anzi, il secolo breve e il vespro lungo:
Chè quercia è quercia, e fungo è sempre fungo.

Porco la zucca
Fitta in parrucca!. .
Che gli diresti mai?
M'inchinerei, l'ossequirei,
5   "Ser Porco, come stai?"

Ahi! guai! per caso mai
Se la coda andasse a male? . . .
Sta tranquillo:
Buon legale
10   Gli farebbe un codicillo.

Salta, ranocchio, e mostrati;
    Non celo pietra in mano:
Merletto in testa e verde vesta,
    Vattene salvo e sano.

5   Rospo lordo, deh non celarti:
Tutto il mondo può disprezzarti,
Ma mal non fai nè mal vo'farti.

Spunta la margherita
Qual astro in sullo stelo,
E l'erbetta infiorita
Rassembra un verde cielo.

Agnellina orfanellina
Giace in cima alla collina,
Fredda, sola, senza madre,—
Senza madre, oimè!
5   Io sarotti e madre e padre,
Io sarò tua pastorella;
Non tremar, diletta agnella,
Io ci penso a te.

Amico pesce, piover vorrà:
Prendi l'ombrella se vuoi star secco.
Ed ecco!
Domani senza fallo si vedrà
5   Lucertolon "zerbino"
Ripararsi dal sol coll'ombrellino.

Sposa velata,
Innanellata,
Mite e sommessa:
Sposo rapito,
5   Insuperbito,
Accanto ad essa:—
Amici, amori,
Cantando a coro,
Davanti a loro
10   Spargete fiori!

Cavalli marittimi
     Urtansi in guerra,
E meglio ci servono
     Quelli di terra.
5   Questi pacifici
Corrono o stanno:
Quei rotolandosi
Spumando vanno.

O marinaro che mi apporti tu?
Coralli rossi e bianchi tratti in su
Dal mar profondo.
Piante non son, nè si scavar da mina:
5   Minime creature in salsa brina
    Fecerne mondo.

Arrossisce la rosa: e perchè mai?
A cagione del sol: ma Sol, che fai?
E tu, Rosa, che t'hai
Che ti fai rosea sì se bene stai?

La rosa china il volto rosseggiato,
    E bene fa:
Il giglio innalza il viso immacolato,
    E ben gli sta.

O ciliegia infiorita,
La bianco rivestita
Dall'Aprile gradita,
Bella sei tu!
5   O ciliegia infruttata,
La verde inghirlandata
La rosso incoronata,
Bella sei tu!

"In tema e in pena addio;
    Addio ma in van, tu sai;
Per sempre addio, cor mio"—
    "E poi più mai."
5   "Oggi e domani addio,
    Nel secolo de'guai
A tutto tempo addio"—
    "E poi più mai."

D'un sonno profondissimo
Dorme la suora mia:
Gli angeli bianchi aligeri
Verranno a trarla via?
5 In sonno profondissimo
Calma e contenta giace:
Un fiore in man lasciamole,
Un bacio in fronte,—e pace!

Ninna nanna, ninna nanna!
Giace e dorme l'agnellina:
Ninna nanna, ninna nanna!
Monna Luna s'incammina:
5 Ninna nanna, ninna nanna!
Tace e dorme l'uccellino:
Ninna nanna, ninna nanna!
Dormi, dormi, O figliolino:
Ninna nanna, ninna nanna!

Capo che chinasi,—
Occhi che chiudonsi,—
A letto, a letto,
Sonnacchiosetto!
5 Dormi, carino,
Fino al mattino,
Dormi, carino.

The Succession of Kings.

William the Norman was brave in the field;
And *Rufus,* his Son, in the chase was killed.
Henry the first early lost his dear Son;
And *Stephen's* battles were bravely won.
5 *Henry the second* his kingdom increased.
Richard the first led Crusades in the East.
John signed Magna Charta at Runnymede.

Henry the third put his seal to the deed.
Brave *Edward the first* the Welsh did subdue.
10 Weak *Edward the second* had foes not a few.
Edward the third to France did aspire,
Whose Son, the Black Prince, died before his Sire.
Richard the second to weakness was prone;
And *Henry the fourth* was placed on his throne.
15 *Fifth Henry* at Agincourt won the field.
Meek *Henry the sixth* was forced to yield,
To *Edward the fourth* who abused his power.
Edward the fifth found a grave in the Tower.
Richard the third was a treacherous friend;
20 By *Henry the seventh* he came to his end.
Henry the eighth had six wives in succession.
Edward the sixth was the hope of the nation;
For ten days reigned his Cousin the Lady Jane.
Queen Mary espoused King Philip of Spain.
25 A reign glorious and long was *Elizabeth's* lot.
James the first shrewdly guessed at the Gunpowder Plot.
Charles the first on a scaffold lost his head;
The Protector Cromwell ruled in his stead.
Richard Cromwell from ruling with joy did retire.
30 *Charles the second* beheld both the Plague and Fire.
For his faith *James the second* the crown did lose;
Which *third William and Mary* did not refuse.
Marlborough fought under good *Queen Anne.*
The Hanover Line with *first George* began.
35 *Second George* overcame the second Pretender.
In the reign of *third George* did Napoleon surrender.
George the fourth was long Regent, but King at last.
Under *William the fourth* the Reform Bill passed.
Good *Queen Victoria*, the last King's Niece,
40 Reigns over England beloved and at peace.

A true Story.   (continued.)

In this great city now the haunt,
Of priest and friar and monk

Where reason sees her ill-starr'd bark,
   By superstition sunk;

5   Where nature's voice by force repress'd,
   Its energy declares,
In demon deeds of wickedness,
   When fear its dagger bares;

In Rome itself there lately dwelt
10   Two sister-maidens fair,
Affianced both to noble youths,
   Of form and virtue rare.

Preparing now for that great step,
   Of weal or woe the seal,
15   Before they joyful give their hands,
   Where purest love they feel;
                  (To be continued)

The two Rossettis (brothers they)
And Holman Hunt and John Millais,
With Stephens chivalrous and bland,
And Woolner in a distant land,
5   In these six men I awestruck see
Embodied the great P.R.B.
D. G. Rossetti offered two
Good pictures to the public view:
Unnumbered ones great John Millais,
10   And Holman more than I can say
*   *   *   *   *   *   *
William Rossetti calm and solemn
Cuts up his brethren by the column.
*   *   *   *   *   *   *

Imitated from the Arpa Evangelica: Page 121.

My Lord, my Love! in pleasant pain
   How often have I said:

Blessed that John, who on Thy Breast
   Laid down his head.
5   It was that contact all Divine
   Transformed him from above,
And made him amongst men the man
   To show forth holy love.

Yet shall I envy blessed John?
10   Nay, not so verily,
Now that Thou, Lord, both Man & God
   Dost dwell in me:
Upbuilding with Thy Manhood's might
   My frail humanity;
15   Yea, Thy Divinehood pouring forth
   In fulness filling me.

Me, Lord, Thy temple consecrate,
   Even me to Thee alone;
Lord reign upon my willing heart
20   Which is Thy throne:
To Thee the Seraphim fall down
   Adoring round Thy house;
For which of them hath tasted Thee,
   My Manna & my Spouse?

25   Now that Thy Life lives in my soul
   And sways & warms it thro',
I scarce seem lesser than the world,
   Thy temple too.
O God Who dwellest in my heart,
30   My God Who fillest me,
The broad immensity itself
   Hath not encompassed Thee.

"T'amo; e fra dolci affanni"—.   p. 121.—

My Lord, my Love!—in love's unrest
35   How often have I said:
"Blessed that John who on Thy Breast
   Reclined his head."
Thy touch it was, Love's Pelican,
   Transformed him from above,

40   And made him amongst men the man
         To show forth holy love!

     Yet shall I envy blessèd John?
         Nay, not so verily,
     While Thou indwellest as Thine own
45   Me, even me:
     Upbuilding with Thy Manhood's worth
         My frail humanity;
     Yea, Thy Divinehood pouring forth,
         In fulness filling me.

50   Me, Lord, Thy temple consecrate,
         Me unto Thee alone;
     Within my heart set up Thy state
         And mount Thy throne:
     The Seraphim in ecstasy
55   Fall prone around Thy house,
     For which of them hath tasted Thee
         My Manna and my Spouse?

     Now Thou dost wear me for a robe
         And sway and warm me thro',
60   I scarce seem lesser than the globe,—
         Thy temple too:
     O God Who for Thy dwelling place
         Dost take delight in me,
     The ungirt immensity of space
65   Hath not encompassed Thee.

     Mr. and Mrs. Scott, and I,
     With Mr. Manson, Editor,
     And of the social Proctors four,
     Agreed the season to defy.

5   We mustered forces at the Rail,
     Struck hands and made our interests one:
     Alas for absent Annie Hayle
     Who should have shared the fare and fun.

Not neighbour Humble and her child
10   —Tho' well-disposed of doubtful force—
But Annie Hayle my verse deplores,
Behatted plump alert and mild.

From Newcastle to Sunderland
Upon a misty morn in June
15   We took the train: on either hand
Grimed streets were changed for meadows soon.

Umbrellas, tarts and sandwiches
Sustained our spirits' temperate flow,
With potted jam, and cold as snow
20   Rough-coated sun-burnt oranges.

1.

Gone to his rest
   Bright little Bouby!
Build green his nest
   Where sun and dew be,
5   Nor snails molest

2.

A cheerful sage,
   Simple, light-hearted:
In ripe old age
   He had departed
10   And ta'en his wage.

3.

Dear for himself;
   Dear for another
Past price of pelf;
   —(Ah, dearest Mother!)—
15   Song-singing elf.

4.
O daisies, grow
    Lightly above him,
Strike root, and blow:
    For some who love him
20 Would have it so.

O Uommibatto
Agil, giocondo,
Che ti sei fatto
Irsuto e tondo!
5   Deh non fuggire
Qual vagabondo,
Non disparire
Forando il mondo:
Pesa davvero
10 D'un emisfero
Non lieve il pondo.

Cor mio, cor mio,
Più non ti veggo, ma mi rammento
Del giorno spento,
    Cor mio.
5   Pur ti ricordi del lungo amore,
Cor del mio core,
    Cor mio?

I said "All's over"—& I made my
Thenceforward to keep silence &
From any hope or enterprise aga
But as one certain day the sap
5   Sun warmed & solaced in its f
So something stirred in me th
And all my hardness broke [illegible fragment]
And hope once more tended [illegible fragment]

I said good bye in hope:
But now we meet again
I have no hope at all
Of anything but pain,
5   Our parting & our meeting
Alike in vain.

Hope on thro' all your life
Until the end, dear Friend.
Live thro' your noble life
10   Where joy & promise blend:
I too will live my life
Until the end.

Long may your vine entwine,
Long may your figtree spread
15   Their paradise of shade
Above your cherished head:
My shelter was a gourd,
And it is dead.

Yet when out of a grave
20   We are gathered home at last,
Then may we own life spilt
No good worth holding fast:—
Death had its bitterness
But it is past.

My Mouse.

A Venus seems my Mouse
Come safe ashore from foaming seas,
Which in a small way & at ease
    Keeps house.

5   An Iris seems my Mouse,
Bright bow of that exhausted shower
Which made a world of sweet-herbs flower
    And boughs.

A darling Mouse it is:—
10   Part hope not likely to take wing,
      Part memory, part anything
          You please.

      Venus-cum-Iris Mouse
      From shifting tides set safe apart,
15   In no mere bottle, in my heart
          Keep house.

      Had Fortune parted us
          Fortune is blind,
      Had Anger parted us
          Anger unkind—
5   But since God parts us
          Let us part humbly
      Bearing our burden
          Bravely & dumbly.

      And since there is but one
10   Heaven, not another,
      Let us not close that door
          Against each other.
      God's Love is higher than mine,
          Christ's tenfold proved,
15   Yet even I would die
          For thee Beloved.

Counterblast on Penny Trumpet.
"When raged the conflict, fierce & hot."

      If Mr. Bright retiring does not please
          And Mr. Gladstone staying gives offence,
      What can man do which is not one of these?
          Use your own common sense.

5   Yet he's a brave man who abjures his cause
          For conscience' sake: let byegones be byegones:

Not *this* among the makers of our laws
    The least & and last of Johns.

    If all our byegones could be piled on shelves
10   High out of reach of penny-line Tyrtaeus!
If only all of us could see ourselves
    As others see us!

A roundel seems to fit a round of days
    Be they the days of upright man or scoundrel:
Allow me to construct then in your praise
    A roundel.
5   [This flower of wit turns out a weed like groundsel:
Yet deign to welcome it, as loftiest bays
    Grown on the shore of Girvan's ocean groundswell.]
Accept the love that underlies the lays;
    Condone the barbarous rhymes that will not sound well
10 In building up, all Poets to amaze,
    A roundel.

Heaven overarches earth and sea,
    Earth-sadness and sea-bitterness;
Heaven overarches you and me:
A little while, and we shall be
5   (Please God) where there is no more sea
    Or barren wilderness.

Heaven overarches you and me
    And all earth's gardens and her graves:
Look up with me, until we see
10 The day break and the shadows flee;
What tho' tonight wrecks you and me,
    If so tomorrow saves?

Sleeping at last, the trouble & tumult over,
Sleeping at last, the struggle & horror past,

Cold & white out of sight of friend & of lover
Sleeping at last.

5   No more a tired heart downcast or overcast,
No more pangs that wring or shifting fears that hover,
Sleeping at last in a dreamless sleep locked fast.

Fast asleep. Singing birds in their leafy cover
Cannot wake her, nor shake her the gusty blast.
10   Under the purple thyme & the purple clover
Sleeping at last.

4th May morning.

My carrier pigeon is a "fancy" pigeon,
Less tangible than widgeon;
A sympathetic love,—yet not a Cupid,
Nor pert nor stupid,
5   Heart-warm & snug tho' May Day deal in zeroes,
A well-known Eros.
On windless wings by flight untired for ever
Outspeed the speeding river,
From Torrington remote to utmost Chelsea
10   (—Do what I tells ye!—)
Carry a heart of love & thanks & blisses,
A beak of kisses,
Past Piccadilly's hills & populous valleys,
Past every human head that more or less is
15   Begirt with tawny tresses,
Past every house, to sumptuous Bellevue Palace;
There greet the courteous Courtneys with politeness,
And the dear Scotts with an affectionate brightness,
And give a kiss to dark-locked Alice.

"Quanto a Lei grata io sono
L'umil dirà semplicità del dono."

THE CHINAMAN.

'Centre of Earth!' a Chinaman he said,
And bent over a map his pig-tailed head,—
That map in which, portrayed in colours bright,
China, all dazzling, burst upon the sight:
5   'Centre of Earth!' repeatedly he cries,
'Land of the brave, the beautiful, the wise!'
Thus he exclaimed; when lo his words arrested
Showed what sharp agony his head had tested.
He feels a tug—another, and another—
10   And quick exclaims, 'Hallo! what's now the bother?'
But soon alas perceives. And, 'Why, false night,
Why not from men shut out the hateful sight?
The faithless English have cut off my tail,
and left me my sad fortunes to bewail.
15   Now in the streets I can no more appear,
For all the other men a pig-tail wear.'
He said, and furious cast into the fire
His tail: those flames became its funeral-pyre.

'Come cheer up, my lads, 'tis to glory we steer!'
As the soldier remarked whose post lay in the rear.

THE PLAGUE

"Listen, the last stroke of death's noon has struck—
   The plague is come," a gnashing Madman said,
   And laid him down straightway upon his bed.
His writhèd hands did at the linen pluck;
5   Then all is over. With a careless chuck
   Among his fellows he is cast. How sped
   His spirit matters little: many dead
Make men hard-hearted.—"Place him on the truck.
Go forth into the burial-ground and find
10   Room at so much a pitful for so many.

One thing is to be done; one thing is clear:
Keep thou back from the hot unwholesome wind,
  That it infect not thee." Say, is there any
  Who mourneth for the multitude dead here?

  How many authors are my first!
    And I shall be so too
  Unless I finish speedily
    That which I have to do.

5 My second is a lofty tree
    And a delicious fruit;
  This in the hot-house flourishes—
    That amid rocks takes root.

  My whole is an immortal queen
10   Renowned in classic lore:
  Her a god won without her will,
    And her a goddess bore.

  Me you often meet
  In London's crowded street,
And merry children's voices my resting-place proclaim.
  Pictures and prose and verse
5   Compose me—I rehearse
Evil and good and folly, and call each by its name.
  I make men glad, and I
  Can bid their senses fly,
And festive echoes know me of Isis and of Cam.
10 But give me to a friend,
    And amity will end,
Though he may have the temper and meekness of a lamb.

So I began my walk of life; no stop
Was possible; or else my will was frail;
Or is it that the first stumblings entail
Weakness no after strength has power to prop?

5   The heart puts forth her boughs; and these we lop
    For very wantonness; until the gale
    Is rank with blood; then our life-portions fail
    And we are fain to share another's sop.
    At first my heart was true and my soul true,
10 And then the outside world believed me false.
    Therefore my sweets grew bitter, and I thrust
    Life back, till it stood still and turned to must.
    Yet sometimes through the great stagnation calls
    Of spirits reach me: is it so with you?

    So I grew half delirious and quite sick,
    And thro' the darkness saw strange faces grin
    Of Monsters at me. One put forth a fin,
    And touched me clammily: I could not pick
5   A quarrel with it: it began to lick
    My hand, making meanwhile a piteous din
    And shedding human tears: it would begin
    To near me, then retreat. I heard the quick
    Pulsation of my heart, I marked the fight
10 Of life and death within me; then sleep threw
    Her veil around me; but this thing is true:
    When I awoke the sun was at his height,
    And I wept sadly, knowing that one new
    Creature had love for me, and others spite.

    On the note you do not send me
    I have thought too long: adieu.
    Hope and fear no longer rend me:—
    Home is near: not news of you.

    CHARON

    In my cottage near the Styx
    Co. and Charon still combine
    Us to ferry o'er like bricks

In a boat of chaste design.
5   Cerberus, thou triple fair,
Distance doth thy charms impair:
Let the passage give to us
Charon, Co., and Cerberus.

CHORUS

Now the passage gives us to
10   Charon, Cerberus, and Co.

FROM METASTASIO

First, last, and dearest,
    My love, mine own,
Thee best beloved,
    Thee love alone,
5   Once and for ever
    So love I thee.

First as a suppliant
    Love makes his moan,
Then as a monarch
10   Sets up his throne:
Once and for ever—
    So love I thee.

CHIESA E SIGNORE

LA CHIESA

Vola, preghiera, e digli
    Perchè Ti stai lontano?
Passeggi Tu frai gigli
    Portando rosa in mano?
5   Non Ti fui giglio e rosa
    Quando mi amasti Tu?
Rivolgiti alla sposa,
    O mio Signor Gesù.

IL SIGNORE

Di te non mi scordai,
10   Sposa mia dolce e mesta:
Se Mi sei rosa il sai,
    Chè porto spine in testa.
Ti diedi e core e vita,
    Me tutto Io diedi a te,
15   Ed or ti porgo aita:
    Abbi fidanza in Me.

LA CHIESA

Vola, preghiera, a Lui,
    E grida: Ahi pazienza!
Te voglio e non altrui,
20   Te senza è tutto senza.
Fragrante più di giglio
    E rosa a me sei Tu,
Di Dio l' Eterno Figlio,
    O mio Signor Gesù.

GOLDEN HOLLY

Common Holly bears a berry
To make Christmas Robins merry:—
Golden Holly bears a rose,
Unfolding at October's close
5   To cheer an old Friend's eyes and nose.

I toiled on, but thou
Wast weary of the way,
And so we parted: now
Who shall say
5   Which is happier—I or thou?

I am weary now
On the solitary way:
But art thou rested, thou?

Who shall say
10   Which of us is calmer now?

Still my heart's love, thou,
In thy secret way,
Art still remembered now:
Who shall say—
15   Still rememberest thou?

COR MIO

Still sometimes in my secret heart of hearts
   I say "Cor mio" when I remember you,
   And thus I yield us both one tender due,
Welding one whole of two divided parts.
5   Ah Friend, too wise or unwise for such arts,
   Ah noble Friend, silent and strong and true,
   Would you have given me roses for the rue
For which I bartered roses in love's marts?
So late in autumn one forgets the spring,
10   Forgets the summer with its opulence,
The callow birds that long have found a wing,
   The swallows that more lately got them hence:
Will anything like spring, will anything
   Like summer, rouse one day the slumbering sense?

My old admiration before I was twenty,—
Is predilect still, now promoted to se'enty!
My own demi-century plus an odd one
   Some weight to my judgment may fairly impart.
5   Accept this faint flash of a smouldering fun,
   The fun of a heavy old heart.

TO MARY ROSSETTI

You were born in the Spring
When the pretty birds sing

In sunbeamy bowers:
Then dress like a Fairy,
5   Dear dumpling my Mary,
In green and in flowers.

Ne' sogni ti veggo,
   Amante ed amico;
Ai piedi ti seggo,
   Ti tengo tuttor.
5   Nè chiedi nè chieggo,
   Nè dici nè dico,
   L' amore ab antico
      Che scaldaci il cor.
   Ah voce se avessi
10   Me stessa a scoprire—
   Ah esprimer sapessi
      L' angoscia e l' amor!
   Ah almen se potessi
      A lungo dormire,
15   Nè pianger nè dire,
         Mirandoti ognor!

TO MY FIOR-DI-LISA

The Rose is Love's own flower, and Love's no less
   The Lily's tenderness.
Then half their dignity must Roses yield
   To Lilies of the field?
5   Nay, diverse notes make up true harmony,
   All-fashioned loves agree:
Love wears the Lily's whiteness, and Love glows
   In the deep-hearted Rose.

Hail, noble face of noble friend!—
   Hail, honoured master hand and dear!—
On you may Christmas good descend
   And blessings of the unknown year

5   So soon to overtake us here.
        Unknown, yet well known: I portend
        Love starts the course, love seals the end.

Hymn

O the bitter shame and sorrow
    That a time could ever be,
When I let the Saviour's pity
Plead in vain, and proudly answered
5   "All of Self, and none of Thee."

Yet He found me; I beheld Him
    Bleeding on the accursed Tree;
Heard Him pray "Forgive them, Father!"
And my wistful heart said faintly
10   "Some of Self, and some of Thee."

Day by day, His tender mercy,
    Healing, helping, full and free,
Sweet and strong, and ah! so patient,
Brought me lower, while I whispered
15   "Less of Self, and more of Thee."

Higher than the highest Heaven,
    Deeper than the deepest sea,
"Lord, Thy love at last hath conquered,
Grant me now my soul's desire
20   None of Self, and all of Thee."

Introduction to Textual Notes

The variant readings given in the textual notes are taken from the extant manuscripts of Christina's poems, the private printing or publication of individual poems during her lifetime, and William Michael Rossetti's 1896 and 1904 editions of her poetry. To some extent his editions are unreliable: many of his spelling, paragraphing, and punctuation variants are not in Christina's extant manuscripts or in versions of the poem published in her lifetime; moreover, he rarely explains the sources of his texts. Nevertheless, I have included his readings because, as her brother, he had access to materials no longer available.

At the beginning of the textual notes for each poem is a headnote listing the manuscripts and printings of the poem and specifying the basic text. Reprints are not listed in the headnotes or cited in the variant notes unless they show a new variant. Editions and reprints are identified by date of publication rather than by title; the titles are given in the listing of editions and reprints herein. An *a* after the date of publication indicates an American edition, and parentheses enclose the dates of reprints. The variants designated 1896s (s = special edition) are recorded only if they differ from the first edition published in that year.

In the textual notes, matter in roman type within square brackets [thus] is supplied by the editor. Italic print within square brackets [*thus*] indicates words or letters deleted, erased, or written over in the manuscripts. Angle brackets <thus> enclose words or letters written in the manuscripts as additions or as replacements for deletions and erasures. Words added in the manuscripts and then deleted are in italic print enclosed in angle brackets and square brackets [<*thus*>]. A solidus represents a line break. The abbreviation for *manuscript* is MS.

A variant within the line is preceded by a pickup word and is followed by a drop word and any punctuation immediately after the drop word.[1] A capitalized variant with no pickup word indicates the beginning of a line.[2] A variant at the end of the line is accompanied by a pickup word and the end-of-line punctuation.[3] If the variation is in the end line punctuation itself, a pickup word precedes it.[4] When a capitalized pickup word occurs within the line, it is accompanied by the preceding word.[5] When a pickup word appears more than once in the line, it is accompanied by the preceding word.[6] If a text contains several variants within the same line, they are presented together in one reading; where the variants are separated by more than two words in the line, empty angle brackets represent the word or words omitted between the variants.[7]

All of the manuscripts and manuscript revisions cited are in ink and in Christina's handwriting unless otherwise indicated. Christina's later pencil changes, her brothers' markings in her manuscripts, and the manuscripts not in her own hand are noted as such.

The following kinds of variants are not registered because they do not seem to perceptibly affect the sound or sense of the poem. I have not recorded the false starts and obvious slips of the pen, which were immediately corrected in the manuscripts. Titles are centered in Christina's manuscripts, but they are aligned at the left margin in this edition. I have eliminated such house practices as setting the first word of the poem in capital letters, and I have not recorded the occurrence of partially printed or missing end-of-line punctuation due to faulty inking, which I found in collating copies of the printed versions of a poem. All variants in words, paragraphing, spelling, and punctuation other than the kinds described above are recorded in the textual notes.

DEATH'S CHILL BETWEEN.

[Composed September 29, 1847. Editions: 1904. The notebook MS, in the handwriting of Christina's sister, Maria Francesca Rossetti, is in the Bodleian Library.

---

1. For example, see the manuscript variant for line 22 of "Death's Chill Between."
2. For example, see the manuscript variant for line 4 of "Death's Chill Between."
3. For example, see the 1850 variant for line 86 of "Repining."
4. For example, see the manuscript variant for line 54 of "Repining."
5. For example, see the manuscript variant for line 33 of "The Offering of the New Law, the One Oblation Once Offered."
6. For example, see the 1850 variant for line 19 of "Repining."
7. For example, see the 1904 variant for line 11 of "Heart's Chill Between."

The poem was published in *Athenaeum*, No. 1094 (October 14, 1848), 1032, and re-printed with revisions in *Beautiful Poetry*, I (1853), 248–49. Basic text: notebook MS. In the MS, lines 8, 26, and 40 are not indented; line 27 is indented two spaces, and line 28 is indented four spaces.]

Title.   MS: Anne of Warwick.
    1853: A LAMENT.
  1. MS: me be a
    1904: not: let
  2. 1848, 1853, 1904: long;
  3. 1848, 1853, 1904: Though the < >
    brittle,
  4. MS: [*Th*] [not indented] <The>
    [indented two spaces] love-cord
  5. MS: would watch a
  6. 1853: a sleeping place.
  7. 1848, 1853, 1904: go,—I
  8. 1848, 1853, 1904: rest.
 13. 1848, 1904: Though with < >
    alone
    1853: Though with
 15. 1848, 1904: moan,—
    1853: moan,
 16. 1848: say "She < > bear:"
    1853: say "she < > bear:"
    1904: say, 'She < > bear.'
 17. 1848, 1904: strong,—
 18. MS: [After line 18 is the following
    stanza:]

    Who hath felt as I have felt?
      Or who grieved as I have grieved?
    When I think how once I knelt
      At his dear side, and believed
    We were joined once and for ever,
    [*And*] [indented two spaces] <And>
      [not indented] that us twain
      none might sever.

 19. 1848: Listen, listen! Everywhere
    1904: Listen, listen!—Everywhere
 22. MS: ye cannot see.
    1904: comes you do

 23. 1848, 1853: Listen, listen!
    Evermore
    1904: Listen, listen!—Evermore
 25. 1848: me; he < > again,—
    1853: again,—
    1904: me! He is < > again,
 26. MS: own husband is
 28. MS: [*Br*] [not indented] <Bring>
    [indented four spaces] wine,
 31. 1848, 1853: harm,—
 32. 1848, 1904: heaviness.
    1853: heaviness,
 36. 1848, 1853: songs:—we
    1904: songs: we
 37. 1848, 1904: weeping?—Yet
    1853: hath talk'd of weeping? Yet
 38. 1848, 1853: heart,
 40. 1848: smart.
    1853: aching, and < > smart.
    1904: smart.—
 41. MS: my Mother, it is vain,
    1848, 1853: —Ah! my mother, 'tis
    1904: Ah, my mother, 'tis
 42. MS: [After line 42 is the following
    stanza:]

    Sorrowing ever for his sake
      I must watch and pray on earth,
    Waiting till the morning break
      Of Creation's second birth.—
    I shall go to him, but he
    Never shall return to me.

    1848: is *not* come
    1853: again!

HEART'S CHILL BETWEEN.

[Composed September 22, 1847. Editions: 1904. The notebook MS, in the hand-writing of Christina's sister, Maria Francesca Rossetti, is in the Bodleian Library. The poem was published in *Athenaeum*, No. 1095 (October 21, 1848), 1056. Basic text: notebook MS.]

Title.   MS: The Last Hope.
  1. 1848, 1904: him, though I
  2. 1848, 1904: me.

  5. 1848: hue,—
    1904: hue—
  7. 1904: o'er—

8. 1848: heart?—
10. 1904: saying—'We <> part,
11. 1848: more."
    1904: friends and <> more':
12. MS: [After line 12 is the following
    stanza:]

I might have wept, I might have prayed,
   I might have told him all;
Have clung to him until he said
   Words he could not recal;
Till his own bride I had been made;—
   His, let what would befal.

1848: —Oh, woman's
13. 1848: done,—
    1904: done:
14. 1904: now:
16. 1904: then I
17. 1848: been,—but
    1904: been—but
19. MS: What while I
    1848: be,
20. 1848, 1904: calm—

21. 1848: me,
    1904: calm: but, if <> me,
23. MS: in my memory
25. 1848: often through the long, long
    night,
    1904: often through the <> night,
28. 1904: fear:
29. 1848, 1904: light,
32. MS: look upon the
33. 1848, 1904: space
34. MS: And hearken to
    1848, 1904: breeze,—
35. 1848, 1904: the burial-place
38. 1848: stupified:
40. 1848, 1904: wide
41. 1904: gone astray:—
42. 1848: Ah, would
43. 1904: peace—
44. 1848, 1904: forget!
46. 1904: is. And yet
47. 1848: Methinks, now, that

REPINING.

[Composed in December, 1847. Editions: 1896, 1904. The notebook MS is in the
Bodleian Library. The poem was published in *The Germ: Thoughts Towards Nature in
Poetry, Literature, and Art,* No. 2 (February, 1850), 111–17. Basic text: notebook MS.]

Title. MS: An Argument.
 1. MS, 1896, 1904: alway through the
 3. 1896, 1904: undertone,
 4. 1850, 1896, 1904: "Come, that
 9. 1850, 1896, 1904: gentle
    turtle-dove
15. 1850: alone save <> she;—
    1896, 1904: alone save <> she:—
17. 1850: wept and
    1896, 1904: wept and <>
    undertone,
18. 1850, 1896, 1904: "Come, that
19. 1850, 1896: followed day, and
    1904: followed day and
21. 1850, 1896, 1904: the moonlight
22. MS: [After line 22 are the
    following lines:]

And when the darkness of the heaven
Before the shining stars was driven,

1896, 1904: to silver-white,

26. MS: His thrilling <throbbing>
    music [The added word is written
    above the line in pencil in Christina's
    hand.]
29. MS: Heard his <the> sweet [The
    added word is written above the
    line in pencil in Christina's hand.]
31. MS: "Arise, O Maid <Damsel rise
    up>; be [The added words are
    written above the line in pencil in
    Christina's hand.]
    1850, 1896, 1904: afraid;
32. 1850, 1896, 1904: For <> last," it
33. MS: trembled though the
    1850: trembled, tho' <> mild;
    1896, 1904: trembled, though the
    <> mild;
34. 1850, 1896, 1904: child;—
37. MS: man, with eyes
39. 1896, 1904: white but

40. 1850, 1896, 1904: glory like <>
veil
42. MS: Through the
1850: room till
1896, 1904: Through the <>
room till
45. 1850: come, I
1896, 1904: come, I prythee stay,
46. 1850, 1896, 1904: That
47. 1850, 1896, 1904: And
48. 1850, 1904: It [A stanza break
follows the line.]
1896: It
49. 1896: answered, "Rise
1904: answered, 'Rise and <> me.
50. MS: [After line 50 are the following
lines, deleted with pencil lines that
were later erased:]

<["*The night is damp, the night is chill,*
"*Hark to the wind upon the hill;*]>

51. MS: go Love? / "stay;
1850: go, friend?
1896, 1904: whither wouldst thou
go, friend?
52. MS: ["*And at*] <Until> the <> day
[The deletion is in pencil. The
added word is written above the
line in pencil in Christina's hand.
After line 52 are the following
lines, deleted in pencil:]

[*"To the far hills and farthest sea*
"I will arise and follow thee."]

1850, 1896, 1904: Until
54. MS: afraid; [After line 54 are the
following lines, deleted with pencil
lines that were later erased:]

<[*"The moon shall light both me and thee,*
"Arise my Love and follow me."]>

1850, 1896, 1904: Of [A stanza
break follows the line.]
56. MS: She <And> passed <> door.
[The added word is written above
the line in pencil in Christina's hand.
After line 56 are the following lines,
deleted in pencil:]

[*And through the night and shadows dim,*
In steadfast love she followed him.]

59. MS: bowed [*beneath his hand;*] [The
deletion is in pencil.]

62. 1850, 1896, 1904: before;
64. 1850, 1896, 1904: bird,
65. 1850, 1896, 1904: footsteps,
fluttered by
66. 1850, 1896, 1904: Where
aspen-trees stood
67. MS: [*As they passed on, at length a
sound*] [The deletion is in pencil.]
68. MS: [*Came trembling on the air
around;*] [The deletion is in pencil.]
69–72. MS: [The following lines are
deleted in pencil:]

[*A sound of speech confused with laughter,*
And happy music hurrying after;
Of lightsome dancing, and of song
The distant echoes bore along;
Of merrymaking since the morn,
Because an infant had been born.]

[On the inside of the back cover of the
notebook is Christina's rough draft
of lines 69–72, written in pencil as
follows:]

The undistinguishable [*noise*] <hum>
Of life; [*low fitful laughs*] <voices> that
<go &> come [The additions
are written above the line.]
[*To them of children   Upon*] the wind
Of busy <eager> men & [*sounds*]
<noises> <[illegible
deletion]> of feet <the
child's> <sweet> [The
addition of "the child's" is
below the line; the illegible
deletion and word "sweet" are
added above the line.]
Low children's [illegible deletion]
<laughter> rang between
Her Trampling <sound <noise> of
trampling feet> [The word
"noise" is added above the
line.]
[*The child's gl*] high laugh & dancing
feet.

70. 1850, 1896, 1904: life, voices
71. 1850, 1896, 1904: men, and
73. 1896, 1904: said, "Wilt
74. 1850: joyfully;
76. MS: "Of sweet communion
1850, 1896, 1904: Of
77. MS: and / "friend;
1850, 1896, 1904: Of
78. MS: end? [After line 78 are the
following lines, deleted in pencil:]

[*"Do thou come with me, and behold*
"And share these blessings manifold."]
1850, 1896, 1904: Is [No stanza
break follows the line.]
80. MS: hillock: "Stay;" [After line 80
are the following lines, deleted in
pencil:]

[*He then said: "all hence thou canst see,*
"But join not yet their revelry."]

81. MS: [*A little*] <It was a> [*village in*
a plain.] [The deletions are in
pencil. The additions are written
above the line in pencil in Christina's
hand. Preceding line 81 are the
following lines, deleted in pencil:]

[*The moon shone down, placid and clear,*
On a few houses scattered near;]

84. 1896, 1904: flowed o'er
85. MS: fine; and round it grew <sent
life up> [The added words are
written above the line in pencil in
Christina's hand.]
1850, 1896, 1904: fine, and
86. MS: Green water plants; and the
birds flew <Green [illegible
additions] & flower cup> [The
added words are written above and
beside the line in pencil in
Christina's hand. After line 86 are
the following lines, deleted in
pencil, below which is a stanza
break:]

[*Above it; and some stayed to drink,*
Standing upon its mossy brink.]

[*Beside one little cottage door,*
Beautiful roses clustered o'er,
The cordial neighbours flocked, to say
Kind speeches on the happy day.
For the young mother with her child
Had just come forth, and blushed and smiled;
And welcomed her friends' gathering,
And the gay wish and whispering.
Even as she spoke the gentle word,
Loud stirring notes again were heard;
Sweet notes and gladly musical
Recalling to the festival;
And one by one the guests withdrew
The merry dancing to renew.]

[*The moon shone bright, the heavens were*
light,

The revelry was at its height;
The dancers panting in their breath
Thought little of the hastening death,
Of the great danger, and the pain
That cometh once, but not again.]

1850, 1896, 1904: and flower-cup.
90. MS, 1896, 1904: rustled through
the
91. 1850, 1896, 1904: head
92. MS: tread, [After line 92 are the
following lines, deleted in pencil:]

[*And every vale, and leafy wood,*
And every silent solitude.]

93. 1850, 1896, 1904: hearken: in
94. MS: [After line 94 are the
following lines, deleted in pencil:]

[*Or do the hills and valleys hail*
The day-dawn, ere the stars grow pale?]

1850, 1896, 1904: together?—
96. MS: Than though a <> fell;
[After line 96 are the following
lines, deleted in pencil:]

[*Thou[gh]* <*tho'*> *each valley found a*
voice
To bid the answering hills rejoice;]

1896, 1904: Than though a
98. MS: [After line 98 are the
following lines, deleted in pencil:]

[*Descending with an angry shock*
From stream to stream, from rock to rock,
Giving one instant's time, to know
But not to fly from overthrow,]

1850, 1896, 1904: flow;—
101. MS: The village and the village
feast, [Written above the line are
illegible pencil additions.]
102. MS: And the glad host and
blithesome guest. [Written above
the line are illegible pencil
additions.]
103. 1850: "Oh! let <> pity fly;
1896, 1904: pity fly!
104. MS: hence Love, thou
1850: hence, friend,
1896, 1904: Let <> hence,
friend,
105. MS: regions still
1850, 1896, 1904: There
106. MS: "Where men resort and find
no ill <these things make not

desolate.> [The added words are
written above the line in pencil in
Christina's hand. After line 106
are the following lines, deleted in
pencil, below which is a stanza
break:]

[*"The silence where was laughter late!*
"The happy hearths made desolate!
"Oh let us seek some distant shore
"Where never death shall grieve us more
"Sudden and sharp; but long desired
"Shall bring sweet rest unto the tired;
"A soft repose, and so like sleep
"The dearest friends shall scarcely /
"weep."]

1850: Where [No stanza break
follows the line.]
1896, 1904: Where
108. 1850, 1896, 1904: said: "Arise
and
110. 1850, 1896, 1904: grass;
112. MS: below, [After line 112 are the
following lines, deleted in pencil:]

[*While the owls hooted in the trees,*
And sighings seemed to swell the breeze.]

115. 1850: face, sometimes
1896, 1904: face sometimes
118. MS: [After line 118 are the
following lines, deleted in pencil,
below which is a stanza break:]

[*The neverceasing voice that spoke*
Of curving waves that broke and broke;
That rose and fell; and evermore
Were broken on the pebbly shore.]

124. MS: [After line 124 are the
following stanzas, deleted in
pencil:]

[*It was a gallant ship and strong,*
Majestically borne along
By the calm waters; and on high
The flags were waving quietly.
Two stood upon the deck; this one
A mother, that, her darling son;
They stood together full of love
Uplooking to the stars above,
Which shone on them on the far sea,
And on the home w<h>ere they would be.
The son might see it nevermore,
Nor the fond mother tread its floor.]

[*The youth is dying, and she knows it;*
The eyes, the sunken cheeks disclose it.

She knows it, yet she does not weep;
The weary one will only sleep
A dreamless slumber; till again
They meet, where is nor care, nor pain,
Nor parting more; and so she still
Smiled sadly with a patient will.
And the boy knew it too; and saw
The coming death with holy awe.
He longed for home; but murmured not
That he might never see the spot
That saw his happy infancy;
It was willed well; so let it be.]

[*As they stood gazing hand in hand*
At once the young heart made a stand;
Then beat again, then paused again;
While a sharp pang of bitter pain
Shot through him; and he reeled and fell
Without a groan, insensible
To earthly care and evil; then
The mother stooped o'er him; and when
She saw that he was dead, she cried
With a loud voice; and vainly tried
To warm the chilly hands, and bring
Life back; and with life suffering.
But when she knew that it was vain,
And that he could not come again,
Kneeling by him she closed his eyes
With low deep sobs and choking sighs.
She prayed for death that comforteth,
With folded hands and hurried breath;
She prayed for death; and ere the day
She with her son was far away.]

126. 1850, 1896, 1904: of the North,
132. 1896, 1904: air,
134. MS: [After line 134 are the
following lines, deleted in pencil:]

[*All stood in fear save she alone*
Whose very heart of hearts was gone;
She knelt in awe, but did not tremble;
She had no terrors to dissemble;
Hoping, with pure hands lifted up,
In paradise that night to sup.
But to be wrecked; and with the shore
In sight; home never seemed before
So dear in its security
As then that tempests rent the sea.]

135. 1850, 1896, 1904: made, and
136. 1896, 1904: scarce!
140. MS: The [*ship*] <ship>; then
[The deletion and restoration are
in pencil.]
1850, 1896, 1904: ship. Then
were

141. 1850, 1896, 1904: the rain hurried forth, and
142. MS: [After line 142 are the following lines, deleted in pencil:]

    [And the hot lightning shone out fiercely;
    And the loud thunders roared, till scarcely
    One man could hear his friend, or hear
    The cries of agonising fear.
    The ocean called to heaven; and back,
    Along a redly changing track,
    The heaven made answer to the sea
    With its great thunders solemnly.
    Flash after flash[;]<!> peal after peal!
    The masts began to rock and reel;
    And through the dim sulphureous air
    Shone out the faces of despair.]

143. MS: [A horizontal pencil line is written between line 143 and the line directly above it.]
    1850, 1896, 1904: together, and
144. MS: [After line 144 are the following lines, deleted in pencil, below which is a stanza break:]

    [One infant on its mothers breast
    Was sleeping with unbroken rest;
    And one, scarce older, at her knee,
    Clapped its small hands, and laughed to see
    The mighty waves that rising higher
    Seemed crested all with floating fire.]

    1850, 1896, 1904: silence, and
145. MS: [Preceding line 145 are the following lines, deleted in pencil:]

    [The ship could bear no more at last;
    The agony of doubt was past.]

    1850: Many half-crazed looked
    1896, 1904: Many half crazed looked
147. 1850, 1896, 1904: forgot friends, foes <> to foes;—
148. MS: and rose; [After line 148 are the following lines, deleted in pencil, below which is a stanza break:]

    [Till down, down, down into the sea
    The mighty wreck sank sullenly.]

149. MS: [Preceding line 149 are the following lines, deleted in pencil:]

    ["I cannot weep, I dare not stay,
    "Oh Love, in mercy come away.]

    1850, 1896, 1904: me! Whom I

150. MS: as though they [After line 150 are the following lines, deleted in pencil:]

    ["And the waves all grow calm; and up,
    "Even in the midst of her cloud cup,
    "The moon is set; nor shuddereth
    "Though shining on the gate of death.
    "To some strong city let us go,
    "Far from the changeful ocean's flow,]

    1850: Are
    1896, 1904: Are <> as though they
151. MS: "[For] <I> in <> earth <there> is [The deletion is in pencil. The additions are written above the line in pencil in Christina's hand.]
    1850, 1896, 1904: In
152. 1850, 1896, 1904: And
153. MS: tempest / "torn,
    1850, 1896: Why <> sea, tempest-torn,
    1904: Why <> sea, tempest- / torn,
154. 1850, 1896, 1904: Bury
156. MS: [The line was deleted with a pencil line and then the pencil line was erased.]
157. MS: any [s]<S>tar; [The line was deleted with a pencil line and then the pencil line was erased.]
    1850, 1896, 1904: not nor any star;
158. 1850, 1896, 1904: far,
160. MS: [After line 160 are the following lines, deleted in pencil, below which is a stanza break:]

    [The path was stony and uneven;
    On either hand stood rocks, nigh riven
    From their firm base, ready to fall;
    And poisonous plants tra[illegible deletion]<il>ed over all.]

    1896: [No stanza break follows the line.]
161. MS: was chill <cold>; but suddenly <till from the South> [The added words are written above the line in pencil in Christina's hand.]
162. MS: hot [and stiflingly] <like sudden drouth> [The deletion is in pencil. The added words are

written above the line in pencil in
Christina's hand.]
1850, 1896, 1904: hot, like <>
drouth,
163. 1850: faces; and
1896, 1904: faces; and <> light,
164. MS: shone through the [After line
164 are the following lines, deleted
in pencil, below which is a stanza
break:]

[*The dew dried up, and evermore* [Above
the line are illegible additions
in pencil.]
A noise came to them far before;
The wail of women's agonies,
And shrieks, and pain-extorted cries.]

1850: red, shone
1896, 1904: red, shone through
the
165. 1850, 1896, 1904: flame
166. 1850, 1896, 1904: death and <>
name.
167. 1850, 1896, 1904: smoke,
168. MS: [After line 168 are the
following lines, deleted in pencil:]

[*They woke in time to feel the fire,*
To know the ruin coming nigher,
To struggle without hope; to hear
The prayers and blasphemies of fear.]

169. 1850: Oh! happy
170. 1896, 1904: away!
173. 1850: not; who
174. MS: [After line 174 are the
following lines, deleted in pencil:]

[*Whose hands are folded quietly*
Upon their breasts in piety;]

175. 1850: Who, dying, said
1896, 1904: increase,
176. 1850, 1896, 1904: let thy servant
178. MS: A [illegible deletion]
[<*shady*>] <shaded> river [The
final addition is written above the
line in pencil in Christina's hand.]
1850, 1896, 1904: near;
180. MS: cold, [After line 180 are the
following lines, deleted in pencil:]

[*That whispered as they lapsed along*
Rush-bordered, an eternal song.
Yet not one day could they obtain
To quench the burning of their pain.]

181. 1850: Was flame-wrapped all
1896, 1904: Was flame-wrapt all
182. MS: all; [After line 182 are the
following lines, deleted in pencil,
below which is a stanza break:]

[*And in the street that scorched their feet*
Did friends and kin pass by and meet.
A woman here with flowing hair
Sought for her lover everywhere;
A mother clasped her child; a bride
Clung trembling to her husband's side,
With large eyes praying silently
For succour in the agony.]

1850: were flame-wrapped all.
1896, 1904: were flame-wrapt all.
183. MS: [*But*] [*w*]<W>hat was
<man's> strength, [The deletions
are in pencil. The added word is
written above the line in pencil in
Christina's hand. The added letter
is written in pencil in Christina's
hand.]
184. MS: [After line 184 are the
following lines, deleted in pencil:]

[*There was no help in love or wealth,*
No hope in youth, no power in health.]

185. 1850, 1896, 1904: prayer, believing
186. 1904: Resigned into a
188. MS: [After line 188 are the
following lines, deleted in pencil:]

[*Then bent the stubborn knees, and then*
Heart-cries went up from haughty men.]

192. MS: [After line 192 is the
following stanza, deleted in
pencil:]

[*And then at length the flames were seen*
To gain the powder magazine;
Then came the explosion, then a cry,
Then silence everlastingly.]

1850, 1896, 1904: still, stood
193. 1850: "Death—death—oh! let
<> from death;
1896, 1904: "Death—death—oh
<> from death!
194. 1850: Where'er <> followeth.
1896, 1904: Where'er <>
followeth;
195. 1850, 1896, 1904: All
196. 1850, 1896, 1904: Remain

197. 1850, 1896, 1904: What <>
     thing? thus
198. 1850, 1896, 1904: To <> eternity;
199. 1850, 1896, 1904: To <> mirth;
200. 1850, 1896, 1904: To <> birth;
201. 1850, 1896, 1904: To <> more;
     to
202. 1850, 1896, 1904: Having <>
     peace.
203. 1850, 1896, 1904: Let <> hence;
     and, even
204. 1850, 1896, 1904: Death
205. 1850, 1896, 1904: Let
206. 1850, 1896, 1904: Those
207. 1850: sighed and <> together.
209. 1850, 1896, 1904: heaven high
     overhead
211. 1850, 1896, 1904: thunder,
213. 1850, 1896, 1904: Forked and
218. MS: [After line 218 are the
     following lines, deleted in pencil:]

     [And in its whisper was the noise
     Of many an agonizèd voice;]

     1850, 1896, 1904: armament:
220. MS: [After line 220 are the
     following lines, deleted in pencil,
     below which is a stanza break:]

     [Yea, full of [illegible deletion] <blood
         and> wounds and pain,
     They looked upon a battle plain.]

     1850, 1896, 1904: were
     down-trodden far <> wide.
221. 1850, 1896, 1904: day
222. MS: [After line 222 are the
     following lines, deleted in pencil,
     below which is a stanza break:]

     [They marched in the cool early hours
     Past fields of corn and banks of flowers,
     O'er weary hills, through darksome woods,
     Through towns and pathless solitudes.
     Cities and villages came out
     And hailed them with a joyful shout;
     The people all were fain to go
     And hear the drums and see the show;
     What mattered it, if on the track
     Were death? if these should not come back?
     If even the young, their day nigh done,
     Now looked their last upon the sun?]

     [The cause of quarrel was not great;
     No wrong; only a jealous hate.
     Two kings were wroth; a weary peace

Had been; but envying's increase
And strife of tongues and angry pride
And hot words spoken on either side
Made peace intolerable; so
The blood of a few churls must flow
To quench the fire of enmity:
It was their portion, verily.]

223. 1850, 1896, 1904: soweth so
227. 1896, 1904: and putrefying flesh;
     1896s: and putrifying flesh;
229. 1904: stifled: stiffened
231. 1850, 1896, 1904: dead: these
232. MS: [The anguish of the wounds they
     bore.] [The deletion is in pencil.
     After line 232 are the following
     lines, deleted in pencil:]

     [The race was run, the journey done,
     The haven and the rest were won.
     In the hot fire they had been tried
     And now were throughly purified.]

     1896s: bore
233. MS: not [weep] <sigh> again,
     1850, 1896, 1904: Behold, they
234. MS: vain, [After line 234 are the
     following lines, deleted in pencil:]

     [Nor mourn the dead and then forget
     But feel a something wanting yet.]

235. 1850, 1896, 1904: them?—is
238. MS: [After line 238 are the
     following lines, deleted in pencil,
     below which is a stanza break:]

     [The weary ones have found repose,
     The sad an easing from their woes,
     The young are saved from coming evil,
     The old have truth for life's false revel,
     The weak are lightened of a load,
     The loving are gone up to God.]

     1850: [No stanza break follows
     the line.]
239. 1850, 1896, 1904: calm; but
242. MS: [After line 242 are the
     following lines, deleted in pencil:]

     [Who saw the far-off wolves appear,
     And heard the vulture hovering near,]

     1850: die.
     1896, 1904: die;
243. MS: [And] <Who> watched [The
     deletion is in pencil. The added
     word is printed above the line in
     pencil.]

245. 1850, 1896, 1904: distance flying
   fast
246. MS: [After line 246 is the
   following stanza, deleted in
   pencil:]

   [*Then came the struggle of the stronger,*
   Striving to live a little longer;
   Then the most weak, life not quite done,
   Shrank as the death-feast was begun;
   The ghastly banquet in which they
   Were given to carrion as a prey.]

247. 1896, 1904: agony.
248. 1850, 1896, 1904: enough," said
250. MS: return [*from*] <to> whence

[The deletion is in pencil. The
added word is written above the
line in pencil in Christina's hand.
After line 250 are the following
lines, deleted in pencil:]

   [*"A very worm formed of the sod,*
   "What was I to dictate to God?
   "Thou gavest that for which I cried;
   "Behold, now I am satisfied.]

   1896, 1904: Let
251. 1850: "Thou, who for
   1896, 1904: Thou who for
252. 1850: me for
   1896, 1904: Forgive me for

NEW ENIGMAS ["NAME ANY GENTLEMAN YOU SPY"]

[Date of composition unknown. Editions: 1896, 1904. The poem was published in
Marshall's Ladies' Daily Remembrancer. For 1850 (London: R. and A. Suttaby and
J. Toulmin, [1850]), 135–36, as the seventh in a series of enigmas by various au-
thors. Christina's copy of the book, containing her holograph revisions, is in the
Princeton University Library. Basic text: 1850 (Christina's copy).]

Title. 1850 (Christina's copy): NEW
   ENIGMAS. / VII. BY
   C.<hristina> [The addition is
   written in pencil. In the right
   margin is written in pencil:]
   <(Jack.)>
   1896, 1904: TWO ENIGMAS / I
1. 1850 (Christina's copy):
   gentleman[, *and he*] <you spy,>
   [The deletion and additions are in
   pencil.]
2. 1850 (Christina's copy): [*Runs a fair*
   chance of being me]; [The deletion is
   in pencil. In the left margin,
   perpendicular to the printed text,
   is written in pencil in Christina's
   hand:]

   <Name any gentleman you spy
   And there's a chance that he is I>

[To the right of the added lines is
written in pencil in Christina's
hand a bracket and the following
words:] <in honour of grammar.
CGR.>
   1896, 1904: is I.
4. 1896, 1904: day.
6. 1896, 1904: befriended.
8. 1896, 1904: dish.
9. 1896, 1904: poor;
11. 1896, 1904: trades—there
12. 1896, 1904: sun.
14. 1896, 1904: same:
15–16. 1850 (Christina's copy): [In the
   right margin beside lines 15 and 16
   is written in pencil in William
   Michael Rossetti's hand:] <1849>

CHARADES ["MY *FIRST* IS NO PROOF OF MY *SECOND*"]

[Date of composition unknown. Editions: 1896, 1904. The poem was published in
Marshall's Ladies' Daily Remembrancer. For 1850 (London: R. and A. Suttaby and
J. Toulmin, [1850]), 140, as the sixth in a series of charades by various authors.
Christina's copy of the book, containing her holograph annotations, is in the Prince-
ton University Library. Basic text: 1850 (Christina's copy).]

Title. 1850 (Christina's copy):
CHARADES. / VI. BY
C.<hristina> [The addition is
written in pencil. To the left of the
subtitle is written in Christina's
hand:] <(Candid).> [At the top of
the page is written in William
Michael Rossetti's hand:]
<Charade>
1896, 1904: TWO CHARADES / I

1. 1896, 1904: My first is <> of my
   second,
2. 1896, 1904: first.
3. 1896, 1904: my whole, I
5. 1896, 1904: more:—If you
7–8. 1850 (Christina's copy): [In the
   right margin beside lines 7 and 8 is
   written in pencil in William
   Michael Rossetti's hand:] <1849>
8. 1896, 1904: my whole.

THE ROSE.

[Composed April 17, 1847. Editions: 1896, 1904. The notebook MS, in the hand-
writing of Christina's sister, Maria Francesca Rossetti, is in the Bodleian Library.
The poem was printed in *Verses: Dedicated to Her Mother* (London: privately printed
at G. Polidori's, 1847), 29. The poem was published in Mary Howitt (ed.), *Pictorial
Calendar of the Seasons Exhibiting the Pleasures, Pursuits, and Characteristics of Country
Life for Every Month in the Year and Embodying the Whole of Aikin's Calendar of Nature*
(London: Henry G. Bohn, 1854), 305. Basic text: notebook MS. In the MS, line 6 is
not indented.]

Title. MS: To a Rose. / Sonnet.
  1854: [untitled]
2. 1847, 1896, 1904: prime,
  1854: prime,—
3. MS: time,
  1896, 1904: perfect fullness in the
  summertime,
4. 1854: asunder,
5. MS: And shew the
6. MS: Thou should'st bloom <>
  clime

7. 1847, 1896, 1904: chilly winter's
  rime,
  1854: Untouch'd by chilly winter's
  rime,
8. 1847, 1896, 1904: flash nor
12. 1847, 1896, 1904: grow:
13. 1847, 1896, 1904: And He who is
  all wise, He
  1854: And He who is all-wise, He

THE TREES' COUNSELLING.

[Composed December 5, 1847. The notebook MS (MS1) is in the Bodleian Library.
A fair copy MS containing lines 38–40 (MS2) is in the University of Kansas Library.
The poem was published in Mary Howitt (ed.), *Midsummer Flowers. For the Young*
(Philadelphia: Lindsay and Blakiston, 1854), 202–203. Basic text: MS1. In the 1854
text, line 12 is indented four spaces and line 28 is not indented.]

Title. MS1: [To the right and slightly
  above the title is written in pencil:]
  <O>
  1854: THE TREES'
  COUNSELLING.
1. 1854: sorrowfully,
2. 1854: Through the cornfields and
4. 1854: shadows:

6. 1854: breeze,
7. MS1: waved [*blew*] <and> blew
8. 1854: rustle through them.
9. 1854: others,
10. 1854: pleasant,
12. 1854: Here
13. 1854: Summer,
14. 1854: Pass <> following:

15. 1854: Little
16. MS1: "Little clouds may
    1854: Little
17. 1854: heaven,
18. 1854: To
19. 1854: When
20. 1854: Full <> her;
21. 1854: And though sometimes, in
    <> night,
22. 1854: Mists <> sight;
23. 1854: She
24. 1854: With

26. 1854: trees, came
29. 1854: Learn <> wood,
30. 1854: That
31. 1854: Go <> thee,
32. 1854: Turn
33. 1854: turned. Behold, the
36. 1854: merely:
37. 1854: wind, not murmuring,
38. 1854: Seemed but
39. 1854: patience, and
40. MS1: merit.
    1854: Shall

"BEHOLD, I STAND AT THE DOOR AND KNOCK."

[Composed December 1, 1851. Editions: 1896, 1904. The notebook MS is in the Bodleian Library. In the 1896 edition, William Michael Rossetti states: "These verses were published in some magazine. I fancy it may have been one named *Aikin's Year*, with which Mary Howitt was connected. If so, I think the poem must be of a date not later than 1852, the publication not later than 1854; and these would be the first verses by Christina which got into print after the cessation of *The Germ* in 1850" (p. 389). The poem is not in Mary Howitt (ed.), *Pictorial Calendar of the Seasons Exhibiting the Pleasures, Pursuits, and Characteristics of Country Life for Every Month in the Year and Embodying the Whole of Aikin's Calendar of Nature* (London: H. G. Bohn, 1854). I have not been able to locate the journal text. Basic text: notebook MS.]

Title. MS: door & knock."
    1896, 1904: BEHOLD, <>
    KNOCK
2. 1896, 1904: love.
3. MS: "O[*h*] [*l*]<Lady>, stay; the
    wind is bitter cold,
    1896: "Oh lady, stay, this
    1904: 'O lady, stay, this
4. MS: "Oh <> the clear frosty [The
    line is indented one-half space.]
5. MS: "I <> feeble, [*old*] <poor>:"—
    1896, 1904: poor."—
7. MS: "Do
    1896, 1904: you; there's <>
    clergyman,"
8. MS: shivering shut the
    1896, 1904: The lady said,
9. MS: gate?—[*w*]<W>ay-worn and
    1896: gate?—Wayworn and pale
    1904: gate?—Way- / worn and pale
10. MS: An ancient man
    1896, 1904: again.
11. MS: "Sweet Lady, <> have
    wandered far,
    1896, 1904: "Kind lady, I

12. MS: "Thro'
13. MS: "Some
    1896, 1904: lodging-place."—
    1896s: lodging-place."
14. 1896: the workhouse very near;
    1904: the work- / house very near;
15. MS: "Go,
    1896, 1904: there"—
16. MS: door upon his
17. MS: gate?—A little child,
18. MS: Her sad look sharpened
    1896, 1904: care.
19. 1896: "Oh lady, save
    1904: 'O lady, save
20. MS: "From sights <> the very air.
    1896, 1904: air:
21. MS: "Have pity
    1896, 1904: good."—
22. 1896, 1904: cry?
23. MS: "I keep
    1896, 1904: not I."
24. MS: She shut the
25. 1896, 1904: heard?
29. 1896, 1904: But who is this, that
    standeth

31. 1896, 1904: This whom thou < >   36. MS: "Now
    succour nor < > in   37. MS: "Three
32. 1896, 1904: teach but < > way.   38. MS: "Three
34. MS: "And   39. MS: "But
35. MS: "Thou   40. MS: "And
    1896, 1904: princess rich < >
    ease—

"GIANNI MY FRIEND AND I BOTH STROVE TO EXCEL"

[Date of composition unknown. The poem was published in *The Crayon*, III (1856), 200–202, as part of the short story "The Lost Titian," and reprinted in *Commonplace, and Other Short Stories* (London: F. S. Ellis, 1870), 161, and *Commonplace, A Tale of To-day; and Other Stories* (Boston: Roberts Brothers, 1870), 200–202. Basic text: 1870.]

1. 1870: 'Gianni   4. 1870: tail.'
3. 1856: indeed, but

THE OFFERING OF THE NEW LAW,
THE ONE OBLATION ONCE OFFERED.

[Composed May 23, 1861. Editions: 1896, 1904. The notebook MS (MS1) is in the British Library. A fair copy MS (MS2), signed "Christina G. Rossetti," is in the Bodleian Library. The poem was published in Orby Shipley (ed.), *Lyra Eucharistica: Hymns and Verses on the Holy Communion, Ancient and Modern; with Other Poems* (London: Longman, Green, Longman, Roberts, and Green, 1863), 48–49, and reprinted with revisions in the second edition of that book (1864), 61–62. Basic text: MS2. In the MS1, 1896, and 1904 texts, no lines are indented.]

Title. MS1: God be merciful to me a   7. MS1: delay;—
    sinner.   1863, 1864: Now, I
    MS2: once [D]<O>ffered.   1896, 1904: delay:—
    1864: The Offering of the New   8. MS1: Today; it
    Law.   1863, 1864: To-day, it < > called
    1896, 1904: THE OFFERING OF   to-day.
    THE NEW LAW   1896, 1904: To-day: it
Opening quotation. MS1, 1864, 1896,   9. MS1: stumble halt < > blind
    1904: [There is no opening   MS2: halt & blind,
    quotation.]   10. MS1: Lo, He < > kind:
    MS2: "Sacrifice & Offering   1896, 1904: Lo He < > kind:
    1863: *Sacrifice and Offering Thou*   11. MS1: soon or < > slow
    wouldest not, but a BODY *hast Thou*   1864: soon or
    prepared Me.   1896, 1904: soon or < > slow—
2. MS1, 1896, 1904: In the palace of   12. MS1, 1864, 1896, 1904: bless I
    < > sky: 14. MS1: Once I chose the love of man;
3. MS1: for [h]<H>is grace   1896, 1904: man:
    1863: Now, I   15. MS1, 1864, 1896, 1904: aside
    1864: Now, I < > for His Grace   17. MS1: Broken re[a]<e>d hath < >
    1896, 1904: for His grace   hand
6. MS1, 1896, 1904: moon: 1896, 1904: hand,

18. 1896, 1904: sand,
20. MS1: without and <> within,—
    1863, 1864: without and
    1896, 1904: without and <>
    within.
21. 1864: Yet, His tree,
    1896, 1904: Yet, His tree, <> root:
22. 1864: Yet, His branch,
    1896, 1904: Yet, His branch, <>
    fruit:
23. MS1: morns
    MS2: eves & morns,
    1864, 1896, 1904: Yet, His sheep,
    <> morns
25. MS1: With [*t*]<T>hine
    [*i*]<I>mage stamped
26. 1864: Find Thy Coin more
    1896, 1904: gold:

28. MS1, 1896, 1904: To Thee Thy
    homesick prodigal.
29. MS1: and [*o*]<O>ffering
    1896, 1904: and offering
30. 1864: bring,
    1896, 1904: bring—
31. MS1, 1896, 1904: None save
32. MS1: of [*t*]<T>hine Own.
    1896, 1904: of Thine own.
33. MS1, 1896, 1904: Broken Body,
    Blood outpoured,
    MS2: Broken Body, Blood
    [*o*]<O>utpoured,
34. MS1: bring, my God, my Lord:
35. MS1, 1864, 1896, 1904: of Life and
36. MS1, 1896, 1904: me Thy board is

THE ELEVENTH HOUR.

[Composed September 5, 1853. Editions: 1896, 1904. The notebook MS is in the
Bodleian Library. The poem was published in *The Victoria Magazine*, II (February,
1864), 317–18. Basic text: notebook MS. In the 1864 text, the opening quotation
marks in lines 24, 33, and 34 are not counted in the paragraphing. In the 1896 and
1904 texts, lines 1, 5, 6, 8, 10, 12, 13, 15, 19, 20, 22, 24, 26, 27, 29, 31, 33, 34, 36, 40,
41, 43, 45, 47, and 48 are indented two spaces, and lines 7, 14, 21, 28, 30, 35, 42, and
49 are not indented.]

Title. 1864: THE ELEVENTH
    HOUR.
    1896, 1904: THE ELEVENTH
    HOUR
1. MS: worn and feeble
2. 1864, 1896, 1904: gate;
3. 1896, 1904: Though no
4. 1896, 1904: Knocking though so
6. 1864, 1896, 1904: of heaven,
10. MS: Blessed [*a*]<A>ngels wonder
13. 1864, 1896, 1904: thicken:
14. 1864, 1896, 1904: is knocking,
    knocking
15. MS: Still the
16. 1864, 1896, 1904: lock:
18. 1864, 1896, 1904: knock.—
23. 1864: Knocketh, prayeth, he:
    1896, 1904: Knocketh, prayeth he:
24. 1864, 1896, 1904: "Lord have
25. 1864: to Thee."
    1896, 1904: When <> to Thee."
26. 1864: unceasing;

27. 1864, 1896, 1904: increasing:
28. MS: me. [After line 28 is the
    following stanza:]

    "Thou, O Lord, hast sought me
        "In the desert place,
    "Borne me on Thy Shoulders,
        "Cheered me with Thy Face:
    "Thou, O Lord, hast led me,
    "Thou, O Lord, hast fed me;
    "Shall I die in sight of grace?"—

    1864: my Lord remember
32. 1864, 1896, 1904: fear:
33. 1864: me—
    1896, 1904: "Jesus, look <> me—
34. 1864: me?—
    1896, 1904: Christ, hast <> me?—
35. 1896, 1904: If <> here."
39. MS: Left without
    1864, 1896, 1904: wall?
41. MS: Arms [*t*]<T>hat sought
42. MS: Bore and kept and loved
    <Held withheld & bore> thro'

[The added words are written
below the line in pencil in Christina's
hand.]
1864: Held, withheld, and <> all.
1896, 1904: Held, withheld, and
bore through all.

43. 1896, 1904: mansion,
45. MS: and budding palm branch,
46. MS: Throne august secure,
47. MS: Angels yet shall bring them;
48. MS: In the eternal kingdom
49. MS: Thou shalt reign for

I KNOW YOU NOT.

[Composed June 26, 1856. Editions: 1896, 1904. The notebook MS is in the British Library. The poem was published in Orby Shipley (ed.), *Lyra Messianica: Hymns and Verses on the Life of Christ, Ancient and Modern; with Other Poems* (London: Longman, Green, Longman, Roberts, and Green, 1864), 28–29, and reprinted with revisions in the second edition of that book (1869), 28–29. Basic text: notebook MS. The poem originally formed part of a poem entitled "'The Chiefest among ten thousand,'" which Christina never published as such. "'The Chiefest among ten thousand'" is presented in its own right in Section 3 of the present volume. In the 1896 text, lines 2, 3, 4, 8, 10, 15, 18, 21, 23, 26, 28, 30, 32, 34, 38, and 39 are indented two spaces; lines 19, 27, 29, 35, and 37 are indented four spaces; and lines 20, 24, and 36 are indented six spaces. In the 1904 text, lines 2, 3, 4, 8, 10, 15, 18, 21, 26, 28, 30, 32, 34, and 38 are indented two spaces; lines 19, 23, 27, 29, 35, and 37 are indented four spaces; and lines 20, 24, 36, and 39 are indented six spaces.]

Title. MS: The Chiefest among ten
thousand. [Below the title is added
in pencil in Dante Gabriel Rossetti's
hand:] <might be shortened>
1896, 1904: I KNOW YOU NOT
1. MS: Thyself the [Preceding line 1
is the following stanza:]

When sick of life and all the world,
How sick of all the earth but Thee,
I lift mine eyes up to the hills,
Eyes of my heart that truly see:
I see beyond all death and ills
Refreshing green for heart and eyes;
The golden streets and gateways
  pearled,
The living trees of paradise.

1864: O Christ
1869, 1896, 1904: O Christ, the
<> living fruit,
1–8. MS: [The stanza is deleted with
a diagonal pencil line.]
2. 1864, 1869, 1896, 1904: The
twelvefold-fruited Tree
4. 1864, 1869: and the Rose;
1896, 1904: The Valley-lily and the
Rose;
5. MS: than Lebanon, [*l*]<T>hou
Root,

1864, 1869, 1896: than Lebanon,
Thou Root;
1904: than Lebanon Thou Root;
6. 1904: grapes Thou
7. MS: of new Wine
1864: O Best, <> red Wine,
1869: O Best, <> red wine,
1896, 1904: O best, Thou <> red
wine,
8. 1869: Keeping thy best wine till
1896, 1904: best wine till
9. 1864: great Price Thyself alone,
1869, 1896, 1904: alone,
9–16. MS: [The stanza is deleted with
a diagonal pencil line.]
10. 1864: the Ruby Thou;
1869, 1896, 1904: ruby Thou;
11. 1864: precious lightning Jasper
1869: precious lightning jasper
stone,
1896: precious lightning Jasper
stone,
1904: lightening Jasper stone,
12. 1864: the Corner spurned before:
1869, 1896, 1904: before:
13. 1864: of Pearl, Thyself the Door:
1869: the Door;

1869: the Door;
1896, 1904: Fair gate of < > the
Door;
14. 1864, 1869: the Way;
1896, 1904: golden street, Thyself
the Way;
15. 1864, 1869, 1896, 1904: now,
16. MS: shall reach Thee in that day.
[After line 16 are the following
stanzas:]

Oh that a dove's white wings I had
To flee away from this distress
For Thou art in the wilderness
Drawing and leading Thine Own love:
Wherefore it blossoms like a rose,
The solitary place is glad;
There sounds the soft voice of the dove
And there the spicy south wind blows.

Draw us, we will run after Thee;
Call us by name, the name we know;
Call her beloved who was not so,
Beulah and blessed Hepzibah:
That where Thou art I too may be
Bride of the Bridegroom heart to heart;
Thou God, my Love, the Fairest art
Where all things fair and lovely are.

1864, 1869: Through Thee
1896, 1904: Through Thee < >
enter heaven one
17. 1864: and Flood;
1869, 1896, 1904: full fount and
flood;
17–24. MS: [The stanza is deleted with
a diagonal pencil line.]
18. 1864, 1869, 1896: calls Thine, as
1904: calls thine, as
19. 1864: forget Thy Sweat and Pain,
20. 1896, 1904: the cross?
21. 1864, 1869, 1896, 1904:
Heart-pierced for
22. 1864, 1869, 1896, 1904: lavished
Blood:
23. 1864, 1869, 1896, 1904: is Thine,
Lord, if < > gain;
24. MS: [After line 24 are the following
stanzas, deleted with a vertical
pencil line:]

[*The sparrow findeth her a house,*
The swallow for her young a nest,
But Thou art far away my Rest,
Thyself my Rest and Thou alone:
No home on earth sufficeth me,
Not Thine Own house most fair to see,

Tho' rich with gold and costly stone,
Painted and ceiled with cedar boughs.]
[*There is a time for all things, saith*
The Word of Truth, Thyself the Word;
And many things Thou reasonest of:
A time for hope so long deferred,
But this is time for [illegible deletion]
<g>*rief and* [t]<f>*ears;*
A time for life, but this is death;
Oh when shall be the time of love
When Thou Thyself shalt wipe our tears?]

1864: lose, Thine
1869: lose, Thine own the
1896, 1904: Or, if < > lose, Thine
own the
25. 1864, 1869: midnight (saith the
Parable)
1896, 1904: the Parable,
25–32. MS: [The stanza is deleted with
a diagonal pencil line.]
26. 1864: A Cry was < > came;
1869, 1896, 1904: came;
27. 1864, 1869, 1896, 1904: in:
28. 1864, 1869, 1896, 1904: rest, shut
< > shame,
29. 1864, 1869: that Feast to win,
1896, 1904: win,
30. 1864, 1869, 1896: cast, and < > lot;
1904: lot;
31. 1864, 1869: divided Heaven from
Hell;
1896, 1904: A gulf divided < >
hell;
32. 1864, 1869, 1896, 1904: said—I
< > not.
33. 1864: door,
1869, 1896, 1904: is this that shuts
< > door,
33–40. MS: [The stanza is deleted with
a diagonal pencil line.]
34. 1864, 1869, 1896, 1904: saith—I
< > not—to
35. 1869, 1896, 1904: wounded hands
and side,
36. MS: long [*before:*] <ago:> [The
deletion and revision are in pencil
in Christina's hand.]
1869, 1896, 1904: The brow
thorn-tortured
37. MS: Yes, This
1864: Yea; This < > grieved, and
bled, and

1869: Yea; this Who
1896, 1904: Yea, This who grieved
38. 1869: This same is
1896, 1904: This same is He who
must
39. 1864, 1869, 1896, 1904: know;
40. MS: [After line 40 are the following
stanzas, the first, second, and fourth
deleted with a vertical pencil line:]

[*When shall Thy coming be, my Lord?*
At midnight? at the cockcrow? when?
Thou Whom the people once abhorred
Art of all nations the Desire:
Thou art as a Refiner's Fire,
As Fuller's Sope to purge and bless;
For Thou shalt judge the sons of men,
Shalt judge the world in righteousness.]

[*But when Thou comest, King of kings,*
Who shall abide Thy triumph day?
Shalt Thou find faith upon the earth,
Loins girt, lamps burning for Thy Sake?
Then will be dreams of frantic mirth
Tho' now it is high time to wake
Or ever earth and earthly things
With a great noise shall pass away.]

From north and south from east and west
Thy sons and daughters all shall flock
Who built their house upon the Rock
And eagle-like renew their strength:
How glad and glorious is their rest
Whom Thou hast purged from fleshly
scum,—
The long-desired is come at length,
The fulness of the time is come.

[*Cast in my lot with theirs, cast in*
The lot of those I love with theirs,
Make those I love not fellow he[*a*]<*i*>*rs*
Heirs of Thy throne Thy love and life:
Teach us to love both foes and friends
With love like Thine which never ends,
For loving and made pure from sin
Must be the Lamb's blood-purchased wife.]

Then the new heavens and earth
shall be
Where righteousness shall dwell indeed:
There shall be no more blight nor need
Nor barrier of the tossing sea;
No sun and moon alternating
For God shall be the Light thereof,
No sorrow more no death no sting
For God shall reign and God is Love.

A CHRISTMAS CAROL.

[Composed August 26, 1859. Editions: 1896, 1904. The notebook MS (MS1) is owned by Mrs. Geoffrey Dennis. A fair copy MS of lines 1–8, signed "C. Rossetti" (MS2), is in the Princeton University Library. MS2 does not appear to be in Christina's handwriting. The poem was published in Orby Shipley (ed.), *Lyra Messianica: Hymns and Verses on the Life of Christ, Ancient and Modern; with Other Poems* (London: Longman, Green, Longman, Roberts, and Green, 1864), 63–64, and reprinted with revisions in the second edition of that book (1869), 81. Basic text: notebook MS. In the 1896 text, line 2 is indented three spaces, lines 3 and 15 are indented two spaces, and lines 5 and 8 are indented four spaces. In the 1904 text, lines 3 and 15 are indented two spaces, and lines 5 and 8 are indented four spaces.]

Title. 1864: Before the paling of the
Stars.
(1869): Before the paling of the
stars.
1. MS2, 1864, 1896, 1904: stars,
2. MS2, 1864, 1896, 1904: morn,
3. MS2: earliest cock<c>row[s],
1864: cockcrow,
1896, 1904: earliest cock-crow
4. MS2: born;
5. 1864: a Stable,
MS2, (1869): a stable,

6. 1864: a Manger,
(1869): a manger,
7. MS2, (1869): world His hands had
8. MS2, (1869), 1896, 1904: a stranger.
9. (1869): and king lay
11. (1869), 1896, 1904: and old lay
13. 1864, 1896, 1904: Saint and Angel,
ox and ass,
14. 1896, 1904: together,
17. 1904: on his Mother's
18. 1864: the Stable cold,
(1869): the stable cold,

19. 1864, 1896, 1904: was He,
20. (1869), 1896, 1904: the fold:
21. 1864, 1896, 1904: with Mary Maid,
    (1869): with Mary maid,
22. 1864, 1896, 1904: hoary,

23. 1864, 1896, 1904: With Saint and
    Angel, ox and ass,
    (1869): With Saint and Angel, ox
    and ass

EASTER EVEN.

[Composed March 23, 1861. Editions: 1896, 1904. The notebook MS is in the British Library. The poem was published in Orby Shipley (ed.), *Lyra Messianica: Hymns and Verses on the Life of Christ, Ancient and Modern; with Other Poems* (London: Longman, Green, Longman, Roberts, and Green, 1864), 251–52, and reprinted with revisions in the second edition of that book (1869), 279–80. Basic text: notebook MS. In the 1864 text, the second and fourth lines of each stanza are indented four spaces.]

2. 1896, 1904: boast:
4. 1896, 1904: host;
5. 1864: his Judgment-hall
7. 1864, 1904: passed them all,
   1896: and past them all,
9. 1864: The Sepulchre made < >
   ponderous Stone,
   (1869): The sepulchre made < >
   ponderous stone,
   1896, 1904: stone,
10. 1864: same Stone, O Priest;
    (1869): same stone, O priest;
    1896, 1904: priest:
11. (1869): the holy One
12. 1896, 1904: east.
13. 1864: the Sepulchre
    (1869): the sepulchre
14. 1896, 1904: death:
15. 1864: the Stone if
    (1869): the stone if
17. 1864: God Almighty, He < > a Seal
    (1869): God Almighty, He < >
    a seal
    1896, 1904: God Almighty, He
18. 1864: a Stone;
    (1869): a stone,
    1896, 1904: stone:
20. 1864: [Below the stanza is a
    horizontal row of five spaced
    asterisks.]
    (1869): [Below the stanza is a
    horizontal row of three spaced
    asterisks.]
    1896, 1904: [There is no line below
    the stanza.]

24. 1864: hair:
25. 1864: Peter, Thomas, Mary
    Magdalene,
26. 1864: The Virgin Unreproved,
    (1869): The Virgin unreproved,
27. MS, 1896, 1904: Joseph and
    Nicodemus
    1864: Joseph with
    (1869): Joseph, with Nicodemus,
    foremost
28. 1864: the Well-beloved,
29. 1864: finest Linen and your Spice,
    (1869): finest linen and your spice,
30. (1869), 1896, 1904: the sacred
    Dead,
32. 1864: The Napkin round
    (1869): The napkin round His
    head;
    1896, 1904: round His head:
33. 1864: the Garden-rock to
    (1869): the garden-rock to
    1896, 1904: the garden-rock to rest:
35. (1869), 1896, 1904: The Sun that
    went
36. 1864: in Strength.
    (1869): in strength.
37. 1864: give Joy for
    (1869): give joy for
39. 1864: Lo! He with Joy shall
    (1869): Lo! He with joy shall < >
    again,
    1896, 1904: Lo He
40. 1864: bring His Sheaves.
    (1869): bring His sheaves.

COME UNTO ME.

[Composed February 23, 1864. Editions: 1896, 1904. The notebook MS is in the British Library. The poem was published in Orby Shipley (ed.), *Lyra Eucharistica: Hymns and Verses on the Holy Communion, Ancient and Modern; with Other Poems* (2nd ed.; London: Longman, Green, Longman, Roberts, and Green, 1864), 5. Basic text: notebook MS.]

Title. MS: Faint yet pursuing.
1. 1864: Oh, for <> by, when
2. 1864: Made His Yoke easy and His Burden light;
   1896, 1904: light!
4. 1896, 1904: Of altar spread <> awful Eucharist:
5. 1864: hopes His Promises sufficed, 1896, 1904: sufficed:
6. 1864: my Soul watched <> day, by night,
   1896, 1904: for Him, by day, by night:

7. 1864, 1896, 1904: lightened and
8. 1864: loss, except
   1896, 1904: the pearl unpriced.
9. 1864: Yet, since <> tender Call, 1896, 1904: Yet, since
10. 1896, 1904: remembers whom I
12. MS: For Hope to whoso runs holds forth a crown,
13. MS: And Faith the walls of Jericho cast down,
    1864: a Crown,
14. 1896, 1904: and Christ is all in

ASH WEDNESDAY.

[Composed March 21, 1859. Editions: 1896, 1904. The notebook MS is owned by Mrs. Geoffrey Dennis. The poem was published in Orby Shipley (ed.), *Lyra Eucharistica: Hymns and Verses on the Holy Communion, Ancient and Modern; with Other Poems* (2nd ed.; London: Longman, Green, Longman, Roberts, and Green, 1864), 355– 56. Basic text: notebook MS.]

Title. MS: [Above the title is written in pencil:] <X>
   1864: Jesus, do I love Thee?
   1896, 1904: ASH WEDNESDAY
3. 1896, 1904: sight,
4. 1864: in Heavenly Light
5. MS: [After line 5 are the following lines, deleted in pencil:]

   [*I have ofttimes knelt me;*
   But have seldom felt Thee
   Make my weakness might,
   Turn my wrong to right,
   Turn my black to white.]

   [In the right margin is written in pencil, perpendicular to the deleted lines:] <leave out> [In pencil is written horizontally between the words "leave" and "out":] <good>
6–9. MS: [Below the deleted lines are the following lines:]

Cherub throngs adore Thee,
Seraphs fall before Thee,
Angels and Archangels, Martyred hosts
   implore Thee:—

9. 1896, 1904: adore Thee.
10. 1864: Blessed She that <> Thee!
    1896, 1904: bore Thee!
11. 1896, 1904: the saints approve
12. 1896, 1904: the virgins love
14. 1896, 1904: hath cleansèd not,
16. 1896, 1904: In thy fruitful lot;
17. 1864: I, fig-tree fruit-unbearing;
    1896, 1904: I, fig-tree fruit-unbearing,
18. 1864, 1896, 1904: Thou, righteous Judge
21. 1864: sound—
    1896, 1904: sound,
22. 1864: Why <> ground?
23. MS: Thy [*l*]<L>ove with
24. 1864: Pleads—Give <> longer.
    1896, 1904: Pleads, "Give

26. 1864: Save Thou shall <> dew;
    1896, 1904: Save Thou shall
27. 1864: with Blood,
    1896, 1904: with blood
28. 1864: good?
29. 1864: Oh, by Thy Gifts that
    <> me,
30. MS: [After line 30 are the following
    lines:]

With Thy Love inflame me,
With Thy Sweetness brim me,
With Thine Arms surround me,
With Thy Goodness crown me,
With Thy Spirit guide me,
With Thy Presence hide me.

    1896, 1904: me.
32. 1864: love Thee;
34. 1864: Love me, and

SPRING FANCIES.

[Part I composed in 1847; Parts II and III composed June 29, 1858. Editions: 1896, 1904 (Parts II and III only). The notebook MS of Part I (MS1), in the handwriting of Christina's sister, Maria Francesca Rossetti, is in the Bodleian Library. A fair copy of Part I (MS2) is in the Princeton University Library. The notebook MS of Parts II and III (MS3) is in the British Library. The poem was published in *Macmillan's Magazine*, XI (April, 1865), 460. Part I is printed in *The Prince's Progress and Other Poems* (1866) as "Spring Quiet"; for text and notes to that poem, see Volume I of the present edition, pp. 120, 270. Basic text: Part I: MS2; Parts II and III: MS3. In the 1896 and 1904 editions, lines 39 and 41 are indented two spaces and line 44 is not indented.]

Title. MS1: The Spring-quiet. [To the
    left of the title is written in pencil:]
    <O / P>
    MS2: "Solitude"
    MS3: Today and Tomorrow.
    1896, 1904: TO-DAY AND
    TO-MORROW
I. MS1, MS2: [There is no section
    number.]
1. 1865: the winter,
2. 1865: the spring,
3. MS1: to the green-wood
    MS2: to the forest
4. MS1: sing:
5. MS1: <Ding a ding dingading>
    [The added line is written in pencil
    in Christina's hand.]
    1865: Ding-ding, ding-a-ding.
6. MS1: the myrtles <whitethorn>
    [The added word is written above
    the line in pencil in Christina's
    hand.]
7. MS1: Singeth the <a> thrush;
    [The added word is written above
    the line in pencil in Christina's
    hand.]
    MS2: Singeth a thrush,
8. MS1: Where the <a> robin [The

    added word is written above the
    line in pencil in Christina's hand.]
    MS2: And a robin
9. MS1: In the holly-bush;
    MS2: In the holly
10. MS1: <with his breast ablush>
    [The added line is written in pencil
    in Christina's hand.]
11–15. MS1, MS2: [Lines 11–15
    constitute the fourth stanza.]
11. MS1: of sweet <fresh> scents [The
    added word is written above the
    line in pencil in Christina's hand.]
12. MS1: the leafy <budding> boughs
    [The added word is written above
    the line in pencil in Christina's
    hand.]
    MS2: the leafy boughs,
13. MS1: Framing <Arching> high
    [The added word is written above
    the line in pencil in Christina's
    hand.]
    MS2: [*Framing*] Arching high
14. 1865: house,
15. MS1: <[illegible deletion] Where
    doves coo the arouse> [The added
    line is written in pencil in Christina's
    hand.]

16–20. MS1, MS2: [Lines 16–20
constitute the third stanza.]
16. MS1, MS2: Where the
18. MS1: [*Where*] <&> is heard
<[*scarce sounds*]> the murmur
<tumult> <an echo> [The
deletions are in pencil. The added
words are written above the line in
pencil in Christina's hand.]
MS2: And is heard an
19. MS1: sea.
20. MS1: <[illegible deletion] Tho' far
off it be.> [The added line is
written in pencil in Christina's
hand. Below the fourth stanza are
the following stanzas:]

Full of sweet scents
  And whispering air
That sayeth softly:
  "We spread no snare;
    <Here or anywhere> [The added
    line is written in pencil in
    Christina's hand.]

"Here dwell in safety,
  Here dwell alone,
With a clear stream
  And a mossy stone."
    <Here make your sad moan.> [The
    added line is written in pencil
    in Christina's hand.]

MS2: [Below the fourth stanza are
the following stanzas:]

Full of fresh scents,
  And whispering air
That sayeth softly:
  "We spread no snare
  "Here or anywhere.

"Here dwell in safety,
  "Here dwell alone,
"With a clear stream
  "And a mossy stone:
"Here make your sad moan.

Christina G. Rossetti

1865: Though far
II. MS3: 1.
1896, 1904: I
22. 1865: flower;
23. MS3: [*I have*] <she has> waited
weeks and weeks [The deletion is
in pencil. The added words are

written above the line in pencil in
Christina's hand. In the right
margin beside lines 23 and 24 is
written in pencil:] <3>
1896, 1904: Earth has waited weeks
and weeks
24. MS3: For this special hour: [Below
line 24 is a pencil line drawn to the
facing left page, on which are
written the following lines in pencil
in Christina's hand:]

<Faint the rainbow comes & goes
In a sunny shower>

1896, 1904: For this special hour:
25. MS3: [*Wake O rosy face and bloom*]
<Curly <headed> catkins
drop—> <[*die*]> [The deletions
are in pencil. The added words
are written in the right margin
in pencil in Christina's hand.]
1896, 1904: Faint the rainbow
comes and goes
26. MS3: [*From thy rosy bower.*] <In an
April shower—> [The deletion is
in pencil. The added words are
written in the right margin in
Christina's hand. Above the
additions to lines 25 and 26 is
written in pencil:] <2>
1896, 1904: On a sunny shower.
27. 1896, 1904: love:
29. MS3: and [*frog*] <[*fish*]> <frog>
[The deletions and additions are in
pencil in Christina's hand.]
30. MS3: To [*frog*] <[*fish*]> <frog>
among [The deletions are in pencil.
The added words are written above
the line in pencil in Christina's
hand.]
31. MS3: Wake, [*and whilst I tell my love*]
<O south wind sweet with spice>
[The deletion is in pencil. The
added words are written above the
line in pencil in Christina's hand.]
1865: Wake, O south-wind sweet
< > spice,
1896, 1904: spice,
32. MS3: [*Blush consenting blushes.*]
<Wake the rose to blushes> [The
deletion is in pencil. The added

words are written below the line in pencil in Christina's hand and retraced in pencil.]
33. MS3: [*All the world is full of change;*] [The deletion is in pencil.]
1896, 1904: Life breaks forth to right and left—
34. MS3: [*Tomorrow may be dreary.*] [The deletion is in pencil.]
1865: To morrow may
1896, 1904: Pipe wild-wood notes cheery.
35–38. MS3: [On the left facing page across from lines 33–34 is written in pencil in William Michael Rossetti's hand:] <Then to #> [At the top of the left facing page is written in pencil:] <#> [Below the sharp symbol are the following lines written in pencil in Christina's hand.]

<Life breaks forth, to right & left
Pipe [illegible erasure] <wild>
woodnotes cheery—
Nevertheless there lie the dead
Fast asleep & weary—>

35. MS3: [*All the world is stuffed with dead*] [The deletion is in pencil.]
1865: forth to <> left,
1896, 1904: Nevertheless there are the dead
36. MS3: [*Fast asleep and weary:*] [The deletion is in pencil.]
1865: the wood-notes cheery:
1896, 1904: Fast asleep and weary—
37. MS3: Today we live, today we love,
1896, 1904: To-day we live, to-day we love,
38. MS, 1896, 1904: Wake and listen, deary.
1865: weary.
III. MS3: 2.
1896, 1904: 2
39. MS3, 1896, 1904: I wish I were dead, my foe,
40. MS3, 1896, 1904: My friend, I wish I were dead,
41. MS3, 1896, 1904: at my tired
42. MS3, 1896, 1904: at my tired
43. MS3, 1896, 1904: the pleasant April
44. 1865: sing:
46. 1896, 1904: of Spring.

"LAST NIGHT."

[Composed probably between October, 1863, and January 15, 1864. Editions: 1896, 1904. The notebook MS is in the British Library. The poem was published in *Macmillan's Magazine*, XII (May, 1865), 48. In the MS, the title, lines 1–9, and lines 33–36 are missing from the notebook. Basic text: title, lines 1–9, and lines 33–36: 1865; lines 10–32: notebook MS. In the 1896 and 1904 texts, lines 1, 2, 4, 5, 8, 9, 10, 13, 16, 17, 18, 20, 21, 22, 24, 25, 26, 28, 29, 30, 32, 33, 34, and 36 are indented two spaces; and lines 3, 7, 11, 15, 19, 23, 27, 31, and 35 are indented four spaces.]

Title. 1896, 1904: LAST NIGHT
9. 1896, 1904: best, speak
11. MS: girls would cry
1865, 1896, 1904: bit,
12. MS: And declare they [Below the line is written in pencil in William Michael Rossetti's hand:] <Begin here>
13. MS: These have been [<*This*>] [<*h*>] <was a> pleasant days <time>, and the days <time> went fast; [The added words are written above the line in pencil in Christina's hand.]
14. MS: while they <it> lasted, but they <it> needn't [The added words are written above the line in pencil in Christina's hand.]
15. MS: [The line is not indented.]
1865, 1896, 1904: wax, and
17. 1865, 1896: me it was:
1904: you? To me it was:
19. MS: fades quite away,
20. MS: As sweet dew

1865, 1896, 1904: steams upward from
21. 1865, 1896, 1904: spring day or
23. 1865, 1896, 1904: oil,
24. MS: pains will relight [Following line 24 is the stanza constituting lines 29–32 of the published text. Below that stanza is the following stanza:]

Broken is broken while the world stands,
Gone is gone tho' one compass seas and lands [illegible end-of-line punctuation]
We shall meet often, but not as we met;

And shake hands, but not as today we loose hands.

[Following the above stanza is the stanza constituting lines 25–28 of the published text.]
25. 1865, 1896, 1904: you:
26. 1865, 1896, 1904: woo.
29. MS: We met first as strangers, we part friend from friend,
30. MS: Each to travel his own path <road> to his own end: [The added word is written above the line in pencil in Christina's hand.]
32. MS: In the quack who sets up
33. 1896, 1904: to Kate—
34. 1896, 1904: mate;

PETER GRUMP / FORSS

[Date of composition unknown. Editions: 1896, 1904. The poem was published in *Argosy*, I (January, 1866), 164, as part of the short story "Hero: A Metamorphosis," and reprinted in *Commonplace, and Other Short Stories* (London: F. S. Ellis, 1870), 209–10, and *Commonplace, A Tale of To-day; and Other Stories* (Boston: Roberts Brothers, 1870), 209–10. Basic text: 1870. In the 1870 text, line 11 is indented two spaces. In the 1896 and 1904 texts, line 10 is not indented and lines 11–15 are indented six spaces. In the 1896s text, lines 8, 11, 12, 14, 16, 18, and 19 are indented four spaces; line 10 is not indented; and lines 13, 15, and 17 are indented six spaces.]

Title. 1896, 1904: FATHER AND LOVER
1. 1896, 1904: [Above line 1 is printed:] FATHER
4. 1896, 1904: Oh would <> there!

9. 1896, 1904: [Above line 9 is printed:] LOVER
19. 1896, 1904: Any more? never more.

HELEN GREY.

[Composed February 23, 1863. Editions: 1896, 1904. The notebook MS is in the British Library. The poem was published in *Macmillan's Magazine*, XIII (March, 1866), 375. Basic text: notebook MS.]

Title. 1866, 1896, 1904: HELEN GREY
2. 1866, 1896, 1904: pout,
3. 1866, 1896, 1904: about,
4. 1866, 1896, 1904: frown, and
8. 1866: wit; you may, perhaps. 1896, 1904: wit; you
9. MS: you're comely, Helen
12. 1866, 1896, 1904: way;

14. 1866: all:
15. 1866, 1896, 1904: heed, you
18. MS: a lower <lowlier> place; [The added word is written above the line in pencil in Christina's hand.] 1866, 1896, 1904: down, and <> place,
19. 1866, 1896, 1904: down, to

IF.

[Composed April 12, 1864. Editions: 1896, 1904. The notebook MS is in the British Library. The poem was published in *Argosy*, I (March, 1866), 336. In the 1904 edition, William Michael Rossetti notes of the poem, "It was afterwards reprinted with the title which I give, sanctioned (I presume) by my sister" (p. 484). Basic text: notebook MS. In the 1896 and 1904 texts, lines 4, 14, 16, 18, 20, 22, and 24 are indented four spaces; and lines 9, 17, 21, and 23 are indented two spaces.]

Title. 1866: IF.
  1896: IF
  1904: HOPING AGAINST HOPE
1. 1866, 1896, 1904: come to-day,
  to-day, to-day,
2. 1866: O, what < > day to-day
  would be!
  1896, 1904: be!
5. 1866: O, little bird, flying, flying,
  flying
  1896, 1904: bird, flying, flying,
  flying
12. 1866, 1896, 1904: him, my love,
  my love!
13. 1866, 1896, 1904: is so cold, so cold,
14. MS: While I [*am*] <sit> here
  1866, 1896, 1904: alone;

15. MS: not like <live> to [The added word is written above the line in pencil in Christina's hand.]
  1866, 1896, 1904: old,
18. 1866, 1896, 1904: lying:
19. MS: [*Perhaps*] <&> he < > come and look <may> [The deletion is in pencil. The added words are written above the line in pencil in Christina's hand.]
  1866, 1896, 1904: dead—
21. 1866, 1896, 1904: two, with < > it,
22. MS: And <&> on [The added word is written above the line in pencil in Christina's hand.]
23. 1866, 1896, 1904: comes, I < > it,

SEASONS. ["OH THE CHEERFUL BUDDING-TIME"]

[Composed January 20, 1863. Editions: 1896, 1904. The notebook MS is in the British Library. The poem was published in *Macmillan's Magazine*, XV (December, 1866), 168–69. Basic text: notebook MS.]

Title. 1866: SEASONS.
  1896, 1904: SEASONS
1. MS: cheerful bud[*i*]<d>ing-time
  1866, 1896, 1904: cheerful
  Budding-time!
2. 1866, 1896, 1904: green,
4. MS: their win[*d*]<t>er screen:
  1866, 1896, 1904: screen;
5. 1866: and "baa,"
7. 1866: Vigorous Nature laughs "Ha, ha,"
  1896, 1904: Vigorous Nature laughs "Ha ha!"
8. 1896, 1904: of Spring.
9. 1866, 1896, 1904: gorgeous
  Blossom-days!
10. 1866, 1896: blow,

11. 1866: in summer-blaze
  1896, 1904: in Summer-blaze
12. 1866, 1896, 1904: Dragon-flies
  flash < > fro;
13. 1896, 1904: keys;
17. 1866, 1896, 1904: shouting
  Harvest-weeks!
18. 1866: Mother earth grown < >
  sheaves
19. 1866, 1896, 1904: seeks;
20. 1866, 1896, 1904: Russet-golden
  pomp
25. 1866: starving Winter-lapse!
  1896, 1904: starving Winter lapse!
26. 1866: dim;
  1896, 1904: hunger-pinched,
  and dim;

27. 1866, 1896, 1904: roots recall their
28. 1896, 1904: grim.
31. MS: windingsheet [The end

punctuation is erased.]
1866, 1896, 1904: a winding-sheet,

HENRY HARDIMAN

[Date of composition unknown. The poem was published in the *Churchman's Shilling Magazine and Family Treasury*, I (May, 1867), 292, as part of the short story "The Waves of this Troublesome World: a Tale of Hastings Ten Years ago," and reprinted in *Commonplace, and Other Short Stories* (London: F. S. Ellis, 1870), 302, and *Commonplace, A Tale of To-day; and Other Stories* (Boston: Roberts Brothers, 1870), 302. Basic text: 1870.]

Title. 1867: "HENRY
    1870: 'HENRY

4. 1867: pain."
  1870: pain.'

WITHIN THE VEIL.

[Composed December 13, 1861. Editions: 1896, 1904. The notebook MS is in the British Library. The poem was published in Orby Shipley (ed.), *Lyra Messianica: Hymns and Verses on the Life of Christ, Ancient and Modern; with Other Poems* (2nd ed.; London: Longmans, Green, and Co., 1869), 393. Basic text: notebook MS.]

Title. MS: One Day.
    1896, 1904: WITHIN THE VEIL
2. MS: Where the ranks
    1869: stand,
    1896, 1904: stand:
4. MS: hair [*comes*] <falls> sweeping
    [The deletion is in pencil. The
    added word is written below the
    line in pencil in Christina's hand.]
    1869: down;

5. 1869, 1896, 1904: brown,
8. MS: [*Sweet*] <Good> to <> and
    [*fair*] <good> to [The deletions
    are in pencil. The added words are
    written above the line in pencil in
    Christina's hand.]
    1869, 1896, 1904: see:
9. 1869: me;
11. MS: not yet half blown
    1869: blown,

PARADISE: IN A SYMBOL.

[Composed November 14, 1864. Editions: 1896, 1904. The notebook MS is in the British Library. The poem was published in Orby Shipley (ed.), *Lyra Messianica: Hymns and Verses on the Life of Christ, Ancient and Modern; with Other Poems* (2nd ed.; London: Longmans, Green, and Co., 1869), 417–18. Basic text: notebook MS. In the 1896 and 1904 texts, lines 7, 9, 10, 15, 19, 25, 27, 29, and 31 are indented two spaces; and lines 8 and 12 are indented four spaces.]

Title. MS: Birds of Paradise. [To the
    left of the title is written in
    pencil:] <X>
    1896, 1904: BIRDS OF PARADISE

5. 1896, 1904: tongue—
6. MS: Windy-winged they
    1896, 1904: Song of songs—they
7. MS: to other calling,

9. MS: to other calling
1896: calling,
12. MS: High out
13. MS: The wings of fire emitted
sparks
14. MS: a [*measured*] <cadenced>
clang, [The added word is in pencil
in Christina's hand.]
1896, 1904: clang:
15. MS: The silver
16. MS: The golden
1896, 1904: rang;
17. 1869, 1896, 1904: whistled through
their

18. 1869: in Heaven they
19. MS: They wheeled and they
flashed out
21. 1869: Mounting, mounting,
mounting
1896, 1904: Mounting, mounting,
mounting still,
22. 1869: skies—
25. 1869: not,
30. MS: best.
1896, 1904: best:—
35. 1869, 1896, 1904: dwell,

"IN JULY / NO GOODBYE"

Date of composition unknown. The poem is part of the short story "Commonplace."
The notebook MS of "Commonplace," dated April, 1870, is in the Princeton University Library. The poem was published in *Commonplace, and Other Short Stories* (London: F. S. Ellis, 1870), 54, and *Commonplace, A Tale of To-day; and Other Stories* (Boston: Roberts Brothers, 1870), 54. Basic text: notebook MS.]

1. MS: "In
1870: 'In
2. 1870: No good-bye;

3. 1870: In August
4. MS: must."
1870: must.'

"LOVE HATH A NAME OF DEATH"

[Date of composition unknown. Editions: 1896, 1904. The poem is part of the short story "Commonplace." The notebook MS of "Commonplace," dated April, 1870, is in the Princeton University Library. The poem was published in *Commonplace, and Other Short Stories* (London: F. S. Ellis, 1870), 79, and *Commonplace, A Tale of To-day; and Other Stories* (Boston: Roberts Brothers, 1870), 79. Basic text: notebook MS. In the 1896 and 1904 texts, lines 2, 3, 5, 6, 7, and 8 are indented two spaces.]

Title. 1896, 1904: LOVE'S NAME
1. 1870: 'Love

4. 1870, 1896, 1904: we, beneath
<> sway,
8. 1870: away.'

"TU SCENDI DALLE STELLE, O RE DEL CIELO"

[Date of composition unknown. The poem is part of the short story "Vanna's Twins," which was published in *Commonplace, and Other Short Stories* (London: F. S. Ellis, 1870), 230, and *Commonplace, A Tale of To-day; and Other Stories* (Boston: Roberts Brothers, 1870), 230. Basic text: 1870.]

1. 1870: 'Tu

6. 1870: amato.'

"ALAS MY LORD"

[Date of composition unknown. Editions: 1904. The poem was published in *Annus Domini: A Prayer for Each Day of the Year, Founded on a Text of Holy Scripture* (London and Oxford: James Parker and Co., 1874), ix–xii. Christina's own copy of the book, containing her holograph addition of lines 19–21, is in the Princeton University Library. Basic text: 1874 (Christina's copy).]

Title. 1904: WRESTLING
2. 1904: the live- / long night
3. 1904: With Thee my God, my strength and my delight?
6. 1904: make Thy face of mercy shine
9. 1904: wonted love, when
11. 1904: about Thine arm, out- / stretcht and
14. 1904: the clenchèd hand
15. 1904: prevailed and
17. 1904: of heaven: he < > again,
18. 1904: lo Thy blessing fell
19–21. 1874 (Christina's copy): [In the left margin is written perpendicular to the text the following stanza in Christina's hand, with a line pointing to the space below line 18:]

<Gulped by the fish,
As by the pit, lost Jonah made his moan;
And Thou forgavest, waiting to atone.>

19. 1904: Gulpt by < > fish
20. 1904: And by < > moan,
28. 1904: Yea Thou
29. 1904: garden prayed,
30. 1904: while like < > wax Thy
32. 1904: faints despite Thy pattern, King of Saints!
33. 1904: Alas alas for me the < > faints!
35. 1904: fast until < > hear Thy voice,
36. 1904: know who hearing it rejoice.
39. 1904: Full fountain of all rapture and all grace.
40. 1904: But, when
41. 1904: made darkness, and
42. 1904: fast and

AN ALPHABET.

[Date of composition unknown. Editions: 1896, 1904. Basic text: 1896. The 1896 text contains the following note to the poem: "This was printed in 1875, with some woodcuts, in some magazine; the headline of the pages is *For Very Little Folks*, which may or may not be the title of the magazine itself. It must be an American publication, as the verses are headed *An Alphabet from England*" (p. 386).]

20. 1904: in July
27. 1896, 1904: is a nut—in
    1896s: is a Nut—in
39. 1904: for Tea

45. 1904: water-bred Whale—
50. 1904: is the Yacca, the
51. 1904: a Zebra, zigzaggèd his

HUSBAND AND WIFE.

[Composed July 12, 1865. Editions: 1896, 1904. The notebook MS (MS1) is in the British Library. A fair copy MS (MS2) is in the Princeton University Library. The poem was published in *A Masque of Poets. Including Guy Vernon, A Novelette in Verse.* No Name Series (Boston: Roberts Brothers, 1878), 42–43. Basic text: MS2.]

Title MS1: [Above the title is written in pencil in Christina's hand:] <No name published in "A Masque of Poets"—C.> [In pencil in the right margin below the title is written:] <X>
MS2: Husband & Wife.
1878: HUSBAND AND WIFE.

2. 1896, 1904: To <> sorrow:
3. 1896, 1904: Oh <> part,
4. MS1, MS2: "For we mayn't meet
   1896, 1904: For we mayn't meet
5. MS1, MS2, 1896, 1904: to force
   your
6. 1896, 1904: And <> life:
7. MS1: part
   1896, 1904: But <> part
8. 1896, 1904: Because
9. MS2: turned her head & tossed
   1896, 1904: tossed her head,
11. MS1: she:
13. MS1, 1896, 1904: "Though I'm
    MS2: might & right
14. 1896, 1904: And
15. MS1: she:
    MS2: never [*kissed*] <loved> you
    1896, 1904: I
18. MS1: and [*glum,*] <dumb,>
    MS2: crossed & dumb
    1896, 1904: dumb,
20. MS1: the stormwinds come.
    1896, 1904: the storm-winds come.

21. MS2: month & day
22. 1878: morn;
23. MS1, 1878, 1896, 1904: leaves,
24. MS1, 1896: lambs been born,
    1878: born,
    1904: lambs been born;
25. 1878: flowers,
28. MS2: white & cold
30. 1896, 1904: Once <> die:
31. 1896, 1904: And
32. 1896, 1904: To
33. 1896, 1904: And <> husband,
    when
34. MS1: "Safe back from
    1896, 1904: Safe back from
35. 1896, 1904: To
36. 1896, 1904: If
38. 1878: vow,
    1896, 1904: Or <> vow,
39. 1896, 1904: But
40. MS2: now.
    1896, 1904: I

MICHAEL F. M. ROSSETTI.

[Composed probably between January 24, 1883, and February 17, 1883. Editions: 1896, 1904. A fair copy MS is owned by Mrs. Geoffrey Dennis. The poem was published in *Athenaeum*, No. 2886 (February 17, 1883), 214. Basic text: fair copy MS. In the MS, below the text of the poem is Christina's signature (Christina G. Rossetti.). In the 1883 text, the poem is printed continuously as one piece divided only by stanza breaks, and below the last line of the poem is printed "Christina G. Rossetti." In the 1896 text, lines 2, 6, 7, 13, 14, 17, 18, 21, 22, 24, 25, 28, and 29 are indented two spaces; lines 4, 8, 15, 19, 23, and 27 are indented four spaces; and lines 10 and 31 are indented six spaces. In the 1896s text, lines 1, 12, 16, 20, 24, 25, 28, and 29 are indented two spaces; lines 2, 4, 6, 8, 15, 19, and 23 are indented six spaces; and lines 5, 7, 13, 14, 17, 18, 21, 22, 27, and 31 are indented four spaces. In the 1904 text, lines 1, 6, 8, 13, 14, 17, 18, 21, 22, 24, 25, 28, and 29 are indented two spaces; and lines 4, 10, 15, 19, 23, 27, and 31 are indented four spaces.]

Title. MS: Michael
Subtitle. MS: *April,* <22.> Born 1881
—— Died 1883. *January,* <24.>
[The additions are written above
the line.]
1896, 1904: Born 22 April 1881;
Died 24 January 1883.
1. 1896, 1904: [Above the line is
   printed:] I
2. 1883, 1896, 1904: word;

3. MS: lofty [illegible deletion]
   <dome>
5. 1896, 1904: [Above the line is
   printed:] 2
6. 1883, 1896, 1904: fled;
9. 1883, 1896: her looking-glass:—
   1904: her looking- / glass:—
12. 1896, 1904: [Above the line is
    printed:] 3
13. 1896, 1904: Alas my

15. 1896, 1904: [No stanza break
 follows the line.]
18. 1896, 1904: Pear-trees will
19. 1896, 1904: [No stanza break
 follows the line.]
22. 1883, 1896, 1904: shoot,

24. 1896, 1904: [Above the line is
 printed:] 4
25. 1883, 1896, 1904: fold,
27. 1883: cold:
 1896, 1904: [No stanza break
 follows the line.]

A SICK CHILD'S MEDITATION

[William Michael Rossetti dates the poem *"Circa* 1885." Editions: 1904. In the 1904 edition, William Michael Rossetti notes of the poem: "Comes from a little Church serial named *New and Old"* (p. 476). I was unable to locate the *New and Old* text of the poem. Basic text: 1904.]

"LOVE IS ALL HAPPINESS, LOVE IS ALL BEAUTY"

[Composed February 24, 1847. Editions: 1904. The notebook MS, in the handwriting of Christina's sister, Maria Francesca Rossetti, is in the Bodleian Library. The poem was published in *Time Flies: A Reading Diary* (London: Society for Promoting Christian Knowledge, 1885), 34, and *Time Flies: A Reading Diary* (Boston: Roberts Brothers, 1886), 48. Basic text: 1885 (Christina's copy). The poem originally formed the last stanza of a poem entitled "Praise of Love," which Christina never published as such. "Praise of Love" is presented in its own right in Part III of the present volume. In the MS, line 5 is indented four spaces. In the 1904 text, no lines are indented.]

Title. 1904: LOVE
 1. MS: happiness, Love is
 2. 1904: hoary;
 3. 1904: duty;

 4. MS: And Love is < > story,
 1904: story,
 5. MS: And leads to endless

"A HANDY MOLE WHO PLIED NO SHOVEL"

[Date of composition unknown. Editions: 1904. The poem was published in *Time Flies: A Reading Diary* (London: Society for Promoting Christian Knowledge, 1885), 40–41, and *Time Flies: A Reading Diary* (Boston: Roberts Brothers, 1886), 55–56. Christina's copy of the English edition, containing her holograph marginalia, is in the University of Texas Humanities Research Center. Basic text: 1885 (Christina's copy).]

Title. 1904: MOLE AND
 EARTHWORM
 1. 1904: handy Mole, who
 3. 1904: in mid- / furrow
 5. 1904: dined, and
 8. 1904: a Worm of
 9. 1904: The Mole turned-on his
 < > eye,

 10. 1904: by.
 11. 1904: The Worm, entrenched < >
 blindness,
 12. 1904: unkindness.
 13. 1904: tunnel,
 15. 1904: plough, its < > pursuing,

"ONE SWALLOW DOES NOT MAKE A SUMMER."

[Date of composition unknown. Editions: 1904. The poem was published in *Time Flies: A Reading Diary* (London: Society for Promoting Christian Knowledge, 1885), 85, and *Time Flies: A Reading Diary* (Boston: Roberts Brothers, 1886), 107–108. Christina's copy of the English edition, containing her holograph marginalia, is in the University of Texas Humanities Research Center. Basic text: 1885 (Christina's copy). In the 1885 text, the opening quotation marks in line 3 extend into the left margin. In the 1904 text, lines 1, 2, 3, 5, 6, 7, 8, 9, and 11 are indented two spaces; and lines 4, 10, and 13 are indented four spaces.]

Title. 1904: ONE SWALLOW DOES   9. 1904: main,
     NOT MAKE A SUMMER   10. 1904: And Winter's woe
 1. 1886: A rose which   11. 1904: glad Summer come
    1904: A rose which < > one Swallow   12. 1904: shore,—
 3. 1904: follow':

"CONTEMPTUOUS OF HIS HOME BEYOND"

[Date of composition unknown. Editions: 1904. The poem was published in *Time Flies: A Reading Diary* (London: Society for Promoting Christian Knowledge, 1885), 129–30, and *Time Flies: A Reading Diary* (Boston: Roberts Brothers, 1886), 159–60. Basic text: 1885 (Christina's copy).]

Title. 1904: A FROG'S FATE   13. 1886: broadwheeled wagon
 2. 1904: and the village-pond,   unawares
 3. 1886: each byway,   1904: A broad-wheeled waggon
    1904: byeway   16. 1904: broke:—
 6. 1904: a Frog.   18. 1904: all!
 7. 1904: yet,   19. 1904: to fame turns < > way;
 8. 1904: wet: 20. 1904: on the hideous highway;
 9. 1904: The night-dew, when < >   21. 1886: familiar byway!"
    come,   22. 1904: gone;
10. 1904: travelled Frog would   23. 1886: The wagoner strode
12. 1885: [Since line 12 is the last line   1904: The Waggoner strode
    on the page, the stanza break that   25. 1886: that wagoner strode on,—
    follows it is an editorial assumption.]   1904: that Waggoner strode on—
    1886: [No stanza break follows the   27. 1904: 'A froggy would < > go.'
    line.]   28. 1904: he,
    1904: more: not [No stanza break   31. 1904: all.
    follows the line.]   32. 1904: mangled Frog abides
                        33. 1904: frog:

A WORD FOR THE DUMB.

[Date of composition unknown. Editions: 1896, 1904. An undated MS letter from Christina to her brother Dante Gabriel Rossetti containing the poem is in the library of the University of British Columbia. The poem was published in *Time Flies: A Reading Diary* (London: Society for Promoting Christian Knowledge, 1885), 138, and *Time Flies: A Reading Diary* (Boston: Roberts Brothers, 1886), 169. Basic text: MS letter.]

Title. MS: <[*A Poor Old Dog.*]> [The
title is added and deleted in
pencil.]
1896, 1904: A POOR OLD DOG
1. 1885, 1886: old dog,
   1896, 1904: old dog
2. 1885: tail a begging in <> need;
   1886, 1896, 1904: need;
3. MS: not [illegible deletion] even
   1885, 1886, 1896, 1904: a frog,
4. MS: too, & that's
   1885, 1886, 1896, 1904: plead;
5. MS: us dozing on
   1885, 1886: Spare puss, who <>
   us, purring <> hearth;
   1896: Spare puss who <> us

dozing on <> hearth;
1904: Spare puss who <> hearth;
6. MS: once so [*merry*] <frisky> & so
   [The deletion is in pencil. The
   added word is written above the
   line in pencil.]
   1885, 1886, 1896, 1904: Spare
   bunny, once <> free;
7. MS: harmless creatures on the
   1885, 1886: earth;
   1896, 1904: harmless creatures
   of the
8. MS: Spare, & be
   1885, 1886: Spare and <>
   spared,—or
   1896, 1904: spared—or

CARDINAL NEWMAN.

[Date of composition unknown. Editions: 1896, 1904. No MS known. The poem was
published in *Athenaeum*, No. 3276 (August 16, 1890), 225. Basic text: 1890.]

Opening quotation. 1896: In <> goest
1904: In <> grave whither <>
goest.

3. 1896, 1904: thy sowing-day, rest
5. 1896, 1904: Yea take
7. 1896, 1904: were spring-tides, set

AN ECHO FROM WILLOWWOOD.

[Date of composition unknown. Editions: 1896, 1904. A fair copy MS, signed
"Christina G. Rossetti," is in the University of Texas Humanities Research Center.
The poem was published in *Magazine of Art*, XIII (September, 1890), 385. A print-
ing of the poem containing Christina's holograph corrections and dated by her
"18/9/88" is in the University of Texas Humanities Research Center; it is desig-
nated "1888" in the textual notes. Basic text: fair copy MS. The 1890 text is in italic
print and is accompanied by a woodcut by C. Ricketts. In the MS, line 11 is indented
two spaces and line 14 is not indented. In the 1888 text, lines 11 and 14 are indented
two spaces and line 13 is not indented.]

Title. 1888: [Above the title is printed:]
Art. Mag. [In the top margin is
written in pencil in Christina's
hand:] <Press>
1890: WILLOWWOOD
1896, 1904: FROM
WILLOW-WOOD
Opening quotation. 1888, 1890: in
willowwood."
1896: in willow-wood."
1904: O <> in willow-wood.

1. MS: he gazed & she,
2. MS: Not hand in hand yet heart in
   heart I
3. MS: Pale & reluctant <> brink
5. MS: she & he,
6. MS: up & sink,
9. 1888: below—
10. MS: for each
    1888: [In the left margin are written
    the words:] <Set back> [The
    words are followed by a wavy

vertical line. Lines 11, 13, and 14
contain holograph brackets
indicating the desired indentation.]
11. MS: Resolute & reluctant
    1888: speech—
12. 1896, 1904: flow,
14. MS: joined, & ah!
    1888: [In vertical lines below the

poem is written in pencil in
Christina's hand:] <Dear Sir /
Everything which depends / on *you*
perfect. / Sincerely yours / CGR- /
18/9/88— / 30 Torrington Sq- /
W.C.>
1896, 1904: ah were

"YEA, I HAVE A GOODLY HERITAGE."

[Date of composition unknown. Editions: 1896, 1904. The poem was published in
Atalanta, IV (October, 1890), [3]. Basic text: 1890. The 1890 text contains a facsimile
of Christina's signature (Christina G. Rossetti) between the title and text of the poem.]

Title. 1896, 1904: YEA I <>
   HERITAGE
5. 1896, 1904: Or, if
7. 1896, 1904: Or, if

8. 1896, 1904: grace.—
10. 1896, 1904: Nay who
11. 1896, 1904: For, though thy

A DEATH OF A FIRST-BORN.

[Composed January 14, 1892. Editions: 1896, 1904. The poem was published in *Literary Opinion*, VII (February, 1892), [227]. Lines 5–8 are printed in E[leanor] V[ere]
B[oyle] (ed.), *A Book of Heavenly Birthdays* (Chicago: A. C. McClurg and Co., [1893]),
23. Basic text: 1892. In the 1892 text, Christina's signature (Christina G. Rossetti) is
reproduced below the text of the poem. In the 1893 text, all the words are printed
in capital letters.]

Title. 1893: [untitled]
   1896, 1904: A DEATH OF A
   FIRST-BORN
Date below title. 1896: 14 January
   1892
   1904: (14 *January* 1892.)

5. 1893: KNELL; —HOPE
   1896, 1904: knell: Hope hears
7. 1896, 1904: Faith, Hope, and
   Love, make
9. 1896, 1904: us, Christ, sole
   consolation,
11. 1896, 1904: all Thy nation

"FAINT, YET PURSUING." / 1.

[Date of composition unknown. Editions: 1896, 1904. The poem was published in
Literary Opinion, II (May, 1892), 67. A facsimile of the proof, with Christina's hand-
written corrections, is in Mackenzie Bell, *Christina Rossetti: A Biographical and Critical
Study* (London: Hurst and Blackett, 1898), 132. Basic text: 1898 (facsimile of the
proof). In the 1898 text, lines 11, 12, and 14 are indented two spaces.]

Title. 1896, 1904: FAINT YET
   PURSUING / I
3. 1896, 1904: be.

6. 1896, 1904: to be through life-long
   scathe.
7. 1896, 1904: while Hope leans on
   Charity,

8. 1896, 1904: while Charity heartens
Faith:
9–14. 1898: [In the left margin is
written in Christina's hand:] <Please
in & out / last 6 lines:—> [The
dash extends into the space
between lines 8 and 9.] / <1
      2
      3
      4
      5
      6>

10. 1898: [The line is missing from the
text. A horizontal line is inserted
between lines 9 and 11 with carets
indicating the left and right
margins, and in the right margin
perpendicular to the text is added
in Christina's hand:] <One while
that ends not and that wearies
not,>
11. 1896, 1904: same.
14. 1896, 1904: tearful Charity to
Love's own

"FAINT, YET PURSUING." / 2.

[Date of composition unknown. Editions: 1896, 1904. The poem was published in *Literary Opinion*, II (May, 1892), 67. A facsimile of the proof, with Christina's hand-written corrections, is in Mackenzie Bell, *Christina Rossetti: A Biographical and Critical Study* (London: Hurst and Blackett, 1898), 132. Basic text: 1898 (facsimile of the proof). In the 1898 text, lines 4, 9, 11, and 14 are indented two spaces, and lines 3 and 10 are not indented.]

Title. 1896: FAINT YET PURSUING
/ II
1904: FAINT YET PURSUING
1–14. 1898: [In the left margin is
written in Christina's hand:]
1
  2
  3
4
5
  6
  7
8
9
  10
    11
  12
13
  14

3. 1896, 1904: desire,
6. 1898: will <∧> me [To the right of
the line is written in Christina's
hand a caret enclosing a comma.]
8. 1898: love <∧> [In the right
margin is written a circle enclosing
a period.]
1896, 1904: on to Love.
9. 1898: golden [*h*]ill, [The deletion
consists of a vertical line through
the letter. To the right of the word
is written in Christina's hand:]
<s/>

"WHAT WILL IT BE, O MY SOUL, WHAT WILL IT BE"

[Date of composition unknown. Editions: 1904. The poem was published in *The Face of the Deep: A Devotional Commentary on the Apocalypse* (London: Society for Promoting Christian Knowledge; New York: E. and J. B. Young and Co., 1892), 35. Basic text: 1892.]

Title. 1904: WHAT WILL IT BE?
1. 1904: soul, what will it be,

4. 1904: revive and rejoice, to rejoice
and to rest?

"LORD, THOU ART FULNESS, I AM EMPTINESS"

[Date of composition unknown. Editions: 1904. The poem was published in *The Face of the Deep: A Devotional Commentary on the Apocalypse* (London: Society for Promoting Christian Knowledge; New York: E. and J. B. Young and Co., 1892), 36. Basic text: 1892.]

Title. 1904: SPEECHLESS
1. 1904: art fullness, I

2. 1904: speechlessness,

"O LORD, I CANNOT PLEAD MY LOVE OF THEE"

[Date of composition unknown. Editions: 1904. The poem was published in *The Face of the Deep: A Devotional Commentary on the Apocalypse* (London: Society for Promoting Christian Knowledge; New York: E. and J. B. Young and Co., 1892), 84. Basic text: 1892. In the 1904 text, line 2 is indented two spaces.]

Title. 1904: PLEADING

2. 1904: plead Thy Love of me:—

"FAITH AND HOPE ARE WINGS TO LOVE"

[Date of composition unknown. The poem was published in *The Face of the Deep: A Devotional Commentary on the Apocalypse* (London: Society for Promoting Christian Knowledge; New York: E. and J. B. Young and Co., 1892), 198. Basic text: 1892.]

A SORROWFUL SIGH OF A PRISONER

[Date of composition unknown. Editions: 1904. The poem was published in *The Face of the Deep: A Devotional Commentary on the Apocalypse* (London: Society for Promoting Christian Knowledge; New York: E. and J. B. Young and Co., 1892), 224. Basic text: 1892.]

2. 1904: dead.

"I SIT A QUEEN, AND AM NO WIDOW, AND SHALL SEE NO SORROW"

[Date of composition unknown. Editions: 1904. The poem was published in *The Face of the Deep: A Devotional Commentary on the Apocalypse* (London: Society for Promoting Christian Knowledge; New York: E. and J. B. Young and Co., 1892), 417. Basic text: 1892. In the 1892 text, the opening quotation marks in line 1 extend into the left margin.]

Title. 1904: SCARLET
1. 1904: sorrow.'
2. 1892: woman, to-day: but < > all to-morrow.
1904: Yea, Scarlet Woman, to-day, but

3. 1892: all to-day without
1904: Scarlet Queen on
4. 1892: thee: to-day must < > of to-morrow.
1904: thee—to-day must end, there

"PASSING AWAY THE BLISS"

[Date of composition unknown. Editions: 1904. The poem was published in *The Face of the Deep: A Devotional Commentary on the Apocalypse* (London: Society for Promoting Christian Knowledge; New York: E. and J. B. Young and Co., 1892), 448. Basic text: 1892. In the 1892 text, the stanzas are printed side by side in a double column. In the 1904 text, lines 3 and 7 are indented eight spaces, and lines 4 and 8 are indented ten spaces.]

Title. 1904: TO-MORROW

"LOVE BUILDS A NEST ON EARTH AND WAITS FOR REST"

[Date of composition unknown. Editions: 1904. The poem was published in *The Face of the Deep: A Devotional Commentary on the Apocalypse* (London: Society for Promoting Christian Knowledge; New York: E. and J. B. Young and Co., 1892), 513. Basic text: 1892.]

Title. 1904: HOMEWARDS			4. 1904: testifies, 'God's will is

"JESUS ALONE:—IF THUS IT WERE TO ME"

[Date of composition unknown. Editions: 1904. The poem was published in *The Face of the Deep: A Devotional Commentary on the Apocalypse* (London: Society for Promoting Christian Knowledge; New York: E. and J. B. Young and Co., 1892), 549. Basic text: 1892. In the 1904 text, lines 2, 5, and 8 are indented two spaces.]

Title. 1904: ALL THINGS

THE WAY OF THE WORLD

[Date of composition unknown. Editions: 1896, 1904. An undated fair copy MS, signed "Christina G. Rossetti," is in the University of Texas Humanities Research Center. The poem was published in *The Magazine of Art*, XVII (July, 1894), 304. Basic text: fair copy MS. The 1894 text is in italic print; and lines 2, 4, 6, and 8 are indented four spaces, and line 7 is indented two spaces.]

Title. 1896, 1904: THE WAY OF THE			1. 1894, 1896, 1904: sea,
  WORLD			5. 1894, 1896, 1904: sea,

BOOKS IN THE RUNNING BROOKS.

[Composed August 26, 1852. Editions: 1896, 1904. The notebook MS is in the Bodleian Library. Basic text: notebook MS. In the 1896 edition, William Michael Rossetti states: "This was printed in some magazine; I know neither the name nor the date of the latter" (p. 380). In the MS, line 10 is indented eight spaces. In the 1896 and 1904 texts, lines 7, 8, 18, 19, 28, 30, 38, 39, 48, 50, 57, and 60 are indented two spaces, and lines 10, 20, 40, and 58 are indented four spaces; line 9 is not indented.]

Title. MS: After a picture in the
Portland Gallery.
1. MS: It < > enough, enough, she
<one> said, [The added word is
written above the line in pencil in
Christina's hand.]
3. MS: I see <spy> a [The added
word is written above the line in
pencil in Christina's hand.]
5. MS: hear the <merry> chime of
sweet Church bells [The added
word is written above the line in
pencil in Christina's hand.]
6. MS: hours.—
1896, 1904: hours."
7. MS: Soft [*falls*] <springs> the
8. 1896, 1904: ground,
11. MS: It < > enough; she
13. MS: I see <watch> a little <flitting>
tender [The added words are
written above the line in pencil in
Christina's hand.]
15. MS: A lamb is grazing <lark is
rising> in the [The added words
are written above the line in pencil
in Christina's hand.]
1896, 1904: grass,
16. MS: nigh.—
1896, 1904: nigh."
17. MS: the fount[illegible erasure]
<ain>
20. 1896, 1904: whitest May.
21. MS: Enough? she
22. MS: doubting: Is
23. 1896, 1904: fair,
24. 1896: O sweetest < > blow?
1904: blow?
25. 1896, 1904: enough—
26. MS: below.—
1896, 1904: below!"
27. MS: shadow trembleth
<stretcheth> [The added word is
written above the line in pencil in
Christina's hand.]
28. MS: On the waters pure;— <From
the hither shore> [The added
words are written in pencil in
Christina's hand below the line in
the margin along the bottom of
the page.]
29. MS: Must it o'ershadow them

<Th[*e*]<ose> waters darken>
[The added words are written in
pencil in Christina's hand above the
line in the margin along the top of
the page.]
1896, 1904: The waters
30. MS: For evermore? <More & more
& more.> [The added words are
written in pencil in Christina's
hand in the margin along the top
of the page.]
31. MS: It < > enough, she
32. MS: weary [*tone:*] <moan:> [The
deletion is in pencil. The added
word is written in pencil in
Christina's hand.]
1896, 1904: listless weary
33. MS: Enough, if <mi[*ng*]<x>ing>
with her [*loving*] friends; [The
deletion is in pencil. The added
word is written above the line in
pencil in Christina's hand.]
1896, 1904: friends:
34. MS: Enough, if
1896, 1904: alone;
35. MS: herself: Not
1896, 1904: enough
36. MS: atone?—
1896, 1904: atone?"
37. MS: cold deep <black> water<s>
[The added word is written above
the line in pencil in Christina's
hand. The added letter is written
in pencil in Christina's hand.]
38. 1896, 1904: there,
39. 1896, 1904: wave
41. MS: says: It < > enough,
43. MS: Enough, to
45. MS: Enough, she < > a want
<lack> [The added word is written
in the right margin in pencil in
Christina's hand.]
46. 1896, 1904: word.
47. MS: and troubled <turbid> [The
added word is written in the right
margin in pencil in Christina's
hand.]
48. 1896, 1904: pass,
50. 1896, 1904: Struggling through the
51. 1896, 1904: Ah will
52. MS: good and <or> ill [The added

word is written above the line in
pencil in Christina's hand.]
1896, 1904: When, calm < > ill,
53. MS: say: It
56. MS: blessed will.—
1896, 1904: blessed Will"?
58. 1896, 1904: rest,

59. MS: Fair <Clear> as [The added
word is written above the line in
pencil in Christina's hand.]
1896, 1904: the sun-track
60. MS: the [*gl*] [illegible erasure]
<purple> West.

GONE BEFORE

[Composed July 12, 1856. Editions: 1896, 1904. The notebook MS is in the British
Library. In the 1896 edition, William Michael Rossetti notes of the poem, "This was
printed in some magazine; I cannot now say which nor when" (p. 382). Basic text:
notebook MS. In the 1896 text, lines 5, 10, 15, 20, 25, and 30 are indented ten
spaces, and lines 8, 11, 12, 13, 16, 17, 18, 21, 22, 24, and 29 are indented two spaces.
In the 1904 text, lines 5, 10, 15, 20, 25, and 30 are indented six spaces, and lines 8,
11, 12, 13, 16, 17, 18, 21, 22, 24, and 29 are indented two spaces.]

Title. MS: "Till thou return."
1. 1896, 1904: rose when < > rarest,
2. 1896, 1904: lily when < > fairest,
3. 1896, 1904: violet sweetest
4. 1896, 1904: snow, cold < > blank,
6. MS: [To the right of the line is
written a cross in pencil.]
1896, 1904: days; she
7. MS: blossoms on the bough or
sweet syringa: [To the right of the
line is written in pencil a cross and
the words *"wont do"* in Dante
Gabriel Rossetti's hand.]

8. MS: she think windy < > more
fair than
17. 1896, 1904: there,—
1896s: there,
18. 1896, 1904: Though it
22. 1896, 1904: grieve, returning
27. 1896, 1904: you, though to < >
fleetest;
29. 1896, 1904: Only, love, I < > you,
30. 1896, 1904: Heart-pierced through
and through.

THE DEAD CITY.

[Composed April 9, 1847. Editions: 1896, 1904. The notebook MS, in the handwrit-
ing of Christina's sister, Maria Francesca Rossetti, is in the Bodleian Library. The
poem was printed in *Verses: Dedicated to Her Mother* (London: privately printed at G.
Polidori's, 1847), 1–10. Basic text: notebook MS. In the 1896 and 1904 editions, the
third and fourth lines of each stanza are indented two spaces.]

Title. MS: The City of Statues.
1896, 1904: THE DEAD CITY
2. 1847: hardihood
11. 1847, 1896, 1904: trees
18. 1847, 1896, 1904: Through the
22. 1847: disaster,
24. 1847: eyes,
25. 1847, 1896, 1904: master.
27. 1847, 1896, 1904: flame;
28. 1847, 1896, 1904: branches
through,

35. 1847, 1896, 1904: solitude:
40. 1896, 1904: Without death's or
sorrow's test.
41. 1896, 1904: O most
42. 1896, 1904: O most
43. 1896, 1904: strife
45. 1896, 1904: marred and
46. 1896, 1904: sun, life-begetting,
49. 1896, 1904: pallid nor
50. 1847, 1896, 1904: forgetting—
51. 1847, 1896, 1904: time;

52. 1847: chime,
53. 1847, 1896, 1904: to be gone;
62. 1847, 1896, 1904: Glancing
    through the <> green,
64. 1896, 1904: trees, and
67. 1847, 1896, 1904: nought; I <>
    sound:
73. 1847, 1896, 1904: ray
77. 1896, 1904: dream—
78. 1896, 1904: fear—
79. 1847, 1896, 1904: saw, as <>
    near,
80. 1847: 'T was in <> gleam,
82. 1847, 1896, 1904: state,
89. 1896, 1904: gradually,
91. 1847, 1896, 1904: Through the
92. 1847, 1896, 1904: shade;
98. 1847, 1896, 1904: fro—
99. 1896, 1904: low,
100. 1847, 1896, 1904: "Go <>
    pride."
102. 1847, 1896, 1904: habitation;
103. 1847, 1896, 1904: tenantless.
107. 1896, 1904: no careworn busy
111. 1847, 1896, 1904: Through the
112. 1847, 1896, 1904: wonderment.
115. 1847, 1896, 1904: astonishment.
117. 1847: Where, amid <> space,
126. 1847, 1896, 1904: way,
127. 1847, 1896, 1904: say,
128. 1847: "Touch <> by
    1896, 1904: "Touch
129. 1847: onwards;" therefore
    1896, 1904: onwards"; therefore
131. 1847, 1896, 1904: desolate.
134. 1847, 1896, 1904: hastened
    through the
136. 1847, 1896, 1904: avenue,
137. 1847, 1896, 1904: view;
138. 1847, 1896, 1904: the sunbeams
    fell
139. 1847, 1896, 1904: founts whose
140. 1847, 1896, 1904: marble basons
    flew.
143. 1847, 1896, 1904: Through the
146. 1847: climbing every where,
    1896: everywhere,
147. 1847, 1896: fair.
    1904: fair;
149. 1847, 1896, 1904: borne
156. 1847, 1896, 1904: went alone,

162. 1847: "Enter <> see,
    1896, 1904: "Enter
164. 1847, 1896, 1904: died."
166. 1896, 1904: Lo a
168. 1896, 1904: tables everything
170. 1896, 1904: rare displayed;
172. 1896, 1904: Practised art makes
176. 1847, 1896, 1904: gold,
180. 1847, 1896, 1904: silver bason
    rolled.
182. 1847, 1896, 1904: streaked and
185. 1896, 1904: rested everywhere.
191. 1847: pear,
192. 1847, 1896, 1904: there,
195. 1896, 1904: fair:
204. 1847, 1896, 1904: between,
206. 1847, 1896: guest,
209. 1847, 1896, 1904: glow not
211. 1847, 1896, 1904: Many
    banqueters were
220. 1847: if spell bound.
    1896, 1904: if spellbound.
222. MS: alone
225. 1847: stone!
    1896, 1904: Lo they <> stone!
228. 1847: smile,
233. MS: Its young age and careless
    heart;
234. 1847, 1896, 1904: apart,
235. MS: a <forwa> look no longer
    flitting. [The added letters are
    written below the line in pencil.]
236. MS: Near them
    1847, 1896, 1904: fair,
242. 1904: a drinking-cup;
243. 1896, 1904: Wine-cup of
245. 1847: no life breath struggling
246. 1847, 1896, 1904: lay and
248. 1847, 1896, 1904: mother,
254. 1847, 1896, 1904: girl whose
255. 1896, 1904: wandered
    roundabout.
256. 1847, 1896, 1904: stillness—none;
260. 1847, 1896, 1904: strange steadfast
    eyes
263. 1847: guest.
    1896: guest.—
    1904: guest—
264. 1847, 1896, 1904: again, the
267. 1847, 1896, 1904: shone,
272. 1847, 1896, 1904: Awed me and
274. MS: much woe and luxury?

THE WATER SPIRIT'S SONG.

[Composed March 4, 1844. The notebook MS, in the handwriting of Christina's sister, Maria Francesca Rossetti, is in the British Library. The poem was printed in *Verses: Dedicated to Her Mother* (London: privately printed at G. Polidori's, 1847), 10–12. Basic text: notebook MS.]

Title. 1847: THE WATER SPIRIT'S
SONG.
4. 1847: lustrously;
6. 1847: gale;
7. MS: murmurs through the
8. 1847: cool refreshing evening
breeze;
10. 1847: tree
11. 1847: repose
13. 1847: deceitfully;
14. 1847: quietly;
19. 1847: sea
22. MS: [No stanza break follows
the line.]
23. 1847: coral
30. 1847: brilliantly.
31. MS: mortal e[*re*]<'er> trod
1847: mortal ee'r trod
34. 1847: door;
42. 1847: isle.
44. MS: With love[*e's sweet*]<ing>
constancy;
1847: constancy,

46. 1847: sea.
47. MS: With <a> fond
50. 1847: rays;
53. 1847: sway,
54. MS: And the [Because line 54 is the
last line on the page, there is no
indication of whether or not a
stanza break is intended to follow
the line.]
55. MS: An[*t*]<d> when
1847: arise
56. MS: the vau[*nte*]<lted> skies,
1847: skies;
58. 1847: the blush-rose forth < >
flings;
60. 1847: dew;
62. MS: greets [*f*]<t>he fresh
1847: away:
64. MS: [*I*]<B>y the
1847: braid;
65. 1847: then, when
66. 1847: motion
67. 1847: sea,

THE SONG OF THE STAR.

[Composed March 19, 1847. Editions: 1896, 1904. The notebook MS, in the handwriting of Christina's sister, Maria Francesca Rossetti, is in the Bodleian Library. The poem was printed in *Verses: Dedicated to Her Mother* (London: privately printed at G. Polidori's, 1847), 12–14. Basic text: notebook MS.]

Title. 1847: THE SONG OF THE
STAR.
1896, 1904: THE SONG OF THE
STAR
1. 1896, 1904: a Star dwelling
5. 1847, 1896, 1904: one,
6. 1904: sun;
7. 1896, 1904: me,
10. 1847: strife;
12. 1896, 1904: No fullness is
18. 1847, 1896, 1904: on to-day,
25. MS: The little birds
29. MS: ripe berries on the bushes
34. 1847, 1896, 1904: loveliness.

37. 1847, 1896, 1904: of the angel
throng
38. 1904: of ecstasy flow
41. MS: will [*gushes*] <bubbles> up
43. 1896, 1904: me,
49. MS: [The punctuation at the end
of the line is illegible.]
51. 1847, 1896, 1904: praise
54. 1896: light,
1904: light;
56. 1896, 1904: immensity;
57. 1847, 1896, 1904: together
59. 1896, 1904: storm nor mist
nor rain,

61. 1896, 1904: On and on and
64. 1847, 1896, 1904: To the heaven
    above

68. MS: love and rejoicing sings,
    [Below the word "rejoicing" a cross
    is added in pencil.]

SUMMER.

[Composed December 4, 1845. Editions: 1896, 1904. A partial MS containing lines 11–14 in Christina's handwriting (MS1) is in the Princeton University Library. The notebook MS (MS2), in the handwriting of Christina's sister, Maria Francesca Rossetti, is in the Bodleian Library. The poem was printed in *Verses: Dedicated to Her Mother* (London: privately printed at G. Polidori's, 1847), 15–17. Basic text: lines 1–10, 15–70: MS2; lines 11–14: MS1. In MS2, lines 5–13, 15, 17–25, 27–29, 31, 33–39, 41, 45, 47, 49–63, 65, 67, and 69 are not indented; and lines 14, 16, 26, 30, 32, 40, 42, 46, 48, 64, 66, 68, and 70 are indented two spaces. In the 1896 text, lines 15, 17–24, 27, and 49–62 are not indented; and line 66 is indented two spaces. In the 1904 text, lines 17–24, 27, and 49–62 are not indented; and line 66 is indented two spaces.]

Title. 1847: SUMMER.
   1896, 1904: SUMMER
2. 1847, 1896, 1904: breeze;
5. 1847: but altogether
6. 1847, 1896, 1904: weather;
8. 1847, 1896: melodiously:
   1904: melodiously;
10. 1847, 1896, 1904: look:
12. MS1: [No stanza break follows
   the line.]
   MS2: [Because line 12 is the last
   line on the page, there is no
   indication of whether or not a
   stanza break is intended to follow
   the line.]
15. 1847, 1896, 1904: bright footpath
   flies
17. 1847: an unconfined tress,
21. 1847, 1896, 1904: flowers;
22. 1847: laughing hours;
   1896, 1904: laughing Hours;
23. 1896, 1904: Heaven and Earth
   make
24. MS2: [Because line 24 is the last line
   on the page, there is no indication

of whether or not a stanza break is
intended to follow the line.]
25. 1847, 1896, 1904: the earth
31. 1847, 1896, 1904: sad
32. MS2: For far off are all traces
36. 1847: kirtle:
   1896, 1904: kirtle.
37. 1847, 1896, 1904: slumbers,
38. 1847, 1896, 1904: numbers—
44. MS2: [No stanza break follows the
   line.]
48. 1847, 1896, 1904: tomb.
50. 1847, 1896, 1904: flies,
51. 1847: foot, and arm, and
   1896, 1904: Hand and
53. 1847, 1896, 1904: hands;
54. 1847: bands;
55. 1847, 1896, 1904: flowers, higher,
   higher,—
62. MS2: [No stanza break follows
   the line.]
63. 1896, 1904: alas they
67. 1896, 1904: seas,
70. 1896, 1904: some far-distant clime.

TO MY MOTHER ON HER BIRTHDAY.

[Composed April 27, 1842. Editions: 1896, 1904. Christina's fair copy (MS1) is in the British Library. The notebook MS (MS2), in the handwriting of Christina's mother, Frances Mary Lavinia Polidori Rossetti, is in the British Library. The poem was printed on a separate card by Christina's grandfather Gaetano Polidori; in the textual notes, variants therein are designated by the word "card." The poem was printed in *Verses: Dedicated to Her Mother* (London: privately printed at G. Polidori's, 1847), 17. Basic text: MS1. In the card, line 1 is indented two spaces; lines 2, 3, 6, and 7 are indented four spaces; and lines 4 and 8 are indented six spaces. In the 1847, 1896, and 1904 texts, lines 4 and 8 are indented two spaces.]

Title. MS2: To my Mother / on the anniversary of her Birth. / Presented with a nosegay. [The first and third lines are indented two spaces.] Card: TO MY MOTHER / ON THE ANNIVERSARY OF HER BIRTH. / April 27. 1842. 1847: TO MY MOTHER. / WITH A NOSEGAY. 1896, 1904: TO MY MOTHER / ON THE ANNIVERSARY OF HER BIRTH / (Presented with a Nosegay)
1. MS1: natal d[y]<a>y MS2: day; Card, 1847, 1896, 1904: To-day's your < > day;

2. MS1: Sweet flowers' I MS2, card: Sweet flow'rs I 1896, 1904: bring:
3. MS2, card, 1847: Mother, accept, I 1896, 1904: Mother, accept < > pray
7. MS2, card, 1847: Receiving, as < > give,
8. MS1: [On the back is added in the handwriting of Christina's mother:] <Written for me April 27th 1842, and given with a nosegay by Christina.> Card: [Below the text of the poem is printed:] CHRISTINA GEORGINA ROSSETTI.

THE RUINED CROSS.

[Composed April 22, 1846. The notebook MS, in the handwriting of Christina's sister, Maria Francesca Rossetti, is in the Bodleian Library. The poem was printed in *Verses: Dedicated to Her Mother* (London: privately printed at G. Polidori's, 1847), 18–19. Basic text: notebook MS. In the 1847 text, the last line of each stanza is indented two spaces.]

Title. 1847: THE RUINED CROSS.
1. MS: bright flowers in
6. 1847: free, and light,
9. 1847: on;
16. MS: [*A*] [indented two spaces] <And> [indented four spaces]
18. MS: [Possible erasure of punctuation at the end of the line.]
25. MS: still, though toilsome
29. 1847: spot . . . . .

31. 1847: ruined cross stood
33. 1847: A cross o'ergrown
34. 1847: A cross fast
35. 1847: The cross she knew, the cross she
39. 1847: that cross,
43. MS: tears[,]
46. MS: Till her young heart 1847: satisfied:
47. 1847: ancient cross is

EVA.

[Composed March 18, 1847. The notebook MS, in the handwriting of Christina's sister, Maria Francesca Rossetti, is in the Bodleian Library. The poem was printed in *Verses: Dedicated to Her Mother* (London: privately printed at G. Polidori's, 1847), 20–22. Basic text: notebook MS. In the MS, line 30 is not indented.]

Title. 1847: EVA. / (SEE MATURIN'S
    "WOMEN.")
4. 1847: a steadfast trust
10. MS: head[,]<.>
12. 1847: oh! still 't is bitter
14. 1847: still.
19. 1847: 'T was in
21. MS: him [*love*] <heal> [The
    revision is in pencil in Christina's
    hand.]
    1847: it:
23. 1847: still.

24. 1847: Nay, it <> whim
25. 1847: woman's steadfast will.
31. MS: Dropping, dropping, dropping
    [illegible erasure] <ever>
38. 1847: Though thy <> bitter
41. 1847: night
48. 1847: sleep
52. 1847: of heaven to win
60. 1847: him heaven's light
63. MS: length [*at*] <in> Heaven.
    1847: in heaven.

LOVE EPHEMERAL.

[Composed February 25, 1845. Editions: 1896, 1904. The notebook MS, in the
handwriting of Christina's sister, Maria Francesca Rossetti, is in the British Library.
The poem was printed in *Verses: Dedicated to Her Mother* (London: privately printed
at G. Polidori's, 1847), 22. Basic text: notebook MS.]

Title. 1847: LOVE EPHEMERAL.
    1896, 1904: LOVE EPHEMERAL
5. MS: soft south[illegible
    deletion]<ern> breeze

7. 1847, 1896, 1904: heaven
8. 1896, 1904: even.
12. MS: Often bre[*eds*]<athes> the
15. 1847, 1896, 1904: away:

BURIAL ANTHEM.

[Composed March 3, 1845. Editions: 1896, 1904. The notebook MS, in the hand-
writing of Christina's sister, Maria Francesca Rossetti, is in the British Library. The
poem was printed in *Verses: Dedicated to Her Mother* (London: privately printed at G.
Polidori's, 1847), 23. Basic text: notebook MS. In the MS, line 5 is indented four
spaces. In the 1847 and 1904 texts, line 2 is not indented, and lines 5, 10, 13, 15, 17,
19, 21, and 28 are indented four spaces. In the 1896 text, lines 2, 5, 10, 13, 15, 17,
19, 21, and 28 are indented five spaces. In the 1896s text, line 2 is indented five
spaces, and lines 5, 10, 13, 15, 17, 19, 21, and 28 are indented four spaces.]

Title. 1847: BURIAL ANTHEM.
    1896, 1904: BURIAL ANTHEM
1. 1896, 1904: Flesh of our flesh,
    bone
2. 1847: one),
    1896, 1904: For <> one—
3. MS: rest has flown,
    1896s: flown
6. 1896, 1904: doubt and want and
    sin and
7. MS: wilt sin "never again".
9. 1896, 1904: distress,—
11. 1847, 1896, 1904: river,
12. 1847, 1896, 1904: ever

15. 1896, 1904: rest
16. 1896, 1904: misery
17. 1847: best:
    1896, 1904: best.
20. MS: [*Struggling*] <Of struggling
    with> our
    1847, 1896, 1904: enemy
21. 1847: dreary,
    1896, 1904: dreary:
23. 1896, 1904: way,
25. 1847, 1896, 1904: desolation;
27. 1847: friend, with thee,
    1896, 1904: our Great Head—and,
    friend, with thee—

SAPPHO.

[Composed September 11, 1846. The notebook MS, in the handwriting of Christina's sister, Maria Francesca Rossetti, is in the Bodleian Library. The poem was printed in *Verses: Dedicated to Her Mother* (London: privately printed at G. Polidori's, 1847), 24.]

Title. 1847: SAPPHO.
 1. 1847: at day dawn, and
 2. 1847: by;

12. MS: Through the
14. 1847: untended, and

TASSO AND LEONORA.

[Composed December 19, 1846. Editions: 1896, 1904. The notebook MS, in the handwriting of Christina's sister, Maria Francesca Rossetti, is in the Bodleian Library. The poem was printed in *Verses: Dedicated to Her Mother* (London: privately printed at G. Polidori's, 1847), 24. Basic text: notebook MS. In the 1847 text, lines 1, 5, and 9 are indented two spaces; and lines 2, 3, 6, 7, 10, and 14 are not indented. In the 1896 text, line 2 is indented four spaces; lines 3, 6, 7, 10, and 14 are not indented; and lines 5 and 9 are indented two spaces.]

Title. MS: Sonnet. / Tasso and
 Leonora.
 1847: TASSO AND LEONORA.
 1896, 1904: TASSO AND
 LEONORA
 2. 1896, 1904: bed,—
 3. 1896, 1904: head,
 4. MS: Though full of brackish water

the rude bowl [A cross is added in pencil to the left of the line.]
 8. MS: strong control[s].
11. 1904: harmonies.
12. MS: what [*melts*] <meets> his [The deletion and revision are in pencil.]
13. 1847, 1896, 1904: Lo! Leonora, with

ON THE DEATH OF A CAT

[Composed March 14, 1846. Editions: 1896, 1904. The notebook MS, in the handwriting of Christina's sister, Maria Francesca Rossetti, is in the Bodleian Library. The poem was printed in *Verses: Dedicated to Her Mother* (London: privately printed at G. Polidori's, 1847), 25–26. Basic text: notebook MS.]

Title. MS: On the death of Aunt Eliza's
 Cat, / aged ten years & a half. [The second line of the title is indented two spaces.]
 1896, 1904: CAT / A <> MINE
 AGED <> HALF
 2. 1847: her cat was
 4. 1847, 1896, 1904: her, belov'd for
 8. 1847, 1896, 1904: call;
 9. 1847, 1896, 1904: mourn with <> breath

11. MS: And whilst you
16. 1847, 1896, 1904: house;
18. 1847, 1896, 1904: pat;
22. 1847: length.
23. 1847, 1896, 1904: side
28. 1896, 1904: as hers that [No stanza break follows the line.]
30. MS: where [*p*]<P>uss doth

MOTHER AND CHILD.

[Composed January 10, 1846. Editions: 1896, 1904. The notebook MS, in the hand-writing of Christina's sister, Maria Francesca Rossetti, is in the Bodleian Library. The poem was printed in *Verses: Dedicated to Her Mother* (London: privately printed at G. Polidori's, 1847), 26. Basic text: notebook MS. In the MS, the stanzas are numbered.]

Title. 1847: MOTHER AND CHILD.
    1896, 1904: MOTHER AND
    CHILD
1. 1847, 1896, 1904: the mother,
2. MS: art thinking
    1847, 1896, 1904: of, my
3. 1847, 1896, 1904: of heaven," he
5. MS: of Heaven<?>", she
    1847, 1896, 1904: of heaven?" she
6. 1847, 1896, 1904: one."
7. 1847: "Oh! I
    1896, 1904: "Oh I
9. 1847, 1896, 1904: child,

10. 1847, 1896, 1904: go,
13. MS: go, mother,
    1847: "Oh! I
    1896, 1904: "Oh I
15. 1847, 1896, 1904: mother;—
16. MS: [After line 16 is the following
    stanza:]
            5
    The little child he died that night,
    The Mother died for sorrow;—
    And they went to the land where the
        flowers never fade,
    And the bright day knows no morrow.

FAIR MARGARET.

[Composed December 28, 1844. The notebook MS, in the handwriting of Christina's sister, Maria Francesca Rossetti, is in the British Library. The poem was printed in *Verses: Dedicated to Her Mother* (London: privately printed at G. Polidori's, 1847), 27–28. Basic text: notebook MS. The MS text contains a short horizontal line below each of the stanzas.]

Title. MS: Song.
Opening quotation. MS: [The quotation
    is not in the text.]
3. 1847: past and
13. 1847: eyes and dark and flashing
16. 1847: sadly
19. 1847: thee

21. 1847: life,—
22. 1847: languish
25. 1847: thee,—
26. 1847: above thee
27. 1847: be—
30. 1847: ONCE bound

EARTH AND HEAVEN.

[Composed December 28, 1844. Editions: 1896, 1904. The notebook MS, in the handwriting of Christina's sister, Maria Francesca Rossetti, is in the British Library. The poem was printed in *Verses: Dedicated to Her Mother* (London: privately printed at G. Polidori's, 1847), 28–29. Basic text: notebook MS. In the 1896 and 1904 texts, lines 1–20 are indented four spaces, lines 21–26 are indented two spaces, and line 28 is indented six spaces.]

Title. 1847: EARTH AND HEAVEN.
    1896, 1904: EARTH AND
    HEAVEN

2. 1847, 1896, 1904: Sunlight deeply
3. 1847, 1896, 1904: riding
5. 1847, 1896, 1904: rushes,

7. MS: White lilies fair, whose
   1847, 1896, 1904: whose dower
8. MS: Is scent as well as flow'r,
   1847, 1896, 1904: and flower,
10. 1847, 1896, 1904: Sunrise from
13. 1847, 1896, 1904: Seaweed, coral,
14. 1847, 1896, 1904: Flowers that < >
    clamber
16. 1847, 1896, 1904: nourish:
18. 1847, 1896, 1904: beauty earth
    is full:

19. 1896, 1904: promised heaven
21. 1847: Yes, for < > in Heaven doth
    dwell,
    1896, 1904: Yes, for < > in heaven
    doth dwell,
24. 1847, 1896, 1904: of earth:
28. MS: [Illegible erasure] <In Heaven
    is Love.>
    1847: is love.
    1896, 1904: In heaven is

LOVE ATTACKED.

[Composed April 21, 1846. Editions: 1896, 1904. The notebook MS, in the hand-writing of Christina's sister, Maria Francesca Rossetti, is in the Bodleian Library. The poem was printed in *Verses: Dedicated to Her Mother* (London: privately printed at G. Polidori's, 1847), 30–31. Basic text: notebook MS.]

Title. 1847: LOVE ATTACKED.
    1896, 1904: LOVE ATTACKED
3. MS: [Illegible deletion] <Warmer
   than> sunny
5. 1847: than music whispers
   1896, 1904: than music whispers,
6. 1896, 1904: day,
10. 1847, 1896, 1904: untrue;
12. 1896, 1904: too.
15. 1896, 1904: soon alas one

16. 1847, 1896, 1904: dies:
25. 1847, 1896, 1904: unrequited,
26. MS: 'Ti[*ll*]<s> still
    1847: 'T is still
31. 1847, 1896, 1904: ages,—
35. 1847: O tell
37. 1847, 1896, 1904: crying,
39. MS: Rose [illegible deletion]
    <from> the
40. 1847, 1896, 1904: "Indifference."

LOVE DEFENDED.

[Composed April 23, 1846. Editions: 1896, 1904. The notebook MS, in the hand-writing of Christina's sister, Maria Francesca Rossetti, is in the Bodleian Library. The poem was printed in *Verses: Dedicated to Her Mother* (London: privately printed at G. Polidori's, 1847), 31–32. Basic text: notebook MS. In the 1847, 1896, and 1904 texts, the second line of each stanza is not indented, and the fourth line of each stanza is indented two spaces.]

Title. 1847: LOVE DEFENDED.
    1896, 1904: LOVE DEFENDED
2. MS: Who has praised
5. MS: who never sees,
7. MS: that has no
11. MS: man trembles not
13. 1847, 1896, 1904: of heaven and
    earth,
16. MS: [*F*] [indented two spaces]
    <For> [indented four spaces] a

17. MS, 1896, 1904: So, though Love
    1847: So tho' love may
20. MS: [After line 20 is the following
    note:] This poem being so closely
    connected with the preceding one,
    has rendered a slight derangement
    of the dates unavoidable.

DIVINE AND HUMAN PLEADING.

[Lines 1–64, 85–88 composed March 30, 1846; lines 65–84 composed February 8, 1846. Editions: 1904 (lines 65–84 only). The notebook MS of lines 65–84 (MS1) and the notebook MS of lines 1–64, 85–88 (MS2), both in the handwriting of Christina's sister, Maria Francesca Rossetti, are in the Bodleian Library. The poem was printed in *Verses: Dedicated to Her Mother* (London: privately printed at G. Polidori's, 1847), 32–35. Basic text: lines 1–64, 85–88: MS2; lines 65–84: MS1. In MS1, line 82 is not indented, and there is a short horizontal line below the title and each stanza. In MS2, line 42 is not indented.]

Title. MS1: Mary Magdalene.
 1847: DIVINE AND HUMAN
 PLEADING.
 1904: MARY MAGDALENE
 1. MS2: prayers![*"*]
 1847: the Saints could
 3. MS2: O[*h*] blessed
12. 1847: [Below line 12 are five spaced
 asterisks.]
13. 1847: calm still
17. 1847: bed:
25. MS2: a holy fire;
 1847: fire,
34. 1847: eyes,
36. 1847: dies:
37. MS2: thy musing hour
41. 1847: pleadings wouldst prefer
42. 1847: me,
43. 1847: To His who is
44. 1847: To His who died
45. 1847: from heaven:
47. 1847: love who waits
49. 1847: know I His long suffering
50. 1847: worth.
52. 1847: earth:
54. 1847: from life's path;
55. 1847: hands—
65. MS1, 1904: She came in deep
 1847: repentance
66. MS1: And knelt
 1847: at His feet
 1904: And knelt < > at His feet

69. MS1, 1904: She had < > away her
 jewels
70. MS1: And her rich
 1847: attire,
 1904: And her rich attire,
71. MS1, 1904: And her breast < >
 holy shame,
 1847: flame
72. MS1, 1904: And her heart
73. MS1, 1904: Her tears
74. MS1: Than her precious
 1847: pearls,—
 1904: Than her precious pearls—
75. MS1: Her tears
 1847: upon His feet
 1904: Her tears < > upon His feet
76. MS1: As she wiped < > with her
 curls.
 1847: wiped them with
 1904: As she wiped them with her
 curls.
77. MS1, 1904: Her youth and her
 beauty
79. MS1, 1904: But she wept
81. MS1, 1904: Trembling
82. MS1: She sought
 1904: She sought < > of Heaven,
83. MS1, 1904: of her ways,
85. MS2: "I went to Him in hope and
 fear,
 1847: to Him,—
87. 1847: intercede.

TO MY FRIEND ELIZABETH.

[Composed March 17, 1846. Editions: 1904. The notebook MS, in the handwriting of Christina's sister, Maria Francesca Rossetti, is in the Bodleian Library. The poem was printed in *Verses: Dedicated to Her Mother* (London: privately printed at G. Polidori's, 1847), 36. Basic text: notebook MS. In the 1904 text, lines 2, 4, and 6 are indented two spaces.]

Title. MS: To E. R.,
1904: TO ELIZABETH READ
Subtitle. MS: some Postage Stamps
for a
1847: WITH SOME POSTAGE
STAMPS TOWARDS A
COLLECTION.
1904: WITH SOME
POSTAGE-STAMPS FOR A
COLLECTION

1. 1847, 1904: accept, I pray,
2. 1904: true:
5. 1847: gay
   1904: black—nor gay
6. 1904: all—is
7. 1847: gladness mixt.
   1904: gladness mixt:
8. 1847: there, perfection
   1904: there—perfection

AMORE E DOVERE.

[Date of composition unknown. Editions: 1896, 1904. The poem was printed in *Verses: Dedicated to Her Mother* (London: privately printed at G. Polidori's, 1847), 37. Basic text: 1847. In the 1896 text, lines 6, 7, 11, 13, 17, 19, and 22 are not indented. In the 1904 text, line 2 is indented two spaces, and lines 6, 7, 11, 13, 17, 19, and 22 are not indented.]

Title. 1896, 1904: AMORE E
DOVERE
2. 1896, 1904: altero:
3. 1896, 1904: No non
5. 1896, 1904: t'amai—

6. 1896, 1904: sai—
20. 1896, 1904: crudeltà.—
23. 1896, 1904: intendo, l'Amore
25. 1896, 1904: Deh placati alfine!

AMORE E DISPETTO.

[Composed August 21, 1846. The notebook MS, in the handwriting of Christina's sister, Maria Francesca Rossetti, is in the Bodleian Library. The poem was printed in *Verses: Dedicated to Her Mother* (London: privately printed at G. Polidori's, 1847), 38–39. Basic text: notebook MS. In the 1847 text, lines 2, 3, 8, 9, 12, 14, 15, 20, 21, 26, 27, 32, 33, 38, and 39 are not indented.]

Title. 1847: AMORE E DISPETTO.
1. 1847: grande amor possente
3. MS: Odi l'umil preghiera
4. MS: D'un [illegible erasure] <tristo
tuo fedel:>
1847: D' un tristo
5. MS: che Lisa altera
6. 1847: crudel!
7. MS: giorno tutto stanco
1847: stanco,
8. MS: sull' erbe il
1847: fianco,
9. MS: Mesto pensava a
10. 1847: ferì.
11. MS: Che mi sembrò sì bella,
1847: bella!—
12. 1847: fuggì.

13. MS: Quando lei vidi
18. MS: M'accorderia pietà.
22. MS: Chinando, s'arrossì;
23. MS: E[illegible erasure]<d io
sclam>ai: Deh
24. 1847: pietà—Cosi. . . .
29. MS: E muto
1847: stetti
30. MS: Quand' ella
31. MS: Non voglio amar nessuno;
32. MS: Ma se vi fosse alcuno
33. MS: Tu nol saresti.
34. MS: Tacque, e da me partì.
36. MS: Amor, dei far cosi;
37. MS: Spirale tu nel core
38. 1847: amore;—
40. MS: se ciò non vuoi far,

LOVE AND HOPE.

[Composed October 9, 1843. Editions: 1896, 1904. The notebook MS, in the handwriting of Christina's sister, Maria Francesca Rossetti, is in the British Library. The poem was printed in *Verses: Dedicated to Her Mother* (London: privately printed at G. Polidori's, 1847), 39–40. Basic text: notebook MS. In the MS, each stanza is numbered, and lines 7 and 9 do not appear to be indented. In the 1847, 1896, and 1904 texts, lines 1, 3, 6, 8, 11, and 13 are indented four spaces; and lines 2, 4, 7, 9, 12, and 14 are indented six spaces.]

Title. 1847: LOVE AND HOPE.
    1896, 1904: LOVE AND HOPE
1. 1847, 1896, 1904: in heaven,—
3. 1847, 1896, 1904: given,—
6. 1847, 1896, 1904: dwelleth,—
7. 1847: not quenched be;
8. 1847, 1896: the life blood welleth,
    1904: welleth,

9. 1847, 1896, 1904: see
10. 1847, 1896, 1904: lips the last—
    fades
11. 1847, 1896, 1904: awaken,
13. MS, 1896, 1904: Though Hope
14. 1847, 1896, 1904: die:
15. 1847, 1896, 1904: For perfect Love
    and perfect bliss shall

SERENADE.

[Composed December 4, 1845. Editions: 1896, 1904. The notebook MS, in the handwriting of Christina's sister, Maria Francesca Rossetti, is in the Bodleian Library. The poem was printed in *Verses: Dedicated to Her Mother* (London: privately printed at G. Polidori's, 1847), 40–41. Basic text: notebook MS. In the 1896 and 1904 texts, lines 5–29 are indented two spaces and line 31 is indented four spaces.]

Title. 1847: SERENADE.
    1896, 1904: SERENADE
1. 1847, 1896, 1904: me: the
2. 1847: bowers;
3. 1847, 1896: me; the
    1904: me: the
4. 1847, 1896, 1904: brilliancy;
6. 1896, 1904: afar.
7. 1847, 1896, 1904: The night wind
    scarce
11. 1847: dove
    1896, 1904: the turtle-dove
12. 1847, 1896, 1904: love.
13. 1847: now 't is the < > balmy hour,
    1896, 1904: balmy hour,

19. 1847, 1896, 1904: brilliantly,
21. 1847, 1896, 1904: slumbered:
23. 1847, 1896, 1904: calm
    Melancholy;—
25. 1847: we love long dead;
    1896, 1904: we love, long dead;
27. 1847, 1896, 1904: Heavenly,
    without
28. 1847: dearest: all < > quiet;
    1896, 1904: dearest: all < >
    quiet—
29. 1847, 1896, 1904: Slumbering the
    < > riot;
30. 1847, 1896, 1904: sea.
31. 1847, 1896, 1904: me.

THE ROSE.

[Composed February 25, 1846. The notebook MS, in the handwriting of Christina's sister, Maria Francesca Rossetti, is in the Bodleian Library. The poem was printed in *Verses: Dedicated to Her Mother* (London: privately printed at G. Polidori's, 1847), 41–42. Basic text: notebook MS. In the MS, there is a short horizontal line below the title and each stanza. In the 1847 text, lines 6–8 and 14–16 are not indented.]

Title. 1847: THE ROSE.   6. 1847: flowing towards the
1. 1847: river,   8. MS: haughty Rosalie.
3. 1847: ever   13. 1847: thriving,
4. 1847: song;   15. 1847: kindliness,
5. MS: in thy onward

PRESENT AND FUTURE.

[Composed November 5, 1846. Editions: 1896, 1904. The notebook MS, in the handwriting of Christina's sister, Maria Francesca Rossetti, is in the Bodleian Library. The poem was printed in *Verses: Dedicated to Her Mother* (London: privately printed at G. Polidori's, 1847), 42. Basic text: notebook MS.]

Title. 1847: PRESENT AND   7. 1847: weariness 't is more.
    FUTURE.   8. 1847, 1896, 1904: fleeting,
    1896, 1904: PRESENT AND   9. 1847, 1896, 1904: long;
    FUTURE   11. 1896, 1904: to evensong.
4. 1847, 1896, 1904: Ever loth to   12. 1847, 1896, 1904: morning
5. 1896, 1904: goodness? is it   15. 1896, 1904: But, though <> it,
6. 1847: Nay, 't is more   16. 1896, 1904: evermore.
    1904: sadness;   17. 1847, 1896s: it

WILL THESE HANDS NE'ER BE CLEAN?

[Composed September 16, 1846. Editions: 1896, 1904. The notebook MS, in the handwriting of Christina's sister, Maria Francesca Rossetti, is in the Bodleian Library. The poem was printed in *Verses: Dedicated to Her Mother* (London: privately printed at G. Polidori's, 1847), 43–44. Basic text: notebook MS. In the 1847 text, lines 3 and 14–37 are not indented, and lines 8 and 47 are indented four spaces. In the 1896 text, lines 4 and 8 are indented eight spaces; lines 20 and 21 are indented two spaces; and line 47 is indented six spaces. In the 1904 text, lines 8 and 47 are indented four spaces, and lines 20 and 21 are indented two spaces.]

Title. MS: To a Murderer.   37. MS: [Because line 37 is the last line
7. 1896, 1904: O deeply-rooted   on the page, there is no indication
22. MS: to [*move*] <wake>, alive [The   of whether or not a stanza break is
    deletion is in pencil. The added   intended to follow the line.]
    word is written above the line in   40. 1896, 1904: And, though <> hell
    pencil.]   and
23. 1847: seem,   41. MS: [*A curse*] <Vengeance>, yet
30. 1847, 1896, 1904: to heaven   [The deletion is in pencil. The
34. 1847, 1896, 1904: fearful shalt   added word is written above the
    thou say   line in pencil.]
36. 1847, 1896, 1904: outcast thou
    shalt be

SIR EUSTACE GREY.

[Composed October 14, 1846. The notebook MS, in the handwriting of Christina's sister, Maria Francesca Rossetti, is in the Bodleian Library. The poem was printed in

Verses: Dedicated to Her Mother (London: privately printed at G. Polidori's, 1847), 45–46. Basic text: notebook MS.]

Title. MS: The Last Words of Sir
Eustace Grey.* [At the bottom of
the page is written:] *See Crabbe.
3. 1847: meanders:
7. 1847: die;
12. 1847: the noontide of

16. MS: the rus[*h*]<tl>ing boughs
[The revision is written in pencil.]
31. 1847: Steadfast as < > above
36. MS: by [*h*]<H>eavenly Love
39. 1847: gloom;
48. MS: Death sweet sleep

THE TIME OF WAITING.

[Composed November 16, 1846. Editions: 1896, 1904. The notebook MS, in the handwriting of Christina's sister, Maria Francesca Rossetti, is in the Bodleian Library. The poem was printed in *Verses: Dedicated to Her Mother* (London: privately printed at G. Polidori's, 1847), 46–49. Basic text: notebook MS.]

Title. MS: Lamentation & Consolation.
1896, 1904: THE TIME OF
WAITING
4. 1847, 1896s: say, "Rejoice to-day,"
1896, 1904: say "Rejoice to-day,"
5. 1847, 1896, 1904: way:
7. 1847, 1896, 1904: say "My
1896s: say, "My
8. 1896, 1904: peace":
16. 1847: ever,—
17. 1847: river,—
18. 1847, 1896, 1904: the sunbeams
quiver.
19. 1847, 1896, 1904: destruction
waxeth bold,
23. 1847, 1896, 1904: ceases
34. 1896, 1904: of humankind;
39. 1847: sorrow drinkiug.

41. 1896, 1904: "Vengeance, Lord!
how
44. 1847: high;
47. 1847, 1896, 1904: The oppressors
shall
48. 1847: great vengeance, which
1896, 1904: great vengeance which
51. 1847, 1896, 1904: again,—
56. 1847, 1896, 1904: Grief and
fear and
57. 1847, 1896, 1904: glorious
resurrection.
58. MS: then a [illegible deletion] night
65. 1847, 1896, 1904: Even to
66. 1896, 1904: Gladness, and
67. 1896, 1904: guiding love alway,
68. 1847, 1896, 1904: everlasting day,

CHARITY.

[Composed September 15, 1844. Editions: 1896, 1904. The notebook MS, in the handwriting of Christina's sister, Maria Francesca Rossetti, is in the British Library. The poem was printed in *Verses: Dedicated to Her Mother* (London: privately printed at G. Polidori's, 1847), 49. Basic text: notebook MS. In the MS, the stanzas are numbered. In the 1847 text, lines 2, 6, and 10 are not indented, and lines 4, 8, and 12 are indented six spaces. In the 1896 and 1904 texts, lines 4, 8, and 12 are indented eight spaces.]

Title. 1847: CHARITY.
1896, 1904: CHARITY
2. 1896, 1904: beauty lying:
6. 1896, 1904: Brightly: yet < > rest
7. 1847: glowing

12. MS: [Below the poem is written the
following note:] The foregoing
verses are imitated from that
beautiful little poem *"Virtue,"* by
George Herbert.

1896: [Below the poem is the   beautiful little poem *Virtue*, by
following note:] (The foregoing   George Herbert.)
verses are imitated from that

THE DEAD BRIDE.

[Composed September 10, 1846. Editions: 1896, 1904. The notebook MS, in the
handwriting of Christina's sister, Maria Francesca Rossetti, is in the Bodleian Li-
brary. The poem was printed in *Verses: Dedicated to Her Mother* (London: privately
printed at G. Polidori's, 1847), 50–51, and in *Our Paper, Being a Monthly Serial for
Private Circulation*, No. 1 (January, 1855), 21. Basic text: notebook MS. In the 1855
text, the last line of each stanza is indented two spaces.]

Title. 1847, 1855: THE DEAD   28. MS, 1847, 1896, 1904: With earth's
    BRIDE.   vanity.
    1896, 1904: THE DEAD BRIDE   29. MS: But, alas!
  3. MS, 1847, 1896, 1904: fleeting, life   1896, 1904: alas, if
    < > frail,   30. 1855: here;
  5. MS: ever:—gone   32. MS: where?—
  7. MS: ever:—who   1855: gladness, where? . . . . . .
19. 1896s: dear   1896, 1904: where? . . .
21. 1855: bride, if   33. 1855: Hush! too
23. 1855: departed,   34. MS: o'er;
24. MS: to d[*l*]<w>ell in   1847: Hush, and
    1855: in heaven.   1855: Hush! and
    1896, 1904: in heaven;   1896, 1904: Hush, and < > o'er.
25. 1847: was fix'd   37. MS: she lay all
    1855: on heaven was   1855: pale,
    1896, 1904: on heaven was fixed   38. MS: her;
26. MS, 1847, 1896, 1904: if charity   39. MS: fleeting, life < > frail,
27. MS, 1896, 1904: Filled her full of 40. MS: Death had found
    light unmixed
    1847: Filled her full of light
    unmix'd

LIFE OUT OF DEATH.

[Date of composition unknown. The poem was printed in *Verses: Dedicated to Her
Mother* (London: privately printed at G. Polidori's, 1847), 51–52. Basic text: 1847.]

THE SOLITARY ROSE.

[Composed March 15, 1847. Editions: 1896, 1904. The notebook MS, in the hand-
writing of Christina's sister, Maria Francesca Rossetti, is in the Bodleian Library.
The poem was printed in *Verses: Dedicated to Her Mother* (London: privately printed
at G. Polidori's, 1847), 52–53. A copy of the book containing Christina's holograph
correction of the poem is owned by Mrs. Roderic O'Conor and is designated "1847
(O'Conor)" in the notes. Another copy of the book containing Christina's holograph

correction of the poem is in the University of Texas Humanities Research Center and is designated "1847 (Texas)" in the notes. Basic text: notebook MS.]

Title. 1847: THE SOLITARY ROSE.
1896, 1904: THE SOLITARY
ROSE
1. 1847, 1896, 1904: happy rose, red
rose, that
3. 1847: Thou art
1847 (O'Conor), 1847 (Texas):
Th[*ou*]<at> art [The revision is in
pencil in both books.]

6. 1847, 1896, 1904: happy rose.
7. 1847, 1896, 1904: What though for
12. 1847, 1896, 1904: happy rose.
13. 1847: peace thou
14. 1896, 1904: thee,
16. 1847, 1896, 1904: leaves nor
18. 1847, 1896, 1904: happy rose.

LADY ISABELLA.

[Composed March 1, 1846. The notebook MS, in the handwriting of Christina's sister, Maria Francesca Rossetti, is in the Bodleian Library. The poem was printed in *Verses: Dedicated to Her Mother* (London: privately printed at G. Polidori's, 1847), 53–54. A copy of the book containing a holograph correction is owned by Mrs. Roderic O'Conor and is designated "1847 (O'Conor)" in the textual notes. Another copy of the book containing a holograph correction and addition is in the University of Texas Humanities Research Center and is designated "1847 (Texas)" in the textual notes. Basic text: notebook MS.]

Title. MS: On Lady Isabella.
1847: LADY ISABELLA.
3. 1847: trouble
4. 1847: the day.
7. 1847: repose
10. 1847: in Heaven
11. 1847: thy fears are
1847 (O'Conor): thy [*f*]<t>ears

are [The revision is in pencil.]
1847 (Texas): thy [*f*]<t>ears are
[The revision is in black ink.]
15. 1847: rest
19. 1847: While yet <> spotless
23. 1847: lustre?
1847 (Texas): lustre?<—> [The
addition is in black ink.]

THE DREAM.

[Date of composition unknown. Editions: 1896, 1904. The poem was printed in *Verses: Dedicated to Her Mother* (London: privately printed at G. Polidori's, 1847), 55–56. Two cancelled leaves (pp. 55–56) from *Verses*, containing what appear to be Dante Gabriel Rossetti's holograph corrections written in black ink and incorporated into the printed text, are in the New York Public Library; in the textual notes, those readings are designated "1847 (cancelled leaves)." Basic text: 1847. In the 1896 and 1904 texts, lines 8, 12, 16, 20, 24, 28, 32, 34, 36, 38, 40, and 42 are indented four spaces.]

Title. 1896, 1904: THE DREAM
3. 1896, 1904: sleep or
15. 1896, 1904: *Thy* happiness
16. 1896, 1904: *My* love
17. 1847 (cancelled leaves): And now

<that> thou [The added word is
written in the right margin.]
19. 1847 (cancelled leaves): And see
[*in*] the [A deletion sign is written
in the right margin.]

21. 1847 (cancelled leaves): sit beneath
it[s] [r]ow, [A deletion sign and the
letter "n" are written in the right
margin.]
22. 1896, 1904: Hearkening the
1896s: Harkening the
29. 1847 (cancelled leaves): say: <">It
<> take it[.]<;> [Quotation
marks are written in the left
margin and a semicolon is written
in the right margin.]

30. 1847 (cancelled leaves): me.<">
[Quotation marks are written in the
right margin.]
1896, 1904: gone—he
31. 1896, 1904: thou shouldst break
33. 1896, 1904: Oh I <> show,
38. 1904: [Below line 38 is a stanza
break.]
39. 1896, 1904: oh how
40. 1896, 1904: seems!
42. 1847 (cancelled leaves): [Below the
text is added:] <1847.>

THE DYING MAN TO HIS BETROTHED.

[Composed July 14, 1846. Editions: 1896, 1904. The notebook MS, in the handwriting of Christina's sister, Maria Francesca Rossetti, is in the Bodleian Library. The poem was printed in *Verses: Dedicated to Her Mother* (London: privately printed at G. Polidori's, 1847), 56–58. Basic text: notebook MS. In the MS, no lines are indented.]

Title. 1847: THE DYING MAN TO
HIS BETROTHED.
1896, 1904: THE DYING MAN
TO HIS BETROTHED
1. 1847: word—'t is all
3. MS: thy perfidy.
4. 1847, 1896, 1904: thou!
9. MS: is [*fleet*]<ebb>ing fast;
12. 1847, 1896, 1904: silence,—still
13. 1847, 1896, 1904: me: for
15. 1896, 1904: pale:
18. 1847: was, bnt never
1896, 1904: was but
19. MS: blessed [illegible erasure]
<moments, ye fleet> fast,
20. MS: latest will be
22. 1847: not, I <> not curs'd
1896, 1904: not, I <> not curst
23. 1847: me:
1896, 1904: me.
25. 1847: first lov'd thee,—
1896, 1904: thee,—
26. 1847: Curse *them!*—Alas! I <>
bless
1896, 1904: Curse *them?*—Alas I
<> bless
27. MS: [Illegible erasure] <In> this
my hour
1847, 1896, 1904: heaviness:—

28. 1896, 1904: distress.
29. 1847, 1896, 1904: thou say'st of
31. 1896, 1904: thee.
33. 1847: love, 't is o'er;
1896, 1904: love, 'tis o'er;
36. 1847: thee; may'st thou
1896, 1904: thee; mayst
38. MS: O<h> may
1847: Oh, may
39. 1847, 1896, 1904: thee,—
41. 1847, 1896, 1904: thy love still
42. 1847, 1896, 1904: everlasting day!
43. 1847: me;—ah!
1896, 1904: me;—ah this
44. 1847, 1896, 1904: side:
45. 1847, 1896, 1904: lower; let
46. MS: thou, my own,
47. 1847, 1896, 1904: love;—I <>
thee:
49. MS: Throughout a bless'd eternity.
50. 1847, 1896, 1904: cover.
51. 1847: for His sake who died
1896, 1904: Oh for His sake who
died
52. MS: more faithful to thy
53. 1847, 1896, 1904: me: Amen.
55. MS: For one short moment think
of me,
1847: me

57. 1847: now, O God! I
58. 1847, 1896, 1904: Thou only,
    Father, <> fail:
60. MS: But yet

1847, 1896, 1904: yet Thy mercy
    shall
61. 1847, 1896, 1904: forgiven;—
63. 1896, 1904: O Christ, who art

THE MARTYR.

[Composed May 24, 1846. Editions: 1896, 1904. The notebook MS, in the handwriting of Christina's sister, Maria Francesca Rossetti, is in the Bodleian Library. The poem was printed in *Verses: Dedicated to Her Mother* (London: privately printed at G. Polidori's, 1847), 59–61. Basic text: notebook MS. In the MS, no lines are indented. In the 1896 and 1904 texts, the first, second, fourth, and fifth lines of each stanza are indented eight spaces.]

Title. 1847: THE MARTYR.
    1896, 1904: THE MARTYR
1. MS: sun has risen!
    1896, 1904: risen—
3. 1847, 1896, 1904: tender,—lead
5. 1847, 1896, 1904: the saints be
    fewer—
6. MS: lost irretrievably.
    1896, 1904: in heaven be
8. 1896, 1904: No nor
9. 1847, 1896, 1904: her down, down;
12. MS: That she might have strength
15. 1847, 1896, 1904: red;
18. MS: dread
21. MS: that His Eye was watching o'er
    1847, 1896, 1904: that His eye
    watched
23. 1847, 1896, 1904: her
24. MS: soul, for love of Him, had
    passed patiently. [After line 24 is
    the following stanza:]

    Now the Judges proffer
    Incense, and they offer
    Life to her, if she will worship their
        divinities;
    But no tears are streaming,
    Love alone is gleaming

From the up-raised glances of her
    speaking eyes.

    1896, 1904: had past, for
25. 1847, 1896, 1904: me,—
26. 1847, 1896, 1904: me,—
28. 1847, 1896, 1904: it,—
30. 1847, 1896, 1904: With the love
    Thou
31. 1847: Quicken'd with
33. MS: She raised up her hands to
    1847: aloud:
    1896, 1904: to heaven, and <>
    aloud:
36. MS: the pure white foldings of
37. 1896, 1904: hope-laden—
39. 1847: no more:—
40. 1847: forgiven,—
41. MS: the road to heaven
    1847: to Heaven,—
    1896, 1904: to heaven,
42. 1847: Through the <> fire, lay
    1896, 1904: fire, lay
47. MS: her form has
48. MS: To a heap of dust;—
50. 1847, 1896, 1904: counting,—
52. 1847, 1896, 1904: her;
53. 1847, 1896, 1904: her;

THE END OF TIME.

[Composed December 9, 1845. Editions: 1896, 1904. The notebook MS, in the handwriting of Christina's sister, Maria Francesca Rossetti, is in the Bodleian Library. The poem was printed in *Verses: Dedicated to Her Mother* (London: privately printed at G. Polidori's, 1847), 61–62. Basic text: notebook MS. The MS contains a short horizontal line below the title and each stanza. In the 1847 text, lines 1, 3, 5, 7, 11, 13, 15, 17, 21, 23, 25, 27, 31, 33, 35, and 37 are indented six spaces; lines 2, 4, 6, 8, 12, 14, 16, 18, 22, 24, 26, 28, 32, 34, 36, and 38 are indented eight spaces; and lines 9, 19, 29, and 39 are not indented. In the 1896 and 1904 texts, lines 1, 3, 5, 7, 11, 13, 15, 17, 21, 23, 25, 27, 31, 33, 35, and 37 are indented ten spaces; and lines 2, 4, 6, 8, 12, 14, 16, 18, 22, 24, 26, 28, 32, 34, 36, and 38 are indented eight spaces.]

Title. 1847: THE END OF TIME.
1896, 1904: THE END OF TIME
6. 1847, 1896, 1904: loved sick bed,
8. 1847, 1896, 1904: dead,—
9. 1847: Hope, hope! Old Time
< > way;
12. 1847: fades e'er night;
16. 1847, 1896, 1904: sea;
17. 1847, 1896, 1904: And Death reigns

18. 1847: Whilst Old Time < > be;—
1896, 1904: be;—
19. 1847: hope! Old Time < > way;
23. MS, 1896, 1904: What though it
25. MS, 1896, 1904: So through all
26. 1847, 1896, 1904: been,
28. 1847, 1896, 1904: mean:—
29. 1847: way;
39. 1847: way;

RESURRECTION EVE.

[Composed April 8, 1847. Editions: 1896, 1904. The notebook MS, in the handwriting of Christina's sister, Maria Francesca Rossetti, is in the Bodleian Library. The poem was printed in *Verses: Dedicated to Her Mother* (London: privately printed at G. Polidori's, 1847), 63–64. A copy of the book containing a holograph correction of the poem is in the University of Texas Humanities Research Center and is designated "1847 (Texas)" in the textual notes. Basic text: notebook MS. In the 1847 text, all of the lines are indented eight spaces. In the 1896 and 1904 texts, lines 1–3, 8–11, 13, 14, 16, 18, 20–26, 28, 30, and 33 are indented six spaces; lines 4–7, 12, 15, 17, 19, 27, 29, 31, and 34 are indented eight spaces; and lines 32 and 35 are indented ten spaces.]

Title. MS: The Resurrection Eve.
1847: RESURRECTION EVE.
1896, 1904: RESURRECTION EVE
1. 1847: resteth; weep not;
1896, 1904: not;
3. 1896, 1904: calm.
6. 1847: Hath no joy
1847 (Texas): Hath [no] joy [The deletion is in pencil, and a deletion sign is written in the margin in pencil.]

13. 1896, 1904: fears appall him,
14. 1847, 1896, 1904: ills befall him;
15. 1847: There 's nought
23. MS: dawning[illegible erasure of punctuation]<:>
1847, 1896, 1904: dawning;
25. 1847, 1896, 1904: the sunbeams,—
27. 1847, 1896, 1904: Of resurrection,
33. 1896, 1904: in heaven,
34. 1896, 1904: The resting-place

ZARA. ["NOW THE PAIN BEGINNETH AND THE WORD IS SPOKEN"]

[Date of composition unknown. Editions: 1896, 1904. The poem was printed in *Verses: Dedicated to Her Mother* (London: privately printed at G. Polidori's, 1847), 64–66. Basic text: 1847.]

Subtitle. 1896, 1904: [There is no subtitle.]

5. 1896, 1904: yea what
6. 1896, 1904: most desolate!

9. 1896, 1904: Yea the
24. 1847: Fnll of
29. 1896, 1904: the heaven no
30. 1896, 1904: the heaven no
32. 1896, 1904: skies:
35. 1896: thunders, deafen, < >

lightnings, blind
1904: thunders, deafen, < >
lightnings, blind me;
36. 1896, 1904: him!
39. 1847: Thongh the
1904: bitter, yet

VERSI.

[Composed October 6, 1849. Editions: 1896, 1904. The notebook MS is in the Bodleian Library. The poem was printed in *The Bouquet, Culled from Marylebone Gardens*, No. 5 (London: printed at the "Bouquet" Press for private circulation, October, 1851), 175. Basic text: notebook MS. In the 1851 text, lines 4, 8, 12, 16, 20, and 24 are indented four spaces.]

Title. 1896, 1904: VERSI
1. 1851: disse,
    1896, 1904: la Madre disse,
2. 1896, 1904: dall' Amore:
3. 1896, 1904: traditore—
5. MS: Non lasciagli sperare [In the right margin are added two illegible lines in pencil.]
6. 1896, 1904: petto,
7. 1896, 1904: gli dà ricetto
11. 1896, 1904: menzognero,
12. MS: [Above the line are two illegible additions written in pencil.]

13. MS: [Above the line is an illegible addition written in pencil.]
15. MS: [Above the line is an illegible addition written in pencil.]
    1851, 1896, 1904: pace,
16. MS: [Beside the line is added an illegible line in pencil.]
17. 1896, 1904: vedo—già
    1896s: vedo—già sai stanca
20. 1896s: chi,
22. 1896, 1904: sinceri—
23. 1851: È se
24. 1851: un di. [Below the text of the poem is printed Christina's pen name:] CALTA.

L'INCOGNITA.

[Date of composition unknown. Editions: 1896, 1904. The poem was printed in *The Bouquet, Culled from Marylebone Gardens*, No. 7 (London: printed at the "Bouquet" Press for private circulation, December, 1851), 216. Basic text: 1851. In the 1896 text, line 5 is indented two spaces, and lines 6 and 7 are not indented. In the 1904 text, lines 2 and 5 are indented two spaces; lines 4 and 8 are indented four spaces; and lines 6 and 7 are not indented.]

Title. 1896, 1904: L'INCOGNITA
3. 1896, 1904: fosse, allor
6. 1896, 1904: ver ma
7. 1896, 1904: la primavera:—

8. 1851: [Below the text of the poem is printed Christina's pen name:] CALTA.
    1896, 1904: Ah l'immagin

"PURPUREA ROSA"

[Date of composition unknown. Editions: 1896, 1904. The poem was printed in *The Bouquet, Culled from Marylebone Gardens*, No. 15 (London: printed at the "Bouquet"

Press for private circulation, August, 1852), 56, as part of a series of letters in Italian entitled "Corrispondenza Famigliare." Basic text: 1852. In the 1896 and 1904 texts, lines 4, 6, 10, and 12 are indented two spaces.]

Title. 1896, 1904: NIGELLA
1. 1896, 1904: rosa,
3. 1896, 1904: bella—

10. 1896, 1904: a sè;
11. 1896, 1904: fiore—

"SOUL RUDDERLESS, UNBRACED"

[Date of composition unknown. Editions: 1896, 1904. Christina's fair copy MS, originally part of a letter to William Michael Rossetti, is in the Princeton University Library. The poem was printed in David Johnston (ed.), *Translations, Literal and Free, of the Dying Hadrian's Address to His Soul* (Bath, England: printed at the "Chronicle" office, for private circulation only, 1876), 49. Basic text: MS. In the 1896 and 1904 texts, lines 2, 3, and 5 are indented four spaces.]

Title. 1876: XII.
   1896, 1904: HADRIAN'S
   DEATH-SONG TRANSLATED
2. MS: friend & guest.
   1876, 1896, 1904: The body's
   friend

3. 1876, 1896, 1904: away to-day?
4. 1876: pale, dis-cased,
5. MS: [Below the poem is written:]
   C.G.R.

"ANIMUCCIA, VAGANTUCCIA, MORBIDUCCIA"

[Date of composition unknown. Editions: 1896, 1904. The poem was printed in David Johnston (ed.), *Translations, Literal and Free, of the Dying Hadrian's Address to His Soul* (Bath, England: printed at the "Chronicle" office, for private circulation only, 1876), 49. Basic text: 1876. In the 1896 text, lines 2, 3, and 5 are indented four spaces.]

Title. 1876: XIII.
   1896, 1904: ADRIANO

HEAVEN.

[Composed in 1842. The notebook MS, in the handwriting of Christina's sister, Maria Francesca Rossetti, is in the British Library. Basic text: notebook MS.]

HYMN. ["TO THE GOD WHO REIGNS ON HIGH"]

[Composed July 2, 1843. Editions: 1896, 1904. The notebook MS, in the handwriting of Christina's sister, Maria Francesca Rossetti, is in the British Library. Basic text: notebook MS. In the 1896 and 1904 texts, lines 2, 4, and 6 are indented two spaces.]

Title. 1896, 1904: HYMN
1. 1896, 1904: the God who reigns
2. 1896, 1904: To the Eternal
3. 1896, 1904: the Blessed Trinity,

4. 1896, 1904: be given,
5. 1896, 1904: sea and
6. 1896, 1904: highest heaven.

CORYDON'S LAMENT AND RESOLUTION.

[Composed in July, 1843. The notebook MS, in the handwriting of Christina's sister, Maria Francesca Rossetti, is in the British Library. Basic text: notebook MS.]

ROSALIND.

[Composed in July, 1843. The notebook MS, in the handwriting of Christina's sister, Maria Francesca Rossetti, is in the British Library. Basic text: notebook MS.]

3. MS: a stag- / hound,
26. MS: I<'>ll compensated

PITIA A DAMONE.

[Composed April 20, 1844. The notebook MS, in the handwriting of Christina's sister, Maria Francesca Rossetti, is in the British Library. Basic text: notebook MS. The MS contains a short vertical line below the title and last line of the poem.]

2. MS: [Illegible erasure] <È gioia> quel
4. MS: [Because line 4 is the last line on the page, there is no indication of whether or not a stanza break is intended to follow it except the absence of a short vertical line below the line of poetry.]

THE FAITHLESS SHEPHERDESS.

[Composed June 17, 1844. The notebook MS, in the handwriting of Christina's sister, Maria Francesca Rossetti, is in the British Library. Basic text: notebook MS.]

8. MS: And [illegible erasure] <arrest> all
17. MS: was murm[u]<'>ring of
19. MS: speak [*from*] <far> above
36. MS: An[illegible erasure]<d arrest> all

ARIADNE TO THESEUS.

[Composed June 18, 1844. The notebook MS, in the handwriting of Christina's sister, Maria Francesca Rossetti, is in the British Library. Basic text: notebook MS.]

Title. MS: [*St. S—— of*] <Ariadne to Theseus.>
1. MS: [Illegible deletion] <Su>nlight to
28. MS: [Below the text of the poem is the following note, enclosed in brackets:] [The reader may perhaps detect in these verses a resemblance to an idea in one of Metastasio's dramas.]

ON ALBINA.

[Composed in June, 1844. Editions: 1896, 1904. The notebook MS, in the handwriting of Christina's sister, Maria Francesca Rossetti, is in the British Library. Basic text: notebook MS.]

Title. 1896, 1904: ON ALBINA
1. 1896, 1904: cheeks
3. MS: gentle Reader, [illegible

erasure] <could it> be
1896, 1904: O gentle reader, could

A HYMN FOR CHRISTMAS DAY.

[Composed June 30, 1844. The notebook MS, in the handwriting of Christina's sister, Maria Francesca Rossetti, is in the British Library. Basic text: notebook MS.]

1. MS: The Shepherds watch[*ed*]
   their
4. MS: the murm[*u*]<'>ring of

8. MS: with [illegible erasure] <love>
   celest[*a*]<i>al glowing.
10. MS: gloom[;]<,> their
14. MS: wend[.]

LOVE AND DEATH.

[Composed July 2, 1844. The notebook MS, in the handwriting of Christina's sister, Maria Francesca Rossetti, is in the British Library. Basic text: notebook MS.]

4. MS: woven [*in*] <of> faint
5. MS: these [illegible erasure] <I'll
   twine> the
6. MS: of th[*ee*]<y> chestnut
9. MS: thee[:]<;>
19. MS: the moon- / beam's deceitful
26. MS: fair[,]<?>

32. MS: [*But*] <All> vain[*ly*] [*he*] <are
    his> struggles
36. MS: hears [illegible erasure] <not>
    the
42. MS: them ro[illegible
    deletion]<lls> each

DESPAIR.

[Composed August 19, 1844. The notebook MS, in the handwriting of Christina's sister, Maria Francesca Rossetti, is in the British Library. Basic text: notebook MS.]

FORGET ME NOT.

[Composed August 19, 1844. Editions: 1896, 1904. The notebook MS, in the handwriting of Christina's sister, Maria Francesca Rossetti, is in the British Library. Basic text: notebook MS.]

Title. 1896, 1904: FORGET ME NOT
1. 1896, 1904: "Forget me not, forget
3. MS: far-off battle<->field
   1896, 1904: far-off battlefield

5. 1896, 1904: Forget me not, forget
6. 1896, 1904: chamber-maid,

EASTER MORNING.

[Composed September 15, 1844. The notebook MS, in the handwriting of Christina's sister, Maria Francesca Rossetti, is in the British Library. Basic text: notebook MS.]

5. MS: summer b[z]<r>eeze is

A TIRSI.

[Composed February 25, 1845. The notebook MS, in the handwriting of Christina's sister, Maria Francesca Rossetti, is in the British Library. Basic text: notebook MS.]

THE LAST WORDS OF ST. TELEMACHUS.

[Composed March 1, 1845. The notebook MS, in the handwriting of Christina's sister, Maria Francesca Rossetti, is in the British Library. Basic text: notebook MS.]

10. MS: without [illegible deletion]
    <praise>—

LORD THOMAS AND FAIR MARGARET.

[Composed April 2, 1845. The notebook MS, in the handwriting of Christina's sister, Maria Francesca Rossetti, is in the British Library. Basic text: notebook MS. The MS contains a short horizontal line below the title and last line of the poem.]

Title. MS: [In the space below the title is a line of illegible erasures.]

1. MS: [Illegible erasure] <Fair Marg'ret sat in her bower,>
2. MS: [Illegible erasure] <Unbraiding of her hair>
3. MS: [Illegible erasure] <When entered in Lord Thomas' ghost,>
4. MS: [Illegible erasure] <And gave her greeting fair.>

14. MS: aye [*must*] <maun> be,
33. MS: fair Marg'ret, oh [illegible deletion]<s>weet Marg'ret,
44. MS: [Below the text of the poem is the following note:] This is imitated from the ballad of "Sweet William's Ghost," in Percy's "Reliques of Ancient English Poetry."

LINES TO MY GRANDFATHER.

[Composed May 1, 1845. Editions: 1904. The notebook MS, in the handwriting of Christina's sister, Maria Francesca Rossetti, is in the British Library. Basic text: notebook MS. In the MS, stanza breaks are indicated by a short horizontal line rather than by an empty space. In the 1904 text, the second and fourth lines of each stanza are indented four spaces.]

Title. 1904: LINES TO MY GRANDFATHER

1–2. Dear Grandpapa,—To be obedient,
6. 1904: My Muse of <> prolific;
12. 1904: venture,
14. MS: The apple<->tree is [The added hyphen is written in red ink.]
15. 1904: red,
16. MS: [Illegible deletion] <With> a
18. MS: The pear<->tree's pure [The

added hyphen is written in red ink.]
26. 1904: The king-cup flowers
31. 1904: fresh Spring air:—
33. 1904: parterre.
34. 1904: concluded;
36. MS: is well- / nigh excluded,
    1904: And, though
38. 1904: beautiful
40–41. 1904: I sign myself—Your dutiful
42. 1904: Affectionate grand-daughter.

CHARADE.

[Composed December 3, 1845. The notebook MS, in the handwriting of Christina's sister, Maria Francesca Rossetti, is in the British Library. Basic text: notebook MS. The MS contains a short horizontal line below the title and last line of the poem.]

   6. MS: [Below the text of the poem is written:] Answer. Sonnet.

HOPE IN GRIEF.

[Composed December 3, 1845. Christina's fair copy (MS1) is in the Princeton University Library. The notebook MS (MS2), in the handwriting of Christina's sister, Maria Francesca Rossetti, is in the British Library. Basic text: MS1. In MS2, lines 6, 10, 12, 16, 18, 24, and 26 are indented two spaces.]

   5. MS2: [*Si*] <Gn>awings that   23. MS2: What, though
  17. MS2: Engulphing, [*wi*] <as>   30. MS2: will [*uprise*] <up-rise> the
     the<y> anguished

LISETTA ALL' AMANTE.

[Composed August 11, 1846. Editions: 1896, 1904. The notebook MS, in the handwriting of Christina's sister, Maria Francesca Rossetti, is in the Bodleian Library. Basic text: notebook MS. In the 1896 text, lines 4, 8, 12, and 16 are indented four spaces, and the remaining lines are not indented. In the 1904 text, line 4 is indented two spaces; lines 8, 12, and 16 are indented four spaces; and the remaining lines are not indented.]

Title. 1896, 1904: LISETTA ALL'   5. 1896, 1904: dimmi e
     AMANTE   13. 1896, 1904: voglio,

SONG. ["I SAW HER; SHE WAS LOVELY"]

[Composed September 27, 1846. The notebook MS, in the handwriting of Christina's sister, Maria Francesca Rossetti, is in the Bodleian Library. Basic text: notebook MS.]

PRAISE OF LOVE.

[Composed February 24, 1847. The notebook MS, in the handwriting of Christina's sister, Maria Francesca Rossetti, is in the Bodleian Library. The final stanza of the poem was published in *Time Flies: A Reading Diary* (see "Love is all happiness, love is all beauty" in Part I herein for that text). Basic text: notebook MS.]

"I HAVE FOUGHT A GOOD FIGHT."

[Composed in July, 1847. Editions: 1896, 1904. The notebook MS, in the handwriting of Christina's sister, Maria Francesca Rossetti, is in the Bodleian Library. Basic text: notebook MS.]

Title. 1896, 1904: I HAVE FOUGHT
   A GOOD FIGHT
  1. 1896, 1904: a steadfast face
  2. 1896: Through the < > to the
    burying- / place?"
    1904: Through the
  6. 1896, 1904: Though thy
 12. 1896: Like a desert-fountain, or

    1904: Like a desert-fountain, or
    < > relief.
15. 1896, 1904: "Though I
16. 1896, 1904: ever, He who
    comforteth."
23. 1896, 1904: the heaven above,
24. 1896, 1904: in His love."

WISHES: / SONNET.

[Composed July 22, 1847. Editions: 1896, 1904. The notebook MS, in the handwriting of Christina's sister, Maria Francesca Rossetti, is in the Bodleian Library. Basic text: notebook MS. In the MS, line 2 is not indented.]

Title. 1896, 1904: WISHES
Subtitle. 1896, 1904: [There is no
    subtitle.]
  1. 1896, 1904: Oh would

  5. 1896, 1904: the wild flowers
    scattered
  9. 1896, 1904: sea—
13. 1896, 1904: But, be

ELEANOR.

[Composed July 30, 1847. Editions: 1896, 1904. The notebook MS, in the handwriting of Christina's sister, Maria Francesca Rossetti, is in the Bodleian Library. Basic text: notebook MS. In the 1896 and 1904 texts, lines 1, 5, 13, 15, and 17 are indented two spaces; and lines 2, 4, 6, 8, 10, 12, 14, 16, 18, 20, 22, 24, 26, 28, 29, 30, and 32 are indented four spaces.]

Title. 1896, 1904: ELEANOR
  6. 1896, 1904: rejoice:
13. 1896, 1904: As though a
21. 1904: hand, her little foot,
25. 1896: But, if < > sang or
    1904: sang or

27. 1896, 1904: As though a
29. 1896, 1904: As though a
31. 1896, 1904: Halfway between < >
    and heaven

ISIDORA.

[Composed August 9, 1847. Editions: 1896, 1904. The notebook MS, in the handwriting of Christina's sister, Maria Francesca Rossetti, is in the Bodleian Library. Basic text: notebook MS. In the MS, lines 20 and 32 are not indented, and line 21 is indented one space.]

Title. 1896, 1904: ISIDORA
Subtitle. 1896, 1904: [There is no
    subtitle.]
  3. 1896, 1904: heed nor heaven
    nor hell
16. 1896, 1904: the accurst control,
19. 1896, 1904: Yea from hell I
23. 1896, 1904: the light that

24. 1896, 1904: the glory of
29. 1896, 1904: Yea thine
31. 1896, 1904: die—
33. 1896, 1904: Thou wouldst gain
34. 1896, 1904: be loth
40. 1896, 1904: ah nothing
41. 1896, 1904: knowest naught of
43. 1896, 1904: thee, none

56. 1896, 1904: words or
58. 1896, 1904: me—But he < > gone!
59. 1896, 1904: back, and
60. 1896, 1904: wilt!—It is
61. 1896, 1904: done,

62. 1896, 1904: Yea the
63. 1896, 1904: won:—
64. 1896, 1904: more:—
68. 1896, 1904: weak, and through my
71. 1896, 1904: care:—

THE NOVICE.

[Composed September 4, 1847. Editions: 1896, 1904. The notebook MS, in the handwriting of Christina's sister, Maria Francesca Rossetti, is in the Bodleian Library. Basic text: notebook MS.]

Title. 1896, 1904: THE NOVICE
1. 1896, 1904: one and
7. 1896, 1904: alter nought
15. 1896, 1904: in hell
16. 1896, 1904: in heaven.
17. 1896, 1904: Yea it < > a
poison-cup

18. MS: quick fire- / draught within;
25. MS: by[illegible deletion]<;>
1896, 1904: by,
27. 1896, 1904: nuts: there
29. 1896, 1904: There autumn leaves

IMMALEE.

[Composed September 21, 1847. Editions: 1896, 1904. The notebook MS, in the handwriting of Christina's sister, Maria Francesca Rossetti, is in the Bodleian Library. Basic text: notebook MS.]

Title. MS: [*Immalee:*] [The deletion is in pencil. Above the title is an illegible pencil erasure.]
1896, 1904: IMMALEE
Subtitle. MS: [/*See Maturin's "Melmoth."*/] / [*Sonnet.*] [The deletions are in pencil. In the top right corner is written a cross and the word "set" in pencil in William Michael Rossetti's hand.]
1896, 1904: [There is no subtitle.]

7. 1896, 1904: fruit and < > strawberry
8. 1896, 1904: nuts and
10. 1904: roof:
13. MS: squirrels [*in the branches almost fly*] <sit perked [*up*] as I pass them by>, [The revisions are written above and beside the line in pencil in Christina's handwriting.]

LADY ISABELLA.

[Composed September 27, 1847. Editions: 1896, 1904. The notebook MS, in the handwriting of Christina's sister, Maria Francesca Rossetti, is in the Bodleian Library. Basic text: notebook MS.]

Title. 1896, 1904: LADY ISABELLA
1. 1896, 1904: warm as summer, fresh as spring,
2. 1896, 1904: as autumn's harvesting,

3. 1896, 1904: the winter's snows;
4. 1896, 1904: in sunlight;
14. 1896, 1904: had Lady Isabel.

NIGHT AND DEATH.

[Composed September 28, 1847. Editions: 1896, 1904. The notebook MS, in the handwriting of Christina's sister, Maria Francesca Rossetti, is in the Bodleian Library. Basic text: notebook MS.]

Title. MS: [To the left of the title is written in pencil:] O
1896, 1904: NIGHT AND DEATH
1. 1896, 1904: the sunlit hours
5. 1896, 1904: measure
16. 1896, 1904: saith
27. 1896, 1904: Though he
28. 1896, 1904: unrest,
29. 1904: breast,

31. 1896, 1904: earth,
32. 1896, 1904: her, are <> worth:
41. 1896, 1904: resigned though desolate;
45. 1904: recompense
50. 1896, 1904: the Angel-uttered chime
53. 1896, 1904: her, and
55. 1896, 1904: flown,

"YOUNG MEN AYE WERE FICKLE FOUND / SINCE SUMMER TREES WERE LEAFY."

[Composed September 30, 1847. The notebook MS, in the handwriting of Christina's sister, Maria Francesca Rossetti, is in the Bodleian Library. Basic text: notebook MS.]

THE LOTUS-EATERS: / ULYSSES TO PENELOPE.

[Composed October 7, 1847. Editions: 1896, 1904. The notebook MS, in the handwriting of Christina's sister, Maria Francesca Rossetti, is in the Bodleian Library. Basic text: notebook MS. In the 1896 and 1904 texts, lines 1, 3, 4, 5, 7, 9, 10, 11, 13, 15, 18, 19, 20, 21, 25, 27–36 are indented two spaces; lines 8, 12, 23, and 24 are indented six spaces; and lines 2, 14, 16, 17, 22, and 26 are indented four spaces.]

Title. MS: [Below the title is the following subtitle:] [<(*an echo from Tennyson*).>] [The addition is in pencil in Christina's hand. The deletion is in pencil.]
1896, 1904: THE LOTUS-EATERS / ULYSSES TO PENELOPE
1. 1896, 1904: a far distant land
5. MS: [*The*] <Cool> evening [The deletion is in pencil. The added word is written above the line in pencil in Christina's hand.]
11. 1896, 1904: a twilight purple rim,
14. MS: soon <it> ceaseth [The added word is written above the line in pencil in Christina's hand.]

15. 1896, 1904: again,—
18. MS: [*Yet*] <But> no [The deletion is in pencil. The added word is written above the line in pencil in Christina's hand.]
20. 1896, 1904: Through the <> flows,
21. 1896, 1904: goes:
23. 1896, 1904: listen hear not:
24. 1896, 1904: But, if <> not—
26. 1896, 1904: the dreams of
27. 1896, 1904: bloweth,
28. 1896, 1904: moweth:
34. 1896, 1904: hot or cold,—

SONNET / FROM THE PSALMS.

[Composed November 7, 1847. Editions: 1896, 1904. The notebook MS is in the
Bodleian Library. Basic text: notebook MS.]

Title. 1896, 1904: SONNET / FROM   3. 1896, 1904: distress:—
   THE PSALMS   8. 1896, 1904: lo the <> spake—
 1. 1896, 1904: All through the <>   11. 1896, 1904: friends or hope or
    awake,   12. 1896, 1904: breast:

SONG. ["THE STREAM MOANETH AS IT FLOWETH"]

[Composed November 7, 1847. Editions: 1896, 1904. The notebook MS is in the
Bodleian Library. Basic text: notebook MS.]

Title. 1896, 1904: SONG   20. 1896, 1904: Hark the
 8. 1896, 1904: help me? who will   21. 1896, 1904: Hark the
 9. 1896, 1904: me: 22. 1896, 1904: dieth:
13. 1896, 1904: sea: 26. 1896, 1904: riot:
16. 1896, 1904: heart-aching,   28. 1896, 1904: beating.
17. 1896, 1904: waking,   29. 1896, 1904: fleeting;
18. 1896, 1904: day-breaking,   30. 1896, 1904: sought—
19. 1904: [A stanza break follows the   31. 1896, 1904: Long unchangeable
    line.]

A COUNSEL.

[Composed November 15, 1847. The notebook MS is in the Bodleian Library. Basic
text: notebook MS.]
 3. MS: Friends hollow- / hearted

THE WORLD'S HARMONIES.

[Composed November 20, 1847. Editions: 1896, 1904. The notebook MS is in the
Bodleian Library. Basic text: notebook MS.]

Title. 1896, 1904: THE WORLD'S   21. MS: Clouds and all the
   HARMONIES   [w]<W>inds
 1. 1896, 1904: Oh listen, listen, for   26. 1896, 1904: eternal chaunt,
 2. 1896, 1904: melody: 29. MS: unseen palace- / gates,
 4. 1896, 1904: blossoms: and   32. 1896, 1904: acceptable:
 7. MS: the [s]<S>ea   33. 1896, 1904: faltering:
    1896, 1904: Oh listen, listen, for   34. 1896, 1904: well:
 8. 1896, 1904: us: 35. 1896, 1904: Yea in
11. 1896, 1904: Lo the   40. 1896, 1904: rejoice:
13. 1896, 1904: look,   41. 1896, 1904: the blessed Spirits
14. 1896, 1904: strong,   42. 1896, 1904: choice:
15. 1896, 1904: giveth life,   44. 1896, 1904: in:
20. 1896, 1904: all: 46. 1896, 1904: win:—
                                          47. 1896, 1904: a Poor Man

Textual Notes

415

LINES / GIVEN WITH A PENWIPER.

[Composed November 20, 1847. The notebook MS is in the Bodleian Library. Basic text: notebook MS.]

THE LAST ANSWER.

[Composed December 2, 1847. Editions: 1896, 1904. The notebook MS is in the Bodleian Library. Basic text: notebook MS. In the 1896 text, line 13 is not indented.]

Title. MS: [Below the title is an erased note written in pencil in William Michael Rossetti's hand:] [<Written to Bouts-rimes>]
1896: THE LAST ANSWER /
(Written to Bouts-rimés)
1904: THE LAST ANSWER /
(Written to Bouts-rimés.)
1. 1896, 1904: eyes.
3. 1896, 1904: Have < > lips," she
4. MS: to [illegible deletion] <arise;>
1896, 1904: Have < > arise.

5. MS: yet he [spoke] <stirred> not; [The deletion is in pencil. The added word is written below the line in pencil in Christina's hand.]
1896, 1904: He < > not: on
6. 1896, 1904: Not
7. 1896, 1904: But
8. MS: fallacies.
1896, 1904: Learned
9. 1896, 1904: me: and
14. MS: statelier
1896, 1904: she meanwhile only

ONE OF THE DEAD.

[Composed December 4, 1847. The notebook MS is in the Bodleian Library. Basic text: notebook MS.]

"THE WHOLE HEAD IS SICK, AND THE WHOLE HEART FAINT."

[Composed December 6, 1847. Editions: 1896, 1904. A separate fair copy (MS1) is in the University of Kansas Library. The notebook MS (MS2), is in the Bodleian Library. Basic text: MS2.]

Title. MS2: and the / "whole
1896: THE WHOLE HEAD IS SICK AND THE WHOLE HEART FAINT
1904: THE WHOLE HEAD IS SICK AND THE WHOLE HEART FAINT.
1. MS1: young <who> say
2. MS1: west;
1896, 1904: to the West,

3. MS1: rest;
4. 1904: for even- / song.
5. MS1, 1896, 1904: hearts, weary
6. MS1: unexpressed:
1896, 1904: longings unexprest;
7. MS1: drest;
10. 1896, 1904: all Nature is
12. 1896, 1904: murmuring:
13. 1896, 1904: say, "The
14. 1896, 1904: perishing."

"I DO SET MY BOW IN THE CLOUD."

[Composed in December, 1847. Editions: 1896, 1904. The notebook MS is in the Bodleian Library. Basic text: notebook MS.]

Title. 1896, 1904: I DO SET MY BOW
  IN THE CLOUD
1. 1896, 1904: me:
2. 1896, 1904: see:
4. 1896, 1904: to home:
8. 1896, 1904: One who is
10. 1896, 1904: me:
12. 1896, 1904: death that <> life:
13. 1896, 1904: me, He
19. 1896, 1904: walls:
21. 1896, 1904: And Angels: yea,

27. 1896, 1904: chasteneth His
  beloved still.
28. 1896, 1904: me: is
29. MS: To f[*ee*]<ee>l that
  1896, 1904: that, when <> rough
30. 1896, 1904: dark and
32. 1896, 1904: have past away
35. 1896, 1904: Behold: He <> a
  haven-rest,
36. 1896, 1904: A sheltering rock, a
  hiding-place,

"O DEATH WHERE IS THY STING?"

[Composed probably between December, 1847, and January 12, 1848. The notebook MS of lines 1–6 is in the Bodleian Library; the rest of the poem was removed from the notebook. Basic text: notebook MS.]

UNDINE.

[Composed January 12, 1848. The notebook MS is in the Bodleian Library. Basic text: notebook MS.]

14. MS: Ol[illegible deletion]<d>   35. MS: the agoni[*s*]<z>ing strife
  thoughts

LADY MONTREVOR.

[Composed February 18, 1848. Editions: 1896, 1904. The notebook MS is in the Bodleian Library. Basic text: notebook MS.]

Title. 1896, 1904: LADY
  MONTREVOR
Subtitle. MS: (See Maturin's "Wild
  Irish Boy."
  1896, 1904: [There is no subtitle.]
1. 1896, 1904: dream—
7. 1896, 1904: sea, and

9. 1896, 1904: And, though young
  spring and summer pass
10. 1896, 1904: And autumn and cold
  winter come again,
12. 1896, 1904: earth, and
13. 1896, 1904: dust, my <>
  complain;—

FLORAL TEACHING.

[Composed February 19, 1848. The notebook MS is in the Bodleian Library. Basic text: notebook MS.]

"DEATH IS SWALLOWED UP IN VICTORY."

[Composed February 20, 1848. Editions: 1896, 1904. The notebook MS is in the Bodleian Library. Basic text: notebook MS. In the MS, all the added quotation marks and all the deletions are in pencil, and the added words are in pencil in Christina's handwriting unless otherwise indicated. In the 1896 and 1904 texts, there are no stanza breaks, and the lines with even numbers are indented two spaces.]

Title. 1896, 1904: DEATH IS SWALLOWED UP IN VICTORY

1. MS: <">Tell <> to [*sit*] <lie> here

2. MS: the [*blossoms*] <cornfields> waving

3. MS: in the [*rosy*] <waxing> Summer <> year?<">
1896, 1904: in the waking summer of

4. MS: <">I [*pass*] <fade> from
1896, 1904: earth, and lo along

5. MS: love [*goeth*] <will fade> away:

6. MS: for [*coldness*] <Autumn> longingly?<">
1896, 1904: for autumn longingly?"

7. MS: <">Yet Autumn [*hath its*] <heareth> fruit[*s, and*] <whilst> day
1896, 1904: "Yet autumn beareth

9. MS: decay.<">

10. MS: <">Decay

11. 1896, 1904: near: behold,

12. MS: Than [*a long life*] <length of days> and [*a long*] <length of> sorrow too.<">

13. MS: <">But
1896, 1904: solitude;

14. 1896, 1904: thee: dost

15. MS: which [*others in vain have*] <in vain have others sued?">

16. MS: <">I <> is [*my*] <mine> only [The added word is retraced in pencil in William Michael Rossetti's hand.]

17. 1896, 1904: me nor

18. MS: deed.<">

19. MS: <">Here
1904: seek it other- / where?

21. MS: many [*pleasant*] <goodly> things and [*f*]<s>weet, [The deleted letter and revised letter are in ink.] <> fair.<">
1896, 1904: things and sweet and

22. MS: <">There
1896, 1904: laughter: in

23. 1896, 1904: lo

24. MS: [*The*] <An> infant's <> birth.<">

25. MS: <">I [*see*] <mark> the

26. MS: hath [*sorrow*] <care> one day, [*on the next*] <& is perplext>
1896, 1904: day and

27. MS: [*May have great gladness in the place of woe.*] <Tomorrow may have joy in place of woe">
1896, 1904: To-morrow may

28. MS: <">Evil
1896, 1904: good: and

29. 1896, 1904: evil: speak <> more:

30. MS: is [*weary*] <wearied> and <> vext.<">

31. MS: <">Is <> no [*wish*] <place> it

32. MS: thou lov[*e*]<'>st, [illegible addition above the line and then erased] and <so> wouldst

33. MS: [*Stay yet*] <Tarry> a little <> door?<">

34. MS: <">I [*shall*] <must> go
1896, 1904: again:

35. MS: But [*the*] <the> friends whom I [*love<d>*] <have> shall

36. MS: And [*we will*] dwell <> without <with me safe from> pain.<">

37. MS: <">Where

38. MS: <Behold> The tombs are [*dark and*] full
1896, 1904: Behold, the <> worms: shalt

39. MS: and [*fly*] <soar> up <> gloriously?<">

40. MS: <">Even <> shine w[*h*]<e> know [The deleted letter and revised letter are in ink.]

41. 1896, 1904: then, changed yet <> same—

42. MS: now.<">
1896, 1904: like Christ, yea being

43. MS: <"Thither> Thou goest [*there*] whence
1896, 1904: thou go'st whence

44. 1896, 1904: not, and in death

45. MS: for [*joy,*] <speech> [*or wealth,*] <sigh> [*or*] fame.<"> [Beside the

line is added in pencil in William
Michael Rossetti's hand:] <speech
or sign or>
  1896, 1904: speech or sign or
46. MS: <">There
47. 1896, 1904: not: and
48. MS: hovereth.<">
49. MS: <">When <> stars [*fail*]
  <fall>, and
  1896, 1904: fall and
51. MS: spent?<">
52. MS: <">The<se> elements shall
  [*cease*] <consummate> their
  [*ancient*] strife,
53. 1896, 1904: scroll,
54. MS: beauty-rife.<">
  1904: re-created, beauty- / rife.'
55. MS: <">Who
57. MS: [*Yea,*] [*w*]<W>ho shall [*live to
  see*] <abide to scan> the [The
  revision is retraced in pencil in
  William Michael Rossetti's hand.]
  <> whole?<">
58. MS: <">He
  1896, 1904: own:
60. MS: hope; [*and*] <who> trusts <>
  alone.<">
  1896, 1904: hope: who <> in Love
  alone."

61. MS: <">Yet
  1896, 1904: thou—the
62. 1896, 1904: rest: think <> it:
63. MS: that <is and> shall be, [*and
  is,*] and <> been.<">
  1896, 1904: be and
64. MS: <">The
65. MS: it [*gladly*] <meekly>? though
66. MS: a [*little*] <moment>, it <>
  shrink.<">
67. MS: <">Satan shall [*rise against*]
  <will wrestle with> thee,
  1896, 1904: thee when
68. MS: and [*he shall*] <Death will>
  bring
69. MS: [*Toward old*] [*s*]<S>ins <to
  remembrance ere> [*before*] thy <>
  part.<">
70. MS: <">In
71. MS: and His [*mighty*] arm <made
  bare> [The added words are
  retraced in pencil in William
  Michael Rossetti's hand.]
72. 1896s: wing,
73. MS: safe[,] [*havened in perfect calm*]
  <at rest & freed from care>.<">

DEATH.

[Composed April 12, 1848. The notebook MS is in the Bodleian Library. Basic text:
notebook MS.]

A HOPELESS CASE. / (NYDIA.)

[Composed April 24, 1848. The notebook MS (MS1) is in the Bodleian Library. A
fair copy, signed "Christina G. Rossetti," (MS2) is in the Princeton University Li-
brary. Basic text: MS2.]

Title. MS1: Nydia. / (See Bulwer's
  "Last days of Pompeii.")
1. MS1: be;
  MS2: All [*day*] <night> I
4. MS1: I have joy in my sleep;
  but, woe
5. MS1: Through the
6. MS1: not; therefore I

7. MS1: potion, that
  MS2: pot[illegible deletion]<ion>
  that
8. MS1: long that pass
11. MS1: pain;—
12. MS1: hope, a
13. MS1: twilight hush is blessedness,
14. MS1: wind and stormy rain.

ELLEN MIDDLETON.

[Composed in May, 1848. The notebook MS is in the Bodleian Library. Basic text: notebook MS.]

ST. ANDREW'S CHURCH.

[Composed June 1, 1848. The notebook MS (MS1) is in the Bodeleian Library. The version of the poem in Christina's 1850 notebook MS of *Maude: Prose & Verse* (MS2) is in the Huntington Library. The poem was printed in *Maude: Prose & Verse, by Christina Rossetti; 1850* (Chicago: Herbert S. Stone, 1897), 67; variants therein are designated "1897a" in the textual notes. Basic text: MS2. In MS1, lines 1, 4, 5, and 8 are not indented; lines 2, 3, 6, 7, 9, and 12 are indented two spaces; and lines 10, 11, 13, and 14 are indented four spaces. In the 1897a text, lines 1, 4, 5, 8, 10, and 13 are indented two spaces, and the remaining lines are not indented.]

Title. MS2, 1897a: [untitled]
  3. MS1: solemnly,
  6. MS1: "What lovest thou
     MS2: "What lov[*e*']<'st> thou
  8. MS1: most blessèd thing."
  11. MS1: to heaven but

MS2: not <to> Heaven,
  1897a: to heaven, but
12. MS1: guard lest
14. MS2: teach.—
  1897a: teach—

GROWN COLD.

[Composed June 18, 1848. The notebook MS is in the Bodleian Library. Basic text: notebook MS.]

ZARA. ["THE PALE SAD FACE OF HER I WRONGED"]

[Composed June 18, 1848. The notebook MS is in the Bodleian Library. Basic text: notebook MS.]

71. MS: long <for> death;

95. MS: [*A*] <Yea, a>t length,

RUIN.

[Composed in 1848. Editions: 1896, 1904. The rough draft (MS1) and a signed fair copy (MS3) are in the Princeton University Library. The notebook MS (MS2) is in the Bodleian Library. Basic text: MS3. In MS1, the text is written in pencil, and no lines are indented. In MS2, lines 11 and 13 are not indented; lines 12 and 14 are indented two spaces; and the revisions and deletions are in pencil in Christina's handwriting unless otherwise indicated. In the 1896 and 1904 texts, line 12 is indented two spaces, and line 13 is not indented.]

Title. MS1: [untitled]
  MS2: [*Bouts rimés*] Sonnets. [The deletion is in pencil, and beside the

title is added in pencil in William Michael Rossetti's hand:] <written to Bouts rimés. Summer 1848.>

1896, 1904: SONNETS/
WRITTEN TO BOUTS-RIMÉS/ I
1. MS1: [*To the anci*] <Amid> the
shadows of an ancient hall
MS2: the shad[*ow*]<e>s of [*an
ancient*] <a deserted> hall
1896, 1904: the shades of
2. MS1: stand thinking on that which
hath <> lost
MS2: stand <&> think[*ing*] on
<much> that [*which*] hath
3. MS1: since any step has crossed
MS2: since [*any*] <other> step has
crossed
1896, 1904: has crost
4. MS1: This time worn floor; the
tapestry
MS2: floor; th[*e*]<is> tapestry
1896, 1904: floor! This tapestry
5. MS1: Wormeaten; & the columns
MS2: Wormeaten; and th[*e*]<ose>
columns
1896, 1904: and these columns
6. MS1: And white in their decay
where <> tossed
MS2: [*And white in*] <Yet
crumbling to> their decay; <>
banners tossed
1896, 1904: banners tost
7. MS1: Thin spider's webs hang[*s*]
now; the bitter

MS2: Thin spider's webs <> now;
the <&> bitter
1896, 1904: now; the bitter
1896s: Thin spider's webs <>
now; the bitter
8. MS1: killed the flower upon <>
wall:
MS2: killed the flower<s> upon
9. MS1: home brimful[*l*] of life
MS2, 1896: home brimful of
MS3: this wa[*ll*]<s> a
1904: home brimfull of
10. MS1: the hope & fear & love <>
youth
MS2: the hope<s> and fear<s>
and
MS3: [*F*]<F>ull of [The capital
letter is made larger in the
revision.]
11. MS1: sound
MS2: sound:—
12. MS1: enshrined & simple truth
MS2: and [*simple*] <kindly> truth;
13. MS1: H[illegible deletion]<ither>
the <> brought [*hith*] his <> wife
14. MS1: here the bridal <> unbound
[Below the poem is written:] 9—
MS2: here the<r> bridal
MS3: [Below the poem is written:]
Christina G. Rossetti.
1896, 1904: here the bridal

"I SIT AMONG GREEN SHADY VALLEYS OFT"

[Composed in 1848. Editions: 1896, 1904. The rough draft (MS1) is in the Princeton University Library. The notebook MS (MS2) is in the Bodleian Library. Basic text: MS2. In MS1, the text is written in pencil and no lines are indented; the last five bouts-rimés are written in ink, apparently in Dante Gabriel Rossetti's hand. In the 1896 and 1904 texts, lines 11 and 14 and indented four spaces.]

Title. MS1: [untitled]
MS2: [The poem is untitled, but it
constitutes the second in a series
entitled in the notebook "Bouts
rimés Sonnets."]
1896, 1904: SONNETS/
WRITTEN TO BOUTS-RIMÉS/
II
1. MS2: [Above the line is added in
pencil:] <2>
1896, 1904: oft,

2. MS1: to echo winds sighing <> woe
3. MS1: grass & flowers <> strong &
sweet below
1896, 1904: below;
4. MS1: Yea I <> tired & the <>
soft
1896, 1904: Yea I <> tired, and
5. MS1: sit & think & never
1896, 1904: think, and <> aloft,
6. MS1: Save [*for*] <to> the [*lights*]
<tops> of

1896: tall poplar-row
1904: tall poplar-/ row
7. MS1: wind whispering [*l*] [*now*]
   <low>
8. MS1: laughed
   1896, 1904: who laught.
9. MS1: bubbles [illegible erasure]
   <near>
   1896, 1904: near,
10. MS1: wandering

11. MS1: look thro'
    1896, 1904: through:
12. MS1: lazy stream[*s*] I
    1896, 1904: Then, sitting <>
    stream, I
13. MS1: thing
14. MS1: [Below the poem is written:]
    7—
    MS2: me honey-/ dew.
    1896, 1904: me honey-dew.

"LISTEN, AND I WILL TELL YOU OF A FACE"

[Composed in 1848. The rough draft (MS1) is in the Princeton University Library. The notebook MS (MS2) is in the Bodleian Library. Basic text: MS2. In MS1, the text is written in pencil, and no lines are indented.]

Title. MS1: [untitled]
   MS2: [The poem is untitled, but it
   constitutes the third in a series
   entitled in the notebook "Bouts
   rimés Sonnets."]
1. MS1: Listen & I
2. MS1: lovely but <> mind
4. MS1: place
6. MS1: Of passion[*s*] many fragrant
   [illegible deletion] <bl>ossoms
   bind

7. MS1: glossy & golden like
8. MS1: grace
9. MS1: *was* [*so*] <so>
10. MS1: heaving
12. MS1: struggling: I
13. MS1: tenderness the <> glow
14. MS1: on not <> believing [Below
    the poem is written:] 9 m

"WOULDST THOU GIVE ME A HEAVY JEWELLED CROWN"

[Composed in 1848. Editions: 1896, 1904. The rough draft (MS1) is in the Princeton University Library. The notebook MS (MS2) is in the Bodleian Library. Basic text: MS2. In MS1, the text is written in pencil, and no lines are indented. In the 1896 and 1904 texts, lines 11 and 12 are indented four spaces.]

Title. MS1: [untitled]
   MS2: [The poem is untitled, but it
   constitutes the fourth in a series
   entitled in the notebook "Bouts
   rimés Sonnets."]
   1896, 1904: SONNETS/
   WRITTEN TO BOUTS-RIMÉS/
   III
1. MS1: [*Wilt*] <Wouldst> thou
   MS2: [Above the line is added in
   pencil:] <3>
2. MS1: mantle & embroidered
3. MS1: Dear child the
   1896, 1904: glorious West

4. MS1: down
6. 1896, 1904: nay give
7. MS1: [*The*] <Pale> violets
8. 1896, 1904: to autumn brown.
10. MS1: careless [illegible erasure]
    <walk,> & an [*an*]
    broidered robe
11. MS1: me; what
    1896, 1904: me. What is <> who
    stept
12. MS1, 1896, 1904: earth more
13. MS1: cinder
14. MS1: globe [Below the poem is
    written:] 8—

"I SAID WITHIN MYSELF: I AM A FOOL"

[Composed in 1848. Editions: 1896, 1904. The rough draft (MS1) is in the Princeton University Library. The notebook MS (MS2) is in the Bodleian Library. Basic text: MS2. In MS1, the text is written in pencil, and no lines are indented. In the 1896 and 1904 texts, lines 12 and 14 are indented four spaces.]

Title. MS1: [untitled]
　　MS2: [The poem is untitled, but it
　　constitutes the fifth in a series
　　entitled in the notebook "Bouts
　　rimés Sonnets."]
　　1896, 1904: SONNETS/
　　WRITTEN TO BOUTS-RIMÉS/
　　IV
1. MS1: [*I said within myself:*] <And
　　yet, when all is said,> I [The
　　deletion and revision are in ink in
　　Dante Gabriel Rossetti's hand.]
　　MS2: [Above the line is added in
　　pencil:] <4> [illegible deletion]
　　1896, 1904: myself: "I am
2. MS1: sigh eve[*r*]<n> [*for*] <once
　　for> that [The deletions and
　　revisions are in ink in Dante
　　Gabriel Rossetti's hand.]
3. MS1: shone
4. MS1: Rejoice—but
　　1896: Rejoice."—But
5. MS1: heart & soul & spirit
6. MS1: with & direct;
7. MS1: memory; & ever & anon

8. MS1: weep [*feeling life is a weary
　　school*] <as a poor child weeps after
　　school> [The deletion and revision
　　are in ink in Dante Gabriel
　　Rossetti's hand.]
　　1896, 1904: weep, feeling
9. MS1: [*There is much noise & bustle in
　　the street*] <Still the same stir goes
　　on: men pass & meet> [The deletion
　　and revision are in ink in Dante
　　Gabriel Rossetti's hand.]
10. MS1: so & it <> now
11. MS1: same & will <> year
12. MS1: Spirit that <> break & wilt
　　<> bow
　　1896, 1904: Spirit that
13. MS1: [*There has*] <Fear not> the
　　cold thou <> heat
14. MS1: wilt but <> fear [Below the
　　poem is written:] 7—
　　MS2: [Below the poem is added in
　　pencil in William Michael Rossetti's
　　hand:] <Here follow[*s*] 5, 6, 7#>
　　1896, 1904: wilt, but

"METHINKS THE ILLS OF LIFE I FAIN WOULD SHUN"

[Composed in 1848. Editions: 1896, 1904. The rough draft MS (MS1) is in the Princeton University Library. A fair copy MS (MS2), signed "Christina G. Rossetti" and dated "21st August 1848," is in the Duke University Library. The notebook MS (MS3) is in the Bodleian Library. Basic text: MS3. In MS1, the text is written in pencil, and no lines are indented. In the 1896 and 1904 texts, lines 11 and 14 are indented four spaces.]

Title. MS1: [untitled]
　　MS2: Bouts rimés.
　　MS3: [The poem is untitled, but it
　　constitutes the sixth in a series
　　entitled in the notebook "Bouts
　　rimés Sonnets."]
　　1896, 1904: SONNETS/
　　WRITTEN TO BOUTS-RIMÉS/
　　VIII

1. MS1: [*Methinks*] the <> life <for
　　care> I [*fain*] would [*s*] shun [The
　　revisions and all but the last deletion
　　are in ink in Dante Gabriel
　　Rossetti's hand.]
　　MS2: shun,
　　MS3: [Above the line is added in
　　pencil:] <[6]> <8>
2. MS1: which [*is*] <though> a blank

[The deletion and revision are in
ink in Dante Gabriel Rossetti's
hand.]
MS2: blank.
1896, 1904: life, which <> blank.

3. MS1: [*Even in my childhood* [*t*]<*o*>*ft*]
<Is life: even when a child> my
[The deletion of the first five words
and the added words are in ink in
Dante Gabriel Rossetti's hand.]
1896, 1904: sank,

4. MS1: done

5. MS1: Among [*my many*]<these
other> friends [The deletion and
revision are in ink in Dante Gabriel
Rossetti's hand.]

7. MS1: Willow-o'er-shadowed [*from
whose lips*] <at whose soul I> [The
deletion and revision are in ink in
Dante Gabriel Rossetti's hand.]
1896, 1904: Willow-o'er-shadowed,
from

8. MS1: sing & run

9. MS1: [*But*] [*often*] <many> times
<since> that [The first deletion

and second revision are in ink in
Dante Gabriel Rossetti's hand.]
MS2: sigh:

10. MS1: [*And*] many <> my [*heart*]
<spirit> have [The deletions and
revision are in ink in Dante Gabriel
Rossetti's hand.]
MS2: times in my heart have I
sought
MS3: times <I> in <> have [*I*]
sought [The deletion and revision
are in pencil in Christina's hand.]

11. MS1: the [*of*] <old> comfort &
not <> yet.
MS2: comfort; and <> yet.
1896, 1904: comfort and <> yet.

12. MS1, MS2: Surely on that

13. MS1: blessed thought
MS2: a blessèd thought,

14. MS1: forget [Below the poem is
written:] 7
MS2: [Below the poem is written:]
(7 minutes) [To the right of the
signature is written:] Brighton.

"STRANGE VOICES SING AMONG THE PLANETS WHICH"

[Composed in 1848. The notebook MS is in the Bodleian Library. Basic text: note-
book MS.]

Title. MS: [The poem is untitled, but it
constitutes the seventh in a series
entitled in the notebook "Bouts
rimés Sonnets."]

"SLEEP, SLEEP, HAPPY ONE"

[Composed November 12, 1848. The notebook MS is in the Bodleian Library. Basic
text: notebook MS.]

Opening quotation. MS: smiled."/
Bla[*ck*]<ke.>

21. MS: is hew[illegible erasure]<n>

WHAT SAPPHO WOULD HAVE SAID HAD HER LEAP
CURED INSTEAD OF KILLING HER.

[Composed December 7, 1848. The notebook MS of lines 1–56 (MS1) is in the
Bodleian Library. A separate notebook leaf containing lines 57–66 (MS2) is in the
Pierpont Morgan Library. Basic text: lines 1–56: MS1; lines 57–66: MS2.]

2. MS1: left it, leav[*e*]<'>st it
5. MS1: O[*h*] blessèd
56. MS1: [In the notebook, a page is

inserted containing lines 57–66
in William Michael Rossetti's
handwriting.]

ON KEATS.

[Composed January 18, 1849. Editions: 1896, 1904. The notebook MS is in the Bodleian Library. Basic text: notebook MS. In the 1896 and 1904 texts, lines 12 and 13 are indented two spaces.]

Title. 1896, 1904: ON KEATS
  2. MS: slumber/ -place
  6. 1896, 1904: daisies; silence,
  7. 1896, 1904: face;
10. 1896, 1904: us? "Here lies one whose name was writ
11. 1896, 1904: In water." While the

12. 1896, 1904: sweet St. Agnes' Eve, while <> springs—
14. MS: [Below the poem is the following note:] For the Eve of Saint Agnes.
    1896, 1904: [Below the poem is the following note:] (Eve of St. Agnes).

HAVE PATIENCE.

[Composed January 23, 1849. Editions: 1896, 1904. The notebook MS is in the Bodleian Library. Basic text: notebook MS. In the 1896 and 1904 texts, lines 24, 26, 32, 34, 46, and 49 are indented four spaces, and lines 37 and 40 are indented six spaces.]

Title. 1896, 1904: HAVE PATIENCE
  3. 1896, 1904: cease. If thou
10. 1896, 1904: again,—
12. 1896, 1904: plain,
13. 1904: and whit'ning
14. 1896, 1904: The gravestones and
16. 1896, 1904: cup
23. 1896, 1904: But, when <> dead
24. 1896, 1904: fallen,
26. 1896, 1904: on,
28. 1896, 1904: it—

31. MS: [*m*]<M>anhood is
33. 1896, 1904: That hath
34. 1896, 1904: This no
39. 1896: last;—
    1904: last—
40. 1904: it:
41. 1896, 1904: deep!—But
46. 1896, 1904: us;
47. 1896, 1904: palm-branches decreed
48. 1896, 1904: crowns to <> meed

TO LALLA, READING MY VERSES TOPSY-TURVY.

[Composed January 24, 1849. Editions: 1896, 1904. The notebook MS is in the Bodleian Library. Basic text: notebook MS.]

Title 1896, 1904: TO LALLA/ READING MY VERSES TOPSY-TURVY
  5. MS: English hieroglyphi[*k*]<c>s
  7. 1896, 1904: you than
12. 1896, 1904: convey.
13. 1896, 1904: silence
20. 1896, 1904: face;

22. 1896, 1904: Tender happy
23. 1896, 1904: pure,
27. 1896, 1904: little Cousin,
30. 1896, 1904: boast:
31. MS: the [*wisest*,] <wiser,> [The deletion and revision are in pencil, apparently not in Christina's hand.]
    1896, 1904: the wiser

SONNET. ["SOME SAY THAT LOVE AND JOY ARE ONE: AND SO"]

[Composed February 6, 1849. The notebook MS is in the Bodleian Library. Basic text: notebook MS.]

THE LAST *COMPLAINT.*

[Composed February 7, 1849. The notebook MS is in the Bodleian Library. Basic text: notebook MS.]

HAVE YOU FORGOTTEN?

[Composed February 16, 1849. The notebook MS is in the Bodelian Library. Basic text: notebook MS. In the MS, the deletions and revisions are in pencil in Christina's handwriting unless otherwise indicated.]

Title. MS: [Below the title is added in pencil in William Michael Rossetti's hand:] <must be Bouts rimés>

3. MS: While [*the*] warm winds sang <hummed to> us

7. MS: <Less> Pleased you less than

8. MS: blushed, <&> seeming<ed> to

12. MS: sounded another<second> chime.

A CHRISTMAS CAROL,/ (ON THE STROKE OF MIDNIGHT.)

[Composed March 7, 1849. Editions: 1896, 1904. The notebook MS (MS1) is in the Bodleian Library. The version of the poem in Christina's 1850 notebook MS of *Maude: Prose & Verse* (MS2) is in the Huntington Library. A fair copy (MS3) is in the Princeton University Library. The poem was printed in *Maude: Prose & Verse, by Christina Rossetti; 1850* (Chicago: Herbert S. Stone, 1897), 77–79; variants therein are designated "1897a" in the textual notes. Basic text: MS3.]

Title. MS1: A Christmas Carol. [To the left of the title is added in pencil:] <P>
MS2, 1897a: [untitled]
MS3: [In the upper left corner of the page is written:] Winter

1896, 1904: A CHRISTMAS CAROL

1. MS1, 1896, 1904: believe:
MS2: "Thank < > believe;
1897a: "Thank

4. MS1, MS2: say,
1896, 1904: so, the < > say,

7. MS1, MS2, 1896, 1904: praise, which
1897a: knelt, full < > praise, which

8. 1897a: not repress, while

10. MS1, MS2, 1896, 1897a, 1904: morn.

12. MS1: little Child:
MS2: a Little Child:
1896, 1904: little child:
1897a: Christ came < > a Little Child:

13. MS2, 1897a: ancient Glory by

14. MS1, 1896, 1904: us and
MS2: us and < > die."—
1897a: us and < > die."

15. MS1, 1896, 1904: thank God? How shall
MS2, 1897a: "How

17. MS1, MS2, 1897a: thus?
1896, 1904: have who loved < > thus?

18. MS1: will [*h*]<H>e take
MS2: us?—

19. MS1, MS2: gold? or
1897a: take Gold? or

20. MS1, MS2, 1896, 1897a, 1904:
    gems? or
21. MS1, 1897a: incense? or
    MS2: incense? or < > myrrh?—
23. MS1, 1896, 1904: ask His will?
24. MS1, MS2, 1896, 1904: learned, we
    MS3: will fulfil[*l*]
    1897a: learned, we < > fulfil,
25. MS1, 1896, 1904: Though He
    MS2, 1897a: Though He < >
    prefer:
26. MS2: messenger?"—
    1897a: messenger?"
27. MS2, 1897a: "Thank
28. MS1, MS2, 1896, 1897a, 1904:
    ground.
29. MS1: road; for
31. MS1: our Messenger: beside,
    1896, 1904: our Messenger beside,
32. MS1: is o[*r*]<u>r [*Gate*] <Door>

and Path and Guide: [The deletion
is in pencil; the added word is
written in pen in Christina's hand.]
MS2, 1897a: our Door and Path and
1896, 1904: our door and path and
Guide:
33. MS1, 1896, 1904: our Offering:
    MS2, 1897a: our Offering;
34. MS2: the Gift That we < >
    bring."—
    1896, 1904: the gift that
    1897a: the Gift. That we < >
    bring—"
35. MS2, 1897a: "Let
36. 1897a: the Lord.
40. MS1: Firstborn of God, and
    MS2: Firstborn of God[,] and Heir
    of Heaven."—
    1897a: First-born of < > and Heir
    of Heaven."

FOR ADVENT.

[Composed March 12, 1849. Editions: 1896, 1904. The notebook MS (MS1) is in the
Bodleian Library. The version of the poem in Christina's 1850 notebook MS of
Maude: Prose & Verse (MS2) is in the Huntington Library. The poem was printed in
Maude: Prose & Verse, by Christina Rossetti; 1850 (Chicago: Herbert S. Stone, 1897),
49–51; variants therein are designated "1897a" in the textual notes. Basic text:
MS2. In MS1 and the 1896, 1897a, and 1904 texts, the second, fourth, sixth, and
eighth through twelfth lines of each stanza are indented two spaces.]

Title. MS2, 1897a: [untitled]
    1896, 1904: FOR ADVENT
 1. MS1, 1896, 1904: waters, falling
    1897a: Sweet, sweet
 2. MS1, 1896, 1904: plain:
 3. MS1: soaring sky-lark, calling
    1897a: Sweet, sweet
 4. MS1, 1896, 1904: again:
 6. MS1, 1896, 1904: rain:
 8. 1896, 1897a, 1904: gain:—
10. 1897a: trees.
11. MS1: a [*far*] <much> more
    pricel [*y*]<ess> worth
12. 1896, 1904: old brown common
13. MS1, 1896, 1897a, 1904: lamb,
    piteously
14. MS1, 1896, 1904: away:
15. MS1: nightingale, retreating

    1896, 1904: Saddest sweetest
    nightingale, retreating
16. MS1, 1896, 1904: day:
18. MS1, 1896, 1904: astray:
19. MS2: was [illegible erasure]
    <rifled> and
20. MS1, 1896, 1897a, 1904: of May:—
21. 1896, 1897a, 1904: trees,
23. MS1: birth;
    1896, 1904: birth:
25. MS1, 1896, 1897a, 1904: the
    never-pausing murmur
26. 1897a: shore;
28. 1896, 1904: bore:
30. 1896, 1904: store:
31. MS1: stars, which < > ceiling,
    MS2: deck [illegible deletion]
    <our> temple's

32. MS1, 1896, 1904: floor:
34. MS1: away;
35. 1896, 1904: cease:
37. 1896, 1904: peace, for
39. MS1: lighted; duly
40. MS2: Fed [illegible erasure]
    <with> oil,
    1896, 1904: oil nor

42. MS1, 1896, 1904: o'er:
43. MS1, 1896, 1904: us:
45. MS1: pray, now, while < > may:
    1896, 1904: now, while < > may:
    1897a: now, while
48. MS1: last trumpet-call
    1896, 1904: last trumpet-call.

TWO PURSUITS.

[Composed April 12, 1849. Editions: 1896, 1904. The notebook MS is in the Bodleian Library. Basic text: notebook MS. In the 1896 and 1904 texts, lines 11 and 13 are indented four spaces.]

Title. 1896, 1904: TWO PURSUITS
1. 1896, 1904: said, "Follow, follow":
   and
   1896s: said "Follow, follow": and
5. 1896, 1904: drink: where
7. 1896, 1904: touch: until

11. 1896, 1904: Called, "Follow,
    follow": and
12. 1896, 1904: a blessed star:
13. MS: sinking s[*p*]<t>eps sustain,
    1896, 1904: Kind steady

LOOKING FORWARD.

[Composed June 8, 1849. Editions: 1896, 1904. The notebook MS (MS1), in the handwriting of Christina's mother, Frances Mary Lavinia Polidori Rossetti, is in the Bodleian Library. The version of the poem in Christina's 1850 notebook MS of *Maude: Prose & Verse* (MS2) is in the Huntington Library. The poem was printed in *Maude: Prose & Verse, by Christina Rossetti; 1850* (Chicago: Herbert S. Stone, 1897), 117–19; variants therein are designated "1897a" in the textual notes. Basic text: MS2. In MS1, no lines are indented. In the 1896 and 1904 texts, the second and sixth lines of each stanza are indented two spaces, and the remaining lines are not indented.]

Title. MS2, 1897a: [untitled]
    1896, 1904: LOOKING
    FORWARD
5. 1897a: dream
6. MS1: of [*the*] <a> Summer
    1896, 1904: a summer sea.
16. 1897a: again:—
19. 1896, 1904: peace! your
21. 1897a: naught.

23. MS1: dance & sing
    1896, 1904: soon, where
25. MS1: live & grow
27. 1904: unseen.
28. 1896, 1904: Then, if
29. MS1: this: poor child,
    1896, 1904: she has her
30. MS2: fruit.—

LIFE HIDDEN.

[Composed July 23, 1849. Editions: 1896, 1904. The notebook MS is in the Bodleian Library. Basic text: notebook MS. In the 1896 and 1904 texts, lines 11 and 12 are indented four spaces.]

Title. 1896, 1904: LIFE HIDDEN
3. 1896, 1904: face,
4. 1896, 1904: there, nor
5. 1896, 1904: light; her

7. 1896, 1904: Seawards, while
9. 1896, 1904: knows; she
10. 1896, 1904: sensible; she
12. 1896, 1904: near, peace

QUEEN ROSE.

[Composed August 13, 1849. Editions: 1896, 1904. The notebook MS is in the Bodleian Library. Basic text: notebook MS. In the MS, the deletions and revisions are in pencil in Christina's hand unless otherwise indicated.]

Title. 1896, 1904: QUEEN ROSE
1. MS: jessamine [is] <shows> like
2. MS: lilies [are] <sway> like
3. MS: [Where darkest leaves and shadows are] <Fair clematis [where] from near & far>
4. MS: [The clematis shows pale and dim] <Sets [Sets] forth its wayward [illegible erasure] tangled whim>;
   1896s: Sets from forth
5. MS: [The violets too are wondrous trim] <Curved meadowsweet blooms rich & dim>;—
6. MS: far. <[How]> <[So fair they are.]>
7. MS: is odo[u]rous; so [The deletion is in ink.]
8. MS: [The] <Maid> lilies
   1896, 1904: Maid-lilies are,
9. MS: where [the hidden violets] <tall meadowsweet [illegible deletion] flowers> grow

1896, 1904: tall meadowsweet-flowers grow
11. MS: can <there> be [sweeter] <more choice> than [all] these?—
12. MS: doth <[That]> bud
13. MS: choose [the] <sweet> jessamine,
14. MS: [And crown themselves with lilies white] <Or weave their lily crown aright>,
   1896, 1904: their lily-crown aright,
15. MS: [The] <Loose> clematis; [and] <or> draw
16. 1896, 1904: clematis, or
17. MS: From [violets in their leafy night] <meadowsweet's [down] clustry downy white>;—
   1896, 1904: From meadowsweets' cluster downy white—
18. MS: The rose, the perfect <[The]>rose
   1896, 1904: perfect rose, be

HOW ONE CHOSE.

[Composed October 6, 1849. Editions: 1896, 1904. The notebook MS is in the Bodleian Library. Basic text: notebook MS.]

Title. 1896, 1904: HOW ONE CHOSE
2. 1896, 1904: are—
4. 1896, 1904: star—
6. 1896, 1904: home, Beloved, for
7. 1896, 1904: home, my Friend,
8. 1896, 1904: us,
9. 1896, 1904: Full of palm-branches or <> crowns,
   1904: Full of palm-branches, or
11. MS: "How [The line is at the top of the page.]
   1896, 1904: it? Let us

14. 1896, 1904: she,
15. 1896, 1904: hope,
27. 1896, 1904: shine through the
28. 1896, 1904: That wrapt her
29. 1896, 1904: passed through
30. MS: reached <the> depths
   1896, 1904: mists, and
32. 1896, 1904: won,
35. 1896, 1904: again,—
41. 1896, 1904: evening,—till
42. 1896, 1904: think, Love, it
43. 1904: 'Nay, seek

SEEKING REST.

[Composed October 10, 1849. Editions: 1896, 1904. The notebook MS is in the Bodleian Library. Basic text: notebook MS.]

Title. 1896, 1904: SEEKING REST
1. MS: [Preceding line 1 are the following stanzas, deleted in pencil:]

[*She knocked at the Earth's greeny door:*
O Mother, let me in;
For I am weary of this life
That is so full of sin:
I look; and, lo, decay and death;
I listen; and a din.]

[*There was a hope I cherished once,*
A longing, a vain dream:
I dreamed it when I thought that men
And things were what they seem;
When the clouds had no gloom for me,
No chill the pale moon-beam.]

[*I never questioned my own heart,*
Asking it what was this
That filled it with a secret store
Of unimagined bliss:
Alas, how could I doubt the source
Of so much happiness?]

[*Unto my soul this vision was*
As a sweet melody;
As tho' birds sang and limpid streams
Welled bubbling to the sea;
As tho' a chime rang evermore
Without monotony.]

[Above line 1 is added in pencil in what appears to be Dante Gabriel Rossetti's hand:] <Begin here>
1896, 1904: said: "The
3. 1896, 1904: she sings and

6. 1896, 1904: overfill."
7. MS: My [s]<S>isters said:
　1896, 1904: said: "Now prythee tell
11. 1896, 1904: us, Sweet:
12. MS: [After line 12 is the following stanza, deleted in pencil:]

[*But evermore I kept my joy*
Hidden in mine own heart;—
I could not show them my life's life:—
So now I bear the smart
Of disappointment; and I strive
To hide it with vain art.]

1896, 1904: thus."
13. 1896, 1904: says: "What
15. 1896, 1904: sorry? Nay, it
16. 1896, 1904: The winter of
17. 1896, 1904: the Springtime comes again,
18. 1896, 1904: appear."
19. 1896, 1904: say: "Come,
21. 1896s: grieve
22. 1896, 1904: Yea haply,
24. 1896, 1904: certainly."
30. MS: [After line 30 is the following stanza, deleted in pencil:]

[*So Mother take me to thyself*
For I am tired in truth:
Where is the profit of my hope?
The gladness of my youth?
The gladness and the profiting
Were vanity in sooth.]

A YEAR AFTERWARDS.

[Composed February 18, 1850. The notebook MS is in the Bodleian Library. Basic text: notebook MS.]

6. MS: her lying <stretched &> still,
　[The added words are in pencil in Christina's hand.]
17. MS: So [f]<o>ften trod
37. MS: [After line 37 is the following stanza, deleted in pencil:]

[*Look at those floating lilies, white*
On the dark waters of the pond

And their own leaves; she was so fond
Of lilies; yet would scarcely take
A single blossom; for she said
It grieved her heart to see them dead.
I recollect one Summer night
I wove a garland for her head
And bade her wear it for my sake;
She wore it till the bloom was gone;
And then made answer: "Pluck no more

"These flowers for me: henceforward I
"Will wait uncrowned till I put on
"Such flowers as Dorothea wore
"When first her footsteps trod the sky."
She ceased; then added timidly:
"Her courage won a soul from earth;—
"Is love sufficient for such things?
"Can simple love possess such worth?—"
I understood her questionings
But would not answer; so we went
On here together, even as you
And I do now: I was content
To walk on silently with her.

Just then a squirrel made a stir
There in that bush, shaking a few
White may leaves down upon her hair;
And the last sun rays touched her brow
Lingering like a glory there;
Her eyes were full of solemn prayer.—
Then I feared that which irks me now.]

49. MS: last [illegible deletion] <a>
    day
57. MS: Of o[f]<f>ten there:
72. MS: A [c]<C>ross formed

TWO THOUGHTS OF DEATH.

[Composed March 16, 1850. Editions: 1896, 1904. The notebook MS is in the Bodleian Library. Basic text: notebook MS.]

Title. 1896, 1904: TWO THOUGHTS
OF DEATH
Subtitles. 1896: I/ II
    1904: I/ 2
3. 1896, 1904: mine, she
5. 1896, 1904: On eyes whereon
7. 1896, 1904: head;
8. 1896, 1904: nothingness,
10. 1896, 1904: green
11. 1896, 1904: the dew-dropping rose
13. 1896, 1904: away,
14. 1896, 1904: Theirs too <> as
    though it
16. MS: because [I still] <still I> loved
    [The indication of reversed order
    is in pencil.]
    1896, 1904: But, because still I
    loved <> memory,
17. 1896, 1904: anemone,

18. MS: upon hea<r>tsease [The
    added letter is in pencil in
    Christina's hand.]
    1896, 1904: lo my
22. 1896, 1904: like heart-pulses.
23. 1896, 1904: flew, far <> sight,—
25. MS: flew [light] <straight> up
    [The revision is in ink in Christina's
    hand.]
    1896, 1904: As though it
26. 1896, 1904: fool, to
28. MS: And [whose day shall] no more
    <shall her day> turn [The deletion
    is in pencil. The added words are
    in pencil in what appears to be
    William Michael Rossetti's hand.]
    1896, 1904: And no more shall her
    day turn

THREE MOMENTS.

[Composed March 23, 1850. Editions: 1896, 1904. The notebook MS is in the Bodleian Library. Basic text: notebook MS. In the 1896 text, lines 4 and 8 are indented six spaces; lines 11–14, 20, 25, 27, 28, 32, 33, 36, 38, 42, 55, and 59 are indented two spaces; and lines 16, 18, 21, and 67 are indented four spaces. The 1904 paragraphing is identical to the 1896 except that line 42 is indented four spaces.]

Title. 1896, 1904: THREE
MOMENTS

1. 1896, 1904: bird,
2. 1896, 1904: Come

3. MS: said: "[illegible erasure] <It is in vain,>
1896, 1904: The Bird said:
4. 1896, 1904: For
5. 1896, 1904: I am
6. 1896, 1904: But
7. 1896, 1904: In
8. 1896, 1904: Far
10. MS: she [illegible deletion]
1896, 1904: bird," said she,
11. 1896, 1904: bitterly.
13. MS: Half s[illegible deletion]<igh>ing pityingly,
15. MS: "Th[*ough*]<o'> [*a*] <thy> bird
1896, 1904: "Though thy < > nevermore,
16. 1896, 1904: Do
17. 1896, 1904: Find < > playfellow,
1896s: Find
18. 1896, 1904: Child,
19. 1896, 1904: Tears
20. 1896, 1904: rose, do
35. 1896, 1904: The
36. 1896, 1904: In
37. 1896, 1904: this,"

40. 1896, 1904: Perhaps,
41. 1896, 1904: And < > said,
43. 1896, 1904: knelt, but
44. 1904: said,
45. 1896, 1904: "Not this, not this!" and
46. 1896, 1904: heart, and < > head,
48. 1896, 1904: "Not this, not this!" tears < > fall;
49. 1896, 1904: this!" it
52. MS: over, [*and*] <when> [The deletion and revision are in pencil in Christina's hand.]
54. 1896, 1904: cried: "O Mother,
55. 1896, 1904: The
56. 1896, 1904: So easily? One single
57. 1896, 1904: Might
58. 1896, 1904: My
59. 1896, 1904: Wasted
61. 1896, 1904: "O Daughter mine, be
62. 1896, 1904: Rejoicing
63. 1896, 1904: Thy
64. 1896, 1904: Once
65. 1896, 1904: But
66. 1896, 1904: Oh
67. 1896, 1904: Oh

ONCE.

[Composed probably between March 23, 1850, and May 10, 1850. The notebook MS (MS1) is in the Bodleian Library. A separate fair copy MS (MS2) is in the Yale University Library. Basic text: MS2. In the 1896 text, the fourth line of each stanza is indented two spaces, and the remaining lines are not indented. In the 1904 text, lines 2, 4, 12, 20, and 28 are indented two spaces; and the remaining lines are not indented.]

Title. MS1: [*A Lady*] <Is and was>.
1896, 1904: IS AND WAS
5. MS1: [After line 5 is the following line, deleted in pencil:] [*And her velvets flushed the floor;*]
MS2: [After line 5 is the following line:] And her velvets flushed the floor;
1896, 1904: wore;
8. 1896, 1904: lilies,
1896s: lilies
12. MS1: [After line 12 is the following line, deleted in pencil:] [In her apron and plain gown,]

MS2: [After line 12 is the following line:] In her apron and plain gown,
14. 1896, 1904: bough, and
16. 1896, 1904: Of Maybloom in
19. MS1: [After line 19 is the following line, deleted in pencil:] [*Pitiful but nothing weak,*]
MS2: [After line 19 is the following line:] Pitiful but nothing weak,
22. MS1, 1896, 1904: lady
23. 1896, 1904: not over loud;
27. MS1, 1896, 1904: direct
28. MS1: <[*Or be angry or suspect;*]> [The deletion is in pencil.

To the right of the line is added
and circled in pencil:] <stet>
1896, 1904: angry or
32. MS1: [After line 32 is the following
stanza, deleted in pencil:]

[All her present pomp of beauty
Had not won me of a truth

If I had not known and loved her
In her simple youth.
Now I cannot change; and yet
Sometimes I almost regret
That we twain have ever met,
Or that I cannot forget.]

THREE NUNS.

[Part 2 composed February 12, 1849; Parts 1 and 3 composed May 10, 1850. Editions: 1896, 1904. The notebook MS of Part 2 (MS1) and the notebook MS of Parts 1, 2, and 3 (MS2) are in the Bodleian Library. The version of the poem in Christina's 1850 notebook MS of *Maude: Prose & Verse* (MS3) is in the Huntington Library. The poem was printed in *Maude: Prose & Verse, by Christina Rossetti; 1850* (Chicago: Herbert S. Stone, 1897), 93–105; variants therein are designated "1897a" in the textual notes. Basic text: MS3. In MS1, the second and third lines of each stanza are indented two spaces. In MS2 and the 1896, 1897a, and 1904 texts, in Part 1 the second and fourth lines of each stanza are indented two spaces; in Part 2 the second and third lines of each stanza are indented two spaces; and in Part 3 the second, fourth, and sixth lines of each stanza are indented two spaces.]

Title. MS1: A Nun.
      1896, 1897a, 1904: THREE NUNS
Part 1. 1896, 1897a, 1904: I
Opening quotation. MS3: non [*so dir*]
      <sadir> perchè." [The revision is
      in pencil.]
      1896: Sospira <> perchè.
      1897a: non sadir perchè."
      1904: Sospira <> core,/ <>
      perchè.
  1. 1896, 1897a, 1904: wall,
  4. 1896, 1904: see:
  5. MS2: come;
      1896, 1904: me, come;
  8. 1896, 1904: Shadow, thou <>
      feet;
      1897a: Shadow, thou
 10. 1896, 1897a, 1904: stainless
      winding-sheet,
 16. 1897a: bird:
 18. 1896: heard.¹ / ¹"Sweetest <>
      seen."—E. B. BROWNING.
      1897a: heard.*/ *"Sweetest <>
      seen."—E. B. Browning.
      1904: heard.¹ / ¹"Sweetest <>
      seen."/ E. B. BROWNING.
 19. 1896, 1904: tree;
 20. 1896, 1904: thee;
 21. MS2: songster sing

22. 1896, 1904: curled,
23. MS2: Tho' men
24. 1896, 1897a: world,
26. 1896, 1904: shorn,
29. 1896, 1904: Here wrapt in
34. MS2: song
      MS3: heart [illegible erasure]
      <sickens>:—sing
      1897a: sickens—sing
35. MS2, 1896, 1904: Blythe bird
      MS3: Bl[y]<i>the bird
37. 1897a: sin;
39. 1897a: begin:
41. MS2: aching, worse <> pain,
      1896, 1904: aching, worse <>
      pain,—
43. MS2, 1896, 1904: Sing; that
45. 1896, 1904: away,
47. MS2: Hyac[y]<i>nths, till
      1896s: Hyacinth, till
50. 1896, 1897a, 1904: wood
51. 1896, 1904: remember long
52. 1896, 1904: stately oaktree stood
      1897a: stately oak-tree stood
53. 1897a: below,
54. 1896, 1904: sight;
55. 1896, 1904: night
56. MS2: Water lilies lay
      MS3: Water<->lilies lay

57. 1897a: child I
58. MS2, 1896, 1904: dream;
59. MS2: nor so[illegible
   erasure]<ug>ht:
   1896: sought;
   1904: found not sought;
62. 1897a: me:
63. 1896, 1904: Ah but <> be!
Part 2. MS1: [MS1 does not contain the
   number.]
   1896, 1897a, 1904: II
   Opening quotation. MS1: [MS1
   does not contain the opening
   quotation.]
   1896, 1904: Sospirerà <> me.
   1897a: "Sospirera d'amore/ <>
   non lodice a
64. MS1: him: yes: where
   MS2: him; yes; where
   1896, 1904: him; yes,
65. MS2: soul:
   1896, 1904: soul;
   1897a: soul,
68. MS1: see.—
   1896, 1904: see:
69. MS1, MS2: stone thou
70. MS1, MS2: him; but
72. MS3: [*I prayed*] [not indented] <I
   prayed> [indented four spaces] for
73. MS3: [*I sacrificed*] [indented four
   spaces] <I sacrificed,> [not
   indented] he
   1896, 1904: bought;
77. MS1, MS2: of nuns; do
   1896, 1904: of nuns: do
78. MS1, 1896, 1904: if when <>
   them
79. MS1, MS2: fire,
   1896, 1904: zeal, and love, kindled
   <> fire,
   1897a: zeal, and <> fire,
81. MS3: not[, *wh*]<? was> my
   1896: not; was
82. 1897a: end,
83. MS1: hope m[*ight*]<ay> not
   1896, 1904: vain;
84. MS1: we [*might*] <may> meet [The
   deletion and revision are in pencil
   in Christina's hand.]
86. MS1: to heaven, in
   1896, 1904: No not
88. MS2, 1896, 1897a, 1904: death, for

90. MS1: breast;
   MS2: breast:
   1896, 1904: The crucifix lies
92. MS2: it thro' my
96. MS1, MS2: chilled; but
   1897a: chilled but
97. MS1: cup:
   1897a: cup,
100. 1896, 1904: Yea the
102. MS3: [*Soon*] [not indented]
   <Soon> [indented four spaces] I
104. MS1, MS2, 1896, 1904: soon with
   <> faith shall
105. MS3: and ce[*e*]<a>se not
106. MS1, MS2: cloud:—
   1896, 1904: cloud—
107. MS3: doth jud[*e*]<g>e.—
   1896, 1897a, 1904: judge—
108. MS1, MS2, 1896, 1904: me: you
110. MS1, 1897a: kept; Eternal
111. MS2: me, tho' mine
112. MS1: the convent ground
   1896, 1904: the Convent-ground
114. 1897a: feet
115. MS1: around:
   MS2, 1896, 1904: around;
116. 1896, 1904: a cross be,
117. MS2: Thro' the
119. MS2, 1896, 1904: pain;
121. MS1: After [*h*]<H>is
   [*l*]<L>ik<e>ness Who
   MS2: After His Lik<e>ness Who
   [The added letter is in pencil.]
   1896, 1904: After His likeness
   who hath
122. MS1, MS2: promiseth)
   MS3: Fait<h>ful is
   1896, 1904: is He who promiseth)
   1897a: promiseth),
123. MS1, MS2, 1896, 1904: satisfied
   therewith.
Part 3. 1896, 1897a, 1904: III
Opening quotation. MS2: "Rispondimi
   cor <> Risponde: Voglio Dio,
   [<*Iddio*>] [The addition is in ink;
   the deletion is in pencil.] / Sospir
   [illegible erasure]<o> per
   1896, 1904: Rispondimi, <>
   Risponde: Voglio Dio, <> per
   Gesù.
124. MS2: a free born bird
   1897a: a free-born bird

126. MS2: That flutters flutters
     evermore
     MS3: That flutters<,> flutters
127. MS2: rest;
     1896, 1904: sings nor <> rest,
130. MS2, 1896, 1904: clouded west.
132. MS2: clay;
     1904: clay
133. 1896, 1904: moan,
135. MS2: Up thro' the
136. MS2, 1896, 1904: Up up <> day
141. 1896, 1904: wise—
142. 1897a: the Living Well,
143. 1897a: rise,
144. 1896, 1904: eyes!
146. 1896, 1904: stand—
     1897a: stand;
148. MS2: heart's [thirsty] <weary>
     land. [The deletion is in pencil;
     the added word is in ink in
     Christina's hand.]
     1896, 1904: land—
151. 1896, 1904: reach heaven's
     strand!
     1896s: reach Heaven's strand!
152. MS2: out
     MS3: Thou [illegible erasure]
     <World> from <> out<,>
     1896, 1904: Thou world from
154. 1897a: things
155. 1897a: old,
156. MS2, 1896, 1904: life
157. 1896, 1897a, 1904: cold;
164. MS2: Which [illegible erasure]
     <others> strive
166. 1897a: rose,
167. MS2: Tho' it
     1897a: see,

169. 1896, 1904: me:
174. 1897a: by night,
175. 1896, 1904: of heaven
177. 1896, 1904: Lo in
     1897a: So, in the New Jerusalem,
178. 1897a: aright,
180. 1896, 1897a, 1904: this world
181. MS2, 1896, 1904: treasure where
182. 1897a: Naught perisheth:
183. 1897a: hair,
185. 1896, 1897a, 1904: fasts, and
186. 1896, 1904: this cross I
188. MS2, 1896, 1904: kept.
190. 1896, 1904: slept:
192. MS2: as I s[illegible
     erasure]<t>ep[t]<'d>;
     MS3: as I step['t]<ped>;
     1896, 1904: as I stept;
193. MS2: wept:
     1896, 1904: The cross was
195. MS2: wife:
     1896, 1897a, 1904: wife,
197. 1897a: eyes and
198. MS2: beauty: my <> failed:
     1896, 1897a, 1904: beauty, my
200. MS2: life;
     1896, 1904: life,—
     1896s: life, [The dash is
     imperfectly printed.]
203. MS2: faint because
     1896, 1904: now, when <> faint
     because
205. 1896, 1904: plead, and say,
206. 1896, 1904: dumb—
207. MS2: The <> say, [c]<C>ome.
     MS3: say, Come."—
     1896, 1904: The Spirit <> say,
     Come.

SONG. ["WE BURIED HER AMONG THE FLOWERS"]

[Composed May 14, 1850. Editions: 1896, 1904. The notebook MS is in the Bodleian Library. Basic text: notebook MS. In the 1904 text, line 12 is not indented.]

Title. 1896, 1904: SONG
11. MS: broke ou[illegible deletion]<r>
    hearts,
    1896, 1904: hearts when
12. 1896, 1904: prayer;
13. 1896, 1904: When, with
14. 1896, 1904: breast,

17. 1896, 1904: flowers;
18. 1896, 1904: while,
19. 1896, 1904: wake and rise,
20. MS: the [self same] <selfsame>
    smile.
    1896, 1904: the self-same smile.

THE WATCHERS.

[Composed May 25, 1850. Editions: 1896, 1904. The notebook MS (MS1) is in the Bodleian Library. A separate fair copy MS (MS2) is in the Yale University Library. Basic text: MS2.]

Title. MS2: The Watchers
    1896, 1904: THE WATCHERS
2. 1896, 1904: sober autumn hours.
3. MS1: Three th[r]<e>re are
6. MS1: [*Which guided her upon her course:*] <For which all else she counted loss> [The deletion and revision are in pencil in Christina's hand.]
    MS2: Which guided her upon her course:
11. 1896, 1904: The holy Cross
14. 1896, 1904: fear:
19. 1896, 1904: Leaf-hidden: so

22. 1896, 1904: rose:
25. 1896, 1904: Though yet
27. 1896, 1904: wings: for
28. 1896, 1904: watches now
30. 1896, 1904: rise:
33. 1896, 1904: Though she
34. 1896, 1904: forget:
37. MS1: [*And*] <Till> when [The deletion and revision are in pencil in Christina's hand.]
    MS2: And when
40. MS1, 1896, 1904: sorrow, as
42. 1896, 1904: in heaven. Amen.

ANNIE. ["ANNIE IS FAIRER THAN HER KITH"]

[Composed September 26, 1850. Editions: 1896, 1904. The notebook MS is in the Bodleian Library. Basic text: notebook MS.]

Title. MS: Annie.[*] [At the bottom of the page is the following:] [*Query: Borrows?*] [The deletions are in pencil.]
    1896, 1904: ANNIE
2. 1896, 1904: kin:
4. 1896, 1904: sin:
6. 1896, 1904: in:
8. 1896, 1904: win!
9. MS: sisters [*are*] <stand> as [The deletion and revision are in pencil in Christina's hand.]
12. 1896, 1904: unclose.

14. 1896: goes;
    1904: goes:
15. MS: tender [illegible erasure] <green>
20. 1896, 1904: blind!
22. MS: never [illegible erasure] <find>
26. 1896, 1904: upon:
27. 1896, 1904: golden harvest-moon
28. 1896, 1904: gone:
31. 1896, 1904: in summertime
33. 1896, 1904: love,
37. 1896, 1904: love,

A DIRGE.

[Composed January 18, 1851. Editions: 1896, 1904. The notebook MS is in the Bodleian Library. Basic text: notebook MS. In the 1896 text, lines 2, 10, 11, and 18 are not indented; lines 3, 8, 16, 19, and 24 are indented two spaces; and lines 5, 6, 13, 14, 21, and 22 are indented four spaces. In the 1904 text, lines 2, 3, 4, 7, 10, 11, 18, and 23 are not indented; lines 5, 6, 13, 14, 21, and 22 are indented four spaces; and lines 16, 19, and 24 are indented two spaces.]

Title. 1896, 1904: A DIRGE
2. 1896, 1904: in Summertime:

7. 1896, 1904: her fast-closed eyes,
11. MS: quickening [*dawn,*] <lying

lorn;> [The deletion and revision
are in pencil in Christina's hand.]
1896, 1904: lorn:
12. 1896, 1904: as though in
17. 1896, 1904: Nay she <> fade,

18. 1896, 1904: fruit:
19. 1896, 1904: the Living Vine, whose
Root
22. 1896, 1904: of ours

SONG. ["IT IS NOT FOR HER EVEN BROW"]

[Composed in 1851. Editions: 1896, 1904. The notebook MS is in the Bodleian Library. Basic text: notebook MS.]

Title. 1896, 1904: SONG
4. 1896, 1904: fair:
5. 1896, 1904: Her tell-tale eyes

10. 1896, 1904: within:
16. 1896, 1904: wings:

A DREAM.

[Composed May 14, 1851. The notebook MS is in the Bodleian Library. Basic text: notebook MS.]

2. MS: lost <love> far
8. MS: [*I*] [indented two spaces] <I>
[not indented]

"A FAIR WORLD THO' A FALLEN."——

[Composed August 30, 1851. Editions: 1896, 1904. The notebook MS is in the Bodleian Library. Basic text: notebook MS.]

Title. 1896, 1904: A FAIR WORLD
THOUGH A FALLEN
2. 1896, 1904: old Fall; and
8. 1896, 1904: comfort?—Hear the
9. MS: and [illegible erasure] <sick at
heart,>

10. 1896, 1904: touch,
12. MS: the bette[*r*]<r> [*part*] <part,>
1896, 1904: For, though I
14. 1896, 1904: much?

ADVENT.

[Composed December 12, 1851. Editions: 1896, 1904. The notebook MS is in the Bodleian Library. Basic text: notebook MS.]

Title. 1896, 1904: ADVENT
2. 1896, 1904: blessed Spirits,
"Come":
3. MS: of Thi[illegible deletion]<n>e
[illegible deletion] <Ow>n flock,
1896, 1904: the lambs of Thine
own flock,
4. MS: [After line 4 is the following
stanza, deleted in pencil:]

[*"Come," to the Saint refraining
His spirit as a child;
"Come," to the sad and troubled soul
Indeed, but undefiled.*]

1896, 1904: little ones, "Come
6. 1904: sent;
10. 1896, 1904: lips though dumb:

ALL SAINTS.

[Composed January 20, 1852. Editions: 1896, 1904. The notebook MS is in the Bodleian Library. Basic text: notebook MS.]

Title. 1896, 1904: ALL SAINTS
2. 1896, 1904: ivory:
3. MS: holy [*m*]<M>other mine,
6. 1896, 1904: exceedingly:
7. 1896, 1904: trespassing,—
8. 1896, 1904: in heaven, set
9. 1896, 1904: voice
10. 1896, 1904: yea answered

11. 1896: "Sing, saith He to the heavens, to earth rejoice:
1904: 'Sing, saith He to the heavens, to earth, Rejoice:
12. 1896, 1904: Thou also lift < > above:
13. 1896, 1904: thee such
14. 1896, 1904: lo His < > is Love."

"EYE HATH NOT SEEN."

[Composed May 1, 1852. Editions: 1896, 1904. The notebook MS is in the Bodleian Library. Basic text: notebook MS.]

Title. 1896, 1904: EYE HATH NOT SEEN ＼
7. 1896, 1904: blest! but
9. 1896, 1904: the light-region where
13. 1896, 1904: wind nor rain
14. 1896, 1904: sun nor snow:
15. 1896, 1904: The Trees of
22. 1896, 1904: in light:
23. 1896, 1904: sad—
25. 1896, 1904: yearning through the
27. 1896, 1904: their best-beloved
33. MS: Sufficing Virgins, [*p*]<P>rophets, Saints,
35. MS: [*Is*] <Shall> be
40. MS: birth[,]<?>
1896, 1904: Through second
43. 1896, 1904: of the sheep,
45. 1896, 1904: leads His own by < > streams—

49. 1896, 1904: the altar comes
51. 1896, 1904: martyred Saints: "How long," they
52. 1896, 1904: "O < > long,
54. 1896, 1904: due?"
55. 1896, 1904: white,
58. 1896, 1904: day—
60. 1896, 1904: said;
61. 1896, 1904: away,
64. 1896, 1904: sleep,
66. 1896, 1904: from Thy face.
67. MS: till [*t*]<T>hy wrath
1904: us, till
69. 1904: and with Magdalene,
72. MS: [*But*] <Who> by [*t*]<T>hy promise [The first deletion and revision are in pencil in Christina's hand.]

ST. ELIZABETH OF HUNGARY.

[Composed June 16, 1852. Editions: 1896, 1904. The notebook MS is in the Bodleian Library. Basic text: notebook MS.]

Title. 1896, 1904: ST. ELIZABETH OF HUNGARY
2. MS: [*In all save in heart*] <Save in heart in all> a [The inversion is indicated in pencil.]
3. 1896, 1904: undefiled,

4. MS: [*She knelt*] <Knelt she> at [The inversion is indicated in pencil.]
1896, 1904: feet:
6. MS: Thin[illegible deletion]<k>ing it

8. MS: Careless [illegible erasure]
   <on> the

10. 1896, 1904: white:
14. 1896, 1904: eyes,

MOONSHINE.

[Composed June 16, 1852. Editions: 1896, 1904. The notebook MS is in the Bodleian Library. Basic text: notebook MS. In the 1896 text, lines 5, 9, 13, 19, 21, 23, 25, 27, 29, 31, 37, 39, 43, 45, 47, 49, 51, 53, 55, 57, 59, 61, and 63 are indented two spaces; and lines 7, 10, 12, 14, 16, 18, 20, 22, 24, 26, 28, 30, 32, 38, 40, 42, 44, 46, 48, 50, 52, 54, 56, 58, 60, and 64 are not indented. The 1904 indentation is identical to the 1896 except that lines 11 and 15 are indented two spaces.]

Title. 1896, 1904: MOONSHINE
6. 1896, 1904: Wilt
7. 1896, 1904: Miles and
8. 1896, 1904: Over <> sea?"
10. 1896, 1904: Truly
11. 1896, 1904: I
12. 1896, 1904: Over
14. 1896, 1904: That
15. 1896, 1904: I
16. 1896, 1904: Love,
18. 1896, 1904: way,
25. MS: Her [look] <smile> rejoices
    [The deletion and revision are in pencil in Christina's hand.]
26. 1896, 1904: mute:
27. MS: [Passing] <She treads> the
    [The deletion and revision are in pencil in Christina's hand.]
37. 1896, 1904: she, "Like

38. 1896, 1904: Shines <> gold":
39. 1896, 1904: she, "I
40. MS: hold.["]
    1896, 1904: In
42. 1896, 1904: awhile;
43. 1896, 1904: My
44. 1896, 1904: In
52. 1896, 1904: fro:
58. MS: [Illegible erasure] <Far across
    the sea;>
    1896, 1904: sea:
60. 1896, 1904: be:
62. MS: Ever [illegible deletion]
    <ha>nd in
63. 1896, 1904: and moonlight
64. MS: For <To> another [The
    addition is in pencil in Christina's
    hand.]

"THE SUMMER IS ENDED."

[Composed September 11, 1852. Editions: 1896, 1904. The notebook MS is in the Bodleian Library. Basic text: notebook MS. In the 1904 text, the fourth and fifth lines of each stanza are indented two spaces.]

Title. MS: is [gone] <ended>."
   1896, 1904: THE SUMMER IS
   ENDED
3. 1896, 1904: Or, if
5. MS: [For] <Once for> my [fair]
   windingsheet. [The deletions and
   revision are in pencil in Christina's
   hand.]
   1896, 1904: my winding-sheet.
7. MS: them [pass] <fade> in [The
   deletion and revision are in pencil
   in Christina's hand.]
8. 1896, 1904: Or, if <> still,

9. MS: [And] <That> they [The
   deletion and revision are in pencil
   in Christina's hand.]
10. 1896, 1904: more, for
13. 1896, 1904: Or, if <> weep,
14. 1896, 1904: on,
15. MS: [After line 15 is the following
    stanza, deleted in pencil:]

    [And lay no stone upon my grave,
    Such honour suits not my degree:
    But if you place one, place a Cross;
      So He Who died to save,
      May He remember me.]

"I LOOK FOR THE LORD."

[Composed September 28, 1852. Editions: 1896, 1904. The notebook MS is in the Bodleian Library. Basic text: notebook MS.]

Title. 1896, 1904: I LOOK FOR THE
LORD
3. 1896, 1904: day;
4. 1896, 1904: things—
6. 1896, 1904: secret water-springs.
12. MS: changeless Par[*d*]<a>dise.

15. 1896, 1904: great;
16. 1896, 1904: dead.
18. MS: As [*t*]<T>hou Thy
22. 1896, 1904: waste:
23. 1896, 1904: Where joy Thou
24. 1896, 1904: And sweetness to

SONG. ["I HAVE LOVED YOU FOR LONG LONG YEARS ELLEN"]

[Composed October 15, 1852. The notebook MS is in the Bodleian Library. Basic text: notebook MS.]

4. MS: you [*sti*] <do> not

A DISCOVERY.

[Composed October 24, 1852. Editions: 1896, 1904. The notebook MS (MS1) is in the Bodleian Library. A separate fair copy (MS2) is in the Princeton University Library. Basic text: MS2.]

Title. MS1: After all.
  1896, 1904: AFTER ALL
1. MS1, 1896, 1904: thought."
2. MS1: still:"—"Yes, <> so;
3. MS1: "Still
4. MS1: "That <> unsought:
  1896, 1904: in heaven alone <>
  unsought:
5. MS1: "Still <> bought."
  1896, 1904: bought."
6. MS1: "[*Nay,*] <Then> chase [The
  deletion and revision are in pencil
  in Christina's hand.]
  MS2: "Nay, chase
8. MS1: "The <> clutches: will <>
  taught?—
  1896, 1904: clutches: will
9. MS1: "You have [*h*]<a> home <>
  broods [*as*] <like> a dove, [The
  second deletion and revision are in
  pencil in Christina's hand.]
  MS2: broods as a
  1896, 1904: dove,
10. MS1: [*"Deep sheltered from the world's*
  loud discontent;] <[*Screened from*

the [illegible deletion] *worlds*
tempestuous]> [The deletion and
revision are in pencil in Christina's
hand. Below line 9 is added in
pencil in William Michael Rossetti's
hand:] <Screened from the weary
world's loud discontent:>
  MS2: Deep sheltered from the
  world's loud discontent,
  1896, 1904: discontent:
11. MS1: "You <> here; you [*look*]
  <wait> for [The deletion and
  revision are in pencil in Christina's
  hand. The added word is repeated
  in pencil above the line, apparently
  in William Michael Rossetti's hand.]
  MS2: here, you look for
  1896, 1904: here: you <> above.
12. MS1: "I
  1896, 1904: went:
13. MS1: "Must
14. MS1: "And <> banishment."
  MS2: [Below the poem is written:]
  Christina G. Rossetti
  1896, 1904: banishment."

FROM THE ANTIQUE.

[Composed December 10, 1852. Editions: 1896, 1904. The notebook MS is in the Bodleian Library. Basic text: notebook MS.]

Title. 1896, 1904: FROM THE
ANTIQUE

2. 1896, 1904: us:

11. 1896, 1904: with fast-closed eyes

"THE HEART KNOWETH ITS OWN BITTERNESS."
["WEEP YET A WHILE"]

[Composed December 23, 1852. Editions: 1896, 1904. The notebook MS is in the Bodleian Library. Basic text: notebook MS. Lines 1–4, 24–34 were published in *Verses* (1893) as "'The day is at hand.'" For text and variants of that poem, see Volume II of the present edition, pp. 297, 456. In the 1896 text, lines 1, 3, 10–14, 16, 18, 21, 22, 24, 27, 29, and 31 are indented six spaces; lines 5–9, 17, 19, 20, 25, 26, 28, 30, and 33 are indented four spaces; and lines 15, 32, and 34 are indented two spaces. The 1904 indentation is the same as the 1896 except that line 2 is indented four spaces, lines 32 and 34 are not indented, and line 33 is indented two spaces.]

Title. 1896, 1904: THE HEART
KNOWETH ITS OWN
BITTERNESS

1–4. MS: [At the opening of the
poem is the following stanza,
deleted in pencil:]

[*Weep, for none shall know
Why sick at heart thou weepest;
Wake and weep, for none shall guess
In thy loneliness
Why thou they vigil keepest.
Weep yet a while;
Weep till the day shall dawn when thou shalt
smile.*]

[Below the text of the poem is the
following stanza, added in pencil in
Christina's hand:]

<Weep yet a while
Weep till that day shall dawn when thou
shalt smile

Watch till the day
When all save only Love shall pass
away.>

[The added lines are interpolated
into the text of the deleted stanza
in pencil in William Michael
Rossetti's hand.]

1. 1896, 1904: yet awhile,—
2. 1896, 1904: smile:
4. 1896, 1904: only love shall
11. 1896, 1904: spring:
15. 1896, 1904: In summertime of
16. 1896, 1904: Heart-sick and
19. 1896, 1904: again:
25. 1896, 1904: weep:
31. 1896, 1904: reap.
32. 1896, 1904: the Lord's own flock
33. 1896, 1904: with His love
34. 1896, 1904: below, who lives

"TO WHAT PURPOSE IS THIS WASTE?"
["A WINDY SHELL SINGING UPON THE SHORE"]

[Composed January 22, 1853. Editions: 1896, 1904. The notebook MS is in the Bodleian Library. Basic text: notebook MS. Lines 78–89 were published in *Verses* (1893) as "'These all wait upon Thee.'" For text and variants of that poem, see Volume II of the present edition, pp. 314, 469–71. In the 1896 text, lines 1, 5–7, 10, 12, 14, 17, 18, 21, 25, 26, 28, 30, 32, 33, 36, 38, 39, 41, 42, 45, 48–50, 52–55, 57, 62, 63, 86, 88, 90–93, 96, 103–105, 109, 110, and 112 are not indented; lines 2, 8, 9,

11, 13, 19, 20, 22, 31, 35, 37, 40, 47, 57, 59, 60, 64, 67, 78, 79, 81, 82, 84, 85, 87, 97, 102, 107, 111, 113, and 118 are indented four spaces; lines 3 and 44 are indented eight spaces; lines 4, 76, 89, 99, and 108 are indented six spaces; and lines 15, 16, 23, 24, 27, 29, 34, 43, 46, 51, 60, 61, 65, 66, 67–75, 77, 80, 83, 94, 95, 106, 114–17, and 119–33 are indented two spaces. The 1904 indentation is the same as the 1896 except that line 2 is not indented.]

Title. 1896, 1904: TO WHAT
PURPOSE IS THIS WASTE?
2. MS: lily [illegible erasure]
 <b>udding in
 1896, 1904: place,
7. 1896, 1904: Hedged-in with
13. 1896, 1904: mouse:
14. 1896, 1904: roots, fit < > fuel,
 roofing
15. 1896, 1904: acorns, and < >
 wheat—
17. MS: [Because line 17 is the last line
 on the page, there is no indication
 of whether or not a stanza break is
 intended to follow the line.]
18. MS: precious pear[*l*]<l> deep
 1896, 1904: pearl deep-buried in
25. 1896, 1904: plumb down-tumbled
 to
30. 1896, 1904: said smiling
31. 1896, 1904: dwells!
33. 1896, 1904: set, though a
34. MS: Already fla[*sh*]<k>ed the
35. 1896, 1904: looked through.
38. 1896, 1904: So, since
43. 1896, 1904: were open to
46. 1896, 1904: tongue, that
48. MS: utter [*l*]<L>ove.
51. 1896, 1904: blessed spirits, chiming
54. 1896, 1904: brushes through the

58. 1896, 1904: shell:
62. 1896: circle roundabout
63. 1896: of heaven, or
 1904: of heaven, or < > a well-/
 spring rise
72. MS: the undefil<e>d,
 1896, 1904: her the
78. 1896, 1904: than ours
89. MS: [Because line 89 is the last line
 on the page, there is no indication
 of whether or not a stanza break is
 intended to follow the line.]
90. 1896, 1904: hidden water-stream
94. 1896, 1904: light:
95. 1896, 1904: the Spring
99. 1896, 1904: mouse
110. 1896, 1904: hymn and incense
111. 1896, 1904: rise:
113. MS: which [*l*]<L>ove accepteth
114. 1904: bird
123. 1896, 1904: us, for
124. MS: [Because line 124 is the last
 line on the page, there is no
 indication of whether or not a
 stanza break is intended to follow
 the line.]
 1904: understood!
132. 1896, 1904: Ah when
133. 1896, 1904: earth?

NEXT OF KIN.

[Composed February 21, 1853. Editions: 1896, 1904. The notebook MS is in the Bodleian Library. Basic text: notebook MS. In the 1896 and 1904 texts, lines 1, 2, 4, 5, 7, 9, 13, and 14 are indented two spaces.]

Title. 1896, 1904: NEXT OF KIN
1. 1896, 1904: sun:
5. 1896, 1904: day:
7. 1896, 1904: be:
9. 1896, 1904: light:
11. 1896, 1904: eyes:

13. MS: mine is [*almost*] <nearly>
 done, [The deletion and revision
 are in pencil in Christina's hand.]
14. 1896s: run.
15. 1896, 1904: head:

"LET THEM REJOICE IN THEIR BEDS."

[Composed March 7, 1853. The notebook MS is in the Bodleian Library. Basic text: notebook MS.]

PORTRAITS.

[Composed May 9, 1853. Editions: 1896, 1904. The notebook MS is in the Bodleian Library. Basic text: notebook MS.]

Title. 1896, 1904: PORTRAITS
2. 1896, 1904: the South,
4. 1896, 1904: mouth:
8. MS: [The stanza below line 8 is missing from the notebook.]
1896, 1904: [Below line 8 is a row of spaced periods representing the stanza missing from the notebook text.]
15. 1896, 1904: heart,
16. 1896, 1904: mine, Good-night.

WHITSUN EVE.

[Composed May 18, 1853. Editions: 1896, 1904. The notebook MS is in the Bodleian Library. Basic text: notebook MS.]

Title. 1896, 1904: WHITSUN EVE
3. 1896, 1904: saileth through the
8. 1896, 1904: pass;
10. MS: up incen[c]<s>e all
1904: night.
12. MS: blessed An[l]<g>els watch
14. MS: Thou [w]<W>ho wert
1896, 1904: Thou who wert

WHAT?

[Composed in May, 1853. Editions: 1896, 1904. The notebook MS is in the Bodleian Library. Basic text: notebook MS. In the MS, deletions and revisions are in pencil in Christina's handwriting unless otherwise indicated. In the 1896 and 1904 texts, lines 1, 5, 7, 9–12, 15, 17, 19, 22, 23, 25, and 26 are indented two spaces; and lines 2–4, 6, 13, 14, 16, 18, and 20 are indented four spaces.]

Title. 1896, 1904: WHAT?
1–6. MS: [A deletion symbol is added and crossed out in the right margin beside the opening stanza.]
7. MS: as [the] <a> dying
8. 1896, 1904: night:
12. MS: [Sweet] <Gay> as [The added word is repeated above the revision, in pencil, apparently in William Michael Rossetti's hand.]
1896, 1904: a cowslip-meadow
14. MS: When <new> day is [just] begun;
1896, 1904: begun:
18. MS: [Fruitful as herb or tree] <Pleasant as budding tree>,
20. 1896, 1904: sea:
21. MS: a [budding] <fragrant> rose
1896, 1904: dew:—
22. MS: sweet, as [thorny] <fruitless> too.
24. 1896, 1904: dream!
26. 1896, 1904: stream!

A PAUSE.

[Composed June 10, 1853. Editions: 1896, 1904. The notebook MS is in the Bodleian Library. Basic text: notebook MS.]
Title. 1896, 1904: A PAUSE

HOLY INNOCENTS.

[Composed July 1, 1853. Editions: 1896, 1904. The notebook MS is in the Bodleian Library. Basic text: notebook MS. In the MS, the deletions and revisions are in pencil in Christina's handwriting.]

Title. 1896, 1904: HOLY
    INNOCENTS
1. 1896, 1904: little Baby, sleep;
3. 1896, 1904: bed, and
6. 1896, 1904: thee:
9. 1896, 1904: The Love which doth
10. 1896, 1904: thee:
13. 1896, 1904: Sleep through the < >
    night,

14. MS: [*Until another dawning*]
    <Christ-kept from snare &
    sorrow>
    1896, 1904: sorrow,
15. MS: [*Bring in the blessed light*]
    <Until thou wake to light>
16. MS: [*Of everlasting morning.*] <&
    love & warmth tomorrow.>
    1896, 1904: warmth to-morrow.

"THERE REMAINETH THEREFORE A REST FOR THE PEOPLE OF GOD."
["COME BLESSED SLEEP, MOST FULL, MOST PERFECT, COME"]

[Composed July 12, 1853. Editions: 1896, 1904. The notebook MS is in the Bodleian Library. Basic text: notebook MS. In the MS, line 2 is not indented.]

Title. 1896, 1904: THERE
    REMAINETH THEREFORE
    A REST FOR THE PEOPLE
    OF GOD
Part 1. 1896, 1904: I
Opening quotation. 1896: Ye < >
    exhortation
    1904: exhortation.'
1. 1896, 1904: Come, blessed < >
    perfect, come:
2. 1896, 1904: Come, sleep,
5. 1896, 1904: Come, happy sleep, to
6. 1896, 1904: control:
9. 1896, 1904: Come, sleep, and
11. 1896, 1904: Come, secret sleep,
    with thine unuttered psalm,

12. 1896, 1904: Safe sheltering in
13. 1896, 1904: Come, heavy
Part 2. 1896, 1904: II
Opening quotation. 1896: Which < >
    children
    1904: children.
17. 1896, 1904: steep:
18. 1896, 1904: goal:
20. 1896, 1904: slumber deep
22. 1896, 1904: Through long
24. 1896, 1904: Lapt in
25. 1896, 1904: My Hands that bled
26. 1896, 1904: My Heart that bled
    < > thy rest:
27. 1896, 1904: everlasting strength,
28. 1896, 1904: upon My breast.

ANNIE. ["IT'S NOT FOR EARTHLY BREAD, ANNIE"]

[Composed August 1, 1853. Editions: 1896, 1904. The notebook MS is in the Bodleian Library. Basic text: notebook MS. In the 1896 and 1904 versions, only the

444   *The Complete Poems of Christina Rossetti*

fifth, eighth, eleventh, fourteenth, and sixteenth stanzas of the poem constitute the text; and lines 27, 45, 61, 91, and 93 are indented two spaces.]

Title. 1896, 1904: A HARVEST
8. MS: [illegible erasure] <In this glorious month of June,>
25. MS: [*The*] <Oh> gate <> blessed [*grave*] <night>, [The deletions and revisions are in pencil in Christina's hand. Above the line is added in pencil in Christina's hand:] <A Harvest. 1- > 1896, 1904: O gate
27. MS: of s[*a*]<h>ame and
37. MS: the shows[, *Annie*,] [The deletion is in pencil.]
43. MS: [Above the line is added in pencil:] <[(*1*)] 2.> [A vertical pencil line is added in the right margin of the stanza.]
46. 1896, 1904: grass:

61. MS: [Above the line is added in pencil:] <[(*2*)] 3.> [A vertical pencil line is added in the right margin of the stanza.]
62. 1896, 1904: unknown:
64. 1896, 1904: undertone:
79. MS: [Above the line is added in pencil:] <[(*3*)] 4.> [A vertical pencil line is added in the right margin of the stanza.]
81. MS: Yet [*I am*] <some are> sick [The deletion and revision are in pencil in Christina's hand.]
91. MS: [Above the line is added in pencil:] <[(*4*)] 5.> [A vertical pencil line is added in the right margin of the stanza.]

SEASONS ["IN SPRINGTIME WHEN THE LEAVES ARE YOUNG"]

[Composed in September, 1853. Editions: 1896, 1904. The notebook MS is in the Bodleian Library. Basic text: notebook MS.]

Title. 1896, 1904: SEASONS
1. 1896, 1904: In Springtime when
4. 1896, 1904: When Summer comes
7. 1896, 1904: In Autumn ere
9. 1896, 1904: these!

10. 1896, 1904: In Winter when
12. MS: And [*pale*] <starved> the [The deletion and revision are in pencil in Christina's hand.]

"THOU SLEEPEST WHERE THE LILIES FADE"

[Date of composition unknown. Editions: 1896, 1904. The notebook MS is in the Bodleian Library. Basic text: notebook MS. In the MS notebook, the poem is the second in a group of ten poems entitled "Odds and Ends." At the end of the group is written, "Copied, September 1853."]

Title. 1896, 1904: BURIED
1. MS: [Above the line is added in pencil, apparently in William Michael Rossetti's hand:] <Buried.>

2. 1896, 1904: not:
6. 1896, 1904: blossom:
7. 1896, 1904: snow—

"I WISH I WERE A LITTLE BIRD"

[Date of composition unknown. Editions: 1896, 1904. The notebook MS is in the Bodleian Library. Basic text: notebook MS. In the MS notebook, the poem is the fourth in a group of ten poems entitled "Odds and Ends." At the end of the group is written, "Copied, September 1853."]

Title. 1896, 1904: A WISH
   1. MS: [Above the line is added in
      pencil, apparently in William

Michael Rossetti's hand:] <A
Wish.>
   2. 1896, 1904: soar;

(TWO PARTED.)

[Date of composition unknown. Editions: 1896, 1904. The notebook MS is in the Bodleian Library. Basic text: notebook MS. In the MS notebook, the poem is the fifth in a group of ten poems entitled "Odds and Ends." At the end of the group is written, "Copied, September 1853."]

Title. 1896, 1904: TWO PARTED
   2. 1896, 1904: Sing
   3. 1896, 1904: Sing
   4. 1896, 1904: Sing <> more."
   5. 1896, 1904: "Sigh <> sore."
   7. MS: love betr[y]<a>yed me,
      1896, 1904: I

   8. 1896, 1904: Was
   9. 1896, 1904: Love,
10. 1896, 1904: "Hark <> sea."
12. 1896, 1904: Still
13. 1896, 1904: Oh
14. 1896, 1904: Or
15. 1896, 1904: "Oh <> sighs!"

"ALL NIGHT I DREAM YOU LOVE ME WELL"

[Date of composition unknown. The notebook MS is in the Bodleian Library. Basic text: notebook MS. In the MS notebook, the poem is the sixth in a group of ten poems entitled "Odds and Ends." At the end of the group is written, "Copied, September 1853."]

(FOR ROSALINE'S ALBUM.)

[Date of composition unknown. Editions: 1896, 1904. The notebook MS is in the Bodleian Library. Basic text: notebook MS. In the MS notebook, the poem is the seventh in a group of ten poems entitled "Odds and Ends." At the end of the group is written, "Copied, September 1853."]

Title. 1896, 1904: FOR ROSALINE'S
      ALBUM

   7. 1896, 1904: see.
   8. 1896, 1904: guest?

"CARE FLIETH"

[Date of composition unknown. Editions: 1896, 1904. The notebook MS is in the Bodleian Library. Basic text: notebook MS. In the MS notebook, the poem is the eighth in a group of ten poems entitled "Odds and Ends." At the end of the group is written, "Copied, September 1853." In the 1896 text, lines 1, 3, 5, and 7 are indented four spaces; line 2 is indented eight spaces; and line 4 is indented two spaces. The 1904 indentation is the same as the 1896 except that line 2 is indented two spaces.]

Title. 1896, 1904: AUTUMN
1. MS: [Above the line is added in
   pencil, apparently in William
   Michael Rossetti's hand:]
   <Autumn>

2. 1896, 1904: Hope and Fear
   together:
4. MS: the Aut[um]<um>n weather.
6. 1896, 1904: Even Care is pleasant:
7. 1896, 1904: When Fear doth
9. 1896, 1904: the turtle-dove:—

(EPITAPH.)

[Date of composition unknown. The notebook MS is in the Bodleian Library. Basic text: notebook MS. In the MS notebook, the poem is the ninth in a group of ten poems entitled "Odds and Ends." At the end of the group is written, "Copied, September 1853."]
4. MS: [Below the poem is written:]
   (Darlaston.)

THE P.R.B.

[Composed November 10, 1853. Editions: 1904. The notebook MS is in the Bodleian Library. The poem was published in William Michael Rossetti (ed.), *Dante Gabriel Rossetti: His Family-Letters with a Memoir* (2 vols.; London: Ellis and Elvey, 1895), I, 138. Basic text: notebook MS. In the 1895 text, lines 2, 3, 5, 7, and 13 are indented two spaces, and lines 4, 6, 8, 9, and 11 are indented four spaces. The 1904 indentation is the same as the 1895 except that line 13 is not indented.]

Title. 1895: THE P.R.B.
      1904: THE P.R.B./ 2
1. 1895: "The <> decadence:
   1904: decadence:
2. 1895, 1904: chops,
6. 1895, 1904: His B's in
7. 1895, 1904: pipe,
9. 1895, 1904: last the champion
   great Millais,

10. 1895: Attaining Academic
    opulence,
    1904: opulence,
11. 1895, 1904: with A.R.A.
12. 1895, 1904: sea;
13. 1895: when over-ripe;
    1904: when over-/ ripe;
14. 1895: consummated P.R.B."

SEASONS. ["CROCUSES AND SNOWDROPS WITHER"]

[Composed December 7, 1853. Editions: 1896, 1904. The notebook MS is in the Bodleian Library. Basic text: notebook MS. In the MS, deletions and revisions are in pencil in Christina's handwriting unless otherwise indicated.]

Title. 1896, 1904: SEASONS
1. MS: [*Primroses and violets wither*]
   <Crocuses & snowdrops wither>,
2. MS: [*Snowdrops and crocuses together*]
   <Violets primroses together>,
   1896, 1904: Violets, primroses
3. MS: Fa[il]<d>ing with the

   fa[il]<d>ing spring
   1896, 1904: the fading Spring
5. 1896, 1904: sweet Summer, pass
6. MS: Stay a[illegible
   deletion]<wh>ile the
   1896, 1904: the harvest-moon:
7. MS: O sweet<est> summer [The

added letters are in ink.]
1896, 1904: sweetest Summer, do
8. 1896, 1904: For Autumn's next
9. 1896, 1904: When Autumn comes
12. MS: the golden <withered> harvest
1896, 1904: the golden
harvest-sheaf.

13. MS: [*Weary*] <Dreary> winter
1896, 1904: Dreary Winter come
<> last:
14. 1896, 1904: past:
15. 1896: sluggish Winter wane
1904: sluggish Winter, wane
16. 1896, 1904: Till Spring and

"WHO HAVE A FORM OF GODLINESS."

[Composed December 18, 1853. Editions: 1896, 1904. The notebook MS is in the Bodleian Library. Basic text: notebook MS. In the 1896 and 1904 texts, lines 11 and 12 are indented four spaces.]

Title. 1896, 1904: WHO HAVE A
    FORM OF GODLINESS
1. 1896, 1904: will:
2. 1896, 1904: Also God's
4. MS: fill[;]<:>
    1896, 1904: fill.
    1896s: fill,

6. 1896, 1904: nest,
7. 1896, 1904: And through hot
9. 1896, 1904: So, when
11. 1896s: brim
12. 1896, 1904: for Him:
13. 1896, 1904: wearied though the
14. 1896, 1904: fainting though the

BALLAD.

[Composed January 7, 1854. Editions: 1896, 1904. The notebook MS is in the Bodleian Library. Basic text: notebook MS. In the 1896 and 1904 texts, lines 7 and 9 are indented two spaces. In the 1896s text, lines 7 and 9 are not indented.]

Title. 1896, 1904: BALLAD
1. 1896, 1904: "Soft
4. 1896, 1904: tree."
5. 1896, 1904: "There's <> if you are
    lonesome,
6. 1896, 1904: rest:
8. 1896, 1904: breast."
9. 1896, 1904: "Fair
12. 1896, 1904: now."
13. 1896, 1904: "I
14. 1896, 1904: breast:
16. 1896, 1904: nest."

17. 1896, 1904: "Faint <> rose, come
18. 1896, 1904: thorn:
19. 1896, 1904: the vesper-bell
20. 1896, 1904: morn."
21. 1896, 1904: There's
24. 1896, 1904: snow:
26. 1896, 1904: grow."
27. 1896, 1904: "But
30. 1896, 1904: Though I <> this."
31. 1896, 1904: "You
34. 1896, 1904: arise:
36. 1896, 1904: of Paradise."

A STUDY. (A SOUL.)

[Composed February 7, 1854. Editions: 1896, 1904. The notebook MS (MS1) is in the Bodleian Library. A fair copy (MS2), signed "Christina G. Rossetti," is in the Princeton University Library. Basic text: MS2. In MS1, the deletions and additions are in pencil in Christina's handwriting unless otherwise indicated.]

Title. MS1: A Soul.
    1896, 1904: A SOUL

1. MS1: pale as parian statues
    MS2: pale as [*p*]<P>arian statues

2. MS1: bay
3. MS1: sway
4. MS1: hand:
6. 1896, 1904: day:
7. MS1, 1896, 1904: steadfast, all
8. MS1: Th[e]<at> foot<->track
   doth not waver on
   MS2: That foot<->track hath
   1896, 1904: foot-track doth not
   waver on
9. 1896, 1904: beacon through the

10. MS1: beacon [in the] <where>
    [wilderness] <storm drift is>,
    1896, 1904: is—
11. MS1: white:
    1896: wonder deathly-white:
    1904: wonder deathly-/ white:
12. MS1: there [steadfast] <patient>
    nerved with [illegible erasure]
    <inner> might, [The second
    revision is in ink.]
    1896, 1904: patient nerved

"THERE REMAINETH THEREFORE A REST."
["VERY COOL THAT BED MUST BE"]

[Composed February 17, 1854. Editions: 1896, 1904. The notebook MS is in the
Bodleian Library. Basic text: notebook MS. Lines 6–10, 21–25 were published as
"The Bourne" in *The Prince's Progress and Other Poems* (1866); for text and variants of
that poem, see Volume I of the present edition, pp. 142, 280. Lines 51–60 were
published as "'There remaineth therefore a Rest to the People of God'" in *Verses*
(1893); for text and variants of that poem, see Volume II of the present edition,
pp. 277, 444. In the 1896 and 1904 versions, the text constitutes only lines 16–20,
31–40, and 51–60.]

Title. MS: [Above the title is added in
pencil in Dante Gabriel Rossetti's
hand:] <Take 2 stanzas>
1896, 1904: THERE
REMAINETH THEREFORE
A REST
6. MS: [Above the line is added in
pencil in Dante Gabriel Rossetti's
hand:] <(1)> [A vertical pencil line
is added in the right margin of the
stanza.]
16. MS: [Above the line is added in
pencil in William Michael Rossetti's
hand:] <a>
17. 1896, 1904: proud—
18. 1896, 1904: crowd:
21. MS: [Above the line is added in
pencil in Dante Gabriel Rossetti's
hand:] <(2)> [A vertical pencil line
is added in the right margin of the
stanza.]
31. MS: [In the right margin of the
stanza is added in pencil in William
Michael Rossetti's hand:] <b>
32. 1896, 1904: sighs:

33. 1896, 1904: eyes:
36. MS: [In the right margin of the
stanza is added in pencil in William
Michael Rossetti's hand:] <c>
38. 1896: rings:
51. MS: [Above the line is added in
pencil in Christina's hand:] <1.>
[In the right margin of the stanza is
added in pencil in William Michael
Rossetti's hand:] <d>
52. 1896, 1904: prayer, and fast!
53. MS: All [is] ful[l]<filled> from
[The deletion and revision are in
pencil in Christina's hand.]
1896, 1904: last:
54. MS: time [is] <gone> past [The
deletion and revision are in pencil
in Christina's hand.]
56. MS: [Bitter cup] <Fear & hope>
and [The deletion and revision are
in pencil in Christina's hand. In the
right margin of the stanza is added
in pencil in William Michael
Rossetti's hand:] <e>
60. 1896, 1904: Struggling, panting

"YE HAVE FORGOTTEN THE EXHORTATION."

[Composed May 10, 1854. Editions: 1896, 1904. The notebook MS is in the Bodleian Library. Basic text: notebook MS. Lines 27–48 were published as lines 1–20 of "'When my heart is vexed I will complain'" in *Verses* (1893); for text and variants of that poem, see Volume II of the present edition, pp. 303, 460. In the 1896 and 1904 texts, lines 1, 2, 5, 7, 9, 11, 13, 16, 19, 20, 22, 23, 29, 33, 41, 45, and 46 are indented four spaces; lines 3, 4, 10, and 12 are indented two spaces; lines 6, 14, 15, 17, 18, 21, 28, 30, 36, 37, 39, 40, 42, 44, 47, and 50 are indented six spaces; and lines 24, 25, 31, 32, 51, and 53 are indented eight spaces.]

Title. 1896, 1904: YE HAVE
    FORGOTTEN THE
    EXHORTATION
2. 1896, 1904: day:
6. 1896, 1904: Ah gone
7. 1896, 1904: Ah dear
8. 1896, 1904: sight!
10. 1896, 1904: above:
13. 1896, 1904: a turtle-dove
16. 1896, 1904: warm but
18. 1896, 1904: heart-deep:
19. 1896, 1904: set:
23. 1896, 1904: sleep:

29. 1896, 1904: The harvest-moon
    shines
30. 1896, 1904: The harvest-time is
32. 1896, 1904: Ah woe < > me!
33. 1896: for harvest-time,
    1904: for harvest-/ time,
37. 1896, 1904: with Seraphim,
38. 1896, 1904: is;
41. MS: give <thee> robes
44. 1896, 1904: door,
50. 1896, 1904: hasten Thine own day
    1896s: hasten thine own day
53. 1896, 1904: begin!

GUESSES.

[Composed June 27, 1854. The notebook MS is in the Bodleian Library. Basic text: notebook MS.]

7. MS: and <felt> that
22. MS: [Illegible deletion] <Hers>elf
    with

FROM THE ANTIQUE.

[Composed June 28, 1854. Editions: 1896, 1904. The notebook MS is in the Bodleian Library. Basic text: notebook MS.]

Title. 1896, 1904: FROM THE
    ANTIQUE
1. 1896, 1904: is, she
3. 1896, 1904: man:
6. 1896, 1904: soul:

10. 1896, 1904: come:
11. MS: [Illegible erasure]
    <Blossoms> bloom
15. 1896, 1904: nothing, while

THREE STAGES./ 1.

[Composed February 14, 1848. Editions: 1904. There are two notebook MSS of the poem, both in the Bodleian Library. The earlier one is designated MS1 in the textual notes; the later one, dated July 25, 1854, is designated MS2. Basic text: MS2.]

Part 1 was published as "A Pause of Thought" in *Goblin Market and Other Poems* (1862); for text and variants of that poem, see Volume I of the present edition, pp. 51, 249. In MS1, the second and third lines of each stanza are not indented, and the fourth line of each stanza is indented two spaces.]

Title. MS1: Lines/ In memory of
Schiller's "Der Pilgrim."
1904: THREE STAGES
Part 1. MS1: [There is no number in
the text.]
1904: I.—A PAUSE OF
THOUGHT
2. 1904: truth:
3. MS1: But [*h*]<y>ears must

7. 1904: for, ever day by day
9. 1904: said 'This <> more;
11. MS1: now, and
1904: peace':
13. 1904: said: 'It
15. MS1: The [*joy*] <peace> of
1904: live?'—
17. 1904: Alas thou
18. 1904: pain:

THREE STAGES./ 2.

[Composed April 18, 1849. Editions: 1896, 1904. There are two notebook MSS of the poem, both in the Bodleian Library. The earlier one is designated MS1 in the textual notes; the later one, dated July 25, 1854, is designated MS2. Basic text: MS2.]

Title. MS1: The End of the First Part.
1896: THE END OF THE FIRST
PART
Part 2. MS1, 1896: [There is no number
in the text.]
1904: 2.—THE END OF THE
FIRST PART
5. 1896, 1904: dream!
6. MS1: pain.
1896, 1904: pain!
14. MS1: sin.
1896, 1904: hopes, are <> sin.
16. MS2: within
17. 1896, 1904: been,

18. MS1: rest.
1896, 1904: ever, will <> rest.
19. MS1, 1896, 1904: cold North wind
20. MS1, 1896, 1904: the West.
21. 1896, 1904: But, where <> stone
22. MS1, 1896, 1904: hermitage:
24. MS1, 1896, 1904: age.
25. MS1: shall [*lay*] <lie> around [The
deletion and revision are in pencil
in Christina's hand.]
1896, 1904: other garden-beds
shall <> around,
26. MS1: thyme.
1896: thyme:
1904: and incense-/ bearing thyme:

THREE STAGES./ 3.

[Composed July 25, 1854. Editions: 1896, 1904. The notebook MS is in the Bodleian Library. Basic text: notebook MS. Lines 9–12 were published as the first stanza of an untitled poem in *Verses* (1893); for text and variants of that poem, see Volume II of the present edition, pp. 276, 442. In the 1896 text, the second and third lines of each stanza are not indented, and the last line of each stanza is indented six spaces. In the 1904 text, the second and third lines of each stanza are not indented.]

Title. 1896: RESTIVE
Part 3. MS: [*3.*] <Restive.> [The
deletion and revision are in pencil,
apparently in William Michael
Rossetti's hand.]

1896: [There is no number in the
text.]
1904: 3
1. 1896, 1904: blow:
2. 1896, 1904: but never more:—

4. MS: [*And*] <Or> watch [The
deletion and revision are in pencil.
After line 4 is the following stanza,
deleted in pencil:]

[*Once and for ever: lapsing without end,*
Lapsing and yet perpetually the same,
Wave after wave, a current without aim—
Where should such current tend?—]

5. MS: <">Oh rest,<"> I thought,
<">in
1896, 1904: dark:
8. MS: [After line 8 are the following
stanzas, deleted in pencil:]

[*Rest out of sight, forgotten, and how cold*
To hope and dear delights of buried youth;
Rest in the darkness, which indeed is truth
Until the earth wax old.]

[*Night came upon the noontide of my day,*
Frost killed my buds fresh opening to the
sun;—
Now I will leap no more, nor p[illegible
erasure]<a>nt, *nor run,*
But toil <plod> *along the way.*]
[The added word is in pencil in
Christina's hand.]

[*My joys are hidden from my sight—amen,*
If mine eyes weep not, who should weep for
these?—
Yet when the axe shall smite all pleasant
trees,
What will it matter then?—]

9. MS: <">The<se> chimes [The
added letters are in pencil in
Christina's hand.]
1896, 1904: last:
10. MS: Th[*e*]<is> sand [The addition
is in pencil in Christina's hand.]
1896, 1904: droppeth through:
13. MS: <">So

14. 1896, 1904: again:
1896s: again.
15. MS: [*Grown dull*] <Gone dead>
alike [The deletion and revision are
in pencil in Christina's hand.]
1896, 1904: pain
16. MS: counterpoise:<"> [After line
16 is the following stanza, deleted
in pencil:]

[*So will I close mine ears and seal mine eyes,*
Grown cold to songs of mirth and summer
light;—
For all is vanity, both depth and height,
Vanity of vanities.—]

1896, 1904: counterpoise."
17. 1896, 1904: heart: and
19. 1896, 1904: myself and
20. 1896: unsought:
21. 1896, 1904: slack,
22. MS: heart [*dreamed*] <slumbered>,
[*and*] may-be [The deletion and
revision are in pencil in Christina's
hand.]
1896, 1904: heart dreamed, and
maybe wandered
24. 1896, 1904: track:
25. MS: to bui[*e*]<l>ding in
26. 1896, 1904: to fullness and < >
scent:
1896s: to fulness and < > scent:
27. 1896, 1904: Ah too my
28. 1896, 1904: fruitful
harvest-sheaves.
29. 1896, 1904: dead;
30. MS: Full [illegible erasure]
<throb> of
1896, 1904: rest.
31. 1896, 1904: Alas I
34. 1896, 1904: song:—

LONG LOOKED FOR.

[Composed August 12, 1854. Editions: 1896, 1904. The notebook MS is in the
Bodleian Library. Basic text: notebook MS. In the MS, deletions and revisions are in
pencil in Christina's hand. In the 1896 and 1904 texts, lines 1, 9, 11, 13, 17, 19, 25,
27, 29, 31, 33, and 39 are indented two spaces; lines 8, 12, and 20 are indented four
spaces; and lines 10, 18, and 36 are not indented.]

Title. 1896, 1904: LONG LOOKED
FOR
3. MS: scarcely [*beat*] <quicken>

4. MS: were her[']s:
6. 1896, 1904: past:
9. MS: then, [*my*] <dear> friends,

14. 1896, 1904: cold;   33. 1896, 1904: not,
21. 1896, 1904: me,   34. 1896, 1904: aside:
    1896s: me   37. MS: may [take] <pluck> a
24. MS: loved [in] <her> long

LISTENING.

[Composed in October, 1854. Editions: 1896, 1904. The notebook MS is in the
Bodleian Library. Basic text: notebook MS. In the 1896 and 1904 texts, lines 6 and
12 are not indented.]

Title. MS: [Two choices.] <Listening.>   She listened with the same heart-joy
    [The deletion and revision are in   To love's dear monotone.]
    pencil in Christina's hand.]
    1896, 1904: LISTENING   11. 1896, 1904: eyes
2. 1896, 1904: alone: 12. 1896, 1904: cheek;
4. MS: [After line 4 is the following   14. MS: [After line 14 are the
    stanza, deleted in pencil:]   following stanzas, deleted in
                                                pencil:]
    [Her hair was golden in the sun,
    Her hair was dove-like in the shade,   [He chose what I had feared to choose—
    She listened to the only [illegible erasure]   (Ah, which was wiser, I or he?)—
    <love>   He chose a love-warm priceless heart,
    That she had ever had.]   And I a cold bare dignity.]

6. 1896, 1904: line: [He chose a life like stainless spring
7. 1896, 1904: bough,   That buds to summer's perfect glow,
8. 1896, 1904: vine: I chose a tedious dignity
10. MS: [After line 10 is the following   As cold as cold as snow:
    stanza, deleted in pencil:]   He chose a garden of delights
                                                Where still refreshing waters flow;
    [She listened like a cushat dove   I chose a barren wilderness
    That never dreamed of life alone;   Whose buds died [illegible erasure]
                                                <years> ago.]

ZARA. ["I DREAMED THAT LOVING ME HE WOULD LOVE ON"]

[Composed January 8, 1855. The notebook MS is in the Bodleian Library. Basic
text: notebook MS.]

8. MS: [Illegible erasure] <And> half

THE LAST LOOK.

[Composed March 23, 1855. Editions: 1896, 1904. The notebook MS is in the
Bodleian Library. Basic text: notebook MS.]

Title. 1896, 1904: THE LAST LOOK   So takes she all her love to heaven
2. 1896, 1904: upon: And none is left for me.]
4. MS: [After line 4 are the following
    lines, deleted in pencil:]   [I will not look upon her face
                                            Her altered face again;
    [So breaks she all the pledges given,   To see the form, but seek to trace
    The hope of joys to be;   The loveliness in vain.

She less is like herself, poor sweet,
  Than is my memory like:—
So cover her from head to feet
  Until the church bells strike.]
[She less is like herself, my love,
  Than is a stately palm
Or voice and softness of a dove
  Where blossoms drop their balm.]
[No stanza break follows the line.]
1896, 1904: [A stanza break follows
  the line.]
6. MS: is th[e]<is> empty [The
  addition is in pencil in Christina's
  hand.]
  1896, 1904: crust:
7. 1896, 1904: dumb, and blind, it
  <> stir,

10. 1896, 1904: shorn:
12. MS: [Between lines 12 and 13 is a
  horizontal pencil line; and in the
  right margin, the following words
  are added in pencil in William
  Michael Rossetti's hand:] <new
  stanza>
  1896, 1904: born. [A stanza break
  follows the line.]
15. MS: lies, [illegible erasure]
  <indeed,>
  1896, 1904: hollow token-lies
  indeed
16. MS: [Illegible erasure] <No
  need>, if

"I HAVE A MESSAGE UNTO THEE."

[Composed March 26, 1855. Editions: 1896, 1904. The notebook MS is in the
Bodleian Library. Basic text: notebook MS. Lines 63–86 were published as "The
Flowers appear on the Earth" in *Verses* (1893); for text and variants of that poem,
see Volume II of the present edition, pp. 319, 475. In the 1896 text, lines 1–4,
6–10, 12–22, 24–34, 36–38, 40, 42, 44–46, 49, 50, 52–60, 62–64, 66–72, 74–76,
78–84, 86–96, 98–106, and 108–10 are indented four spaces; lines 5, 23, 47, 51,
61, 73, 85, 97, 107, and 111 are indented two spaces; lines 11 and 35 are not inden-
ted; and lines 39, 41, 43, 48, 65, 77, and 112 are indented six spaces. The 1904 in-
dentation is the same as the 1896 except for lines 63–86, which are omitted from
the 1904 version.]

Title. 1896, 1904: I HAVE A
  MESSAGE UNTO THEE
Subtitle. 1896, 1904: (WRITTEN IN
  SICKNESS)
4. 1896, 1904: blows:
5. 1896, 1904: The water-lily, silver
6. 1896, 1904: living fair <> light: [A
  stanza break follows the line.]
7. MS: [Illegible erasure] <Sweet
  jasmine branches> trail
  1896, 1904: Sweet jasmine-branches
  trail
8. MS: dusky star[illegible erasure]
  <ry> veil:
10. 1896, 1904: degree:
11. 1896, 1904: I only
16. 1896, 1904: dews:
17. 1896, 1904: Then water-lilies ever
18. 1896, 1904: river:
22. 1896, 1904: sing:

26. 1896, 1904: pluck:
28. 1896, 1904: For honey-bees to
32. 1896, 1904: down:
45. MS: Oh [illegible erasure]
  <bloom> that
  1896, 1904: O bloom
  1896s: Oh bloom
46. MS: Oh blossom<s> [illegible
  erasure] <quite gone> past,
  1896, 1904: O blossoms
  1896s: Oh blossoms
49. 1896, 1904: Your work-day fully
54. 1896, 1904: chime,—
56. 1896, 1904: heaven;
58. 1896, 1904: Through the <>
  lapse.
61. 1896, 1904: Delights through
  heaven's
64. 1896: wreath:
66. 1896: In garden-plots of

69. 1896: whose hoped-for sweet
71. 1896: Ah what
72. 1896: ease?
74. 1896: meet!
80. 1896: away:
84. 1896: air:
92. 1896, 1904: reap:
94. 1896, 1904: patient harvest-gain.
98. 1896: Shall
    1904: Shall < > vain?
100. 1896, 1904: But
101. 1896, 1904: Better
102. 1896, 1904: Our
103. MS: "Than o[*l*]<n>ly plucked
    1896, 1904: Than

104. 1896, 1904: The
105. 1896, 1904: Not
106. 1896, 1904: Hymns < > a
    holly-bush.
107. MS: ["*Be*] [not indented] < "Be>
    [indented two spaces] wise
    1896, 1904: Be
108. MS: ["*Suck*] [not indented]
    < "Suck> [indented two spaces]
    sweets
    1896, 1904: Suck < > tree,
109. 1896, 1904: To < > flown:
110. 1896, 1904: So
111. 1896, 1904: Your
112. 1896, 1904: But

COBWEBS.

[Composed in October, 1855. Editions: 1896, 1904. The notebook MS is in the Bodleian Library. Basic text: notebook MS. In the MS, deletions and revisions are in pencil in Christina's hand.]

Title. 1896, 1904: COBWEBS
2. 1896, 1904: wind nor
3. 1896, 1904: valleys: but
4. MS: Stretches [*for*] <thro' long
   unbroken> miles
   1896, 1904: Stretches through long
   < > away,
8. MS: the [*silent*] <sluggish> air
   1896, 1904: While through the
6. 1896, 1904: Broodeth: no
7. MS: flow [*is*] <are> there
8. 1896, 1904: bud-time, no
   leaf-falling, there < > aye:—

10. 1896, 1904: space:
11. 1896, 1904: life through all < >
    land
12. MS: [*No future hope*] <And loveless
    sea>; no trace
13. 1896, 1904: toil-won resting-place,
14. MS: [*For ever and for ever evermore*]
    <No future hope no fear for
    evermore>.
    1896, 1904: hope, no

UNFORGOTTEN.

[Composed November 20, 1855. Editions: 1896, 1904. The notebook MS is in the Bodleian Library. Basic text: notebook MS.]

Title. 1896, 1904: UNFORGOTTEN
1. 1896, 1904: O unforgotten!
2. 1896, 1904: saith.
5. 1896, 1904: O unforgotten!
9. 1896, 1904: is:—
10. 1896, 1904: longer? Time is < >
    span,
11. 1896, 1904: The dalliance-space of
    < > man:

12. 1896, 1904: can?
14. 1896, 1904: space:
15. 1896, 1904: *Now* shadows darkening
    < > face;
16. 1896, 1904: *Then* glory
17. 1896, 1904: spirit,
18. 1896, 1904: now, yea broken, for
    < > while—
19. 1896, 1904: by mile,

20. 1896, 1904: the Eternal Smile.
21. 1896, 1904: O joy eternal!
22. 1896, 1904: O youth
23. 1896, 1904: blessed Angels saw,

26. 1896, 1904: yet, O all-surpassing peace:
31. 1896, 1904: the new-sown field
33. 1896, 1904: thee:

AN AFTERTHOUGHT.

[Composed December 18, 1855. Editions: 1896, 1904. The notebook MS is in the Bodleian Library. Basic text: notebook MS. In the 1896 and 1904 texts, lines 2–5, 16, 17, 20–22, 25, 28, 30, 32, 34, 38–41, and 44–47 are indented two spaces; and lines 26, 33, and 35 are indented four spaces.]

Title. 1896, 1904: AN AFTER-THOUGHT
1. 1896, 1904: garden Paradise!—
5. 1896, 1904: intensely star-inlaid?
8. 1896, 1904: eyes?
10. 1896, 1904: choicer garden-nest,
12. MS: child [*has*] <is> laid [The deletion and revision are in pencil in Christina's hand.]
    1896, 1904: in,—
15. 1896, 1904: all,
16. 1904: worth,
18. 1896, 1904: fall?

20. 1896, 1904: supremely broken-hearted
22. 1904: peace!
26. 1896, 1904: For the bitter fall.
28. 1896, 1904: love:
34. 1896, 1904: sword,
35. 1896, 1904: still,
48. MS: [Illegible erasure] <Of days and months> and years
51. 1896, 1904: Of Paradise, that
54. 1896, 1904: away!
56. 1896, 1904: past,

TO THE END.

[Composed December 18, 1855. Editions: 1896, 1904. The notebook MS is in the Bodleian Library. Basic text: notebook MS. In the 1896 and 1904 texts, lines 11, 15, 21, 25, 27, 31, 35, 47, and 65 are indented two spaces; and line 68 is not indented. The 1896s indentation is the same as the 1896 except that line 68 is indented two spaces.]

Title. 1896, 1904: TO THE END
6. 1896, 1904: rest:
7. 1896, 1904: the bright-eyed heartsease
8. 1896, 1904: best:
11. 1896, 1904: O bird that flyest eastward
12. 1896, 1904: land,
13. 1896, 1904: thou light on
18. 1896, 1904: eyes,
21. 1896, 1904: to heaven
23. 1896, 1904: pilgrim through the
29. 1896, 1904: holy fellow-servant sent

32. 1896, 1904: as ours,
44. 1904: good?
45. 1896, 1904: Lulling, lulling
46. 1896, 1904: While Death's strong
47. 1896, 1904: behind his back,
49. 1896, 1904: Till through sleep
56. 1896, 1904: from heaven:
    1896s: from Heaven:
57. 1896, 1904: for heaven sevenfold
    1896s: for Heaven sevenfold
58. 1896, 1904: seven:
61. 1896, 1904: in heaven,
    1896s: in Heaven,
62. 1896, 1904: love;

"ZION SAID."

[Composed December 31, 1855. Editions: 1896, 1904. The notebook MS is in the Bodleian Library. Basic text: notebook MS.]

Title. 1896, 1904: ZION SAID
2. 1896, 1904: distress?
3. 1896, 1904: changed, growing < >
   and less,
4. 1896, 1904: me through all < >
   old?
6. 1896, 1904: fail through weariness:

8. MS: [Illegible erasure] <On> me;
   1896, 1904: me: behold, O Lord, O
   Love, behold!
9. 1896, 1904: indeed—
11. 1896, 1904: Thou who hast < >
    bleed:
12. 1896, 1904: in:

MAY.

[Composed December 31, 1855. Editions: 1896, 1904. The notebook MS is in the Bodleian Library. Basic text: notebook MS. In the MS, deletions and revisions are in pencil in Christina's hand. In the 1896 and 1904 texts, line 2 is a continuation of line 1; lines 1, 4, 5, 7, 12, 17, 19, 20, 22, 23, and 30 are indented two spaces; lines 3, 6, 8, 13–16, 18, 24, 27–29, and 32 are indented four spaces; and lines 25 and 26 are indented six spaces.]

Title. MS: [*A colloquy*] <May>.
   1896, 1904: MAY
1. MS: Sweet [*love*] <Life> is
   1896, 1904: "Sweet < > dead."—
   "Not
5. 1896, 1904: snow,
8. 1896: nay,
   1904: nay.
9. 1896, 1904: see:
11. 1896, 1904: me."
12. MS: But [*love*] <Life> is
    1896, 1904: "But < > me:
13. MS: <The worn-out year was
    failing>
    1896, 1904: failing,
14. MS: <West winds took up a
    wailing>
15. MS: [*I*] <To> watch[*ed*] his
16. MS: [*Cold*] <Bare> poplars [*stood
    up*] <shivered> tall
17. MS: [*While yew trees crouched to see*]/
    And [*fair*] <lank> vines [*bowed the
    knee*] <stretched to see>;
    1896, 1904: see.
19. MS: [*Is built of cold hard*] <Was
    frozen of earth like> stone
    1896, 1904: of earth-like stone
20. 1896, 1904: overgrown:
21. MS: [*The*] <Chill> darkness

wrap[*s*]<ped> him
   1904: pall,
22. 1896, 1904: alone."
23. 1896, 1904: "How
26. MS: every [*mossy*] <mossgrown>
    bank
    1896: bank,
    1904: every moss-grown bank,
29. MS: With [*roses*] <may flowers>
    white
    1896, 1904: With May-flowers
    white
30. MS: my [*silver lily*] <tender
    heartsease> bed;
    1896: tender heartsease-bed:
    1904: tender heartsease-/ bed:
31. MS: my [*bough*] <branch> to
32. MS: [After line 32 is the following
    stanza, deleted in pencil:]

    [*Oh loth to comprehend,
      Deep rooted in a lie
    Your heart is dead, my friend;
      Not love, he cannot die.
    Your eye is dim, your ear
    Is dull and slow to hear:
      Love's fountain runs not dry,
      Love's bloom shall not pass by,
    He nor begins nor hath an*[illegible
         erasure] *end
    But fills eternity.*]

    1896: tread."

RIVER THAMES(?).

[Composed February 7, 1856. Editions: 1896, 1904. The notebook MS (MS1) is in the Bodleian Library. A separate fair copy (MS2), signed "Christina G. Rossetti," is in the Princeton University Library. Basic text: MS2.]

Title. MS1: By the Water.
    1896, 1904: BY THE WATER
2. MS1: Lily laden to
    1896, 1904: sea:
6. MS1: [After line 6 is the following stanza:]

    And if there were a fairy boat
    And if the river bore us
    We should not care for all the past
    Nor all that lies before us,
    Not for the hopes that buoyed us once
    Nor for the fears that tore us.

    1896: [After line 6 is the following stanza:]

    And if there were a fairy boat
    And if the river bore us,
    We should not care for all the past
    Nor all that lies before us,
    Not for the hopes that buoyed us once
    Not for the fears that tore us.

1904: [After line 6 is the following stanza:]

    And if there were a fairy boat
    And if the river bore us,
    We should not care for all the past
    Nor all that lies before us,
    Not for the hopes that buoyed us once,
    Not for the fears that tore us.

7. 1896, 1904: river
8. MS1, 1896, 1904: by,
9. MS1: lilies
    1896, 1904: Rocking, rocking
10. MS1, 1896, 1904: and I:
13. MS1: But, ah,
    1896, 1904: ah where
15. MS1, 1896, 1904: lilies
18. MS1: And, ah,
    1896, 1904: ah where < > friend?

A CHILLY NIGHT.

[Composed February 11, 1856. Editions: 1896, 1904. The notebook MS is in the Bodleian Library.]

Title. 1896, 1904: A CHILLY NIGHT
1. 1896, 1904: night,
6. 1896, 1904: Middle-aged, young,
11. 1896, 1904: moonlight,
12. 1896, 1904: ground:
14. 1896, 1904: they leaped without
18. 1904: wind.
20. 1896, 1904: day:
24. 1896, 1904: see:
27. 1904: spoke;
28. 1896, 1904: word,
37. 1896, 1904: words,
38. 1896, 1904: hear;
49. MS: and [*f*]<d>ead had
    1896, 1904: dead had failed,

"LET PATIENCE HAVE HER PERFECT WORK."

[Composed March 12, 1856. Editions: 1896, 1904. The notebook MS is in the Bodleian Library. Basic text: notebook MS. In the 1896 text, lines 1–3, 5–7, 11–13, 15, 16, 19, 20, 22–24, 26–29, and 31–34 are indented two spaces; lines 4, 14, and 21 are indented four spaces; and lines 8, 10, 18, 25, and 30 are indented six spaces. The 1904 indentation is the same as the 1896 except that line 35 is indented two spaces and line 37 is indented four spaces.]

Title. 1896, 1904: LET PATIENCE
    HAVE HER PERFECT WORK
4. 1896, 1904: Though it < > early
    Spring.

5. 1896, 1904: buds half-blown,
6. 1896, 1904: sown:
9. 1896, 1904: alone:
15. 1896, 1904: no moon-glories are,
17. 1896, 1904: Beams through night
20. 1896, 1904: alone,
23. 1896, 1904: mate,
28. 1896s: bright,
30. MS: [Below the line is a horizontal pencil line and the following words

added in pencil in William Michael Rossetti's hand:] <new stanza>
1896, 1904: [A stanza break follows the line.]
31. 1896, 1904: Ah better
33. 1896, 1904: unknown:
34. 1896, 1904: Till, time <> gone,
36. MS: [A]<W>hile patience
37. 1896, 1904: the harvest-land of

A MARTYR.

[Composed April 23, 1856. Editions: 1896, 1904. The notebook MS is in the Bodleian Library. Basic text: notebook MS.]

Title. 1896, 1904: A MARTYR
2. 1896, 1904: doubt:
3. 1896, 1904: asleep though her
4. 1896, 1904: shout:
5. 1896, 1904: again,
9. 1896, 1904: lost:
10. 1896, 1904: drouth:

11. 1896: safe resting-place
1904: safe resting-/ place
12. 1896, 1904: toward the South.
14. 1896, 1904: round:
15. 1896, 1904: nest,
21. 1896, 1904: rough, but
23. 1896, 1904: my God,—

IN THE LANE.

[Composed May 3, 1856. Editions: 1896, 1904. The notebook MS is in the Bodleian Library. Basic text: notebook MS.]

Title. 1896, 1904: IN THE LANE
1. 1896, 1904: me,
2. 1896, 1904: Pleasant summer bringing,
3. 1896, 1904: leaf,
4. 1896: singing. [A stanza break follows the line.]
1904: singing. [Line 4 is the last line on the page.]

5. 1896, 1904: [The line is omitted from the text.]
6. 1896, 1904: [The line is omitted from the text.]
9. 1896, 1904: day,
10. 1896, 1904: dreamy.
13. 1896, 1904: hedge,
14. 1896, 1904: river,
17. 1896, 1904: home,

ACME.

[Composed May 9, 1856. Editions: 1896, 1904. The notebook MS is in the Bodleian Library. Basic text: notebook MS.]

Title. 1896, 1904: ACME
1. 1896, 1904: awhile:
2. 1896, 1904: as though I <> forget;
3. 1896, 1904: fret,
1896s: [The last word of the line is omitted.]

4. 1896, 1904: smile,
5. MS: in <the> sunlight
7. 1896, 1904: path: O sorrow, slumber,
9. 1896, 1904: strength,
12. 1896, 1904: edge.
13. 1896, 1904: last: beneath

A BED OF FORGET-ME-NOTS.

[Composed June 17, 1856. Editions: 1896, 1904. The notebook MS is in the British Library. Basic text: notebook MS.]

Title. 1896, 1904: A BED OF
FORGET-ME-NOTS
1. 1896, 1904: Is Love so
2. 1896, 1904: rear Forget-me-not
3. 1896, 1904: a garden-plot?—
11. 1896, 1904: rule:

12. MS: [Illegible erasure] <Hath curb or call an answer got?—>
13. 1896, 1904: be Forget-me-not.
16. 1896: a fixed star,
21. 1896, 1904: is Forget-me-not and Love.

THE CHIEFEST AMONG TEN THOUSAND.

[Composed June 26, 1856. The notebook MS is in the British Library. Basic text: notebook MS. Lines 1–8, 33–40, and the deleted eighth stanza of the MS text were published in *Verses* (1893) as "'I will lift up mine eyes unto the Hills'"; for text and variants of that poem, see Volume II of the present edition, pp. 271, 437. The first, second, third, sixth, and seventh deleted stanzas of the MS text (that is, those stanzas deleted with a diagonal pencil line) were published as "I know you not" in Orby Shipley (ed.), *Lyra Messianica: Hymns and Verses on the Life of Christ, Ancient and Modern; with Other Poems* (1864); "I know you not" is presented in Section 2 of the present volume.]

Title. MS: [Below the title is added in pencil in Dante Gabriel Rossetti's hand:] <might be shortened>
8. MS: [After line 8 are the following stanzas, deleted with a diagonal pencil line:]

[*Thyself the Vine with living Fruit,*
The twelvefold fruited Tree of Life,
The Balm in Gilead after strife,
The valley Lily and the Rose:
Stronger than Lebanon, [*t*]<*T*>*hou Root,*
Sweeter than clustered grapes, Thou Vine;
Oh Best, Thou Vineyard of new Wine
Keeping Thy best Wine till the close.]

[*Pearl of great price Thyself alone*
And ruddier than the ruby Thou,
Most precious lightening Jasper Stone,
Head of the corner spurned before;
Fair Gate of pearl, Thyself the Door,
Clear golden Street, Thyself the Way,
By Thee we journey toward Thee now
Thro' Thee shall reach Thee in that day.]

24. MS: [After line 24 are the following stanzas—the first, fourth, and fifth deleted with a horizontal pencil line; the second, third, sixth, and seventh deleted with a vertical pencil line:]

[*I thirst for Thee, full Fount and Flood,*
My heart calls Thine as deep to deep:
Dost Thou forget Thy sweat and pain,
Thy provocation on the Cross?
Heart pierced for me, vouchsafe to keep
The purchase of Thy lavished Blood;
The gain is Thine Lord if I gain,
Or if I lose Thine Own the loss.]

[*The sparrow findeth her a house,*
The swallow for her young a nest,
But Thou art far away my Rest,
Thyself my Rest and Thou alone:
No home on earth sufficeth me,
Not Thine Own house most fair to see,
Tho' rich with gold and costly stone,
Painted and ceiled with cedar boughs.]

[*There is a time for all things, saith*
The Word of Truth, Thyself the Word;
And many things [*t*]<*T*>*hou reasonest of:*
A time for hope so long deferred,
But this is time for [illegible
         deletion]<*g*>*rief and*
         [*t*]<*f*>*ears;*
A time for life, but this is death;
Oh when shall be the time of love
When Thou Thyself shalt wipe our tears?]

[*At midnight, saith the parable,*
A cry was made, the Bridegroom came:
Those who were ready entered in;
The rest shut out in death and shame

Strove all too late that feast to win
Their die was cast and fixed their lot,
A gulph divided heaven from hell,
The Bridegroom said, 'I know you not.']

[*But Who is This That shuts the door*
And saith 'I know you not' to them?
I see the wounded Hands and Side,
The Brow thorn-tortured long [*before:*]
<*ago:*> [The deletion and
revision are in pencil in
Christina's hand.]
Yes, This Who grieved and bled and died,
This Same is He Who must condemn;
He called, but they refused to know,
So now He hears their cry no more.]

[*When shall Thy coming be, my Lord?*
At midnight? at the cockcrow? when?
Thou Whom the people once abhorred
Art of all nations the Desire:
Thou art as a Refiner's Fire,
As Fuller's Sope to purge and bless;
For Thou shalt judge the sons of men,
Shalt judge the world in righteousness.]

[*But when Thou comest, King of kings,*
Who shall abide Thy triumph day?
Shalt Thou find faith upon the earth,
Loins girt, lamps burning for Thy Sake?
Then will be dreams of frantic mirth
Tho' now it is high time to wake
Or ever earth and earthly things
With a great noise shall pass away.]

32. MS: [After line 32 is the following
stanza, deleted with a vertical
pencil line:]

[*Cast in my lot with theirs, cast in*
The lot of those I love with theirs,
Make those I love not fellow he[*a*]<*i*>*rs*
Heirs of Thy throne Thy love and life:
Teach us to love both foes and friends
With love like Thine which never ends,
For loving and made pure from sin
Must be the Lamb's blood-purchased wife.]

"LOOK ON THIS PICTURE AND ON THIS."

[Composed July 12, 1856. Editions: 1896, 1904. The notebook MS is in the British
Library. Basic text: notebook MS. In the 1896 edition, William Michael Rossetti
states, "In my sister's MS. this poem is a rather long one, forth-six [*sic*] triplets; I
have reduced it to twenty-three—omitting those passages which appear to me to be
either in themselves inferior, or adapted rather for spinning out the theme than
intensifying it" (p. 382). In the 1896 and 1904 texts, lines 1, 3, 4, 16, 28, 30, 49, 50,
56, 57, 85, 104, 105, 107, 108, and 114 are indented two spaces.]

Title. MS: [Below the title is an illegible
erasure.]
1896, 1904: LOOK ON THIS
PICTURE AND ON THIS
1. 1896, 1904: true:
3. MS: But [*now I hate myself*] <I hate
myself now> Eva [The inversion is
indicated in pencil.]
1896, 1904: But I hate myself now,
Eva, when
6. 1896, 1904: You, my saint, lead
<> heaven, she
7–15. MS: [The lines are deleted with
pencil.]
1896, 1904: [The lines are not in
the text.]
16. 1896, 1904: stately:—in
18. 1896, 1904: devils, but
21. 1896, 1904: music, all

22–27. MS: [The lines are deleted with
pencil.]
1896, 1904: [The lines are not in
the text.]
28. MS: ask, <">why
1896, 1904: But you ask, "Why
struggle?
30. MS: sup.<">—
1896, 1904: temptation, for <>
sup."
32. 1896, 1904: passion, silent
33. 1896, 1904: dove, my
34–42. MS: [The lines are deleted with
pencil.]
1896, 1904: [The lines are not in
the text.]
44. 1896, 1904: burdensome:
45. 1896, 1904: a winding-sheet,
pulseless, at peace, and

46–48. MS: [The lines are deleted with pencil.]
1896, 1904: [The lines are not in the text.]
49. 1896, 1904: heart, barred <> door:
50. 1896, 1904: before:
52. 1896, 1904: lies:
55. 1896, 1904: regret:
56. 1896, 1904: the marriage-guests are
57. MS: with [illegible erasure] <joy eternal as we had> never
59. MS: together [illegible erasure] <stretched> here
1896, 1904: feet:
60. 1896: one winding-/ sheet.
1904: one winding-sheet.
61–69. MS: [The lines are deleted with pencil.]
1896, 1904: [The lines are not in the text.]
66. MS: man you lov[']<e>d, you
71. 1896, 1904: silent? Weep before <> despair:—
72. 1896, 1904: patience, wings
73–84. MS: [The lines are deleted with pencil.]
1896, 1904: [The lines are not in the text.]
85. 1896, 1904: saint:
86. 1896, 1904: bent:
88–96. MS: [The lines are deleted with pencil.]
1896, 1904: [The lines are not in the text.]
97. 1896, 1904: you? Never from <> this:
98. 1896, 1904: bliss:
100–102. MS: [The lines are deleted with pencil.]

1896, 1904: [The lines are not in the text.]
103. 1896, 1904: last!
104. 1896, 1904: past—
106. 1896, 1904: then: I loved, the <> charms:
107. 1896, 1904: first time, last time, lie <> heart, my
108. 1896, 1904: time, as
109–11. MS: [The lines are deleted with pencil.]
1896, 1904: [The lines are not in the text.]
112. 1896, 1904: yet:
113. 1896, 1904: Listen, love, I
114. 1896, 1904: face, in
115. 1896, 1904: grieve:
116. 1896, 1904: home through death <> life: but
117. 1896, 1904: heaven's love, O love, can
118. 1896, 1904: with heart-truth above
1896s: Fully, freely, fondly, with heart-truth above
120. 1896, 1904: heads, forgiving
121. 1896, 1904: not one!—One look more—too late, too late!
122. 1896, 1904: hate:
123. 1896, 1904: of Love the
124. 1896, 1904: rest: day
125. 1896, 1904: ray:
127. 1896, 1904: dumb—
129. 1896, 1904: speak; what <> say?—what
130. 1896, 1904: left, and
131. 1896, 1904: white—
133–35. MS: [The lines are deleted with pencil.]
1896, 1904: [The lines are not in the text.]

"NOW THEY DESIRE."

[Composed August 13, 1856. Editions: 1896, 1904. The notebook MS is in the British Library. Basic text: notebook MS.]

Title. 1896, 1904: NOW THEY DESIRE
1. 1896, 1904: slept,
2. 1896, 1904: unknown:

3. MS: There [illegible erasure] <hearts> are
4. 1896, 1904: Alone or
6. 1896, 1904: truth:

7. 1896, 1904: seem,
10. 1896, 1904: never tempest-tost:
17. 1896, 1904: a Love which fills
18. 1896, 1904: requite:
19. 1896, 1904: fire it draws
21. 1896, 1904: For it we <> strife,
22. 1896, 1904: yearn, we
23. 1896, 1904: Lo in the far-off land
24. 1896, 1904: Doth it not <> us?
25. 1896, 1904: O fair, O fair
    Jerusalem,
26. 1896, 1904: fair, how
27. 1896, 1904: thy Jasper-gem
31. MS: royal [*e*]<E>lders on

32. 1896, 1904: manifold?
33. 1896: Fair City of
    1904: Fair City of <> the Bride
35. 1896, 1904: thee loving-eyed,
36. 1896, 1904: Sun-girdled, happy
38. 1896, 1904: Blood-cleansed,
    blood-purchased once:
39. MS: fair g[*l*]<r>ound is
40. 1896, 1904: sons!
42. 1896, 1904: thine:
44. 1896, 1904: the very Vine:
46. 1896, 1904: praise,
47. 1896, 1904: O fair, O fair
    Jerusalem,

A CHRISTMAS CAROL, FOR MY GODCHILDREN.

[Composed October 6, 1856. Editions: 1896, 1904. The notebook MS is in the British Library. Basic text: notebook MS. In the 1896 and 1904 texts, lines 1, 5, 7, 9, 23, 29, 31, 35, 37, and 51 are indented two spaces; and the lines with even numbers are indented four spaces.]

Title. 1896: A CHRISTMAS CAROL/
    For my Godchildren
    1904: A CHRISTMAS CAROL/
    For my Godchildren.
1. 1896, 1904: The Shepherds <> an
    Angel,
2. 1896, 1904: The Wise Men had
9. 1896, 1904: in His bosom
10. 1896, 1904: track:
13. MS: my [*g*]<G>uiding Star,
    1896, 1904: my guiding star,
14. 1896, 1904: My beacon-light in
16. 1896, 1904: uneven:
17. MS: me <to> that
    1896, 1904: He, true light, leads
19. 1896, 1904: Those Shepherds
    through the
22. 1896, 1904: sleep,
23. 1896: singing "Glory glory"
25. 1896, 1904: me, His

27. 1896, 1904: be His own in
29. 1896: their "Glory glory"
    1904: their 'Glory glory'
31. 1896, 1904: The Wise Men left
32. 1896, 1904: by morn,
33. 1896, 1904: myrrh,
38. 1896: like God's book,
    1904: like God's book;
39. 1896, 1904: good Wise Men
42. 1896, 1904: took!
43. 1896, 1904: Lord, I
47. 1896, 1904: Lord, make
48. 1896, 1904: holier;
50. 1896, 1904: unite,
51. 1896: my "Glory glory"
    1904: my 'Glory glory'
52. 1896, 1904: white;
53. 1896: All "Glory glory" given
    1904: All 'Glory glory' given
54. 1896, 1904: Through all

"NOT YOURS BUT YOU."

[Composed October 27, 1856. Editions: 1896, 1904. The notebook MS is in the British Library. Basic text: notebook MS. In the 1896 and 1904 texts, lines 11 and 14 are indented four spaces.]

Title. 1896, 1904: NOT YOURS BUT
    YOU

1. 1896, 1904: "He
2. 1896, 1904: prayer:

3. MS: court [*have*] <wear> crowns
   [The deletion and revision are in
   pencil in Christina's hand.]
   1896, 1904: hair:
4. 1896, 1904: subtle Cherubim;
5. 1896, 1904: intense Seraphim
6. 1896, 1904: lightnings through the
   air.
7. 1896, 1904: bare,
8. 1896, 1904: dim."—
9. 1896, 1904: "Give <> youth."—"I
   <> rod,

10. 1896, 1904: me."—
11. 1896: "Give <> life."—"I <> by
    breath,
    1904: 'Give <> life.'—'I <> by
    breath;
12. 1896, 1904: so give I Thee."—
13. 1896, 1904: "Give <> love."—"So
14. MS: me [illegible deletion] <ev>en
    to
    1896, 1904: death."

AN ANSWER.

[Composed November 26, 1856. The notebook MS is in the British Library. Basic text: notebook MS. The first page of the MS is missing from the notebook.]

SIR WINTER.

[Composed November 28, 1856. Editions: 1896, 1904. The notebook MS is in the British Library. Basic text: notebook MS. In the 1896 edition, William Michael Rossetti states, "Mr. Swynfen Jervis, a friendly acquaintance of our father, wrote a quatrain and a half entitled *Sir Winter;* and he appears to have got Christina to complete the little poem. Christina finished quatrain two, and wrote five others. The third of these five reverts to the idea of '*Sir* Winter'; so I omit it, as being extraneous to the character of her own composition: it has no poetical value" (p. 382).]

Title. 1896, 1904: WINTER
1–8. 1896, 1904: [The lines are not
   in the text.]
9. MS: with ch[*f*]<a>ffinch and
   [Above the line is added in pencil
   in William Michael Rossetti's hand:]
   <Begin here/ Winter./ 1>
11. 1896, 1904: force,
12. 1896, 1904: the spice-teeming
    southlands
    1896s: the spice-teaming southlands
13. MS: [Above the line is added in
    pencil:] <2>

14. 1896, 1904: eat:
15. 1896, 1904: hedge,
17–20. MS: [The lines are deleted with
    pencil.]
    1896, 1904: [The lines are not in
    the text.]
21. MS: [Above the line is added in
    pencil:] <3>
25. MS: [Above the line is added in
    pencil:] <4>
    1896, 1904: But, since

IN AN ARTIST'S STUDIO.

[Composed December 24, 1856. Editions: 1896, 1904. The notebook MS is in the British Library. Basic text: notebook MS.]

Title. 1896, 1904: IN AN ARTIST'S
   STUDIO
1. 1896, 1904: his canvases,
2. 1896, 1904: leans:

464   The Complete Poems of Christina Rossetti

5. MS: ruby [g]<d>ress,
6. 1896, 1904: freshest
   summer-greens,
7. 1896, 1904: angel—every canvas
   means
10. 1896, 1904: him,

12. MS: Not [worn] <wan> with [The
    deletion and revision are in pencil
    in Christina's hand.]
14. MS: but as [illegible erasure]
    <sh>e fills

INTROSPECTIVE.

[Composed June 30, 1857. Editions: 1896, 1904. The notebook MS is in the British Library. Basic text: notebook MS.]

Title. 1896, 1904: INTROSPECTIVE
2. 1896, 1904: and again:
6. 1896, 1904: bent:
12. 1896: long to-come.
    1904: long to-/ come.
14. 1896, 1904: tell;

15. MS: soul I [illegible erasure] <talk
    with> thee
    1896, 1904: soul, I < > thee,
16. MS: the [illegible erasure] <sight>
18. 1896, 1904: wrung:
19. 1896, 1904: must,

"THE HEART KNOWETH ITS OWN BITTERNESS."

[Composed August 27, 1857. Editions: 1896, 1904. The notebook MS is in the British Library. Basic text: notebook MS. Lines 1–8, 49–56 were published in *Verses* (1893) as "'Whatsoever is right, that shall ye receive'"; for text and variants of that poem, see Volume II of the present edition, pp. 267, 435.]

Title. 1896, 1904: THE HEART
    KNOWETH ITS OWN
    BITTERNESS
8. 1896, 1904: enough?
9. 1896: say "enough" on earth—
   1904: earth—
10. 1896: "Enough" with < > heart?
    1904: heart?
11. 1896, 1904: birth,
14. 1896, 1904: new:
23. 1896, 1904: sum—
25. 1896, 1904: receive!
27. 1896, 1904: leave,
28. 1896, 1904: whole.

33. 1896, 1904: pin,
34. 1896, 1904: breath:—
38. 1896, 1904: do:
41. 1896, 1904: strait:
42. 1896, 1904: pour, you < > hold.—
43. 1896, 1904: wait,
44. 1896, 1904: sealed through heat
45. 1896, 1904: years:
50. 1896, 1904: stuff:—
51. 1896, 1904: seen, nor < > heard
52. 1896: full "enough":
53. MS: the s[p]<e>parating sea,
54. 1896, 1904: heart:

"REFLECTION".

[Composed September 8, 1857. Editions: 1896, 1904. The notebook MS (MS1) is in the British Library. A fair copy MS (MS2), signed "Christina G. Rossetti," is in the Princeton University Library. Basic text: MS2. In MS2, lines 5 and 35 are not indented. In the 1896 and 1904 texts, the last line of each stanza is not indented.]

Title. MS1: Day Dreams.
1896, 1904: DAY-DREAMS
1. 1896, 1904: Gazing through her
2. MS1: my [*cold*] <soul's> dear
1896, 1904: soul:
5. 1896, 1904: control.
10. 1896, 1904: feet?
11. MS1, 1896, 1904: answers,
12. 1896, 1904: Gazing, gazing
14. MS1: [Illegible erasure]
<Ceda>red sunlit hill;
19. MS1: a [*pained*] <mere> surprize,
1896, 1904: mere surprise,
20. MS1: slow [*golden mists arise?*]
<mists do rise & rise> [The
deletion and revision are in pencil
in Christina's hand.]
1896, 1904: and rise?
21. MS1: for:
1896, 1904: for,
22. MS1: peace:
1896, 1904: peace,
24. MS1: ease:
1896, 1904: ease,
26. MS1: [*Answer me, O self-forgetful*—]
<So she sits and [*never*]
<doth not> answer[*s*]> [The
words "doth not" are added in
pencil in Christina's hand.]
27. MS1: [*Or of what beside?*—] <With
her dreaming eyes>
28. MS1: [*Is it day-dream of a maiden,*]
<With her languid look delicious>

29. MS1: [*Vision of a bride,*] <Almost
Paradise,>
1896, 1904: Almost paradise,
30. MS1: [*Is it knowledge, love, or pride?*]
<Less than happy, over-wise.>
1896, 1904: happy, over-wise.
32. 1904: beside?
33. MS1, 1896, 1904: it day-dream of
35. MS1: [*I*] [not indented] <Is>
[indented two spaces] it
36. 1896, 1904: sits through all
39. MS1: day;
41. 1896, 1904: secret,
45. MS1: for no or yes?—
1896, 1904: for no or yes?
46. MS1: burial
47. MS1: dead;
1896, 1904: Though, when
49. MS1: her [*golden*] <royal> head,
[The deletion and revision are in
pencil in Christina's hand.]
51. MS2: [*I will give her stately burial,*]
<I will give her stately burial,>
52. MS1: Stately [*monument;*] <willow
branches bent;> [The deletion and
revision are in pencil in Christina's
hand.]
MS2: [*Stately monument*] <Willow
branches bent;>
1896, 1904: Stately willow-branches
bent:

A COAST-NIGHTMARE.

[Composed September 12, 1857. Editions: 1896, 1904. The notebook MS (MS1) is
in the British Library. A fair copy MS (MS2), signed "Christina G. Rossetti," is in the
Princeton University Library. In MS1, lines 5–36 are missing from the notebook.
The 1896 and 1904 texts contain only lines 1–4, 37–40. In the 1896 and 1904 texts,
lines 1, 4, and 40 are indented four spaces; and line 2 is not indented.]

Title. MS1: A Nightmare.
<—Fragment> [The addition is in
pencil in William Michael Rossetti's
hand.]
1896, 1904: A NIGHTMARE/
FRAGMENT
1. MS1: a [*love*] <friend> in [The
deletion and revision are in pencil
in Christina's hand.]

2. MS1: lost—
1896, 1904: me how
3. MS1: Blood-red sea-weeds drip
< > that coast-land
4. MS1: and tost.
1896, 1904: and tost. [Below the
line is a horizontal row of spaced
periods.]
35. MS2: sleep, [*he like a trump*] <his

trumpet voice> compel[s] me [The
deletions and revision are in red
pencil in Christina's hand and
retraced in red ink.]

37. MS1: wake he [rides] <hunts> me
[The deletion and revision are in
pencil in Christina's hand.]
1896, 1904: wake he <> nightmare:
38. MS1: up my

'FOR ONE SAKE.'

[Composed October 25, 1857. Editions: 1896, 1904. The notebook MS is in the British Library. Basic text: notebook MS.]

Title. MS: <'>For one Sake.<'> [The
addition is in pencil.]
1896, 1904: FOR ONE SAKE
1. 1896, 1904: by,
2. 1896, 1904: stars.

4. 1896, 1904: why:
9. 1896, 1904: alone to-night, and
10. 1896, 1904: eventide:
11. 1904: before.
12. 1896, 1904: weep:

MY OLD FRIENDS.

[Composed July 16, 1858. Editions: 1896, 1904. The notebook MS (MS1) is in the British Library. A fair copy MS (MS2), signed "Christina G. Rossetti," is in the Princeton University Library. Basic text: MS2. Lines 1–3, 13–15, 17–19, 75–77 were published as an untitled poem in Verses (1893); for text and variants of that poem, see Volume II of the present edition, pp. 306, 462. Lines 41–46 were published as "'Then whose shall those things be?'" in Verses (1893); for text and variants of that poem, see Volume II of the present edition, pp. 272, 438.]

Title. MS1: A Burthen.
1896, 1904: A BURDEN
2. MS1, 1896, 1904: dew is cool
6. 1896, 1904: yet:
11. MS2: wintry [M]<m>ay—
1896, 1904: wintry May—
12. MS1: [After line 12 is the following
stanza:]

They lie asleep with us, and take
Sweet rest altho' our heart should ache,
Rest on altho' our heart should break—
                                    Miserere.

1896, 1904: [After line 12 is the
following stanza:]

They lie asleep with us, and take
Sweet rest although our heart should
ache,
Rest on although our heart should
break—
                                    Miserere.

21. 1896, 1904: them, and
24. 1896, 1904: Sursum Corda.
26. 1896, 1904: see,

29. MS1, 1896, 1904: we think them
31. MS1, 1896, 1904: shall be glorious
as a star?—
33. MS1: Where chill or
1896, 1904: Where chill or <>
rise,
34. MS1, 1896, 1904: in the depth of
Paradise
36. MS1: [After line 36 is the following
stanza:]

Safe as a hidden brooding dove,
With perfect peace within, above,
They love and look for perfect love—
                                    Hallelujah.

1896, 1904: [After line 36 is the
following stanza:]

Safe as a hidden brooding dove,
With perfect peace within, above,
They love, and look for perfect love—
                                    Hallelujah.

38. MS1: rest;
42. MS1, 1896, 1904: Our houses

45. MS1, 1896, 1904: grasping more
    and seeking more
46. MS1: at the door?—
    1896, 1904: While Death stands
    <> at the door?—
49. MS1: And sick at
    1896, 1904: And sick at <> thirst,
    I
53. MS1, 1896, 1904: Sweet love, the
    one sufficiency
54. MS1, 1896, 1904: For all the
    longings that
56. MS1, 1896, 1904: happy they alone
57. 1896, 1904: love! I <> to spot:
60. MS1: life; nay,
    1896, 1904: nay verily.
61. 1896, 1904: me,
65. MS1, 1896, 1904: Are heaped and
    <> to him who
66. 1896: year's harvest-sheaves?—
    1904: year's harvest-/ sheaves?—

68. 1896, 1904: life, yet
    1896s: life yet
69. MS1: Hush throbbing heart and
    sobbing breath:
    MS2: Hush painful heart and
    labouring breath: <I sought life as
    but a breath> [The addition is in
    pencil in Christina's hand.]
    1896, 1904: Hush, throbbing heart
    and sobbing breath!
71. 1896, 1904: before:
74. MS1: *Hallelujah*
75. MS1, 1896, 1904: Our friends, our
    kinsfolk, great and small,
76. MS1: Our loved, our best beloved
    of all:
    1896, 1904: Our loved, our best
    beloved of all,
77. MS2: They w[illegible
    deletion]<a>tch across

"YET A LITTLE WHILE".

[Composed August 6, 1858. Editions:1896, 1904. The notebook MS is in the British Library. Basic text: notebook MS. Lines 13–24 were published as "'Vanity of Vanities'" in *Verses* (1893); for text and variants of that poem, see Volume II of the present edition, pp. 315, 472. Lines 37–48 were published as an untitled poem in *Verses* (1893); for text and variants of that poem, see Volume II of the present edition, pp. 265, 433.]

Title. 1896, 1904: YET A LITTLE
    WHILE
2. MS: [*T*] [out to left margin] <To>
    [indented two spaces] sit
4. 1896, 1904: continually:
5. 1896, 1904: to ecstasy
8. 1896, 1904: moon,
9. 1896, 1904: cordial June:
11. 1896, 1904: and aches,
12. 1896, 1904: wane, most
14. MS: an [*a*]<A>utumn leaf
17. 1896, 1904: when Spring-twigs
    gleamed

23. 1896, 1904: sings:
26. 1896, 1904: life:
30. 1896, 1904: full—death's
34. 1896, 1904: blast:
35. 1896, 1904: that, past
36. 1896, 1904: ache, did
37. 1896, 1904: *We* have
37–48. MS: [The lines are deleted in
    pencil. In the right margin is
    added in pencil:] <stet>
43. 1896, 1904: *You* have
46. 1896, 1904: long: while
47. 1896, 1904: climbs,

"ONLY BELIEVE."

[Composed probably between August 6, 1858, and October 15, 1858. Editions: 1896, 1904. The notebook MS is in the British Library. Basic text: notebook MS. The last page of the MS is missing from the notebook. Lines 35–62 were published as "'What good shall my life do me?'" in *Verses* (1893); for text and variants of that poem, see Volume II of the present edition, pp. 294, 454. The 1896 and 1904 texts contain only lines 1–34. In the 1896 and 1904 texts, lines 1, 2, 4, 8, 10, 12, 15–19, 23, 29–31, and 33 are indented four spaces; lines 5–7, 9, 11, 13, 14, 20–22, 24, 26, 27, and 32 are indented two spaces; and line 28 is indented six spaces. In the MS, the added quotation marks are in pencil.]

Title. 1896, 1904: ONLY BELIEVE
4. 1896, 1904: sleeping.
5. MS: <">Is
   1896, 1904: "Is
7. MS: death?<">
   1896, 1904: death?"
8. MS: <">White
   1896, 1904: "White <> dove,
11. MS: twilights.<">
    1896, 1904: twilights."
12. MS: <">Is
    1896, 1904: "Is
13. MS: tresses?<">
    1896, 1904: tresses?"
14. MS: <">There
    1896, 1904: "There
16. MS: rare.<">
    1896, 1904: rare."
17. MS: <">Are
    1896, 1904: "Are
18. MS: these?<">
    1896, 1904: these?"
20. MS: <">To
    1896, 1904: "To
20. 1896s: trees

1904: [A stanza break follows the line.]
21. 1896, 1904: wildernesses,
24. MS: and bough.<">
    1896, 1904: and bough."
25. MS: <">Who <> nest?<">
    1896, 1904: "Who <> nest?"
26. MS: <">Heart with
    1896, 1904: "Heart with
31. 1896, 1904: ease,—
32. 1896, 1904: west,
33. 1896, 1904: south,
34. MS: drouth.<">
    1896, 1904: drouth."
35. MS: <">How <> wait?<">
36. MS: <">There
39. MS: Dust to dust, clod to
    [*g*]<c>lod
42. MS: years.<">
43. MS: <">Their
51. MS: grave?<">
52. MS: <">Lies
60. MS: down.<">
61–62. MS: [The lines are deleted in pencil.]

"RIVALS."/ A SHADOW OF SAINT DOROTHEA.

[Composed November 11, 1858. Editions: 1896, 1904. The notebook MS (MS1) is in the British Library. A fair copy MS (MS2), signed "Christina G. Rossetti," is in the Princeton University Library. Basic text: MS2. Lines 1–19 were published as part of a poem entitled "'As cold waters to a thirsty soul, so is good news from a far country'" in *Verses* (1893); for text and variants of that poem, see Volume II of the present edition, pp. 284, 448. In the 1896 text, lines 1, 9, 18, 22, 26, 28, and 29 are indented two spaces; lines 6, 34, and 37 are not indented; lines 10, 11, 16, 17, 19–21, 24, 30, 35, and 36 are indented four spaces; and lines 13, 14, 23, and 31 are indented six spaces. In the 1904 text, lines 1, 9, 16, 20, 24, and 30 are indented two spaces; lines 6, 25, 27, 34, and 37 are not indented; lines 10, 11, 23, 31, 35, and 36 are indented four spaces; and lines 13 and 14 are indented six spaces. In MS1, the added quotation marks are in pencil. MS1 and the 1896 and 1904 texts contain opening quotation marks only at the beginning of each stanza.]

Title. MS1: A shadow of Dorothea.
   1896, 1904: A SHADOW OF
   DOROTHEA

Subtitle. MS1, 1896, 1904: [There is no subtitle in the text.]
1. MS1: <">Golden-haired,

lily-white,
1896, 1904: "Golden-haired,
lily-white,
2. 1896, 1904: lilies?
5. MS1: is your<r> hair
8. MS1: desire?—<">
　　1896, 1904: desire?"
9. MS1: <">I
10. 1896, 1904: red:
15. MS1: pluck palm-branches in <>
　　land.<">　　　　　　　\
　　1896, 1904: pluck palm-branches
　　in <> land."
16. MS1: <">Is
　　1896, 1904: to heaven
17. 1896, 1904: tread?
22. 1896, 1904: wise,
23. MS1: dead?—<">
　　1896, 1904: dead?"

24. MS1: <">There
　　1896, 1904: a heavenward stair—
28. MS1, 1896, 1904: root
29. MS1: [Illegible erasure] <With
　　healing le>aves and <> fruit
　　1896, 1904: fruit
30. MS2: In [*M*]<m>usical Heaven
　　1896, 1904: musical heaven-air:
31. MS1: there.—<">
　　1896, 1904: there."
32. MS1: <">I
34. MS1: you.<">—
　　1896, 1904: you."
35. MS1: <">Nay, choose
　　1896, 1904: "Nay, choose
36. MS1: or lo[illegible erasure]<th:>
　　1896, 1904: or loth:
37. MS1: too.—<">
　　1896, 1904: too."

A YAWN.

[Composed November 11, 1858. The notebook MS is in the British Library. Basic text: notebook MS. Lines 11–25 were published as "By the Sea" in *Goblin Market, The Prince's Progress, and Other Poems* (1875); for text and variants of that poem, see Volume I of the present edition, pp. 191, 297.]

8. MS: safe [*a*]<A>rk,

FOR H. P.

[Composed January 16, 1859. Editions: 1896, 1904. The notebook MS is in the British Library. Basic text: notebook MS.]

Title. 1896, 1904: FOR HENRIETTA
　　POLYDORE
1. 1896, 1904: sea

7. 1896, 1904: To-day in toil, to-night
　　in
8. 1896, 1904: Be best beloved and

"THEN THEY THAT FEARED THE LORD
SPAKE OFTEN ONE TO ANOTHER."

[Composed August 26, 1859. The notebook MS is owned by Mrs. Geoffrey Dennis. Basic text: notebook MS. Lines 1–8 were published as part of a poem entitled "'Thy Friend and thy Father's Friend forget not'" in *Verses* (1893); for text and variants of that poem, see Volume II of the present edition, pp. 202, 408.]

"WHAT GOOD SHALL MY LIFE DO ME?"

[Composed August 27, 1859. Editions: 1896, 1904. The notebook MS is owned by Mrs. Geoffrey Dennis. Basic text: notebook MS.]

Title. 1896, 1904: WHAT GOOD
    SHALL MY LIFE DO ME?
1. 1896, 1904: life: yet
2. 1896, 1904: scope.
4. 1896, 1904: sun) through light,
5. 1896, 1904: Through dark, for
    <> all, read aright,
6. 1896, 1904: Is Love, for Love
13. 1896, 1904: beneath: beside,
14. 1904: grows myriad-/ eyed
17. 1896, 1904: shone:
18. 1896, 1904: upon:
20. 1896, 1904: words:
21. 1896, 1904: winged ecstasies of
23. 1896, 1904: not?
25. 1896, 1904: dead, and fit,
26. 1896, 1904: pit,
30. 1896, 1904: begetteth Love?

31. 1896, 1904: distils:
32. 1896, 1904: subtle fountain-rills
33. 1896, 1904: hills,
34. 1896, 1904: fertilize:
35. 1896, 1904: cries,
36. 1896, 1904: satisfies:
37. 1896, 1904: space: Love
38. 1896, 1904: poles,
39. 1896, 1904: aureoles:
40. 1896, 1904: sun: Love through the
41. 1896, 1904: arc:
42. 1896: spark:
    1904: the glow-/ worm's spark:
43. 1896, 1904: great: Love <> small:
44. 1896, 1904: wall:
46. MS: who [know] <taste> that
50. 1896, 1904: ear,

THE MASSACRE OF PERUGIA.

[Composed probably between August 27, 1859, and November 18, 1859. The note-book MS is owned by Mrs. Geoffrey Dennis. Basic text: notebook MS. The lines following those given in the text are missing from the notebook.]

"I HAVE DONE WITH HOPE"

[Composed probably between August 27, 1859, and November 18, 1859. The note-book MS is owned by Mrs. Geoffrey Dennis. Basic text: notebook MS. The lines preceding and following those given in the text are missing from the notebook.]

PROMISES LIKE PIECRUST.

[Composed April 20, 1861. Editions: 1896, 1904. The notebook MS is in the British Library. Basic text: notebook MS.]

Title. 1896, 1904: PROMISES LIKE
    PIE-CRUST
2. 1896, 1904: you:
6. 1896, 1904: go:
10. 1896, 1904: one:

15. 1896, 1904: glass,
18. 1896, 1904: again:
20. 1904: chain.
22. 1896, 1904: less:

BY THE WATERS OF BABYLON.

[Composed December 1, 1861. Editions: 1896, 1904. The notebook MS is in the British Library. Basic text: notebook MS.]

Title. 1896, 1904: BY THE WATERS
     OF BABYLON
4. 1896, 1904: sleep:
6. 1896, 1904: gone:
10. 1896, 1904: The willow-trees grow

14. 1896, 1904: gone:
26. 1896, 1904: Though the
28. 1896s: dust;
31. 1896, 1904: dust,

BETTER SO.

[Composed December 13, 1861. Editions: 1896, 1904. The notebook MS is in the British Library. Basic text: notebook MS. Lines 13–24, 31–36 were published as an untitled poem in *Verses* (1893); for text and variants of that poem, see Volume II of the present edition, pp. 309, 466. The 1904 text contains only lines 1–12, 25–30 of the poem. In the 1896 text, lines 2, 8, 14, 20, and 29 are indented four spaces; lines 5, 10, 11, 16, 17, 22, 23, 26, 27, 32, and 35 are indented six spaces; and lines 6, 7, 9, 18, 31, and 36 are indented two spaces. In the 1904 text, lines 2, 8, and 29 are indented four spaces; lines 5, 10, 11, 26, and 27 are indented eight spaces; and lines 6, 7, and 9 are indented two spaces.]

Title. 1896, 1904: BETTER SO
2. MS: [*F*] [not indented] <Fast>
     [indented two spaces] asleep
3. 1896, 1904: Though the
4. 1896, 1904: Though the
5. 1896, 1904: past:
7. 1896, 1904: weep, whilst death-bells
     toll,
16. MS: [*Now*] <Just> at [The deletion
     and revision are in pencil in
     Christina's hand.]

18. MS: For [*that*] <one> dear [The
     deletion and revision are in pencil
     in Christina's hand.]
30. MS: thy [illegible erasure] <feet>
     on
32. 1896: thou shouldst say:
33. MS: <">O [The addition is in
     pencil.]
36. MS: took <">—? [The addition is
     in pencil.]
     1896: took"?

OUR WIDOWED QUEEN.

[Composed December 16, 1861. Editions: 1896, 1904. The notebook MS is in the British Library. Basic text: notebook MS.]

Title. 1896, 1904: OUR WIDOWED
     QUEEN
10. MS: [*St*]<St>rengthen her
14. 1896, 1904: bereft:
16. 1896, 1904: Beggared though
     much

18. 1896, 1904: weeps:
22. 1896, 1904: move:
25. 1896, 1904: soul possest
26. 1896, 1904: she fulfil her
27. 1896, 1904: call her blest,
28. 1896, 1904: her Husband praise.

IN PROGRESS.

[Composed March 31, 1862. Editions: 1896, 1904. The notebook MS is in the British Library. Basic text: notebook MS. In the 1896 and 1904 texts, lines 11 and 12 are indented four spaces.]

Title. 1896, 1904: IN PROGRESS
4. MS: And [*deep*] <dim> dried [The
deletion and revision are in pencil
in Christina's hand.]

11. MS: certainly[*:*]<.>
12. MS: may [*some*] <one> day [The
deletion and revision are in pencil
in Christina's hand.]

"OUT OF THE DEEP."

[Composed December 17, 1862. Editions: 1896, 1904. The notebook MS is in the
British Library. Basic text: notebook MS. In the 1896 and 1904 texts, lines 11 and 13
are indented four spaces; and line 12 is indented two spaces.]

Title. 1896, 1904: OUT OF THE
DEEP
1. 1896, 1904: Have mercy, Thou my
God—mercy, my God!
2. 1896, 1904: by day.
3. 1896, 1904: there, I
5. 1896, 1904: tedious desert-path
long
6. 1896, 1904: will Thy judgment
judge me, yea or nay?

7. 1896, 1904: grace: but
8. 1896, 1904: shod—
9. 1896, 1904: still Thou haunt'st me,
12. 1896, 1904: All-faithful Thou,
13. MS: traitor s[*hr*]<lu>nk back
1896, 1904: Myself: I
14. 1896, 1904: repent—help

FOR A MERCY RECEIVED.

[Composed January 13, 1863. Editions: 1896, 1904. The notebook MS is in the Brit-
ish Library. Basic text: notebook MS. Lines 31–40 were published as "'As a king,
. . . . unto the King'" in *Verses* (1893); for text and variants of that poem, see Volume
II of the present edition, pp. 248, 426.]

Title. 1896, 1904: FOR A MERCY
RECEIVED
1. 1896, 1904: Thank God who
spared
3. MS: stands, [*O*] <Thou> Faithful
[The deletion and revision are in
pencil in Christina's hand.]
5. 1896, 1904: length: once
7. MS: and b[*a*]<e>ar the
9. 1896, 1904: wing:
13. MS: were [illegible erasure]
<labour>, failure,
14. 1896, 1904: lag,
18. MS: O Thou [*t*]<T>hat art
1896, 1904: O Thou that art < >
seek,
20. 1896, 1904: forth Thy hand to
21. 1896, 1904: Through many < >
have I past,

23. 1896, 1904: now Thy hand hath
24. 1896, 1904: Lord, help < > last:
27. 1896, 1904: back,
29. 1896, 1904: by love doth
30. 1896, 1904: pay love is
32. MS: as [*k*]<K>ing with
1896, 1904: as king with king
34. 1896, 1904: cry:
35. 1896, 1904: bring:—
36. 1896, 1904: loves: though soiled
37. 1896, 1904: yore.
38. MS: [*Whoever*] <Who ever>
[separated with a solidus written in
pencil] came
39. 1896, 1904: By thee? Do,
1896s: By Thee? Do,

SUMMER. ["COME, CUCKOO, COME"]

[Composed February 5, 1863. Editions: 1896, 1904. The notebook MS (MS1) is in the British Library. A separate fair copy MS (MS2), signed "Christina G. Rossetti," is in the Princeton University Library. Basic text: MS2. In the 1896 and 1904 texts, lines 1, 2, 4–6, 8–10, 12, 14, 16–18, 20, and 24 are indented four spaces; and line 22 is not indented.]

Title. MS1: June.
    1896, 1904: JUNE
1. 1896, 1904: cuckoo, come:
2. 1896, 1904: swallow:
3. MS1: welcome; when you
    1896, 1904: welcome! when you
4. MS1, 1896, 1904: follow:
5. MS1, 1896, 1904: June the <>
    months
6. 1896, 1904: too,

10. 1896, 1904: riper:
12. MS1: its woo[*l*]<d>land piper:
13. MS1: the maple tops
    1896, 1904: the maple-tops
17. MS1: year [*might*] <would> stand
20. MS1: <N>Or further [The added
    letter is in pencil in Christina's
    hand.]
    MS2: Or further
22. MS1, 1896, 1904: seven,

A DUMB FRIEND.

[Composed March 24, 1863. Editions: 1896, 1904. The notebook MS is in the British Library. Basic text: notebook MS. In the 1896 and 1904 texts, the second and third lines of each stanza are not indented.]

Title. 1896, 1904: A DUMB FRIEND
1. 1896, 1904: young:
7. 1896, 1904: All through the
10. 1896, 1904: it tost
11. MS: rattling [*blast*] <gale>, or
    [The deletion and revision are in
    pencil in Christina's hand.]
    1896: frost:
    1904: gale or

13. MS: round [illegible erasure]
    <green head> with
14. 1904: by.
15. 1896, 1904: age: and
18. 1896, 1904: see,
19. 1896, 1904: me,
26. 1896, 1904: in summer-heat give
27. 1896, 1904: winter: when

MARGERY.

[Composed October 1, 1863. Editions: 1896, 1904. The notebook MS is in the British Library. Basic text: notebook MS. Lines 31–35 were published as the first five lines of an untitled poem in *Verses* (1893); for text and variants of that poem, see Volume II of the present edition, pp. 308, 465.]

Title. 1896, 1904: MARGERY
3. 1896, 1904: head;
4. 1896, 1904: be:
8. MS: have [*hel*] <tried> a
    1896, 1904: plan:
22. 1896, 1904: cares,
27. 1896, 1904: grief:
28. 1896, 1904: leaf;

29. 1896, 1904: smiled:
32. 1896, 1904: out,
33. MS: and [*hedged*] <snared> us
    [The deletion and revision are in
    pencil in Christina's hand.]
    1896: us roundabout,
    1904: us round-/ about,
40. MS: Her [*pine and*] <blossom>

fade [The deletion and revision are   42. MS: leave b[*l*]<e>hind
in pencil in Christina's hand and   47. 1896, 1904: while:
retraced by William Michael   52. 1896, 1904: for,
Rossetti.]

IN PATIENCE.

[Composed March 19, 1864. Editions: 1896, 1904. The notebook MS is in the British Library. Basic text: notebook MS. Lines 9–16 were published as an untitled poem in *Verses* (1893); for text and variants of that poem, see Volume II of the present edition, pp. 296, 455.]

Title. 1896, 1904: IN PATIENCE   5. 1896, 1904: Though sad
2. MS: Who [*all*] <this> my [The   6. 1896, 1904: song:
   deletion and revision are in pencil   7. 1896, 1904: Though dim
   in Christina's hand.]   8. 1896, 1904: At evening-time there
   1896, 1904: given: 11. 1896s: pray

SUNSHINE.

[Composed May 31, 1864. Editions: 1896, 1904. The notebook MS (MS1) is in the British Library. A separate fair copy MS (MS2), signed "Christina G. Rossetti," is in the Princeton University Library. Basic text: MS2. In MS1, the last line of each stanza is indented four spaces.]

Title. 1896, 1904: SUNSHINE   7. 1896, 1904: world,
1. 1896, 1904: heart,   8. MS1, 1896, 1904: know."
2. 1896, 1904: sink: 9. MS2: [*I*] <Now i>f of
3. 1896, 1904: world,   10. MS1: less;
4. MS1, 1896: think."   11. MS1, 1896, 1904: tell:
   1904: think.   12. MS1, 1896, 1904: You guess.
6. 1896, 1904: glow):

MEETING.

[Composed June 11, 1864. Editions: 1896, 1904. The notebook MS is in the British Library. Basic text: notebook MS. Lines 19–24 were published as lines 11–16 of an untitled poem in *Verses* (1893); for text and notes of that poem, see Volume II of the present edition, pp. 277, 445. In the 1896 and 1904 texts, lines 4, 8, 10, 11, 13, 15, 16, and 18–24 are indented four spaces; lines 6 and 12 are indented six spaces; and line 14 is not indented.]

Title. 1896, 1904: MEETING   8. 1896, 1904: see to-morrow's light:
1. 1896, 1904: shall live, we live: 9. 1896, 1904: again:
2. 1896, 1904: shall die, we die: 10. 1896, 1904: But to-night,
3. 1896, 1904: live we <> again: good-night.
4. 1896, 1904: But to-night, good-bye. 11. 1896, 1904: Good-night, my
7. MS: sleep, we Shall wake   13. 1896, 1904: part:
   1896, 1904: sleep we   14. 1896, 1904: pain:

18. 1896, 1904: To-morrow you
19. 1896, 1904: for:
20. 1896, 1904: meet.

21. 1896, 1904: for:
23. MS: parting [*f*]<b>efore
    1896, 1904: before,

"NONE WITH HIM."

[Composed June 14, 1864. Editions: 1896, 1904. The notebook MS is in the British Library. Basic text: notebook MS.]

Title. 1896, 1904: NONE WITH HIM
1. 1896, 1904: bear to live,
2. 1896, 1904: fro?
5. 1896, 1904: truth Thou cam'st to show.
   1896s: Thy face, to <> truth Thou cam'st to show.

6. MS: didst [*t*]<T>hou bear
7. 1896, 1904: pain?
8. 1896, 1904: astonishment, past by,
10. 1896, 1904: whom Thy blood was <> vain.
15. 1896, 1904: death, Thy

UNDER WILLOWS.

[Composed July 27, 1864. Editions: 1896, 1904. The notebook MS is in the British Library. Basic text: notebook MS. In the 1896 and 1904 texts, lines 2, 4, 8, 11, 16, 20, and 24 are indented four spaces; lines 10, 14, 18, and 22 are not indented; and line 12 is indented six spaces. In the 1904 text, lines 4, 8, 16, 20, and 24 are indented four spaces; line 12 is indented six spaces; and lines 14, 18, and 22 are not indented.]

Title. 1896, 1904: UNDER WILLOWS
3. 1896, 1904: waves,
6. MS: welladay[*?*]<!>
11. 1896, 1904: awhile:
12. 1896, 1904: by,—

13. 1896, 1904: tune:
19. 1896, 1904: raves.
21. 1896, 1904: cold:
22. 1896, 1904: past:

A SKETCH.

[Composed August 15, 1864. Editions: 1896, 1904. The notebook MS is in the British Library. Basic text: notebook MS. In the 1904 text, the fifth and sixth lines of each stanza are not indented.]

Title. 1896, 1904: A SKETCH
2. MS: wear [*plumes*] <wings> to
   [The deletion and revision are in pencil in Christina's hand.]
   1896, 1904: stir;
3. 1896, 1904: fur,
4. 1896, 1904: below:
6. 1896, 1904: coat: he's <> men:
7. MS: quill [*becomes*] <is cut to> a
   [The deletion and revision are in pencil in Christina's hand and retraced by William Michael Rossetti.]

9. 1896, 1904: speech.
11. 1896, 1904: whole;
12. 1896, 1904: part, so
13. MS: tho' pa[*r*]<t>ent plain,
    1896, 1904: whole though patent plain,—
18. MS: nothing h[illegible deletion]<i>d for
19. 1896, 1904: day:
20. 1896, 1904: But, since <> say,
21. 1896, 1904: "Where? What?" and

IF I HAD WORDS.

[Composed September 3, 1864. Editions: 1896, 1904. The notebook MS is in the British Library. Basic text: notebook MS.]

Title. 1896, 1904: IF I HAD WORDS
Title.
20. 1896, 1904: dry:
21. 1896, 1904: Though there
23. MS: Then [I]<i>f I

25. 1896, 1904: dove,
27. 1896, 1904: out Love,
29. 1896, 1904: to Love, my rest—
30. 1896, 1904: To Love, my

WHAT TO DO?

[Composed August 4, 1865. Editions: 1896, 1904. The notebook MS is in the British Library. Basic text: notebook MS. In the 1896 and 1904 texts, the last line of each stanza is indented four spaces.]

Title. 1896, 1904: WHAT TO DO?
1. 1896, 1904: O my
7. 1896, 1904: coverlet,

8. 1896, 1904: wattle,
12. 1896, 1904: moan:
14. 1896, 1904: sleeping,

YOUNG DEATH.

[Composed November 3, 1865. Editions: 1904. The notebook MS is in the British Library. Basic text: notebook MS. Lines 16–21 and 36–41 were published as "'Is it well with the child?'" in *Verses* (1893); for text and variants of that poem, see Volume II of the present edition, pp. 292, 453. In the MS, a vertical pencil line is added in the right margin of lines 16–21 and 36–41. In the 1904 text, lines 16–21 and 36–41 are omitted; and lines 15, 25, 29, 31, and 35 are indented four spaces.]

Title. 1904: YOUNG DEATH
1. 1904: Lying a-dying—
5. 1904: pleasure:
6. 1904: passion,
9. 1904: loathing.
12. 1904: flashes,
15. 1904: [Below the line is a horizontal row of spaced periods.]
22. 1904: in the room, the upper,
24. 1904: New-bathed from
25. 1904: gazing:

27. 1904: praising.
28. 1904: weeping
29. 1904: fear or
30. 1904: more or sleeping
31. 1904: night or
33. 1904: Of saints, or thirst or hunger:
34. 1904: more strong,
35. 1904: [Below the line is a horizontal row of spaced periods.]

IN A CERTAIN PLACE.

[Composed March 6, 1866. Editions: 1896, 1904. The notebook MS is in the British Library. Basic text: notebook MS. In the 1896 text, lines 2, 5, and 16 are indented four spaces; and lines 4, 6, 8, 12–14, and 17–28 are indented two spaces. In the 1904 text, lines 4, 5, and 16 are indented four spaces; and lines 6, 8, 12–14, and 17–28 are indented two spaces.]

Title. 1896, 1904. IN A CERTAIN
    PLACE
1. MS: found [*l*]<L>ove in
3. 1896, 1904: bed,
10. 1896, 1904: before:
11. 1896, 1904: Or, if

14. 1896, 1904: of to-morrow:
16. MS: [Because line 16 is the last on
    the page, there is no indication of
    whether or not a stanza break is
    intended to follow the line.]

"CANNOT SWEETEN."

[Composed March 8, 1866. Editions: 1896, 1904. The notebook MS is in the British
Library. Basic text: notebook MS. In the 1896 and 1904 texts, line 27 is indented
two spaces.]

Title. 1896, 1904: CANNOT
    SWEETEN
1. 1896, 1904: "If <> in,
2. 1896, 1904: black?"
3. 1896, 1904: "Because
4. 1896, 1904: back!"
5. 1896, 1904: "If <> in,
6. 1896, 1904: wine is red?"
7. 1896, 1904: "Because <> goings,
8. 1896, 1904: Red, red is <> tread."
9. 1896, 1904: "Slew you mother
10. 1896, 1904: by?"
11. 1896, 1904: "Not father, and
12. 1896, 1904: eye."

13. 1896, 1904: "Slew you sister
14. 1896, 1904: part?"
15. 1896, 1904: "Not brother
17. 1896, 1904: "He loved me because
18. 1896, 1904: had:
19. 1896, 1904: because he loved me:
21. 1896, 1904: "Yet <> loving,
25. 1896, 1904: "I
29. 1896, 1904: "So
32. 1896, 1904: Blacker, redder
33. 1896, 1904: "Cold <> heavy:
35. 1896, 1904: cleaner,
36. 1896, 1904: Dropping, dropping,
    dropping <> it."

OF MY LIFE.

[Composed May 15, 1866. Editions: 1896, 1904. The notebook MS is in the British
Library. Basic text: notebook MS. In the 1896 and 1904 texts, the second, third, and
fourth lines of each stanza are not indented, and the fifth line of each stanza is in-
dented two spaces.]

Title. 1896, 1904: OF MY LIFE
2. 1896, 1904: Through the
7. 1896, 1904: Through the
8. 1896, 1904: delight,
11. 1896, 1904: might, I <> die:

12. MS: My soul[*s*] should
14. MS: sweet sou[*ls*]<ls> sing
    1896, 1904: say—
16. 1896, 1904: might, I <> die:

"YES, I TOO COULD FACE DEATH AND NEVER SHRINK"

[Date of composition unknown. Editions: 1904. The version of the poem in Chris-
tina's 1850 notebook MS of *Maude: Prose & Verse* is in the Huntington Library. The
poem was printed in *Maude: Prose & Verse, by Christina Rossetti; 1850* (Chicago: Her-
bert S. Stone and Company, 1897), 10; variants therein are designated "1897a" in
the textual notes. It was also printed in *Maude: A Story for Girls, by Christina Rossetti*

478   *The Complete Poems of Christina Rossetti*

(London: James Bowden, 1897), 5–6; variants therein are designated "1897" in the
textual notes. Basic text: notebook MS. In the 1897a text, lines 1, 4, 5, 8, 10–12, and
14 are indented two spaces. In the 1904 text, lines 1, 4, 5, and 8 are not indented;
and lines 2, 3, 6, 7, 10, and 12 are indented two spaces.]

Title. 1904: ENDURANCE
 1. 1904: shrink.
 6. MS: the [*grave*] <deep> [illegible
    erasure] <grave, nor drowse,>
    though
    1904: drowse tho' it
 7. 1897a: knife,
 8. 1897a: courage, as
    1904: home:—this <> courage, as
 9. 1904: do.

10. 1904: done: to
11. 1897a: heart-sicknesses;
    1904: of heart-/ sicknesses.
12. MS: [*Of the daily*] <Each day's>
    experience [illegible erasure]
    <testifies of this:>
    1904: this.
13. MS: but good [*states*] <lives> are
    1904: few:
14. 1897, 1897a, 1904: lees?

"WOULD THAT I WERE A TURNIP WHITE"

[Date of composition unknown. Editions: 1896, 1904. The version of the poem in
Christina's 1850 notebook MS of *Maude: Prose & Verse* is in the Huntington Library.
The poem was printed in *Maude: Prose & Verse, by Christina Rossetti; 1850* (Chicago:
Herbert S. Stone and Company, 1897), 27; variants therein are designated "1897a"
in the textual notes. It was also printed in *Maude: A Story for Girls, by Christina Rossetti*
(London: James Bowden, 1897), 19–20; variants therein are designated "1897" in
the textual notes. Basic text: notebook MS. In the 1896 and 1904 texts, lines 1 and 4
are indented two spaces; lines 2, 3, and 7 are indented four spaces; and lines 5, 8,
10, 12, and 14 are not indented. In the 1897 text, line 11 is not indented, and line 12
is indented four spaces. In the 1897a text, lines 1, 4, 5, 8–10, and 14 are indented
two spaces; and lines 11 and 12 are not indented.]

Title. 1896, 1904: X*a*
 8. MS: Or fre[z]<e>zing traveller
 9. 1896, 1904: were straw-catching as
    <>drown
    1897, 1897a: were straw-catching as
10. 1896, 1897, 1904: swim),
    1897a: landsman I, who <> swim),

11. 1904: sink,—
12. 1897: writing; I
13. 1897: gown,
14. MS: With deep-cu[*t*]<t>
    scollop[*p*]ed edges

"I FANCY THE GOOD FAIRIES DRESSED IN WHITE"

[Date of composition unknown. Editions: 1896, 1904. The version of the poem in
Christina's 1850 notebook MS of *Maude: Prose & Verse* is in the Huntington Library.
The poem was printed in *Maude: Prose & Verse, by Christina Rossetti; 1850* (Chicago:
Herbert S. Stone and Company, 1897), 28–29; variants therein are designated
"1897a" in the textual notes. It was also printed in *Maude: A Story for Girls, by Chris-
tina Rossetti* (London: James Bowden, 1897), 21; variants therein are designated
"1897" in the textual notes. Basic text: notebook MS. In the 1896 and 1904 texts,
lines 1, 4, and 8 are not indented; lines 2, 3, 6, 7, 10, and 14 are indented two spaces;
and lines 11 and 12 are indented four spaces. In the 1897 text, line 11 is not in-
dented, and line 12 is indented four spaces. In the 1897a text, lines 1, 4, 5, 8, 10, and
14 are indented two spaces; and lines 11 and 12 are not indented.]

Title. 1896, 1904: X*b*
1. MS: "I <> good fa<i>ries dressed
2. 1896, 1897a: like moonbeams
   through
   1904: like moonbeams through
   <> black,
5. 1896, 1904: faded autumn-leaves
   from

1897a: faded autumn leaves <>
sight,
7. 1904: ample bean-/ pod sack
9. MS: Or [*holding a poor*] <fishing for
   a> fly
12. MS: Or dy<e>ing the
14. 1896, 1904: rim.

"SOME LADIES DRESS IN MUSLIN FULL AND WHITE"

[Date of composition unknown. Editions: 1896, 1904. Christina's rough draft (MS1) is in the Princeton University Library. The version of the poem in her 1850 notebook MS of *Maude: Prose & Verse* (MS2) is in the Huntington Library. The poem was printed in *Maude: Prose & Verse, by Christina Rossetti; 1850* (Chicago: Herbert S. Stone and Company, 1897), 29–30; variants therein are designated "1897a" in the textual notes. It was also printed in *Maude: A Story for Girls, by Christina Rossetti* (London: James Bowden, 1897), 22; variants therein are designated "1897" in the textual notes. Basic text: MS2. In MS1, the text is written in pencil, and no lines are indented. In the 1896 and 1904 texts, lines 1, 4, 5, and 8 are not indented; lines 2, 3, 6, 7, 10, and 14 are indented two spaces; and lines 11 and 12 are indented four spaces. In the 1897 text, line 11 is indented four spaces. In the 1897a text, lines 1, 10, 11, and 14 are not indented; and lines 4, 5, 8, 9, and 13 are indented two spaces.]

Title. 1896, 1904: X*c*—VANITY FAIR
1. MS1: full & [*right*] <white>,
   1897a: "Some
2. MS1: Some gentleman in <>
   succinct & black;
3. MS1: Some patronize a waggon,
   some
   1896, 1904: Some patronize a
4. MS1: painted brougham only right
5. MS1: [Illegible deletion] <Youth>
   is <> always su[*h*]<c>h a <>
   sight
   1897: sight:
6. MS1: back
7. MS1: in a great coat like [*a*]<a>
   sack
9. MS1: the [*earth*] <world> were
   1896, 1904: drown,

10. MS1: teach <to> swim
    1897: swim;
11. MS1: sink
12. MS1: pink
13. MS1: roses [*a*]<&> geraniums
    <> gown
    1897, 1904: gown:
    1897a: their gowns:—
14. MS1: to [*t*]<T>he Basin, pole
    them <o'er> the rim. [Below the
    line is written:] 7 M.
    MS2: rim."—
    1896, 1904: rim.
    1897: rim."
    1897a: to the Basin, poke <> rim.

AUTUMN. ["FADE TENDER LILY"]

[Date of composition unknown. Editions: 1904. The version of the poem in Christina's 1850 notebook MS of *Maude: Prose & Verse* (MS1) is in the Huntington Library. A separate fair copy (MS2), signed "Christina G. Rossetti," is in the Princeton University Library. The poem was printed in *Maude: Prose & Verse, by Christina Rossetti; 1850* (Chicago: Herbert S. Stone and Company, 1897), 120; variants therein are designated "1897a" in the textual notes. It was also printed in *Maude: A Story for Girls, by Christina Rossetti* (London: James Bowden, 1897), 79; variants therein are designated "1897" in the textual notes. Basic text: MS2.]

Title. MS1, 1897, 1897a: [untitled]
1904: WITHERING
1. MS1, 1897, 1897a, 1904: Fade,
tender
2. MS1, 1897, 1904: Fade, O
1897a: Fade, Oh crimson
3. MS1, 1897, 1897a, 1904: flower,
5. MS1, 1897, 1897a, 1904: Go, chilly
6. 1897, 1904: Come, O
1897a: Come, Oh Winter

7. MS1: green stalks die [*w*]<a>way
1897, 1897a, 1904: green stalks die
10. MS1, 1897, 1897a: withering.
MS2: on [illegible deletion]
withering:
12. MS1: pleasant Spring.—
1904: pleasant spring.

IL ROSSEGGIAR DELL' ORIENTE

[Composed from December, 1862, to August, 1868. Editions: 1896, 1904. Christina's fair copy MS is in the British Library. Basic text: MS.]

Title. MS: Il rosseggiar dell' Oriente/
Canzoniere/ di/ Cristina G.
Rossetti./ "All' Amico Contano"—.
1896: IL ROSSEGGIAR DELL'
ORIENTE/ Canzoniere all' Amico
lontano

1904: IL ROSSEGGIAR DELL'/
ORIENTE/ Canzoniere all' Amico
lontano.

1./ AMOR DORMENTE?

[Composed in December, 1862. Editions: 1896, 1904. Christina's fair copy MS is in the British Library. Basic text: MS.]

Title. 1896, 1904: I/ AMOR
DORMENTE?
1896s: I/ AMOR DORMENTE

3. 1896, 1904: già m' uccise il
5. 1896, 1904: per l' altra vita

2./ AMOR SI SVEGLIA?

[Composed in January, 1863. Editions: 1896, 1904. Christina's fair copy MS is in the British Library. Basic text: MS.]

Title. MS: Amor [*s*]<S>i sveglia?
1896, 1904: 2/ AMOR SI
SVEGLIA?
3. 1896, 1904: Amor t' insinua
"Spera"—
5. 1896, 1904: S' "Ama" ti dice
Amore,

6. 1896, 1904: S' ei t' incoraggia,
amico,
9. 1896, 1904: Anzi quel
11. 1896, 1904: spero:
1896s: spero;

3./ SI RIMANDA LA TOCCA-CALDAJA.

[Composed probably between January, 1863, and January, 1867. Editions: 1896, 1904. A separate unsigned MS of the poem (MS1) is in the Princeton University Library. Christina's fair copy MS (MS2) is in the British Library. Basic text: MS2.]

Title. MS1: [There is no number above the title.]
1896, 1904: 3/ SI RIMANDA LA TOCCA-CALDAJA

2. 1896, 1904: D' ereditar l' oggetto
3. 1896, 1904: Ch' una fiata
5. 1896, 1904: più l' usar non

4./ "BLUMINE" RISPONDE:

[Composed in January, 1867. Editions: 1896, 1904. Christina's fair copy MS is in the British Library. Basic text: MS.]

Title. 1896, 1904: 4/ BLUMINE RISPONDE
1. 1896, 1904: S' io t' incontrassi nell' eterna pace,
3. 1896, 1904: S' io t' incontrassi in < > maledetto,
7. 1896, 1904: dì m' aspetto

9. 1896, 1904: tempo; e
10. 1896, 1904: mondo.
11. MS: mi s[a]<o>gno quel
12. 1896, 1904: me, "Doman
13. 1896, 1904: Doman < > ma s' ami tu
14. 1896, 1904: fondo?

5./ "LASSÙ FIA CARO IL RIVEDERCI"—.

[Composed in January, 1867. Editions: 1896, 1904. Christina's fair copy MS is in the British Library. Basic text: MS. In the 1896 and 1904 texts, lines 3, 5, 9, and 11 are not indented; and lines 4 and 10 are indented two spaces.]

Title. 1896: 5/ Lassù < > rivederci
1904: 5/ Lassù < > rivederci.
4. 1896, 1904: me; chè cieche
7. 1896: Lascia ch' io dica
1904: Lascia ch' io dica, 'Le
8. 1896, 1904: Come

10. 1896, 1904: Lascia ch' io dica ancor, "Con
11. 1896, 1904: Giorno
12. 1896, 1904: Lungo
13. 1896, 1904: Al < > là dell' inverno primavera."

6./ "NON SON IO LA ROSA MA VI STETTI APPRESSO."

[Composed in April, 1867. Editions: 1896, 1904. Christina's fair copy MS is in the British Library. Basic text: MS. In the 1896 text, line 9 is indented two spaces.]

Title. 1896: 6/ Non < > appresso
1904: 6/ Non appresso.
6. 1896, 1904: dicendo,—
7. 1896, 1904: fia quand' io mi
9. 1896, 1904: Ma s' egli vi sarà quand' io vi

10. 1896, 1904: S' egli m' accoglie col
12. MS: rosa a[l]<r>rossirà nel
1896, 1904: viso:—

7./ "LASSUSO IL CARO FIORE"—.

[Composed in April, 1867. Editions: 1896, 1904. Christina's fair copy MS is in the British Library. Basic text: MS.]

Title. 1896: 7/ Lassuso <> caro Fiore
    1904: 7/ Lassuso <> caro Fiore.
1. 1896, 1904: Se t' insegnasse Iddio
2. MS: proprio [a]<A>mor così,
5. 1896, 1904: chiama,
6. 1896, 1904: dì";—

7. 1896, 1904: che t' ama
13. 1896, 1904: duol ch' è stato
14. 1896, 1904: Domanderai "Dov' è?"
21. MS: L'[a]<A>mata tanto
23. 1896, 1904: E l' alma tua

8./ SAPESSI PURE!

[Composed in May, 1867. Editions: 1896, 1904. Christina's fair copy MS is in the British Library. Basic text: MS.]

Title. 1896, 1904: 8/ SAPESSI PURE
3. 1896, 1904: che facc' io

4. 1896, 1904: È ch' ognor penso
5. 1896, 1904: Pensando, a

9./ IDDIO C'ILLUMINI!

[Composed in May, 1867. Editions: 1896, 1904. Christina's fair copy MS is in the British Library. Basic text: MS. In the 1896 text, the last line of each stanza is indented six spaces. In the 1904 text, the last line of each stanza is indented eight spaces.]

Title. 1896, 1904: 9/ IDDIO
    C' ILLUMINI
5. 1896, 1904: Calcando l' uno
    inusitata
6. MS: Seguendo l'al[r]<t>ro il
    1896, 1904: Seguendo l' altro il
10. 1896, 1904: sia ch' io ti
11. 1896, 1904: allor d' averci detto

13. 1896, 1904: Quanto t' amavo e
14. 1896, 1904: Esprimer quell' amor
    che
23. MS: alfin? [s]<S>oltanto il <> si
    sch<i>ude
24. 1896, 1904: D' un sole
27. MS: Gesù, [c]<C>he sconosciuto
    1896, 1904: Gesù, che sconosciuto

10./ AMICIZIA:/ "SIRROCCHIA SON D'AMOR"—.

[Composed in August, 1867. Editions: 1896, 1904. Christina's fair copy MS is in the British Library. Basic text: MS.]

Title. 1896: 10/ AMICIZIA/ Sirocchia
    son d' Amor
    1904: 10/ AMICIZIA/ Sirocchia
    son d' Amor.
3. 1896, 1904: Abitan l' uno e l' altra in

9. MS: Oggi e<d> ancor
    1896, 1904: per l' amicizia,
13. MS: gran deliz<i>a,
    1896, 1904: Giorno d' amor, giorno

11./ "LUSCIOUS AND SORROWFUL"—.

[Composed in August, 1867. Editions: 1896, 1904. Christina's fair copy MS is in the British Library. Basic text: MS. In the 1896 and 1904 texts, lines 2, 4, and 6 are indented four spaces.]

Title. 1896: 11/ Luscious <> sorrowful
1904: 11/ Luscious <> sorrowful.
1. 1896, 1904: Uccello delle rose

2. 1896, 1904: Uccel d' amore,
5. 1896, 1904: Fido all' infido, tieni

12./ "OH FORZA IRRESISTIBILE/ DELL'UMILE PREGHIERA"—.

[Composed in September, 1867. Editions: 1896, 1904. Christina's fair copy MS is in the British Library. Basic text: MS.]

Title. 1896: 12/ O forza <> /
Dell' umile preghiera
1904: 12/ O forza <> / Dell' umile
preghiera.
1. 1896, 1904: darò, Gesù
2. 1896, 1904: quello ch' amo più,
3. 1896, 1904: Accettalo, Signor
11. 1896, 1904: fanno,
12. MS: [Illegible erasure] <"Padre
perdona l>or, ch' essi
1896, 1904: Padre, perdona lor,
ch' essi non sanno."

13. MS: sa [*q*]<Q>uello che
14. MS: [Because line 14 is the last one
on the page, it is impossible to
determine if a stanza break is
intended to follow the line.]
1896, 1904: pure T' amerà s' uno
gl' insegna.
18. 1896, 1904: è vanita fuorchè
24. 1896, 1904: D' amore amabil

13./ FINESTRA MIA ORIENTALE.

[Composed in October, 1867. Editions: 1896, 1904. Christina's fair copy MS is in the British Library. Basic text: MS. In the 1896 and 1904 texts, lines 15, 16, 19, 24, and 26 are indented six spaces; and lines 17, 18, 20–23, and 25 are indented eight spaces.]

Title. 1896, 1904: 13/ FINESTRA
MIA ORIENTALE
Subtitle. MS: [The following subtitle
is enclosed in brackets:] [In
mal[*i*]<a>ttia.]
1896, 1904: [IN MALATTIA]
1. 1896, 1904: verso l' oriente,
3. 1896, 1904: lati dell' aurora;
5. 1896, 1904: te l' occhio languente,
8. 1896, 1904: T' ama, ti
11. 1896, 1904: raccolgo,—

14. MS: [Because line 14 is the last one
on the page, it is impossible to
determine if a stanza break is
intended to follow the line.]
17. 1896, 1904: U' si facesse
20. 1896, 1904: [No stanza break
follows the line.]
22. MS: [Illegible erasure] <Co>l cor
23. 1896, 1904: D' essere amato
26. 1896, 1904: S' infiorirebbe.

14./ [EPPURE ALLORA VENIVI.]

[Composed in February, 1868. Editions: 1896, 1904. Christina's fair copy MS is in the British Library. Basic text: MS. In the 1896 text, lines 2 and 6 are indented six spaces, and line 5 is indented four spaces. In the 1904 text, line 2 is indented four spaces.]

Title. 1896, 1904: 14/ EPPURE
ALLORA VENIVI

1. 1896, 1904: O tempo
5. 1896, 1904: te foss' io,

15./ PER PREFERENZA.

[Composed in March, 1868. Editions: 1896, 1904. Christina's fair copy MS is in the British Library. Basic text: MS. In the MS, the first two stanzas are written in parallel columns, with the third stanza centered below them. In the 1896 text, line 2 is indented four spaces; lines 3, 6, 7, 10, 11, 14, 15, 18, 19, 22, and 23 are not indented; and lines 4 and 8 are indented two spaces. In the 1904 text, lines 4, 8, 12, 16, 20, and 24 are indented two spaces; and lines 3, 6, 7, 10, 11, 14, 15, 18, 19, 22, and 23 are not indented.]

Title. 1896, 1904: 15/ PER
PREFERENZA
1. MS: [Above the line is added an arrow and the following word written perpendicular to the text:] <Supposto>
5. MS: t'amano [illegible erasure] <di> dritto
1896, 1904: Che t' amano di
6. 1896, 1904: D' amor contento
9. MS: [Above the line is added an arrow and the following word written perpendicular to the text:] <Accertato>
10. 1904: Veder di quando

15. 1896, 1904: che l' amo alfine—
16. 1896: M' ama egli
1904: M' ama egli < > sa?
17. MS: [In the left margin is added an arrow and the following word:] <Dedotto>
18. 1896, 1904: Dell' altro, al
20. MS: tutto [illegible deletion] <o> nulla*
1896, 1904: tutto o nulla[1] a te;
21. 1896, 1904: troppo vo' lagnarmi
22. 1896, 1904: Ch' or stai
1896, 1904: [1]Ma < > / Quel ch' io sarò

16./ OGGI

[Composed in March, 1868. Editions: 1896, 1904. Christina's fair copy MS is in the British Library. Basic text: MS. In the 1896 text, line 2 is indented four spaces. In the 1904 text, lines 4 and 8 are indented two spaces.]

Title. 1896, 1904: 16/ OGGI
2. 1896, 1904: Ch' io non t' amassi, O Caro:
6. 1896, 1904: fai l' amaro;

7. 1896, 1904: mi dai,
1896s: mi dài,
8. 1896, 1904: do l' amore.

17./ [SE FOSSI ANDATA A HASTINGS.]

[Composed in March, 1868. Editions: 1896, 1904. Christina's fair copy MS is in the British Library. Basic text: MS. In the 1896 text, line 2 is indented four spaces. In the 1904 text, line 2 is indented two spaces.]

Title. 1896, 1904: 17/ [There is no title below the number.]

1. 1896, 1904: do l' addio,
6. 1896, 1904: Di quando

18./ RIPETIZIONE.

[Composed in June, 1868. Editions: 1896, 1904. Christina's fair copy MS is in the British Library. Basic text: MS. In the 1896 text, lines 4 and 8 are indented eight spaces.]

Title. 1896, 1904: 18/ RIPETIZIONE
1. MS: Cre[illegible deletion]<de>a
   di

6. 1896, 1904: e vo' ridirlo ancora.
8. 1896, 1904: Fino all' aurora.

19./ "AMICO E PIÙ CHE AMICO MIO"—.

[Composed in August, 1868. Editions: 1896, 1904. Christina's fair copy MS is in the British Library. Basic text: MS. In the 1896 and 1904 texts, lines 12 and 14 are indented two spaces.]

Title. 1896: 19/ Amico < > mio
   1904: 19/ Amico < > mio.
1. 1896, 1904: volge l' altro mio
4. 1896, 1904: grida, e
5. MS: Ma l'a[illegible erasure]<spro
   duolo> fummi
   1896, 1904: Ma l' aspro duolo

11. 1896, 1904: non m' è duol
14. 1896, 1904: tu m' ami dillo < > te
   ch' io t' amo.

20./ "NOSTRE VOLUNTÀ QUIETI VIRTÙ DI CARITÀ"—.

[Composed in August, 1868. Editions: 1896, 1904. Christina's fair copy MS is in the British Library. Basic text: MS.]

Title. MS: di car[illegible
   deletion]<it>à"—.
   1896: 20/ Nostre < > quieti/ Virtù
   < > carità
   1904: 20/ Nostre < > quieti/ Virtù
   < > carità.
5. MS: un '[n]<N>o' volendo

1896: diede un "No" volendo un
   "Sì"
6. MS: Vole[d]<n>do e
   1904: ridir?)
11. 1896, 1904: occhi vo' levar,
14. MS: [*Ed ogni creatura in carità.*]
   <Ed il creato tutto in carità.>

21./ [SE COSÌ FOSSE.]

[Composed in August, 1868. Editions: 1896, 1904. Christina's fair copy MS is in the British Library. Basic text: MS. In the 1896 and 1904 texts, lines 4 and 8 are indented six spaces.]

Title. 1896: 21/ Se < > fosse
   1904: 21/ Se < > fosse.

6. 1896, 1904: virtù d' amor,
7. 1896, 1904: Nell' altro mondo

BY WAY OF REMEMBRANCE.
["REMEMBER, IF I CLAIM TOO MUCH OF YOU"]

[Composed in 1870. Editions: 1896, 1904. Christina's fair copy MS is in the British Library. Basic text: MS.]

Title. 1896, 1904: BY WAY OF
   REMEMBRANCE
3. 1896, 1904: end—
6. 1896, 1904: poor, and

7. 1896, 1904: lend,
11. MS: B[y]<e>yond the
12. MS: Is dea[lt]<lt> to

BY WAY OF REMEMBRANCE.
["WILL YOU BE THERE? MY YEARNING HEART HAS CRIED"]

[Composed in 1870. Editions: 1896, 1904. Christina's fair copy MS is in the British Library. Basic text: MS.]

1. 1904: cried.
5. 1904: another, dearer,
6. 1896, 1904: jubilee,

9. 1896, 1904: Yea,
13. 1896, 1904: sake,

BY WAY OF REMEMBRANCE. ["IN RESURRECTION IS IT AWFULLER"]

[Composed October 23, 1870. Editions: 1896, 1904. The rough draft MS (MS1) is in the Princeton University Library. Christina's fair copy MS (MS2) is in the British Library. Basic text: MS2. In MS1, the text is written in pencil, and no lines are indented.]

1. 1896, 1904: In Resurrection is
2. MS1, 1896, 1904: or of the Each—
3. MS1: All all have of all nations < >
   speech
   1896s: kins, of < > nations, of
4. MS1: Or [*of each*] <one clasp> one
   of every him & her?
   MS2: of [illegible deletion] <him
   and> him [illegible deletion] <&>
   her?
   1904: of *him* and *him* and *her?*
5. MS1: When animated earth begins
   1904: stir,
6. MS1: Here there beyond beyond
   [*reason*] <reach> beyond reach
7. MS1: When every
   1896, 1904: beach,

8. MS1: or dead in life some
   seafarer?—
   1896, 1904: dead-in-life, some
9. MS1: resurrection on < > days
   1896, 1904: In Resurrection, on
10. MS1: The day < > earth
11. MS1: again
    1896, 1904: In Resurrection may
12. MS1: more to part or die or suffer
    pain
13. MS1: sorrow one so < > mirth
14. MS1: our Hallelujah songs
    1896, 1904: our resurrection-songs
    of

BY WAY OF REMEMBRANCE.
["I LOVE YOU AND YOU KNOW IT—THIS AT LEAST"]

[Composed in 1870. Editions: 1896, 1904. Christina's fair copy MS is in the British Library. Basic text: MS.]

3. 1896, 1904: it, and
4. 1896, 1904: feast:
6. 1896, 1904: plain.

7. MS: a [illegible deletion] <roll>ing
   moon
   1896, 1904: wane—
9. 1896, 1904: when Love folds

VALENTINES FROM C.G.R.

[Composed from 1876 to 1886. Editions: 1896, 1904. Christina's fair copy MS is in the British Library. Basic text: MS. In the MS, at the end of the series is added the following note in pencil in Christina's handwriting: "These *Valentines* had their origin from my dearest Mother's remarking that she had never received one. I, her CGR, ever after supplied one on the day= & so far as I recollect it was a *surprise* every time, she having forgotten all about it in the interim."]

Title. MS: Valentines/ from/ C.G.R.
1896, 1904: VALENTINES TO
MY MOTHER

VALENTINES FROM C.G.R./
["FAIRER THAN YOUNGER BEAUTIES, MORE BELOVED"]

[Composed in 1876. Editions: 1896, 1904. Christina's fair copy MS is in the British Library. Basic text: MS. In the 1896 text, line 12 is indented six spaces.]

Title. 1896, 1904: 1876
1. MS: [Above the line is added in pencil in William Michael Rossetti's handwriting:] <Valentines to my Mother>

2. 1896, 1904: wife,
4. 1896, 1904: life;
7. 1896, 1904: Raising and making
8. 1896, 1904: grace:
9. 1896, 1904: welcome, and with

A VALENTINE, 1877.

[Composed in 1877. Editions: 1896, 1904. Christina's fair copy MS is in the British Library. Basic text: MS. In the 1896 and 1904 texts, lines 1–5, 8–11, 13, 14, and 16 are indented two spaces.]

Title. 1896, 1904: 1877
8. MS: the sa[n]<m>e,—

16. MS, 1896, 1904: same./ C.G. for
M.F.R.
1896s: same.

1878.

[Composed in 1878. Editions: 1896, 1904. Christina's fair copy MS is in the British Library. Basic text: MS. In the 1896 and 1904 texts, lines 9 and 11 are indented four spaces, and line 12 is indented six spaces.]

Title. 1896, 1904: 1878
1. 1896, 1904: Blessed Dear and Heart's Delight,
2. 1896, 1904: Companion, Friend, and Mother mine,

3. 1896, 1904: fears and love
4. 1896, 1904: stand and sing
5. 1904: Where angels form
10. 1896, 1904: Human love and Love Divine,—

1879.

[Composed in 1879. Editions: 1896, 1904. Christina's fair copy MS is in the British Library. Basic text: MS. In the 1896 and 1904 texts, lines 2–6 and 12 are indented two spaces; lines 7 and 11 are indented four spaces; and lines 8 and 9 are indented six spaces.]

Title. 1896, 1904: 1879
1. MS: [On the page opposite the text
of the poem is written:] To the
Queen of Hearts
1896, 1904: mine,

3. 1896, 1904: endear,—
8. 1896, 1904: a-wooing,
9. 1896, 1904: Billing and cooing,—

1880.

[Composed in 1880. Editions: 1896, 1904. Christina's fair copy MS is in the British Library. Basic text: MS. In the 1896 and 1904 texts, line 2 is indented six spaces, and lines 4 and 6 are indented two spaces.]

Title. 1896, 1904: 1880
1. MS: [On the page opposite the text
of the poem is written:] The Queen
of Hearts
4. 1896, 1904: on flower.
5. 1896, 1904: Through shower and
shine

7. 1896, 1904: Through shine,
through shower,
8. 1896, 1904: Through summer's
flush, through autumn's fading

ST. VALENTINE'S DAY/ 1881.

[Composed in 1881. Editions: 1896, 1904. Christina's fair copy MS is in the British Library. Basic text: MS. In the 1896 and 1904 texts, lines 2, 4, 5, and 9 are indented four spaces; line 7 is indented two spaces; and line 10 is indented six spaces.]

Title. 1896, 1904: 1881
1. MS: [On the page opposite the text
of the poem is written:] The Queen
of Hearts.

5. 1896, 1904: hours."
8. 1896, 1904: in heaven above

A VALENTINE/ 1882.

[Composed in 1882. Editions: 1896, 1904. Christina's fair copy MS is in the British Library. Basic text: MS. In the 1904 text, lines 12 and 14 are not indented, and line 13 is indented two spaces.]

Title. 1896, 1904: 1882
1. MS: [On the page opposite the text
of the poem is written:] The Queen
of Hearts.
4. 1896, 1904: dove;
6. 1896, 1904: above;

9. 1896, 1904: brought holly then;
10. 1896, 1904: frailer snowdrops
shivering;
11. 1896, 1904: thought—
12. 1896, 1904: I her < > duteous
Valentine—

FEBRUARY 14. 1883.

[Composed in 1883. Editions: 1896, 1904. Christina's fair copy MS is in the British Library. Basic text: MS.]

Title. 1896, 1904: 1883
1. MS: [On the page opposite the text
of the poem is written in purple
crayon:] The Queen of Hearts
1896, 1904: change and loss,

2. 1896, 1904: heart and eyes
3. 1896, 1904: bear and painful
6. 1896, 1904: rejoices, having

1884.

[Composed in 1884. Editions: 1896, 1904. Christina's fair copy MS is in the British
Library. Basic text: MS.]

Title. 1896, 1904: 1884
1. MS: [On the page opposite the text
of the poem is written:] The Queen
of Hearts
1896, 1904: joy and grief,

2. 1896, 1904: hope and fear:
5. 1896, 1904: But, since
8. 1896, 1904: You guide, and I

1885./ ST. VALENTINE'S DAY.

[Composed in 1885. Editions: 1896, 1904. Christina's fair copy MS is in the British
Library. Basic text: MS. In the 1896 text, lines 1, 5, 9, and 13 are indented two
spaces; and lines 2, 4, 6, 8, 10, 12, 14, and 16 are indented four spaces. In the 1904
text, lines 1, 5, 9, 13, and 16 are indented two spaces; and lines 2, 4, 6, 8, 10, 12, and
14 are indented four spaces.]

Title. 1896, 1904: 1885
1. MS: [On the page opposite the text
of the poem is written:] The Queen
of Hearts
2. 1896, 1904: winter through,

4. 1896, 1904: do;
6. 1896, 1904: wind and storm
9. 1896, 1904: You and I,
10. 1896, 1904: winter through,
14. 1896, 1904: olive and the

1886/ ST. VALENTINE'S DAY.

[Composed in 1886. Editions: 1896, 1904. Christina's fair copy MS is in the British
Library. Basic text: MS.]

Title. 1896, 1904: 1886
1. MS: [On the page opposite the text
of the poem is written:] The Queen
of Hearts.

3. 1896, 1904: hour,
4. 1896, 1904: [A stanza break follows
the line.]
8. 1896, 1904: treasure, O

"AH WELLADAY AND WHEREFORE AM I HERE?"

[Date of composition unknown. Editions:1896, 1904. Christina's rough draft MS is
in the Princeton University Library. Basic text: MS. In the MS, the text of the poem
is written in pencil. In the 1896 and 1904 texts, lines 2, 3, 6, 7, 10, and 13 are in-
dented two spaces; and lines 11 and 12 are indented four spaces.]

Title. 1896, 1904: SONNETS/
  WRITTEN TO BOUTS-RIMÉS/
  VI
2. 1896, 1904: day, I sit and think—
3. MS: I wat<c>h the < > it [s] sink
  1896, 1904: sink,
4. 1896, 1904: soul-light, though the
  < > clear.
5. 1896, 1904: folly, it
6. 1896, 1904: Madness, to

7. MS: despair <&> yet [*fear to*]
  <not> break
  1896, 1904: despair, and yet
10. 1896, 1904: hope, and tremble
  thus,
11. 1896, 1904: day and miss < > ever.
12. 1896, 1904: broken, they
13. 1896, 1904: Say, "She < > us,
14. MS: [Below the poem is written:] 8
  minutes
  1896, 1904: hand."

"ALONG THE HIGHROAD THE WAY IS TOO LONG"

[Date of composition unknown. Christina's rough draft MS is in the Princeton University Library. Basic text: MS. In the MS, the text of the poem is written in pencil.]

1. MS: Along the high[*way*]<road>
  the [*road*] <way> is
3. MS: you take a c[*er*]<he>rry stick
7. MS: so [*I*]<in> good
9. MS: are c[*a*]<h>anged friend
11. MS: heart: [*a*]<i>nto your

12. MS: [Illegible deletion] <Oh>
  listen
13. MS: these shad[*ows*]<es that> have
14. MS: of ma[*ny*]<ny> suns. [Below
  the poem is written:] 6m.

"AND IS THIS AUGUST WEATHER? NAY NOT SO"

[Date of composition unknown. Editions: 1896, 1904. Christina's rough draft MS is in the Princeton University Library. Basic text: MS. In the MS, the text of the poem is written in pencil. In the 1896 and 1904 texts, lines 2, 3, 6, 7, 10, and 13 are indented two spaces; and lines 11 and 12 are indented four spaces.]

Title. 1896, 1904: SONNETS/
  WRITTEN TO BOUTS-RIMÉS/
  VII
1. 1896, 1904: weather? Nay, not so.
3. 1896, 1904: down! and hark
4. 1896, 1904: pace and slow
5. 1896, 1904: linger, being
7. MS: wet [illegible deletion] <for>
  that:
  1896, 1904: grandeur—it's
8. MS: drear [*we*]<se>ason cares
9. 1896, 1904: And, since < > is
  August, all

10. 1896, 1904: allowable; winter
  foregone
11. MS: glad [*f*] <w>armth more
  1896, 1904: sunlight and of < >
  warmth more.
13. MS: rain[*drops as they press down*]<.
  Hath the sun ever shone>
  1896, 1904: shone?
14. MS: [Below the poem is written:]
  6—
  1896, 1904: up! there

"FROM EARLY DAWN UNTIL THE FLUSH OF NOON"

[Date of composition unknown. Christina's rough draft MS is in the Princeton University Library. Basic text: MS. In the MS, the text of the poem is written in pencil.]

10. MS: The [*bosom of the*] sea <is full
    of life & beauty,> [*with*] how
11. MS: [Illegible deletion] <The
    grand waves leap up—as tho' full
    of> sense,

12. MS: [*Trust me*] <A> better
14. MS: [Below the poem is written:]
    8m

"I SEEK AMONG THE LIVING & I SEEK"

[Date of composition unknown. Editions: 1896, 1904. Christina's rough draft MS is
in the Princeton University Library. Basic text: MS. In the MS, the text of the poem
is written in pencil, with some ink revisions apparently in Dante Gabriel Rossetti's
handwriting. In the 1896 and 1904 texts, lines 2, 3, 6, 7, 10, and 14 are indented two
spaces; and lines 11 and 12 are indented four spaces.]

Title. 1896, 1904: SONNETS/
WRITTEN TO BOUTS-RIMÉS/
V
1. MS: I [*seek*] <sought> among
[The deletion and revision are in
ink in Dante Gabriel Rossetti's
hand.]
1896, 1904: I sought among < >
living, and I
2. 1896, 1904: dead, for
3. MS: I [*find*] <found> at last &
th[*e*]<*o*>se ha[*ve*]<d> quite run
[*th*] through [All the revisions but
the last one are in ink in Dante
Gabriel Rossetti's hand.]
1896, 1904: I found at last, and
those had quite
4. 1896, 1904: love; and friendship
< > weak,
5. MS: [*And*] <Too> cold [The
deletion and revision are in ink in
Dante Gabriel Rossetti's hand.]
1896, 1904: Too cold < > speak,
6. MS: my [*sorrow*] <heart want> to
[*cold*] <smooth> listeners [The
second revision is in ink in Dante
Gabriel Rossetti's hand.]
1896, 1904: my heart-want to
smooth listeners
7. MS: [*Will*] <Would> wonder
[The deletion and revision are in
ink in Dante Gabriel Rossetti's
hand.]
1896, 1904: Would wonder < >
bear and do—

8. MS: [*No tears shall sully my
unfurrowed*] <Hot shame shall dry
no tears upon my> cheek [The
revision is in ink in Dante Gabriel
Rossetti's hand.]
1896, 1904: Hot shame shall dry
no tears upon my cheek.
9. MS: [*T*]<S>o when
1896, 1904: So, when < > other
dust,
10. 1896, 1904: decay,
11. MS: cease [*to be & rot*] <like a
mere thought> [The deletion and
revision are in ink in Dante Gabriel
Rossetti's hand.]
1896, 1904: ease and cease like a
mere thought,—
12. MS: [*The*] <Those> whom I love[*d*]
thinking [*of*] <on> me [The
second and third revisions are in
ink in Dante Gabriel Rossetti's
hand.]
1896, 1904: whom I loved,
thinking on me, shall
13. MS: we [illegible deletion] <must>
1896, 1904: saying, "Now
14. MS: we [*go & play.*] <laugh
to-day.> [The deletion and
revision are in ink in Dante Gabriel
Rossetti's hand. Below the poem is
written:] 8—
1896, 1904: we laugh to-day."

"O GLORIOUS SEA THAT IN EACH CLIMBING WAVE"

[Date of composition unknown. Christina's rough draft MS is in the Princeton University Library. Basic text: MS. In the MS, the text of the poem is written in pencil.]

3. MS: earth [*have*] <oft> at
4. MS: [Illegible erasure] <And> not
5. MS: the [*ancient*] <mighty> winds
8. MS: [*You have*] <Thou hast> recalled
10. MS: they we[*re*]<ar>

12. MS: be [illegible deletion] <seasoned> well
13. MS: to [*we*] bear:—
14. MS: men: [*g*]<G>o back [Below the poem is written:] 8m.

"OH THOU WHO TELL'ST ME THAT ALL HOPE IS OVER"

[Date of composition unknown. Christina's rough draft MS is in the Princeton University Library. Basic text: MS. In the MS, the text of the poem is written in pencil.]

1. MS: who [illegible erasure] <tell'st> me
5. MS: [*A*]<R>ound &
8. MS: good [*s*]<t>ruth a
9. MS: [*O*] <Oh> take
10. MS: [*And*] <As> thou hast [illegible erasure] <ta'en> thy

12. MS: were [illegible erasure] <worse> than
14. MS: [Below the poem is written:] 8—

"SURELY THERE IS AN ACHING VOID WITHIN"

[Date of composition unknown. Christina's rough draft MS is in the Princeton University Library. Basic text: MS. In the MS, the text of the poem is written in pencil.]

2. MS: [*Within man*] <Man's spirit> unto
3. MS: unveiled [illegible deletion] <a>nd freely
4. MS: Would [*show*] <open> to

5. MS: [Illegible deletion] <And> folly
10. MS: Our o[*n*]<w>n selves
11. MS: on [*gr*] grace;
14. MS: [Below the poem is written:] 8.

"THE SPRING IS COME AGAIN NOT AS AT FIRST"

[Date of composition unknown. Christina's rough draft MS is in the Princeton University Library. Basic text: MS. In the MS, the text of the poem is written in pencil.]

7. MS: [Illegible erasure] <Hopes> all
8. MS: & curs[*ed*]<t>.
11. MS: did [*the*] <once>: when

13. MS: & [illegible erasure] <fill> the
14. MS: [Below the poem is written:] m5

"WHO SHALL MY WANDERING THOUGHTS STEADY & FIX"

[Date of composition unknown. Christina's rough draft MS is in the Princeton University Library. Basic text: MS. In the MS, the text of the poem is written in pencil.]

8. MS: Shall [illegible deletion]
   <know> all.

13. MS: is [*t*]<l>ined with
14. MS: [Below the poem is written:] 7

"YOU WHO LOOK ON PASSED AGES AS A GLASS"

[Date of composition unknown. Christina's rough draft MS is in the Princeton University Library. Basic text: MS. In the MS, the text of the poem is written in pencil, with some ink revisions apparently in Dante Gabriel Rossetti's handwriting.]

1. MS: [Illegible erasure] <You> who
2. MS: [*Glass*] <To shadow> forth
6. MS: And [illegible deletion]
   <solemn> sun
10. MS: hopeful [*pile*] <dream> [The deletion and revision are in ink in Dante Gabriel Rossetti's hand.]

11. MS: about i[*n*]<t> in
12. MS: [*And*] <For> if
13. MS: All [*of*] <as> the < > to [*smile*] <beam> [The second revision is in ink in Dante Gabriel Rossetti's hand.]
14. MS: [Below the poem is written:] 9

"ANGELI AL CAPO, AL PIEDE"

[Date of composition unknown. Editions: 1896, 1904. The copy of *Sing-Song* containing Christina's holograph MS of the poem is owned by Mrs. Roderic O'Conor; the text is written on p. 1, above "Angels at the foot." Basic text: MS.]

Title. 1896, 1904: NINNA-NANNA/ I/
[ANGELS AT THE FOOT]

1. 1896, 1904: piede;

"AMAMI, T'AMO"

[Date of composition unknown. Editions: 1896, 1904. The copy of *Sing-Song* containing Christina's holograph MS of the poem is owned by Mrs. Roderic O'Conor; the text is written on p. 2, above "Love me,—I love you." Basic text: MS. In the 1896 text, line 8 is not indented.]

Title. 1896, 1904: NINNA-NANNA/
2/ [LOVE ME, I LOVE YOU]
1. 1896s, 1904: Amami, t' amo,
4. 1896: [Because the line is the last on the page, it is impossible to determine if a stanza break is

intended to follow the line.]
1904: [A stanza break follows the line.]
5. 1896, 1904: Mamma t' abbraccia,
6. 1896, 1904: chiama;
8. 1896, 1904: chi t' ama.

"E BABBO E MAMMA HA IL NOSTRO FIGLIOLINO"

[Date of composition unknown. Editions: 1896, 1904. The copy of *Sing-Song* containing Christina's holograph MS of the poem is owned by Mrs. Roderic O'Conor; the text is written on p. 3, above "My baby has a father and a mother." Basic text: MS. In the 1896 and 1904 texts, lines 2, 4, and 5 are indented six spaces.]

Title. 1896, 1904: NINNA-NANNA/
3/ [MY BABY HAS A FATHER
AND A MOTHER]

2. 1896, 1904: bambino.

"S'ADDORMENTÒ LA NOSTRA FIGLIOLINA"

[Date of composition unknown. Editions: 1896, 1904. The copy of *Sing-Song* containing Christina's holograph MS of the poem is owned by Mrs. Roderic O'Conor; the text is written on p. 4, above "Our little baby fell asleep." Basic text: MS. In the 1896 and 1904 texts, lines 2, 4, and 6 are indented four spaces.]

Title. 1896, 1904: NINNA-NANNA/   1. 1896, 1904: S' addormentò la < >
4/ [OUR LITTLE BABY FELL   figliolina,
ASLEEP]   3. 1896, 1904: mattina.

"CUCCURUCÙ! CUCCURUCÙ!"

[Date of composition unknown. Editions: 1896, 1904. The copy of *Sing-Song* containing Christina's holograph MS of the poem is owned by Mrs. Roderic O'Conor; the text is written on p. 5, above "'Kookoorookoo! kookoorookoo!'" Basic text: MS. In the 1896 and 1904 texts, lines 4, 6, and 8 are not indented, and line 5 is indented two spaces.]

Title. 1896, 1904: NINNA-NANNA/   4. 1896, 1904: ciel s' ammanta.
5/ [KOOKOOROOKOO,   5. 1896, 1904: Cuccurucù—
KOOKOOROOKOO]   cuccurucù—
1. 1896, 1904: Cuccurucù—   6. MS: un gorgh<e>ggiare:
cuccurucù—   1896, 1904: gorgheggiare.
2. 1896, 1904: All' alba il < > canta.   7. 1896, 1904: Chicchirichì—
3. 1896, 1904: Chicchirichì—   chicchirichì—
chicchirichì—

"OIBÒ, PICCINA"

[Date of composition unknown. Editions: 1896, 1904. The copy of *Sing-Song* containing Christina's holograph MS of the poem is owned by Mrs. Roderic O'Conor; the text is written on p. 6, above "Baby cry." Basic text: MS. In the 1896 and 1904 texts, line 4 is not indented. In the 1896s text, lines 4 and 6 are not indented.]

Title. 1896, 1904: NINNA-NANNA/   4. 1896, 1904: de':
6/ [BABY CRY]   5. 1896, 1904: tre,
1. 1896, 1904: Ohibò piccina   6. 1896, 1904: finita.
2. 1896, 1904: atterrita!

"OTTO ORE SUONANO"

[Date of composition unknown. Editions: 1896, 1904. The copy of *Sing-Song* containing Christina's holograph MS of the poem is owned by Mrs. Roderic O'Conor; the text is written on p. 7, above "Eight o'clock." Basic text: MS. In the 1896 and 1904 texts, lines 1–3 and 8 are indented two spaces; and lines 4–6 are indented four spaces.]

Title. 1896, 1904: NINNA-NANNA/   1. 1896, 1904: suonano—
7/ [EIGHT O'CLOCK]   2. 1896, 1904: postino:

4. 1896: [Because the line is the last on the page, it is impossible to determine if a stanza break is intended to follow the line.]

1904: [A stanza break follows the line.]
8. 1896, 1904: V' è per

"NEL VERNO ACCANTO AL FUOCO"

[Date of composition unknown. Editions: 1896, 1904. A separate fair copy of the first version (MS1) is in the University of British Columbia Library. The copy of *Sing-Song* containing Christina's holograph MS of the poem (MS2) is owned by Mrs. Roderic O'Conor; the text is written on p. 8, the first version above "Bread and milk for breakfast," and the alternate version below. Basic text: MS2. In the 1896 text, lines 1 and 4 are indented four spaces; line 2 is indented six spaces; and line 3 is indented two spaces.]

Title. MS1: "Bread & milk for breakfast"—.
1896, 1904: NINNA-NANNA/ 8/ [BREAD AND MILK FOR BREAKFAST]
2. 1896, 1904: minestra,

4. 1896, 1904: Ch' ei pur
5. 1896, 1904: [OVVERO]
6. 1896: S' affaccia un < > finestra—
1904: finestra—
7. 1896, 1904: Vieni vieni < > minestra.

"GRAN FREDDO È INFUORI, E DENTRO È FREDDO UN POCO"

[Date of composition unknown. Editions: 1896, 1904. The copy of *Sing-Song* containing Christina's holograph MS of the poem is owned by Mrs. Roderic O'Conor; the text is written on p. 9, above "There's snow on the fields." Basic text: MS. In the 1896 and 1904 texts, lines 3 and 4 are indented two spaces.]

Title. 1896, 1904: NINNA-NANNA/ 9/ [THERE'S SNOW ON THE FIELDS]
5. 1896, 1904: bere e fuoco
6. 1896, 1904: tetto o panni in < > intenso—

7. MS: Ah [*che*] mi <si> [*duole*] <stringe> il cor mentr[*e*]<'io> ci
1896, 1904: cor mentre io ci penso.

"SCAVAI LA NEVE,—SÌ CHE SCAVAI!"

[Date of composition unknown. Editions: 1896, 1904. The copy of *Sing-Song* containing Christina's holograph MS of the poem is owned by Mrs. Roderic O'Conor; the text is written on p. 11, above "I dug and dug amongst the snow." Basic text: MS.]

Title. 1896, 1904. NINNA-NANNA/ 10/ [I DUG AND DUG AMONGST THE SNOW]
1. 1896, 1904: neve—sì < > scavai—

2. 1896, 1904: mai.
4. 1896, 1904: [No stanza break follows the line.]

"SÌ CHE IL FRATELLO S'HA UN FALCONCELLO"

[Date of composition unknown. Editions: 1896, 1904. The copy of *Sing-Song* containing Christina's holograph MS of the poem is owned by Mrs. Roderic O'Conor; the text is written on p. 13, above "Your brother has a falcon." Basic text: MS.]

Title. 1896, 1904: NINNA-NANNA/ 2. 1896, 1904: suora:
11/ [YOUR BROTHER HAS A 6. 1896, 1904: figliolino:
FALCON]
 1. MS: fratello [illegible deletion]
  <s'ha un> falconcello, <(*s'ha un*)>
  1896, 1904: fratello s' ha un

"UDITE, SI DOLGONO MESTI FRINGUELLI"

[Date of composition unknown. Editions: 1896, 1904. A separate fair copy MS (MS1) is in the University of British Columbia Library. The copy of *Sing-Song* containing Christina's holograph MS of the poem (MS2) is owned by Mrs. Roderic O'Conor; the text is written on p. 14, above "Hear what the mournful linnets say." Basic text: MS2. In MS1, line 6 is indented two spaces. In the 1896 and 1904 texts, line 6 is indented six spaces.]

Title. MS1: "Hear what the mournful 1. 1896, 1904: fringuelli:—
linnets say"—.   6. MS1: Bel nido rotondo.
1896, 1904: NINNA-NANNA/ 12/
[HEAR WHAT THE
MOURNFUL LINNETS SAY]

"AHI CULLA VUOTA! ED AHI SEPOLCRO PIENO"

[Date of composition unknown. Editions: 1896, 1904. The copy of *Sing-Song* containing Christina's holograph MS of the poem is owned by Mrs. Roderic O'Conor; the text is written on p. 15, above "A baby's cradle with no baby in it." Basic text: MS.]

Title. 1896, 1904: NINNA-NANNA/ 1. 1896, 1904: vuota ed
13/ [A BABY'S CRADLE WITH 3. 1896, 1904: in paradiso ameno,
NO BABY IN IT]

"LUGUBRE E VAGABONDO IN TERRA E IN MARE"

[Date of composition unknown. Editions: 1896, 1904. The copy of *Sing-Song* containing Christina's holograph MS of the poem is owned by Mrs. Roderic O'Conor; the text is written on p. 18, above "O wind, why do you never rest." Basic text: MS.]

Title. 1896: NINNA-NANNA/ 14/ [O WIND, WHY DO YOU NEVER
WIND WHY DO YOU NEVER REST?]
REST?]   3. 1896, 1904: fin dall' occidente,
1904: NINNA-NANNA/ 14/ [O

"AURA DOLCISSIMA, MA DONDE SIETE?—"

[Date of composition unknown. Editions: 1896, 1904. The copy of *Sing-Song* containing Christina's holograph MS of the poem is owned by Mrs. Roderic O'Conor; the text is written on p. 26, above "O wind, where have you been." Basic text: MS.]

Title. 1896: NINNA-NANNA/ 15/ [O
WIND WHERE HAVE YOU
BEEN?]
1904: NINNA-NANNA/ 15/ [O
WIND, WHERE HAVE YOU
BEEN?]
1. 1896, 1904: "Aura <> siete?"
1896s: "Aura <> ma dondo siete?"

2. 1896, 1904: "Dinfra<>
mammole—non
3. 1896, 1904: adocchiar l' erbetta
4. 1896, 1904: trovar l' ascosa
mammoletta.
6. 1896, 1904: mammoletta."

"FOSS'IO REGINA"

[Date of composition unknown. Editions: 1896, 1904. The copy of *Sing-Song* containing Christina's holograph MS of the poem is owned by Mrs. Roderic O'Conor; the text is written on p. 33, beside "If I were a Queen." Basic text: MS. In the 1896 and 1904 texts, lines 3 and 5 are indented four spaces; lines 4 and 8 are indented six spaces; and line 7 is not indented.]

Title. 1896, 1904: NINNA-NANNA/
16/ [IF I WERE A QUEEN]
1. 1896, 1904: "Foss' io regina,
4. 1896, 1904: M' inchinerei." [No
stanza break follows the line.]

5. 1896, 1904: "Ah foss' io re!
7. 1896, 1904: Sì che
8. 1896, 1904: farei."

"PESANO RENA E PENA"

[Date of composition unknown. Editions: 1896, 1904. The copy of *Sing-Song* containing Christina's holograph MS of the poem is owned by Mrs. Roderic O'Conor; the text is written on p. 34, above "What are heavy? sea-sand and sorrow." Basic text: MS. In the 1896 and 1904 texts, lines 1 and 2 are indented four spaces; line 4 is indented six spaces; and line 6 is indented two spaces.]

Title. 1896, 1904: NINNA-NANNA/
17/ [WHAT ARE HEAVY?
SEA-SAND AND SORROW]

"BASTA UNA NOTTE A MATURARE IL FUNGO"

[Date of composition unknown. Editions: 1896, 1904. The copy of *Sing-Song* containing Christina's holograph MS of the poem is owned by Mrs. Roderic O'Conor; the text is written on p. 40, above "A toadstool comes up in a night." Basic text: MS.]

Title. 1896, 1904: NINNA-NANNA/
18/ [A TOADSTOOL COMES UP
IN A NIGHT]

3. 1896, 1904: Anzi il <> lungo,
1896s: Anzi il <> e il vesprolungo,

"PORCO LA ZUCCA"

[Date of composition unknown. Editions: 1896, 1904. A separate fair copy MS (MS1) is in the University of British Columbia Library. The copy of *Sing-Song* containing Christina's holograph MS of the poem (MS2) is owned by Mrs. Roderic O'Conor; the text is written on p. 42, beside "If a pig wore a wig." Basic text: MS2. In the 1896 and 1904 texts, lines 3 and 5 are indented two spaces.]

Title. MS1: "If a pig wore a wig"—.
    1896, 1904: NINNA-NANNA/ 19/
    [IF A PIG WORE A WIG]
1. MS1: Porco, la
1–2. 1896: "Porco la zucca fitta in
    parrucca! . . .
    1904: 'Porco la zucca fitta in
    parrucca! . . .
2. MS1: parrucca,
3. MS1: gli faresti mai?—
    1896: mai?"
    1904: mai?'
4. MS1: l'ossequirei:
    1896: "M' inchinerei,
    l' ossequierei—
    1904: 'M' inchinerei,
    l' ossequierei—

5. MS1: stai?—
    1896: 'Ser <> stai?'" [No stanza
    break follows the line.]
    1904: "Ser <> stai?'" [No stanza
    break follows the line.]
6. 1896: "Ahi guai per
    1904: 'Ahi guai per
7. MS1: male?—
    1896: male?" . . .
    1904: male?' . . .
8–9. 1896: "Sta tranquillo—buon
    legale
    1904: 'Sta tranquillo—buon
    legale
10. 1896: codicillo."
    1904: codicillo.'

"SALTA, RANOCCHIO, E MOSTRATI"

[Date of composition unknown. Editions: 1896, 1904. The copy of *Sing-Song* containing Christina's holograph MS of the poem is owned by Mrs. Roderic O'Conor; the text is written on p. 56, above "Hopping frog, hop here and be seen." Basic text: MS.]

Title. 1896, 1904. NINNA-NANNA/
    20/ [HOPPING FROG, HOP
    HERE AND BE SEEN]

4. 1896, 1904: [No stanza break
    follows the line.]
7. 1896, 1904: mal vo' farti.

"SPUNTA LA MARGHERITA"

[Date of composition unknown. Editions: 1896, 1904. The copy of *Sing-Song* containing Christina's holograph MS of the poem is owned by Mrs. Roderic O'Conor; the text is written on p. 57, above "Where innocent bright-eyed daisies are." Basic text: MS. In the 1896 and 1904 texts, lines 2 and 4 are indented two spaces.]

Title. 1896, 1904: NINNA-NANNA/
    21/ [WHERE INNOCENT
    BRIGHT-EYED DAISIES ARE]

3. 1896, 1904: E l' erbetta infiorita

"AGNELLINA ORFANELLINA"

[Date of composition unknown. Editions: 1896, 1904. The copy of *Sing-Song* containing Christina's holograph MS of the poem is owned by Mrs. Roderic O'Conor;

the text is written on p. 61, above "A motherless soft lambkin." Basic text: MS. In the 1896 and 1904 texts, lines 4 and 8 are indented two spaces.]

Title. 1896, 1904: NINNA-NANNA/
22/ [A MOTHERLESS SOFT
LAMBKIN]

3. 1896, 1904: madre,
4. 1896, 1904: madre ohimè!
1896s: madre ohime!

"AMICO PESCE, PIOVER VORRÀ"

[Date of composition unknown. Editions: 1896, 1904. The copy of *Sing-Song* containing Christina's holograph MS of the poem is owned by Mrs. Roderic O'Conor; the text is written on p. 64, above "When fishes set umbrellas up." Basic text: MS. In the 1896 and 1904 texts, lines 1 and 2 are indented two spaces; line 3 is indented six spaces; and line 5 is indented four spaces.]

Title. 1896, 1904: NINNA-NANNA/
23/ [WHEN FISHES SET
UMBRELLAS UP]
1. 1896, 1904: vorrà;

2. 1896, 1904: Prendi l' ombrello se
4. 1904: si vedra
5. 1896, 1904: Lucertolon zerbino
6. 1896, 1904: sol coll' ombrellino.

"SPOSA VELATA"

[Date of composition unknown. Editions: 1896, 1904. The copy of *Sing-Song* containing Christina's holograph MS of the poem is owned by Mrs. Roderic O'Conor; the text is written on p. 90, above "A ring upon her finger." Basic text: MS. In the 1896 and 1904 texts, lines 4, 5, 8, and 9 are indented two spaces.]

Title. 1896, 1904: NINNA-NANNA/
24/ [A RING UPON HER
FINGER]
2. MS: In[n]anellata, [The deletion is
in pencil.]
1896, 1904: Inanellata,

6. 1896, 1904: essa.
8. 1904: coro
10. 1896, 1904: fiori.

"CAVALLI MARITTIMI"

[Date of composition unknown. Editions: 1896, 1904. A separate fair copy MS (MS1) is in the University Of British Columbia Library. The copy of *Sing-Song* containing Christina's holograph MS of the poem (MS2) is owned by Mrs. Roderic O'Conor; the text is written on p. 94, beside "The horses of the sea." Basic text: MS2. In MS1 and the 1896 and 1904 texts, lines 6 and 8 are indented two spaces.]

Title. MS1: "The horses of the sea"—.
1896, 1904: NINNA-NANNA/ 25/
[THE HORSES OF THE SEA]
6. MS1: stanno,
1896, 1904: stanno;
6–7. [In an undated letter (now in the
University of British Columbia
Library) to Dante Gabriel
Rossetti, Christina writes:
"'—rotolandosi, spumando,

vanno'—gave, I thought,
something of the accumulative
on-come of the waves, mounting
on each other's backs: otherwise
I am not aware of any reason
against 'spumanti' as you suggest;
or one might obliterate the
sound yet more by making it
'spumosi'—."]

"O MARINARO CHE MI APPORTI TU?"

[Date of composition unknown. Editions: 1896, 1904. A separate fair copy MS (MS1) is in the University of British Columbia Library. The copy of *Sing-Song* containing Christina's holograph MS of the poem (MS2) is owned by Mrs. Roderic O'Conor; the text is written on p. 95, beside "O sailor, come ashore." Basic text: MS2. In MS1, lines 3 and 6 are indented two spaces. In the 1896 and 1904 texts, lines 3 and 6 are indented six spaces.]

Title. MS1: "O Sailor come ashore"—.
1896, 1904: NINNA-NANNA/ 26/
[O SAILOR, COME ASHORE]
1. MS1: O Marinaro, che <> tu?—
1896, 1904: "O marinaro, che <> tu?"

2. 1896, 1904: "Coralli
4. MS1: si trovaro in mina:
1896, 1904: son nè
6. 1896, 1904: mondo."

"ARROSSISCE LA ROSA: E PERCHÈ MAI?"

[Date of composition unknown. Editions: 1896, 1904. The copy of *Sing-Song* containing Christina's holograph MS of the poem is owned by Mrs. Roderic O'Conor; the text is written on p. 111, above "The rose with such a bonny blush." Basic text: MS. In the 1896 text, line 3 is indented four spaces. In the 1904 text, line 3 is indented six spaces.]

Title. 1896, 1904: NINNA-NANNA/
27/ [THE ROSE WITH SUCH A
BONNY BLUSH]
1. 1896: Arrossice la rosa—e
1904: rosa—e

2. 1896, 1904: ma, sol, che
3. 1896, 1904: tu, rosa, che t' hai

"LA ROSA CHINA IL VOLTO ROSSEGGIATO"

[Date of composition unknown. Editions: 1896, 1904. The copy of *Sing-Song* containing Christina's holograph MS of the poem is owned by Mrs. Roderic O'Conor; the text is written on p. 112, above "The rose that blushes rosy red." Basic text: MS. In the 1896 and 1904 texts, lines 2 and 4 are indented eight spaces.]

Title. 1896, 1904: NINNA-NANNA/
28/ [THE ROSE THAT BLUSHES
ROSY RED]

2. 1896, 1904: bene fà:
4. 1896, 1904: gli stà.

"O CILIEGIA INFIORITA"

[Date of composition unknown. Editions: 1896, 1904. A separate fair copy MS (MS1) is in the University of British Columbia Library. The copy of *Sing-Song* containing Christina's holograph MS of the poem (MS2) is owned by Mrs. Roderic O'Conor; the text is written on p. 113, above "Oh, fair to see." Basic text: MS2. In MS1 and the 1896 and 1904 texts, lines 4 and 8 are indented two spaces.]

Title. MS1: "Oh fair to see"—.
　1896, 1904: NINNA-NANNA/ 29/
　[OH FAIR TO SEE]
2. MS1: La bianco<->rivestita
　1896, 1904: La bianco-rivestita,
3. 1896, 1904: [The line is not in the
　text.]
4. 1896, 1904: tu.

6. MS1: La verde<->inghirlandata,
　1896, 1904: La
　verde-inghirlandata,
7. MS1: La
　rosso<->[*corono*]<->incoronata,
　1896, 1904: La rosso-incoronata,
8. 1896, 1904: tu.

"'IN TEMA E IN PENA ADDIO"

[Date of composition unknown. Editions: 1896, 1904. The copy of *Sing-Song* containing Christina's holograph MS of the poem is owned by Mrs. Roderic O'Conor; the text is written on p. 120, above "'Goodbye in fear, goodbye in sorrow." Basic text: MS. In the 1896 and 1904 texts, lines 4 and 8 are indented four spaces.]

Title. 1896, 1904: NINNA-NANNA/
　30/ [GOOD-BYE IN FEAR,
　GOOD-BYE IN SORROW]
1. MS: "In [*p*]<t>ema e
　1896, 1904: addio,

3. 1896, 1904: mio."
6. 1896, 1904: secolo de' guai
7. 1896, 1904: addio."

"D'UN SONNO PROFONDISSIMO"

[Date of composition unknown. Editions: 1896, 1904. The copy of *Sing-Song* containing Christina's holograph MS of the poem is owned by Mrs. Roderic O'Conor; the text is written on p. 127, above "Baby lies so fast asleep." Basic text: MS.]

Title. 1896, 1904: NINNA-NANNA/
　31/ [BABY LIES SO FAST
　ASLEEP]
1. 1896: D' un sonno
　1904: 'D' un sonno

4. 1904: via?'
5. 1904: 'In
8. 1896: fronte—e pace.
　1904: fronte—e pace.'

"NINNA NANNA, NINNA NANNA!"

[Date of composition unknown. Editions: 1896, 1904. The copy of *Sing-Song* containing Christina's holograph MS of the poem is owned by Mrs. Roderic O'Conor; the text is written on p. 129, above "Lullaby, oh, lullaby!" Basic text: MS. In the 1896 and 1904 texts, lines 2, 4, 6, and 8 are indented two spaces.]

Title. 1896, 1904: NINNA-NANNA/
　32/ [LULLABY OH LULLABY]
1. 1896, 1904: Ninna-nanna,
　ninna-nanna,
2. 1896, 1904: dorme l' agnellina.
3. 1896, 1904: Ninna-nanna,
　ninna-nanna,
4. 1896, 1904: Monna Luna
　s' incammina.

5. 1896, 1904: Ninna-nanna,
　ninna-nanna,
6. 1896, 1904: dorme l' uccellino.
7. 1896, 1904: Ninna-nanna,
　ninna-nanna,
8. 1896, 1904: Dormi, dormi, o
　figliolino.
9. 1896, 1904: Ninna-nanna,
　ninna-nanna.

"CAPO CHE CHINASI,—"

[Date of composition unknown. Editions: 1896, 1904. The copy of *Sing-Song* containing Christina's holograph MS of the poem is owned by Mrs. Roderic O'Conor; the text is written on p. 130, beside "Lie a-bed." Basic text: MS. In the 1896 and 1904 texts, lines 5 and 7 are not indented.]

Title. 1896, 1904: NINNA-NANNA/
    33/ [LIE A-BED]
  1. 1896, 1904: chinasi,
  2. MS: Oc[illegible

    erasure]<c>h[illegible
    deletion]<i> che
    1896, 1904: chiudonsi—
  6. 1896, 1904: mattino,—

THE SUCCESSION OF KINGS.

[Date of composition unknown. Christina's unsigned fair copy MS is in the Princeton University Library. Basic text: MS.]

Title. MS: [In the upper right margin
    is added in pencil in William
    Michael Rossetti's hand:]
    <Unpublished/ (very early)>
  7. MS: signed Magna Charta [illegible
    erasure]<t> Runnymede.

32. MS: Which [*Willia*]<*third*> William
34. MS: [In the right margin is added
    in pencil in William Michael
    Rossetti's hand:] <? 46>

A TRUE STORY.

[Date of composition unknown. The MS fragment, in the handwriting of Christina's mother, Frances Mary Lavinia Polidori Rossetti, is in the University of Kansas Library. Basic text: MS. On the reverse side of the MS, William Michael Rossetti has written: "These are early poems (say 1847) by Christina G. Rossetti. The handwriting at back is my mother's."]

  8. MS: dagger [illegible deletion]
    <bares;>

"THE TWO ROSSETTIS (BROTHERS THEY)"

[Composed September 19, 1853. Editions: 1904. The MS, which forms part of a letter, is in the University of British Columbia Library. Basic text: MS.]

Title. 1904: THE P.R.B./ I
  1. MS: two Rossettis <(>brothers
  3. MS: [*And*] <With> Stephens
  4. MS: [Illegible deletion] <And>
    Woolner
    1904: land—
  8. 1904: view;
  10. 1904: say. [A stanza break follows

    the line; the asterisks are not in the
    text.]
  11. 1904: William Rossetti, calm <>
    solemn,
  12. MS: his br[*o*]<e>th[*ers*]<ren> by
    1904: [There are no asterisks below
    the line.]

IMITATED FROM THE ARPA EVANGELICA: PAGE 121.

[Date of composition unknown. Editions: 1896, 1904. A fair copy of lines 1–32 (MS1), signed "Christina G. Rossetti," is in the Princeton University Library. A fair copy of lines 33–65 (MS2), signed "C.G.R.," is in the British Library. Basic text: lines 1–32: MS1; lines 33–65: MS2. In the 1896 edition, William Michael Rossetti notes, "In our father's volume of religious poems, *L' Arpa Evangelica* (1852), there is a composition named *Nell' Atto della Communione*, in three parts. The third begins with the words—'T' amo, e fra dolci affanni,' and is the one which Christina here translates in two separate versions. The date which I give is conjectural; I assume the translation to have been made not long after our father's death" (pp. 389–90). In MS1, the first and second stanzas are written side by side on the front of the sheet, and the third and fourth stanzas are written side by side on the back of the sheet. In the 1896 and 1904 editions, lines 33–65 are presented as the "First Version," and lines 1–32 are presented afterward as the "Second Version."]

Title. 1896, 1904: HYMN AFTER
     GABRIELE ROSSETTI
2. 1896, 1904: said,
3. 1896, 1904: "Blessed that John
     who on Thy breast
4. 1896, 1904: head."
5. 1896, 1904: all divine
10. 1896, 1904: Nay not
11. 1896, 1904: both Man and God,
15. 1896, 1904: forth,
16. 1896, 1904: In fullness filling
19. 1896, 1904: Lord, reign
24. 1896, 1904: My Manna and my
25. 1896, 1904: that Thy life lives
26. 1896, 1904: sways and warms it
     through,
29. 1896, 1904: O God, who dwellest
30. 1896, 1904: My God who fillest
32. MS1: [In the bottom left margin of
     the sheet is added in pencil in
     William Michael Rossetti's hand:]
     <Circa 1855>

33. 1896: T' amo e <> affanni
     1904: T' amo e <> affanni.
34. 1896: My Lord, my Love! in
     1904: My Lord, my love! in
35. 1896, 1904: said,
36. 1896, 1904: on Thy breast
41. 1896, 1904: love.
42. 1896, 1904: envy blessed John?
43. 1904: Nay not
44. MS2: [Illegible deletion] <While>
     Thou
48. 1896, 1904: Yea Thy
49. 1896, 1904: In fullness filling
54. 1896s: in ecstacy
56. 1896, 1904: tasted Thee,
59. 1896, 1904: me through,
60. 1896, 1904: globe,
62. 1896, 1904: O God, who for Thy
     dwelling-place

"MR. AND MRS. SCOTT, AND I"

[Date of composition unknown. The MS, which is owned by Mr. Robert H. Taylor, is in the Princeton University Library. Basic text: MS.]

9. MS: Not [illegible erasure]
     <neighbour> Humble

"GONE TO HIS REST"

[Date of composition unknown. The unsigned fair copy MS is in the Princeton University Library. Basic text: MS. In the MS, above the border enclosing the text of the poem is added in pencil in an unidentified hand: "Feb' 6. 1869." Below the border is added in pencil in an unidentified hand: "On the death of AB's chaffinch Bouby." The MS text is written in double columns, the first two stanzas in the left column and the last two stanzas in the right.]

20. MS: [In the right corner below   unidentified hand:] <Christina
     the line is added in pencil in an   R.>

"O UOMMIBATTO"

[Date of composition unknown. Editions: 1896, 1904. The MS is in the Princeton University Library. Basic text: MS. In the MS, the poem is written in pencil, over which the text is recopied in ink. In the 1896 and 1904 texts, lines 2, 4, 6, 8, and 11 are indented two spaces.]

Title. 1896, 1904: L' UOMMIBATTO   is written in pencil. In the lower
  1. 1904: O UOMMIBATTO,   right margin is added in pencil in
 10. 1896, 1904: D' un emisfero   William Michael Rossetti's hand:]
 11. MS: [Illegible erasure] [*immenso*]   <[*C 69*]>/ <[*Circa*] 1869.>
     <Non lieve il> pondo! [The line

"COR MIO, COR MIO"

[Date of composition unknown. Editions: 1896, 1904. The MS is in the Princeton University Library. Basic text: MS. In the MS, the text is written in pencil. In the 1896 and 1904 texts, lines 2, 3, and 6 are indented two spaces; and lines 4 and 7 are indented four spaces.]

Title. 1896, 1904: COR MIO   pencil in William Michael Rossetti's
  7. MS: [Below the poem is added in   hand:] <[*C 70*]/ Circa 1870>

"I SAID 'ALL'S OVER'—& I MADE MY"

[Date of composition unknown. The partial MS is in the Princeton University Library. Basic text: MS. In the MS, the text of the poem is written in pencil, over which the text is recopied in ink. The text is deleted with diagonal lines written in ink.]

  7. MS: & all [written in pencil]   8. MS: & hope [written in pencil]

"I SAID GOOD BYE IN HOPE"

[Date of composition unknown. Editions: 1896, 1904. The MS is in the Princeton University Library. Basic text: MS. In the MS, the poem is written in pencil, over which the text is recopied in ink. In the 1896 text, lines 2, 3, 8, 10, and 21 are indented two spaces; and lines 6, 12, 18, and 24 are indented four spaces. In the 1904 text, lines 2, 3, 8, 10, and 21 are indented two spaces; and lines 6, 12, 18, and 24 are indented six spaces.]

Title. MS: [In the upper right corner
   of the MS is added in William
   Michael Rossetti's hand:]
   <Meeting.>
   1896, 1904: MEETING
1. 1896, 1904: said good-bye in hope;
2. 1896, 1904: But, now <> again,
4. 1896, 1904: pain,—
5. 1896, 1904: parting and our
7. 1896, 1904: on through all
8. 1896, 1904: dear friend:
9. MS: [*Life*] Live thro'
   1896, 1904: Live through your

10. 1896, 1904: joy and promise
   blend—
11. MS: will li[*f*]<v>e my
14. 1896, 1904: your fig-tree spread,
19. MS: [Illegible deletion] <Yet>
   when
   1896, 1904: Yet, when
23. 1896, 1904: bitterness,
24. MS: past [Below the poem is added
   in pencil in William Michael
   Rossetti's hand:] <C 75>/ <Circa
   1875>

MY MOUSE.

[Composed January 1, 1877. Editions: 1896, 1904. The fair copy MS, signed
"C.G.R.," is in the British Library. Basic text: MS.]

Title. 1896, 1904: MY MOUSE
3. 1896, 1904: way and at
7. 1896, 1904: of sweet herbs flower
13. 1896, 1904: Venus-cum-Iris
   Mouse,

16. MS: [Below the line is written:]
   New Year 1877.

"HAD FORTUNE PARTED US"

[Date of composition unknown. Editions: 1896, 1904. A fair copy MS, signed
"C.G.R.," is in the Princeton University Library. Basic Text: MS. In the MS, the text
is written in pencil. In the 1896 and 1904 texts, lines 1, 3, 5, and 7 are indented two
spaces; and lines 2, 4, 6, 8, 10, 12, 14, and 16 are indented four spaces.]

Title. MS: [Above the poem is added
   in pencil in William Michael
   Rossetti's hand:] <Parted.>
   1896, 1904: PARTED
1. 1896, 1904: us,
2. 1896, 1904: blind;
3. 1896, 1904: us,
6. 1896, 1904: humbly,
8. 1896, 1904: Bravely and dumbly.

11. MS: not [*shut*] <close> that
16. MS: [In the lower left corner of
   the MS is written in pencil:] Una
   replica/ Lo vedesti, Cor mio. [In
   the right margin is added in pencil
   in William Michael Rossetti's hand:]
   <Circa 1880>
   1896, 1904: thee, Beloved.

COUNTERBLAST ON PENNY TRUMPET.

[Date of composition unknown. Editions: 1896, 1904. The MS is in the British Li-
brary. Basic text: MS.]

Title. 1896, 1904: COUNTERBLAST
   ON PENNY TRUMPET

Subtitle. MS: <"When raged the
   conflict, fierce & hot.">

506 The Complete Poems of Christina Rossetti

1896, 1904: [The subtitle is not in
the text.]
1. 1896, 1904: please,
4. MS: [Below line 4 is the following
deleted stanza:]

[*"I never said I loved you, John"—not you!*
Nor gift nor grace of hi[m]<s> makes
him your toast:
Or if you toast, under an aspect new
In effigy to roast.]

1896s: [No stanza break follows the
line.]
8. 1896, 1904: least and last
12. MS: [Below the poem is written:]
C<.>G<.>R<.>/ *see* St. James's
Gazette/ July 21.1882./ (*motive* a
Poem).

"A ROUNDEL SEEMS TO FIT A ROUND OF DAYS"

[Date of composition unknown. A fair copy MS is in the University of British Co-
lumbia Library. Basic text: MS.]

11. MS: [Below the poem is written:]
W.B.S. spurns the birthday
(Sept.12.1887) tribute of CGR:

tableau visible to the "fine frenzied"
mental eye.

"HEAVEN OVERARCHES EARTH AND SEA"

[Date of composition unknown. Editions: 1896, 1904. Christina's rough draft (MS1)
is in the Princeton University Library. A fair copy MS (MS2) is in the Bodleian Li-
brary. Basic text: MS2. In MS1, the text is written in pencil with some ink revisions,
and no lines are indented.]

Title. MS1: [Above the poem is added
in pencil in William Michael
Rossetti's hand:] <Heaven
over-arches>
1896, 1904: HEAVEN
OVERARCHES
1. MS1: earth & sea
2. MS1: Earth sadness & sea
bitterness
1896, 1904: sea-bitterness.
3. MS1: you & me
4. MS1: while & we
1896, 1904: while and < > be—
5. 1896, 1904: Please God—where
6. MS1: Nor [*parting has distress*]
<barren wilderness.>
1896, 1904: Nor barren
7. MS1: you & me
1896, 1904: me,

8. MS1: gardens & her graves
1896, 1904: graves.
9. MS1: me = [*we both shall see*] <until
we see> [The revision is in ink.]
10. MS1: break & the < > flee
1896, 1904: flee.
11. MS1: What [*if today*] <tho' night>
wrecks you & me [The revision is
in ink.]
1896, 1904: What though to-night
wrecks < > me
12. MS1: [*So that*] <If so> tomorrow
[The revision is in ink. Below the
poem is added and deleted in
pencil in William Michael Rossetti's
hand:] <[*C 93*]>
1896, 1904: so to-morrow saves?

"SLEEPING AT LAST, THE TROUBLE AND TUMULT OVER"

[Date of composition unknown. Editions: 1896, 1904. The unsigned fair copy MS is
in the British Library. Basic text: MS. On the back of the MS is added in pencil in

William Michael Rossetti's hand: "13/2/95—I found these verses at Christina's house, in a millboard-case containing some recent memoranda &c—nothing of old date—The verses must I think be the last that C. ever wrote—perhaps late in 1893, or early in 94/ WMRossetti." In the 1896 and 1904 texts, lines 2, 5, 7, and 9 are indented two spaces; and lines 4 and 11 are indented six spaces.]

Title. 1896, 1904: SLEEPING AT
    LAST
  1. 1896, 1904: trouble and tumult
  2. 1896, 1904: struggle and horror
  3. 1896, 1904: Cold and white, out
    < > friend and of lover,

  5. MS: more [*of*] <a> tired
  6. MS: pangs that wring[*s*] or
10. 1896, 1904: thyme and the

4TH MAY MORNING.

[Date of composition unknown. The fair copy MS, signed "C.G.R.," is in the Princeton University Library. Basic text: MS.]

10. MS: (<—>Do
17. MS: with polite[illegible
    deletion]<n>ess,

"'QUANTO A LEI GRATA IO SONO"

[Date of composition unknown. The fair copy MS, signed "C.G.R.," is in the Princeton University Library. Basic text: MS.]

THE CHINAMAN.

[William Michael Rossetti dates the poem "1842." Editions: 1904. The poem was first published in William Michael Rossetti (ed.), *Dante Gabriel Rossetti: His Family-Letters, with a Memoir by William Michael Rossetti* (2 vols.; London: Ellis and Elvey, 1895), I, 79. Basic text: 1895.]

Title. 1904: THE CHINAMAN
  1. 1895: "'Centre
  4. 1904: sight;

11. 1904: soon, alas, perceives.
18. 1895: funeral-pyre."

"'COME CHEER UP, MY LADS, 'TIS TO GLORY WE STEER!'"

[William Michael Rossetti dates the poem "*Circa* 1845." Editions: 1904. The poem was first published in William Michael Rossetti (ed.), *Dante Gabriel Rossetti: His Family-Letters, with a Memoir by William Michael Rossetti* (2 vols.; London: Ellis and Elvey, 1895), I, 78. Basic text: 1895.]

Title. 1904: COUPLET
  1. 1895: "'Come
    1904: steer'—

2. 1895: rear."

THE PLAGUE

[William Michael Rossetti dates the poem *"August* 1848." Editions: 1896, 1904. Basic text: 1896.]

Title. 1896, 1904: IX—THE PLAGUE

"HOW MANY AUTHORS ARE MY FIRST!"

[William Michael Rossetti dates the poem *"Spring* 1849." Editions: 1896, 1904. Basic text: 1896. William Michael Rossetti notes that the charade was published in *Marshall's Ladies' Daily Remembrancer* (1850), but I was unable to find it in that work.]

Title. 1896: TWO CHARADES/ II
       1904: TWO CHARADES/ 2

"ME YOU OFTEN MEET"

[William Michael Rossetti dates the poem *"Spring* 1849." Editions: 1896, 1904. Basic text: 1896. William Michael Rossetti notes that the enigma was published in *Marshall's Ladies' Daily Remembrancer* (1850), but I was unable to find it in that work.]

Title. 1896: TWO ENIGMAS/ II
       1904: TWO ENIGMAS/ 2

"SO I BEGAN MY WALK OF LIFE; NO STOP"

[The poem is appended to a letter dated August 31, 1849. The poem was published in William Michael Rossetti (ed.), *The Family Letters of Christina Georgina Rossetti, with some Supplementary Letters and Appendices* (London: Brown, Langham; New York: Scribner's Sons, 1908), 8. Basic text: 1908.]

"SO I GREW HALF DELIRIOUS AND QUITE SICK"

[The typescript letter containing the poem is dated September 24, 1849. Editions: 1904. William Michael Rossetti's typescript of the poem is in the Princeton University Library. Basic text: typescript. In the 1904 text, lines 2, 3, 6, 7, 10, 11, and 13 are indented two spaces.]

Title. 1904: A BOUTS-RIMÉS
       SONNET
  1. typescript: sick<,> [The comma is
     added by hand.]
  2. 1904: And through the
  3. typescript: fin<,> [The comma is
     added by hand.]
     1904: Of monsters at
  4. 1904: clammily. I

  6. 1904: din,
 10. 1904: me. Then sleep
 11. 1904: true.
 12. 1904: height;
 13. typescript: And I [*slept*] <wept>
     sadly‡<,> knowing [The semicolon
     is typed over the letter. The
     deletion and additions are done by
     hand.]

"ON THE NOTE YOU DO NOT SEND ME"

[The typescript letter containing the poem is dated January 18, 1850. William Michael Rossetti's typescript of the poem is in the Princeton University Library. Basic text: typescript. In the letter, which is addressed to William Michael Rossetti, Christina states, "Will you recite to Gabriel the following admonitory stanza:—" Following the poem she adds: "The last line is a little mystic. Never mind."]

CHARON

[William Michael Rossetti dates the poem "*June* 1853." Editions: 1896, 1904. Basic text: 1896. In the 1904 edition, William Michael Rossetti notes, "When first published (1896), the verses were entitled by me *Near the Styx;* but I now gather that Christina's own name for them was *Charon*" (p. 491).]

Title. 1896: NEAR THE STYX

FROM METASTASIO

[William Michael Rossetti dates the poem "1857—or earlier rather than later" in the 1896 edition, and "1868 or rather earlier" in the 1904 edition. Editions: 1896, 1904. Basic text: 1896.]

3. 1904: best belovèd,

CHIESA E SIGNORE

[William Michael Rossetti dates the poem "perhaps towards 1860." Editions: 1896, 1904. Basic text: 1896.]

9. 1896s: scordai

GOLDEN HOLLY

[William Michael Rossetti dates the poem "*Circa* 1872." Editions: 1896, 1904. Basic text: 1896.]

"I TOILED ON, BUT THOU"

[William Michael Rossetti dates the poem "*Circa* 1875" in the 1896 edition, and "*Circa* 1884" in the 1904 edition. Editions: 1896, 1904. Basic text: 1896. In the 1896 and 1904 editions, lines 1, 3, 6, 8, 11, 13, and 15 are indented two spaces; lines 2, 7, and 12 are indented four spaces; and lines 4, 9, and 14 are indented six spaces.]

Title. 1896, 1904: WHO SHALL SAY?

COR MIO

[William Michael Rossetti dates the poem "*Circa* 1875." Editions: 1896, 1904. Basic
text: 1896. Christina incorporated lines 9–14 into a sonnet entitled "Later Life./
18," which she published in *A Pageant and Other Poems* (1881); for text and notes to
that poem, see Volume II of the present edition, pp. 146, 390.]

3. 1896s: due

"MY OLD ADMIRATION BEFORE I WAS TWENTY"

[William Michael Rossetti dates the poem "*Spring* 1882." Editions: 1904. The poem
was published in William Bell Scott, *Autobiographical Notes of the Life of William Bell
Scott* (2 vols.; New York: Harper and Brothers, 1892), I, 314. Basic text: 1892.]

Title. 1904: TO WILLIAM BELL
  SCOTT
  1. 1904: twenty

2. 1904: se'enty.
6. 1892: heart. C.G.R.

TO MARY ROSSETTI

[William Michael Rossetti dates the poem "*Circa* 1887." Editions: 1904. Basic text:
1904.]

"NE' SOGNI TI VEGGO"

[William Michael Rossetti dates the poem "*Circa* 1890." Editions: 1896, 1904. Basic
text: 1896.]

Title. 1896, 1904: SOGNANDO [In
  the 1896 edition William Michael
  Rossetti notes, "I give this title to
  two stanzas which I find written by
  Christina into a copy of our father's

book of sacred poems—*Il Tempo,
  ovvero Dio e l' Uomo, Salterio,* 1843"
  (p. 394).]
8. 1904: [A stanza break follows the
  line.]

TO MY FIOR-DI-LISA

[William Michael Rossetti dates the poem "1892." Editions: 1896, 1904. Basic text:
1896. In the 1904 text, lines 2, 4, 6, and 8 are indented four spaces.]

5. 1904: harmony;

"HAIL, NOBLE FACE OF NOBLE FRIEND."

[The poem is appended to a letter dated December 19, 1885. The poem was first
published in Lona Mosk Packer, "Christina Rossetti and Alice Boyd of Penkill
Castle," *Times Literary Supplement,* June 26, 1959, p. 389. Basic text: 1959.]

HYMN ["O THE BITTER SHAME AND SORROW"]

[Date of composition unknown. The fair copy MS, which does not appear to be in Christina's handwriting, is in the Princeton University Library. Basic text: MS.]

5. MS: none of Thee.
18. MS: last ha[s]<th> conquered,

20. MS: "None [Below the poem is written:] Christina Rossetti.

Appendixes to Volume III

A. *Extant Indexes from Christina Rossetti's Manuscript Notebooks of Poetry* *

April 27, 1842–December 3, 1845

[The MS notebook is in the British Library. The index, which is in the handwriting of Christina's sister, Maria Francesca Rossetti, follows p. 62 of the notebook.]

Index.

December 4, 1845–September 11, 1846

[The MS notebook is in the Bodleian Library. The index, which is in the handwriting of Christina's sister, Maria Francesca Rossetti, follows p. 58 of the notebook.]

Index.

*In the MSS, the indexes are written in a single column that spans the notebook page.

September 16, 1846–April 17, 1847

[The MS notebook is in the Bodleian Library. The index, which is in the handwriting of Christina's sister, Maria Francesca Rossetti, follows p. 63 of the notebook.]

Index.

[April,] 1847–December, 1847

[The MS notebook is in the Bodleian Library. The index follows p. 63 of the notebook.]

Index.

December, 1847–June 1, 1848

[The MS notebook is in the Bodleian Library. The index follows p. 61 of the notebook.]

Index.

———

June 18, 1848–April 28, 1849

[The MS notebook is in the Bodleian Library. The index follows p. 62 of the notebook.]

Index.

———

May 15, 1849–May 14, 1850

[The MS notebook is in the Bodleian Library. The index follows p. 63 of the notebook.]

Index

May 25, 1850–May 18, 1853

[The MS notebook is in the Bodleian Library. The index follows p. 68 of the notebook.]

Index.

———

May, 1853–June 28, 1854

[The MS notebook is in the Bodleian Library. The index follows p. 70 of the notebook.]

Index.

July 25, 1854–May 9, 1856

[The MS notebook is in the Bodleian Library. The index follows p. 78 of the notebook.]

Index.
———

June 17, 1856–December 13, 1856

[The MS notebook is in the British Library. The index follows p. 79 of the notebook.]

Index.

———

December 18, 1856–June 29, 1858

[The MS notebook is in the British Library. The index follows p. 64 of the notebook (p. 64 of the notebook is now in the Huntington Library).]

Index.

———

June 29, 1858–February 15, 1859

[The MS notebook is in the British Library. The index follows p. 64 of the notebook.]

Index.

———

March 23, 1861–March 24, 1863

[The MS notebook is in the British Library. The index follows p. 78 of the notebook.]

Index

———

April 24, 1863–August 26, 1864

[The MS notebook is in the British Library. The index follows p. 78 of the notebook.]

Index.

Verses [1893]

[The MS notebook is in the King's School. The index follows the title page of the notebook. The index of first lines follows p. 373 of the notebook.]

Index.

Index of First Lines.

B. Corrections and Additions to Volume I

p. 308

THE GERMAN-FRENCH CAMPAIGN.

[A rough draft MS of lines 25–28 is in the Princeton University Library. In the rough draft, the text is written in pencil below "In resurrection is it awfuller," and no lines are indented.]

25. MS: Oh thou King terrible < > strength & building
26. MS: Thy <terrible> [illegible deletion] <future on> thy past
27. MS: Tho he dr the last <the K of Shisak>
28. MS: Yet shall dr at the last

p. 310

PARADISE.

[The poem was published in Orby Shipley (ed.), *Lyra Messianica: Hymns and Verses on the Life of Christ, Ancient and Modern; with Other Poems* (2nd ed., London: Longmans, Green, and Co., 1869), 365–66.]

Title. 1869: Paradise: in a Dream. [The title is in Gothic print.]
22. 1869: rest:
34. 1869: look, within;
38. 1869: green palm-branches many-leaved—
44. 1869: touch, and handle, and
47. 1869: the Saints,

C. Corrections and Additions to Volume II

p. 394

THE DESCENT FROM THE CROSS.

[A partial MS containing the last several words of each line is in the Princeton University Library. In the MS, the text is in pencil, written over in ink.]

1. MS: [*fills*] <thrills> with awe [The deletion and revision are in ink.]
2. MS: ce above,
3. MS: a flaw
4. MS: e of Love?
5. MS: less clod
6. MS: e sufficed
7. MS: of God,
8. MS: sus Xt.

p. 397

"A HELPMEET FOR HIM."

[The poem was published in *"New and Old:" For Seed-Time and Harvest,* XVI (January, 1888), 22.]

5. 1888: overlaid,
6. 1888: might,
7. 1888: Firm she stands tho' sometime dismayed.

p. 400

"ALONE LORD GOD, IN WHOM OUR TRUST AND PEACE"

[The notebook MS is in the King's School.]

1. MS: trust & peace,
2. MS: love & our
4. MS: begin & cease,
8. MS: Bending & stretching
10. MS: patience & desire,
11. MS: loving so & so <> pray:
12. MS: Thy Will be

p. 401

"SEVEN VIALS HOLD THY WRATH: BUT WHAT CAN HOLD"
[The notebook MS is in the King's School.]
  8. MS: the Same, & Manifold.
12. MS: in & comforted:

"WHERE NEITHER RUST NOR MOTH DOTH CORRUPT."
[The notebook MS is in the King's School.]
  6. MS: treasure & our
  8. MS: life & deathlier
11. MS: rise & go
13. MS: gourds & past

"AS THE SPARKS FLY UPWARDS."
[The notebook MS is in the King's School.]
Title. MS: ["*The*"] [illegible deletion] <"As"> the < > fly upward."
  2. MS: hope & passionate
  3. MS: aspiring, & aspire
  7. MS: mount & still
10. MS: nothing: they
11. MS: Onward & upward < > that blessed place
12. MS: his God, & soul

"LORD, MAKE US ALL LOVE ALL: THAT WHEN WE MEET"
[The notebook MS is in the King's School.]
  5. MS: around Thy blessed Feet,

"O LORD, I AM ASHAMED TO SEEK THY FACE"
[The notebook MS is in the King's School.]
  6. MS: heart & bid
13. MS: Devil & shifting world & fleshly

"IT IS NOT DEATH, O CHRIST, TO DIE FOR THEE"
[The notebook MS is in the King's School.]
  5. MS: Thyself Who Wast & Art & Art
  7. MS: hand
  8. MS: Loving & loved
  9. MS: not death, & therefore
10. MS: Nor silence silence; & I
14. MS: bundle, & a

p. 402

"LORD, GRANT US EYES TO SEE AND EARS TO HEAR"
[The notebook MS is in the King's School.]
  1. MS: see & ears < > hear
  2. MS: love & minds
  4. MS: hope, & filial
  6. MS: Before Thee heart in heart & hand
  8. MS: waters & as

9. MS: us what Thou wilt, & what
10. MS: Deny, & fold < > in [*t*]<T>hy peaceful
13. MS: jasper & with

"CRIED OUT WITH TEARS."
[The notebook MS is in the King's School.]
Title. MS: with tears."
8. MS: tardy & too tepid & too
14. MS: me & Eye

"O LORD ON WHOM WE GAZE AND DARE NOT GAZE"
[The notebook MS is in the King's School.]
1. MS: we gaze & dare
3. MS: love, & living
4. MS: long & lengthening
5. MS: prayer & praise,
7. MS: men & me,
8. MS: darkness & amend
10. MS: treasure & our
14. MS: with Thee & heart

"I WILL COME AND HEAL HIM."
[The notebook MS is in the King's School.]
Title. MS: come & heal
2. MS: ruth & shame,
3. MS: self-contempt & blame:
4. MS: harp & palm & aureole
6. MS: poor & blind & lame;
9. MS: priceless Blood; & therefore
11. MS: of [*me:*] <Thee:>

"AH LORD, LORD, IF MY HEART WERE RIGHT WITH THINE"
[The notebook MS is in the King's School.]
8. MS: Because Thy [illegible deletion] Love
9. MS: hope & comfort
10. MS: Remembering Thy Cradle & Thy
14. MS: loved, & much

"THE GOLD OF THAT LAND IS GOOD."
[The notebook MS is in the King's School.]
8. MS: hear & worship & behold.
10. MS: day & is

"WEIGH ALL MY FAULTS AND FOLLIES RIGHTEOUSLY"
[The *Verses* notebook MS (MS2) is in the King's School.]
1. MS2: faults & follies
2. MS2: Omissions & commissions,
10. MS2: work & hastening
13. MS2: own Heart, & overweigh

p. 403

"LORD, GRANT ME GRACE TO LOVE THEE IN MY PAIN"
[The notebook MS is in the King's School.]
   3. MS: foundation & my hill;

"LORD, MAKE ME ONE WITH THINE OWN FAITHFUL ONES"
[The notebook MS is in the King's School.]
   2. MS: love Thee & are
   3. MS: break & till < > flee
   4. MS: alms & orisons:
   5. MS: toils & him who runs
   8. MS: moons & suns.
 13. MS: unknown well-known

"LIGHT OF LIGHT."
[The notebook MS is in the King's School.]
   1. MS: our Light Whom
   2. MS: discern & gaze
   5. MS: see;
 12. MS: heat & cold

"THE RANSOMED OF THE LORD."
[The notebook MS is in the King's School.]
   2. MS: Incense & joy & gold;
   6. MS: sins & tears;
   8. MS: flaws & fears.
   9. MS: faints & fails
 11. MS: hopes & hails
 13. MS: faith & pure

"LORD, WE ARE RIVERS RUNNING TO THY SEA"
[The notebook MS is in the King's School.]
   2. MS: waves & ripples

p. 404

"AN EXCEEDING BITTER CRY."
[The notebook MS is in the King's School.]
   1. MS: Contempt & pangs & haunting
   8. MS: thorn & grief & scorn,
   9. MS: ruin & regret.
 14. MS: My Lord & God
 16. MS: desolate & unsufficed?

"O LORD, WHEN THOU DIDST CALL ME, DIDST THOU KNOW"
[The notebook MS is in the King's School.]
   2. MS: disheartened thro' & thro',
   4. MS: cucumbers & melons
   7. MS: How [*weak my efforts were, how few,*] <married I was & withered too,>
   9. MS: Timid & rash, hasty & slow?

13. MS: love & impotent
16. MS: Good Lord Who
18. MS: arise & do
20. MS: knew."

"THOU, GOD, SEEST ME."
[The notebook MS is in the King's School.]
  2. MS: Exposed & open
17. MS: Challenge & prove
20. MS: self & make
22. MS: guilt, & still
23. MS: trust & pray."—

"LORD JESUS, WHO WOULD THINK THAT I AM THINE?"
[The notebook MS is in the King's School.]
  7. MS: last & heaven

"THE NAME OF JESUS."
[The notebook MS is in the King's School.]

"LORD GOD OF HOSTS MOST HOLY AND MOST HIGH"
[The notebook MS is in the King's School.]
  1. MS: of Hosts most Holy & most High,
11. MS: sin & death & suffering
15. MS: live & gain

p. 405
"LORD, WHAT HAVE I THAT I MAY OFFER THEE?"
[The notebook MS is in the King's School.]
  2. MS: pray Thee, & see.—
  7. MS: ones & the
  8. MS: one & all.—
10. MS: crushed & hard:

"IF I SHOULD SAY 'MY HEART IS IN MY HOME'"
[The notebook MS is in the King's School.]
  4. MS: treasure, dwells
  5. MS: heart: this Truth & this
10. MS: beauty & desirability.
11. MS: O Lord Whose

"LEAF FROM LEAF CHRIST KNOWS"
[The notebook MS is in the King's School.]
  5. MS: Star & star
14. MS: is & what
16. MS: spirits & all

"LORD, CARRY ME.—NAY, BUT I GRANT THEE STRENGTH"
[The notebook MS is in the King's School.]
  2. MS: walk & work [*T*]<t>hy way
  4. MS: weak, & bid
  8. MS: flesh can, & what

"LORD, I AM HERE.—BUT, CHILD, I LOOK FOR THEE"
[The notebook MS is in the King's School. In the MS, the lines with
even numbers are indented two spaces.]
  2. MS: Elsewhere & nearer
  5. MS: test & see
  14. MS: made & rule

"NEW CREATURES; THE CREATOR STILL THE SAME"
[The notebook MS is in the King's School.]
  2. MS: For ever & for
  5. MS: same: & still
  7. MS: us, & still
  9. MS: wounded Hands: & Thou
  10. MS: clasp & cling
  11. MS: fast & not
  14. MS: old & still

p. 406

"KING OF KINGS AND LORD OF LORDS."
[The notebook MS is in the King's School.]
  Title. MS: "King of kings, and
  2. MS: love Thee: King
  4. MS: All Cherubs & all < > south & north,
  5. MS: east & west
  7. MS: fashionings;
  8. MS: south & north,
  9. MS: east & west,
  14. MS: life & resurrection

"THY NAME, O CHRIST, AS INCENSE STREAMING FORTH"
[The notebook MS is in the King's School.]
  1. MS: as [*ointment is poured*] <incense streaming> forth
  2. MS: Sweeten[*ing*]<s> our
  3. MS: south & from
  5. MS: is Amen & Yea.
  7. MS: Shepherd & Door, our Life & Truth & Way:—

"THE GOOD SHEPHERD."
[The notebook MS is in the King's School.]
  5. MS: joys
  6. MS: eat & drink
  8. MS: Ninety [*a*]<&> nine?—
  9. MS: stay my bleeding
  10. MS: hush my pleading
  11. MS: death & clomb
  12. MS: gall & wormwood
  13. MS: bud [*m*]<M>y joys

14. MS: sake & good
16. MS: Ninety & nine.

"REJOICE WITH ME."
[The notebook MS is in the King's School.]
5. MS: cost Thee![—]

"SHALL NOT THE JUDGE OF ALL THE EARTH DO RIGHT?"
[The notebook MS is in the King's School. In the MS, lines 4 and 8 are indented four spaces.]
3. MS: life & light?
5. MS: turn & sift & see,
8. MS: Remember, Lord, & do.

"ME AND MY GIFT: KIND LORD, BEHOLD"
[The notebook MS is in the King's School.]
1. MS: Me & my
3. MS: fire & gold
4. MS: [*Me*] [indented four spaces] <Me> [indented two spaces] & my
5. MS: Myself & mine
11. MS: Me & my

p. 407

"HE CANNOT DENY HIMSELF."
[The notebook MS is in the King's School. In the MS, the last three lines of each stanza are indented two spaces.]
1. MS: is Love, & doeth
7. MS: heart
15. MS: Come & see."

"SLAIN FROM THE FOUNDATION OF THE WORLD."
[The notebook MS is in the King's School.]
2. MS: behold & see:

"LORD JESU, THOU ART SWEETNESS TO MY SOUL"
[The notebook MS is in the King's School.]

"I, LORD, THY FOOLISH SINNER LOW AND SMALL"
[The notebook MS is in the King's School.]
1. MS: low & small,
4. MS: asked, [*w*]<W>hat lack
11. MS: More & yet
20. MS: thee, & still
21. MS: grace & breath.
22. MS: up & do.—
23. MS: end, & certify
25. MS: die & have
30. MS: measure & the
33. MS: thou Me.—

538 *Appendix C*

"BECAUSE HE FIRST LOVED US."
[The notebook MS is in the King's School.]
Title. MS: [*"Because He first loved us."*] <"Because He first loved us.">
  [The revision is written on the line above the erasure.]
  1. MS: hungry, & Thou
  5. MS: for [*m*]<M>y sake;
  6. MS: them & Me:
  10. MS: wait & pray:
  14. MS: heart & hand <> them & Me:
  15. MS: thou shalt ask, & shalt

"LORD, HAST THOU SO LOVED US, AND WILL NOT WE"
[The notebook MS is in the King's School.]
  1. MS: us: & will
  2. MS: heart & mind & strength & soul,
  4. MS: desiring [*t*]<T>hee?
  5. MS: saints, cry
  7. MS: many [*c*]<C>rowns, beyond
  8. MS: Ninety & nine
  11. MS: with Thee & in

p. 408

"AS THE DOVE WHICH FOUND NO REST"
[The notebook MS is in the King's School.]
  6. MS: ruin & wrack,
  12. MS: save;
  13. MS: sun & the

"THOU ART FAIRER THAN THE CHILDREN OF MEN."
[The notebook MS is in the King's School.]
  1. MS: lily, & the

"AS THE APPLE TREE AMONG THE TREES OF THE WOOD."
[The notebook MS is in the King's School.]
Title. MS: [Illegible erasure] <"As the Apple Tree among the trees of the wood.">
  3. MS: sweetness & fragrance
  4. MS: another's & thorns
  5. MS: comely & colourless,

"NONE OTHER LAMB, NONE OTHER NAME"
[The notebook MS is in the King's School.]
  3. MS: guilt & shame,
  7. MS: want & woe,

"THY FRIEND AND THY FATHER'S FRIEND FORGET NOT."
[The *Verses* notebook MS (MS2) is in the King's School.]
Title. MS2: "Thy Friend & thy
  5. MS2: spent & rotting
  7. MS2: tired & sore.

8. MS2: pleasures & enlarge
9. MS2: desire, & famished
12. MS2: far & near
13. MS2: us & found & paid
16. MS2: For us, & holds

p. 409

"SURELY HE HATH BORNE OUR GRIEFS."
[The *Verses* notebook MS (MS2) is in the King's School.]
9. MS2: a lookingglass as
10. MS2: Christ's Face & man's
14. MS2: comes,—& listens

"THEY TOIL NOT, NEITHER DO THEY SPIN."
[The notebook MS is in the King's School.]
7. MS: love; & some

p. 410

"DARKNESS AND LIGHT ARE BOTH ALIKE TO THEE"
[The notebook MS is in the King's School.]
1. MS: Darkness & light
4. MS: light & present
9. MS: gulf & fountain
12. MS: find, & finding

"AND NOW WHY TARRIEST THOU?"
[The notebook MS is in the King's School.]
Title. MS: now[,] why
2. MS: my God, to Thee:
9. MS: stint & sorrow,
10. MS: day & not
14. MS: far:
20. MS: risen & striven & now

"HAVE I NOT STRIVEN, MY GOD, AND WATCHED AND PRAYED?"
[The *Verses* notebook MS (MS2) is in the King's School.]
1. MS2: my God, [*have I not*] <& watched &> prayed[,]<?>
4. MS2: that [*t*]<T>hou canst
7. MS2: grope & grasp
8. MS2: sight & reach
9. MS2: [*And*] [indented two spaces] <And> [not indented] piteous men & women
10. MS2: [*Whis*] [indented four spaces] <Whispering> [indented two spaces] & wistful
11. MS2: [*Thou*] [indented four spaces] <Thou> [indented two spaces] Who
12. MS2: turn & look
13. MS2: shame
14. MS2: angels & to

"GOD IS OUR HOPE AND STRENGTH."
[The notebook MS is in the King's School.]
Title. MS: our Hope & Strength."
  1. MS: Tempest & terror below: but
  3. MS: billows & flames <> noise,—& where
  4. MS: joys, & death & destruction
  5. MS: death, & Jesus
  6. MS: sought & the
  7. MS: call & recall,
  9. MS: abound & to
  10. MS: on Thee face unto Face, & respond

p. 411

"DAY AND NIGHT THE ACCUSER MAKES NO PAUSE"
[The notebook MS is in the King's School.]
  1. MS: Day & night
  2. MS: Day & night
  3. MS: Good & Evil
  7. MS: our Jesu makes

"O MINE ENEMY"
[The notebook MS is in the King's School.]
  1. MS: enemy,
  5. MS: free & far
  6. MS: sun & star
  7. MS: prepared & spacious
  10. MS: heart & break;

"LORD, DOST THOU LOOK ON ME, AND WILL NOT I"
[The notebook MS is in the King's School.]
  1. MS: me, & will
  4. MS: him & often
  9. MS: look & love <> in Th[y]<in>e Eyes,
  10. MS: Thy heart is <> day & night,
  13. MS: see & love

"PEACE I LEAVE WITH YOU."
[The notebook MS is in the King's School.]
  1. MS: Tumult & turmoil, trouble & toil,
  3. MS: grudge & never
  5. MS: O my King & my

"O CHRIST OUR ALL IN EACH, OUR ALL IN ALL!"
[The *Verses* notebook MS (MS2) is in the King's School.]
  7. MS2: Follow Thy foot track, hearken
  12. MS2: me, & darkness

p. 412

"BECAUSE THY LOVE HATH SOUGHT ME"
[The notebook MS is in the King's School.]
2. MS: All mine is Thine & Thine

"THY FAINTING SPOUSE, YET STILL THY SPOUSE"
[The notebook MS is in the King's School.]

"LIKE AS THE HART DESIRETH THE WATER BROOKS."
[The notebook MS is in the King's School.]
Title. MS: as the h[*e*]<a>rt desireth
2. MS: heart;
9. MS: look, & win
10. MS: frighted & faint.
13. MS: gifts & with
17. MS: Yearning & thrilling
19. MS: unknown untold,

"THAT WHERE I AM, THERE YE MAY BE ALSO."
[The notebook MS is in the King's School.]
Title. MS: am, <there> ye
2. MS: morning-glories & heartsease & unexampled
4. MS: so:
7. MS: the worn out eyes;
9. MS: so:
11. MS: O Lord Christ Whom < > love & desire
12. MS: O Lord Christ Who
14. MS: so:

"JUDGE NOT ACCORDING TO THE APPEARANCE."
[The notebook MS is in the King's School.]
1. MS: Lord, [*grant us*] <purge our> eyes
7. MS: word

"MY GOD, WILT THOU ACCEPT AND WILL NOT WE"
[The notebook MS is in the King's School.]
1. MS: accept, & will

p. 413

"A CHILL BLANK WORLD. YET OVER THE UTMOST SEA"
[The notebook MS is in the King's School.]

"THE CHIEFEST AMONG TEN THOUSAND."
[The notebook MS is in the King's School.]
8. MS: heart faints & the

ADVENT SUNDAY.
[The notebook MS is in the King's School.]
Title. MS: Advent Sunday. [The title is written in pencil and retraced in ink.]
2. MS: lamps & garlands

    4. MS: midnight black <> pitch
   11. MS: Veiled she
   14. MS: a Dove's, & she's
   19. MS: ablaze & garlands

ADVENT.
[The notebook MS is in the King's School. In the MS, lines 2, 4, 5, 7, 9, and 11 are indented two spaces.]
Title. MS: Advent. [The title is written in pencil and retraced in ink.]
    1. MS: old yet

"SOONER OR LATER: YET AT LAST"
[The notebook MS is in the King's School.]
Title. MS: Advent. [The title is written in pencil and retraced in ink.]
   19. MS: earth & sea
   20. MS: great & small;
   26. MS: name
   27. MS: hissing & a
   31. MS: blossoms, & to
   37. MS: Lord God of Mercy & of

CHRISTMAS EVE.
[The notebook MS is in the King's School.]
Title. MS: Christmas Eve.
   10. MS: sing & bells

p. 414
CHRISTMAS DAY.
[The notebook MS is in the King's School.]
Title. MS: Christmas Day. [The title is written in pencil and retraced in ink.]
    3. MS: their King
    9. MS: innocent & mild
   10. MS: sod,
   11. MS: And Jesus Christ the Undefiled
   15. MS: White & ruddy,
   16. MS: you & me.
   19. MS: stirred
   22. MS: music & melody:
   24. MS: Carol we & worship

CHRISTMASTIDE.
[The notebook MS is in the King's School.]
Title. MS: Christmastide.
    4. MS: Star & Angels
   10. MS: yours & love
   11. MS: to God & all
   12. MS: plea & gift & sign.

ST. JOHN, APOSTLE.
    [The notebook MS is in the King's School.]
    Title. MS: St. John, Apostle. [The first two words of the title are
        written in pencil and retraced in ink.]
      3. MS: finish li[v]<f>e never
      4. MS: Eagle & sun
      6. MS: peace & joy

"'BELOVED, LET US LOVE ONE ANOTHER,' SAYS ST. JOHN"
    [The notebook MS is in the King's School.]
    Title. MS: St. John, Apostle. [The first two words of the title are
        written in pencil and retraced in ink.]
      6. MS: past & gone;

HOLY INNOCENTS.
    [The notebook MS is in the King's School.]
    Title. MS: Holy Innocents. [The title is written in pencil and retraced
        in ink.]

"UNSPOTTED LAMBS TO FOLLOW THE ONE LAMB"
    [The notebook MS is in the King's School.]
    Title. MS: Holy Innocents. [The title is written in pencil and retraced
        in ink.]
      7. MS: them, & even

p. 415

EPIPHANY.
    [The notebook MS is in the King's School.]
    Title. MS: Epiphany.
      4. MS: prophecy & star
      6. MS: down & worship,
      8. MS: began."—
     13. MS: Both Good & Great:
     15. MS: Low lying desolate?"—
     16. MS: down & worship,
     22. MS: Myrrh: no
     31. MS: frankincense & gold:
     33. MS: Good will doth
     35. MS: stars & seraphs
     37. MS: Flutters & coos
     38. MS: And Dove & Lamb & Babe
     39. MS: Come, all mankind, come, all

EPIPHANYTIDE.
    [The notebook MS is in the King's School.]
    Title. MS: Epiphanytide.
      2. MS: Shamefaced & trembling
      3. MS: O First & with
      5. MS: sin & from < > down & worship

8. MS: O Faithful Lord & [*Tru*] True! < > us & do,
9. MS: free
10. MS: Heart & soul & spirit < > all & worship

SEPTUAGESIMA.
[The notebook MS is in the King's School.]
Title. MS: Septuagesima. [The title is written in pencil and retraced in ink.]
　　1. MS: more, & the
　　2. MS: more, & the
　　3. MS: more, & a
　　9. MS: more, & the
　10. MS: more, & life's
　11. MS: more, & the

SEXAGESIMA.
[The notebook MS is in the King's School.]
Title. MS: Sexagesima. [The title is written in pencil and rewritten in ink on the line above.]
Opening quotation. MS: [The opening quotation is written over the title that is in pencil.]
　　5. MS: is & cradle
　　9. MS: the harvest field which
　15. MS: earth: & once

"THAT EDEN OF EARTH'S SUNRISE CANNOT VIE"
[The notebook MS is in the King's School. In the MS, the last line of each stanza is indented four spaces.]
Title. MS: Sexagesima. [The title is written in pencil and retraced in ink.]
　10. MS: sun & moon
　11. MS: hath God & Lamb
　15. MS: Triumph & rest.
　16. MS: Hail, Eve & Adam, < > death & shame!
　17. MS: death, & Jesu's
　19. MS: Hail Adam & hail

p. 416

QUINQUAGESIMA.
[The notebook MS is in the King's School.]
Title. MS: Quinquagesima [The title is written in pencil and retraced in ink.]
　　7. MS: learns & teaches:
　13. MS: Oh teach
　14. MS: love & learn.

"PITEOUS MY RHYME IS"
[The notebook MS is in the King's School.]
Title. MS: Quinquagesima. [The title is written in pencil and retraced in ink.]

1. MS: [*Piteous my rhyme is*] [not indented] <Piteous my rhyme is>
   [indented two spaces]
2. MS: love & pain,
6. MS: is
12. MS: pain
13. MS: again
19. MS: is & does & can

ASH WEDNESDAY.
[The notebook MS is in the King's School. In the MS, lines 4 and 8 are
indented four spaces.]
Title. MS: Ash Wednesday. [The title is written in pencil and retraced
   in ink.]
1. MS: sin
2. MS: great; [illegible deletion] <&> if
7. MS: tell [*t*]<T>his all,

"GOOD LORD, TODAY"
[The notebook MS is in the King's School.]
Title. MS: Ash Wednesday. [The title is written in pencil and retraced
   in ink.]
5. MS: curse:
8. MS: pity tho'

LENT.
[The notebook MS is in the King's School.]
Title. MS: Lent. [The title is written in pencil and retraced in ink.]
1. MS: first
2. MS: distress
3. MS: hunger & thirst
5. MS: spend & be
6. MS: watch & to pray,
7. MS: Life & Death

EMBERTIDE.
[The notebook MS is in the King's School.]
Title. MS: Embertide. [The title is written in pencil and retraced in ink.]
7. MS: sat & faint,
13. MS: sin & sorrow,

p. 417

MID-LENT.
[The notebook MS is in the King's School.]
Title. MS: Mid Lent. [The title is in pencil and written over in ink.]
2. MS: good & best:
6. MS: nest:
7. MS: heart being
8. MS: hope for
10. MS: wakening & of
12. MS: pursued & hath < > faint:

13. MS: speed
14. MS: [*Still faint*] [indented two spaces] <Still faint> [indented four spaces] yet

PASSIONTIDE.
[The notebook MS is in the King's School.]
Title. MS: Passiontide. [The title is written in pencil and retraced in ink.]
  1. MS: of Thy Love, dear Lord <Love, dear Lord> [retraced over originals], that
  3. MS: cold & poor, <> for Thy State,
  8. MS: grace heaven's bowers.
  9. MS: once"—& still
  13. MS: seek & wait"—
  15. MS: "Come & repent: come & amend:
  16. MS: —Christ passeth by - - - -
  17. MS: come—& I—& I. Amen.

PALM SUNDAY.
[The notebook MS is in the King's School.]
Title. MS: Palm Sunday. [The title is written in pencil and retraced in ink.]
Opening quotation. MS: treadeth the Winepress of the Fierceness & Wrath of
  1. MS: eyes, & see
  2. MS: the Tree,
  3. MS: sake & athirst
  4. MS: there
  5. MS: thorns & bleeding
  6. MS: all & glad
  12. MS: thee & will
  15. MS: unbridgeable & near!
  17. MS: boundless Sacrifice:
  24. MS: trust Me still & love
  27. MS: shamed & uncomforted.
  28. MS: day,
  29. MS: heart even
  30. MS: in love, trust on, love on, & pray."

MONDAY IN HOLY WEEK.
[The *Verses* notebook MS (MS2) is in the King's School. Editions: 1896.]
Title. MS2: Monday in Holy Week. [The title is written in pencil and retraced in ink.]
  1896: FOR UNDER A CRUCIFIX
  1. 1896: sake;
  3. 1896: pain;
  4. MS2: rend my [*h*]<H>eart again?
  1896: thou pierce My [A stanza break follows the line.]
  5. MS2: thorns & shameful

7. MS2: Bore my Cross
1896: Gave up glory, broke My will,—
8. 1896: And canst thou reject Me still?

TUESDAY IN HOLY WEEK.
[The notebook MS is in the King's School.]
Title. MS: Tuesday in Holy Week. [The title is written in pencil and
retraced in ink.]
1. MS: By Thy longdrawn anguish
3. MS: mercy & atone
5. MS: Thou who thirsting
6. MS: mankind & all <> love & me,
7. MS: love & see
8. MS: mankind & all <> love & me.

p. 418

WEDNESDAY IN HOLY WEEK.
[The notebook MS is in the King's School.]
Title. MS: Wednesday in Holy Week. [The title is written in pencil and
retraced in ink.]
2. MS: Preaching & teaching, <> to & fro,
8. MS: curse & an

MAUNDY THURSDAY.
[The notebook MS is in the King's School.]
Title. MS: Maundy Thursday. [The title is written in pencil and
retraced in ink.]
Opening quotation. MS: said . . . . Should <> cheereth God & /
"man, & go
2. MS: trees, "We will <> thing:
5. MS: curve & droop, <> climb & cling:
6. MS: buffeting.
7. MS: heads & sing,
9. MS: I a king, & thou a king, & what
11. MS: swayed & murmured
12. MS: Stooped & drooped
13. MS: earth & lay
15. MS: life & put <> death: & lo!
17. MS: triumphing[illegible deletion of punctuation]<,>—
18. MS: I a king, & thou a king, & this

GOOD FRIDAY MORNING.
[The notebook MS is in the King's School.]
Title. MS: Good Friday morning. [The first two words of the title are in
pencil and written over in ink.]
5. MS: the World triumphant,
9. MS: Up my
11. MS: carried

GOOD FRIDAY.
> [The notebook MS is in the King's School. In the MS, lines 4 and 8 are
> indented eight spaces.]
> Title. MS: Good Friday. [The title is written in pencil and retraced
>> in ink.]
>> 1. MS: Lord Jesus Christ grown
>> 5. MS: upon Thee & make
>> 6. MS: heaven & earth
>> 7. MS: earth & heaven,

GOOD FRIDAY EVENING.
> [The notebook MS is in the King's School.]
> Title. MS: Good Friday evening. [The first two words of the title are
>> written in pencil on the line below the complete title, which is in ink.]
> Opening quotation. MS: [The opening quotation is written over the
>> words of the title that are in pencil.]
>> 3. MS: pierced & broken
>> 5. MS: faint goodwill,
>> 7. MS: more, & still
>> 8. MS: More & yet

p. 419
"A BUNDLE OF MYRRH IS MY WELL-BELOVED UNTO ME."
> [The notebook MS is in the King's School.]
> Title. MS: Good Friday. [The title is written in pencil and repeated in
>> ink on the line above.]
> Opening quotation. MS: "A bundle of myrrh is my Wellbeloved unto
>> me." [The opening quotation is written over the title that is in
>> pencil.]
>> 2. MS: dear Lord, assi[n]<g>ned to
>> 3. MS: Ours lowly statured crosses;
>> 6. MS: small
>> 7. MS: Easy & light, <> great & ponderous.
>> 9. MS: racking & emulous:—

EASTER EVEN.
> [The notebook MS is in the King's School.]
>> 1. MS: over & gone,
>> 2. MS: finished" & the
>> 5. MS: silence & of
>> 6. MS: cave & entrance
>> 15. MS: break & the
>> 16. MS: The Shaking & the

OUR CHURCH PALMS ARE BUDDING WILLOW TWIGS.
> [The notebook MS is in the King's School.]
> Title. MS: Easter Even.
> Opening quotation. MS: Our Church Palms are budding willow twigs

5. MS: north & south, <> east & west,
7. MS: laughed, & Faith

EASTER DAY.
[The notebook MS is in the King's School.]
Title. MS: Easter Day. [The title is written in pencil and retraced in ink.]
13. MS: her song birds,
18. MS: day & ours.

EASTER MONDAY.
[The *Verses* notebook MS (MS2) is in the King's School.]
Title. MS2: Easter Monday. [The title is written in pencil and retraced in ink.]
10. MS: died & good
14. MS: life & death
15. MS: wax & wane;
18. MS: on [illegible deletion] <&> wane.

p. 420

EASTER TUESDAY.
[The notebook MS is in the King's School. In the MS, lines 5 and 7 are indented two spaces, and line 6 is not indented.]
Title. MS: Easter Tuesday. [The title is written in pencil and retraced in ink.]
2. MS: amen & yea
8. MS: lamps being
9. MS: watch & pray:

ROGATIONTIDE.
[The notebook MS is in the King's School.]
Title. MS: Rogationtide. [The title is written in pencil and retraced in ink.]
1. MS: wheat
2. MS: others [illegible deletion] eat.
5. MS: be
7. MS: more

ASCENSION EVE.
[The notebook MS is in the King's School.]
Title. MS: Ascension Eve. [The title is written in pencil and retraced in ink; on the line below it is an illegible pencil erasure, possibly the word "Ascension."]
2. MS: whom Thou has formed
5. MS: speak & grant
6. MS: come to us & grant
9. MS: living & of
13. MS: earth & up <> heaven,

ASCENSION DAY.
   [The notebook MS is in the King's School.]
   Title. MS: Ascension Day.
     2. MS: souls & wills
     7. MS: not life. Remember, Lord, & see,
    10. MS: one longdrawn anguish
    15. MS: for Him; while
    17. MS: do His Will, & doing
    18. MS: spend & to
    24. MS: Strenuous & strong.
    27. MS: to Heaven,—

p. 421

WHITSUN EVE.
   [The notebook MS is in the King's School.]
   Title. MS: Whitsun Eve. [The title is written in pencil and retraced
     in ink.]
     3. MS: afar stumbling & marred & small
     5. MS: sin & sorrow
     7. MS: love & rest; < > to Thee, & call
     8. MS: rest & love.

WHITSUN DAY.
   [The notebook MS is in the King's School.]
   Title. MS: Whitsun Day.
     1. MS: wind & sight
     2. MS: flesh & blood < > spirit & fiery
     3. MS: in Christ's & the
     5. MS: life & shame for their boa[t]<s>t,
     7. MS: as death & stronger

WHITSUN MONDAY.
   [The notebook MS is in the King's School.]
   Title. MS: Whitsun Monday. ["Whitsun M" is written in pencil on the
     line below the title.]
   Opening quotation. MS: [The opening quotation is written over the
     title that is in pencil.]
     2. MS: be
     3. MS: for ever & ever & ever
     7. MS: for ever & ever & ever
     8. MS: flows & abides.
    11. MS: for ever & ever & ever
    15. MS: for ever & ever & ever
    16. MS: flows & is
    19. MS: for ever & ever & ever

WHITSUN TUESDAY.
[The notebook MS is in the King's School.]
Title. MS: Whitsun Tuesday. [The title is written in pencil and retraced in ink.]
   1. MS: Lord Jesus Christ our Wisdom & our
   2. MS: reveal & wisely
   4. MS: to Thy Will Whose Will
   6. MS: envy & too
   7. MS: dove-hearted & dove-eyed,
   8. MS: Soft-voiced, & satisfied
 10. MS: silver & of
 12. MS: past & gone:"
 13. MS: love & dove,

TRINITY SUNDAY.
[The notebook MS is in the King's School.]
Title. MS: Trinity Sunday. [The title is written in pencil and retraced in ink.]
   1. MS: My [*g*]<G>od, Thyself
   2. MS: And love Thy Will & love
 11. MS: told:
 13. MS: Is, Was, & Is
 14. MS: remainest; yea & yea!

CONVERSION OF ST. PAUL.
[The notebook MS is in the King's School.]
Title. MS: [*St. Paul*] [written in pencil] <Conversion of St. Paul.> [written in ink]
   2. MS: Arise & wash
   3. MS: head & wash

p. 422
"IN WEARINESS AND PAINFULNESS ST. PAUL"
[The notebook MS is in the King's School. In the MS, lines 4 and 11 are indented two spaces.]
Title. MS: St. Paul.
   1. MS: weariness & painfulness
   2. MS: Served God & pleased
   3. MS: on & can <> one & all
   4. MS: weariness & painfulness[.]<,>
   5. MS: faith & hope
   7. MS: trust & bless,
   8. MS: Weep & rejoice,
   9. MS: hands, & forward
 11. MS: weariness & painfulness.

VIGIL OF THE PRESENTATION.
[The notebook MS is in the King's School.]
Title. MS: Vigil of the Presentation. [The title is written in pencil and
retraced in ink.]
1. MS: Long & dark <> dim & short
5. MS: nights & days,

FEAST OF THE PRESENTATION.
[The notebook MS is in the King's School.]
Title. MS: [*Presentation*] [written in pencil] <Feast of the
Presentation.> [written in ink]
2. MS: Infant & Lamb
3. MS: A Virgin & two
7. MS: Freeman & bondman, <> king & queen,
8. MS: candles & with
11. MS: offered Thee
13. MS: frankincense & myrrh;
16. MS: snowdrops & my

THE PURIFICATION OF ST. MARY THE VIRGIN.
[The notebook MS is in the King's School.]
Title. MS: The Purification of St. Mary the Virgin. [The title is written
in ink over illegible pencil writing.]
2. MS: [*Was*] [indented two spaces] <Was> [not indented] such
7. MS: The Essence & Author
9. MS: spotless & holy & mild;
12. MS: Her God & Redeemer & Child.

VIGIL OF THE ANNUNCIATION.
[The notebook MS is in the King's School.]
Title. MS: Vigil of the Annunciation. [The title is written in ink over
illegible pencil writing.]
3. MS: flesh & time:—
10. MS: strife & anguish
14. MS: watch & pray,—

p. 423

FEAST OF THE ANNUNCIATION.
[The notebook MS is in the King's School.]
Title. MS: Feast of the Annunciation. [On the line below the title is
written in pencil:] Annunciation
5. MS: is [*Man*] mankind's <> flower[,]<:>

"HERSELF A ROSE, WHO BORE THE ROSE."
[The notebook MS is in the King's School. In the MS, lines 5, 10, 15,
and 20 are indented two spaces.]
Title. MS: [*Annunciation*] [written in pencil] <Feast of the
Annunciation.> [written in ink]
2. MS: the Rose & felt

5. MS: slept & woke <> night & morn.
15. MS: good & ill.
16. MS: grace & love,
17. MS: beauty & of life & death:
18. MS: hope & love & faith
20. MS: Spouse, [s]<S>ister, Mother,"

ST. MARK.
[The notebook MS is in the King's School.]
Title. MS: St. Mark.
3. MS: hands & knees
7. MS: breadth & length

ST. BARNABAS.
[The notebook MS is in the King's School. In the MS, line 13 is in-
dented two spaces and line 14 is indented four spaces.]
Title. MS: St. Barnabas.
Opening quotations. MS: left / "hand."—Acts 21.3. / <>
contrary."—Acts 27.4.
3. MS: That Chosen Vessel,
4. MS: Proclaimed the Gentiles [a]<&> the
8. MS: love, & sigh
9. MS: in lifelong exile
10. MS: hands, & commune
13. MS: sighted Cyprus; & once

VIGIL OF ST. PETER.
[The notebook MS is in the King's School.]
Title. MS: [*St. Peter*] [written in pencil] <Vigil of St. Peter.> [written
in ink]
5. MS: me thro' & thro'
7. MS: on me, Lord, & make

ST. PETER.
[The notebook MS is in the King's School.]
Title. MS: St. Peter.
2. MS: To Peter: & he
9. MS: Lord, Lover of Thy Peter, & of

p. 424
"ST. PETER ONCE: 'LORD, DOST THOU WASH MY FEET?'"
[The notebook MS is in the King's School.]
Title. MS: St. Peter.
2. MS: stand & knock
4. MS: Bolted & barred,
6. MS: within & dancing <> mock;
9. MS: knocking. Still I
11. MS: heart & make

"I FOLLOWED THEE, MY GOD, I FOLLOWED THEE"
[The notebook MS is in the King's School.]
Title. MS: St. Peter.
   4. MS: back [illegible deletion] on
   9. MS: perforce, & silently
   12. MS: weak & small
   13. MS: be
   14. MS: Sinning & sorrowing—
   24. MS: plumb & see
   25. MS: depth & height.
   29. MS: Blinded & rash;
   40. MS: heart & die.
   43. MS: wrings & comforts
   48. MS: silently:
   56. MS: hart the water brooks I
   64. MS: pierce Thee & me:
   66. MS: throne & kingdom;

VIGIL OF ST. BARTHOLOMEW.
[The notebook MS is in the King's School.]
Title. MS: [*V. St. Bartholomew*] [written in pencil] <Vigil of St.
   Bartholomew.> [written in ink]
   1. MS: hearts & eyes:
   3. MS: watch & weep.
   4. MS: wake & rise
   5. MS: vigil & are
   12. MS: withheld & all

ST. BARTHOLOMEW.
[The notebook MS is in the King's School.]
Title. MS: St. Bartholomew.
   4. MS: call, & we

ST. MICHAEL AND ALL ANGELS.
[The notebook MS is in the King's School.]
Title. MS: SS. Michael & All Angels.
Opening quotation. MS: <"Ye that excel in strength.">
   1. MS: Service & strength, God's Angels & Archangels;
   2. MS: fires, & lamps
   3. MS: highest & from
   6. MS: serve, & Powers
   8. MS: Flames fire-out-flaming, chill
   9. MS: scant & dim
   11. MS: Sacred & free
   18. MS: laud & magnify

VIGIL OF ALL SAINTS.
[The notebook MS is in the King's School.]
Title. MS: [*V All Ss*] [written in pencil] <Vigil of All Saints.> [written in ink]
   8. MS: reap & rest & smile

p. 425

ALL SAINTS.
[The notebook MS is in the King's School. In the MS, lines 11 and 13 are indented four spaces and line 14 is indented two spaces.]
Title. MS: [*All Ss*] [written in pencil] <All Saints.> [written in ink]
   2. MS: Numbered & treasured
   4. MS: things & Jerusalem
   6. MS: rest & understand;
   8. MS: outward, thro' & thro'.
 11. MS: others & rejoice:
 13. MS: All love & only

ALL SAINTS: MARTYRS.
[The notebook MS is in the King's School.]
Title. MS: [*All Ss*] [written in pencil] <All Saints: Martyrs.> [written in ink]
   3. MS: luminous & lovely
   7. MS: heart & eyes
   8. MS: throne & diadem.
 10. MS: that is & is
 12. MS: love & fires
 14. MS: the Father, Son, & Holy

"I GAVE A SWEET SMELL."
[The notebook MS is in the King's School.]
Title. MS: All Saints.

"HARK! THE ALLELUIAS OF THE GREAT SALVATION"
[The notebook MS is in the King's School.]
Title. MS: All Saints.
   9. MS: the [*g*]<G>reat Captain < > salvation
 10. MS: truth may

A SONG FOR THE LEAST OF ALL SAINTS.
[The notebook MS is in the King's School.]
Title. MS: A Song for the Least of all Saints.
   1. MS: is they key < > life & death,

SUNDAY BEFORE ADVENT.
[The notebook MS is in the King's School.]
Title. MS: Sunday before Advent. [The title is written in pencil and retraced in ink.]
   6. MS: musical

7. MS: Sweet never ending waters
9. MS: unplumbed unspanned,
10. MS: great & small,

p. 426

"LOVE LOVETH THEE, AND WISDOM LOVETH THEE"
[The notebook MS is in the King's School.]
1. MS: Love loveth Thee, & wisdom
4. MS: was & is & is to be.
5. MS: Wisdom & love
9. MS: Wisdom & love & rest,
13. MS: have & harp & aureole,
14. MS: rest, love—& lo!

"LORD, GIVE ME LOVE THAT I MAY LOVE THEE MUCH"
[The notebook MS is in the King's School.]
3. MS: worship & adore
8. MS: perfect having
13. MS: longer brighter lovelier

"AS A KING, ... UNTO THE KING."
[The notebook MS is in the King's School.]
1. MS: grace & dignify
4. MS: cry
5. MS: offering,
6. MS: heart tho' soiled & bruised,
7. MS: heart tho' < > before:
8. MS: came & was
10. MS: do, & make

p. 427

"O YE WHO LOVE TODAY"
[The notebook MS is in the King's School.]
10. MS: face

"LIFE THAT WAS BORN TODAY"
[The notebook MS is in the King's School. In the MS, the last stanza is written in two columns, lines 17–20 on the left side of the page, and lines 21–24 on the right.]
7. MS: live & give
11. MS: counts & mounts
15. MS: name, & flame
19. MS: cloud & shroud,
20. MS: peaceful [illegible deletion]<d>ove.
23. MS: Eyesight & light

"PERFECT LOVE CASTETH OUT FEAR."
[The notebook MS is in the King's School.]
1. MS: fear
2. MS: love,

"HOPE IS THE COUNTERPOISE OF FEAR"
[The notebook MS is in the King's School.]
    5. MS: sunshine & with
    8. MS: sere
  10. MS: hymn so sweet & clear
  11. MS: He seems
  12. MS: resurrection & of

"SUBJECT TO LIKE PASSIONS AS WE ARE."
[The notebook MS is in the King's School.]
Title. MS: [*"Of like Passions with ourselves."*] <"Subject to like Passions as
    we are.">
    9. MS: is anguish yet
  10. MS: delight:
  12. MS: meet but <> sunder with

p. 428

"EXPERIENCE BOWS A SWEET CONTENTED FACE"
[The notebook MS is in the King's School.]
    7. MS: sun & moon & rain & rainbow
  11. MS: peace & patience
  12. MS: While Hope, who
  13. MS: forth & backward <> hair

"CHARITY NEVER FAILETH."
[The notebook MS is in the King's School.]
Title. MS: never faileth."
    2. MS: around & rage
    3. MS: beyond tempest far
    6. MS: be,

"THE GREATEST OF THESE IS CHARITY."
[The notebook MS is in the King's School.]
    4. MS: veiled,—
    5. MS: slackened & our
    9. MS: Nay!—love
  10. MS: Flushing & sweet
  12. MS: faith & hope,
  13. MS: of New Jerusalem
  14. MS: full & where the palm tree blows.

"ALL BENEATH THE SUN HASTETH"
[The notebook MS is in the King's School.]
    1. MS: [*All that hath begun wasteth,*] / <All beneath the sun hasteth[;],>
  10. MS: goad & rein,

"IF THOU BE DEAD, FORGIVE AND THOU SHALT LIVE"
[The notebook MS is in the King's School.]
    1. MS: forgive & thou
    2. MS: forgive & be

3. MS: gracious & forgive,
5. MS: die & not

"LET PATIENCE HAVE HER PERFECT WORK."
[The notebook MS is in the King's School.]
4. MS: of or < > hear
11. MS: himself [*al*] & all
13. MS: ebb & swell,

p. 429

"PATIENCE MUST DWELL WITH LOVE, FOR LOVE AND SORROW"
[The notebook MS is in the King's School.]
1. MS: for Love & Sorrow
6. MS: shade & hold
7. MS: thee; & lo!

"LET EVERYTHING THAT HATH BREATH PRAISE THE LORD."
[The notebook MS is in the King's School.]
Title. MS: "Let every thing that
7. MS: must fail & fail

"WHAT IS THE BEGINNING? LOVE. WHAT THE COURSE?
LOVE STILL"
[The notebook MS is in the King's School.]
6. MS: you & me.

"LORD, MAKE ME PURE"
[The notebook MS is in the King's School.]
2. MS: art,

"LOVE, TO BE LOVE, MUST WALK THY WAY"
[The notebook MS is in the King's School.]
4. MS: still & pray.
11. MS: Faithless & hopeless
15. MS: her myrtle leaf,

"LORD, I AM FEEBLE AND OF MEAN ACCOUNT"
[The notebook MS is in the King's School.]
1. MS: feeble & of
4. MS: hear & grace
5. MS: hear & see

"TUNE ME, O LORD, INTO ONE HARMONY"
[The notebook MS is in the King's School.]
3. MS: love & melody,
8. MS: Devil & world, < > flee;
9. MS: flesh, & arm

p. 430

"THEY SHALL BE AS WHITE AS SNOW."
[The notebook MS is in the King's School.]
2. MS: own sight & God's

5. MS: wrong & love
10. MS: guilt, & for

"THY LILIES DRINK THE DEW"
[The notebook MS is in the King's School.]
2. MS: rill, & I
6. MS: Bows & fulfils
7. MS: rest & play
13. MS: pure & temperate,
14. MS: betimes & late,
15. MS: love & praise
17. MS: be
18. MS: Spotless & sweet,

"WHEN I WAS IN TROUBLE I CALLED UPON THE LORD."
[The notebook MS is in the King's School.]
1. MS: bleeds & bears
2. MS: hopes & waits
3. MS: fears & cares,
6. MS: O Gracious Lord & kind,
8. MS: And sta[u]nch & bind?

"GRANT US SUCH GRACE THAT WE MAY WORK THY WILL"
[The notebook MS is in the King's School.]
2. MS: words & walk
3. MS: Profound & calm < > deep & still:
5. MS: hastening & not
7. MS: Content & fearless
10. MS: river & each

"WHO HATH DESPISED THE DAY OF SMALL THINGS?"
[The notebook MS is in the King's School.]
1. MS: recluse & sweet,
5. MS: While half awakened Spring
6. MS: bleak & bare,
7. MS: Daisies & violets
8. MS: bloom & make

"DO THIS, AND HE DOETH IT."
[The notebook MS is in the King's School.]
Title. MS: this, & he
6. MS: heart & glad
7. MS: low
11. MS: so

p. 431
"THAT NO MAN TAKE THY CROWN."
[The notebook MS is in the King's School.]
3. MS: yea, & He
7. MS: faithful challenging

9. MS: us & to
10. MS: heaven & earth

"YE ARE COME UNTO MOUNT SION."
[The notebook MS is in the King's School.]
1. MS: Fear, Faith, & Hope
2. MS: Prudence, Obedience, & Humility
5. MS: Faith & Humility <> grave & strong;
6. MS: Prudence & Hope
12. MS: Weans them & [illegible deletion] <woos> them
13. MS: stem
15. MS: being their's in
16. MS: to Love, & so
19. MS: on Love & mirror

"SIT DOWN IN THE LOWEST ROOM."
[The notebook MS is in the King's School.]
Title. MS: lowest [*place."*] <room.">
6. MS: place:
8. MS: S[illegible deletion]<i>t low,

"LORD, IT IS GOOD FOR US TO BE HERE."
[The notebook MS is in the King's School. In the MS, lines 12 and 14
are indented four spaces and line 13 is indented two spaces.]
1. MS: patience & that
3. MS: the longdrawn shadows
9. MS: gracious & how
12. MS: pale & careful

"LORD, GRANT US GRACE TO REST UPON THY WORD"
[The notebook MS is in the King's School.]
3. MS: unruffled & unstirred,
5. MS: burden & this
8. MS: flesh & blood

"A VAIN SHADOW."
[The notebook MS is in the King's School.]
2. MS: Mouldy, wormeaten, grey:
6. MS: froth & the
8. MS: was & shall
9. MS: is & passes

p. 432

"LORD, SAVE US, WE PERISH."
[The notebook MS is in the King's School.]
9. MS: Turn [illegible deletion] not

"WHAT IS THIS ABOVE THY HEAD"
[The notebook MS is in the King's School.]
4. MS: pearls & golden
6. MS: day & night

11. MS: up & perishing;
14. MS: Tinsel & paint.
18. MS: Beauty & youth
26. MS: her death pall
29. MS: befooled & slow

BABYLON THE GREAT.
[The notebook MS is in the King's School.]
1. MS: she & ill-favoured,
9. MS: upon her; for
12. MS: When at < > desire
13. MS: vest & gold & gem & pearl

"STANDING AFAR OFF FOR THE FEAR OF HER TORMENT."
[The notebook MS is in the King's School.]
4. MS: foulness & besottedness.
5. MS: friend? hath [*sheno*] she no clinging
6. MS: all:
12. MS: Somewhat, & lo!

"O LUCIFER, SON OF THE MORNING!"
[The notebook MS is in the King's School.]

"ALAS, ALAS! FOR THE SELF-DESTROYED"
[The notebook MS is in the King's School.]
3. MS: Sink down & die

p. 433

"AS FROTH ON THE FACE OF THE DEEP"
[The notebook MS is in the King's School.]
4. MS: day & a

"WHERE THEIR WORM DIETH NOT, AND THE FIRE IS NOT QUENCHED."
[The notebook MS is in the King's School.]
Title. MS: dieth not, & the
1. MS: tempest & storm
3. MS: more, & love
4. MS: tempest & storm;
7. MS: tempest & storm.

"TOLL, BELL, TOLL. FOR HOPE IS FLYING"
[The notebook MS is in the King's School.]

"EARTH HAS CLEAR CALL OF DAILY BELLS"
[The *Verses* notebook MS (MS2) is in the King's School.]
2. MS2: gloom & star,
8. MS2: Of Earth & Heaven: its
10. MS2: sit & gaze,

p. 434
    "ESCAPE TO THE MOUNTAIN."
       [The notebook MS is in the King's School.]
        1. MS: within, & saw
        2. MS: Upward, & saw
        3. MS: Downward, & saw darkness & flame
        6. MS: darkness & devouring
        8. MS: death & shame.
      10. MS: of far off day:—
      11. MS: happy [*in*]<th>at endure,

    "I LIFE MINE EYES TO SEE: EARTH VANISHETH"
       [The notebook MS is in the King's School.]
        2. MS: eyes & [*bow*] <bend> my
        3. MS: down, & face
        9. MS: a palmbranch tree,

    "YET A LITTLE WHILE."
       [The notebook MS is in the King's School.]
        2. MS: earth & main.
        3. MS: live & die,
        4. MS: revive, & rise
        5. MS: how long? Oh long

    "BEHOLD, IT WAS VERY GOOD."
       [The notebook MS is in the King's School.]
        5. MS: declare:
        7. MS: home & cast
        8. MS: tree
        9. MS: low sit
      10. MS: more, in

p. 435
    "WHATSOEVER IS RIGHT, THAT SHALL YE RECEIVE."
       [The *Verses* notebook MS (MS2) is in the King's School.]
        2. MS2: once, & fallen
      15. MS2: join & no

    "THIS NEAR-AT-HAND LAND BREEDS PAIN BY MEASURE"
       [The notebook MS is in the King's School. In the MS, the last line of
       each stanza is indented four spaces.]
        1. MS: near-at-hand <land> breeds
        7. MS: sobbing & sighing:
        8. MS: speech & sweet
      10. MS: errors & follies:
      13. MS: Up & away,
      18. MS: For ever & ever;
      22. MS: Come & laugh

p. 436

"WAS THY WRATH AGAINST THE SEA?"
[The notebook MS is in the King's School.]
 3. MS: high & passing
 9. MS: sea! God's Wisdom worketh
 11. MS: high, & passing

"AND THERE WAS NO MORE SEA."
[The notebook MS is in the King's School.]
 1. MS: above & from
 2. MS: near & far,
 3. MS: life & out
 7. MS: Heaven & earth & sea
 14. MS: sweetest gladdest best at
 15. MS: peace & smile;
 18. MS: lot & love

"ROSES ON A BRIER"
[The notebook MS is in the King's School.]
 11. MS: still, & earn

"WE ARE OF THOSE WHO TREMBLE AT THY WORD"
[The notebook MS is in the King's School.]
 3. MS: curbed & spurred:
 7. MS: wants & woes.

"AWAKE, THOU THAT SLEEPEST."
[The notebook MS is in the King's School.]
 4. MS: stiffness & starkness!
 7. MS: Far far
 9. MS: life & to
 11. MS: men & up

"WE KNOW NOT WHEN, WE KNOW NOT WHERE"
[The notebook MS is in the King's School.]
 5. MS: athirst & thirsty
 6. MS: We know & know

p. 437

"I WILL LIFT UP MINE EYES UNTO THE HILLS."
[The *Verses* notebook MS (MS2) is in the King's School. In the MS, the fourth and eighth lines of each stanza are indented four spaces.]
 1. MS2: life & all
 2. MS2: [*When*] <How> sick
 5. MS2: death & ills
 6. MS2: heart & eyes,
 7. MS2: streets & gateways
 13. MS2: grief & fears;
 15. MS2: Oh when

17. MS2: new Heavens & Earth
21. MS2: sun & moon

p. 438

"THEN WHOSE SHALL THOSE THINGS BE?"
[The *Verses* notebook MS (MS3) is in the King's School.]
2. MS3: here, & seek
3. MS3: treasure, & add <> to field
4. MS3: And heap to heap & store
5. MS3: grasping more & seeking

p. 441

"HIS BANNER OVER ME WAS LOVE."
[The notebook MS is in the King's School.]
1. MS: attain
3. MS: doubt & no
5. MS: gems & gold & inlets

"BELOVED, YIELD THY TIME TO GOD, FOR HE"
[The notebook MS is in the King's School.]
3. MS: for His Love, & be
4. MS: Beatified pa[t]<s>t earth's

"TIME SEEMS NOT SHORT"
[The notebook MS is in the King's School.]
4. MS: bear & strike
7. MS: out & see
8. MS: within sphere time
13. MS: sole battleground of right & wrong:

"THE HALF MOON SHOWS A FACE OF PLAINTIVE SWEETNESS"
[The notebook MS is in the King's School.]
2. MS: Ready & poised
9. MS: incompleteness

"AS THE DOVES TO THEIR WINDOWS."
[The notebook MS is in the King's School.]
1. MS: east & the
2. MS: north & the south with
7. MS: ruin & wrong.

p. 442

"OH KNELL OF A PASSING TIME"
[The notebook MS is in the King's School.]
5. MS: night & when
6. MS: Moon & sun pass
11. MS: numbered, & day

"TIME PASSETH AWAY WITH ITS PLEASURE AND PAIN"

[The notebook MS is in the King's School.]

1. MS: pleasure & pain,
2. MS: cypress & bay,
3. MS: wealth & with <> balm & a

"THE EARTH SHALL TREMBLE AT THE LOOK OF HIM."

[The notebook MS is in the King's School.]

2. MS: thee & brought
3. MS: Always everywhere thy
5. MS: music & mirth?
7. MS: hunger & thirst
9. MS: heaven & breathe
10. MS: of harvest & infinite

"TIME LENGTHENING, IN THE LENGTHENING SEEMETH LONG"

[The notebook MS is in the King's School.]

7. MS: to be & be & be,
11. MS: up & strained & shooting
16. MS: here & still

"ALL FLESH IS GRASS."

[The notebook MS is in the King's School.]

1. MS: a life, & then
9. MS: life, & then

"HEAVEN'S CHIMES ARE SLOW, BUT SURE TO STRIKE AT LAST"

[The *Verses* notebook MS (MS2) is in the King's School.]

7. MS2: suffer, & a

p. 444

"THERE REMAINETH THEREFORE A REST TO THE PEOPLE OF GOD."

[The *Verses* notebook MS (MS2) is in the King's School.]

2. MS2: Work & vigil, prayer & fast,
5. MS2: begun.
6. MS2: Fear & hope & chastening
9. MS2: Heat & burden

p. 445

"PARTING AFTER PARTING."

[The *Verses* notebook MS (MS3) is in the King's School. In the MS, lines 11–16 constitute a separate poem.]

2. MS3: loss & gnawing
4. MS3: [A stanza break follows the line.]

p. 446

"THEY PUT THEIR TRUST IN THEE, AND WERE NOT
CONFOUNDED." / I.
    [The notebook MS is in the King's School.]
    Title. MS: in Thee, & were <> confounded." / 1.
      2. MS: While Time & Death

"THEY PUT THEIR TRUST IN THEE, AND WERE NOT
CONFOUNDED." / II.
    [The notebook MS is in the King's School.]
    Title. MS: 2.
      3. MS: is; & we
      7. MS: holds & weighs
    10. MS: where & when,

"SHORT IS TIME, AND ONLY TIME IS BLEAK"
    [The notebook MS is in the King's School.]
      1. MS: Short is time, & only
      6. MS: Pray & watch & pray, <> up & meek;

FOR EACH.
    [The notebook MS is in the King's School.]
      2. MS: Weak & watery
      3. MS: Day & night
      9. MS: Snares & pits
    10. MS: fallen so

FOR ALL.
    [The notebook MS is in the King's School.]
      1. MS: harvest is pa[*t*]<s>t, his
      2. MS: Hope & fear
      8. MS: earth & ocean

p. 447

"THE HOLY CITY, NEW JERUSALEM."
    [The notebook MS is in the King's School.]
    Title. MS: "The Holy City, [*n*]<N>ew Jerusalem."
      2. MS: pearl & gem:
    13. MS: matins & her
    17. MS: flower & fruit <> trees
    19. MS: clear & calm
    20. MS: with the Palm
    21. MS: triumph & for food & balm.
    22. MS: Jerusalem where
    24. MS: to Jerusalem
    27. MS: first & last, <> great & small,
    28. MS: by one, home one & all.

"WHEN WICKEDNESS IS BROKEN AS A TREE"
[The notebook MS is in the King's School.]
3. MS: sand
12. MS: harps & songs

"JERUSALEM OF FIRE"
[The notebook MS is in the King's School.]
2. MS: gold & pearl & gem,
9. MS: A palm branch from

"SHE SHALL BE BROUGHT UNTO THE KING."
[The notebook MS is in the King's School.]
7. MS: forgotten & sorrowful memories,
10. MS: won & with

"WHO IS THIS THAT COMETH UP NOT ALONE"
[The notebook MS is in the King's School.]
5. MS: of Kings' daughter,
8. MS: Her eyes a dove's eyes & her
10. MS: saints & angels

p. 448

"WHO SITS WITH THE KING IN HIS THRONE? NOT A SLAVE BUT
A BRIDE"
[The notebook MS is in the King's School.]
2. MS: all Greatness & Grace
6. MS: whirlpool & Dragon's
9. MS: Lo, Dragon laments & Death
10. MS: of Peace, & her

ANTIPAS.
[The notebook MS is in the King's School.]
3. MS: in God's Presence worshipped
8. MS: be love with love & light with light,

"BEAUTIFUL FOR SITUATION."
[The notebook MS is in the King's School.]
2. MS: lovely, & whose
3. MS: all angels sing;
5. MS: Saluting [*l*]<L>ove with palmbranch in
8. MS: Set wide, & where
12. MS: beloved, & thither
13. MS: heart & set < > face, & go
14. MS: pursuing home

"LORD, BY WHAT INCONCEIVABLE DIM ROAD"
[The notebook MS is in the King's School.]
8. MS: groans & totters
12. MS: Yea but
13. MS: body & refreshed

"AS COLD WATERS TO A THIRSTY SOUL, SO IS GOOD NEWS FROM A FAR COUNTRY."
[The *Verses* notebook MS (MS3) is in the King's School.]
10. MS3: Lilies & roses
14. MS3: Sweet scented from
15. MS3: we sing amid
16. MS3: gather palm branches."
20. MS3: bower & blossom
21. MS3: steep & straight
22. MS3: trees
23. MS3: sing & wait
24. MS3: gather palm branches."

p. 450

"CAST DOWN BUT NOT DESTROYED, CHASTENED NOT SLAIN"
[The notebook MS is in the King's School.]
1. MS: slain:—
3. MS: I who
8. MS: faster & my
13. MS: Fear & desire & pangs & ecstasies;
14. MS: Yea th[*e*]<us> they

"LIFT UP THINE EYES TO SEEK THE INVISIBLE"
[The notebook MS is in the King's School.]
9. MS: purblind & deafened,

"LOVE IS STRONG AS DEATH."
[The notebook MS is in the King's School.]

"LET THEM REJOICE IN THEIR BEDS."
[The notebook MS is in the King's School.]
5. MS: discloses
6. MS: work save waiting done.
7. MS: stars while
8. MS: Resting for
12. MS: O Lord God the

"SLAIN IN THEIR HIGH PLACES: FALLEN ON REST"
[The notebook MS is in the King's School.]
1. MS: Slain [*th*] in
7. MS: gifts & graces.
8. MS: oh twine heaven's

"WHAT HATH GOD WROUGHT!"
[The notebook MS is in the King's School.]
2. MS: contented & free
3. MS: very far off, & far
4. MS: them. One King & one
5. MS: harmonious & strong,
6. MS: One King & one love & one s[*o*]<h>out of

p. 451

"BEFORE THE THRONE, AND BEFORE THE LAMB."
> [The notebook MS is in the King's School.]
> Title. MS: "Before the Throne, & before
>> 3. MS: moon & unswayed
>> 5. MS: ring

"HE SHALL GO NO MORE OUT."
> [The notebook MS is in the King's School.]
> Title. MS: go [*out*] no more[."]<o>ut."
>> 5. MS: death & doubt & sin;
>> 6. MS: with & all
>> 7. MS: life skin

"YEA, BLESSED AND HOLY IS HE THAT HATH PART IN THE FIRST RESURRECTION!"
> [The notebook MS is in the King's School.]
>> 1. MS: blessed & holy
>> 2. MS: gaze even we
>> 3. MS: lustre of God & of
>> 4. MS: blessed & holy
>> 7. MS: scattered & peeled, < > sifted & chastened & scourged & set
>> 9. MS: is that King & that
>> 11. MS: blessed & holy

"THE JOY OF SAINTS, LIKE INCENSE TURNED TO FIRE"
> [The notebook MS is in the King's School.]
>> 7. MS: in all, & all
>> 8. MS: is love & love
>> 9. MS: white & all
>> 10. MS: gold & thrones
>> 12. MS: glass & fire
>> 13. MS: young, & none

"WHAT ARE THESE LOVELY ONES, YEA, WHAT ARE THESE?"
> [The notebook MS is in the King's School.]
>> 3. MS: [*Cast*] <Stripped> off < > ease
>> 7. MS: cease
>> 9. MS: harps, & wherefore

p. 452

"THE GENERAL ASSEMBLY AND CHURCH OF THE FIRSTBORN."
> [The notebook MS is in the King's School.]
> Title. MS: "The General Assembly [illegible deletion] <&> Church
>> 2. MS: glory & Thy
>> 5. MS: Raptures & voices
>> 6. MS: Love & are
>> 9. MS: Matrons & mothers
>> 10. MS: Wise & most

11. MS: who making merry lead
13. MS: change & chance,
15. MS: reproduce [*o*]<O>ne Countenance,
17. MS: hungry & athirst

"EVERY ONE THAT IS PERFECT SHALL BE AS HIS MASTER."
[The notebook MS is in the King's School.]
 9. MS: all
11. MS: clings & trusts & worships,
13. MS: which prompting < > obedience
15. MS: the great & small.

"'AS DYING, AND BEHOLD WE LIVE!'"
[The notebook MS is in the King's School.]
 1. MS: dying, & behold
 7. MS: prayer & sighing.

"SO GREAT A CLOUD OF WITNESSES."
[The notebook MS is in the King's School.]
 1. MS: known, & lift
 6. MS: sing & while
 7. MS: in, & more, & yet more, & again
 8. MS: open entrance door.
11. MS: them, & speak

"OUR MOTHERS, LOVELY WOMEN PITIFUL"
[The notebook MS is in the King's School.]
 2. MS: life & death;
 6. MS: walked much
 7. MS: hoped despite < > slips & scathe,
 8. MS: joy & confident
 9. MS: can see:

"SAFE WHERE I CANNOT LIE YET"
[The notebook MS is in the King's School.]
 3. MS: fume & the
 6. MS: frost & the
 7. MS: storm & the sun;

p. 453
"IS IT WELL WITH THE CHILD?"
[The *Verses* notebook MS (MS2) is in the King's School.]
Title. MS2: the Child?"
 5. MS2: fetched & carried,
 6. MS2: betrothed & married.
 8. MS2: Meek eyed & simple,

"DEAR ANGELS AND DEAR DISEMBODIED SAINTS"
[The notebook MS is in the King's School.]
 1. MS: Dear Angels & dear
 4. MS: quest

    5. MS: moulds & paints
    7. MS: undermines & taints
    8. MS: sin & sloth
    9. MS: Sloth, & a lie, & sin:
  11. MS: Th[*e*]<at> heart [*that*] <which> being
  12. MS: rose & ran
  13. MS: When Christ life-giver roused
  14. MS: rise & run & rest

"TO EVERY SEED HIS OWN BODY."
[The notebook MS is in the King's School.]
    5. MS: must [*life*] live afresh, & must
    7. MS: goal;
  12. MS: Each dovelike soul

p. 454
"WHAT GOOD SHALL MY LIFE DO ME?"
[The *Verses* notebook MS (MS2) is in the King's School.]
  10. MS2: change & smiles & tears.
  12. MS2: Rejoice & grieve,
  13. MS2: fear, & die?
  18. MS2: Lies & shows
  20. MS2: hope & sleep
  30. MS2: rest & leap.

p. 455
"HER SEED; IT SHALL BRUISE THY HEAD."
[The notebook MS is in the King's School.]
  10. MS: earth, & undismayed

"JUDGE NOTHING BEFORE THE TIME."
[The notebook MS is in the King's School.]
    8. MS: love & to
  10. MS: patient & approve:

"HOW GREAT IS LITTLE MAN!"
[The notebook MS is in the King's School.]
    2. MS: moon & stars
    9. MS: Ah rich man! ah poor
  13. MS: things man,
  17. MS: Little & great

"MAN'S LIFE IS BUT A WORKING DAY"
[The *Verses* notebook MS (MS2) is in the King's School.]
    6. MS2: green & robes
    7. MS2: A longdrawn breath,

p. 456

"IF NOT WITH HOPE OF LIFE"
[The notebook MS is in the King's School.]
3. MS: tremendous lifelong strife
7. MS: fear & hope
10. MS: watch & ward;

"THE DAY IS AT HAND."
[The *Verses* notebook MS (MS2) is in the King's School.]
Title. MS2: "The Day is
7. MS2: love & [illegible deletion] <st>int not deep

p. 457

"ENDURE HARDNESS."
[The notebook MS is in the King's School.]
2. MS: burgeon & to
4. MS: With [illegible deletion] <flakes> [illegible deletion] <& sprays
of snow>
5. MS: coldness & thro'

"WHITHER THE TRIBES GO UP, EVEN THE TRIBES
OF THE LORD."
[The notebook MS is in the King's School.]
16. MS: all Saints & rest

"WHERE NEVER TEMPEST HEAVETH"
[The notebook MS is in the King's School.]

"MARVEL OF MARVELS, IF I MYSELF SHALL BEHOLD"
[The notebook MS is in the King's School.]
4. MS: least & last
6. MS: saints my
8. MS: darkness & cold

"WHAT IS THAT TO THEE? FOLLOW THOU ME."
[The *Verses* notebook MS (MS3) is in the King's School.]
Title. MS3: thou Me."
2. MS3: saith, "Wait & bear."
12. MS3: hour?
15. MS3: choice & only

p. 458

"WORSHIP GOD."
[The notebook MS is in the King's School.]
2. MS: near":
3. MS: prayer & tear
5. MS: thorned & thistled
7. MS: brutes, & envious
8. MS: Unliving & undying
9. MS: said, "Worship Me: & give
10. MS: child": now

"AFTERWARD HE REPENTED, AND WENT."
[The notebook MS is in the King's School.]
Title. MS: "Afterward[s] he repented, & went."
5. MS: but just, & Thou

p. 459

"ARE THEY NOT ALL MINISTERING SPIRITS?"
[The notebook MS is in the King's School.]
8. MS: on & pray
9. MS: Obedient & at

"OUR LIFE IS LONG. NOT SO, WISE ANGELS SAY"
[MS2 does not appear to be in Christina's handwriting. The *Verses* note-book MS (MS3) is in the King's School.]
1. MS3: so wise
4. MS3: so the <> protest
5. MS3: consolation & of
8. MS3: spent."
9. MS3: Repent & work today, work & repent.
13. MS3: wait & long
14. MS3: hope & freed
16. MS3: for thirtythree
17. MS3: to Thee
18. MS3: art there

p. 460

"LORD, WHAT HAVE I TO OFFER? SICKENING FEAR"
[The notebook MS is in the King's School.]
11. MS: us & not

"JOY IS BUT SORROW"
[The notebook MS is in the King's School. In the MS, lines 1, 3, 5–8, 10, and 12–14 are not indented, and lines 2, 4, 9, and 11 are indented two spaces.]
7. MS: fair & frail.

"CAN I KNOW IT?—NAY.—"
[The notebook MS is in the King's School.]
4. MS: ever & aye.—
7. MS: heart & pray
13. MS: past May day
27. MS: a palm branch pray;

"WHEN MY HEART IS VEXED I WILL COMPLAIN."
[Lines 1–20 composed May 10, 1854. The notebook MS (MS1) is in the Bodleian Library. The *Verses* notebook MS (MS2) is in the King's School. Lines 1–20 originally formed part of a longer poem entitled "'Ye have forgotten the exhortation,'" which Christina never published as such. "'Ye have forgotten the exhortation'" is presented in its own right in Volume III of the present edition.]

Title. MS1: "Ye have forgotten the exhortation."
1. MS1: *Angel* / The [The word "*Angel*" is centered above the line.
   Preceding line 1 are the following stanzas:]

Angel

Bury thy dead, dear friend,
Between the night and day;
Where depths of summer shade are cool,
And murmurs of a summer pool
And windy murmurs stray:—

Soul

Ah, gone away,
Ah, dear and lost delight,
Gone from me and for ever out of sight.

Angel

Bury thy dead, dear love,
And make his bed most fair above;
The latest buds shall still
Blow there, and the first violets too,
And there a turtle dove
Shall brood and coo:—

Soul

I cannot make the nest
So warm, but he may find it chill
In solitary rest.

Angel

Bury thy dead heart-deep;
Take patience till the sun be set;
There are no tears for him to weep,
No doubts to haunt him yet:
Take comfort, he will not forget:—

Soul

Then I will watch beside his sleep;
Will watch alone,
And make my moan
Because the harvest is so long to reap.

MS2: look & see,
3. MS1: The harvest moon shines full and clear,
   MS2: The full orbed harvest
4. MS1: time is near,
5. MS1: cheer:—
6. MS1: *Soul* / Ah, <> me; [The word "*Soul*" is centered above the
   line.]
   MS2: "Ah woe
8. MS1: to chime.
9–14. MS1:

Angel

But One can give thee heart, thy Lord and his,
Can raise both thee and him
To shine with Seraphim
And pasture where the eternal fountain is.

Can give thee of that tree
Whose leaves are health for thee;
Can give <thee> robes made clean and white,
And love, and all delight,
And beauty where the day turns not to night.

12. MS2: heart & shining
14. MS2: rivers & the
15–20. MS1:

Who knocketh at His door
And presseth in, goes out no more.
Kneel as thou hast not knelt before—
The time is short—and smite
Upon thy breast and pray with all thy might:—

[Below line 20 is the following stanza:]

Soul

O Lord, my heart is broken for my sin:
Yet hasten Thine Own day
And come away.
Is not time full? Oh put the sickle in,
O Lord, begin.

18. MS2: That ever open door
19. MS2: short) & smite
20. MS2: breast, & pray

p. 461

"PRAYING ALWAYS."
[The notebook MS is in the King's School.]
  2. MS: one:
  4. MS: up & hark!
  6. MS: After midday, in
  7. MS: one:
  8. MS: Day fall has
 11. MS: noon & night,
 15. MS: brothers & O sisters? Pause & pray.

"AS THY DAYS, SO SHALL THY STRENGTH BE."
[The notebook MS is in the King's School.]
  6. MS: night & scarcely

"A HEAVY HEART, IF EVER HEART WAS HEAVY"
[The notebook MS is in the King's School.]
  4. MS: do & dare
  6. MS: blossom & stood
  9. MS: Leafless & bloomless
 12. MS: leaps & lightens
 14. MS: sing, & see

"IF LOVE IS NOT WORTH LOVING, THEN LIFE IS NOT WORTH LIVING"

[The notebook MS is in the King's School.]

3. MS: storing & gifts
5. MS: death-cold, & life-heat
6. MS: offering & vainer
9. MS: rot;

"WHAT IS IT JESUS SAITH UNTO THE SOUL?"

[The *Verses* notebook MS (MS3) is in the King's School. The poem was published in *Maude: A Story for Girls* (London: James Bowden, 1897), 79–80; variants therein are designated "1897" in the textual notes. It was also published in *Maude: Prose & Verse by Christina Rossetti; 1850* (Chicago: Herbert S. Stone and Co., 1897), 120–21; variants therein are designated "1897a" in the textual notes. In the 1897 text, lines 1, 4, 5, 8, 10, and 13 are indented four spaces, and the remaining lines are not indented. In the 1897a text, lines 1, 4, 5, 8, 10, 11, and 13 are indented two spaces, and the remaining lines are not indented.]

1. 1897a: soul?—
2. MS3: the Cross, & come & follow
   1897: come, and
   1897a: the Cross and come, and
3. 1897, 1897a: This word < > all; no man
4. MS3: a Cross yet
   1897, 1897a: Without the Cross, wishing to win the
5. MS3: up, & brace
   1897, 1897a: Then take it < > up, setting thy
7. 1897: Beyond thy utmost strength: take it; for He
   1897a: Beyond thy utmost strength: take it, for He
8. 1897, 1897a: Knoweth when thou art weak, and will control
9. MS3: today, & let
   1897: The powers of darkness that thou need'st not fear.
   1897a: The powers of darkness that thou needst not fear.
10. 1897, 1897a: He will be with thee, helping, strengthening,
11. 1897, 1897a: Until it is enough: for lo, the day
12. 1897: Cometh when He shall call thee: thou shalt hear
    1897a: Cometh when He shall call thee: thou shall hear
13. MS3: Suffer & work & strive
    1897: His Voice that says: "Winter is past, and Spring
    1897a: His voice that says: "Winter is past, and Spring
14. 1897, 1897a: Is come; arise, My Love, and come away."

p. 462

"THEY LIE AT REST, OUR BLESSED DEAD"

[The *Verses* notebook MS (MS3) is in the King's School.]

8. MS3: wept & eyes
10. MS3: great & small,
12. MS3: salt sea wall.

p. 464

"YE THAT FEAR HIM, BOTH SMALL AND GREAT."
[The notebook MS is in the King's School. In the MS, the last line of each stanza is indented two spaces.]
Title. MS: small & great."
17. MS: tears & sighing,

"CALLED TO BE SAINTS."
[The notebook MS is in the King's School.]
1. MS: steep & high
5. MS: hail & grace

p. 465

"THE SINNER'S OWN FAULT? SO IT WAS"
[The *Verses* notebook MS (MS2) is in the King's School.]
3. MS2: Dogged us & hedged
8. MS2: lagged & would
10. MS2: mend & pray.

p. 466

"WHO CARES FOR EARTHLY BREAD THO' WHITE?"
[The notebook MS is in the King's School.]

"LAUGHING LIFE CRIES AT THE FEAST,—"
[The *Verses* notebook MS (MS2) is in the King's School.]
3. MS2: beast?"—

"THE END IS NOT YET."
[The notebook MS is in the King's School.]
2. MS: prayer & praise,
3. MS: old & great <> small
5. MS: nights & many
8. MS: called & death
10. MS: wall

"WHO WOULD WISH BACK THE SAINTS UPON OUR ROUGH"
[The *Verses* notebook MS (MS2) is in the King's School.]
12. MS2: hear & see?
18. MS2: rest, & good

p. 467

"THAT WHICH HATH BEEN IS NAMED ALREADY, AND IT IS KNOWN THAT IT IS MAN."
[The notebook MS is in the King's School.]
Title. MS: already, & it <> known that it is [*m*]<M>an."
1. MS: known & weighed
6. MS: song & spoken
7. MS: lovelier loftier
11. MS: death: wh[illegible deletion]<at fi>re shall

"OF EACH SAD WORD WHICH IS MORE SORROWFUL"
  [The notebook MS is in the King's School.]
 5. MS: mourn: & lo!
 9. MS: wise & saints
 10. MS: shape steppingstone, or

"I SEE THAT ALL THINGS COME TO AN END." / I.
  [The notebook MS is in the King's School.]
  Title. MS: end"—: / 1.
 1. MS: sun & planets fly
 2. MS: wind & storm & seasons
 3. MS: live & while
 5. MS: roar
 6. MS: cry
 8. MS: silence by & bye:
 9. MS: cold & hoar!

p. 468

"BUT THY COMMANDMENT IS EXCEEDING BROAD." / II.
  [The notebook MS is in the King's School.]
  Title. MS: "But Thy [c]<C>ommand[illegible deletion]<m>ent is < >
    broad." / 2.
 3. MS: watch & pray & weep
 7. MS: long & rough & plain.
 8. MS: Sow & reap:
 9. MS: Time & earth & life
 10. MS: laugh & reap

SURSUM CORDA.
  [The notebook MS is in the King's School.]
 1. MS: hearts[,]<.>" "We
 6. MS: stoop, Lord, & take
 8. MS: Stoop, Lord, & hearken, hearken, Lord, & do,
 9. MS: will & take < > heart & take

"O YE, WHO ARE NOT DEAD AND FIT"
  [The notebook MS is in the King's School.]
 1. MS: dead & fit
 5. MS: earth & heaven
 8. MS: poles
 18. MS: up & wonder & draw
 21. MS: love & cast

"WHERE SHALL I FIND A WHITE ROSE BLOWING?—"
  [The *Verses* notebook MS (MS2) is in the King's School.]
 5. MS2: snow & a
 19. MS2: winter & now
 22. MS2: Winter & sorrow
 23. MS2: winter & no

p. 469

"REDEEMING THE TIME."
[The notebook MS is in the King's School.]
  5. MS: flower & not
  6. MS: flower & not
  7. MS: Arise & sow & weed:

"NOW THEY DESIRE A BETTER COUNTRY."
[The notebook MS is in the King's School.]
  5. MS: watch & pray;
  6. MS: praying:
  7. MS: pale & grey.
  9. MS: his dreamworld flushed
 10. MS: weighing

A CASTLE-BUILDER'S WORLD.
[The notebook MS is in the King's School.]
Title. MS: A Castle-Builder's World.
Opening quotation. MS: confusion, & the
  5. MS: men & women
  6. MS: flocks & shoals;
  7. MS: Flesh-&-bloodless hazy < > there
  8. MS: orbs & poles;
  9. MS: Flesh-&-bloodless vapid

"THESE ALL WAIT UPON THEE."
[The *Verses* notebook MS (MS2) is in the King's School. In the MS, lines 1, 2, 4, 5, 7, 8, and 12 are indented two spaces.]
  3. MS2: birds & insects
  7. MS2: least & last

p. 471

"DOETH WELL . . . DOETH BETTER."
[The notebook MS is in the King's School.]
Title. MS: well . . . . doeth
  6. MS: "us" & spoke
  7. MS: substantial while
  9. MS: rest tho' < > toss & rend
 10. MS: heart & keeps

"OUR HEAVEN MUST BE WITHIN OURSELVES"
[The *Verses* notebook MS (MS2) is in the King's School. In the MS, the last line of each stanza is indented six spaces.]
  2. MS2: home & heaven < > faith,
  5. MS2: wall
  8. MS2: gem & flower.

p. 472

"VANITY OF VANITIES."
[The *Verses* notebook MS (MS2) is in the King's School.]
2. MS2: an [*a*]<A>utumn leaf

p. 473

"THE HILLS ARE TIPPED WITH SUNSHINE, WHILE I WALK"
[The notebook MS is in the King's School.]
2. MS: dim & cold:
6. MS: glory, & the
8. MS: sunny hill tops I,
14. MS: Sunshine & song,

"SCARCE TOLERABLE LIFE, WHICH ALL LIFE LONG"
[The notebook MS is in the King's School.]
1. MS: tolerable life, whic[illegible deletion]<h> all
2. MS: dread [*by one dread*] of
5. MS: me [*t*]<,> this
6. MS: grows & dwindles
8. MS: lengthened & its
10. MS: lived, & yet
12. MS: life immortal ever

"ALL HEAVEN IS BLAZING YET"
[The notebook MS is in the King's School.]
13. MS: chose & choose
15. MS: life who[*s*] seems

p. 474

"BALM IN GILEAD."
[The notebook MS is in the King's School.]
6. MS: watering, [illegible deletion] weeding,

"IN THE DAY OF HIS ESPOUSALS."
[The notebook MS is in the King's School.]
2. MS: Sinks & rises & loves & longs
3. MS: temperate zones & torrid
9. MS: Queens in throngs & damsels
10. MS: tones & mysteries
11. MS: That [*s*]<S>ong of

"SHE CAME FROM THE UTTERMOST PART OF THE EARTH."
[The notebook MS is in the King's School.]
2. MS: wisdom & of
6. MS: speech & mien;
9. MS: face & her

"ALLELUIA! OR ALAS! MY HEART IS CRYING"
[The notebook MS is in the King's School.]

"THE PASSION FLOWER HATH SPRUNG UP TALL"
[The notebook MS is in the King's School.]
    2. MS: east & west

GOD'S ACRE.
[The notebook MS is in the King's School.]
    2. MS: darkness & cold;
    3. MS: sweet & how
    5. MS: balm, [*balsam*] <myrtle> & heliotrope
    6. MS: watch & there
    7. MS: the Sun which
    8. MS: Each & all

p. 475
"THE FLOWERS APPEAR ON THE EARTH."
[The *Verses* notebook MS (MS2) is in the King's School.]
    7. MS2: [*Or bride's*] [not indented] <Or bride's> [indented two spaces]
    whose hoped for sweet
  12. MS2: night & morning
  20. MS2: love & resurrection.
  21. MS2: fair

p. 476
"THOU KNEWEST . . . THOU OUGHTEST THEREFORE."
[The notebook MS is in the King's School.]
Title. MS: knewest . . . . thou
    5. MS: bed & shroud:
    9. MS: was & low,
  10. MS: strong enough & high
  12. MS: did & prospered,
  13. MS: little doing

"GO IN PEACE."
[The notebook MS is in the King's School.]
    6. MS: will & can;

"HALF DEAD."
[The notebook MS is in the King's School. In the MS, the second line of
each stanza is indented two spaces.]
    4. MS: O Christ my <> oil & wine
    6. MS: Me ever Thine, & Thee
    7. MS: saints & sinners,
    8. MS: great & small:
  13. MS: prayer & vow
  14. MS: now- - -

"ONE OF THE SOLDIERS WITH A SPEAR PIERCED HIS SIDE."
[The notebook MS is in the King's School.]
Title. MS: a [s]<S>pear pierced
3. MS: from Thee & me:
9. MS: Another, & another—

p. 477

"WHERE LOVE IS, THERE COMES SORROW"
[The notebook MS is in the King's School.]

"BURY HOPE OUT OF SIGHT"
[The notebook MS is in the King's School.]
2. MS: it & no
4. MS: growing & well:
19. MS: day & its
20. MS: more & no

A CHURCHYARD SONG OF PATIENT HOPE.
[The notebook MS is in the King's School. In the MS, lines 4 and 8 are indented six spaces.]
3. MS: thee & me!—

"ONE WOE IS PAST. COME WHAT COME WILL"
[The notebook MS is in the King's School.]
2. MS: ended & made
9. MS: pain & fear & poisonous

"TAKE NO THOUGHT FOR THE MORROW."
[The notebook MS is in the King's School.]
1. MS: Who knows? God knows: & what
2. MS: well & best.
12. MS: west

"CONSIDER THE LILIES OF THE FIELD."
[The notebook MS is in the King's School.]
7. MS: earth & air:
8. MS: us & wear.

"SON, REMEMBER."
[The notebook MS is in the King's School. The poem was published in *"New and Old;" For Seed-Time and Harvest*, XVII (October, 1889), 274. In the 1889 text, lines 11 and 14 are indented two spaces.]
Title. 1889: LAZARUS LOQUITUR.
1. MS, 1889: I, laid
2. 1889: not, I
3. MS: Hungry & thirsty, sore & sick & bare,
4. MS: Dog-comforted & crumbs-solicitous:
7. 1889: Thus, a <> wonder, thou <> care;
8. 1889: And, be <> not seen, I

10. MS: songs & trumpet
    1889: worm, angel
12. 1889: alas, but
13. MS: Fire & an

p. 478
"HEAVINESS MAY ENDURE FOR A NIGHT, BUT JOY COMETH IN
THE MORNING."
[The notebook MS is in the King's School.]
 7. MS: off a<->dying from
21. MS: calls & soon
22. MS: sweet & true.
24. MS: delights & charities,

"THE WILL OF THE LORD BE DONE."
[The notebook MS is in the King's School.]
12. MS: ours, & keep

"LAY UP FOR YOURSELVES TREASURES IN HEAVEN."
[The notebook MS is in the King's School.]
 5. MS: pleasure
 7. MS: treasure

"WHOM THE LORD LOVETH HE CHASTENETH."
[The notebook MS is in the King's School.]
 3. MS: hands & urge
10. MS: rise & greet

"THEN SHALL YE SHOUT."
[The notebook MS is in the King's School.]
 2. MS: sing,
 8. MS: sing & say.
16. MS: Our love song while

p. 479
"EVERYTHING THAT IS BORN MUST DIE"
[The notebook MS is in the King's School.]
 3. MS: balance low or high
 6. MS: Hope & fear
 7. MS: Height & depth
 9. MS: on homebound wing:

"LORD, GRANT US CALM, IF CALM CAN SET FORTH THEE"
[The notebook MS is in the King's School.]
 4. MS: sea
 7. MS: east & west, <> south & north,

CHANGING CHIMES.
[The notebook MS is in the King's School.]
Title. MS: [*"Thou shalt hear a Voice behind Thee."*] [written in pencil]
    <Changing Chimes.> [written in ink]

3. MS: up & act:
4. MS: Watch alway,—watch & pray,—watch alway[,]<.>—
6. MS: aught was lacked [*good will*] <goodwill> was
7. MS: Alas, [*good will*] <goodwill> is
9. MS: Watch & act,—watch & pray,—watch alway.

"THY SERVANT WILL GO AND FIGHT WITH THIS PHILISTINE."
[The notebook MS is in the King's School.]
Title. MS: "Thy [*s*]<S>ervant will go & fight
9. MS: Devil & Death & Hades,

"THRO' BURDEN AND HEAT OF THE DAY"
[The notebook MS is in the King's School.]
1. MS: burden & heat
2. MS: hands & the
3. MS: stay
4. MS: burden & heat!
7. MS: is [illegible deletion] fleet.
8. MS: show [*g*] lengthening & grey,
11. MS: burden & heat?

"THEN I COMMENDED MIRTH."
[The notebook MS is in the King's School.]
2. MS: life & all
5. MS: nature & well
6. MS: man & beast,

p. 480

"SORROW HATH A DOUBLE VOICE."
[The notebook MS is in the King's School.]

"SHADOWS TODAY, WHILE SHADOWS SHOW GOD'S WILL"
[The notebook MS is in the King's School.]
4. MS: marvels & whose
5. MS: course & deep
7. MS: not over bright;
10. MS: garland thee & bid
11. MS: choirs & glance

"TRULY THE LIGHT IS SWEET."
[The notebook MS is in the King's School.]
4. MS: rise & shine,
7. MS: beauty & delight,
12. MS: Oh well < > thee & happy

"ARE YE NOT MUCH BETTER THAN THEY?"
[The notebook MS is in the King's School.]

"YEA, THE SPARROW HATH FOUND HER AN HOUSE."
[The notebook MS is in the King's School.]

Title. MS: the Sparrow hath < > her a<n> house."

5. MS: sparrows & swallows,

7. MS: chapel & nest,

8. MS: wish & a will & a

10. MS: alone & in

"I AM SMALL AND OF NO REPUTATION."
[The notebook MS is in the King's School.]
Title. MS: small & of
5. MS: fear & I

"O CHRIST MY GOD WHO SEEST THE UNSEEN"
[The notebook MS is in the King's School.]

p. 481
"YEA, IF THOU WILT, THOU CANST PUT UP THY SWORD"
[The notebook MS is in the King's School.]
1. MS: sword:

"SWEETNESS OF REST WHEN THOU SHEDDEST REST"
[The notebook MS is in the King's School.]
4. MS: men:
6. MS: earth & under

"O FOOLISH SOUL! TO MAKE THY COUNT"
[The notebook MS is in the King's School.]
2. MS: falls & much
4. MS: storm & carry

"BEFORE THE BEGINNING THOU HAST FOREKNOWN THE END"
[The notebook MS is in the King's School.]
2. MS: birthday the deathbed was
7. MS: defend, arise to [*fr*] befriend,

"THE GOAL IN SIGHT! LOOK UP AND SING"
[The notebook MS is in the King's School.]
1. MS: up & sing,
5. MS: [*Let be the*] [not indented] <Let> [indented two spaces] <be>
[written above the line] <the> left,
10. MS: Hail! Life & Death & all

"LOOKING BACK ALONG LIFE'S TRODDEN WAY"
[The notebook MS is in the King's School.]
2. MS: Gleams & greenness
3. MS: melts & mellows
5. MS: Rose & purple & a

Indexes

INDEX OF TITLES

INDEX OF FIRST LINES